Search Engine Optimization

ALL-IN-ONE

FOR

DUMMIES®

A Wiley Brand

Third Edition

by Bruce Clay

Search Engine Optimization All-in-One For Dummies®, Third Edition

Published by:
John Wiley & Sons, Inc.
111 River Street
Hoboken, NJ 07030-5774
www.wiley.com

For general information on our other products and services, please contact our Customer Care Department within the U.S. at 877-762-2974, outside the U.S. at 317-572-3993, or fax 317-572-4002. For technical support, please visit www.wiley.com/techsupport.

Wiley publishes in a variety of print and electronic formats and by print-on-demand. Some material included with standard print versions of this book may not be included in e-books or in print-on-demand. If this book refers to media such as a CD or DVD that is not included in the version you purchased, you may download this material at http://booksupport.wiley.com. For more information about Wiley products, visit www.wiley.com.

Library of Congress Control Number: 2015947060

ISBN: 978-1-118-92175-3

ISBN 978-1-118-92176-0 (ebk); ISBN ePDF 978-1-118-92177-7 (ebk)

Manufactured in the United States of America

10 9 8 7 6 5 4 3 2

Contents at a Glance

Table of Contents

Introduction

*I*nternet marketing is a dynamic marketing channel because of its accuracy and ease in tracking traffic. It also generates new opportunities for communication and marketing at breakneck speeds.

In the early days of the Internet, search engines evolved to bring the web to users who were looking for sites, products, and like-minded users. These days, savvy marketers know that showing up on search engine results pages is a fruitful way to reach potential new customers. But landing your business's website in that precious spot high on the results pages is far from guaranteed. Search engine optimization (SEO) grew out of the need to persuade search engines that your site offers the best content for a particular topic.

Search engine optimization isn't a difficult discipline, but it is complex because of its many different parts that you need to tweak and adjust so that they work in harmony. And as far as marketing disciplines go, SEO is a wildly moving target. This latter quality makes a book on search engine optimization a challenging undertaking, often requiring a focus on broad concepts rather than specifics. Many of those specifics change or even fade away so often that they can need to be replaced or updated a hundred times just while this book is being updated for the newest edition.

To keep pace with the unavoidably fluctuating nature of SEO recommendations and search engine guidelines, your business needs to avoid chasing search engine algorithms. Instead, your goal should be simply to present your pages as the most relevant for a given search query. Resist the urge to assume that one aspect of search engine optimization is more important than another. Keep in mind that to succeed, all the various aspects of your SEO endeavors need to work together.

About This Book

Throughout this book, we reference tools as well as experts (ourselves and others) in the field. Search engine marketing (SEM), as an industry, is very active and excels at knowledge sharing. Although we cover the basics here, we strongly urge you to take advantage of the community that has developed since search engine marketing began. Truly, without the SEM community, we couldn't have written this book.

We hope that you keep this book near at hand, picking it up when you need to check for answers. For that reason, we attempt to make each minibook stand on its own. If something falls outside the scope of a particular minibook, or requires a mention in one but more detail in another, we refer you to the correct chapter or minibook for more information.

Search engine optimization has grown and changed over the years, along with the search engines themselves, and it continues to change at such a fast pace that sometimes the tools and features of the search engines become outdated even soon after this book's publication. For example, over the course of writing this book, Google changed the name of its webmaster tools platform from Google Webmaster Tools to Google Search Console, and modified the layout of local search results pages multiple times. This changeability means that you may have to research the most current tools and features available to you at at any given moment.

This book uses the following conventions, as follows:

✦ Text appears in brackets when it represents a search query that an Internet user might type into a search engine's search box, like this: [when is Mother's Day].

✦ Web addresses and programming code appear in `monofont`. If you're reading a digital version of this book on a device connected to the Internet, you can click or tap the web address to visit that website, like this: `www.dummies.com`.

Foolish Assumptions

We wrote this book for a particular sort of person. We assume that you, the one holding this book, are a small-business owner who's pretty new to Internet marketing. You might have a website, or maybe you're thinking about finally diving into this online thing; either way, we presume that you've already figured out how to turn on your computer and connect to the Internet.

We also assume that you're either somewhat familiar with the technologies that power websites or that you have access to someone who is. HTML, JavaScript, Flash, and other technologies are broad topics on their own. We don't expect you to know everything there is to know about JavaScript programming or Flash, but we also don't spend time explaining them to you. If you don't know how to program in these technologies, find a super-smart programmer to help you in your journey of developing your business's online presence. For a primer, you may want to seek out the *For Dummies* titles devoted to these topics.

Icons Used in This Book

 This icon calls out suggestions that help you work more effectively and save time.

 Try to keep items marked with this icon in mind while you optimize your website. Sometimes we offer a random tidbit of information, but more often than not, we talk about something that you'll run into repeatedly, so you should remember it.

 SEO can get pretty technical pretty fast. If you're not familiar with the terminology, it can start to sound like gibberish. We marked the sections where we get extra-nerdy with this icon so that you can be prepared. If these sections go over your head, don't worry: You can move on without understanding every nuance.

 If you see a Warning, take extra care. This icon denotes the times when getting something wrong can nuke your site, tank your rankings, and just generally devastate your online marketing campaign.

Beyond the Book

Because SEO and the Internet are always growing and changing, we encourage you to keep your knowledge of Internet marketing fresh through reading and research beyond these pages. We have written a lot of extra content that you won't find in this book, and that we will update as strategies and tactics change. Go online to find the following:

✦ **The Cheat Sheet at**

    www.dummies.com/cheatsheet/searchengineoptimizationaio

Bookmark this Cheat Sheet in your web browser so that you can easily access server status codes, advanced search operators, and an SEO checklist while you're tuning up your website. The SEO checklist is a quick-hits guide to making sure that every element on a web page helps your page rank. Use the advanced search operators to search Google, Bing, and Yahoo like a power user, filtering results to just the websites or types of pages you're looking for. And have the server status codes handy as you check that your web server is behaving.

✦ **Online articles covering additional topics at**

    www.dummies.com/extras/searchengineoptimizationaio

In the online Web Extras, we expand on some of the tools and how-to steps that we mention in the book. You'll find in-depth instructions on using the free Keyword Suggestion tool to capture new search traffic; how to use the SEO Multi-Page Information tool, another free tool created by Bruce Clay, Inc.; use a checklist for making sure that your website is optimized to be mobile friendly; find some tips for enlivening content that could otherwise be boring; how to use the Free Link Analysis Report tool; explore new options for top-level domains; and find out how to set goals in Google Analytics. And finally, if you've read about international SEO and business opportunities in Asia, Latin America, and Europe but need some more help deciding if it's right for your business, you can get some help with that decision here.

✦ **Updates to this book, if we have any, are at**

    `www.dummies.com/extras/searchengineoptimizationaio`

Where to Go from Here

The best thing about this book is that you can go anywhere from here. Although we've written it like a regular instruction manual that you can read from beginning to end, we also want you to be able to use it as a reference or a go-to guide for tricky problems. So, start anywhere you want. Jump into mobile website design or take a crack at creating great content for blogs and social media.

If you're brand new to SEO, we recommend that you start at the beginning. After that, it's up to you. Good luck and have fun. Just because this is business doesn't mean that you can't enjoy the ride.

Book I
How Search Engines Work

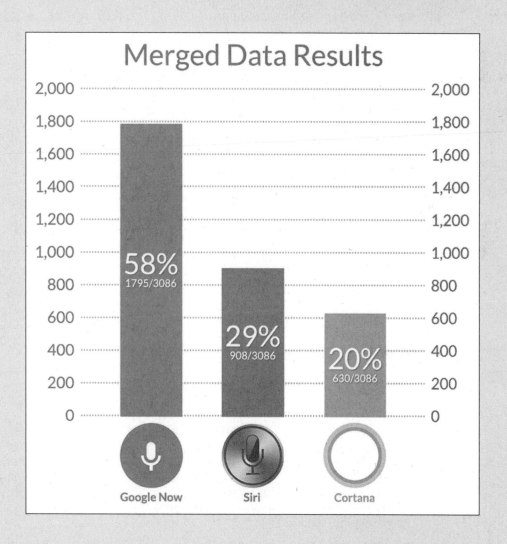

Merged Data Results

58%
1795/3086

29%
908/3086

20%
630/3086

Google Now   Siri   Cortana

Contents at a Glance

Chapter 1: Putting Search Engines in Context

In This Chapter

✔ Identifying search engine users

✔ Discovering why people use search engines

✔ Pinpointing elements for getting high keyword rankings

✔ Defining relationships between search engines

The Internet offers a world of information, both good and bad. Almost anything a person could want is merely a few taps on a screen or a couple clicks of a mouse away. A good rule of thumb for the Internet is if you want to know about something or purchase something, there's probably already a website just for that. The catch is actually *finding* it. This is what brings you to this book. You have a website. You have hired what you hope is a crack team of designers and have unleashed your slick, shiny, new site upon the web, ready to start making money. However, there is a bit of a problem: Nobody knows that your site exists. How will people find your website? The most common way that new visitors will find your site is through a search engine. A *search engine* is a web application designed to hunt for specific keywords and group them according to relevance. It used to be, in the stone age of the 1990s, that most websites were found via directories or word-of-mouth. Somebody linked to your website from his website, or maybe somebody posted about it on one of his newsgroups, and people found their way to you. Search engines such as Google, Yahoo, and Bing were created to cut out the middleman and bring your user to you with little hassle and fuss.

In this chapter, we show you how to find your audience by giving you the tools to differentiate between types of users, helping you sort out search engines, identifying the necessary elements to make your site prominent in those engines, and giving you an insider look at how all the search engines work together.

Identifying Search Engine Users

Who is using search engines? Well, everyone. A significant amount of all visitor traffic to websites comes from search engines. Unless you are a household name like eBay or Amazon.com, chances are people won't know where you are unless they turn to a search engine and hunt you down. In fact, even the big brands get most of their traffic from search engines. Search engines are the biggest driver of traffic on the web, and their influence only continues to grow.

But although search engines drive traffic to websites, you have to remember that your website is only one of a half trillion websites out there. Chances are, if someone does a search, even for a product that you sell, your website won't automatically pop up in the first page of results. If you're lucky and the query is targeted enough, you might end up somewhere in the top 100 of the millions of results returned. That might be okay if you're only trying to share your vacation photos with your family, but if you need to sell a product, you need to appear higher in the results. In most cases, you want the number one spot on the first page because that's the result everyone looks at and that most people click.

In the following sections, you find out a bit more about the audience available to you and how to reach them.

Figuring out how much people spend

The fact of the matter is that people spend money on the Internet in increasing numbers. It's frightfully easy: All you need is a credit card, a computer with an Internet connection, and something that you've been thinking about buying. The U.S. Commerce Department reports that in 2014, e-commerce spending in the United States was over $300 billion (`https://www.internetretailer.com/2015/02/17/us-annual-e-retail-sales-surpass-300-billion-first-ti`). Combine that with the fact that Americans spend an average of 5 to 6 minutes of every hour online doing online shopping, and you're looking at a viable means of moving your product. To put it simply, "There's gold in them thar hills!"

So, now you need to get people to your website. In real estate, the most important thing is location, location, location. On the web, instead of having a prime piece of property, you need a high listing on the *search engine results page* (SERP). Your placement in these results is referred to as your *ranking*. You have a few options when it comes to achieving good rankings. One, you can make your page the best it can be and hope that people will find it in the section of the search results normally referred to as the organic rankings; or two, you can pay to appear in one of the advertising slots, identified on the search results page as ads. In the middle of 2014, it was projected that by the end of the year, marketers would spend more than $135 billion on Internet ads worldwide (http://www.emarketer.com/Article/Digital-Ad-Spending-Worldwide-Hit-3613753-Billion-2014/1010736).

While paying for ads is one way to get your business in front of Internet users, *search engine optimization* (SEO), when properly done, helps you to design your website in such a way that when a user does a search, your pages appear in the unpaid (that is, *organic*) results, in a top spot, you hope. Your main focus in this book is finding out about SEO, but because there is some overlap, you pick up a bit of paid search marketing knowledge here and there along the way.

Knowing your demographics

In order to get the most bang for your SEO buck, you need to know the demographics of your web visitors. You need to know who's looking for you, because you need to know how best to promote yourself. For example, if you're selling dog sweaters, advertising in biker bars is probably not a great idea. Sure, there might be a few Billy Bob Skullcrushers with a cute little Chihuahua in need of a cashmere shrug, but statistically, your ad would probably do much better in a beauty salon. The same goes for your website in a search engine. Gender, age, and income are just a few of the metrics that you want to track in terms of identifying your audience. Search engine users include slightly more male than female users across the board. Of the major search engines, Bing attracts the smallest percentage of users over the age of 55. Search engines even feed their results into other search engines, as you can see in our handy-dandy Search Engine Relationship Chart in the section "Understanding the Search Engines: They're a Community," later in this chapter. Table 1-1 breaks down user demographics across the three most popular search engines for your reference.

Table 1-1   User Demographics Across Major Search Engines

	Google Search	*Yahoo Search*	*Bing Search*
Female	47.8%	47.4%	48.7%
Male	52.2%	52.6%	51.3%
18–34	35%	33.5%	35.3%
35–54	40.6%	42%	43.1%
55+	24.4%	24.6%	21.5%
Less than $30K/year	27.4%	27.6%	28.4%
$30K–$100K/year	53.8%	53.8%	52.5%
More than $100K/year	18.8%	18.7%	19%

For the month of July 2013 (via Compete.com)

These broad statistics are just a start. You need to know who *your* search engine visitors are, because demographic data helps you effectively target your desired market. This demographic distribution is often associated with search query *keywords*. Think of your keywords as the words that best indicate what your website content is about and that search engine visitors might use to search for what your website offers. A search engine looks for these keywords when figuring out which web pages to show on the SERP. (For an in-depth look at choosing keywords, check out Book II, Chapter 2.) Basically, your keywords are the words searchers might actually use in a *search query* — what they type (or speak) into a search engine — or what the engine thinks the searcher *intended* to search for. If you are searching for something like information on customizing classic cars, for example, you might type [classic custom cars] into the search field. (***Note:*** Throughout the book, we use square brackets to show the search query. You don't actually type the brackets into the search field.) Figure 1-1 displays a typical search engine results page for the query [classic custom cars].

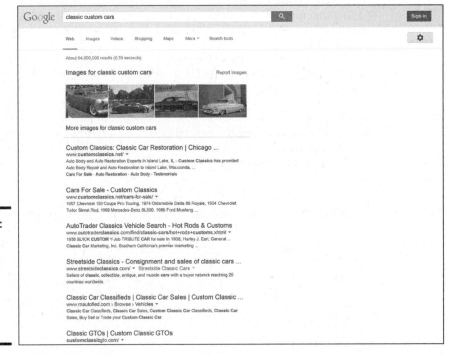

Figure 1-1:
Keyword
query in
a search
engine:
[classic
custom
cars].

Simply put, the search engine goes to work combing its index for web pages about these keywords and returns with the results it thinks will best satisfy you. As a website creator, therefore, if you have a product that's geared toward a certain age bracket, toward women more than men, or toward any other demographic, you can tailor your keywords accordingly. You want to choose keywords that appeal to the right audience. For example, on the classic custom cars website, you might say convertible, open-air, top-down, roadster, drop top, or rag top (all synonyms for convertible), depending on which terms people in your target demographic use. It may seem inconsequential, but trust us, this is important if you want to be ranked well for targeted searches.

Figuring Out Why People Use Search Engines

We've already established that a *lot* of people use search engines. But what are people looking for when they use them? Are they doing research on how to restore their classic car? Are they looking for a place that sells parts for classic cars? Or are they just wanting to kill time watching videos that show custom cars racing? The answer is yes to all the above. A search engine is there to scour the billions upon billions of websites out there in order to get you where you need to go, whether you're doing research, going shopping, or just plain wasting time.

Research

Most people who use a search engine for research purposes. They are generally looking for answers, or at least for data with which to make a decision. They're looking to find a site to fulfill a specific purpose. Someone doing a term paper on classic cars for his or her Automotive History 101 class would use a search engine to find websites with statistics on the number of cars sold in the United States, instructions for restoring and customizing old cars, and possibly communities of classic car fanatics out there. Companies would use a search engine to find websites their clients commonly visit and even to find out who their competition is.

Search engines are naturally drawn to information-rich, research-oriented sites and usually consider them more relevant than shopping-oriented sites, which is why a lot of the time the highest listing for the average query is a Wikipedia page. *Wikipedia.com* is an open-source online reference site that has a lot of searchable information, tightly cross-linked with millions of links from other websites (backlinks). *Open source* means that anyone can have access to the text and edit it. Wikipedia is practically guaranteed to have a high ranking on the strength of its site architecture alone. (We go over site architecture in depth in Book IV.) Wikipedia is an open-source project; thus, information should be taken with a grain of salt as there is no guarantee of accuracy. This brings us to an important lesson of search engines — they base "authority" on the quality of your content and the quality, relevance, and quantity of other sites linking to your site — that's what positions your site as an authority in the eyes of the search engine. Accuracy of information is not one of their criteria; notability is. Search engines are prone to confusing popularity with expertise, though they are improving in this area.

In order to take advantage of research queries, you need to gear your site content toward things that would be of interest to a researcher. In-depth how-to articles, product comparisons and reviews, and free information are all things that attract researchers to your site.

Shopping

Many people use a search engine to shop. After the research cycle is over, search queries change to terms that reflect a buying mindset. Phrases like "best price" and "free shipping" signal a searcher in need of a point of purchase. Optimizing your web page to meet the needs of that type of visitor results in higher *conversions* (actions taken by a user who meets a sales or business goal) for your site. As we mention in the preceding section, global search engines such as Google tend to reward research-oriented sites, so your pages have to strike a balance between sales-oriented terms and research-oriented terms.

Although Google and Bing do integrate products right into their regular search results, shopping is where specialized engines also come into the picture. Although you can use a regular search engine to find what it is you're shopping for, some people find it more efficient to use a search engine geared directly toward buying products. Some websites out there are actually search engines just for shopping. Amazon.com, eBay, Alibaba, and Shopping.com are all examples of shopping-only engines. And Google has its own shopping platform called Google Shopping. When you type in a query for the particular item you are looking for, your results include the actual item instead of websites where the item is sold. For example, say you're buying a book on Amazon.com. You type the title into the search bar, and it returns a page of results. Now, you have the option of either buying it directly from Amazon.com, or, if you're on a budget, clicking over to the used book section. Booksellers provide Amazon.com with a list of their used stock, and Amazon.com handles all the purchasing, shipping, and ordering info. With shopping searches on Bing and Google, all those results can also be shown, mixed in with ads, so you can jump to Amazon.com, eBay, or Mike's Bookshop just as easily. And as with all things on the Internet, odds are that somebody, somewhere, has exactly what you're looking for. Figure 1-2 displays a results page from a Google Shopping search.

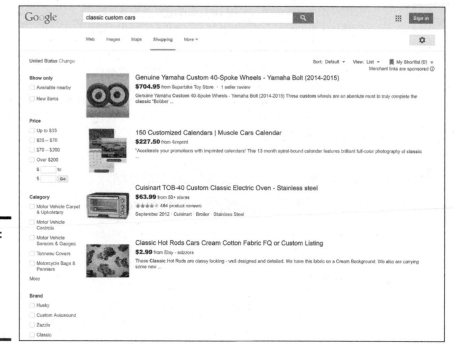

Figure 1-2:
A typical
Google
Shopping
search
results
page.

Entertainment

Research and shopping aren't the only reasons to visit a search engine. The Internet is a vast, addictive, reliable resource for consuming your entire afternoon, and lots of users out there start with the search engines to find ways of entertaining themselves. They look up things like videos, movie trailers, games, and social networking sites. Technically, it's also research, but it's research used strictly for entertainment purposes. A child of the '80s might want to download an old-school version of the *Oregon Trail* video game onto her computer so she can recall the heady days of third grade. It's a quest made easy with a quick search on Google. Or if you want to find out what those wacky young Hollywood starlets are up to, you can turn to a search engine to bring you what you need.

If you're looking for a video, odds are it's going to be something from YouTube, much like your research results are going to include a Wikipedia page. YouTube is another excellent example of a site that achieves high listings on results pages, especially in Google (which owns YouTube). This immensely popular video-sharing website enables people with a camera and a working email address to upload videos of themselves doing just about anything, from talking about their day to shaving their cats. The videos themselves have keyword-rich listings in order to be easily located in video searches, plus videos show up in regular web search results as well, so videos provide lots of ranking opportunities. Many major companies have jumped on the YouTube bandwagon, creating channels for their companies (a YouTube *channel* is a specific account housing many videos). Record companies use channels to promote bands, production companies use them to unleash the official trailers for their upcoming movies, and even your business can produce videos that can be seen by searchers everywhere (not just in a theater near you).

Discovering the Necessary Elements for Getting High Keyword Rankings

If the mantra of real estate is location, location, location, and the very best location on the web is on page one of the search engines, you need to know the SEO elements that can get you there. A good place to start is with keywords.

Search engines use advanced processes to categorize and analyze keyword usage and other factors in order to figure out what each website is about and bring searchers the web pages they're looking for. The more relevant your keywords and content are to the user's query and intent, the better chance your page has of ranking in a search engine's results. Keeping the keywords clear, precise, and simple helps the search engines do their job a whole lot faster. If you're selling something like customized classic cars, you should probably make sure your text includes keywords like *classic cars, customized cars, custom classic Mustangs,* and so forth, as well as clarifying words like *antique, vintage, automobile,* and *restored.* You can read more about how to choose your keywords in Book II.

In the following sections, you get a broad, brief overview on how you get a higher rank than the other guy who's selling restored used cars. You need to know the basics, or you can't do targeted SEO.

The advantage of an SEO-compliant site

Having an SEO-compliant website entails tailoring your website so that it follows search engine guidelines *and* communicates clearly what it's about and in a way search engines can understand. Basically, you want search engine spiders to easily digest all the juicy content in your website and not find any red flags along the way. Communicating well with search engines includes optimizing your page titles and metadata (the page title, description tag and keywords tag are collectively known as metadata) so that they contain (but aren't stuffed with) relevant keywords for your subject. Also, make sure that your web pages contain searchable text and not just pretty Flash animations and images (because search engines have limited capability to understand non-text content), and that all your images contain an `Alt` *attribute* (a description of an image) with brief text that describes the content of the image. You also need to be sure that all your internal content as well as your links are organized in a hierarchical manner that allows both search engines and users to easily understand what a site is about. You want to be sure to optimize every single one of these elements. Use this list (individual items are covered later in this book) to get yourself organized:

✦ `Title` tag

✦ `Meta Description` tag

✦ `Meta Keywords` tag

✦ Heading tag(s)

✦ Textual content

✦ `Alt` attributes on all images

✦ Fully qualified links

✦ Sitemaps (both XML and HTML, as explained in Book VI)

✦ Text navigation

✦ `Canonical` elements

✦ Structured data markup

✦ URL structure (file naming, limiting parameters)

✦ Ordered and unordered lists

✦ JavaScript/CSS externalized

✦ Robots text (`.txt`) file

✦ Web analytics

✦ Keyword research (technically a process — see Book II)

✦ Link development

✦ Image names

✦ Privacy statement

✦ Contact information

✦ Dedicated IP address

Defining a clear subject theme

Another way of getting a high keyword ranking is having a clear subject-matter theme to the site. If you're selling kits to customize classic cars, keeping your website focused on the topic of classic car customization not only makes it easier for users to navigate your site and research or purchase what they need, but it also increases your credibility and your chances of ranking for related keyword queries. Search engine spiders are programs that crawl the World Wide Web to search for and index data. The more similarly themed keywords you have on your pages, the better. It's the nature of a search engine to break up a site into subjects that add up to an overall theme for easy categorization, and the more obvious your site theme is, the higher your results will be.

It's kind of like going to an all-you-can-eat buffet and deciding you want to get a salad. You, the search engine, immediately go to the salad corner of the buffet because it's been clearly labeled, and from there, you can do your breakdowns. You want romaine lettuce, croutons, parmesan cheese, and Caesar dressing, so you go to where they keep the lettuce, the trimmings, and the dressings in the salad bar section. It's easy to find what you want if everything is grouped accordingly. But if the restaurant stuck the dressing over with the mashed potatoes, you'd have trouble finding it because salad dressing and potatoes don't normally go together. Similarly, when you keep your website content organized with everything in its proper place, the search engine views your content with clarity, understanding what you're about — which in turn improves your credibility as an expert and gives you a better chance to rank. *Siloing* is a way of structuring your content and navigational links in order to present a clear subject-matter theme to the search engines. For more on this technique, refer to Book II, Chapter 4 as well as the entirety of Book VI.

Focusing on consistency

Methodical consistent implementation is the principle that says that when you update your website, you should do it the same way every time. Your site should have a consistent look and feel over time without massive reorganizations at every update. In order for a search engine to maintain efficiency, you need to keep related content all placed in the same area.

It is confusing to customers to have things constantly changing around. Search engines and visitors to your website face the same challenge as a restaurant patron. Getting back to our salad bar analogy from the preceding section, the restaurant owner shouldn't scatter the salad dressings according to the whims of his buffet designer, randomly moving things every time he gets in a new topping or someone discontinues one of the old dressings.

You also need to keep all your updating processes consistent. That way, if something goes wrong during your next update, you can pinpoint what went wrong where without too much hassle, since you update things the same way every time.

Building for the long term

You need to consider your persistence for the long term. How long will your website be sticking around? Ideally, as with any business, you want to build it to last without letting it fall behind and look dated. Relevancy to the current market is a big part of this, and if your site is behind the times, it's probably behind your competitors. The technology that you use to build your website is inevitably going to change as the Internet advances, but your approach to relevancy should remain the same, incorporating new technologies as they arise. In the early days of the web, for example, frames were used to build sites, but that looks very outdated now. A few years ago, *splash pages* (introductory pages, mostly built in Flash and providing little content or value to the user) were very popular. Today, they are discouraged because the search engines cannot typically see much of the content behind the Flash programming and therefore don't know what the page is about. Web developers and designers should use code that is compatible with the search engines. The Internet is an ever-changing entity, and if you're not persistent about keeping up with the times, you might fall by the wayside.

Understanding the Search Engines: They're a Community

You'll be happy to hear there are really only a few search engines that you need to consider in your SEO planning. Each search engine appears to be a unique company with its own unique service. When people choose to run a search using Google, Yahoo, Bing, Ask.com, or any of the others, they might think they've made a choice between competing services and expect to get varying results. But they'd be surprised to find out that under the surface, these seeming competitors are often actually working together — at least on the data level.

Google's stated purpose is to "organize the world's information." When you think about the trillions of web pages that exist, multiplying and morphing every day, it's hard to imagine a more ambitious undertaking. It makes sense, then, that not every search engine attempts such a daunting task itself. Instead, the different search engines share the wealth when it comes to indexed data, much like a community.

You can see at a glance how this community works. Figure 1-3 shows how the major players in the search engine field interact.

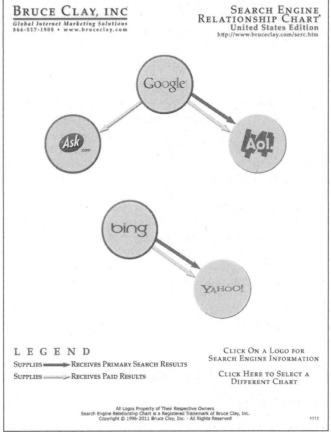

Figure 1-3:
The Search
Engine
Relationship
Chart
depicts the
connections
between
search
engines.

Chart courtesy of Bruce Clay, Inc.

A look back: Search engines in the beginning

Bruce Clay first published his Search Engine Relationship Chart® in 2000. Back then, more major players were in the search game, and things were, to say the least, somewhat cluttered. The chart had 26 companies on it: everyone from Yahoo to Magellan to that upstart Google. Fifteen of those companies took their primary results from their own indexes; five of those supplied secondary results to other engines. Without a road map, it was an impossible task to keep it all straight. But over the years, things changed. What was once a cluttered mess is now a tidy interplay of a select group of companies. This figure shows what the very first Search Engine Relationship Chart looked like.

Note: To see an interactive view of how the search engine landscape changed over time, check out www.bruceclay.com/serc_histogram/histogram.htm.

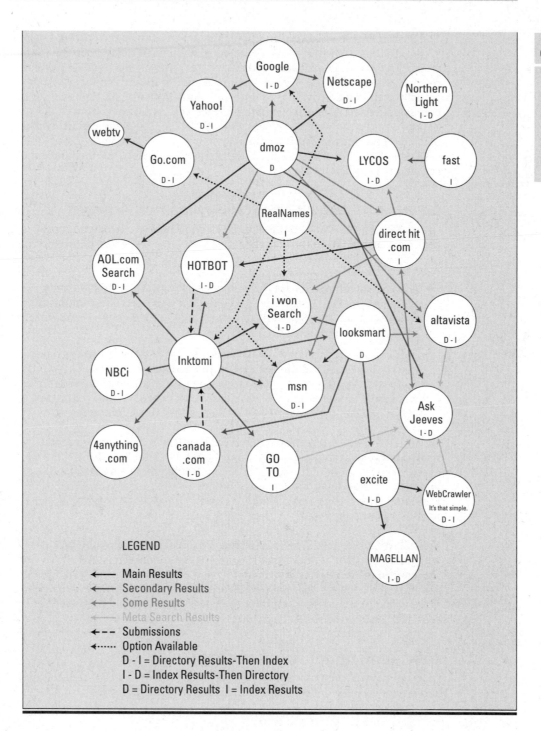

LEGEND

← Main Results
← Secondary Results
← Some Results
← Meta Search Results
←- - - Submissions
←······ Option Available
   D - I = Directory Results-Then Index
   I - D = Index Results-Then Directory
   D = Directory Results I = Index Results

The Search Engine Relationship Chart (subject to change; the current chart is at `www.bruceclay.com/serc/`) includes all the major players in the United States. The arrows depict search results data flowing from supplying sites to receiving sites. Only two players — Google and Bing — are suppliers. They actually gather and provide search results data, both organic and paid. Ask. com maintains its own organic data but receives paid listings from Google. Yahoo, on the other hand, receives its organic data but generates its own paid ads. The chart makes it clear that when you do a search on Yahoo, for instance, the order of the results is determined by Yahoo, but the indexed results are supplied by Bing.

Looking at search results: Apples and oranges

One more thing to know about search results: There are two main types. Figure 1-4 points out that a search engine can show these two different types of results simultaneously:

✦ Organic search results are the web page listings that search engines find most relevant to the user's search query and perceived intent. SEO focuses on getting your website ranked high in the organic search results (also called *natural* results).

✦ Paid results are basically advertisements. — the website owners have paid to have their web pages and products display for certain keywords, so these listings show up when someone runs a search containing those keywords. (For more on the whys and hows of paid results, you can read about pay per click advertising in Chapter 4 of this minibook.)

On a search results page, you can tell paid results from organic search results because search engines set apart the paid listings, putting them above or to the right of the primary results, giving them a shaded background or border lines, labeling the column as "ads" or "sponsored," or providing other visual clues. Figure 1-4 shows the difference between paid listings and organic results.

Typical web users might not realize they're looking at apples and oranges when they get their search results. Knowing the difference enables a searcher to make a better informed decision about the relevancy of a result. Additionally, because the paid results are advertising, they may actually be more useful to a shopping searcher than a researcher (remembering that search engines favor research results).

How do they get all that data?

Okay, so how do they do it? How do search engines keep track of everything and pop up results so fast? Behold the wonder of technology!

Paid results

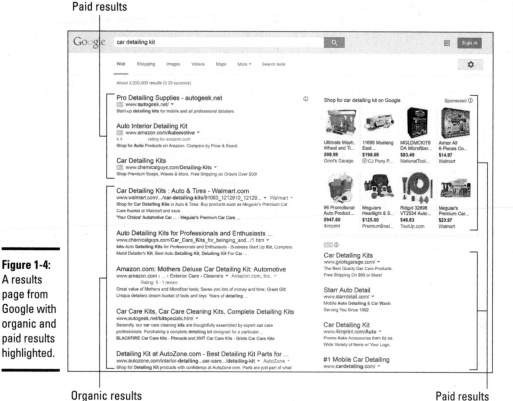

Figure 1-4:
A results
page from
Google with
organic and
paid results
highlighted.

Organic results

Paid results

Gathering the data is the first step. An automated process (known as *spidering*) constantly crawls the Internet, gathering web-page data into servers. Google calls its spider *Googlebot;* you could refer to the data-gathering software processes as *spiders, robots, bots,* or *crawlers,* but they're all the same thing. Whatever you call them, they pull in masses of raw data and do so repeatedly. This is why changes to your website might be seen within a day or might take up to a few weeks to be reflected in search engine results.

In the second step, search engines have to index the data to make it usable. *Indexing* is the process of taking the raw data and categorizing it, removing duplicate information, and generally organizing it all into an accessible structure (think filing cabinet versus paper pile).

For each query performed by a user, the search engines apply an *algorithm* — basically a math equation (formula) that weighs various criteria about a web page and generates a ranking result — to decide which listings to display and in what order. The algorithms might be fairly simple or multilayered and complex.

At industry conferences, Google representatives have said that their algorithm analyzes more than 200 variables to determine a web page's search ranking to a given query. You're probably thinking, "What are their variables?" Google won't say exactly (and neither will the other engines), and that's what makes SEO a challenge. But we can make educated guesses.

So, can you design a website that gets the attention of *all* the search engines? The answer is yes, to an extent, but it's a bit of an art. This is the nuts and bolts of SEO, and what we attempt to explain in this book.

Chapter 2: Meeting the Search Engines

In This Chapter

⊾ **Finding common threads among the engines**

⊾ **Meeting the major and minor search engines**

⊾ **Finding your niche in the vertical engines**

⊾ **Understanding metasearch engines**

*A*ll search engines try to make their results the most relevant. They want to make you happy, because when you get what you want, you're more likely to use that search engine again. The more you use them, the more money they make. It's a win/win situation. So when you do your search on classic car customization and find what you're looking for right away instead of having to click through five different pages, you'll probably come back and use the same search engine again.

In this chapter, you meet the major search engines and discover their similarities and differences, get familiar with the difference between organic and paid results, and gain a better understanding of how the search engines get their organic results. Plus, you find out about the search engines' paid search programs and get help deciding whether metasearch engines have a place in your SEO campaign.

Finding the Common Threads among the Engines

To keep their results relevant, all search engines need to understand the main subject of a website. You can help the search engines find your website by keeping in mind the three major factors they're looking for:

✦ **Content:** Content is the meat and bones of your website. It's all the information your website contains, not just the words but also the *Engagement Objects* (the images, videos, audio, interactive technologies, and so on that make up the visual space). Your page's relevancy increases based upon your perceived expertise. And expertise is based on useful, keyword-containing content. The *spiders,* the software the search engines use to read your website, also measure whether you have enough content that suggests you know what it is you're talking about. A website with ten pages of content is going to rank lower than a website with ten thousand pages of content, assuming that they are equally relevant.

✦ **Popularity:** The Internet is a little like high school in that you are popular as long as a lot of people know you exist and are talking about you. Search engine spiders are looking for how many people are linking to your website, along with the number of outgoing links you have on your own site. Google really loves this factor.

✦ **Architecture:** If you walk into a grocery store and find everything stacked haphazardly on the shelves, it's going to be harder to find things, and you might just give up and go to another store that's better organized. Spiders do the same thing. As we mention in Chapter 1 of this minibook, search engines love Wikipedia because of how it's built. It's full of searchable text, `Alt` attribute text, and keyword-containing hyperlinks that support terms used on the page.

You also have some control over two variables that search engines are looking at when they set the spiders on you. One is your site's *response time,* which is how fast your server is and how long it takes to load a page. If you're on a server that loads one page per second, the bots request pages at a very slow rate. A second seems fast to us, but it's an eternity for a bot that wants five to seven pages per second. If the server can't handle one page per second, imagine how long it would take the bots to go through 10,000 pages. In order not to crash the server, spiders request fewer pages; this puts a slow site at a disadvantage to sites with faster load times. Chances are bots will index sites on a fast server more frequently and thoroughly than sites on a slow server. Page speed has become very important to Google in particular and so deserves some attention. We discuss improving page and site speed in depth in Book VII, Chapter 1.

The second variable is somewhat contested. Some SEOs believe that your rank could be affected by something called *bounce rate,* which measures how often someone clicks on a page and immediately hits the Back button. The search engines can detect when a user clicks on a result and then clicks on another result in a short time. If a website constantly has people loading the first page for only a few seconds before hitting the Back button to return to the search results, it's a good bet that the website is probably not very satisfying. Remember, engines strive for relevancy and user experience in their results, so they most likely consider bounce rate when they're determining rankings.

So if all search engines are looking at these things, does it matter if you're looking at Bing versus Google versus Yahoo? Yes, it does, because all search engines evaluate subject relevance differently. The big players have their own algorithms that measure things in a different way than their competition.

So something that Google thinks belongs on Page 1 of listings may or may not pop up in the Top Ten over on Bing.

Getting to Know the Major Engines

It's time to meet the three major search engines: Google, Bing, and Yahoo. As we said earlier, they all measure relevancy a bit differently. Google might rank a page of content as more relevant than Bing does, so Google's results pages could look quite different from Bing's results pages for the same search query. Meanwhile, Yahoo uses Bing's index of the web and ranking algorithm to serve organic and much of its paid search listings. For this reason, deciding which search engine is best is often subjective. It all depends on whether you find what you're looking for.

Organic versus paid results

One of the major ways search engines are differentiated is how they handle their organic versus paid results. *Organic results* are the web pages that the search engines find on their own using their spiders. *Paid results* (also called *sponsored listings*) are the listings that the site owners have paid for. In web searches, paid results usually appear as ads along the top or right side of the window, but they also can appear lower on the page, among or below organic listings. Paid results don't necessarily match your search query either. Here's how this happens.

Companies can bid on almost any keyword for which they want to get traffic (with some legal exceptions). The *bid price* needed to have an ad show in the SERP is based on many factors, including competition for the keyword, traffic on the keyword, and, at least in Google's case, the quality of the *landing page*. The better-constructed the landing page (the web page that a visitor receives after clicking an ad), the lower the minimum bid price. This doesn't have to be an exact match. Businesses often bid on keywords that are related to their products in hopes of catching more visitors. For example, if a visitor searches for tickets to Sports Team A, a *sponsored* (paid) link might show up advertising Sports Team B. This is what's happening below in Figure 2-1. Ticketmaster has bid on [Lakers tickets] as a keyword in order to advertise tickets for a different team, the LA Clippers, and clicking the sponsored link takes you to a page for buying Clippers tickets. The ad for Boston Celtics Tickets operates the same way. The organic links, however, should all take you to sites related to Lakers tickets.

Paid results are quite different from organic results. Generally, people click on organic results rather than paid results. You can't buy your way to the top of organic results. You can only earn your way there through effective search engine optimization.

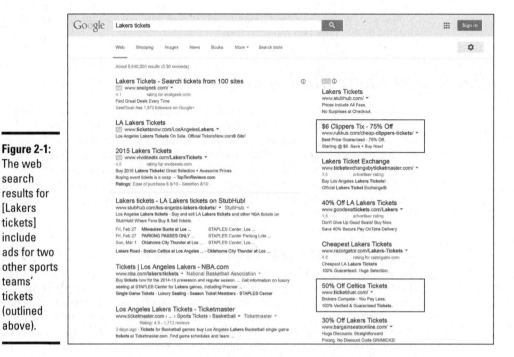

Figure 2-1:
The web search results for [Lakers tickets] include ads for two other sports teams' tickets (outlined above).

Table 2-1 lists the major search engine players (in order of their appearance) and the attributes of each, for comparison. The following sections introduce you to each search engine in more detail and talk about its organic results and paid advertising services.

Table 2-1   **U.S. Search Engine Comparison Table**

Engine Name	Organic	Paid (Desktop)	Paid (Mobile)
Yahoo	Yes. Uses Bing's index and algorithm	Yes. Uses Bing Ads	Yes. Yahoo Gemini
Google Spider name: Googlebot	Yes	Yes. Google AdWords	Yes. Google AdWords
Bing Spider name: Bingbot	Yes	Yes. Bing Ads	Yes. Bing Ads

Yahoo

In 1994, two electrical engineering graduate students at Stanford University, David Filo and Jerry Yang, created Yahoo, a search engine and network of properties that has undergone much change in its 20-year history. For many years, Yahoo has outsourced its search function to other providers like Google and, today, Bing.

Organic results

In 2010, Yahoo made a deal with Bing to power its search engine and pay per click program. That means that the organic search results in Yahoo use Bing's ranking algorithm and Bing's index of the web.

Paid results

Because Yahoo no longer provides its own paid results for desktop searches, in order to advertise on Yahoo's network, you must use Microsoft Bing Ads (and get two-for-one exposure).

Mobile advertising is a different story. In 2014, Yahoo migrated to Yahoo Gemini, its own mobile ad marketplace. The strategy appears to be paying off; its third-quarter earnings place Yahoo in third place for total mobile ad revenue, behind Google and Facebook but, surprisingly, ahead of Twitter.

Google

Google began as a research project by two other Stanford University students, Larry Page and Sergey Brin, in January 1996. They officially incorporated as Google in September 1998.

Organic results

Over time, Google has developed into the powerhouse of the search engine realm. Here are just some of the reasons why Google is the king of search engines and shows no signs of giving up the crown:

✦ **Highly relevant:** Google's relevancy is one of its strongest suits thanks to its analysis of site backlinks and on-site content on the one hand, and its understanding of user intent on the other.

✦ **PageRank:** PageRank is a famous part of Google's search algorithm. PR is a numerical weight assigned to a website in order to measure its importance, based on backlinks.

✦ **Enormous index:** Google has indexed billions of pages on the Internet. In addition, Google search's semantic-based algorithm and integration with other Google products (such as Gmail, Google+, YouTube, and Google Drive) give it a wide vantage point for seeing the connections between concepts, people, and other entities on the web.

✦ **Advanced technology:** Google is the undisputed leader, technologically speaking. Its algorithms aggressively weed out spam from its results, and its Knowledge Graph far outpaces the other engines' capability to understand a searcher's intent. You learn more about the Knowledge Graph and how it affects search results in Chapter 3 of this minibook.

✦ **Brand recognition:** Google is so recognized for search that the brand name is used as a verb and listed in dictionaries (as in, "I Googled this the other day . . .").

✦ **Most-visited web property:** Google is the number one search engine worldwide (except in China, where Baidu reigns, and Russia, where Yandex tops the list). In the United States, Google has more of the search market than all the other search engines combined, netting more than two-thirds of all search engine traffic (see Table 2-2; `http://www. comscore.com/Insights/Press_Releases/2014/3/comScore_ Releases_February_2014_U.S._Search_Engine_`).

Table 2-2   **comScore Explicit Core Search Share Report, U.S. (August versus July 2014)***

Core Search Entity	July 2014	August 2014	Share Change
Total Explicit Core Search	100.0%	100.0%	None
Google Sites	67.4%	67.3%	−0.1
Microsoft Sites	19.3%	19.4%	0.1
Yahoo Sites	10.0%	10.0%	0.0
Ask Network	2.0%	2.0%	0.0
AOL, Inc.	1.3%	1.3%	0.0

*"Explicit Core Search" excludes contextually driven searches that do not reflect specific user intent to interact with the search results.

Paid results

Google has a service called Google AdWords that regulates its paid results for desktop and mobile. It's a pay per click advertising model that lets you create your own ads, choose the keyword phrases you want your ad to appear for, and set your bid price and budget. Google ranks its ads based on the ad's bid amount and *Quality Score* — a combined measure of the ad's relevance, landing-page experience, and expected *click-through rates,* or how often the ad is clicked. Google AdWords can also help you create your ads if you're stuck on how to do so.

After your AdWords ads are set up, Google matches your ads to the right audience within its network, and you pay only when your ad is clicked. Google provides gives an ever-increasing number of ways to target your ad audience, such as by demographics like gender, age group, annual household income, ethnicity, and number of children in the household. AdWords also allows you to do location-based targeting and *day-parting,* which limits the display of your advertisement to certain times of the day. Recently, Google introduced "In-market audiences" targeting, which lets you leverage Google's understanding of consumer behavior patterns and find people who are actively researching products like yours.

You can potentially get a lot of exposure for your paid ads. The Google AdWords distribution network lets you advertise on Google search sites and affiliates like AOL and Ask.com. Mobile and tablet ads are also centrally managed through AdWords.

Google also offers the ability to publish ads on the Google Display Network. Consisting of more than two million websites, videos, and mobile apps, the Display Network also includes Google sites such as Gmail, YouTube, and Blogger. Owners can earn money by enrolling in Google's AdSense program to allow advertisements on their sites, apps, or video content. AdSense ads generate revenue for the site owners based on factors such as clicks or impressions.

Bing

Bing (previously named MSN Search and Microsoft Live Search) is a search engine designed by Microsoft that competes with Google and Yahoo. It's currently the second-most-used general search engine in the United States.

Organic results

In addition to providing rich, blended SERP results on par with Google's, Bing differentiates itself through features like its daily full-screen home page image, a longer list of search results per page, and a rewards program that lets people earn points that can be redeemed for gift cards just for using Bing. Bing Search also lets users easily modify the search results based upon any location they would like the search to appear from.

Paid results

Microsoft's paid program is called Bing Ads, and reports are that it offers advertisers an extremely good *return on investment* (ROI). Like Google, Bing ranks its ads based on keyword bid price and ad quality. Microsoft also lets you place adjustable bids based on demographic details. For example, a mortgage lead from an adult with a higher income might be worth more than an equivalent search by someone who is young and still in college.

Checking Out the Rest of the Field: AOL and Ask.com

The five biggest search engines worldwide right now are Google, Yahoo, Bing, Baidu (a Chinese search engine), and Yandex (a Russian search engine — see Book IX, Chapter 2 for more information on Baidu and Yandex), with Google taking home the lion's share. But other smaller engines that draw a pretty respectable number of hits are still operating.

AOL

AOL has been around in some form or another since 1983. Today AOL provides some services such as email, chat, and its own search engine. AOL gets all its search engine results from Google, both organic and paid.

If you want to appear in an AOL search, you must focus on Google. AOL uses the Google index results in its search engine.

Ask.com

Ask.com (some of you may remember it as Ask Jeeves) pioneered *blended search* (the integration of different content types, such as images, videos, news, blogs, books, maps, and so on, onto the search results page) but failed to gain any significant market share from the larger three engines (Google, Bing, and Yahoo). Ask.com changed its market strategy and now considers itself an "answer engine," rather than a search engine. Ask.com generates comprehensive results answering question-focused search queries, pulling information from third-party directories, feeds, Q&A forums, and Google's organic results.

Ask.com gets most of its paid search ads from Google AdWords. Ask.com does have its own internal ad service, but it places internal ads above the Google AdWords ads only if it feels the internal ads will bring in more revenue.

Finding Your Niche: Vertical Engines

We've been talking mostly about *general search engines,* whose specific purpose is to scour everyone and everything on the web and return results to you. But there's also another type of search engine known as a vertical search engine. *Vertical search engines* are search engines that restrict their search either by industry, geographic area, or file type. Google has several vertical search engines listed in the upper-left corner of its home page for images, apps, and so forth. So when you type [jam] into Google's Images search, it only returns pictures of jam instead of web pages. The three main types of vertical search engines are detailed in the following sections.

Industry-specific

Industry-specific vertical search engines serve particular types of businesses. The real estate industry has its own search engines like Realtor.com (www. realtor.com) and Zillow.com (www.zillow.com), which provide housing listings, and companion sites like HomeAdvisor.com, which is for home improvement contractors. If you want to conduct searches related to the medical industry, you can use WebMD.com (www.webmd.com), a search engine devoted entirely to medical questions and services. Questions about Hollywood stars and anyone ever connected with movie-making can be answered at IMDB.com, which stands for Internet Movie Database. If you are searching for legal services, FindLaw.com (www.findlaw.com) and Lawyers.com (www.lawyers.com) can help you search for an attorney by location and practice.

Niche engines like these deliver less traffic but make up for it in the targeted nature of traffic. Visitors who access your site using niche engines are prequalified because they're looking for exactly your type of site.

Local

A *local search engine* is an engine specializing in websites that are tied to a limited physical area also known as a *geotargeted area.* Basically, this type of engine is looking for things in your general neck of the woods. In addition to their main indexes, the major search engines have local-only indexes that they integrate into their main results, like Google My Business and Bing Places. Businesses submit a *local listing* to the search engines, which includes information about the local business such as its name, address, city, phone number, categories the business may be searched under, and so on. That means the site could pop up if someone's looking for that type of business within its geographic area.

A searcher might specify a ZIP code, city, or other geographic qualifier in a search query to find geotargeted results, such as [Milwaukee chiropractor]. However, Google and Bing can pretty reliably understand the intent of a search. If the engine thinks the searcher wants to find a nearby business, it displays local listings right in the search results. For example, a search for [dry cleaners] brings up website links to businesses near the searcher, even though no location was specified in the query.

Local results take up a lot of SERP space and often rank above the organic results. To be clear, these local results are still served up "organically" by the local search algorithm, but the local results may take precedence over what we have come to know in the past as the top organic results. Searches performed on a smartphone or other mobile device tend to have even more local results, since the majority of queries people speak or type into mobile devices are thought to have local intent. See Chapter 4 of this minibook for examples of several types of local results.

Many large cities have their own local search engines. Yahoo Local and Local.com are the most well known local-only engines. Internet directories like YellowPages.com, SuperPages.com, DexKnows.com, and YellowBook. com are also out there clamoring for your local search queries.

File type-specific

Certain search engines devote themselves to just one type of file — videos, photographs, or other. Rather than limiting traffic, being a file type-specific engine creates traffic because visitors know exactly what they're going to get. The video-only engine YouTube.com, for example, reports some astonishing statistics: More than 1 billion people visit YouTube each month, watching more than 6 billion hours of video and uploading an average of 100 hours of video per minute. In fact, YouTube's traffic makes it the second most popular website in the world, behind only Google (http://www.youtube.com/yt/press/statistics.html). There are other video engines as well, including Blinkx.com, Metacafe.com, and Hulu.com; Hulu specializes in the video niche of television shows and movies.

Image searches performed on Google, Bing, or Yahoo return images from all over the web. But there are also many successful image-only search engines, like PicSearch.com and CC (Creative Commons) Search (search. creativecommons.org), which comb the Internet looking for images that match your criteria. Sites like Flickr.com are image-sharing sites, where users can upload their photos and specify how they may be used. Other sites have their own stock of images that users can search for and download (either for free or for a fee based on the user's intended use), such as `GettyImages.com`, `iStockphoto.com`, `Fotolia.com`, and `Dreamstime.com`, just to name a few.

As a website owner, one way to leverage these specialty engines is to upload content that will attract searchers looking for images or videos. You can learn more about strategies with images and videos in Book V, Chapter 2.

Discovering Internal Site Search

Say you're writing an article and you need to reference something in the *New York Times*. The *New York Times* website (`www.nytimes.com`) keeps an archive of online articles, but because you can't remember the date the article was published, you'd have a long trek through the online archives. Luckily, it has its own internal site search engine that enables you to look up articles using keywords and filters. Any search engine that's *site-specific*, meaning it searches just that website, is an *internal site search engine.*

Larger websites with thousands of pages employ these internal site search engines as an easy way of browsing their archives. A very small site probably doesn't need an internal search, but most e-commerce sites with more than a few products should consider implementing one.

Techniques that help you rank in general search engines also help your users when they need to find something on your site using an internal search. A good internal search can be the difference between making a sale and visitors leaving in frustration. To get started quickly, Google offers a hosted internal search solution as well as an enterprise-level solution. See `https://www.google.com/enterprise/search/products/gss.html` for more information.

Understanding Metasearch Engines

Another breed of search engine to be aware of is a *metasearch engine.* Metasearch engines do not maintain a database of their own, but instead combine results from multiple search engines. The advantage they tout is a twist on "bigger is better" — the more results you see in one fell swoop, the better. The sites Dogpile.com (`www.dogpile.com`) and DuckDuckGo.com (`www.duckduckgo.com`) top the list of metasearch engines. When you run a

A brief history of metasearch

Metasearch engines have passed their heyday. In the old days (1996, if you're curious, which is approximately 10,000 B.C. in Internet years), dozens of different search engines were still in their growth stages. None had indexes that encompassed the whole Internet. Because every search engine had only a piece of the pie, metasearch engines that could dish up the whole thing at one time served a real purpose. Now, however, the big search engines all have fairly exhaustive indexes with billions of listings with usable and relevant results, and, as we cover in Chapter 1 of this minibook, there's already a lot of indexed-data sharing going on. When you run a search in any of today's major search engines, you can be sure that you're seeing most of the applicable organic results and many of the paid ones.

The metasearch engines today rank very low in total market share compared to the three big players. According to comScore statistics (at the time of writing), Google sites (which include Google search and YouTube) have 67.5 percent of the search market share in the United States and a majority of web searches globally. In the United States, the three big guys combined (Google, Yahoo, and Bing) make up more than 90 percent market share. Ask.com and AOL take most of the remaining few percentage points.

search on Dogpile, it pulls and displays results from four of the largest global engines (including Google and Yahoo) in one place. DuckDuckGo's marketing proposition is that it respects searchers' privacy by not tracking their search behavior, but pulls from many different search engines and key sites to present non-personalized search results.

After pulling results from multiple search engines, the metasearch engines retain the top ranked results from the separate search engines and present the user with the top results. This is different from applying an algorithm, as the indexed search engines do (an *algorithm* is a mathematical equation that weighs many specific criteria about each web page to generate its ranking result, as we discuss in Chapter 1 of this minibook). Metasearch engines take more of a filtering approach to all the indexed data gathered from the other search engines. Ads appear at the top and bottom, with organic "Web Results" in the middle of the page. We've found metasearch engines helpful for keeping track of which competitors buy paid results for which keywords. (You can read more about paid results in Book I, Chapter 4). Figure 2-2 shows you a results page from the Dogpile metasearch engine.

Figure 2-2:
The Dogpile
metasearch
engine
results
page.

Chapter 3: Recognizing and Reading Search Results

In This Chapter

✓ **Reading the search engine results page**

✓ **Understanding the search results page and why rank position matters**

✓ **Identifying how mobile users search**

✓ **Discovering the effects of blended search**

✓ **Understanding the effect of Google's Knowledge Graph**

✓ **Discovering the impact of semantic search and Hummingbird**

*I*n Chapter 2 of this minibook, we discuss organic versus paid results: *organic results* being the listings that are ranked by perceived merit by a search engine, and *paid results* (also called sponsored results or sponsored links) being purchased ads that appear along with the organic results. In this chapter, you discover what the rest of the results page means, find out about what gets the most attention on a search page, how search results appear for mobile searchers, and how search engines are adapting to the rising use of voice search.

Reading the Search Engine Results Page

Say that Mother's Day is coming up and you want to buy your mother a nice bouquet of roses. (Good for you! No wonder Mom always liked you best.) After going to Google and typing your [bouquets] search query into the box, you're presented with a results page. The results page contains many different listings containing the *keyword,* or search word, [bouquets], sorted according to what Google thinks is most relevant to you. Figure 3-1 shows a Google results page for the query [bouquets].

Take a look at the different parts of the page shown in Figure 3-1. (Note that we're using a Google results page because Google gets the lion's share of traffic. Plus, there isn't much difference between Google's results-page layout and those of Yahoo and Bing.)

Search verticals   Time the search took

Search box   Page count   Organic results   Map results

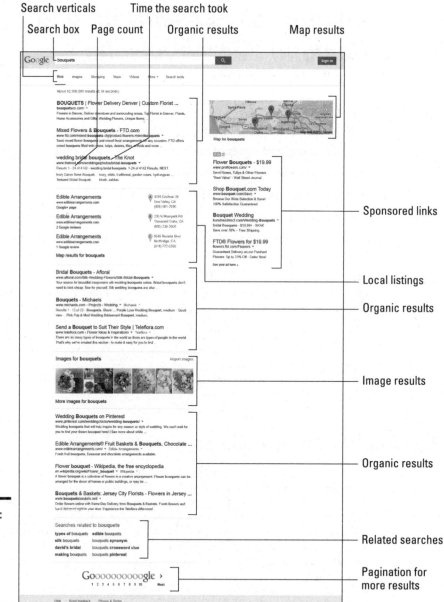

— Sponsored links

— Local listings

— Organic results

— Image results

— Organic results

— Related searches

— Pagination for more results

Figure 3-1:
A typical Google search results page.

✦ **Search Box:** The box where you type your *search query,* or whatever it is that you're looking for. In this case, it's bouquets.

✦ **Search Verticals:** Links to the *vertical search engines,* the specialized ones that narrow your search to a specific type of result, such as images or news. Clicking one of these links takes you to a results page with only images or only shopping results, for instance.

✦ **Page Count:** The number of web pages Google found that matches your search query in some way. In Figure 3-1, we have a lot of pages in our results.

✦ **Time Search Took:** How long the search engine took to retrieve your results.

✦ **Organic Results:** The listing results from a general search of Google's index, with algorithms applied to determine relevance.

✦ **Ads:** The paid advertising links. These are marked as "Ads" (or sometimes "Sponsored") and usually appear to the right of the organic listings or above them.

✦ **Local Map Results ("local pack"):** Local businesses considered to be relevant to the query, pulled from Google's local index.

✦ **Map:** Visual map of the local area with markers to show where all the local map result listings are located.

✦ **Images:** Picture files that match your query. These come from Google's Images vertical engine. Clicking the text link would take you to the vertical search results; in this case, a page containing only images of bouquets.

✦ **Related Searches:** Other topics that contain your query or other searches Google thinks might be relevant.

✦ **Pagination:** Links to the additional pages of results.

✦ **Sign In:** Google encourages users to be signed in to their Google accounts, which enables the search engine to track their behavior and personalize their results. When you are signed in, you'll see your picture and a different set of buttons in the upper-right corner.

Other SERP Features: There are *many* additional display options that Google might include on a given search results page. In fact, it's hard to get the same SERP twice! Some of the most innovative features come from what Google calls its *Knowledge Graph,* which is a database of information connecting people, places, and things; we explain more about this later in the chapter.

Understanding How People Look at Search Results

Knowing what is on the results page is important, but so is understanding how people read it. As it turns out, there is actually a predictable pattern in the way people read a results page. Eye-tracking studies show that, just as Google's SERP has changed a lot over the past decade, people's behavior when viewing results has similarly evolved.

Back in 2005, a ground-breaking study was conducted to track people's eye movements while reading a typical search engine results page. The study, done by Enquiro Research, which was later acquired by Mediative, discovered a pattern that it called the *Golden Triangle.* The Golden Triangle identified on a visual heat map how people's eyes scan a results page and how long they look at a particular result before moving on. Figure 3-2 shows that originally, people reading a SERP tended to start in the upper-left corner and move down the page, and then out to the right when a title caught their attention. This eye-tracking pattern forms a triangle (or an F, as another research organization, the Nielsen Norman Group, observed in its 2006 study). For many years, the top three positions got almost all the user's attention, with a little bit given to the middle of the page, and almost none for the last few results on the page.

Times have changed, and so has the way users view search engine results. After acquiring Enquiro, the company Mediative followed up the research with a new eye-tracking study in September 2014. It found that a searcher's gaze often travels outside the Golden Triangle area looking for what seems most relevant. Because Google's SERP format can be different with every search, it's no wonder people have learned to scan a greater portion of the page to find what they need.

As an example, the heat map in Figure 3-3 shows how searchers look at a desktop SERP that includes a local pack and map. Notice that the eye pattern goes down the page and over to the map on the right. The most time is spent looking at the top listings in each of the various display formats down the page: two paid ads at the top of the page, the reviews section, the top two local listings, and the first organic listing below the local pack.

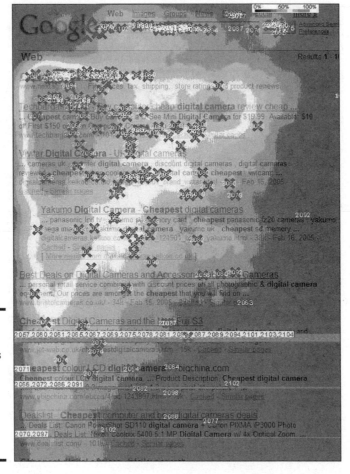

Figure 3-2:
Enquiro
dubbed this
2005 eye-
tracking
study's
results the
Golden
Triangle.

The SERP pictured in Figure 3-3 is just one possible configuration. Also, Mediative's study found that today's searcher tends to view more of the listings but spend less time looking at each one (1.17 seconds compared to just under 2 seconds in 2005, according to the study). Searchers also tend to look farther down the page, perhaps because smartphones have conditioned people to scroll vertically. Whatever the reason, Google SERPs have taught people to check out more than just the top-left results. That means more opportunity to be seen in the SERPs — though your listing has only about a second to make a good impression.

Searcher behavior on mobile devices is another thing entirely. As we mention earlier, people routinely and quickly scroll down. But that doesn't mean that the ranking advantage is spread evenly among the top results.

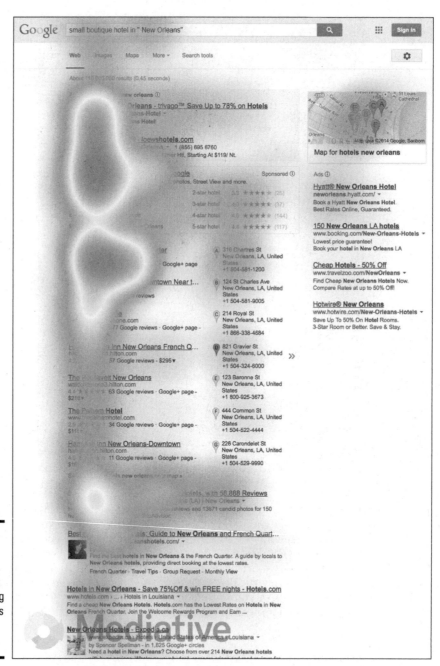

Figure 3-3:
A heat
map from
Mediative's
eye-tracking
study shows
a different
pattern.

Identifying Mobile Users' Search Patterns

At the start of 2014, it finally happened: Internet use via mobile devices actually exceeded desktop Internet usage in the U.S. for the first time. Face it, everyone has a smartphone these days, and people are increasingly using those handy devices, tablets like the iPad and the new midsize range of *phablets* (oversized phone-tablet devices) to go online.

Website owners need to take this trend seriously. If your website is not mobile-friendly, you're probably already losing business, or turning off potential customers. People are not as forgiving as they once were with a slow-loading page or a site that doesn't resize well on a small screen. If that's a concern, you can find lots of help optimizing your site for mobile users over in Book IV, Chapter 3. But here, we look at how users view search on a mobile device.

Mobile SERP features

Mobile devices range from smartphones to tablets, with many different sizes of screens. Because the viewing area on a mobile device is usually much smaller than a desktop computer screen, users have gotten used to scrolling quickly to see more. Sometimes not much shows in the initial view. Figure 3-4 contains iPhone results of a search for [Lakers tickets] using the Google search app.

Figure 3-4: Mobile search results on an iPhone.

In this instance, the search for [Lakers tickets] turned up two ads sitting squarely at the top, blocking nearly all the organic results below them. Unlike with a desktop SERP, the searcher cannot just scan to find a relevant listing. The only remedy is to scroll down.

Eventually, this search results set displays lots of organic listings plus additional SERP elements such as images and news article links. But it takes some finger scrolling to see them.

Mobile's impact on ranking

It turns out that searcher behavior is a lot different on a mobile device, and this difference puts ranking positions in a slightly new light.

A very interesting study by seoClarity looked at *click-through rates* (the percentage of time a user clicks on a listing) on desktop versus mobile SERPs. The study tracked clicks over a three-month period (June–August 2014), a period that avoids much seasonal fluctuation. Figure 3-5 shows the results of the study in two line graphs — one showing the CTR (click-through rate) for all the different ranking positions on desktop SERPs, and the second for mobile SERPs.

In the top graph, desktop click-throughs show the typical curve we'd expect to see — the top ranking position gets the most clicks, with the remaining rankings descending in click-throughs from there. So being No. 2 is better than being No. 3, No. 3 is better than No.4, and so on down the page.

Not so for the mobile SERP. The study found that CTR does not follow a predictable linear pattern from one ranking position to the next. The top spot still receives the most clicks, and the second position the second highest number of clicks. But the next best place to be is No. 4, according to the study, followed by No. 5. The third position's CTR falls in a trough, with the same low CTR as No. 6.

Another interesting thing to note: Look at how many more click-throughs the top-ranking position gets on a mobile SERP versus desktop — 27.7 percent of mobile users clicked the first result, compared to only 19.3 percent on a desktop SERP! Doesn't that make you want to rank in mobile search?

Understanding how changes to the search results page and different search platforms can affect traffic and click-throughs is important. Even when the SERPs change in look and feel, you can make an educated guess about the effect of those changes based on the trends discussed in this section. Keeping up with the changing SERPs and how to fine-tune your optimization campaign in response is an important part of SEO.

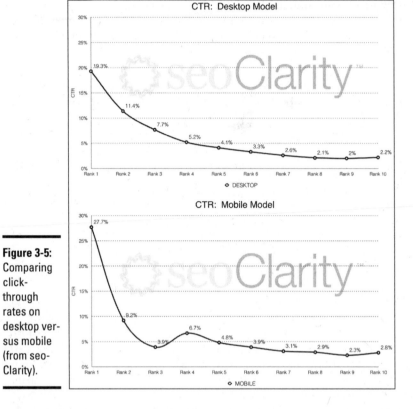

Discovering the Features of a Search Results Page

We've already covered how search engines can display various types of content besides just text links on a results page. In this section, you dig deeper into what makes up all those different elements, which ones you as a site owner can influence, and what it all means to you as you aim your SEO campaigns.

Blended results

The term *blended results* (dubbed *Universal search* by Google) refers to the integration of results from many different verticals into a SERP. Google started this trend years ago, and now all the major engines blend together different types of results. The intent of this blending is to increase the chance that the results will satisfy the user's needs.

Most SERPs today contain blended results. In fact, about 81 percent of Google searches bring back a blended SERP, based on a December 2013 study by Searchmetrics. The study revealed that videos and images show up the most often, as Table 3-1 shows.

Table 3-1	Universal Search Integrations in Google.com
Vertical Result Type	*Frequency of Appearance in SERPs (Market Share)**
Videos	14 percent
Images	35 percent
News	6 percent
Shopping	44 percent
Maps	1 percent

*Note: Market shares add up to more than 100 percent because SERPs can contain more than one type of blended result.

Effects of blended search

You can see why blended search impacts search engine optimization in a big way. The eye-tracking research shows how people skip around a SERP in order to find what they're looking for. Adding an image to the search results, especially one that pops up high on the page, leads searchers' eyes to jump to it, making the spots above it on the page not as important as they used to be. That means that, in a blended results page with an image, instead of being the No. 1 or No. 2 result, you might actually be happier in the No. 4 spot, under the image where the eye will naturally jump to next.

Knowledge Graph

The *Knowledge Graph* is a database system launched by Google in May 2012. Beyond just storing facts, the Knowledge Graph connects information about various *entities* (people, places, and things) to understand how they are related. The Knowledge Graph enables Google to take all those facts in its database and start to make sense of the connections between them. Not only does this type of understanding help the search engine decipher what a searcher is asking for, it also affects the results.

Effects of the Knowledge Graph on SERPs

Knowledge Graph elements show up in all kinds of ways on Google SERPs. With such a vast knowledge repository, Google often takes the direct route and displays just what (it thinks) the searcher wants to know right on the results page. Users benefit because they can get a quick answer to their question without even leaving Google. Website owners have mixed feelings about the Knowledge Graph, because while it's possible to get your own site quoted or linked to from within a KG element, more often Google seems to be competing with websites for clicks. We talk more about how to deepen your site content to hold your own against the Knowledge Graph in Book V, Chapter 3.

Figure 3-6 shows an example of the Knowledge Graph at work. Searching for the query [flights from Los Angeles to Paris] brings up a SERP that displays no organic listings above the fold at all. Ads appear at the top and right column, as usual. Below that is an interactive Knowledge Graph element that lets you choose your travel dates and see flight choices and prices. Organic web links for Kayak, Expedia, and the rest of the usual travel sites do appear on this SERP but are visible only if the user scrolls below the Knowledge Graph feature.

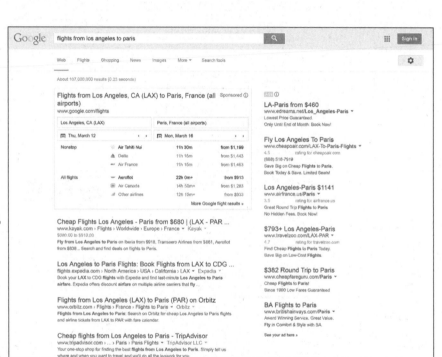

Figure 3-6: An interactive Knowledge Graph element in a Google.com SERP.

Other Knowledge Graph features take up less space or are arranged in a less obstructive way (from an SEO point of view). For example, Figure 3-7 shows a Google SERP for the query [Los Angeles Angels of Anaheim]. The engine interprets what the searcher might be after, and the search engine dishes up organic links to websites about this baseball team with blended results from the Google Images and News vertical engines as well as the following Knowledge Graph elements:

✦ Game information about the team's next scheduled game

✦ Stadium picture, map and background information, as well as user reviews and links to search results pages about upcoming events

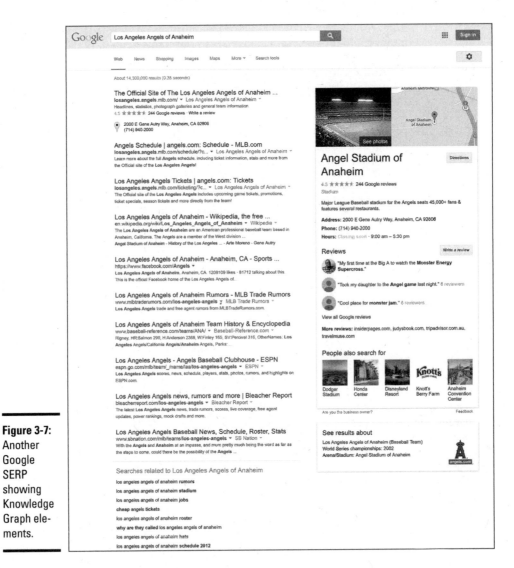

Figure 3-7: Another Google SERP showing Knowledge Graph elements.

Hummingbird and the semantic search revolution

On September 26, 2013, Google dropped a bombshell on the search industry: It announced that its search algorithm had been completely rewritten and had been live for over a month already. The startling thing was that the transition had been so seamless, virtually no one had noticed! Nevertheless, under the hood, the new algorithm (named *Hummingbird*) revolutionized Google's approach.

When Hummingbird flew in, the old way of just matching up strings of char-acters in a search query to web pages containing those character strings went out the window. With Hummingbird, Google's method changed "from strings to things." Hummingbird transformed Google from a search engine into a knowledge engine.

The search engine's goal, as always, is to make search results more rel-evant to the user's actual intent. But the new way of doing that which Hummingbird ushered in is more broadly known as *semantic search*. In a semantic search world, the search engine begins with user intent and tries to understand the query itself, not just the keywords in the query. Basically, a semantic search engine tries to understand the meaning and context just as a human would. Next, semantic search technology seeks to extract enti-ties from its database as answers and display personalized search results that are just right for the individual user.

Effects of Hummingbird on search

Earlier in this chapter, we tell you about how the Knowledge Base has changed search results by using injected answers right alongside the ads, blended results, and organic listings. That's happening across the board in the main SERPs for the majority of text and voice searches across all types of devices. With Hummingbird's semantic search technology, Google has been able to improve the accuracy of those answer boxes and other KG ele-ments. But Hummingbird has had an even greater effect on how people enter a search.

Hummingbird paved the way for *voice search*, or the ability to search by speaking a query into a search engine using a smartphone or other device. The ability to understand spoken search queries in terms of user intent and contextual meaning, such as are found in spoken conversation, is an advanced application of semantic search.

Consider how you'd talk to your friend about a movie you want to see. "Did you see the trailer for 'Awesome Flick II' yet?" you might say as an opener. When your friend responds, you can continue discussing the movie — the lead actors, why you're excited, the special effects, where it's playing, and so on. In all that conversation, you probably never say "Awesome Flick II" again (hopefully not!). But your friend isn't confused by your wanton use of pro-nouns; the conversation topic remains clear.

Imagine being able to talk to a computer that way. Semantic search is revolu-tionizing how people search because they can interact not in keywords, but in conversational style. And this is especially true for mobile.

Mobile use is growing across the globe, and with it the number of searches performed on a smartphone or tablet. In response, the search engines and mobile device providers are cranking out software to win the race to provide the best user experience. A big part of that is how well the device can provide answers to a user's questions.

Not surprisingly, Google's version of voice-assisted search is currently way out in front of the pack. (See the sidebar "Meet the voice assistants" for details.) Because Google has access to data not only from search, but also from other Google properties, including YouTube, Google Drive, Gmail, Google+, and more, it's likely to continue setting the standard in semantic search.

Meet the voice assistants

With semantic search, people can now talk to a search engine just like they would to a person. Well, almost. But the *voice assistants*, the software that can interpret your spoken language (using voice-recognition technology) and understand your meaning well enough to give an answer or perform some other task (based on the underlying Knowledge Graph), are getting more intelligent all the time.

If you haven't tried speaking a search into your smartphone, you're missing out. It's a bit mind-blowing to be able to converse with a computer program. For instance, you could ask, "When was Abraham Lincoln president?" After the voice assistant replies, you can ask a series of follow-up questions such as "How old was he when he died?", "Who was his wife?", "Where was she from?" and so on. Though you never mention the key term "Lincoln" again, the voice assistant can understand your meaning, just like in a human conversation.

The three main voice assistants are:

✓ **Google Now** — on Google Android devices

✓ **Siri** — on Apple devices such as iPhone

✓ **Cortana** — on Microsoft Bing/Windows devices, such as Windows phone

Each of them can work only as well as its underlying knowledge base can interpret a spoken query. To test this and find out which voice assistant's knowledge box was the most accurate, an October 2014 study by Eric Enge of Stone Temple Consulting compared how the three different voice assistants handled thousands of queries specifically chosen to trigger a knowledge box element (also known as an *answer box*) in the results. In the following figure reprinted from the study results, you see how often the knowledge boxes tracked completely answered the query.

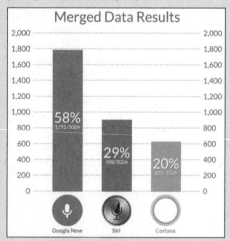

The study found Google Now to be the clear winner, providing the most accurate and relevant information.

Chapter 4: Getting Your Site to Appear in the Right Results

In This Chapter

✔ Seeking traffic as your real goal

✔ Avoiding spam

✔ Understanding how behavioral searching impacts your ranking

✔ Introducing intent-driven search

✔ Using vertical search engines to your advantage

✔ Getting into local search results

✔ Signing up for paid ads in the various search engines

*I*f the Internet were a mall, Google would be the biggest department store and Yahoo and Bing would be the smaller ones in between. But a mall is more than just its department stores: You can also shop in dozens of specialty stores, food venues, merchant carts, and so on. In this chapter, you meet the specialty stores of searching, the vertical engines, and find out how to make sure your product (your site) displays on those stores' shelves.

In this chapter, you discover how to put your products in front of customers by changing your focus to traffic, not ranking; discover how to avoid spam tactics that could hurt your site; and gain an understanding how personalized searches change what your audience sees on the search results page. You also find out about how to get into the local search results and how to get started with a pay per click campaign in the main engines.

Seeking Traffic, Not Ranking

First, a couple of reminders are in order. Your search engine optimization efforts, if done well, can earn your site a higher ranking in search results pages. However, do not confuse the means with the end. Keep in mind your real goal — getting lots and lots of interested people to visit your site. What you really want to do is drive more web traffic your way, and ranking represents just one means for achieving that end. In this chapter, you discover another reason to set your sights on traffic rather than ranking — technological advances (namely personalization and semantic search) are causing ranking to become less important.

Avoiding Spam

Here's the second important reminder: Be sure that you are earning that traffic, not attempting to cheat to get it. In the search engine world, cheating is known as spam. *Spam* involves deliberately building web pages, links, or signals that try to trick a search engine into offering inappropriate, redundant, or poor-quality search results. Spam is not only unethical but also can cause your site to be penalized or even removed from an index entirely. So you definitely want to know how to avoid it.

Here's a basic spam illustration: Site A is well written, content-rich, and exceptionally relevant for the search query [sailboat rigging]. Site B is not as well written, not as content-rich, and not as relevant. Site B implements a few spam tactics to trick the engine into believing that Site B's more relevant, and suddenly Site B outranks Site A for searches on [sailboat rigging]. What's the end result? It lowers users' satisfaction with the relevancy of their search results in that search engine, hurts the user experience because they don't find what they need, and slaps the face of those working at the search engine company who are responsible for making sure that users actually see relevant content and are happy.

Is it any wonder that the search engines enforce anti-spam rules? It's one thing to want to improve the quality, presentation, and general use of keyword phrases on your web page; it's an entirely different thing to attempt to trick the engines into giving you higher rankings without providing the real goods. (Because spam, whether intentional or unintentional, can get your site in trouble, refer to Chapter 6 of this minibook for some specific spam techniques to avoid.)

A note about spam: Spam is largely based on perception. For example, when you get email that you do not want, you consider it spam even though you might have opted to receive email from that company. However, if you're planning a trip and get email about your travel destination, you don't think of that email as spam, even if it was unsolicited. Your interest makes the email not spam. (*Note:* Search engines do the same thing by targeting ads to the user's interest. This leads to more clicks and higher user satisfaction surrounding advertising. But we digress . . . .)

In the SEO world, it's the search engine's perception that counts. The search engine can act as judge and jury, so even the appearance of spam must be guarded against in order to protect your website's good standing and rankings. You learn more about penalties and how to avoid them in the next chapter of this minibook.

Understanding Personalized Search's Impact on Ranking

Have you ever noticed that your search results usually differ from another person's search results — even when you both type the same query into the same search engine? This is a scenario that is becoming more and more common. Before you think this means that search engine optimization is completely futile and throw your hands up in exasperation, read on. Here's what's really going on.

To make each searcher's results as relevant as possible, it makes sense that search engines would want to continually improve their capability to understand the intent, context, and all the other clues related to each search. That involves getting to know the searcher, the query, and the results better.

Search engines use a combination of techniques to *personalize* the results page for each searcher and each query. One primary method that search engines use to know the searcher part of the equation better is called *behavioral search,* which refers to customizing a results page based on the user's previous search behavior. Behavioral search tracks the searches you've run, sites you've visited, and files you've downloaded, so the search engine can adjust new search results to include items that will interest you. But behavioral data is only part of the complex set of signals that contribute to personalized results.

Search engines can individually customize search results based on the user's

✦ Recent search behavior

✦ Location

✦ Web history

✦ Demographic information

✦ Community

Personalization means that the major search engines use a lot more than just keyword ranking to determine the order of results. This is down to the individual-user level. With behavioral search and other forms of personalization, results revolve around users, not a single boiler plate algorithm.

Behavioral targeting particularly affects the *paid results* you see (that is, ads or sponsored links that site owners have paid the search engine to display on results pages, based on keywords). For instance, if you run a search for [coffee mugs] followed by a search for [java], the search engine throws in a few extra paid results for coffee-related products at the top or sides of the page.

Even if you're not logged in, the data from your search history may influence your search engine results, making your search results different from what you would see if you were a new searcher for [java]. Your previous search for [coffee mugs] influenced the search engine to assume you meant [java] as in coffee, rather than the computer language.

Personalizing results by location

Thanks to some fairly simple (and occasionally inaccurate) technology, search engines can tell where you are! Your computer's IP address identifies your approximate city location to a search engine, which can then personalize your search results to include local listings for your search terms. This technique, often called *geotargeting,* comes into play the most when you search for items that involve brick-and-mortar businesses or services that need to be provided locally (for example, searches for the terms [furniture reupholstery] or [house painters] would bring up some local businesses mixed in with the other results).

Personalizing results by web history

Search engines can further understand searchers' intentions by looking at their personal *web history,* or the records of their previous searches and the websites they've visited or bookmarked. How far back the records go is unclear, although Google once stated that it anonymizes the data after 18 months. It's important to note that Google can only track your web history between sessions while you're signed in to your Google account. Because the extra services like free email and customizable home pages are truly wonderful, many people have these accounts and may not realize their surfing behavior is being recorded.

Google does give you ways to delete your web history or block the data collection; however, there is no way to prevent Google from personalizing your results within a *session.* A session is any time you perform multiple searches from within the same browser window without closing it entirely and clearing cookies. Google will always tailor your results based on the searches you have already done in a single session.

Want to see your own web history the way it's stored in Google's database? You might be surprised at how much of a trail you've left behind. Here's where you can go to view your private web history: `https://history. google.com/`.

Personalizing results by demographics

Search engines often know demographic information about you, such as your gender, age, home address, or city, as well as your interests. You may provide this information to them when you first sign up for an account. Search engines can't get this data without your consent. However, lack of direct input doesn't mean they're not going to try to infer information about you based on what you have told them. Your income could be assumed based on your location, or your gender could be assumed based on your search history. They also learn about you by tracking what you do within their site. For instance, if you do a search on their map and, for map-searching convenience later, mark your home address as your starting location, the search engine reasonably assumes that that's where you live.

Personalizing results based on Google products

If you're signed in to your Google account while searching, Google may include information relevant to your search query that is pulled from:

✦ Gmail

✦ Google Calendar

✦ Google+

This has practical applications as well as one very powerful SEO opportunity. First, on a practical note, it might be convenient for you to see upcoming events pulled from your own personal Google Calendar within search results. You can query [my events] to see a SERP full of your own private events, or type [what time is my next flight] to see flight information, to give just two examples pulled from Google Calendar.

The integration between Google Search and Google+ (the engine's social network) creates powerful community building and SEO benefits. The way your Google+ activity can impact SERPs is this: Your results can include any relevant content that's visible to you in Google+, such as posts from people in your circles and links that those people recommend (by clicking +1). These results show up only for you; however, consider the ripple effect. If someone who has a lot of followers on Google+ recommends your post or web page with a link, anyone who has that influencer circled may see your listing show up in his or her personalized results, assuming that the person searches for a relevant query. So even if your listing doesn't rank, it still might show up on the first page of the SERPs for a lot of people. You can learn more about Google+ and other advantages of social networks in Book VI, Chapter 5.

Opting out of personalized results

All these personalization techniques enable search engines to target your search results more specifically to your individual needs. If this results in more relevant listings, it may not be a bad thing. (At least that's the position the search engines take.)

You might want to opt out of personalized results because of privacy concerns. But in addition, when you're evaluating keywords and doing SEO research, you don't want the results to reflect your personal biases. You want to see the results that most people see, most of the time.

 You have ways to opt out of personalization in Google. Most important, you need to be signed out. Google's Web History feature tracks you only while you're signed in to your Google account, so if you sign out, it's turned off — until you sign in again. However, the search engine can still *customize* your results even if you're signed out, unless you also disable that feature. Google does offer a Yes/No switch to turn personalization off altogether, and it offers ways to delete history records or pause tracking temporarily, but all these options are a little buried. To find them, go to Google Help and find the topic "Search and browse privately." Turning off Web History does not prevent Google from applying behavioral search targeting to your searches based on session behavior. To turn off all result customization, choose Disable Customizations Based on Search Activity from `http://google.com/history/optout` while signed out of your Google account.

Using News, Images, Books, and Other Search Verticals to Rank

The major general search engines (like Google, Yahoo, or Bing) have categories in which users can search for specific types of content, such as images or shopping result. Getting your content to show up in these categories, or verticals, is fairly simple and requires little extra work. Ranking well is another story. Ranking in a vertical is a lot like ranking in a general search engine. To optimize images, video, shopping, news, books, and apps, you must tailor your listing so that certain attributes are even more specific. In the next few sections, we highlight the most important attributes for ranking in each vertical.

Video

With the advances in streaming technology and faster Internet connection speeds, video is becoming more and more popular as time goes on. Like increasing the rank of your website, you can use similar techniques to make sure your video has a chance of achieving a high ranking.

Getting search engine ranking for your video is as simple as this:

+ **Place keywords in the metadata of a video.** *Metadata* is descriptive text, containing mostly keywords, that can be placed in the HTML of the video file. You want this text to both describe the video and give the spiders something to look at.

✦ **Place keywords in your video's filename.** Remember to keep your keywords for both the metadata description and the filename specific and relevant.

✦ **Use YouTube (**www.youtube.com**) to host your video.** YouTube was acquired by Google, so any video on YouTube gets spidered and indexed a lot faster than it would on other video-hosting sites.

✦ **Link from your video to your website.** This could help drive up your site's traffic and ranking. Of course, you especially benefit from this strategy if the video you post becomes popular (but don't ask what makes a video popular, because not even Hollywood can predict accurately what people will like).

✦ **Include text about the video in the page area surrounding the video link, if possible.** Keep in mind that video, along with images, can be spidered. Spiders can read and index the metadata and the text surrounding the video, as long as the text is descriptive of the video, full of keywords, and relevant to a user's search. In Figure 4-1, note the title and description, which contain relevant keywords. Remember, Google loves this.

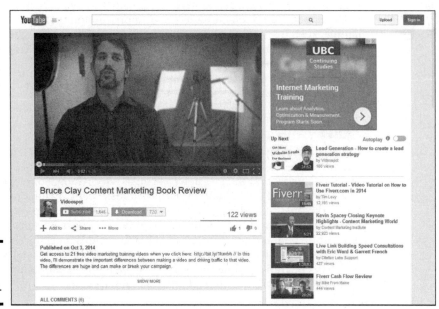

Figure 4-1:
Your video
on YouTube.

Keep in mind that because YouTube is a separate site, the video is not considered "your" content. You want to host the video on your own site as well so that you get credit for it as part of your content. Always link back to your site in the description of the video and in the video file itself.

Images

You can apply many of the tips we state in the previous section to images, as well. Images and video can be identified by topic as long as the text surrounding them relates to the image or video. Spiders are also looking at the filename, so instead of naming your image file `00038.jpg`, call it `redporsche.jpg` or something equally descriptive. Definitely include `Alt` attribute text for every image on your website. `Alt` *attributes* are used to describe an image for users who are using screen readers or when an image does not display. In some browsers, this text becomes user-visible when they move their mouse over the image. Spiders also read and index the `Alt` attribute text. Because people (and spiders) read it (it's required by disabilities laws supporting visually impaired users), it's worth the effort to write something meaningful. For example, the HTML of the image of the red Porsche could look like this:

```
<img src="redporsche.jpg" alt="Red 2005 Porsche with leather
    interior">
```

A short, simple, descriptive phrase is all you need for the `Alt` attribute. Stuffing it with keywords, however, is considered evil and might get your site dropped (see Book I, Chapter 6 for more info on that point). Keep it simple, keep it short, and keep it to the point. Consider the size of the image as a guideline: Smaller images probably only need a couple words to explain what they are. Larger images might require several words. Don't go overboard. If you have paragraphs of information about the image, consider putting that on the web page as content.

News

Getting into a news vertical is a bit tricky. You might have a company website with a news section that you frequently update with articles and recent events, yet it won't rank in a news vertical. Why? Google only considers a site a news site if it is updated multiple times a week by multiple authors and is devoted to nothing but news. Your company News page, for example, would not be considered for inclusion in Google News because even though it might be updated several times a week, it resides on a site that also sells products or services. Compare this to a site like SearchEngineLand.com, which is updated multiple times a day by many different authors and exists to do nothing more than report search-industry news.

The only way to make your company news available for news searches is to distribute your article and hope that a journalist gets intrigued enough to write about it. The primary ways to distribute news are press releases and social media. To issue a press release, you can choose from a variety of different news wire services (PR Newswire, PRWeb, eReleases, and so on); the fees vary depending on the length of your article, the geographic region you want to cover, and other factors. After you submit your press release, it's available for any news agency to pick up and publish, increasing your company exposure and potentially your site traffic.

TIP

You can monitor who picks up your news either by using the optional tools provided by your news wire service or by creating a free Google Alert. You can sign up for a Google Alert at www.google.com/alerts and enter your company name, keywords, or other descriptor for your search terms. Google then automatically emails you whenever an article relevant to your keywords hits the web!

Shopping

Google's Shopping vertical engine no longer includes organic listings, so the only way you can get your products to rank there is by paying for a *PLA,* or a Google product listing ad. Organic shopping-related listings do appear in regular web searches, although even there, ads are by far the most prominent results. Having *rich snippets,* which are extra pieces of information displayed with your SERP listing such as price, rating, and so on, can help make your listing stand out. (You learn more about how to get rich snippets in Book IV, Chapter 4.) Having a video, image, or news article talk about you is another indirect way to show up. For example, the Google SERP in Figure 4-2 shows paid ads at the top and all down the right side; however, in the left column you can see an organic listing for the brand manufacturer's site at the top, and then a couple news articles, followed by several organic listings from retail sites.

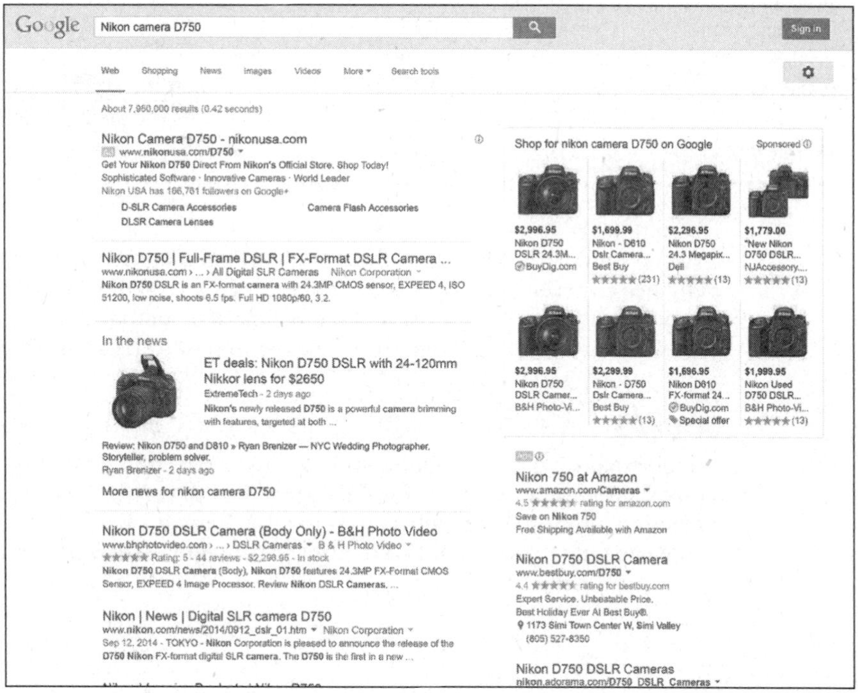

Figure 4-2:
Shopping results can appear organically in Google's main web search, but not in the Shopping vertical.

Over at Bing, shopping results no longer appear in a separate vertical at all. In 2013, Bing merged shopping results into its main web search. As Figure 4-3 shows, when you do a search that Bing thinks has shopping intent, the SERP just automatically includes paid and organic results as well as a "snapshot" of products you might like in the right-hand column.

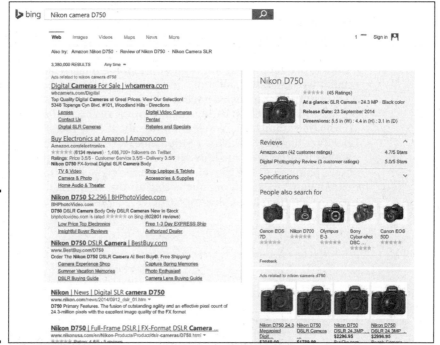

Figure 4-3: Bing shopping results (paid and organic) display within the main web search only.

Yahoo retains the only true shopping vertical among the big three search engines (`https://shopping.yahoo.com/`). Organic shopping results may appear among ads, and products may link to a comparison of many different retailers, as in the "Choose from 5 stores" results shown in Figure 4-4.

Books

Google has a vertical engine dedicated to books. If you've published a book, this is great news for you. Because specialized, vertical results are often blended into the main web search results, having a book increases your chances for ranking in both the Books and regular search engines.

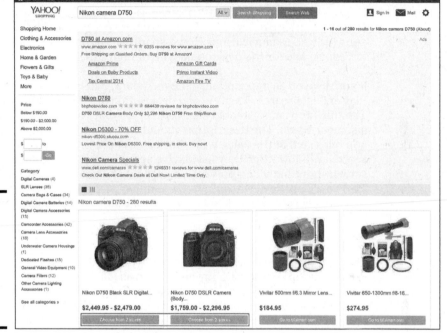

Figure 4-4:
Yahoo has
the only
true shop-
ping verti-
cal engine
among the
big three.

Google says that it chooses results "out of millions of books, including pre-views and text, from libraries and publishers worldwide." It is not stated exactly what communicates to Google that a book exists and needs to be indexed. Even if you self-publish a book, the publishing service you use should assign an *ISBN* (a unique book identification number). Selling the book on Amazon.com or another major book retailer's site probably ensures that Google's spiders find it. Also, you can create a page about your book on your website and include *structured data,* which means marking up the book title, author, and other fields with specific codes that spiders can read. (More on structured data in Book IV, Chapter 4.)

Apps

Another vertical engine currently found only in Google indexes *apps,* which are software applications that can be downloaded onto a mobile (or some-times desktop) device. In the mobile ecosystem, apps are all the rage; they can help you do almost anything — track your expenses, monitor your sleep cycles, watch videos, play games, and lots more.

Having a vertical engine just for searching apps means that Google takes its popularity seriously. In fact, Google also operates the *Google Play* (https://play.google.com) store, where people can find and purchase apps (as well as movies, music, and so forth), so there's also money in apps for Google and for the developers who optimize their apps to be found there.

If you develop an app, optimize the metadata to help it be found in Google Play and in a search. The title and description are the most important parts. The title (app name) should clearly identify what your app is and possibly also your brand. The description should describe in a nutshell what your app does so that the value it provides shows above the fold, the view users see in a window when they first arrive at a page before scrolling down. The screen shots and video preview you provide help convince users to download your app. Reviews, ratings, the number of installs, and the length of time people keep it installed are also strong signals for ranking apps.

Maps

Map search is an ever-evolving technology, with Google in the lead. Try this: Run a desktop search for a product (such as [Nikon D750]) in Google's main web search and then click Maps. Unfazed, Google takes the addresses of any retailers including in the organic results and plots them (complete with business details, customer reviews, and so on) on a map. Typically, people search for a business name or category or an address using Maps.

Mobile is where map searching really shines. When you're out and about and suddenly need caffeine, finding the nearest coffee shop is just a voice search away — and the results come back with a map and directions, based on your current location. In fact, the search engines figure that someone on a mobile device (especially a smartphone) is far more likely to want a nearby business, so mobile search results contain a much higher percentage of local map results than do traditional desktop searches.

Showing Up in Local Search Results

You now know that local searches provide another playing field for your website to attract potential customers. Better yet, they give you a much smaller field, where your business has an excellent chance of being a star player.

Making sure that your business shows up in a map search and/or local results starts with setting up your business profile in the major search engines. Being consistent with your business name, address, and phone number is important, as is specifying the categories of products or services you offer. You want to send the clearest possible signals of what your business provides. The following sections show step-by-step instructions (which are accurate at the time of this writing) for getting your site to show up in local-oriented searches. Note that there is no charge for submitting a basic local listing, so think of it as free advertising!

Getting your site into the local engines has another benefit. The traffic for local term searches in a broad-base engine (such as Google) far outweighs the traffic you get from a local-only search engine. Search engines such as Google, Yahoo, and Bing are the first stop for a consumer in search of a solution. However, listing your business in the local search engines also ensures that your site shows up for general searches that include *geo-targeting* (search queries that contain a city, ZIP code, or other geographic term). For example, if you have a florist's shop in the Bronx, your shop's website would come up when someone searches for [Bronx florist].

Getting into Google My Business

Much like its main search index, Google My Business is the most popular local vertical out there. Submitting your site to Google My Business enables you to show up for local queries, appear on Google Maps for searches there, and, of course, appear for relevant general queries via blended search when Google detects that a local result is appropriate. Here is a step-by-step guide to getting your site listed in Google My Business:

1. **Go to Google My Business (**`www.google.com/business/`**), and then click the Get on Google button.**

   First you'll find out whether your business is already listed. You can also do a regular search in Google for your company name, and if your business already has a local listing, it will show up in the results. This can happen when Google has put your business on its map. But it may still be open to public editing if you haven't yet verified ownership.

2. **Sign in to your Google account (if you aren't already signed in). Then enter your business name (and address) to find it on the map.**

3. **If your listing is there, click it and proceed to verify ownership (if you see View Dashboard, it's already verified).**

4. **If your listing isn't there yet, click Add Your Business. Complete the business setup form. You'll then follow the instructions to verify that you are the business owner.**

Be sure to enter the same *NAP* (name, address, phone number) for your business every time. That means that if we use "Bruce Clay, Inc." in one local engine and then carelessly enter "BruceClay Incorporated" in another, we just confuse the search engines and possibly impact our ability to rank in local search. Being accurate with your local profiles up front can prevent a lot of hassle trying to correct inconsistencies across all the various sites and databases later.

Getting into Yahoo Local

Yahoo (`www.yahoo.com`) is an extremely popular home page for many people on the web; as a result, Yahoo's local product receives a fair amount of traffic. Like Google, Yahoo also integrates its local results into a map search and incorporates them in blended search results. Follow these simple steps to increase your site's exposure for relevant local searches:

1. **Check Yahoo Local (`http://local.yahoo.com`) to see whether your business is already listed. Enter your company name or type of business, enter your city or ZIP code, and click the Search button.**

2. **Scan the results to see if your business is already listed. If not, go to** `https://smallbusiness.yahoo.com/local-listings`.

3. **Click Sign In near the top of the page and sign in to your Yahoo account.**

   (You have a Yahoo account if you've ever created a free email or My Yahoo account.) If you are a new user, click Sign In and then Create Account.

4. **Go to the Local Marketing section of Yahoo Small Business (`https://smallbusiness.yahoo.com/local-listings`). Scroll down to Try Local Basic Listing for Free and click the Sign Up button.**

   Figure 4-5 shows what the pop-up sign-up form looks like after you click the Sign Up button to try local basic listing for free. Fill out the sign-up forms as accurately and completely as possible. Be accurate and consistent with your name, address, and phone number — three elements so crucial to online visibility for local or brick-and-mortar businesses that the industry has an acronym for them, NAP.

5. **You'll see an option to sign up for Yahoo Localworks (for $29.99 a month) or list only on Yahoo for free. Click the link "No thanks! I only want to list my business on Yahoo."**

   Use the following form to complete your Yahoo Basic Listing for your business, adding a business email and website address, and then clicking the Submit button. You'll be given an option of ways to verify your listing, so choose your preferred method from the options of call, text, or postcard mailer.

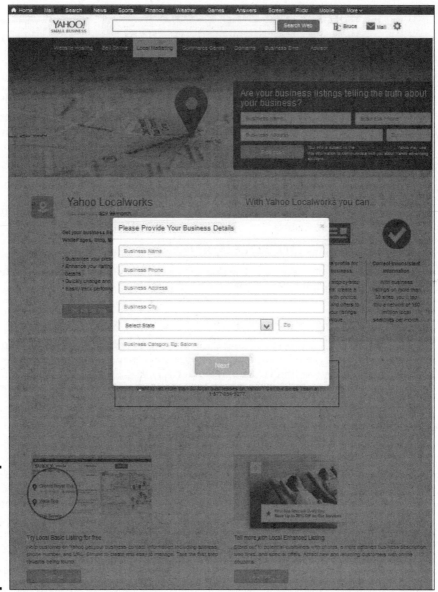

Figure 4-5:
The sign-up form to include your business in Yahoo Local.

Yahoo offers a basic listing for free, but if you want to add coupons, photos, a logo, and so on, you have to upgrade to an "enhanced" listing with a small monthly fee.

Getting into Bing Places

Microsoft's local product is the new kid on the block, but this scrappy underdog is worth the effort it takes to sign up. Follow these step-by-step directions to get into the local results and capture a new market:

1. **Go to** `https://www.bingplaces.com/` **and click Get Started.**

2. **Enter your country/region and then search for your business by the phone number, name, or location. If your business is found, select it. If it isn't found, you will see a Create New Business button.**

3. **You need to sign in to your Microsoft account.**

   Sign up if you don't have an account.

4. **Complete the online forms by following the instructions; then submit your listing.**

5. **Choose the most appropriate categories.**

   Wait two or three weeks for verification via postal mail or choose the option for verification via email.

Using other resources to aid local ranking

In addition to submitting your website to the big three search engines directly, you ought to know about the other highly visible places where people can find you online. Especially if you're a local business and need to attract customers in your local geographic area, don't miss out on directories and review sites.

Local directories

Consider getting yourself listed in niche local directories such as Citysearch, Yellowpages.com, Superpages, and more. Google and the other search engines use these smaller directories as signals to their local algorithm, and the search engines consider your inclusion in these directories as further verification of the trustworthiness of your business. Additionally, local-oriented sites often rank well for targeted terms, which can bring you even more traffic. You can use sites such as Yext (`http://www.yext.com/`) or Moz Local (`https://moz.com/local`) to monitor your listings on your own.

Review sites

Reviews can make or break a local business today. People have always instinctively looked for community consensus to help them make decisions, but with reviews and ratings showing up in searches now as the norm, it's never been easier to find out what people think. As a business owner, reviews give you credibility not only to prospective customers but also to a search engine. Google wants to show users the "best" listings, and reviews and ratings can influence ranking. That's especially true for people running a search on a mobile device.

Being found on a popular review site (such as Yelp.com and many others) can also give you increased visibility in the SERPs. Consider the results Google provides for the search [chinese restaurants] in Figure 4-6. "Szechuwan Garden Restaurant" shows up no less than four times — twice in the local carousel at the top of the page, and twice in the web listings — all organically! That's because in addition to ranking for its own website, the restaurant has a review page on Urbanspoon.com that also ranks.

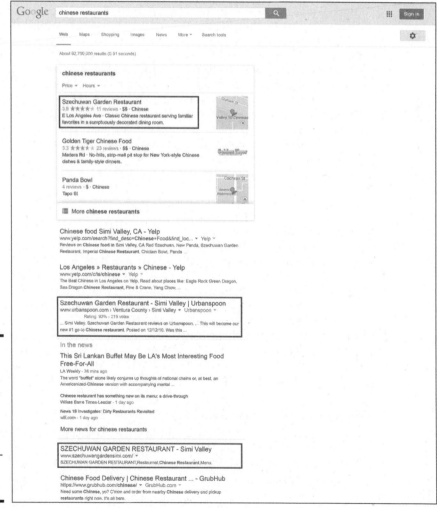

Figure 4-6: In local search results, reviews of your business can rank in addition to your own listing.

There are definitely right and wrong ways to get customers to review your business online. You should never coerce or reward anyone for doing it, or the review site itself may penalize your business. That means no offering a free drink for writing a review, and no setting up a computer for your customers to use to submit a review while they're in your store. Still, you can inform people that you are in a particular review site in case they want to add their comments, and you can display Yelp's or another review site's logo somewhere near your checkout area, as gentle reminders.

Making the Most of Paid Search Results

We briefly go over paid search results in Book I, Chapter 2 for Google, Yahoo, and Bing. If you're wondering what the difference between them is, think of it as similar to buying a commercial on television. Running a commercial during the biggest sporting event of the year is going to be much more expensive than running it at 3 a.m. on a local station. The same is true for buying an ad on Google versus buying an ad on one of the less-trafficked search engines. It will be cheaper on the smaller engines, sure, but the odds of someone seeing it are going to be about as low as the price. Price also depends on the popularity of the keyword being bid on. Your best bet for the widest reach when you're getting started with PPC ads is to advertise on one of the three larger engines. Keep in mind that for the most visibility possible, you should probably advertise on as many as you can. In the following sections, we break PPC ads down for you in terms of how to buy on each of the engines, how much you'll be paying, and who is going to see your ad.

Google AdWords

Google AdWords (http://www.google.com/adwords/) is Google's paid search program. It lets you create your own ads, choose your keywords, set your maximum bid price, and specify a budget. If you're having trouble creating ads, Google has a feature to help you create and target your ads. It then matches your ads to the right audience within its network, and you pay only when your ad is clicked. How much you pay varies greatly depending on the keyword because competition drives the bid price. For instance, a keyword like *mesothelioma,* the cancer caused by asbestos, runs about $56 per click. Lawyers love this one because a case could arguably net them hundreds of thousands of dollars, so it's worth getting the one case per hundred clicks, and multiple competitors drive the price up through bidding wars.

Signing up for Google AdWords

You can create an AdWords account for free, choosing a maximum *cost-per-click* (how much you are willing to pay when your ad is clicked) ranging from one cent on up. Google provides a calculator for determining your daily budget, along with information on how to control your costs by setting limits. Google also has stringent editorial guidelines designed to ensure ad effectiveness and discourage spam. Many payment options are available, including automatic and manual payments (via credit or debit card) and monthly invoicing, which requires a credit line.

Placement options

With Google AdWords, you have three placement options available to you. The most common is for your ads to appear on Google search engine results pages based on a keyword trigger. The second option allows your site to show up in the search results pages of Google's distribution partners like AOL and Ask.com. The third option is site-targeted campaigns in which you can have your ads show up on sites in Google's Display Network (via Google's AdSense publisher platform). Display campaigns can be based on a cost-per-1,000-impressions model (a CPM model — the M stands for *mille* and is a holdover from the old printing press days), or a traditional CPC (cost-per-click) model.

Google also offers demographic targeting, allowing advertisers to select gender, age group, annual household income, ethnicity, and children/no children in the household, which allows advertisers to better target their ads across the Google Display Network.

Most people want to advertise on Google because their ad has a chance of appearing across a wide range of websites, like AOL, HowStuffWorks, Ask. com (U.S. and U.K.), T-Online (Europe), Tencent (China), and thousands of others worldwide. Notice in Figure 4-7 how the ads on a Google SERP are targeted to the query in the same way the organic results are.

The major benefits of Google AdWords PPC advertising are

+ **An established brand:** Google gets the most searches (67 percent in August 2014).
+ **Strong distribution network.**
+ **Both pay-per-click and pay-per-impression cost models.**
+ **Site targeting:** For both text and image ads.
+ **Costs automatically reduced:** Google reduces the cost to the lowest price required to maintain your ad's position.
+ **Immediate listings:** Typically, ads go live within 15 minutes.
+ **No minimum monthly spending or monthly fees.**
+ **Daily budget visibility.**

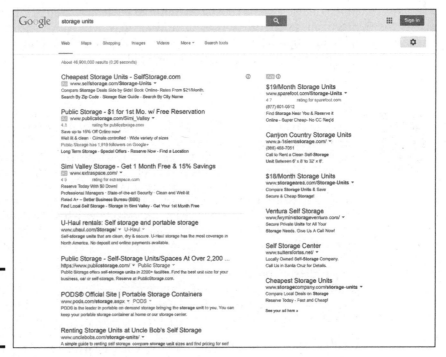

Figure 4-7: A sampling of Google ads.

✦ **Multiple ads:** You can create additional ads to test the effectiveness of your messaging.

✦ **Keyword suggestion tool:** This tool helps provide keyword search and cost estimates.

✦ **Conversion tracking:** This feature helps advertisers track campaign performance by tracking "conversions," or desired actions that you want your visitors to complete when they are on your website.

Yahoo

Because Yahoo switched to using the Bing index and search marketing inventory, you can now buy Yahoo paid listings through Bing Ads. Check out the following section to see how you can advertise in Bing and Yahoo by using the same service.

Bing

Bing's paid search program is called Bing Ads (http://advertise. bingads.microsoft.com/en-us/home). Like Google, Bing Ads offers a keyword research and optimization tool, based in Excel, which enables you to conduct in-depth keyword research. This tool is called Bing Ads Intelligence Tool (`http://advertise.bingads.microsoft.com/en-us/cl/257/training/bing-ads-intelligence-tool`).

Bing Ads

Signing up for Bing Ads is free. You pay only when someone clicks your ad, with cost-per-click bids starting as low as $0.01/click. You can import your search campaign by uploading spreadsheets, or you can even import campaigns from Google AdWords!

Placement options

Bing Ads allows you to target your ads based on user demographics, such as gender, marital status, age, and so forth. On top of that, Bing Ads allows you to run your ads on specific days of the week or certain times of day. If you have an ad that targets teenagers, for example, you can choose to have your ad run after 3 p.m. on weekdays and all day on weekends in order to achieve higher visibility. Like Google, Bing Ads shows search ads in Bing search results. In addition, Bing Ads, much like AdWords, allows advertisers to show Display ads, which show on websites that are opted into the Bing/Yahoo Network.

Bing is the latest engine to have done studies proving that audiences exposed to both search and display ads together deliver a greater positive *brand lift* (that is, user recall and positive associations with the brand) than either type of campaign can yield on its own.

Figure 4-8 shows a typical search ad (top) and a typical display ad (bottom).

These are some of the benefits of Bing Ads:

✦ **Demographic targeting:** Allows you to target specific demographics.

✦ **Cost by segmentation:** Adjusts cost per click to target demographics.

✦ **Search and display ads:** Provides a useful tool for small businesses.

✦ **Tools:** Contains keyword search and optimization tools.

✦ **Reach:** Makes your ads appear on Microsoft's content network, which now includes Yahoo properties, including Yahoo Search.

✦ **Conversion rates:** Typically returns better ROI than other paid search solutions.

✦ **Lower costs:** The cost of bidding on a keyword to have your ad show up is usually lower than Google.

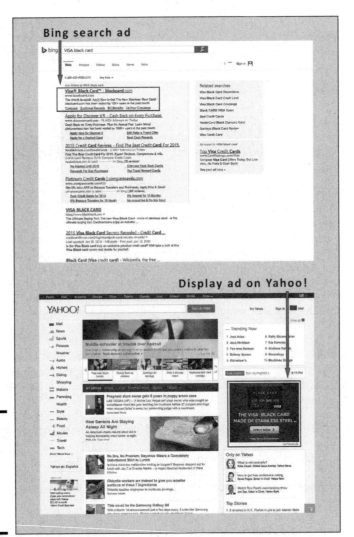

Figure 4-8:
A Bing
search ad
(top) and a
display ad
on Yahoo
(bottom).

Chapter 5: Knowing What Drives Search Results

In This Chapter

✔ **Searching like a power user**

✔ **Using advanced operators to supercharge your search engine optimization**

✔ **Finding specific file types in the vertical search engines**

✔ **Capturing more conversions using the long-tail approach**

✔ **Using Google Instant search suggestions as an intelligence tool**

*I*n this chapter, you discover how to use the search engines like a pro through the use of advanced operators. You also learn how to use vertical engines to get specialized results. You see why it's imperative to capture the so called *long tail* of search, and how predictive searches like Google Instant can be used as a tool to help you turn your site into a search magnet. The expert-searcher skill set definitely complements your role as a search engine optimizer, so we're devoting a whole chapter to it. At the end of this chapter, you get to apply your newfound skills to enhancing your site with keywords targeted for your audience.

A typical search returns many results (commonly in the millions) and may include lots of irrelevant listings. Because search engines find what you tell them to search for, an overly large result set can be chalked up to a too-broad *search query* (the terms typed into the search box). You probably already know some simple techniques for narrowing a search, such as adding more specific terms (such as [bass fishing vacations] instead of just [bass fishing]) or including quotation marks around words that must be an exact phrase. For instance, searching for ["bass fishing vacations"] in quotation marks reduces the result set to just a few hundred listings, compared to more than 600,000 without the quotes. You may even know to click the Advanced Search link to access additional search fields that let you specify what to exclude as well as include. We offer more tips along this line in this chapter.

Using Advanced Search Operators

Search engines have come up with additional tools called *advanced search operators* to give power users even more control when searching. Advanced search operators are special terms that you can insert in your search query to find specific types of information that a general search can't provide. Several of these operators provide useful tools for SEO experts as well as others who want very specific information or who want to restrict their search to very specific sources. These operators have a particular meaning to each of the different search engines, but not all engines accept the same operators.

Type the advanced search operators at the beginning of your search query, followed by a particular *domain name* (the base URL of a website, such as `www.bruceclay.com`). This type of query modifies the search to dig deeper into the engine's *algorithms* (the mathematical formulas the search engine uses to weigh various factors and establish a website's relevance to a search). The returned page provides entirely different results than the average search.

For example, say you type this query into a Google search box (substituting your own website domain name from *yourdomain.com*): [site:www.*yourdomain.com*]. The Google results page includes a list of the web pages that are indexed from your website only. In this particular case, the advanced operator used is [site:], followed by the site's domain name. (You can't put a space between the operator and the domain name.)

You have numerous operators at your fingertips that can provide significant and useful information. If you use the [site:] operator by typing [site:] into the search box before the domain name, the search engine results tell you how many pages that particular domain and its sub-domains contain, and lists those pages. Those results can also provide information on pages that have been indexed more than once, which in turn provides information regarding duplicate content. It also provides information about pages that are being dropped out of the search engines. You can see how powerful this can be for SEO!

You can also put additional search terms in your query. For example, this search would list all the pages on the given website: [site:www.bruceclay.com]. If you were looking for something specific on the site, however, you could add more search terms to the end. For instance, to find pages on the website that contain the word *training,* type this: [site:www.bruceclay.com training].

Table 5-1 shows several advanced operators for Google, Yahoo, and Bing and describes their use.

Table 5-1			**Advanced Search Operators for Power Searching on Google, Yahoo, and Bing**
Google	*Yahoo*	*Bing*	*Result*
cache:			Shows the version of the web page from the search engine's cache.
related:			Finds web pages that are similar to the specified web page.
info:			Presents some information that Google has about a web page.
define:	**define:** or **definition:**	**define:** or **definition:**	Provides a definition of a keyword. You must insert a space between the colon and the query in order for this operator to work in Yahoo and Bing.
stocks:	**stocks:**	**stocks:**	Shows stock information for ticker symbols. (***Note:*** Enter ticker symbols; don't type websites or company names.)
site:	**site:**	**site:**	Finds pages only within a particular domain and all its sub-domains.
allintitle:			Finds pages that include all query words as part of the indexed Title tag.
intitle:	**intitle:**	**intitle:**	Finds pages that include a specific keyword as part of the indexed Title tag. You must include a space between the colon and the query for the operator to work in Bing.
allinurl:			Finds a specific URL in the search engine's index. (***Note:*** You must include **http://** in the URL you enter.)
inurl:			Finds pages that include a specific keyword as part of their indexed URLs.
	inbody:	**inbody:**	Finds pages that include a specific keyword in their body text.
"[phrase]"	**"[phrase]"**	**"[phrase]"**	Finds instances of the exact phrase within the quotation marks everywhere it appears within the search engine's index. (***Note:*** Substitute [phrase] in the search operator with the exact phrase you're searching for.)

(continued)

Table 2-1 *(continued)*

Google	Yahoo	Bing	Result
-	-	-	Removes results that contain the word following the minus sign. (**Note:** This search operator is added on to the keyword or phrase being searched for. It should follow the search query. For example, the query [site:www.bruceclay.com-training] will give you all indexed web pages on the domain without the word training on the page.)

Combining operators for turbo-powered searching

Whether you're an SEO expert or just now gleaning the basics of the search engine optimization industry, you may often find that you need to combine some of the commands to pinpoint the information you need.

For example, say you want to determine how many pages on a site have a particular keyword phrase in their `Title` tag (one of the HTML tags contained in the HTML code that appears at the top of a web page). Because `Title` tags are weighted quite heavily in most search engines' algorithms, this information would be very useful in your search engine optimization work. Fortunately, you can combine multiple search operators to find information such as keyword phrases in `Title` tags.

To find out how many pages on a site have a particular keyword phrase, you could type the following query in either Google or Yahoo: [site:www.*sampledomain.com* intitle:*keyword phrase*].

Your query is basically asking, "Within the site, how many pages have this keyword phrase in their `Title` tags?"

However, keep in mind that many combinations of basic and advanced search operators do *not* always work. For example, you cannot combine a [site:] command in Google with an [allintitle:] search, as we have here: [site:www.*sampledomain.com* allintitle:*keyword phrase*]. This query doesn't always work.

A few types of search operators can never be used in combination with another operator. For your reference, we include them here:

✦ Every Google [allin:] operator

✦ Operators that request special information (for example, [define:], [stocks:], and so on)

✦ Search operators that are specific to a page ([cache:], [related:], [url:], and so on)

Discovering which combinations work and which ones don't is a matter of trial and error.

Searching for images

When you do search engine optimization, you want to know how to find specific types of files quickly. The vertical search engines and other file-type-specific sites (such as YouTube for videos) can make your life easier when you're looking for image files, video files, news articles, blog posts, or maps. And if you can find the specific file, you can be sure it has been indexed by the search engine.

To search for image files, click the Images link located near the search text box on all the major search engines, and then type your search terms in the new search text box and click the Search button. This type of search restricts your search results to show only image files (file types such as JPEG and GIF, which include photos, diagrams, drawings, stars, lines . . . basically, any static graphic on a web page).

Besides the entertainment value of seeing tons of pictures on any subject, image searches also give you an easy way to make sure that the images on your website have been indexed by the search engine. For example, if you have a photo of a ten-gallon jar of peanut butter on your website, you can search for it by clicking Images and then typing descriptive text about your image, like [peanut butter jar]. If your webmaster gave the image an Alt attribute (text that displays in place of an image if it cannot display for some reason — for more details, see Book IV, Chapter 1) like "Ten-gallon peanut butter jar," you can use the Alt attribute as your search query. If the search engine spidered your website and found the image, it also should have indexed the Alt attribute. To really target your search, first tell the search engine to look only within your website: [site:www.*yourdomain*.com "Ten-gallon peanut butter jar"]. Using quotation marks around the query tells the search engine to return only pages with that exact text on them.

Searching for videos

Videos are being used more and more inside websites. Sites like YouTube store millions of videos that can be watched by anyone, anywhere, on nearly any subject. You can search within these sites for videos, but you can also do a broader video search using a vertical search engine.

From the Google, Yahoo, or Bing search page, click the Videos link near the search text box, and then type your search terms into the new search text box and click the Search button. Your results include only video files that the search engine has indexed and that match your search terms.

Searching for news

In the same way that you can run an image or video vertical search, you can click a News link on the major search engines near the search text box to find news articles. The search engines consider a *news site* to be a site that has multiple authors and frequent postings.

In Google, the News vertical search engine keeps only articles published within the last 30 days. If you want to search for any news older than that, you can select a custom date range by clicking the Search tools button and then using the time and date drop-down menu to select "Custom range."

Searching with maps

We probably don't need to say much about map searches because anyone who has ever needed directions has probably already used them. Online mapping is a fast-moving industry for which the technology continues to advance at lightning speed. Companies spend a lot of money and time to improve their interactive maps because visual map tools attract visitors in droves. What's good for you, though, is that maps are more than a tool for driving directions; they're also a great way to perform a local search.

Finding news through a regular search

You sometimes see news items appear in the results of the regular Google search page (not Google News). One way is to enter a search query that reads like a headline of a recent event. For instance, if you enter [man invents self-washing car] and this world-shattering news has just broken, your results very likely consist mostly of newspaper article links. Also, search engines blend news stories into a regular search results page if the search engine's algorithm considers a recent story highly relevant to your search. In a blended search, Google usually places the news item in the first or fourth position on the search results page.

Click the Maps link at Google, Yahoo, or Bing, and you see a large map image topped by a simple search field. This is a friendly, visual interface for finding a local dry cleaner, an orthodontist, or a pet groomer. The search field is very flexible; you can enter a type of business, a specific company name, an address, or just a city. When your business shows up in a local search, a user can see not only your information on the left but also your location pinpointed on a map. (**Note:** If your business does not show up, see Book I, Chapter 4 for how the search engines find and select news search results.)

Understanding Long-Tail Queries

You want to attract a lot of people to your website. But you don't want just quantity — you want quality traffic. You want to attract visitors who come and stay a while and find what they're looking for on your site. What you really need are customers. In the world of search engine marketing, site visitors who become customers are called *conversions*. They came, they looked, they bought. They were converted.

When you design your website for search engine optimization, keep in mind that you want high conversion rates, not just high traffic. You need to consider the long-tail phenomenon (a term coined by Chris Anderson in an October 2004 *Wired* magazine article and frequently discussed in SEO circles ever since).

The *long tail* is a statistical concept that says items in comparatively low demand can nonetheless add up to quite large volumes. For example, a large bookstore sells dozens of books from the bestseller lists every day. These popular titles make up only about 20 percent of the store's inventory, yet their sales amount to more than half of the bookstore's total revenue. The slower, incremental sales of the remaining 80 percent of the store's inventory typically generate the other half of the store's sales. Individually, no one book sells a large number of copies, but added together, the revenue is substantial.

You can apply the long-tail concept when you're choosing keywords for your website. The graph in Figure 5-1 represents different keywords (across the horizontal axis) and the quantity of searches, or traffic, that each keyword generates (up the vertical axis). The keywords that have high potential traffic appear at the left end of the graph, followed by keywords that are less frequently searched. The potential traffic drops off in what looks like a long tail while you move to the right.

 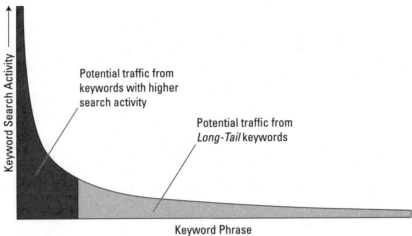

Figure 5-1: Long-tail traffic is incremental traffic that, when added together, brings greater return than head terms.

Keyword Search Activity

Potential traffic from keywords with higher search activity

Potential traffic from *Long-Tail* keywords

Keyword Phrase

Don't ignore the long-tail traffic. In our bookstore example, this would be the equivalent of emptying all the shelves except for the bestsellers' table — cutting revenue substantially.

Think about focusing your keywords for your target audience. You want to use some specialized phrases in your keywords to attract long-tail traffic. A specialized keyword phrase might be three, four, five, or more words in length. A person coming to your website after searching for [compact rechargeable cordless widgets] would be more likely to purchase the item on your site than a person who had just searched for [widgets]. You might not have very many searches for that phrase, but the few who did search for it saw your listing (because it moved way up in the search engine results) and became conversions.

For more in-depth information on keyword selection, see Book II, Chapter 2.

Using Predictive Search as a Research Assistant

When you start typing a query into a Google search box, you may have noticed that the search engine offers up common searches that start with the letters you've already typed. Google is trying to make it easier on searchers by predicting the query they're looking for. This search enhancement is called Google Instant, and it has been around since 2010. Google Instant has proven to be extra helpful for people using their smartphones to search, because typing on a smartphone's touchscreen isn't always easy, and selecting a query from a list of suggestions makes for a good search experience, provided that the query you're looking for, or something similar, is among the suggestions.

Figure 5-2 is a screenshot from a mobile device used to search Google for [peanut butter]. Notice that a list of searches has populated below the search bar. These are popular searches that start the same as the letters or words that have been typed into the search box already.

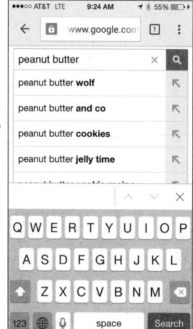

Figure 5-2: Google Instant shows you a list of queries that you might be looking for based on what you've typed in the search box so far.

Mobile devices and Google Instant in particular have changed how people search. When Google shows common and popular searches, it influences future searches. You know that people search for the suggested searches Google lists in Google Instant, so target those queries in your SEO efforts. Use the suggested searches as a keyword research tool. Start typing keyword phrases you're targeting and see whether Google adds any phrases you didn't know about to the list. Now, as an expert searcher, you've got an edge for doing market research, keyword analysis, and much more.

Chapter 6: Spam Issues: When Search Engines Get Fooled

In This Chapter

✓ Finding out about the different types of search engine spam

✓ Understanding the consequences of using spam

✓ Avoiding search engine penalties

✓ Being wary of guaranteed results and other false promises

✓ Understanding ethical SEO

*W*hen you hear the word *spam,* what comes to mind? You probably think of all those annoying emails with their poorly worded and often obscene messages that clutter your inbox daily. That's spam, all right, but there's another kind of spam that's directed at search engines.

In this chapter, you find out about spam techniques that some websites use to fool or trick the search engines into delivering a higher listing on the results page. Any time you think you can achieve higher rankings by deceiving the search engines, you'd better think again! Google and the other engines get better all the time at sniffing out spam, and the penalties can be harsh. Even inadvertent spam can get a website in trouble, so in this chapter we go over some of the more popular and dangerous methods that have been used. Then we delve into the guidelines search engines use to define what they consider spam, as well as our search engine optimization (SEO) code of ethics to help keep you and your site in the clear.

Understanding What Spam Is

When you normally think of spam, the first thing that comes to mind is either the canned meat product or the junk email that's clogging up your inbox. (Or the Monty Python skit . . . "Spam, spam, spam, spam" . . . ahem.) When we here in SEO-land talk about spam, however, we mean something a little different than meat by-products, unwanted emails, or British comedy troupes. Search engine *spam* (also sometimes known as *spamdexing*) is any tactic or web page that is used to deceive the search engine into a false understanding of what the whole website is about or its importance. It can be external or internal to your website, it may violate the search engines' policies directly, or it may be a little bit sneakier about its misdirection. How spam is defined depends on the *intent* and *extent*. What is the intent of the tactic being used, and to what extent is it being used?

If you stuff all your *metadata* (text added into the HTML of a page describing it for the search engine) full of *keywords* (words or phrases relating to your site content that search engines use to determine whether it's relevant) with the sole intent of tricking the search engine so that your page will receive a higher page rank on the results page, that's spam. Also, if you do that all over your website, with your `Alt` *attribute text* (text used to describe an image for the search engine to read), your links, and keywords, trying to trick the search engine *spider* (the little programs that search engines use to read and rank websites) into giving you the highest rank possible, it's a little harder to claim to the search engine that it was simply an accident and it was done out of ignorance.

Most technologies that are used in the creation, rendering, and design of websites can be used to trick the search engines. When a website tries to pull a fast one, or the search engines even so much as *perceive* it did, the search engines consider that website spam. Search engine companies do not like spam. Spam damages the reputation of the search engine. They're working their hardest to bring you the most relevant results possible, and spam-filled pages are not what they want to give you. Users might not use the search engine again if they get spammy results, for starters. So if someone's caught spamming, that person's site could be penalized or removed entirely from the search engine's *index* (the list of websites that the search engine pulls from to create its results pages).

You can report spam if you run across it by contacting the search engines (see the "Reporting Spam" section near the end of the chapter).

Discovering the Types of Spam

In the following sections, we talk a little about what types of spam there are in SEO-land and what *not* to do in order to keep your site from getting penalized or even pulled out of the engines by accident.

Spam is any attempt to deceive the search engines into ranking a page when it does not deserve to be ranked. In the following sections, we describe spam that is known to be detected and punished by the search engines.

Do not attempt any of the discussed methods, because they will result in your site being branded as a spammer. This chapter is not meant to cover every type of spam out there on the web. It's just meant to give you the knowledge you need to recognize when a tactic might be venturing down the wrong path. Spammers use other advanced techniques that may also be detectable by the search engines, so avoid any attempt to deceive the search engines.

Hidden text/links

One of the more obvious ways to spam a site is to insert hidden text and links in the *content* of the web page (the content of a site being anything that the user can see). All text has to be visible to the user on the site. Hidden content can be defined as text that appears within the rendered HTML code that is not visible on the page to the user without requiring user-interaction in order to see it. Hidden text can simply be a long list of keywords, and the hidden links increase the site's popularity. Examples of using hidden text and links are

✦ **White text/links on a white background:** Putting white text and links on a white background renders the text invisible to the user unless the text is highlighted by right-clicking on the mouse. Spammers can then insert keywords or hyperlinks that the spiders read and count as relevant.

✦ **Text, links, or content that is hidden by covering it with a layer so that it is not visible:** This is a trick that people use with CSS. They hide spiderable content under the page that can't be seen with the naked eye or by highlighting the page.

✦ **Positioning content off the page's view with CSS:** This is another programming trick spammers use.

✦ **Links that are not clickable by the user:** Creating a link that has only a single 1-x-1 pixel as its anchor, that uses the period on a sentence as the anchor, or that has no anchor at all. There's nothing for a user to click, but the engine can still follow the link.

Using invisible or hidden text is a surefire way to get your site *banned* so that it no longer shows up in the engines. The reasoning behind this is that you would want all your content visible to the user, and any hidden text is being used for nefarious purposes.

Figure 6-1 shows what we mean by hidden text on a background. Usually, you find this as white text on a white background, but it could be any color as long as it's not visible to a user (black on black, gray on gray, and so on). This is spam and will get your site banned.

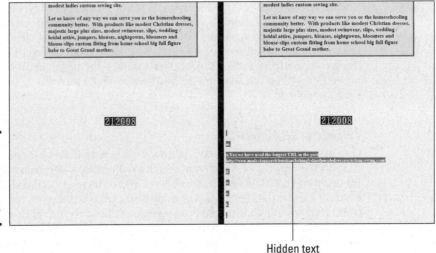

Figure 6-1:
An example
of white text
on a white
background.

Hidden text

Doorway pages

A *doorway page* is a web page submitted to search engine spiders that has been designed to satisfy the specific algorithms for various search engines but is not intended to be viewed by visitors. Basically they do not earn the rankings but instead deceive the search engines into rankings by design and keyword-stuffing tricks that you'd never want to put on a page for a user to see. Doorway pages are there to spam the search engine *index* (the database of information from which search engines draw their primary results) by cramming it full of relevant keywords and phrases so that it appears high on the results page for a particular keyword, but when the user clicks it, he or she is automatically redirected to another site or page within the same site that doesn't rank on its own.

Doorway pages are there only for the purpose of being indexed, and there is no intention for anyone to use those pages. Sometimes more sophisticated spammers build a doorway page with viewable, relevant content in order to avoid being caught by the search engine, but most of the time a doorway page is made to be viewed only by a spider. Doorway pages are often used in tandem with deceptive redirection, which we discuss in the following section.

Deceptive redirection

Has this ever happened to you? You do a search for a cartoon you used to love as a kid, and you click one of the links on the results page. But instead of the page you were expecting, you get an entirely different website, with some very questionable content. What just happened? Behold the headache that is deceptive redirection. *Deceptive redirection* is a type of coded command that redirects the user to a different location than what was expected via the link that was clicked.

Spammers create shadow page/domains that have content that ranks for a particular *search query* (the words or phrase you type into the search text box), yet when you attempt to access the content on the domain, you are redirected to a shady site (often having to do with porn, gambling, or drugs) that has nothing to do with your original query.

The most common perpetrators of deceptive redirects are also a spam method: doorway pages. Most doorway pages redirect through a `Meta` *refresh command* (a method of instructing a web browser to automatically refresh the current web page after a given time interval). Search engines are now issuing penalties for using `Meta` refresh commands, so other sites will trick you into clicking a link or using JavaScript (a computer programming language) to redirect you. Google now considers any website that uses a `Meta` refresh command or any other sneaky redirect (such as through JavaScript) to be spam.

Not all redirects are evil. The intent of the redirect has to be determined before a spam determination can be made. If the page that you are redirected to is nothing like the page expected, it is probably spam. If you get exactly what you expect after a redirect, it probably isn't spam. We discuss a lot more about redirects in Book VII, Chapter 3.

Cloaking

Another nefarious form of spam is a method called cloaking. *Cloaking* is a technique in which the content presented to the search engine spider is different from that presented to the user's browser, meaning that the spiders see one page while you see something entirely different. Spammers can cloak by delivering content based on the *IP addresses* (information used to tell where your computer or server is located) or the *User-Agent HTTP header* (information describing whether you're a person or a search engine robot) of the user requesting the page. When a user is identified as a search engine spider, a server-side script delivers a different version of the web page, one that contains content different from the visible page. The purpose of cloaking is to deceive search engines so they display the page when it would not otherwise be displayed.

Like redirects, cloaking is a matter of intent rather than always being evil. There are many appropriate uses for this technique. News sites use cloaking to allow search engines to spider their content while users are presented with a registration page. Sites selling alcohol require users to verify their age before allowing them to view the rest of the content, while search engines pass unchallenged.

Unrelated keywords

Unrelated keywords are a form of spam that involves using a keyword that is not related to the image, video, or other content that it is supposed to be describing in the hopes of driving up traffic. Examples include putting unrelated keywords into the `Alt` attribute text of an image, placing them in the metadata of a video, or placing them in the `Meta` tags of a page. Not only is it useless, but it also gets your site pulled if you try it.

Keyword stuffing

Keyword stuffing occurs when people overuse keywords on a page in the hopes of making the page seem more relevant for a term through a higher keyword frequency or density. Keyword stuffing can happen in the metadata, `Alt` attribute text, and within the content of the page itself. Basically, going to your `Alt` attribute text and typing **porsche porsche porsche porsche** over and over again is not going to increase your ranking, and the page will likely be yanked due to spam.

There are also much sneakier methods of using keyword stuffing: using hidden text in the page, hiding large groups of repeated keywords on the page (usually at the bottom, far below the view of the average visitor), or using HTML commands that cause blocks of text to be hidden from user sight.

Link farms

You might envision a "link farm" as a pastoral retreat where docile links graze in rolling green pastures, but alas, you would be wrong. A *link farm* is any group of websites that *hyperlink* (a link to another part of the website) to all the other sites in the group. Remember how Google loves links and hyperlinks and uses them in its algorithm to figure out a website's popularity? Most link farms are created through automated programs and services. Search engines have combated link farms by identifying specific attributes that link farms use and filtering them from the index and search results, including removing entire domains to keep them from influencing the results page.

Not all link exchange programs are considered spam, however. Link exchange programs that allow individual websites to selectively exchange links with other relevant websites are not considered spam. The difference between these link exchange programs and link farms is the fact that the site is selecting links relevant to its content, rather than just getting as many links as it can get to itself.

Reporting Spam

Fighting spam is a top priority for the search engines. Google alone has a squadron of PhDs who do nothing but identify and combat spammers and their techniques. Fighting spam is important to Google because its business depends on presenting reliable, relevant results when you search. This is why its spam filters are getting better all the time.

The major search engines have posted quality guidelines to spell out what webmasters should and shouldn't do — stuff like avoiding hidden text or hidden links, not loading pages with irrelevant keywords, and so forth. The search engines also encourage people to submit a spam report about sites that violate their quality guidelines and cross the line into spam. You should report spam when you see it. Eliminating search engine spam makes the world of SEO a fairer place, and searchers around the world get better results.

Google

Google has two ways to submit a spam report:

✦ Registered Search Console users can submit an authenticated spam report form at www.google.com/webmasters/tools/spamreport?pli=1. Google promises to investigate every spam report submitted by a registered Search Console user.

✦ Anyone can fill out an unauthenticated spam report form located at www.google.com/contact/spamreport.html. Google reportedly assesses every unauthenticated report in terms of its potential impact and investigates "a large fraction" of these reports, as well.

Figure 6-2 shows the many categories of spam report forms that are available in Google.

Bing

Bing doesn't have a spam report form at a specific URL, but there is a way to report spam nonetheless. Click the Feedback link either in the lower-right corner of Bing.com, or in the footer of any Bing results page. You can type your complaint in a simple text box, as shown in Figure 6-3. Be sure to mention "spam" in your message, click Dislike, and provide the essential details, like the URL and the query you used, so that Bing can research the issue.

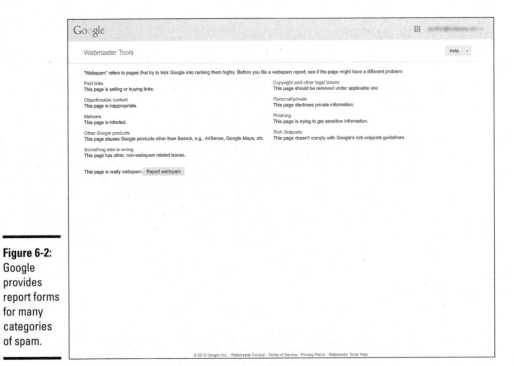

Figure 6-2:
Google provides report forms for many categories of spam.

Figure 6-3:
You can report spam using the feedback form in Bing.

Avoiding Being Evil: Ethical Search Marketing

We didn't spend this chapter describing spam just so that unscrupulous users could run out and use it. Sure, the spam might bump their page rank for a little while, but they will be caught, and their site will be penalized or pulled from the index entirely. So why use it?

For too long, many SEO practitioners were involved in an arms race of sorts, inventing technology and techniques in order to achieve the best rankings and get the most clients. Unfortunately, some developed more and more devious technology to trick the search engines and beat the competition. Thus we have two types of techniques used in SEO:

✦ **White hat:** This includes all SEO techniques that fall into the ethical realm. White-hat techniques involve using relevant keywords, descriptive `Alt` attribute text, simple and clear metadata, and so on. White-hat techniques clearly comply with the published intent of the various search engine quality guidelines.

✦ **Black hat:** These are the SEO techniques we describe in this chapter (among others that we haven't covered). Black-hat techniques are sneaky and devious, and they attempt to game the engines to promote content not relevant to the user. These techniques are deceptive and generally break (or at least stretch) the search guidelines, commonly leading to spam penalties that are painful at best and devastating at worst.

With the search engines implementing aggressive antispam programs, the news is out: If you want to get rankings, you have to play well within the rules. And those rules are absolutely "No deception or tricks allowed." Simply put, honest relevancy wins at the end of the day. All other approaches fade away.

Generally, the search engines all adhere to a code of conduct. Little things do vary from search engine to search engine, but the general principle is the same:

✦ Keywords should be relevant, applicable, and clearly associated with page body content.

✦ Keywords should be used as allowed and accepted by the search engines (placement, color, and so on).

✦ Keywords should not be utilized too many times on a page (frequency, density, distribution, and so on). The use should be natural for the subject.

✦ Redirection technology (if used) should facilitate and improve the user experience. But understand that this is almost always considered a trick and is frequently a cause for penalties or removal from an index.

✦ Redirection technology (if used) should always display a page where the body content covers the expected topic and contains the appropriate keywords (no bait and switch).

You *can* get back into a search engine's good graces after getting caught spamming and penalized or yanked out of the index. It involves going through your site and cleaning it up, removing all the spam issues that caused it to get yanked in the first place, and resubmitting your pages for placement into the index. Don't expect an immediate resubmission, though. You have to wait in line with everyone else.

Search engine penalties

The search engines tweak their algorithms all the time in a continuous effort to improve the quality of search results. Google has said it makes more than 500 changes a year — that's more than once per day! Many changes are minor, but others aggressively attack one form of spam or another, causing major consequences for websites trying to rank. When the dust settles, both winners and losers emerge.

Within the SEO industry, we call any sudden and noticeable demotion in search engine ranking a *penalty*. Penalties can be assigned either manually or as the result of an algorithm change, but the resulting drop in traffic and revenue feels the same to the website owner. Search engines have human quality raters who can review a website and assign a *manual action* if they find that the site violates their quality guidelines. That's what search engines call a "penalty." But sites can also get hit with an *algorithmic penalty* when an algorithm change redefines what's okay to do and they are suddenly caught outside the new stricter boundaries. Just as in musical chairs when the music stops, a site that has been happily playing the game can suddenly find itself without a place to sit in the SERPs.

Google's major algorithm updates have resulted in massive algorithmic penalties (as well as an arguably much cleaner SERP). For some reason, the updates are usually named after cute black-and-white animals. You find out more about how to avoid these penalties individually in their appropriate topic sections throughout this book. Table 6-1 lists the whole menagerie and explains the types of spam tactics or low-quality content each update targets.

Table 6-1	Major Google Penalty-Related Updates	
Update	*Release Dates*	*Purpose*
Panda	February 2011; several subsequent updates	Reward quality content and penalize sites with thin or shallow content
Penguin	May 2012; periodic updates every 6–12 months	Penalize sites that have link spam or too many low-quality links to a site
Page Layout	January 2012	Penalize sites with too much advertising above the fold
Payday Loans	June 2013; two updates in 2014	Target spammy sites and queries, such as [payday loans], [casinos], [viagra]
Pigeon	July 2014	Improve local search results in Google Maps and Web searches

Realizing That There Are No Promises or Guarantees

Say that you know that you won't use spam in order to increase your page ranking in the search engines. You understand that it's unethical and is more trouble than it's worth. But at the same time, you need to increase your page rank. The simple solution is to hire an SEO organization to do the optimizing for you. But beware: Although you might not use spam, there's a chance than an unscrupulous SEO practitioner will.

A code of ethics applies to people in the search engine optimization industry. Beware of those who promise or guarantee results to their clients, allege a special relationship with a search engine, or advertise the ability to get priority consideration when they submit to a search engine. People who make these claims are usually lying. Remember, there is no way to pay your way into the top of the search results page. Yahoo does have a program called Search Submit Pro where, for a fee, you can submit your page and be guaranteed that the Yahoo spider will crawl your site frequently, but Yahoo doesn't guarantee rankings, and it's the only large engine with this sort of program (see Chapter 2 of this minibook for more details). Also avoid those that promise link popularity schemes or promise to submit your site to thousands of search engines. These do not increase your ranking, and even if they do, it's not in a way that would be considered positive, and the benefits, if any, are usually short-lived.

Unfortunately, you are responsible for the actions of any company you hire. If an SEO company creates a web page for you using black-hat tactics, you are responsible and your site could be pulled entirely from the search engine's index. If you're not sure about what your SEO company is doing, ask for clarification. And remember, like in all things, *caveat emptor.* Buyer beware.

Following the SEO Code of Ethics

The discussion of any SEO code of ethics is like a discussion on politics or religion: There are more than two sides, all sides are strongly opinionated, and seldom do they choose the same path to the same end. Most search engine optimization (SEO) practitioners understand this code of ethics, but not all practitioners practice safe SEO. Too many SEO practitioners claim a bias toward surfers, or the search engines, or their clients (all are appropriate in the correct balance), and it is common for the SEO pros to use the "whatever it takes" excuse to bend some of the ethical rules to fit their needs. This does not pass judgment; it simply states the obvious.

Although the industry as a whole hasn't adopted an official code of ethics, the authors of this book have drafted a specific code that we pledge to adhere to with respect to our clients. We have paraphrased this code here, but you can read the original at `www.bruceclay.com/web_ethics.htm`:

✦ Do not intentionally do harm to a client. Be honest with the client and do not willfully use technologies and methods that are known to cause a website's removal from a search engine index.

✦ Do not intentionally violate any specifically published and enforced rules of search engines or directories. This also means keeping track of when policies change and checking with the search engine if you're unsure of whether the method or technology is acceptable.

✦ Protect the user visiting the site. The content must not mislead, no "bait and switch" tactics (where the content does not match the search phrase) should be used, and the content should not be offensive to the targeted visitors.

✦ Do not use the continued violation of copyright, trademark, servicemark, or laws related to spamming as they may exist at the state, federal, or international level.

✦ All pages presented to the search engine must match the visible content of the page.

✦ Don't steal other people's work and present it as your own.

✦ Don't present false qualifications or deliberately lie about your skills. Also, don't make guarantees or claim special relationships with the search engine.

✦ Treat all clients equally and don't play favorites.

✦ Don't make false promises or guarantees. There is no such thing as a guaranteed method of reaching the top of the results page.

✦ Always offer ways for your clients to settle disputes. There will be competition among your clients' websites. Make sure there's a way to mediate conflict if it ever comes up.

✦ Protect your clients' confidentiality and anonymity of your clients with regard to privileged information and any testimonials supplied by your clients.

✦ Work to the best of your ability to honestly increase and retain the rankings of your client sites.

In a nutshell? Don't be evil. Spammers never win, and winners never spam. What works in the short term won't work forever, and living in fear of getting caught is no way to run a business.

Book II
Keyword Strategy

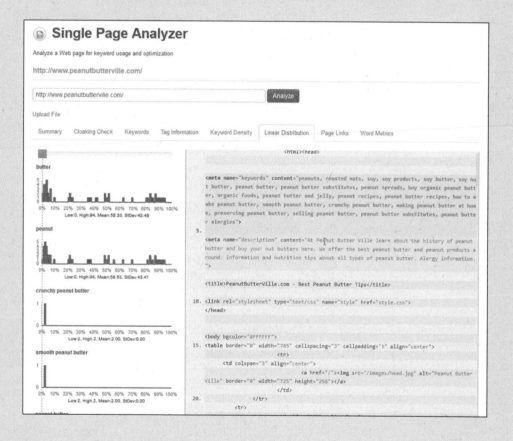

Go to www.dummies.com/extras/searchengineoptimizationaio for an article about using the free Keyword Suggestion tool to capture new search traffic.

Contents at a Glance

Chapter 1: Employing Keyword Research Techniques and Tools

In This Chapter

- ✔ Discovering your site theme
- ✔ Brainstorming for keywords
- ✔ Creating a keyword-based outline
- ✔ Choosing related keywords
- ✔ Researching keywords by niche
- ✔ Evaluating keywords

In this chapter, we talk about picking and choosing your keywords. This is an extremely important step. You might say the mantra of search engines should be "keywords, keywords, keywords." Search engine *spiders* (the bots that go through your page gathering web page data) are looking for keywords that match or closely relate to the search query. A *keyword* is a specific word or phrase a search engine looks for in its index (the list of websites it looks at during a search), based on what the user typed as the search query. For example, [cars] could be a keyword for a website that deals with restoring classic cars.

It seems simple enough: Just figure out a couple of great keywords and go! Unfortunately, there's more to picking keywords than that. Say you've got a website that specializes in selling custom-made classic automobiles. But the site isn't receiving the *traffic* (number of visitors) it should. Here's a tip: Think about what kind of keywords you used in your website. You might be using general keywords like [automobiles] and [vehicles], but how many people actually type in a search query of [classic automobiles]? Nine times out of ten people are going to be looking for [classic cars]. Little distinctions like this can make a big difference in the traffic your website receives.

This chapter shows you how to pick good, solid, relevant keywords. You discover that one of the first things you must do is to identify the theme of your website. Second, you sit down and brainstorm all the keywords you think fit your theme. And we're not talking five or ten keywords here: We're talking dozens or hundreds or thousands. Then we talk about creating a good outline for those keywords and researching your market to find out what the competition is doing and what your potential customers are searching for. We also discuss culling unproductive keywords so that you can focus on the most relevant ones.

Remember, relevancy = higher ranking = more traffic for your website.

Discovering Your Site Theme

The first thing you need to figure out is your website's theme. The *theme* is the main thing that your site is about. It's the central concept of whatever your site is doing on the web. Again, it seems simple enough, but it's very important to know *exactly* what it is that you're about. If you have a website that specializes in selling customized classic cars, you need to figure out exactly what that means, narrowing down the kinds of cars you consider to be classic, the types of customization you do, and so forth. Also consider where it is that you'll be going with this website. Think about whether you only want to handle classic cars, or if you might also want to broaden your scope and include newer models. Be thinking about whether there's a broad enough market out there for customized classic cars, decide whether you might include both domestic and foreign cars, newer cars, and so on.

You also need to think about your service area. Are you a local-only business, or could you take things to a national or international level? Try to break it down in very specific terms.

Write down the things that you feel your website is about, and all the things that your site *is not* about. So, if you're creating a site about customized classic cars, you would write things like

✦ We work on only classic cars built from 1950–1970.

✦ The cars we work on are American-made; no foreign vehicles.

✦ Customization means we do paint, chrome, and upholstery.

✦ We do engine work or can install an entirely new engine if necessary.

✦ We do not install "banging" stereos; that's the guy down the road.

✦ We are a local business, but are willing to accept clients from out of town and out of state.

Brainstorming for keywords

After your theme is clear in your mind and you've clarified what your business is really about, you have a good starting point for your keyword brainstorming sessions.

Brainstorming is an appropriate first step for choosing good keywords. At this point, there are no bad keywords; you just want to compile a big list of possibilities. Here are some possible viewpoints to consider and questions you can ask yourself:

+ **Natural language:** What would I search for to try to find my product?

+ **Customer mindset:** How do regular people talk about the products or services I offer?

+ **Industry jargon:** What do the experts call my products or services?

**Book II
Chapter 1**

Employing
Keyword Research
Techniques and
Tools

Write down whatever you think would be the major keywords you will be using. Ask your friends, relatives, associates, employees, and coworkers. It's a matter of throwing things at the wall to see what sticks and what doesn't. Figure 1-1 shows a simple mind map. Tools like this can help you come up with new topics and concepts that might relate to your site.

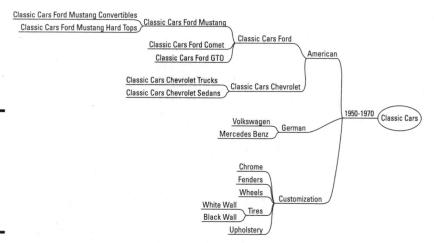

Figure 1-1:
Brain-
storming
your
keywords
with a map
outline.

Building a subject outline

After you have a large list of keywords that you might want to use, your next step is to create an outline using those keywords. Start with the broadest ones at the top level and break the list into categories and subcategories, getting more specific as you go deeper.

A keyword outline for a customized classic cars website could look something like this list. Notice how the keywords build on each other as you delve deeper into the subject:

Classic cars

Classic cars 1950–1970

Classic cars American

Classic cars Ford

    Classic cars Ford Mustang

        Classic cars Ford Mustang convertibles

        Classic cars Ford Mustang hard tops

    Classic cars Ford Comet

Classic cars Chevrolet

    Classic cars Chevrolet trucks

    Classic cars Chevrolet sedans

Classic cars German

Classic cars Volkswagen

Classic cars Mercedes Benz

Classic cars customization

    Classic cars customization paint

    Classic cars customization chrome

    Classic cars customization fenders

    Classic cars customization wheels

    Classic cars customization tires

        Classic cars customization tires white wall

        Classic cars customization tires black wall

    Classic cars customization upholstery

You can see how the breakdown in the preceding list goes from very broad terms to more specific terms. These all represent things that people might search for when they are looking up classic cars, or customization, or both, and can all be used as keywords. This is a very small, simple outline. You can go into even more breakdowns and come up with even more specific keywords as appropriate for your site.

Remember to list as many keywords that relate to your theme as you can. The broader base you have to work with, the better chances you have of identifying good, solid, relevant keywords.

Choosing theme-related keywords

Now, take your nice, long list of hundreds of potential keywords and go through and match them to your theme. Figure out whether you will be doing custom work for a Ford Anglia as opposed to Ford Mustangs, and whether you want to include Dodge at all. Also start thinking about keyword phrases, like [Ford Mustang convertible] or [1960s Ford Mustang hardtops]. Qualifiers, such as [convertible] or [1960s], thrown in at the beginning and end of a main keyword, turn it into a keyword phrase, and they help you figure out how narrow you want the search to be. This is especially important if you have a local business because you want to rank for the local search query, such as [Poughkeepsie classic car customization]. When you feel as though you have some good usable keywords, drag out your thesaurus and look up synonyms for those words. Anything that relates to your keyword or has the same meaning is another good keyword.

Book II
Chapter 1

Employing
Keyword Research
Techniques and
Tools

Doing Your Industry and Competitor Research

Now it's time to check out the competition. With any business, it's an important step in getting a feel for the market. With industry research, you need to know what keywords your competitors are using in their content and what kind of traffic they're getting. One of the easiest ways is to look them up on the search engines. Use the keywords you came up with during your brainstorming session and plug them into the query window. Google bolds your search terms in the search results, so pay attention to those words and the text surrounding them. Google also provides you with disambiguation options when appropriate, as in a "Did you mean . . . ?" phrase. In Figure 1-2, the search for [classic car customization] returns 1,400,000 results. The top 10 results returned are worth mining for keyword ideas.

Check out the highest listings and make note of the keywords they use on their pages. The websites that have the highest rank are your competition for those keywords, and to have such a high listing on the search engine, they're obviously doing something right. For a really in-depth look at how to do research on your competition, check out Book III.

After you've identified who your competitors are, it's time to do some research. Look at any print materials they've put out, along with what's on their websites. Pay attention to how they market themselves and what words they use to describe themselves. This is important especially if you're looking to draw industry traffic to yourself or obtain links from other industry sites. Look at their sites' navigation, check out their metadata, and read their content and press.

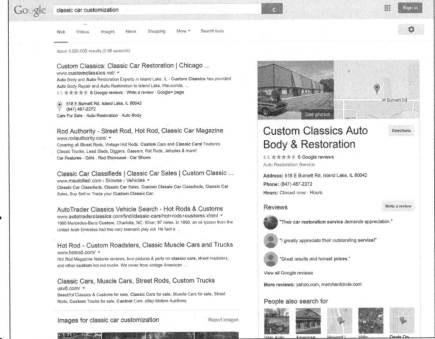

Figure 1-2:
A Google
search
result for
[classic car
custom-
ization].

Researching Client Niche Keywords

After you know what keywords your competition is using, it's time to start thinking about what your targeted visitors are using to search for your products or services. The language the industry uses and the language the customer uses are often two entirely different things. For example, people in the auto industry use the words *auto* or *vehicle,* but the guy on the street is not going to refer to his Ford as his auto: He's going to call it his car. The same goes for search queries. Most people are not looking for [classic automobiles]; they're going to be looking for [classic cars].

You can find out what the man on the street is saying by actually going to the man on the street. Check out Internet forums, interest groups, and newsgroups that relate to your business and make note of what people are writing in their posts. What words do they use when referring to your type of business or the product that you sell? Those can be used as keywords for your website. Talk to your clients. Communication is key to figuring out what they're looking for.

Also, pay attention when people call your business and ask questions. Those are the kinds of questions that people are asking the search engine. One person's slightly questionable phrasing can be another person's usable keyword.

Checking Out Seasonal Keyword Trends

Some keywords retain their popularity and relevance throughout the year, like [Ford Mustang] or [California]. Others see rises and spikes throughout the year due to seasonal trends. Holidays are a good example. More people buy Christmas tree ornaments in December than in July, and the majority of costume sales happen before Halloween. The same is true of the actual seasons themselves because people look for things at certain times of the year. More people look for bathing suits in the months before summer and for snowboards in the winter (see Figure 1-3).

 You can use tools provided by the search engines to see keyword spikes and trends. Take advantage of end-of-the-year reports such Google Zeitgeist (www.google.com/press/zeitgeist), along with Google Trends (www.google.com/trends), which measures how often a keyword is used during a given day, providing the most popular examples and measuring when the spikes happen.

You may find it important to note spikes and trends in your keywords: While certain things immediately come to mind during a given holiday (for example, *flowers* and *chocolate* for Valentine's Day), other keywords and keyword phrases that are much more loosely connected might spike during that time period as well. Around February 14, you might notice a rise in searches for engagement rings, vacation listings for second honeymoons, and wedding-related searches. Restaurant searches and hotel listings also probably spike, along with clothing, shoes, and jewelry. As we explain in the section "Brainstorming for keywords," earlier in this chapter, one broad high-traffic term can be broken down into specific, small-traffic terms. These more specific terms are every bit as relevant as the broad term, and they generally have less competition. Remember the long tail when considering possible keywords.

Seasonal keywords are important to keep track of because you can use them to tailor your site to draw in that seasonal traffic. Many stores receive the bulk of their revenue from seasonal purchases, so it's a good thing to keep seasonal traffic in mind when building your website.

Book II
Chapter 1

Employing
Keyword Research
Techniques and
Tools

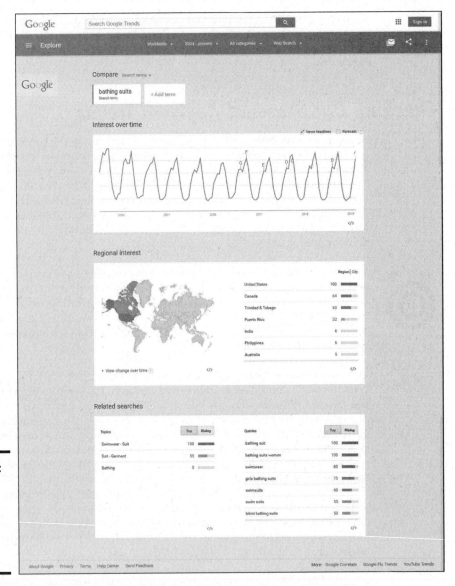

Figure 1-3:
Google Trends showing seasonal keyword trends.

Evaluating Keyword Research

After you've done your research and your brainstorming, you have, with luck, acquired a good long list of keywords that can be used. Now it's time to figure out which ones you'll actually be using.

In figuring out how often your keywords are searched for, you can use a variety of tools for keyword evaluation. Using some of these tools, you can monitor how often a certain keyword is searched, what the click-through rates are, and whether it would be a good, usable keyword to keep. Some tools you have to pay for, but there are free ones out there. A couple of examples:

✦ **Google Keyword Planner:** Google has its own keyword research tool, shown in Figure 1-4. You have to have a Google AdWords account to access the Keyword Planner keyword research tool located at `https://adwords.google.com/keywordplanner`. (Microsoft has a keyword tool as well, which also requires you to establish an account. Find the tool login page at `www.bing.com/toolbox/keywords`.) Note that the Keyword Planner gives you additional suggestions based on seed keywords, competitiveness of keywords, and average number of searches for keywords. What's really cool are the different ways of breaking down keyword popularity by mobile devices and location of searchers.

✦ **Search Engine Optimization/KSP:** Bruce Clay, Inc., provides a free keyword tool at `www.bruceclay.com/seo/combining-keywords.htm`. Simply type your keywords into the Please Enter Keywords box and click the Run KSP button. You'll get keyword counts, plus demographic information.

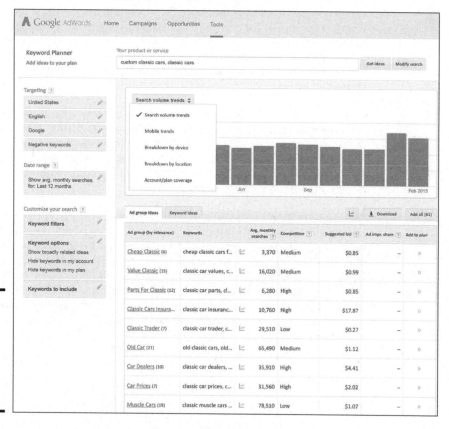

Figure 1-4:
The Google AdWords free keyword research tool.

The following services are paid services, so you have to cough up a little bit of cash for them. They actually do research and check out your competition for you, so they might be something you want to invest in. That doesn't mean you get out of doing the brainstorming and researching yourself; they just make it easier. Here are some paid services:

✦ **SEOToolSet:** In addition to the free tools offered by Bruce Clay, Inc., you can also subscribe to a suite of fully integrated SEO tools. Far more robust than the free version, the Pro version of the SEOToolSet is available for $89.00 per month for up to two domains (`www.bruceclay.com/seo/tools.htm`).

✦ **Wordtracker** (`www.wordtracker.com`): A keyword tracking service that you have to pay for, but they do offer free trials. Several monthly and annual pricing plans are available starting at $27 per month.

✦ **Keyword Discovery** (`www.keyworddiscovery.com`): Made by Trellian, this is another paid keyword tracking tool. You can subscribe for $199.95 a month.

You need to cull the least relevant keywords from the list right away. If your business is customizing only American cars as opposed to foreign ones, you can do away with words like [foreign], [Anglia], and [Volkswagen]. Don't worry: You've still got a pretty big list to choose from. You're just narrowing the focus a bit. When you're clipping out keywords, remember that keywords that are supportive of a strong branding exercise, that result in sales more often than other keywords, or that have very high profit margins should all be retained.

Using the tools and brainstorming methods we describe in this chapter, you can come up with a pretty sizable list of keywords. Using the keyword tracking tools, you can also get rid of a bunch of irrelevant, low-traffic keywords right away and pick a good list to focus on. Remember, you're not looking for five or ten keywords: You're looking for hundreds of good keywords, depending on the size of your site.

Although it might seem like a good idea to concentrate on the broadest, most general keywords out there, it's actually not. What you want are keywords that give you conversion. A keyword that brings 60 visitors to your site, 10 of whom make a purchase, is much more desirable than a generic keyword that brings in thousands of visitors who only come in, blink, and then hit Back on their browser. Statisticians attribute this to the fact that people use generic keywords when gathering information and more specific keywords when they're ready to open their wallets. We explain this phenomenon more in Chapter 2 of this minibook.

Chapter 2: Selecting Keywords

In This Chapter

✔ Selecting proper keyword phrases

✔ Reinforcing versus diluting your site theme

✔ Selecting subject categories

✔ Choosing high-traffic and high-conversion keywords

✔ Optimizing with keywords for natural language-based search

In this chapter, we take that nice long list of keywords discussed in Chapter 1 of this minibook and select the best keywords of the bunch. (If you haven't yet put together such a list, what are you waiting for? Do it now!) In this chapter, you discover what makes a good keyword phrase, especially in terms of a *search query* (the words you type into the search engine's Search box). We also explain the deal with subject categories and how they help you choose your keywords. Also, we talk about high-traffic keywords and high-conversion keywords, as well as the difference between the two. After you understand the concept behind using keywords on your website to match search queries, you learn about *semantic search* (a method by which search engines rank results to best match word meaning, as opposed to exact keyword matching).

Selecting the Proper Keyword Phrases

When you're doing a search, you must use the proper phrase as a search query. Just like a *keyword* is a single word used as a search query, a *keyword phrase* is two or more words typed as a search query. For example, [Poughkeepsie classic car customization] is a good example of a keyword phrase.

Search engine users find what they are looking for by searching for specific keywords or keyword phrases and choosing the most relevant result. You want your site to have as many opportunities to be included in those search results as possible. In other words, you should try to use every keyword phrase that you think someone might search for in order to find your site.

Usually when people do a search, they type in a keyword phrase rather than just a single keyword. In fact, the vast majority of search queries are three words or longer. So, having keyword phrases on your site increases your website's chance of appearing higher on the page rank (because more keywords match the search query). The *click-through rate* (how many people click your listing to go to your site) also increases when more words match the search query. Your *conversion rate* (how many visitors actually purchase something, sign up, or take whatever action is appropriate on your site) also increases because you're more likely to have what the user is looking for.

Search engine users are becoming more savvy as time goes on, and they know that a single keyword is probably going to be too broad a search to return the results they're looking for. A good example is what happens when you do a search for [security]. You might be in need of a security guard service, but doing a quick search on Google by using the keyword [security] gives you results as varied as the Wikipedia article on security, the Department of Homeland Security, the Social Security Administration, and many listings for computer security software. Using the keyword phrase [security guard service Poughkeepsie], on the other hand, turns up map results that list local businesses, two local business sites for hiring security guards, and a couple of news articles about security services in Poughkeepsie.

You can see why it's a good idea to have proper keyword phrases, and not just single keywords, on your web pages. You could use the keyword phrase [Poughkeepsie classic car customization] as a heading for your paragraphs, place it in the `Heading` tags (HTML tags used for paragraph headings), or use it as the title of your web page (by using the `Title` tag in the HTML code).

It is best to use simple, everyday language that searchers are likely to type in. As a general rule, we recommend including multiple uses of each keyword phrase, enough to be prominent on the page without forcing your keywords into your content. Mention each keyword a couple of times while making sure that the way you use those keywords still sounds natural. Additionally, you should avoid using only general phrases; be sure to include detailed descriptive words, as well. If your keywords are too general, they likely have to compete with too many others targeting the same keywords. However, if your keywords are too specific, few people search for those terms, resulting in few potential visitors. It's a balancing act, and the rules aren't hard and fast. You need to find the right mix for your site by finding the keywords that not only bring traffic but bring traffic that actually converts — in other words, you want to put out the bait that brings in the right catch.

When putting keywords in the content of your site, make sure the words surrounding those keywords are also good, searchable keywords. For example

✦ Classic car customization in Poughkeepsie

✦ Reupholstery for classic Mustangs

✦ Chrome, wheels, and paint for classic automobiles

✦ New York State classic cars

These can all be used as headings for paragraphs or as links to their own pages. Remember, search engines also look for keywords in *hypertext links* (where clicking a word or phrase takes you to another page on the web) within the page, and using a search phrase within the hyperlink leads to a higher search rank for that phrase.

You should also still include *stop words* (very common words such as *the, a, to, if, who,* and so forth, which serve to connect ideas but don't add much in the way of meaning to your content) in your search phrases. Google had removed stop words from its indexes for several years, but it now uses them to deliver much more precise search results. Plus, you don't want your website text to sound like machine language — "Come shop classic cars customization all your needs Poughkeepsie." Instead, you want your website to sound like properly written English (or whatever language your audience is using): Your true readers are real people, after all. You also don't want to give the search engines the impression that you're *keyword stuffing* — over-using keywords in the text thinking it will help with ranking; they're expecting natural-sounding text, which means full sentences with natural keyword usage.

Reinforcing versus Diluting Your Theme

If you have a list of thousands of keywords that apply to your website (we tell you how to create this list in Chapter 1 of this minibook), unfortunately, you probably can't use *all* those keywords — not unless you have a site that has hundreds or thousands of pages, anyway. And even if you do have a site that huge, it's best to reduce the list somewhat: There is such a thing as too many keywords. What you want are keywords that are going to enhance your site theme and not dilute it.

Imagine that your website is a jar full of black marbles. That's a very focused theme with very focused keywords, so your site ranks high for searches for [black marbles]. Because you never talk about anything but black marbles, it's inherently obvious to search engines and visitors that your site is an expert on black marbles. Imagine that the jar of black marbles in Figure 2-1 is your site.

Figure 2-1:
Your site
is clearly
about black
marbles.

Perhaps you also sell white marbles on your site. If you just add the different-colored marbles, with no order or emphasis, it becomes harder to say that your site is focused on black marbles. You're starting to dilute your focus. The search engine still ranks it pretty high for [black marbles] because this theme is still very obvious. You might even rank for [white and black marbles]. But your rank for [black marbles] drops because your focus is now not explicitly clear. Figure 2-2 shows how a mixed-up jar of marbles doesn't seem to be about either black or white marbles, in particular, although it's still clearly about marbles.

Figure 2-2:
A jar of mixed black-and-white marbles.

Similarly, if you add gray marbles to the mix, you further dilute the black-marble theme of the jar. The search engines still rank you for [marbles], but your rankings for [black marbles] and [white marbles] are much lower or gone entirely. Your site isn't about just black marbles anymore. The more colors you add — blue, green, red, pink, tiger's eye, clear, silver — the more diluted your theme of black marbles becomes. Figure 2-3 shows how adding more colors makes black marbles less of an obvious focus.

By picking a clear site theme (in this case, black marbles) and removing all the marbles not associated with that theme, you bump up your website's search ranking because the search engine can clearly deduce that your site is all about black marbles. (**Note:** You *can* rank well for lots of different themes successfully by using a technique called *siloing*. For more on how to silo your site, refer to Chapter 4 of this minibook. Detailed instructions on siloing can be found in Book IV.)

Keeping in mind that you want a clearly defined theme, take your nice, long list of keywords and choose the ones that represent your site's theme the best. Say your site theme is Classic Car Customization. Keywords that you would definitely need to use would be [classic], [car], and [customization]. But don't forget the industry-standard words. When experts want to link to other resources, they use industry jargon to do their searches. So, research both your industry and the people on the street, so you can attract both kinds of traffic. Also include [auto], [automobile], and [vehicle] in your keywords because those words are industry terms, even though users are more likely to search for [cars] than [automobiles].

Focusing only on keywords that are very broad, high-traffic terms can lead to you not achieving a high ranking in the search engines and not getting good conversions from what traffic you do get. People tend to look for broad search terms only when they're first doing information gathering; they use much more specialized terms or phrases when they're getting ready to make a purchase. Broad search terms can bring people to your website, but make sure you also have much more specific keywords that go along with them as well.

Make sure that the specific keywords match your site theme and don't dilute it. For example, if you run a classic American car customization business in Poughkeepsie, tossing in keywords such as [Anglia], [Ferrari], [Italian], and so forth could actually do more harm than good because the business doesn't deal with foreign cars. You don't want to draw traffic for traffic's sake; you want people to actually stay and visit your site. Unless your website makes money simply by the number of visitors (like sites that make their money from selling ads based on page views), you want to attract people who won't immediately hit the Back buttons on their browsers.

Figure 2-3:
White, black, and gray marbles mixed together.

Here are some things to remember when you're picking keywords:

✦ **Clarity:** Are the keywords clear and concise?

✦ **Relevance:** Do the keywords relate to what you're actually offering on your website? (False advertising is *never* a good idea.)

✦ **Categorization:** Can the keywords be grouped into understandable keyword phrases?

✦ **Audience appropriateness:** Do the keywords give a good mix of both industry standards and what your clients use in their searches?

✦ **Targeted keywords:** Are the keywords specific to your product? Three-, four-, even five-word phrases are best.

Start weeding out what won't work for you using the preceding criteria and taking into account the traffic and return on investment the keyword brings. This can be a pretty time-consuming process, but you can take steps during the brainstorming process (see Chapter 1 of this minibook) to make this as painless as possible.

Picking Keywords Based on Subject Categories

Having a clear site theme, plus many relevant keywords, is a good start. But now you're going to have to break it down into smaller categories in order to best organize your website and all those keywords you picked out. In Chapter 1 of this minibook, you can make an outline of your list of keywords, grouping them into categories and subcategories.

The high-level terms represent broad keywords, and then they're broken into longer, much more specific keywords as you go down the outline. Using this detailed outline, you can arrange your subject categories for your website. You want to have distinct subject categories for your website because those categories help you when you *silo* (or theme) your website's contents. A website that has grouped or related keywords and links allows a search engine to return results more quickly, which in turn equals a higher page ranking for that website.

High-traffic keywords

The next step you want to take with your keywords list is to determine which ones generate a high amount of traffic and which ones have a high conversion rate. High traffic keywords are the keywords that bring the most people to your site.

With a high-traffic keyword, you want not only to bring people to your website but also to keep them there. If your word brings in a lot of traffic, but there's also a high *bounce rate* (people who stay at the landing page only briefly and then hit Back on the browser), you have a problem. A high bounce rate indicates one or more of the following issues:

✦ The keyword isn't relevant for your web page.

✦ The text on the web page isn't relevant enough to the keyword.

✦ The content or layout of the web page doesn't hold a user's interest.

✦ The page loads too slowly, so a user loses patience and abandons the page before that page fully renders.

In any case, you want to look closely at the page with the particular keyword in mind and make appropriate improvements. Keywords that have a high bounce rate do not yield many conversions, and therefore do not generate any revenue (unless you have a website where you make money based on page views alone). If anything, high bounce rate keywords can cost you money by requiring a lot of site hardware and *bandwidth* (the speed data moves to and from your site) to support all the extraneous traffic.

What we recommend to help you analyze your keywords is to use a spreadsheet program like Microsoft Excel. Excel comes along with most Microsoft Office packages, so if you have Microsoft Word, chances are you already have Excel. Microsoft Excel allows you to arrange and compare data in rows and columns, similar to a paper ledger or accounts book. We're going to talk about Microsoft Excel, but there are other spreadsheet programs out there like Google Sheets and PlanMaker. You can also try the open-source Open Office program from the Apache Software Foundation.

We suggest that you copy your entire keyword list and paste it into column A of an Excel spreadsheet, so you end up with a simple list of keywords, one per row. Depending on how big your list is, you may want to create a new tab for each subject category, separating their keywords into more manageable spreadsheets. Setting up a keywords spreadsheet comes in handy when you're keeping track of which keywords are working and which ones aren't. Not an Excel whiz? Check out *Excel 2016 For Dummies,* by Greg Harvey (John Wiley & Sons, Inc.).

Now you can use the remaining columns (B, C, and so on) to store data about each keyword. The first piece of data you need to find is an estimate of how many times people search for the keyword each day.

You can use free tools like Bruce Clay, Inc.'s Search Engine Optimization/KSP tool to measure daily search activity for specific keyword phrases on the Internet across the major search engines. It's not just guesswork; you can see actual counts!

In the previous chapter, we list tools that are available online for checking search activity by keyword (and many other search engine optimization-related tasks).

Keep in mind that the results from any keyword research tool are only estimates and should be taken as general guidelines. However, they give you a general indication of activity levels. For instance, if the keyword research tools say that Keyword A supposedly has 20,000 searches a day and Keyword B only 200, you can look at the numbers proportionally and trust that although the actual counts may vary, relatively speaking, Keyword A is searched 100 times more frequently than Keyword B.

On your spreadsheet, label column B **Searches** or **Activity.** Using a keyword research tool, enter your keywords and fill in the daily search activity count in column B for each keyword (shown in Figure 2-4). You may find it tedious to try out each keyword and copy the resulting activity number into your spreadsheet, but this data will be extremely useful for you in evaluating your keywords and improving your search engine optimization. You need benchmarks and figures, not just guesses, to make sure that you're optimizing your site for the right keywords.

Figure 2-4:
A keyword spreadsheet lets you compare data for each keyword.

	A	B	C
1	Query	Searches	Volume
3	pga	5244	11.08230719
4	pga.com	2583	6.610499028
5	freegolfinfo	64	4.147764096
6	golf tips	1884	3.046014258
7	golf	176386	1.62022035
8	pga tour	4142	1.360985094
9	michigan football	5105	0.777705768
10	golf swing	1596	0.777705768
11	pga golf	1406	0.712896954
12	pga championship	504	0.583279326
13	mgoblue	311	0.583279326
14	putting tips	133	0.518470512
15	golf shank	22	0.453661698
16	michigan wolverines	2587	0.453661698
17	golf lessons	463	0.453661698
18	us open	6077	0.388852884
19	online golf tips	8	0.388852884
20	university of michigan	4948	0.32404407
21	golf schools	1657	0.32404407
22	how to play golf	394	0.32404407
23	free video golf lessons	5	0.32404407
25	stratton	976	0.259235256
26	swing plane	15	0.259235256

High-conversion keywords

You want to figure out what keywords are going to draw buyers, versus just window shoppers, to your website. It's nice to get a lot of traffic, but it's better to get conversions; and it's best to have both *ROI* (return on investment) and high traffic. A *high-conversion keyword* is a keyword that brings you a lot of sales, sign-ups, entrants, or whatever action you consider a conversion on your site. A high-conversion keyword also could be a high-traffic keyword (see the preceding section), but not necessarily so.

A low traffic keyword may be okay if it is also a high conversion keyword. For example, if you have a keyword that brings only ten visitors a year, but one of those visitors becomes a sale that equals half a million dollars, that's a good keyword. You wouldn't want to remove that keyword from your site for a minute! Sometimes these types of keywords are called *elephant words* — big words that are so laborious to type and so obscure in usage that only a very serious searcher would think of entering it in a query. One elephant word is *mesothelioma,* which is the type of cancer that results from asbestos poisoning. Law firms love *mesothelioma* as a keyword, because even though it doesn't bring them a huge amount of traffic, people searching for the term usually mean business, and even one legal case can generate a huge amount of revenue. On the other hand, if you optimize for a keyword that brings you a million visitors and only one conversion that isn't worth much money, it's time to consider dropping that keyword phrase unless that term is a branding term for you and you want to keep it for the name recognition.

Understanding Keyword-Based Search versus Semantic Search

Earlier you learned that search engines use keywords to match results to queries. However, that's not entirely true. Search engines were first developed to use a ranking system that rewards pages by how closely the words in the query match the words on a page. The more exactly the query phrase matches a phrase repeatedly used on your web page the more likely your web page is to be delivered to a searcher as a relevant result.

There are problems with a strict keyword-based ranking system, though. First, it's easy to manipulate this kind of system with keyword spam. And perhaps more important, searchers are moving away from stilted keyword phrase-type queries like [classic car parts Poughkeepsie] and toward natural language queries like [who sells classic car parts in Poughkeepsie?]. A major driver in this shift is the prevalence of mobile Internet use and queries spoken into smartphones via the voice assistants introduced in Book I, Chapter 3.

In order to deliver the best results for queries in a natural language format, search engines developed technology that understands the connection between words, or semantic search.

By understanding the connections between words, search engines build *entities.* An entity is a person, place, or thing, as a search engine understands it, and entities are understood in connection to other entities. For instance, the entity Abraham Lincoln is connected to the entity of the White House and the entity of the American Civil War — a person, place, and thing, respectively, each with a history and multitude of facts that are much more than keywords strung together. In fact, Google often describes semantic search and the entities behind it as a move to a system of "things, not strings" (of keywords).

How to optimize with keywords in light of semantic search

How does semantic search affect what you do to help your website rank? It makes it especially important that full sentences are used and that keywords are included in a natural way that doesn't feel forced or overdone. Focus on covering a topic in a thorough and complete way rather than hitting a keyword quota. If the web page is indeed about the keyword, that keyword will necessarily be included in the text, along with other words and phrases associated with the topic. Seek to develop your website into an authoritative resource for the topic you cover. Provide useful and helpful resources that cover a topic in depth. Search engines rank subject matter experts highly, rewarding sites on qualifications it refers to as *E-A-T* (expertise, authority, and trust).

In practical terms, optimizing your web pages with targeted keywords is a process that helps content writers and website owners make sure that their website is on target, supporting the overall website theme and purpose. Keywords are helpful for guiding web page content and making it clear what the page is about. Choosing keywords and optimizing pages for them requires a certain amount of guesswork, science, finesse, and practice. The process has few hard and fast rules — for each item, you must weigh the pros and cons and make a lot of decisions. Over time, you develop a feel for search engine optimization and it becomes easier. However, it's extremely important to both track and test your keywords as you develop your website. This process is ongoing, so be patient and let yourself go through the learning curve. And remember that the kinds of tools and analytics you've begun to use in this chapter are an SEO's best friend.

Chapter 3: Exploiting Pay Per Click Lessons Learned

In This Chapter

✔ **Analyzing pay per click campaigns**

✔ **Testing keywords through pay per click ads**

✔ **Building your brand with pay per click ads**

✔ **Eliminating low click-through keywords**

✔ **Overlapping paid ads with organic ranking to reduce costs**

*B*uying pay per click ads can be a useful part of your overall search engine optimization strategy. *Pay per click ads* are paid ads that appear in a Sponsored Links section on a search results page (the site owners have negotiated with the search engine to display the search results page when a user searches for certain keywords). Pay per click ads can complement the work you're doing to move your listing up in the *organic results* (the normal search results). And because it's relatively fast to set up pay per click ads, they can be an easy way to jump-start your website's performance in search results.

To buy a pay per click ad, go to the chosen search engine's paid search website (we cover these sites in Book I, Chapter 4) and bid on a particular keyword phrase for which you want your ad to appear. From then on, the search engine tracks how many times people click your ad and bills you monthly for the total clicks. Generally, the highest bidders are awarded the top positions on the search results (though with Google, some relevance factors do affect the order). For more information on buying pay per click ads, you can pick up a copy of *Pay Per Click Search Engine Marketing For Dummies,* by Peter Kent (John Wiley & Sons, Inc.). In this chapter, you learn why these ads are useful to your search engine optimization efforts and how to use them to build your brand and reduce your cost of conversion.

Analyzing Your Pay Per Click Campaigns for Clues about Your Site

You can use pay per click (PPC) ads to provide clues that help you optimize your website for organic results, such as

✦ Which keywords bring *traffic* (lots of visitors) to your site

✦ Which keywords don't bring traffic to your site

✦ Which keywords bring the right kind of visitors to your site (for example, ones that convert to customers)

✦ Some real traffic volume numbers from that search engine for a particular keyword

What's nice about using PPC ads for this kind of research is that you can test ads scientifically. (*Note:* It's difficult to set up scientific tests of keywords in the natural search rankings because the search engine's methods are largely a secret and their algorithms are constantly in flux.) With PPC ads, you can control which ads appear for which keywords, and you can set up comparison tests. For example, you could test

✦ **Two different versions of an ad:** To see which wording draws more people

✦ **An ad that appears for two different keywords:** To find out which keyword is more effective

The various statistics and analytical tools offered by Google AdWords and Bing Ads are a nice benefit to purchasing paid ads through these search engines. The data you collect through them helps you refine your website's theme(s) and keywords. In turn, this knowledge helps you improve your site's ranking in organic search results, as well as paid results, by targeting better keywords for your pages.

Keep in mind that pay per click campaigns require constant monitoring and revision. Bid prices can fluctuate, and you have to make adjustments based on the performance of your ads. Over time, you must change your listings, removing the underperformers and adding new ones. You want to identify keywords that are costing far more than the profits they generate and discontinue them, while keeping track of these lessons learned to apply them to your natural search engine optimization as well. For these reasons, it is important to use the search engines' analytics tools mentioned previously to measure the effectiveness of your ads and to harvest data that helps you optimize your campaign.

Be aware that pay per click data does not necessarily represent how the same keywords would behave in natural search results; it only provides clues. However, it's a step in the right direction. Organic search engine optimization can take months of trial and error to produce results. By comparison, a pay per click campaign benefits you immediately with listings placed on the first page of search results, an increase in traffic, and some useful data. These benefits can help start your SEO efforts off quickly and give you some good indications of what might be the best keywords for your site.

Brand building

You want your company name to be seen and recognized in your industry without becoming generic — that's *branding*. When you think Nike, you think of a lifestyle, not merely a pair of running shoes. When your company is branded, it becomes a search keyword all by itself. Successful branding associates you with your particular industry so tightly that you're nearly synonymous. The key word here is *nearly,* of course. You don't want to have your brand name become so watered down that you lose control of how people use it. For instance, when you sneeze, do you reach for a tissue or a Kleenex? When you need a paper copied, do you photocopy it or Xerox it? A recent brand struggling with this problem is Google. It's been fighting to remind people that you're not "Googling your blind date," you're "performing a search on your blind date by using Google." Walking that line is probably a long way down the road for most businesses, however.

You can build awareness of your brand instantly by purchasing pay per click ads. Every time your company name shows up visibly in search results for a particular search query, it helps to build your brand. If your business is selling classic custom cars, you can make your name appear on search results for [classic custom cars] simply by bidding for that keyword phrase with the search engines. Although you might need to do months of search engine optimization work to bring your listing up to the first page in the natural search results, pay per click ads give you a way to increase your branding right away.

We usually recommend that clients buy ads for their own company names. You'd be amazed how many companies don't show up in natural search results for their own names. This is brand nonexistence, at least on the web. If you want to generate brand awareness, taking out PPC ads on your branded terms is a quick fix that should be on your to-do list. And if your company already does rank well in the natural search results for your branded terms, including a PPC ad as well only strengthens your branding. According to studies done by Microsoft, companies with the top organic spot and the top paid listing receive a greater brand lift than those appearing in either location alone.

When you're building your brand name, make sure your brand goes first in the `Title` tags on your website. For example, a page on our company site could have a `Title` tag that looks like this:

```
<title>Bruce Clay, Inc. - Search Engine Optimization
    Services</title>.
```

When you put your brand name first, it shows up first in your search results listing (as well as at the top of the browser window when someone is on your site). This exposure helps to give your brand a sense of authority. Be aware, however, that this does sacrifice some relevancy in the mind of the user when searching on non-branded terms.

Identifying keywords with low click-through rates

Pay per click ads let you easily test different keywords. Write your ads by using good marketing copy that's highly relevant to the keyword phrase you're bidding on in a search engine's paid search. After you've accomplished that, you can find out which keywords yield the most *click-throughs* (when people click the link) and *conversions* (when people not only visit your site, but also buy what you offer). Conversely, you can weed out those keywords that have low click-through and conversion rates.

After all, just being listed on a search results page is of little value if people don't click through to your site. With pay per click ads, you can find out which search terms work best at generating the kind of traffic you need. Broad search terms such as [cars] are probably not a good place to put your ad money. First of all, these types of broad terms are heavily searched, which makes the bidding for them more competitive. The per-click cost for a broad term would be very high (measured by price per click times traffic) and might not be worth it. Also, although [cars] is searched frequently, the click-through rate is very low. Even if someone does click your listing and visit your site, broad search queries tend to have low conversion rates because the people usually are just seeking general information and not ready to take action, such as making a purchase.

As a best practice, bid on everything that has a positive ROI and test, test, test — always test . . . never stop.

You want keywords that specifically draw people to your site and result in conversions. Here are a few facts you can keep in mind:

+ Approximately 70 percent of search queries contain at least three words.

+ People tend to use short, one- or two-word search queries for information gathering; those searches usually don't convert into customers.

✦ When users refine their search by using longer queries, they tend to be more seriously looking for a product or service.

✦ In general, users are getting more sophisticated and using more refined searches (meaning they type in longer search queries).

When choosing good keywords for your site, keep in mind the long-tail effect we cover in Book I, Chapter 5. The *long tail* is a statistical concept that says items in comparatively low demand can nonetheless add up to quite large volumes. The idea is that longer, more specific keyword phrases may not get a lot of traffic, but when people do search for them, the likelihood of click-through and conversion is quite high. Take our classic custom cars website example. A long-tail keyword phrase such as [1965 Ford Mustang GT] might make an excellent keyword phrase for a pay per click ad linked right to the Ford Mustang page on the website. Although the phrase might not get searched very often, someone typing in this search query would probably be a serious shopper — or, at the very least, will find exactly what she's looking for on your web page.

You want to purchase long-tail keyword phrases for pay per click ads for several reasons:

✦ They're relatively cheap to buy because fewer sites bid on them.

✦ The *bounce rate* (percentage of people who click a listing but then bounce right back to the search results by clicking the Back button) tends to be low because your web page closely relates to the search query.

✦ Fewer searches mean fewer clicks, so your costs remain low.

✦ The pay per click ads let you test different keyword phrases and find out what people search for that leads them to your site.

✦ You can apply what you figure out with your pay per click ads directly to optimize your website for effective keywords, which can help you rank highly in organic search results. Your ranking may go up fairly easily for these long-tail keywords because they're less competitive.

✦ Long-tail traffic adds up, and that makes it attractive.

If you have ads that people aren't clicking, the keyword might not be the problem. A low click-through rate could be due to a number of factors:

✦ Your ad copy may not be written well.

✦ Your ad may not be relevant to the search term.

✦ The audience your ad is targeting is not the same audience searching for the keywords that you associate with the ad.

Because there are several variables, it may be difficult to pinpoint exactly why a given ad has a low click-through rate. You can actually learn more from ads with high click-through rates than you can from those that underperform. If you've found a winning combination of ad copy and relevant keyword terms and it's bringing the right kind of traffic to your website, you have marketing gold. By all means, apply the same types of keywords to your website to improve your organic search engine optimization, as well.

Reducing Costs by Overlapping Pay Per Click with Natural Keyword Rankings

Pairing your search-engine-optimization work with a pay per click campaign often yields the best results. Don't do just one or the other. If you have the budget, doing both organic SEO and pay per click together is the best strategy.

Research supports the use of PPC ads, in addition to organic search results, that rank for your targeted keywords. If your company name appears in two places on the results page, you get higher impact and brand awareness — and more clicks on both the ad and the listing — than you would if only one appeared in the results. Studies have shown that when your company listing appears in the organic results *and* in a paid ad on the first results page, people get the impression that your company is an expert. As a result, they click your organic listing far more often than they would if no pay per click ad appeared. See Figure 3-1 for an example of a search ad paired with an organic ranking.

You benefit when your pay per click ads work in conjunction with a high page ranking in the organic results. It's interesting to note that when both display, although click patterns depend upon the keyword, some studies have shown that clicks go up for both the listing and the ad. Nevertheless, most people click the organic listing, rather than the paid ad. Either way, you're still generating more traffic to your site by having both an ad and a good ranking.

In addition to perceived expertise and more click-throughs, your company earns better brand recognition by appearing in two places on the search results page. And on a practical level, your site also controls more real estate on the page — leaving less room for competitors.

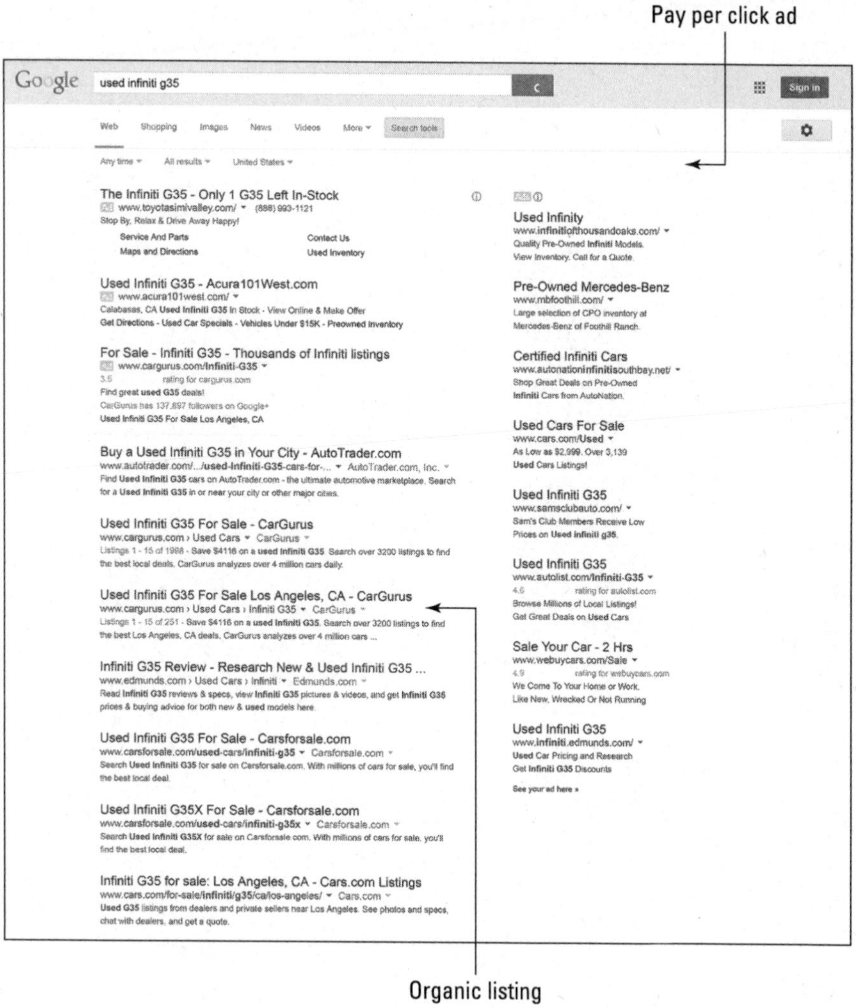

Pay per click ad

Figure 3-1:
Displaying
a paid ad
as well as
an organic
listing, as
CarGurus.
com has in
this exam-
ple, raises a
company's
perceived
expertise,
branding,
and click-
throughs.

Organic listing

Chapter 4: Assigning Keywords to Pages

In This Chapter

✔ **Knowing what search engines see as keywords**

✔ **Planning your site's themes**

✔ **Creating landing pages that attract and hold visitors**

✔ **Organizing your site into subject categories**

✔ **Consolidating themes for maximum ranking value**

*I*f you've read Chapters 1 through 3 of this minibook, you've already done a lot of the prep work for assigning keywords to pages. In this chapter, you use all that research and prep work as we explain how you can assign keywords in a way that helps make your website most accessible to search engines. You want to make it as easy as possible for the search engines to find out what your site is about because the more relevant your site is to a user's search query, the higher your site is likely to show up in the search results.

Understanding What a Search Engine Sees as Keywords

In this section, we take a step back first and talk about what search engines really see as keywords. When someone enters a search query, the search engine looks for those words in its index. Here are some general things the search engine looks for:

✦ Web pages that contain the exact phrase.

✦ Web pages that have all the words of the phrase in close proximity to each other.

✦ Web pages that contain all the words, although not necessarily close together.

✦ Web pages that contain other forms of the words (such as *customize* instead of *customization*). This is called *stemming*.

+ Web pages that have links pointing to them from other pages, in which the link text contains the exact phrase or all the words in a different sequence.

+ External web pages that link to this site from a page that is considered to be about the same keyword.

+ Web pages that contain the words in special formatting (bold, italics, larger font size, bullets, or with heading tags).

The preceding list gives you some of the clues a search engine would use to determine your site's keywords. They are not listed in order of priority, nor do they represent an exhaustive list (because the search engines keep their methods a secret). All mystery aside, the search engine's main goal is to give users the most relevant results. If a search engine cannot clearly connect a user's query to keywords on your web page, it won't include your site in the search results.

You should also put each page's keywords into its `Meta` keywords *tag* (part of the HTML coding for your web page). Opinions are divided within the SEO industry on this point, however. Around 2005, the search engines said they would no longer weigh the keywords tag heavily, if at all, because so many webmasters had abused it by cramming it full of words that didn't pertain to their sites. Although this obviously lessened the overall importance of the keywords tag, it has been our experience that a keywords tag containing appropriate phrases that are also used in the page content definitely helps your web page to rank highly. In addition, Google recently recommended that sites use the keywords tag to list common misspellings of company names or products. This confirms that Google does indeed consider the keywords tag in some searches.

Planning Subject Theme Categories

Search engines rank individual pages but they do look for overall site-wide themes in determining how relevant your web page is to a search query. As a general rule, the home page should use more broad-range terms, and the supporting pages should use more specific and targeted terms that help support the home page. By using this method, you enable the search engines to understand and index your site's contents because this is the organization they're expecting. And better indexing means better inclusion on search results.

Here's a general guideline about keywords, topics, and themes: A web page's first paragraph should introduce its keywords. If a keyword is repeated in every paragraph, it's a *topic*. If the website has multiple (we recommend six or more) interconnected pages related to the topic, we consider that a *theme*. Search engines consider a site with multiple pages of unique, informative content on a theme to be highly relevant.

You need to choose a main theme for your website. What is your whole website about? For instance, our classic custom cars website might have a main site theme of *custom cars* or *classic cars.* Which one makes the most sense depends on two things: which theme most accurately fits the business and vision of the website, and which theme is searched for the most. To find out which phrase gets the most searches, you need to use a keyword research tool such as those covered in Chapter 2 of this minibook. Here, we suffice to say that the phrase [classic cars] receives about four times the number of searches that [custom cars] does, so we use *classic cars* as our main site theme.

The preceding example points out an important principle: You should not plan your site theme and structure based solely on what makes sense to you. Instead, do research to find out how people search, and lay out your website accordingly. This is essential to your design.

Assuming that you want your site to rank high in searches for its major theme, you want to

✦ Make sure your site theme is included in your home page's `Title` tag and `Meta` tags (HTML code located at the top of a web page — we show you how this is done in Book IV).

✦ Use your site theme in your page content so that the search engines interpret the theme as keywords for your web page. Making your theme part of the keywords helps your web page come up in searches for those keywords. (You learn more about keyword strategy in Chapter 5 of this minibook.)

After you've got your main site theme, you need to organize the site content. If you already have a website, try to view it with fresh eyes because the current organizational structure might not be the most conducive to good search engine ranking. In our experience, many websites are disjointed arrays of unrelated information with no central theme. Your site may not be that bad, but as you read through the recommendations in this chapter, you may find that you're light on content, have too much of the wrong type of content, or need to do some major reorganization. As Figure 4-1 shows, you need to figure out how best to divide your site into subject categories.

Look at all the content, products, services, and so on that your website offers. Is all the stuff on your site well organized into categories and subcategories? Do those breakdowns match the way people search for what you offer? Depending on the size of your website and the diversity of its subject matter, you could have a single site-wide theme or a structure with hundreds of subject theme categories and subcategories. Some keyword research is in order here as well to make sure you're dividing up the information according to how people search. For instance, the classic cars website could separate

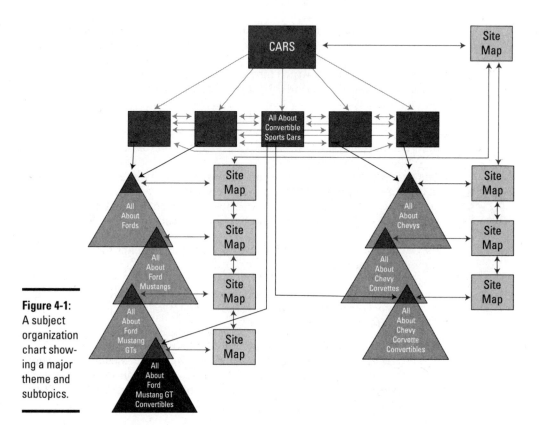

Figure 4-1:
A subject organization chart showing a major theme and subtopics.

its content either by body type (sedans, coupes, convertibles, vans, and so on), by make (Chevrolet, Ford, Oldsmobile, and so on), by year of manufacture (1950, 1951, 1952, and so on), or by some other method. It turns out that people don't usually search for cars by body type, such as [sedan cars], or by year, such as [1959 Oldsmobiles]. Instead, most people looking for cars search by make and model, like [Oldsmobile 98]. For maximum ranking in search engines, therefore, this website ought to organize its contents by make, and then by model. Of course, based on how people search in your industry, your subcategories will vary.

Choosing Landing Pages for Subject Categories

You should organize your website into categories not just because it's neater that way but also so that your site can rank well for any of its subject themes. Rather than having all inbound links point to your home page only, you should create an array of highly targeted pages representing all your categories. For each subject category in your website, you want to choose a landing page.

A *landing page* acts as the primary information page for a subject category. It's the page where all *hypertext links* (text that can be clicked to take the user to another web page) related to that subject should point. Your website's landing pages present the all-important first impression to site visitors. You want to make sure your landing pages not only put your best foot forward but also interest visitors enough to entice them to go further and hopefully convert to customers. Landing pages have to look good to users *and* search engines.

The primary subjects for our classic cars website are the different makes of cars, and each one needs a landing page. The Ford landing page needs to contain some general information about Ford cars; a separate Oldsmobile landing page should contain some information about Olds cars, and so on. Your landing pages need to have enough content so that people reaching them from a search engine feel satisfied that they've come to the right place. You want the content to engage visitors enough so that they want to stay. You also need your landing pages to link to other pages on your site that offer more detailed information within the subject category and lead to opportunities to buy, sign up, or take whatever action your site considers a conversion.

Organizing Your Primary and Secondary Subjects

Search engines look for depth of content. Your landing pages should each have at least three or four pages of supporting information that they link to. These subpages need to be within the same theme as the landing page that they support. Having several subpages linked from each landing page that all talk about the same subject theme reinforces your theme and boosts your landing page's perceived expertise on the subject.

Now that you've decided on primary subjects for your website, each with its own landing page, you need to decide whether further stratification is needed. Do you have natural subcategories under your primary subject categories? If so, you probably want to create landing pages for this second tier, as well. For our classic cars website, the secondary subjects under each car manufacturer would be the different models of cars, and we'd create a landing page for each model. So the Ford landing page could link to individual landing pages for Ford Mustang, Ford Falcon, Ford Thunderbird, and so on.

The concept of organizing a website's content into distinct subject categories, each with its own landing page and supporting pages, is called *siloing*. Refer back to the diagram in Figure 4-1 to see how our classic cars website could be arranged into silos.

A note about links

Hypertext links (also known as just *hyperlinks*) that lead to each landing page should contain your page's keywords. You want the linked text that the user clicks (the *anchor text*) to be meaningful. Google keeps track of links to determine the relevancy of each of your web pages. The link Ford Mustang Information and Pricing gains you a lot more points than Click Here because your page is not really about Click Here — it's about Ford Mustangs. You definitely want to use good, keyword-rich anchor text for links going to landing pages in your website. You don't have as much control over the links that other websites use to link to your pages, but as much as possible, try to have those links also show descriptive anchor text.

Here are a few recommendations for building landing pages:

✦ Keep each landing page's content focused on its particular subject category.

✦ Make the content engaging — consider including video, audio, images, or dynamic elements along with highly relevant text (not in place of it!).

✦ Customize the keywords on each landing page to reflect that page's subject theme.

✦ Be sure to include the keywords in the page content as well as in the Meta tags.

✦ Include links to secondary pages in the same category.

✦ Don't include links to secondary pages under different subject categories. (See the "A note about links" sidebar for more about the effective use of links.)

Understanding Siloing "Under the Hood"

Now that you understand the importance of grouping content on your site, you might be wondering how to accomplish it. If you have a gigantic website with thousands of pages that need to be reorganized, don't panic. You can do your siloing in two ways. Either can be successful, but you get the most bang from your buck by doing both:

✦ **Physical silos:** Ideally, the physical structure of your site — the directories or folders — should reflect your silo organization. This is the simplest, cleanest way to do it, and it keeps everything nicely organized as your website grows. With this organization, you want the top-level folders to be your primary subject categories, the next-level folders to contain the secondary subject categories, and so forth. So a directory structure for our classic cars site might look something like Figure 4-2.

Figure 4-2: A siloed directory structure in Windows Explorer.

Arranging the physical directories to match your siloing scheme is fine if you have the luxury of starting a site from scratch or if your site is small enough to move things around without too much pain and effort. However, if you have a very large site or a very stubborn *Content Management System* (*CMS;* software that helps you create, edit, and manage a website), you need a more flexible solution.

✦ **Virtual silos:** Websites that cannot adjust their directory structures can accomplish siloing by creating *virtual silos.* Instead of moving related web pages into new directories, virtual silos connect related pages using links. You still need to have one landing page per subject, and you need links on each landing page to identify the sublevel pages within that subject's silo. So no matter how the directories are set up for our classic cars website, the Ford landing page would have links to the Ford Falcon, Ford Mustang, and Ford Thunderbird pages. Because search engine spiders follow the links as they move through a website, this virtual silo organization does not confuse the spiders, no matter how your underlying files and folders are set up.

✦ **Doing both:** Incorporating both virtual and physical silos can be very powerful for a site that has pages that should exist in more than one silo or category. For a complete overview of siloing and architecture, refer to Book VI.

Consolidating Themes to Help Search Engines See Your Relevance

In order to rank well in search results for a particular keyword phrase, your website must provide related information that is organized in clear language that search engines understand. When your textual information has been stripped away from its design and layout, does it measure up to be the most relevant aggregate information compared to that of other sites? If so, you have a high likelihood of achieving high rankings and attracting site visitors who are researching and shopping for products and services that you offer.

As we mention in Chapter 2 of this minibook, we often explain the importance of creating subject silos by using the analogy that most websites are like a jar of marbles. A search engine can decipher meaning only when the subjects are clear and distinct. Take a look at the picture of the jar of marbles in Figure 4-3.

Figure 4-3:
A typical website is a jumbled mixture of items, like this jar of marbles.

The jar in Figure 4-3 contains black marbles, white marbles, and gray marbles all mixed together, with no apparent order or emphasis. It would be reasonable to assume that search engines would classify the subject only as *marbles.* (By the way, the marbles are used quite a lot in this book as we explain concepts and refine your understanding of developing themes. Learn to love them.)

If you separated each group of marbles into its own jar (or website), they would be classified as a jar of black marbles, a jar of white marbles, and a jar of gray marbles (see Figure 4-4).

Figure 4-4:
Each jar (or site) is clearly about one color of marbles: black, white, and gray.

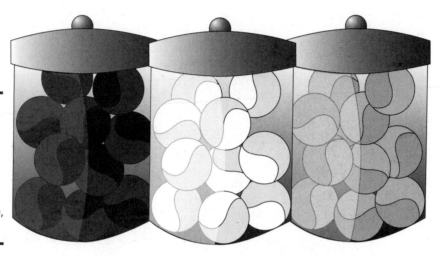

However, if you wanted to combine all three marble colors into a single jar, you could create distinct silos within the site that would allow the subject themes to be *black marbles, white marbles, gray marbles,* and finally the generic term *marbles.* (See Figure 4-5.) Most websites never clarify the main subjects they want their site to become relevant for. Instead, they try to be all things to all people.

Your goal, if you want your site to rank for more than a single generic term, is to selectively decide what your site is and is not about. Rankings are often damaged in three major ways:

+ By having too little content for a subject on your website

+ By including irrelevant content that dilutes and blurs your theme

+ By choosing keywords that are not well matched to your theme

Do you have your themes poorly defined, spread out in pieces over a number of different pages? Or are you mixing dissimilar items together on a page so that no central theme emerges (similar to the first jar of marbles in

Figure 4-3)? Both of these cases may be preventing the search engines from seeing your web pages as relevant to your keywords. If your website is not currently ranking well for a keyword phrase, consider both possible causes. You may have too little content for a theme, in which case you need to increase the number of pages that contain keyword-rich content on that subject. Conversely, if you have irrelevant or disorganized content, you might need to consolidate your subject themes by separating and concentrating them into silos, like the marbles in Figure 4-5.

Figure 4-5:
A website
can contain
multiple
subjects
if they are
clearly
organized
into silos.

Chapter 5: Adding and Maintaining Keywords

In This Chapter

✔ **Figuring out keyword densities**

✔ **Adjusting keywords**

✔ **Updating keywords**

✔ **Using tools to aid keyword**

*I*f you've been doing what we suggest in the previous four chapters of this minibook, you've brainstormed, done your research, categorized your keywords, and created *landing pages* (the web page the user comes to when clicking a link) for your subject categories. So now what? Now you actually get to add keywords.

There is an art to placing keywords on your website. You can't simply type **car, car, car, car, car, car** again and again. For one thing, that's considered spam and will get your site pulled from the search engine index. (For our purposes, *spam* is any type of deceptive web technique meant to trick a search engine into offering inappropriate, redundant, or poor-quality search results. For more details, see Book I, Chapter 6.) For another thing, a user who sees "car, car, car, car . . . " would immediately hit Back on the browser window because your site is obviously not going to be of any use to him. Remember, you want to *keep* people on your website so that they will stick around and be converted from a visitor to a customer (or however your website defines a conversion). To do that, you have to create searchable, readable content for your website.

But what do you do with those keywords we make you gather in Chapter 1 of this minibook? In this chapter, we talk about how to distribute them on your pages and how to determine the number of times you need to use them. We also discuss how to maintain your keywords. Unfortunately, the Internet is ever changing, and so is the market. To maintain your relevancy, you also have to adjust and update your keywords regularly, both in importance and frequency. But not to worry: There are tools out there that help you measure your keywords' performance and analyze your competition's keywords, and we show you how to use them.

Understanding Keyword Frequency and Distribution

Keyword *frequency* and *distribution* are two factors that marketers look closely at in SEO land. Keyword *frequency* refers to the number of times a keyword is used on a web page. Any word (or phrase) is considered a keyword if it's used at least twice on the page. (Note that search engines do not include stop words such as *and, the, a,* and so forth as keywords, although they may be part of keyword phrases.)

Keyword *distribution* measures whether a keyword is evenly distributed throughout the page and the site. It's important to make sure that your keywords appear throughout the page but especially right up front because search engine spiders generally put more weight on the first 200 words, including words in your navigation, headings, and so on. Make sure to remember to sprinkle the keywords evenly throughout the page in a normal writing fashion. Natural-sounding text is easier to read and scores better with search engines.

You can visualize keyword distribution if you imagine all the content of a web page arranged horizontally in a box, so that the beginning of the page is at the far left and the last words on the page are at the right edge. Figure 5-1 shows the distribution of a keyword on a given page. These charts show how often a keyword phrase [peanut butter] occurs many times near the beginning of the page, a couple of times near the middle of the page, with another sprinkling of uses near the end. Although a more even distribution would be better, search engines could tell from this distribution that the word [peanut butter] is an important keyword for this web page.

Figure 5-1: A linear distribution chart for a keyword across a web page.

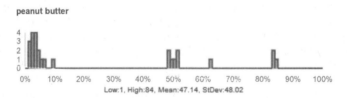

In order to have proper keyword distribution, you can't clutter up your page with keywords or just dump them on the page. When writing your text, form sentences that use those keywords. Remember what we said about keyword phrases as well. Search engine users are getting more sophisticated these days and they're entering search queries that contain four or more words instead of just two or three. If you're a good writer, you're going to have to tame some of those habits you learned while writing papers. Good writers are encouraged to use synonyms and rephrase things to keep from being too repetitive. This makes a document easier to read, surely, but it won't help with your site rankings. Because your search engine ranking is going to be measured using a math equation, it's better to think of your site in terms of supplying the equation with numbers.

For instance, if you want to rank high for a query like [classic cars], you're going to have to keep using the words *classic cars* in your page instead of using *these* and *them* and so forth. Use discretion when doing this; otherwise, your page could become unpleasant to read. A good example of how to properly spread keywords is this book. Notice how many times we say a particular word, like *keyword,* and how we distribute it through the text. We don't say "Choose your keywords during your keyword research for keyword optimization purposes using keyword tools." That level of repetition is unnatural-sounding. Instead, we mention keywords every now and then, when it's appropriate. On the other hand, we don't just say *keyword* once and then spend the rest of our time trying to find flowery ways to refer to keywords. Your competition is a good way to get an idea of what looks natural to search engines. For more on how to analyze your competition's pages, read Book III, Chapter 1.

Book II
Chapter 5

Adding and
Maintaining
Keywords

Remember that search engines count every instance of a word on a web page (except if that word appears in a graphic — computers can't "read" images). This includes all words in the article text plus words in headings, navigation elements, links, and HTML tags. Here's an example, and remember this is just a recommended guideline, of how you might evenly distribute a main keyword throughout a page that had 750 words divided into five paragraphs:

+ Once in the `Title` tag

+ Once or twice in the description `Meta` tag (in the HTML code)

+ Once or twice in the keywords `Meta` tag (in the HTML code)

+ Once in the first sentence of *on-page* (user visible) text

+ Twice in the first 200 words (including the first sentence)

+ Once each in paragraphs two, three, and four

+ Once or twice in the last paragraph

On the flip side, there is such a thing as using too many keywords — that's how you venture into the realm of spam through keyword stuffing. (Refer back to spam definitions in Book I, Chapter 6.) Remember our sample sentence about keywords from a few paragraphs ago? That's a stuffed sentence. There's no guaranteed magic number for keyword frequency, but it's a good rule of thumb to keep your keywords below 5 percent of the total number of words on the page. The better way to do it is to make it sound natural as compared to your competition. Use a keyword too often, and you could trip an alarm on a keyword-stuffing filter. Keywords repeated too often also work against user retention and could bring down the conversion rate. For a commercial website, you want to keep customers around so they'll make purchases, and you risk driving them away with too much repetition. For an informational or reference website, the goal is to have as many visitors as possible stick around and read the information available. Badly written text does not make someone want to stay on your website. Figure 5-2 shows a made-up example of a web page with keyword stuffing.

Want to make sure a search engine doesn't miss your keywords? You can draw more attention to keywords by applying special formatting, such as strong (`strong`) or emphasis (`em`), changing the font size, or using `Heading` tags. Putting them in the page titles (in the HTML `Title` tags) and the description and keywords `Meta` tags (also in the HTML code) is also recommended.

Figure 5-2:
This web page need-lessly repeats the keyword [peanut butter]. Not only is this bad writing, but also it could be considered keyword stuffing.

Adjusting Keywords

After you optimize your website for your selected keywords, be aware that your job is not done. Search engine optimization involves continual monitoring, testing, and tracking. You need to keep track of how your keywords are performing as you go along. If a keyword is not drawing in as much traffic as you think it should be, or it's drawing in the wrong kind of traffic (visitors who don't convert), it's time to go in and change it. (This is why you do a bunch of research into your competition, and look up synonyms while you're at it.)

If a keyword is not working out, sitting around and hoping it eventually will is not going to increase your ranking. SEO is not an exact science; it requires tweaking, fixing, and adjusting things. If one keyword is not working for you, perhaps its synonym might. If you find that you're getting traffic but no conversions, that's a sign that you need to look deeper into whether this is a useful keyword or if you're just wasting time trying to fight that battle.

It's more than okay to go in and adjust your keywords as needed. Do some testing between different keywords and compare the results to find your best performers. If a word's not working for you, stop using it! There are words out there that *will* bring your targeted audience, and all you need to do is make the proper adjustments to find them.

Updating Keywords

The thing about keyword maintenance is that it's not an exact science. There is no one guaranteed keyword out there that will always bring you a ton of traffic today and into the future. For one thing, no one knows what the Internet will look like two years from now, let alone five or ten. Vernacular changes very rapidly. In 2000, Google was a small upstart search engine; today, Google so dominates the industry that it's become a word in the dictionary and is often used as a verb. You can't stay still in the online world. Things that are common sense to us today might not stay that way.

For example, in the late '90s, you used a cellular telephone. Nowadays, it's a cell phone. If you're abroad, you don't use a cell phone, you use a mobile. A term that made sense as a keyword five years ago might not make sense today. The moral of the story is that you can't do your keyword research once and then say you're done. You have to keep researching as you go along, especially if you're making plans for the long term.

Using Tools to Aid Keyword Placement

Just as there are tools for measuring how often a keyword is searched (which we cover in Chapter 4 of this minibook), there are also tools out there that aid you in researching keyword frequency and distribution on a certain page. You want to use these tools to check out the competition. You need to know not only what keywords your competitors are using but also in what frequency.

There are a couple of ways you can go about this. You can count the keywords by hand and probably drive yourself nuts. Or you can use a helpful tool called the Single Page Analyzer. The *Single Page Analyzer* measures and analyzes how effectively `Meta` tags are written, how often you are using your intended keywords compared to the total number of words on your web page, and other useful word metrics about the page. This tool measures frequency and prominence and graphs the distribution of keywords. Figures 5-3, 5-4, and 5-5 show a few things about a page's keywords reported by the Single Page Analyzer of the SEOToolSet.

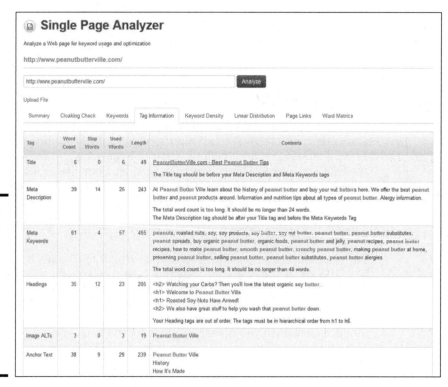

Figure 5-3: The Single Page Analyzer looks at a page's `Meta` tags and highlights the use of keywords.

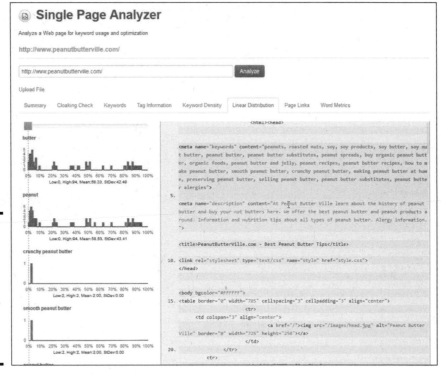

Figure 5-4:
The Single Page Analyzer reports the linear distribution of a keyword on a page.

Book II
Chapter 5

Adding and
Maintaining
Keywords

Using a page analyzer allows you to analyze competing web pages that are currently ranking in order to see what the search engines prefer and why. We also advise you to keep track of the results using an Excel spreadsheet (see Chapter 2 of this minibook for more details on that). This is something you should do periodically in order to keep track of the progress of your competition.

You can find many page analyzers out there, but the one we discuss is available within SEOToolSet Lite, which you can subscribe to for free at http://www.seotoolset.com/tools/plans-pricing/. To use it, choose Single Page Analyzer from the Page Analysis menu, and then simply type your website's URL into the query window. Click the Analyze button, and after a minute, you see a results page like the one shown in Figures 5-3, 5-4, and 5-5 for our training site, www.peanutbutterville.com.

The Single Page Analyzer shows your SEOToolSet `Meta` tag information under the Tag Information tab, as shown in Figure 5-3.

In this section of the report, under the heading Contents, you can see all the text the Single Page Analyzer found in your `Title` tag and `Meta` tags for this page. `Title` tags are what you name your web pages in the HTML coding of the site. Placing a keyword or keywords in your page titles is very important. The `Meta` description and keywords tags are other items in the HTML code

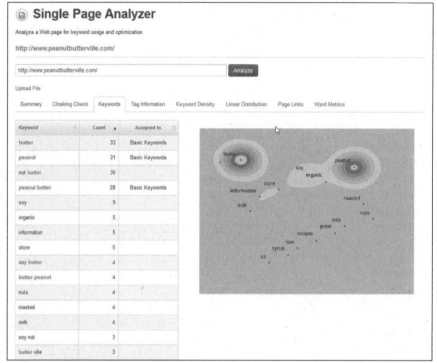

Figure 5-5:
The Single
Page
Analyzer
also maps
prominent
words used
on the page
in relation to
one another.

at the top of each page. These are not visible to the user, but search engine spiders read them and use the words in these fields to help determine how relevant your web page is and where it should be ranked for search queries.

The Single Page Analyzer can let you know whether a title is too long or too short, too many or not enough keywords are used, and you're in danger of a spam violation.

The next two tabs on the report reveal important information about keywords used on the page. For instance, you can see all the words and phrases that appear frequently on the page by using the Keyword Density tab. And the Linear Distribution tab shows how the Single Page Analyzer visualizes the linear distribution of your intended keywords throughout the page, as shown in Figure 5-4. Bigger bumps on the graph mean the keyword was used a lot in that part of the page.

In Figure 5-5, you see the prominent words used on a page in a visualization like a topographical map (under the Keywords tab). Words that are used the most appear as high elevations, or darker colors. How closely associated those words seem to be in the page's content is represented by how closely the words are positioned on the map. The keyword map lets you see, at a glance, whether the page is hitting its primary keyword targets.

Using the SEOToolSet for a broader view

Similar to the Single Page Analyzer is a *multipage analyzer,* which measures the keyword density of multiple web pages so that you can check out what your competition does and compare it with your own website. Reading a multipage analyzer is a lot like reading a single-page analyzer, so we don't break that one down separately for you. Unfortunately, multipage analyzers are generally available only as a paid option (for example, you'd need to sign up for SEOToolSet Pro to use our Multi Page Analyzer tool), but they are very useful. We cover how to mimic the multipage analyzer in Book III, Chapter 2.

There are no guarantees when it comes to SEO. The tools we describe in this chapter are just that, tools — they can only help you do a task more easily, not tell you what to do. Search engine optimization is not only about keywords, either. If you only adjust your keywords, you only upgrade your page to an okay page instead of an excellent page. Competitor research (Book III), site design (Book IV), content (Book V), linking (Book VI), site environment (Book VII), and analysis (Book VIII) are all vital components of succeeding.

The more practice you have with researching, updating, and maintaining keywords, the less you need tools like the Single Page Analyzer. When you have more experience, you can look at a page and see if the keyword density needs tweaking, but it takes practice and patience to get to that point!

Maintaining keywords is only one part of search engine optimization. The gold standard of a website is to achieve algorithmic immunity. *Algorithmic immunity* means that your page is the least imperfect it can be, across the board. So if the search engines' algorithms were to change (as they do frequently), say, lessening the importance of links and stressing the importance of on-page factors, your website wouldn't be affected because it's optimized across the board. Keywords are important, certainly, but there are also many other factors to consider before your page is the least imperfect it can be.

Book III
Competitive Positioning

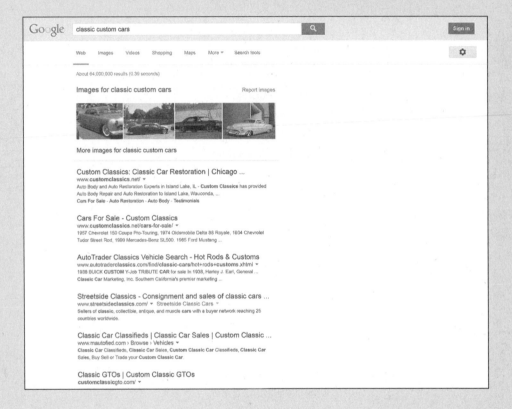

Go to www.dummies.com/extras/searchengineoptimizationaio to find out about using a valuable free tool, the SEO Multi-Page Information tool created by Bruce Clay, Inc., which gives you a report about the elements of a web page.

Contents at a Glance

Chapter 1: Identifying Your Competitors

In This Chapter

✔ **Getting to know your competition**

✔ **Figuring out the real competition**

✔ **Knowing your strengths and weaknesses**

✔ **Looking at conversion in a competitive market**

✔ **Discovering the difference between conversion and traffic**

A s with any business, you need to know what you're up against. Knowing who your competition is and figuring out how to beat them are the hallmarks of good business planning. Online businesses are like any business in that regard, but online and traditional businesses have some slight differences in how you build a competitive strategy, especially when it comes to search engine optimization.

In this chapter, we discuss how to figure out who your competition is and how to make their strengths and weaknesses work for you. You figure out how to research who your competitors are for the coveted top search engine rankings. Also, your competition in the brick-and-mortar world might not be the same as your competitors online. Finally, it's one thing to know your competition; it's another to put that information to use. Not to worry: We've got you covered in this chapter.

Getting to Know the Competition

With any business, you want to feel out the market. Whom are you competing with, and how are they doing? This is important because it gives you an idea of how to run your own business. If others are succeeding in your market space, they're doing something right. You also need to know what other people are doing wrong so that you can capitalize on that and avoid their mistakes.

Say that your business is customizing classic cars. You restore, repaint, and rev up any old model American car. To figure out your competition, sit down and think about the kind of competitors you think would be in your market. Who is your competition? Other classic car customization places. Other people who do paint and body work. Other businesses that offer simple customization services. Write them all down, even ones you think would be only loosely connected. Figure 1-1 is a brainstorming graph of your business and what you do that links your competition to you.

Figure 1-1: A bubble graph is a good organizational technique for assessing your competition.

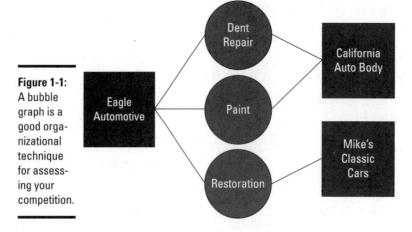

Research all these other companies and consider the following questions about these areas of their businesses:

+ **Tactics:** How do they advertise?

+ **Similarities:** What services do they offer that are similar to yours?

+ **Differences:** What services do they offer that are different?

+ **Success rate:** Do they get more or less business than you?

+ **Opportunities:** What are some of the things they are doing that you could be doing, too?

This approach is a good way to start market research. You also need to remember to continue doing this because businesses, and especially Internet businesses, are subject to changing their tactics and offerings. Every market differs, but you probably want to do a review of your competitors four to six times a year.

The other important thing to keep in mind about researching your competition using the search engines is just how much a search engine's results can differ in a day. And because different search engines use different algorithms, the page Google ranks number one — say, [classic car customization] — could be in an entirely different position over on Yahoo and in yet another position for Bing. You have no guarantee that all three engines even have the same page indexed.

Another problem is that sometimes a spider has not crawled a page in the index for more than two weeks (or longer). Although two weeks is not a long time to us, in those two weeks, that website could have been taken offline, been completely redone to reflect changes in the business, or had screwy code attached to attain a higher rank for the site. Search engines are not infallible, so it's best to continue to research the competition often to maintain the most up-to-date information possible.

Also, the playing field changes between the brick-and-mortar world and the online business world, so make a list and check it multiple times. Just because you have a cross-town rival for your business doesn't mean that he's online or that you won't have other competitors to worry about. In the real world, you see competitors coming. Online, they appear from nowhere. You have to be vigilant.

Figuring Out the Real Competition

Part of knowing whom you're competing against is knowing who is actually drawing the customers you want and who is just limping along, especially when it comes to search engine optimization. Who you think your competition should be and who actually pops up on those search results pages are sometimes two completely different things.

Doing a quick search on Google for your business's *keywords* (the words people use when doing a search) might turn up those that you think of as your competition, as well as others that are completely out of the blue. Book II tells you how to pull together a keyword list that gives you a good starting point for finding your competition. Take a typical search, as in Figure 1-2, which shows the SERP (search engine results page) for [classic car customization].

The search results page yields a mixture of listings for websites related to the search term:

✦ Classic car classifieds

✦ Customization and restoration businesses

✦ Classic car magazines

✦ Videos from classic car shows

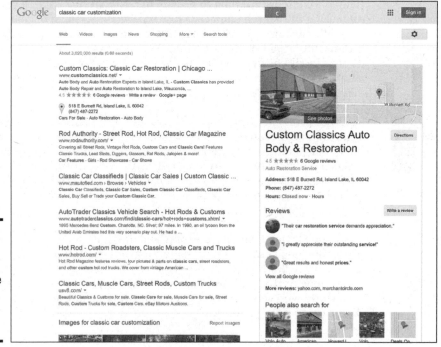

Figure 1-2:
A Google search results page for [classic car customization].

Note the different types of businesses. Are they what you'd thought they'd be? These sites represent the true competition in the search engine world for [classic car customization] because they're ranking high for those keywords. Try out other, more specialized keywords as well, and make note of who's ranking for them. Are they actual classic-car-related businesses like our example? Or are they something that's only tangentially related to classic car customization?

Another good idea is to do a search for your actual business name to see if your brand is ranking. If you don't occupy the number one position for your business name, find out who does and what they're doing to rank higher. Because if they've got the spot you want, by using *your name,* they're obviously doing something right.

For example, going back to your car customization business, say that your biggest competitor in your hometown is Bob's Customized Classics. Bob is everywhere you look. He's got print ads, he's got billboards, and he's got a *really* annoying commercial. He markets himself very well. But when you go online and do an online search for your keywords [classic car customization], Bob is nowhere to be found. In fact, you find out that Bob doesn't even have a website! What you see ranking number one for your most important keyword phrase is Motormouth Mabel's Classic Car Boutique down in Boca Raton.

Mabel's website is gorgeous. It has an SEO-friendly design, is full of spiderable content, doesn't have Flash, and contains plenty of high-quality links — it's even optimized for mobile devices (read more about mobile optimization in Book IV, Chapter 3). Mabel, not Bob, is your real competition when it comes to the Internet because when people do a search in the search engines, they're going to go to her instead of Bob. So although Bob is your competition in the brick-and-mortar world of your hometown, Mabel's the one you need to be studying if you want to get anywhere with your online presence.

Your other competitors might not even be related to classic car customization products or services, but because they rank high for your keywords, you should study them to understand their online methodology. After you know their tactics, you can figure out how to beat them. If you're doing searches for a keyword and none of the competitors are even in the same ballpark in terms of your business, you might have a keyword that isn't appropriate to your business, and you should reconsider optimizing for it.

Knowing Thyself: Recognizing Your Business Advantages

Part of being able to market yourself is actually understanding your business and your niche. This might seem like common sense, but the truth is a lot of businesses out there can't decide exactly what they are and what they're selling. Knowing what your strengths and weaknesses are gives you a huge advantage because you can work on reducing your weaknesses while emphasizing your strengths.

The first part of knowing yourself is figuring out what you do best. In our example, you customize classic cars, certainly. But maybe what you do best is repair work. You can take a rusted-out hunk of a Comet and have it up and running within weeks, with a shiny new paint job to boot. So one of the strengths you would play to on your website is restoration. Emphasize that on your website. Have a section devoted entirely to car restoration, with subsections linking to that.

The lighter side of competitive research

Doing competitive research can also be a good way to think up new tools, tricks, or toys to add to your website to attract users. You may discover that your competitors are writing confusing "How-To" articles that would be much clearer as instructional videos. Or they may have an article listing the latest baby names, which could easily be turned into a fun tool — take the initiative and create it. Users love interactive content. Be continuously looking for creative ways to make your site more interesting and more useful to your visitors.

Think about what makes you different than Bob or Mabel. Bob does restoration as well, but he doesn't have an Internet presence like you do. That's a point for you and gives you an advantage over Bob. Mabel has a gorgeous, SEO-friendly website, but she doesn't have much on that website about actual car restoration, so there's an advantage point for you to build on.

Knowing what your weaknesses are is also very important. Mabel's got a great website. Your website is not as good (yet). She's also a national business, while you are still fairly local. Those might be points you want to build on in order to make yourself equal with your competition. Streamline your website, and filter out or downplay your weaknesses. If necessary, completely take your site down and rebuild it from scratch.

Be aware of what makes you different. If you offer a service that many other people are offering, what makes you stick out from the rest of the pack? Do you offer other services that the competition doesn't? Are you quicker or more efficient? Make sure to keep a note of these differences when researching the competition. What are they doing, and how do you do it better? Or how will you do it better? Make yourself valuable to the customer.

Compare your website to your competition's: You have to make yourself equal before you can set yourself apart. Make sure you match what your competition offers in your own way and then provide content that explains why you're unique, more trustworthy, and better overall. In other words, make it obvious that you're the first choice to fit the visitor's needs. *You* know that you are made of awesome; now you just have to convince everyone else.

Looking at Conversion as a Competitive Measure

When you go through your competitors' sites, you're essentially looking for anything they have that gives them an advantage — any special content that appeals only to a certain sector or that is attracting links. Obviously, you're not using their sites as a blueprint to copy, but there's something about venturing off your own website and seeing things from a visitor's eye that can alert you to holes you would have missed otherwise.

If you are bringing your business online, you're going to want a return on your investment. If you have a shopping site, you want sales. If you have an information site, you want people to hang out and read your content. If you're advertising a newsletter, you want people to sign up for it. These user responses are examples of *conversions* (the actions that a website wants visitors to take). Getting conversions, not just visitors, is your goal if you have a website.

Your keywords are an important part of this. A good, relevant keyword for which your site ranks highly brings people to your site, and if your bottom line depends on the number of *page views* you're getting (how many people are viewing your website), you're pretty much set. However, if your keywords aren't providing you with conversions, they could be actually doing you more harm than good. Keywords that aren't generating conversions won't pay for the time, labor, or the bandwidth they take up.

Here is a conversion checklist to help you decide whether your keywords are effective:

✦ Is your keyword bringing in traffic?

✦ Is that traffic bringing you conversions?

✦ Are you able to sustain yourself based on those conversions? For example, say you have a keyword that brings only one or two conversions a year, but those conversions are worth two million dollars each. That keyword is a keeper.

✦ Is this a great keyword for branding or for an emerging product area? The only reason to keep a keyword that isn't earning you money is if that keyword has value as a brand or future investment.

Conversions also depend on your competition. You want to do better than the other guy. It's a simple fact of marketing. But you want higher conversions versus high traffic. A website that pulls in 1,200 visitors per month but has only three conversions is less of a threat than a website that has 10 visitors a month but six conversions. Your goal is to achieve high traffic numbers with a high conversion rate. Your competition is the guy who already figured out how to do that.

Recognizing the Difference between Traffic and Conversion

While you're looking at your competitors, make sure that you're also looking at which keywords are making sales versus drawing lots of window shoppers. Take note of how specialized they are. People search for broader terms when they're still doing their research and more specialized terms when they're getting ready to make a purchase. Your competitor who is ranked high for a general keyword might not be raking in the sales like the competitor dominating all the niche terms. Sometimes it takes users a lot of time and research to make a purchasing decision, so conversions may be slow to happen on broad terms.

Mabel's Classic Car Boutique might have a fantastic, high-ranking website, but if she has very few conversions, she's not really someone you should be looking at when trying to set the bar for yourself in the competitive market. High traffic does not always equal a high conversion rate.

Although a website may be high ranking and well designed for prime search engine optimization, it's pretty much moot if the site does not provide what the user is looking for. If your site's revenue depends entirely on traffic, you want a lot of traffic. But even in that scenario, you also want that traffic to stay around and visit the other pages within your site. Web pages with a lot of traffic and a high *bounce rate* (which means the visitor didn't check out more than one page on the site or look at the main site for longer than a few seconds) aren't web pages with a high conversion rate.

On the flip side, you might have a website that provides a newsletter, and the only way to get conversions is to convince people to sign up for your newsletter. A lot of traffic is good, yes, but it matters only if the people who are coming to your site do what you want them to do. If no one signs up for your newsletter, you get no conversions.

Along the same lines, if you have a keyword that draws in a lot of traffic but doesn't provide you with very many conversions, the keyword could be more trouble than it's worth. It's using up bandwidth and server space to handle all the traffic, not to mention all the time and effort you spent doing your SEO, but it's not providing you with any income.

A good example of the difference between a lot of traffic and actual conversions is a company we know that needed some optimizing. This company did well for itself in the mail order business, but not so well online. Its website was not at all search engine–friendly. After determining that changing the site's technology was not an option, the company created a research or content site, as a sister site to the original, that was designed to draw in traffic and then send people to the actual, not-optimized website, where they could make purchases. For a while, this worked well, with increased traffic and sales, until the company decided to pull down the sister site because the company felt it was drawing traffic away from its original site! Never mind that the sister site was designed to bring in traffic in order to create conversions for the original site.

The lesson here is that the company shot itself in the foot by confusing traffic with conversions. The sister site increased its sales by drawing in the window shoppers and funneling the true customers to the original website. Keep this in mind while checking your *server logs* (records that measure the amount of traffic your site receives), and don't freak out if you're not getting insanely huge numbers. If you're making a lot of sales, it really doesn't matter.

Determining True Competitors by Their Measures

Knowing your competition is very important. In terms of competition, you have three basic types: the local brick-and-mortar business, the online powerhouse, and the large corporate brand name. These are all different markets and need to be treated differently in terms of competing with them. What you need to do after doing the research on your competition is to figure out whom you're really competing against. Look at all the information you've gathered. Is Bob, your local business competitor, your main competition, or is it Mabel's online website? Or are you competing against the big kids on the block, like Ford and Chevy? It all depends on who you are and what you're trying to sell. Bob is not your competition online because he doesn't even have a website! Mabel pops up first in the search engine results, but she doesn't do quite what you do. And as for the large corporations, it's probably not even worth trying to compete with them for their broad terms.

Consider another example. Say that your brother owns his own car customization business, but he restores only Volkswagen vans. He doesn't want to rank for the term [Volkswagen] because his is a specialized business and Volkswagen is too broad a term. Most people searching for [Volkswagen] alone would probably not be looking to restore a Volkswagen van. If he were to focus solely on the keyword [Volkswagen], it would do him more harm than good because the term is too broad and is already a brand name. What he would want to do is rank for the keyword phrase [Volkswagen van restoration] or [Volkswagen bus restoration].

Brands are something to watch out for. Most people doing a search for [Nike], for example, are not actually looking for running shoes. They're looking for the brand itself. Trying to rank for the keyword [Nike] is probably not in your best interest because Nike markets a brand more than it does a singular product. If you were trying to sell running shoes while also trying to rank for the keyword [Nike], it's probably not going to work very well. You are much better off concentrating on your niche market than trying to tackle the big brands.

So assume that you've crossed out the big corporations and the smaller businesses that aren't really relevant to what you're doing. You've got a list of web pages that are your true competition. They're the ones that customize classic cars, just as you do, and rank high on the search engine results page. So how are they doing it?

There are tools out there to help with determining how your competition is doing. comScore (`www.comscore.com`), Compete (`www.compete.com`), and Hitwise (`http://www.experian.com/hitwise/`) are three such websites that offer tools designed for online marketers, giving them statistics and

**Book III
Chapter 1**

Identifying Your
Competitors

a competitive advantage. These tools measure or gauge Internet traffic to websites. They collect Internet usage data from panels, toolbars, and ISP log panels. Essentially, they can measure who's coming in to your website and from where. They also can gauge your competition. They can tell you how much your competition is bidding for a certain keyword, how much they spent on that keyword, and more. They can also track your brand name. They're statistical tools that online advertisers and site owners use to rank sites in various categories on estimated traffic.

Unfortunately, all these services charge a fee for their services. They actually cost a pretty penny. Compete starts at $249 per month for an individual plan. Hitwise and comScore do not publish their pricing. All three are useful tools for measuring the traffic to your site and where that traffic came from, along with the traffic on your competitors' websites.

Sweating the Small Stuff

Take advantage of what you can control. Every little piece of information counts, whether it's market research, what kind of traffic your competition is getting, what keywords they're using, or something else. *Do* sweat the small stuff: It really counts in search engine optimization.

But don't get discouraged because of all the competition out there: Many companies out there don't know *anything* about search engine optimization. Most major companies don't even bother with it. Your competition probably doesn't know as much as you know at this point, and you can use that to your advantage.

Chapter 2: Competitive Research Techniques and Tools

In This Chapter

✔ Finding out how to equal your high-ranking competitors

✔ Calculating what your site needs to gain high ranking

✔ Running a Page Analyzer

✔ Using Excel to help analyze your competition

✔ Discovering other tools for analyzing your competitors

✔ Diving into SERP research

*I*f you followed our suggestions in Chapter 1 of this minibook, you spent some time finding out who your real competitors are on the web, and you might have discovered that they are quite different from your real-world, brick-and-mortar competitors. You also found out that for each of your main keyword phrases, you probably have a different set of competitors. If you're starting to feel overwhelmed and thinking that you'll never be able to compete in such a busy, complicated marketplace, take heart! In this chapter, we show you how to get "under the hood" of your competitors' sites and find out why they rank so well.

Realizing That High Rankings Are Achievable

No matter what type of market your business competes in — whether broad-based or niche, large or small, national or local, corporate or home-based — you can achieve high rankings for your Internet pages by applying a little diligence and proper search engine optimization (SEO) techniques.

Your site may not be coming up at the top of search engine results for a specific keyword (yet), but someone else's is. The websites that do rank well for your keywords are there for a reason: The search engines find them the most relevant. So in the online world, those pages are your competitors, and you need to find out what you must do to compete with them. What is the barrier to entry into their league? You need a model for what to change, and analyzing the pages that do rank well can start to fill in that model.

The top-ranking web pages are not doing things perfectly. That would require that they know and understand every single one of Google's more than 200 ranking signals and are targeting them perfectly, which is highly improbable. However, the websites that rank highly for your keyword are working successfully with the search engines for the keyword you want. The web pages that appear in the search results may not be perfect, but if they rank at the top, they are the least imperfect of all the possible sites indexed for that keyword. They represent a model that you can emulate so that you can join their ranks. To emulate them, you need to examine them closely.

Getting All the Facts on Your Competitors

Identifying your competition on the web can be as easy as typing your main keywords into Google and seeing which pages rank above your own. (***Note:*** If you know that your audience uses another search engine heavily, run your search there as well. But with a market share of more than 64 percent in the U.S. and even higher globally, we think Google offers the most efficient research tool.)

You want to know which web pages make it to the first search engine results page. After you weed out the Wikipedia articles and other non-competitive results, what are the top four or five web pages listed? Write down their web addresses (such as www.wiley.com) and keep them handy. Or, if you did more in-depth competition gathering, which we explain in Chapter 1 of this minibook, bring those results along. We're going to take you on a research trip to find out what makes those sites rank so well for your keywords.

You need to know as much as you can about the web pages that rank well for your keywords. The types of things you need to know about your competitors' websites can be divided into three categories:

✦ On-page elements (such as content and `Title` tags and metadata)

✦ Links (incoming links to the page from other web pages, which are called *backlinks,* as well as outbound links to other pages)

✦ Site architecture

One basic strategy of SEO is this: Make yourself equal before you set yourself apart. But you want to analyze the sites that rank well because they are the least imperfect. You can work to make your site equal to them in all the ranking factors you know about first. When your page can play on a level field with the least imperfect sites, you'll see your own rankings moving up. After that, you can play with different factors and try to become *better* than your competition and outrank them. That's when the fun of SEO really starts! But we're getting ahead of ourselves.

Calculating the Requirements for Rankings

As you look at your keyword competitors, you need to figure out what it takes to play in their league. What is the bare minimum of effort required in order to rank in the top ten results for this keyword? In some cases, you might decide the effort required is not worth it. However, figuring out what kind of effort *is* required takes research. You can look at each of the ranking web pages and see them as a human does to get an overall impression. But search engines are your true audience (for SEO, anyway), and they are deaf, dumb, and blind. They can't physically experience the images, videos, music, tricks, games, bells, and whistles that may be on a site. They can only read the site's text, count everything that can be boiled down to numbers, and analyze the data. To understand what makes a site rank in a search engine, you need research tools that help you think like a search engine.

Table 2-1 outlines the different research tools and procedures we cover in this chapter for doing competitor research. Although SEO tools abound, you can generally categorize them into several basic types of information-gathering: on-page factors, web server factors, relevancy, and site architecture. For each category of information gathering, we've picked out one or two tools and procedures to show you.

**Book III
Chapter 2**

**Competitive
Research
Techniques
and Tools**

Table 2-1 Information-Gathering Tools for Competitor Research

Tool or Method	Type of Info the Tool Gathers
Page Analyzer	On-page SEO elements and content
Server Response Checker	Web server problems or health
Google [link:domain.com] query	Expert relevancy and popularity (how many links a site has)
Yahoo Site Explorer	Expert relevancy and popularity
View Page Source	Content, HTML (how clean the code is)
Google [site:domain.com] query	Site architecture (how many pages are indexed)
Microsoft Excel	Not an information-gathering tool, but a handy tool for tracking all the data for analysis and comparison

Of the three types of information you want to know about your competitors' web pages — their on-page elements, links, and architecture — a good place to start is the on-page elements. You want to find out what keywords your competitors use and how they're using them, look at the websites' content, and analyze their other on-page factors.

Behind every web page's pretty face is a plain skeleton of black-and-white HTML called *source code*. You can see a web page's source code easily by choosing Source or Page Source from your browser's View menu. If you understand HTML, you can look under the hood of a competitor's web page. However, you don't have to understand HTML for this book, or even to do search engine optimization. We're going to show you a tool that can read and digest a page's source code for you and then spit out some statistics that you'll find very useful.

We do recommend that you know at least *some* HTML or learn it in the future: Your search engine optimization campaign will be a great deal easier for you to manage if you can make the changes to your site on your own. You can check out the many free HTML tutorials online, such as the one by W3Schools (`http://www.w3schools.com/html/`), if you need a primer on HTML.

Cleaning up the on-page elements of your website alone may give you a lot of bang for your SEO buck. Because they're on your own website, where you have a lot of control, changes such as modifying your `Meta` tags should take little effort. Often sites see major leaps in their search engine ranking just by fixing what's out of whack in their web pages.

You may be tempted, in the early stages of your research, to conclude that a competitor's site doesn't deserve its high rankings. But don't. As you continue to collect data, you will discover why it ranks well. Gathering accurate data, and plenty of it, can mean the difference between drawing brash conclusions and forming an effective strategy.

Grasping the tools for competitive research: The Single Page Analyzer

The Single Page Analyzer tool tells you what a web page's keywords are (by identifying every word and phrase that's used at least twice) and computes their density. *Keyword density* is a percentage indicating the number of times the keyword occurs compared to the total number of words in the page. We also cover the Single Page Analyzer in Book II, Chapter 5, as it applies to analyzing your own website. When you run a competitor's page through the Single Page Analyzer, it lets you analyze the on-page factors that help the web page rank well in search engines. Subscribers to SEOToolSet Pro can simply run the Multi Page Analyzer, but for those just using the Single Page Analyzer included with a free subscription to SEOToolSet Lite, we've included a step-by-step process to build a comparison tool for yourself.

Because you're going to run the Single Page Analyzer report for several of your competitors' sites and work with some figures, it's time to grab a pencil and paper. Better yet, open a spreadsheet program such as Microsoft Excel, which is a search engine optimizer's best friend. Excel comes with most Microsoft Office packages, so if you have Word, chances are you already have Excel, too. Microsoft Excel allows you to arrange and compare data in rows and columns, similar to a paper ledger or accounts book. (We talk about Microsoft Excel, but you might have another spreadsheet program such as Google Sheets, and that's fine, too.)

Here's how to set up your spreadsheet:

1. **In Excel, open a new spreadsheet and name it** Competitors.

2. **Type a heading for column A that says** URL **or something that makes sense to you.**

   In this first column, you're going to list your competitors' web pages, one per row.

3. **Under column A's heading, type the URL (the web page address, such as** www.bruceclay.com**) for each competing web page (the pages that are ranking well in search results for your keyword phrase), one address per cell.**

   You can just copy and paste the URLs individually from the search results page if that's easier than typing them.

Now you're ready to run the Single Page Analyzer report for each competitor. You can use the free version of this tool available through our website. Here's how to run the Page Analyzer:

1. **Go to** www.seotoolset.com/tools/free-tools/.

2. **In the Single Page Analyzer section, enter a competitor's URL (such as** www.competitor.com**) in the Page URL text box.**

3. **Click the Run Page Analyzer button and wait while the report is prepared.**

While you run this report for one of your own competitors, we're going to use a Single Page Analyzer report we ran on a competitor for our classic custom cars website. The whole report contains a lot of useful information (including ideas for keywords you might want to use on your own site), but what we're trying to gather now are some basic counts of the competitor's on-page content. So we want you to zero in on a row of data that begins with "Used Words," about halfway down the report and shown in Figure 2-1, which shows a quick summary of some important page content counts.

Book III
Chapter 2

Competitive
Research
Techniques
and Tools

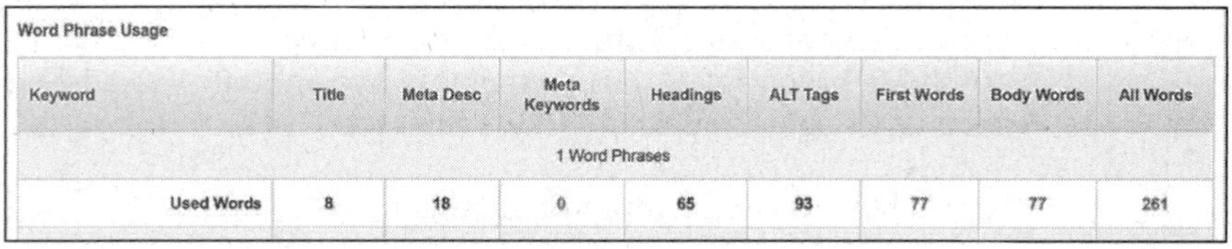

Figure 2-1:
The summary row of a competitor's on-page elements from a Single Page Analyzer report.

Word Phrase Usage								
Keyword	Title	Meta Desc	Meta Keywords	Headings	ALT Tags	First Words	Body Words	All Words
			1 Word Phrases					
Used Words	8	18	0	65	93	77	77	261

Next, you're going to record these summary counts in your spreadsheet. We suggest you create some more column headings in your spreadsheet, one for each of the following seven bold items (which we also explain here):

✦ **Title:** Shows the number of words in the page's `Title` tag (which is part of the HTML code that gets read by the search engines).

✦ `Meta` **Description:** Shows the number of words in the description `Meta` tag (also part of the page's HTML code).

✦ `Meta` **Keywords:** Shows the number of words in the keywords `Meta` tag.

✦ `Headings:` The number of headings in the text (using HTML heading tags).

✦ `ALT` **Tags:** The number of `Alt` attributes (descriptive text placed in the HTML for an image file) assigned to images on the page.

✦ **Body Words:** The number of words in the page text that's readable by humans.

✦ **All Words:** The total number of words in the page content, including onscreen text plus HTML tags, navigation, and other.

Now that you have the first several columns labeled, start typing in the counts from the report for this competitor. Run the Single Page Analyzer report for each of your other competitors' URLs. You're just gathering data at this point, so let yourself get into the rhythm of running the report, filling in the data, and then doing it all over again. After you've run the Single Page Analyzer for all your competitors, you should have a spreadsheet that looks something like Figure 2-2.

After you gather some raw numbers, what can you do with them? You're trying to find out what's "normal" for the sites that are ranking well for your keyword. So far you've gathered data on eight different factors that are part of the search engines' ranking systems. Now it's just simple math to

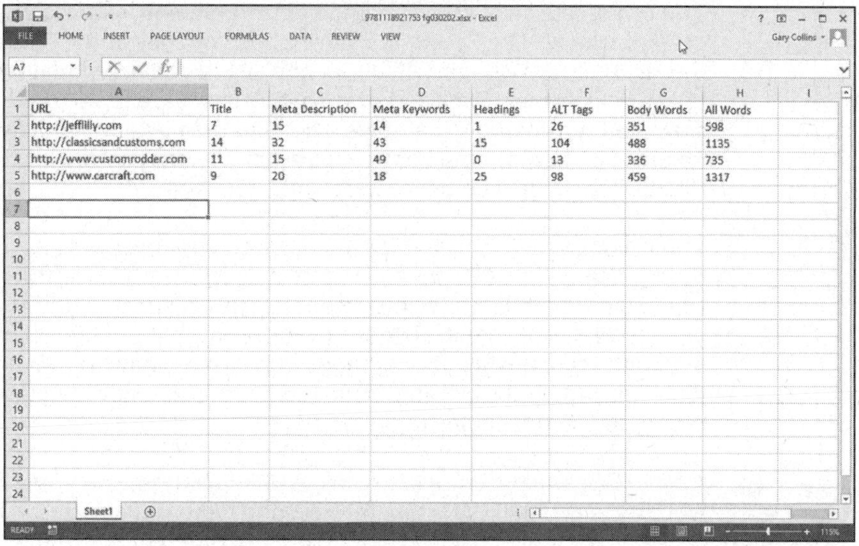

Figure 2-2:
The spreadsheet showing data gathered by running the Single Page Analyzer.

calculate an average for each factor. You can do it the old-fashioned way, but Excel makes this super-easy if you use the AutoSum feature (found in the Formulas toolbar). Click to highlight a cell below the column you want to average and then click formulas, then AutoSum, and then Average. When you select Average, Excel automatically selects the column of numbers above the field containing the average calculation, so press Enter to approve the selection. Your average appears in the highlighted field, as shown in Figure 2-3.

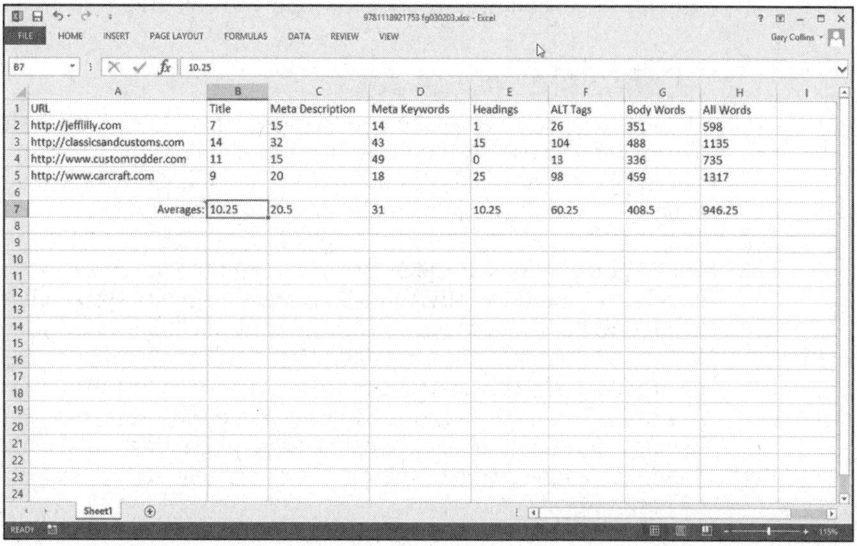

**Book III
Chapter 2**

**Competitive
Research
Techniques
and Tools**

Figure 2-3:
Excel's tools let you compute averages effortlessly.

You can create an average for each of the columns in literally one step. (You can see why we like Excel!) In Figure 2-3, if you look at the outlined cell to the right of the Average cell, notice the slightly enlarged black square in the lower-right corner. Click and drag that little square to the right, all the way across all the columns that have data, and then let go. Averages should now display for each column because you just copied the AutoSum Average function across all the columns where you have data.

You can next run a Single Page Analyzer on your own website and compare these competitor averages to your own figures to see how far off you are from your target. For now, just keep this spreadsheet handy and know that you've taken some good strides down the SEO path of information gathering. In Chapter 3 of this minibook, we go into depth, showing you how to use the data you gathered here, and begin to plan the changes to your website to raise your search engine rankings.

A Multi Page Analyzer makes short work of analyzing all your competitors' web pages at once. Unfortunately, we don't know of any free versions of this tool, but you can subscribe to a number of different SEO tool vendors online that provide this and many other worthwhile tools for a fee, including the SEOToolSet.

Discovering more tools for competitive research

Beyond the Single Page Analyzer, there are some other tricks that you can use to size up your competition. Some of this may seem a little technical, but we introduce each tool and trick as we come to it. We even explain what you need to look for. Don't worry: We won't turn you loose with a bunch of techie reports and expect you to figure out how to read them. In each case, there are specific items you need to look for (and you can pretty much ignore the rest).

Mining the source code

Have you ever looked at the underside of a car? Even if it's a shiny new luxury model fresh off the dealer's lot, the underbelly just isn't very pretty. Yet the car's real value is hidden there, in its inner workings. And to a trained mechanic's eye, it can be downright beautiful.

You're going to look at the underside of your competitors' websites, their source code, and identify some important elements. Remember that we're just gathering facts at this point. You want to get a feel for how this web page is put together and notice any oddities. You may find that the page seems to be breaking all the best-practice rules but somehow ranks well anyway — in a case like that, it's obviously doing something else very right (such as having tons of high-quality backlinks pointing to the page). On the other hand, you might discover that this is a very SEO-savvy competitor that could be hard to beat.

To look at the source code of a web page, do the following:

1. **View a competitor's web page (the particular page that ranks well in searches for your keyword, which may or may not be the site's home page) in your browser.**

2. **From the View menu, choose Source or Page Source (depending on the browser).**

As you look at the source code, keep in mind that the more extra stuff it contains, the more diluted the real content becomes. For good search engine ranking, a web page needs content that's as clean as possible. Too much HTML, script, and coding can slow down page loading time, bog down the search engine spiders, and most importantly, dilute your keyword content and reduce your ranking. Webmasters may not agree with this principle, but from an SEO perspective, a web page should be a lean, mean, content-rich machine. Want to see if your competitor is doing things right? Look for these types of best practices:

✦ Use an external *CSS* (Cascading Style Sheet) file to control formatting of text and images. Using style sheets eliminates font tags that clutter up the text. Using a CSS that's in an external file gets rid of a whole block of HTML code that could otherwise clog the top section of your web page and slow everything down (search engines especially).

✦ JavaScript code should also be off the page in an external JS file (for the same clutter-busting reasons).

✦ Get to the meat in the first hundred lines. The actual text content (the part users read in the Body section) shouldn't be too far down in the page code. We recommend limiting the code above the first line of user-viewable text overall.

You want to get a feel for how this web page is put together. Pay attention to issues such as:

✦ **Doctype:** Does it show a Doctype at the top? If so, does the Doctype validate with W3C (World Wide Web Consortium) standards? (*Note:* We explain this in Book IV, Chapter 4 in our recommendations for your own website.)

✦ **Title, description, keywords:** Look closely at the Head section (between the opening and closing `Head` tags). Does it contain the `Title`, `Meta` description, and `Meta` keywords tags? If you ran the Single Page Analyzer for this page, which we describe how to do in the section "Grasping the tools for competitive research: The Single Page Analyzer," earlier in this chapter, you already know these answers, but now notice how the tags are arranged. The best practice for SEO puts them in this order: title, description, keywords. Does the competitor's page do that?

Book III
Chapter 2

Competitive
Research
Techniques
and Tools

✦ **Other `Meta` tags:** Also notice any additional `Meta` tags ("`revisit after`" is a popular and perfectly useless one) in the Head section. Webmasters can make up all sorts of creative `Meta` tags, sometimes with good reasons that may outweigh the cost of expanding the page code. However, if you see that a competitor's page has a hundred different `Meta` tags, you can be pretty sure it doesn't know much about SEO.

✦ **Heading tags:** Search engines look for heading tags such as `H1`, `H2`, `H3`, and so forth to confirm what the page is about. It's logical to assume that a site will make its most important concepts look like headings, so these heading tags help search engines determine the page's keywords. See whether and how your competitor uses these tags. (We explain the best practices for heading tags in Book IV, Chapter 1, where we cover good SEO-friendly site design.)

✦ **Font tags, JavaScript, CSS:** As we mention in the previous set of bullets, if these things show up in the code, the page is weighted down and not very SEO-friendly. Outranking pages with a lot of formatting code might end up being easier than you thought.

Seeing why server setup makes a difference

Even after you've checked out the source code for your competitor's pages (which we talk about in the preceding section), you're still in information-gathering mode, sizing up everything you can about your biggest competitors for your chosen keywords. The next step isn't really an on-page element; it's more the foundation of the site. We're looking beyond the page now at the actual process that displays the page, which is on the server level. In this step, you find out how a competitor's server looks to a search engine by running a server response checker utility.

Generally, an SEO-friendly site should be free of server problems such as improper *redirects* (a command that detours you from one page to another that the search engine either can't follow or is confused by) and other obstacles that can stop a search spider in its tracks. When you run the server response checker utility, it attempts to crawl the site the same way a search engine spider does and then spits out a report. In the case of our tool (available at no charge as part of the SEOToolSet at `www.seotoolset.com`), the report lists any indexing obstacles it encounters, such as improper redirects, robot disallows, cloaking, virtual IPs, block lists, and more. Even if a page's content is perfect, a bad server can keep it from reaching its full potential in the search engine rankings.

You can use any server response checker tool you have access to, but we're going to recommend ours because we know it works, it returns all the information we just mentioned, and it's free. Here's how you can run the free SEOToolSet Server Response Checker:

1. **Go to** `www.seotoolset.com/tools/free-tools/`.

2. **Under the heading Check Server Page, enter the URL of the site you want to check in the Your URL text box, and then click the Check Response Headers button.**

The SEOToolSet Check Server Page tool reads the robots text (`.txt`) file on a website, which contains instructions for the search spiders when they come to index the site. Because you don't want the first thing a search engine finds to be a File Not Found error, you definitely want to have a robots text file on your own website. Even an empty file is preferable to having *no* file at all. Search engines always check for one, and if no file exists, your server returns a File Not Found error. (More on robots text files in Book VII, Chapter 1.)

When we run the Check Server Page report for a classic cars competitor site, the report looks like Figure 2-4.

CHECK SERVER PAGE

When search engine spiders visit your website, it's important to make sure they can crawl around easily and index the maximum number of pages possible. Use the Check Server Page tool to quickly verify the spiderability of your site. After reading the server's response headers, the tool reports any potential roadblocks that could cause a problem for search engine spiders. You can run it anytime as a precaution, but it's especially useful before you submit your site to search engines for indexing new content.

Knowing what's under your server's hood can help you keep your site humming. A clean server ensures the best possible environment for search engine indexing as well as user experience.

Enter the URL of any web page to run the Check Server Page tool below. Redirects (301 redirects are OK, but all other types are not recommended) and any problems detected will include the server error codes and other details, so you can resolve issues that could impact your website's ranking and visibility in search results.

Your URL:

www.classiccars.com

[Check Response Headers]

SEOToolSet™ Server Header Check Report

Header	Value
Status	301 - Moved Permanently (http://www.classiccars.com/) → 200 - OK (http://classiccars.com/)
content-length	89490
x-powered-by	ASP.NET
set-cookie	Cobrand=default; path=/; _ASPXANONYMOUS=ChMGSRo5wb4Fwi8BKBt-g4Tiihoa87g8XYSOjb8JYEisZAfDeA2jyu8uquCD2KhnsfTaHkLqhVe4z3b8mYShCej7KBTVymQvCCCzbMQtxX00p-sw2_IJlFCNTghZiJ6tzP_zdddjdmYADgG1forYTg2; expires=Thu, 27-Aug-2015 08
x-aspnet-version	4.0 30319
server	Microsoft-IIS/8.5
connection	close
cache-control	private
date	Thu, 18 Jun 2015 21
p3p	CP="CAO PSA OUR"
content-type	text/html; charset=utf-8

Other Info

Original URL	http://www.classiccars.com/
DNS IP	Address: 138.91.157.119
Ping	Failed (Average Ping Time: 0ms)

Figure 2-4: The Check Server Page report for a competitor's web page.

Book III Chapter 2

Competitive Research Techniques and Tools

In the report shown in Figure 2-4, you can see that it has a `Sitemap.xml` file, which serves to direct incoming bots. The more important item to notice, however, is the number 200 that displays in the Header Info section. This is the site's server status code, and 200 means that its server is A-okay and is able to properly return the page requested.

Table 2-2 explains the most common server status codes. These server statuses are standardized by the World Wide Web Consortium (W3C), so they mean the same thing to everyone. The official definitions can be found on its site at `http://www.w3.org/protocols/rfc2616/rfc2616-sec10.html` if you want to research further. We go into server code standards in greater depth in Book IV. Here, we boil down the technical language into understandable English to show you what each server status code really means to you.

Table 2-2		Server Status Codes and What They Mean	
Code	*Description*	*Definition*	*What It Means (If It's on a Competitor's Page)*
200	Okay	The web page appears as expected.	The server and web page have the welcome mat out for the search engine spiders (and users too). This is not-so-good news for you, but it isn't surprising either because this site ranks well.
301	Moved Permanently	The web page has been redirected permanently to another web page URL.	When a search engine spider sees this status code, it simply moves to the appropriate other page.
302	Found (Moved Temporarily)	The web page has been moved temporarily to a different URL.	This status should raise a red flag. Although there are supposedly legitimate uses for a 302 Redirect code, they can cause serious problems with search engines and could even indicate something malicious is going on. Spammers frequently use 302 Redirects.
400	Bad Request	The server could not understand the request because of bad syntax.	This could be caused by a typo in the URL. Whatever the cause, it means the search engine spider is blocked from reaching the content pages.

Code	Description	Definition	What It Means (If It's on a Competitor's Page)
401	Unauthorized	The request requires user authentication.	The server requires a login in order to access the page requested.
403	Forbidden	The server understood the request, but refuses to fulfill it.	Indicates a technical problem that would cause a roadblock for a search engine spider. (This is all the better for you, although it may be only temporary.)
404	Not Found	The web page is not available.	You've seen this error code; it's the `Page Can Not Be Displayed` page that displays when a website is down or nonexistent. Chances are that the web page is down for maintenance or having some sort of problem.
500 and higher	Miscellaneous Server Errors	Individual errors are defined in the report.	The 500–505 status codes indicate that something's wrong with the server.

The other thing you want to glean is whether the page is *cloaked* (the page shows one version of a page's content to users but a different version to the spiders). Enter the site URL you want to check into the SEO Cloaking Checker tool (also located at www.seotoolset.com/tools/free-tools/). This software tool runs through the site, identifying itself as different services, including Mozilla Firefox, Googlebot, and Bingbot, to ensure that they all match (see Figure 2-5).

**Book III
Chapter 2**

Competitive Research Techniques and Tools

Figure 2-5:
Cloaking info from the SEO Cloaking Checker report.

SEO CLOAKING CHECKER

Cloaking refers to the practice of showing one version of a web page to humans, but a different version to search engine spiders. For search engine optimization, cloaking is generally considered bad practice and should be avoided. Search engines want to index what the user sees, and can get pretty suspicious and even levy penalties if they think something deceptive is going on.

Enter your site below to check for cloaking in the eyes of various search engines and web browsers. If you find any cloaking issues, we suggest you investigate and resolve them appropriately.

URL:
www.bruceclay.com

Check for Cloaking

SEOToolSet® Page Cloaking Report

To manually detect whether a competitor's site uses *cloaking,* you need to compare the spiderable version to the version that you are viewing as a user. So do a search that you know includes that web page in the results set, and click the cached link under that URL when it appears. This shows you the web page as it looked to the search engine the last time it was spidered. Keeping in mind that the current page may have been changed a little in the meantime, compare the two versions. If you see entirely different content, you're probably looking at cloaking.

Tracking down competitor links

So far, we've been showing you how to examine your competitors' on-page elements and their server issues. It's time to look at another major category that determines search engine relevance: backlinks.

Backlinks, also known as inbound links, are incoming hyperlinks from one web page to another site.

Why do search engines care so much about backlinks? Well, it boils down to the search engines' eternal quest to find the most relevant sites for their users. They reason that if another web page thinks your web page is worthy of a link, your page must have value. Every backlink to a web page acts as a vote of confidence in that page.

The search engines literally count these "votes." It's similar in some ways to an election, but with one major exception: Not every backlink has an equal vote. Backlinks that come from authorities in your subject area will have greater weight than those that do not. For example, if you have a site about search engine optimization, a backlink from Search Engine Land (a popular digital marketing news website) will carry more weight than a backlink from your neighbor's blog about pet care. However, that backlink from the pet care blog would be valuable to a pet store's website. The value of a backlink depends on where it's pointing. You can read more about how linking works in Book VI.

In the search engines' eyes, the number of mentions and backlinks to a web page increases its expertness factor (and yes, that is a word, because we say so). Lots of backlinks indicate the page's popularity and make it appear more trustworthy as a relevant source of information on a subject. This alone can cause a page to rank much higher in search engine results when the links come from related sites.

You can find out how many backlinks and mentions your competitors have:

✦ **Using tools:** There are a number of paid tools, such as Link Detox (www.linkdetox.com) and Majestic (https://majestic.com), that let you analyze your competitors' links. Majestic also provides a free plug-in (`https://majestic.com/majestic-widgets/plugins`) that provides backlink data for any page you visit, including the number of backlinks and the quality of those backlinks.

✦ **Using Google:** In the regular search box on `www.google.com`, type the query **["domain.com" -site:*domain.com*]**, substituting the competing page's URL for `domain.com`, and click the Google Search button. This returns all pages that mention your site, usually as a link (and if it isn't, you can ask the site to make it a link!). You can also use **[link:domain.com]** but the numbers are less accurate.

You may want to run these tests for both `www.domain.com` and `domain.com` (the second time, without the `www.` in front). Sites may have these URLs as separate web pages. Searching with the non-www version produces results from www and non-www pages, plus any other sub-domains the site may be using.

There is, unfortunately, no tool that provides a comprehensive list of all a competitor's backlinks. You can, however, look at the numbers to get an idea, proportionately, of how many inbound links each web page has that's outranking yours. The numbers aren't really accurate in themselves, but they give you a gauge for comparison. For instance, if you're trying to optimize your classic custom cars web page for the same keyword as a page that has 12,000 backlinks to it, and your page has only 50, you know it's going to be an uphill battle. In fact, you might decide that optimizing that page for that keyword isn't where you want to spend your energy, but we cover making those kinds of decisions in Chapter 3 of this minibook.

In any event, you want to track your competitors' backlink counts; this is very useful raw data. We suggest adding more columns to your competitor-data spreadsheet and recording the numbers given by Google and/or tools in columns so that you can compare your competitors' numbers to your own.

Sizing up your opponent

If you walk onto a battlefield, you want to know how big your opponent is. Are you facing a small band of soldiers or an entire army with battalions of troops and air support? This brings us to the discussion of the website as a whole, and what you can learn about it.

So far we've focused a lot on the individual web pages that rank well against yours. But each individual page is also part of a website containing many pages of potentially highly relevant supporting content. If your competition has an army, you need to know.

**Book III
Chapter 2**

Competitive
Research
Techniques
and Tools

To find out how big a website is, you can use a simple Google search with the `site:` operator in front of the domain, as shown in Figure 2-6. At Google.com, enter [**site:*domain.com***] in the search box (leaving out the square brackets, and using the competitor's domain) and then click Google Search. The number of results tells you how many pages on the site have been indexed by Google — and what you're up against. You can also use this exact same process on Bing.

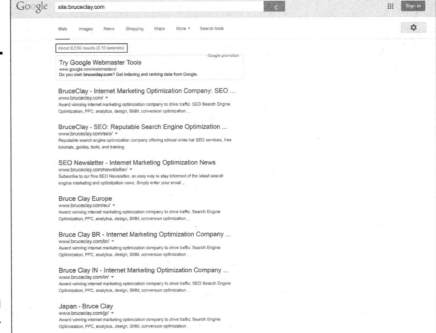

Figure 2-6:
By searching for [site: bruceclay.com], you can identify how many pages Google has indexed for a site. In the case of www.bruceclay.com, we see Google has indexed 6,530 pages.

For performance reasons, Google doesn't display all the indexed pages, but omits the ones that seem most like duplicates. If you truly want to see all the indexed listings for a site, you can navigate to the very last results page of your [site:] query and click the option to Repeat the Search with the Omitted Results Included. (Even then, Google shows only up to a maximum of 1,000 listings.) Pull out your competitor-data spreadsheet again and record the total number of indexed pages (filtered and total) for each site in new columns.

Comparing your content

You've been pulling in lots of data, but data does not equal analysis. Now it's time to run research tools on your own web page and find out how you compare to your competition.

Run a Single Page Analyzer report for your web page, and compare your on-page elements to the figures you collected in your competitor-data spreadsheet (as we describe in the earlier section, "Grasping the tools for competitive research: The Single Page Analyzer"). Next, check your own backlink counts using Google and Yahoo. (See the earlier section, "Tracking down competitor links," for details on how to do this.) Record all the numbers with today's date so that you have a benchmark measurement of the "before" picture before you start doing your SEO.

After you have metrics for the well-ranked pages and your own page, you can tell at a glance how far off your page is from its competitors. The factors in your spreadsheet are all known to be important to search engine ranking, but they aren't the *only* factors, not by a long shot. Google has more than 200 factors in its algorithm, and they can change constantly. However, having a few that you can measure and act on gives you a starting place for your search engine optimization project.

Penetrating the Veil of Search Engine Secrecy

Book III Chapter 2

The search engines tell you a lot, but not the whole story. Search engines claim that the secrecy surrounding their algorithms is necessary because of malicious spammers, who would alter their sites deceptively for the sole purpose of higher rankings. It's in the search engines' best interests to keep their methods a secret; after all, if they published a list of do's and don'ts, and just what their limits and boundaries are, then the spammers would know the limits of the search engines' spam catching techniques. Also, secrecy leaves the search engines free to modify things any time they need to. Google changes its algorithm frequently. For instance, Matt Cutts of Google said the search engine makes more than 500 changes to the algorithm per year. No one knows what changed, how big the changes were, or when exactly they occurred. Instead of giving out the algorithm, search engines merely provide guidelines as to their preferences. This is why we say that SEO is an art, not just a science: Too many unknown factors are out of your control, so a lot of finesse and intuition are involved.

Competitive Research Techniques and Tools

Other factors can complicate rankings as well. Here's a brief list of factors, which have nothing to do with changes on the websites themselves, that can cause search engine rankings to fluctuate:

✦ The search engine changed its algorithm and now weighs factors differently.

✦ The search engine may be testing something new (a temporary change).

✦ The index being queried is coming from a different data center. (Google, for instance, has many data centers in different locations, which may have different versions of the index.)

✦ The search engine had a technical problem and restored data temporarily from cache or a backup version.

✦ Data may not be up-to-date (depending on when the search engine last crawled the websites).

Diving into SERP Research

You can use the search engines to help you analyze your competitors in many ways. You're going to switch roles now and pretend for a moment that the high-ranking site is yours. This helps you better understand the site that is a model for what yours can become.

Start with a competitor's site that's ranking high for your keyword in the search engine results pages (SERPs). You want to find out why this web page ranks so well. It may be due to one of the following:

✦ **Backlinks:** Find out how many backlinks the web page has. Run a search at Google for ["www.*domain.com*/page.htm" =site:*domain.com*], substituting the competitor's web page URL for *domain.com*. The number of results is an indicator of the site's popularity with other web pages. If it's high, and especially if the links come from related industry sites with good PageRank themselves, backlinks alone could be why the page tops the list.

✦ **Different URL:** Run a search for your keyword on Google to see the results page. Notice the URL that displays for the competitor's listing. Keeping that URL in mind, click the link to go to the active page. In the address bar, compare the URL showing to the one you remembered. Are they the same? Are they different? If they're different, how different? Although an automatic redirect from `http://domain.com` to `http://www.domain.com` (or vice versa) is normal, other types of swaps may indicate that something fishy is going on. Do the cache check in the next bullet to find out whether the page the search engine sees is entirely different than the one live visitors are shown.

✦ **Cached version:** If you've looked at the web page and can't figure out why it would rank well, the search engine may have a different version of the page in its *cache* (its saved archive version of the page). Whenever the search engine indexes a website, it stores the data in its cache. Note that some websites are not cached, such as the first time a site is crawled or if the spider is being told not to cache the page (using the `Meta` robots `noarchive` instruction) or if there is an error in the search engine's database.

To see the cached version of a page, follow these steps:

1. **Run a search on Google for your keyword.**

2. **Click the drop-down icon next to the URL and click Cached.**

3. **View the cached version of the web page.**

   At the top of the page, you can read the date and time it was last spidered. You can also easily view how your keywords distribute throughout the page in highlighted colors.

You can also view a cached version of a page on Bing following the same steps.

**Book III
Chapter 2**

**Competitive
Research
Techniques
and Tools**

Chapter 3: Applying Collected Data

In This Chapter

⊾ Applying best practices to your page construction

⊾ Identifying what's natural for your competitors

⊾ Sizing up what engagement objects you need

⊾ Building your link equity with a little help from your competitors

⊾ Examining how your competitors organize their content

⊾ Applying your analysis to help with content siloing

Your real competitors online are the sites that show up at the top of the results whenever someone searches for your *keywords* (words or phrases that people enter as a search query), not necessarily the big name brand in your industry. So if you want your classic car customization business to rank well in the search engines, for example, you can run searches for your main keywords to see who your competition is.

If you just finished the exercises in Chapters 1 and 2 of this minibook, you should have a spreadsheet full of data on your top competitors. Looking at the web pages that the search engines find most relevant for your keywords is a crucial step in your search engine optimization (SEO). Looking at them, you can find out what's "natural" for your competition. For example, you could find that all the top-ranked web pages have more than 1,000 words of text. You can be pretty sure that if you're going to rank well for that keyword, you're going to have to beef up your page's content to match the competition.

Search engines include many different page factors in their *algorithms* (in this context, formulas for determining a web page's relevance to a key-word), which they use to decide the order in which web pages are listed on a search engine results page (SERP). For each ranking factor, it's impossible to know exactly what the search engine considers to be a "perfect" score. But you can look at the top ranking sites for clues because they're most consistently ranked for top keyword categories. Of the more than 200 different ranking signals in Google's algorithm, some are known, but many remain a mystery. For all the known ranking factors, the sites that rank well are the ones that are the "least imperfect" in the search engine's eyes. So it's a good idea to try to make yourself equal to them before you try to set yourself apart.

In this chapter, you take the data you've gathered on your top competitors and apply it to your own website. In other words, you're going to figure out how to make yourself equal to and then better than your competition. We talk about the best practices for some of these page elements, which help you make good decisions on how far to go in making yourself equivalent. You also look beyond page elements to other data about your competitors, including their *backlinks* (incoming links to a web page), their content structure, and what kinds of images, videos, and other types of objects they have on their sites to engage users. All this helps you understand what you need to do to make your site compete in the search engines.

Sizing Up Your Page Construction

It's time to look at your own website and see how it's measuring up. Examine your main landing pages, which are the pages best suited for searchers looking for your main keywords. You generally need a minimum of one landing page with at least five secondary or supporting pages/articles dedicated to each of your main keywords so that users searching for those keywords click your link and arrive at a page that delivers just what they're looking for. You should also have secondary keywords on those pages, but the point is to have focused content that has the main keyword distributed throughout.

Landing page construction

The way your landing pages are put together matters to search engines and helps them determine the relevance of each page. The engines count everything that can be quantified, like the total number of words, how many times your keywords are repeated on the page *(prominence)*, and so forth. It pays to make your page construction line up with what the search engines consider to be optimal for each of these elements as much as possible.

In Chapter 2 of this minibook, we explain how to do research on your top competitors using the Page Analyzer tool's report (which compiles statistics about a web page such as its *keyword density,* a percentage indicating the number of times the keyword occurs compared to the total number of words in the page). We recommended that you put your data in a spreadsheet like the one in Figure 3-1, which pulls together stats from four different competitors' web pages.

Figure 3-1:
Spreadsheet showing competitor data from a Single Page Analyzer report.

URL	Title	Meta Description	Meta Keywords	Headings	ALT Tags	Body Words	All Words
http://jefflilly.com	7	15	14	1	26	351	598
http://classicsandcustoms.com	14	32	43	15	104	488	1135
http://www.customrodder.com	11	15	49	0	13	336	735
http://www.carcraft.com	9	20	18	25	98	459	1317
Averages: 10.25	20.5	31		10.25	60.25	408.5	946.25

Notice that there are seven columns of data for each competitor, and the numbers they contain are straight off of the Single Page Analyzer report. Also notice the Averages row at the bottom, which is simply the *mean* (or average) of each column. It's a pretty simple way to figure out what's considered normal (or "natural") for the top-ranking competitors for your keyword, in the search engines' eyes. These seven categories represent on-page elements that you can compare to your own web page.

After you study your competitors, it's time to run your own web pages through the Single Page Analyzer to get your starting figures for comparison. Here's how to run the Single Page Analyzer:

1. **Go to** www.seotoolset.com/tools/free-tools/.

2. **In the Single Page Analyzer tool, enter your page's URL (such as** www.yourdomain.com/pageinprogress.html**) in the Page URL text box.**

3. **Click the Run Page Analyzer button and wait until the report displays.**

Keep in mind that for each item, the best practices just give you a starting point for your analysis. As we mentioned, the top sites are imperfect, so there is room to vary your analysis because your goal is first becoming equal to and then better than your competition. Your market may require certain page elements to be much shorter or longer than the guidelines recommend. Remember that your page construction should make you competitive for

**Book III
Chapter 3**

Applying Collected Data

your keywords and make judgment calls backed up by real-world results. SEO requires ongoing monitoring and tweaking because the nature of rankings is transitory. Search engine rankings fluctuate, and you have to make tweaks to adapt. Your target number for each element can be changed over time as you get more of a feel for what the search engines consider most relevant.

After you have your data in hand, you can dig into your analysis. In this list, we cover what we consider to be the SEO best practice for each item and how it lines up with the competitors' natural usage based on the averages in Figure 3-1. Knowing those two things, you can decide what to do on your own page (these numbers are examples only; your industry will be different):

- ✦ **Title:** The `Title` tag is a line of HTML you put in the Head, or top, section of a web page's HTML code:

  - **Best practice:** Six to 12 words (up to approximately 65 characters).

  - **Competitors' average:** 10.25 words.

  - **Recommendation:** Because the search engines are rewarding these sites with top rankings and those sites' natural averages fall within best practices, you should make your `Title` tag ten words in length.

- ✦ **Meta description:** The `Meta` description is another HTML tag that goes in the Head section of a web page:

  - **Best practice:** Twelve to 24 words (up to 156 characters)

  - **Competitors' average:** 20.5 words.

  - **Recommendation:** The top-ranking sites seem to be following best practices here, so go ahead and match them by putting 20 or 21 words in your `Meta` description tag.

- ✦ **Meta keywords:** The `Meta` keywords tag also goes in the Head section and gives you a place to list all your keywords for the page:

  - **Best practice:** 24 to 48 words in length.

  - **Competitors' average:** 31 words.

  - **Recommendation:** They've done it again, falling within best practice guidelines. You should make your `Meta` keywords tag about 31 words long.

- ✦ **Headings:** This refers to the number of heading tags on the page (which are `h#` formatting tags applied to headings and subheadings):

  - **Best practice:** There's no minimum/maximum guideline for heading tags; however, you should have a single `H1` tag at the top of the page for your main headline because search engines look for this. Use `H2`, `H3`, and so on throughout the page for subheadings that help break up the text in natural places.

- **Competitors' average:** 10.25 tags. However, notice that the competitors don't agree on this: Their Heading counts are 1, 15, 0, and 25.

- **Recommendation:** Where you have one or two competitors that are completely out of range of the rest, you shouldn't try to match the average. Follow the bulk of the sites or best practices instead.

✦ **Alt tags:** `Alt` attributes are alternate text attached to images that briefly describes the image to search engines (and users). In the Single Page Analyzer, the `Alt` tags figure represents the total number of words included in `Alt` attributes on the page:

- **Best practice:** For every image, you should include an `Alt` attribute (incorporating keywords, if appropriate). The length of the `Alt` attribute depends on the size of the image but should not exceed 12 words per image for the largest images. (See Book V, Chapter 2 for the mathematical rule of thumb for this.)

- **Competitors' average:** 60.25 words.

- **Recommendation:** There's a wide disparity between the four sites (26, 104, 13, 98). You should probably follow the best practices rather than the average here.

✦ **Body words:** This refers to the number of words in the Body section, which is the part between the beginning and ending `Body` tags, or the main page content that users see. The count excludes *stop words* (little words like *a, an, but,* and others that the search engines disregard):

- **Best practice:** You should fall within the range of your competitors, but a landing page needs at least 400 to 500 words of readable content as a general rule to establish its relevance to a keyword.

- **Competitors' average:** 408.5 words.

- **Recommendation:** All the competitors' pages have a similar count, falling within best practices, so this average is probably a sweet spot you'll want to match or slightly exceed.

✦ **All words:** This is the total number of words in the page minus stop words (so it includes the Body section as well as other sections that may or may not be visible to users):

- **Best practice:** There's no minimum or maximum guideline here, so match your competitors as long as they're in keeping with other SEO best practices (such as keeping the HTML code uncluttered, and so on).

- **Competitors' average:** 946.25 words.

- **Recommendation:** Aim to have sufficient text in the Body section and to keep your HTML clean. This number usually takes care of itself.

Want more info on page construction? See Book V, Chapter 3 for additional recommendations on building effective, SEO-friendly page elements.

**Book III
Chapter 3**

Applying Collected Data

Content

To make sure that your landing pages have enough focused content to be considered relevant for their main keywords, you want to examine the distribution of keywords on a page. You can do this by looking in the search engine's *cache* (stored version of a page). Google's cached text-only version of a web page is the best way to see how much content the search engines have actually *indexed* (included in their database of web pages, from which they pull search results).

Pull up Google's cached text version of a page and then follow these steps:

1. **Press the Control key and the F key simultaneously.** (On a Mac, press Command and F.)

2. **Type the keyword or keyword phrase and press Enter.**

3. **Select Highlight All and discover an at-a-glance view of the keyword distribution on the page.**

This text-only view is what Google sees, and your keywords are highlighted. This view is useful because

✦ You can find out how much text Google indexed.

✦ You can see visually how many times you used each keyword.

✦ You can tell how evenly you distributed the keyword throughout the page.

If you find that the page has very little textual content that can actually be read by the search engines, your design might be relying too much on non-text elements like images or Flash. (*Adobe Flash* is a multimedia software program used for building animated and interactive elements for the web.) Although these elements may be good for your users, they're not very readable to a search engine. In general, landing pages need a *lot* of text-based content so search engines can figure out what they're all about.

The Single Page Analyzer report further breaks down how keywords are used on a web page. It identifies all the single- and multiword keyword phrases. It also tells you whether the keywords are used in all the right places (for instance, search engines expect any word used in the Title tag to also appear in the Meta description tag, in the Meta keywords tag, and throughout the page).

For more help using the Single Page Analyzer to optimize your landing pages, see Book V, Chapter 3.

Engagement Objects

Before leaving the subject of page construction, there's a hot topic you need to know about: engagement objects. *Engagement objects* are non-text elements such as images, videos, audio, or interactive elements on a web page that help engage users. Not only do they make your page more interesting to a user, but they are also now becoming increasingly important as a search engine ranking factor.

With the rise of *blended search* (also known as *Universal Search* in Google), search engine results pages (SERPs) are now able to show a combination of different types of files to a searcher. So a search for [1969 Ford Mustang] can return photos, videos, and so on, in addition to website links, all on the same SERP (as shown in Figure 3-2).

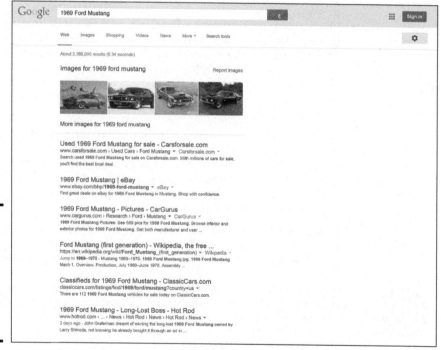

**Book III
Chapter 3**

**Applying Collected
Data**

Figure 3-2:
Blended
search
results
combine
many differ-
ent types of
listings.

The search engines (particularly Google) want to provide the most relevant and engaging results to their users, so having Engagement Objects on your website can actually make you rank higher in search results than your competitors.

Take a look at your top competitors' web pages as a user would and notice their Engagement Objects. Keep your own website in mind so you can make a list of things you might need to add. Besides getting an overall feel for how these sites engage their users, look to see how extensively they incorporate Engagement Objects such as

✦ **Images:** Notice the number of photos, infographics, illustrations, diagrams, charts, and so on. Also pay attention to size. Larger images with good `Alt` attribute text and good surrounding text can get indexed and actually returned as a search result themselves, so notice whether the competitor has anything like this.

✦ **Video:** Video is extremely important these days for getting noticed on the web. The best method is to embed the video right into your landing page and also upload it or a portion of it to a video-sharing site like YouTube. Include a keyword-rich description and a link back to your site, and you'll probably get traffic as a result. Consider this: YouTube's internal search function now gets more total searches than Yahoo or Bing. Depending on how you look at it, that means YouTube is the second most visited search engine in its own right. Obviously, YouTube's site search isn't a true search engine, but you better believe that the traffic is true traffic. If your competitors haven't been savvy enough to upload videos to YouTube and embed videos on their sites yet, here's a good way to one-up them. Being where people can find you is critical.

✦ **Audio:** Look for embedded audio files within the site, which is another type of element that's good for user engagement. Audio files are expected on music-industry sites, but other sites might benefit from a creative use of audio, as well. Google can now parse soundtracks and generate text of the words that can be subsequently indexed. This clearly shows that audio is a valid content form.

✦ **Flash:** Flash files (SWF) are not recommended, from an SEO point of view. A site built completely in Flash, in particular, can't be very competitive in searches because it lacks sufficient text content and may be slow to load.

There are many other types of engagement objects, and there is a lot more to say about the best ways to include them on your web pages. Please see Book V, Chapter 7 to get more information.

Learning from Your Competitors' Links

What else can you learn from your competitors? You can find out who's linking to them.

Besides your page construction, another big factor in your search engine ranking is your *link equity,* which is the value of all the backlinks coming to your web pages. The search engines consider every link to your web page to be a "vote" for that page. The more votes your page has, the more "expert" your page appears to be. Based on the links pointing to your site, the search engines either increase or decrease how relevant your site is for particular keyword searches. The quality of your backlinks also matters; one testimonial-grade link from an authoritative website in your field is an important endorsement and can be worth more than thousands of links from unrelated and inconsequential sites in terms of your link equity.

You want to have a natural variety of backlinks to your landing pages, from sites with a range of different link equity values themselves. However, it's good to keep in mind what the gold standard is so that you can recognize a nugget when you see one and go after it. The most ideal backlinks come from a web page that is

+ Well-established (that is, an older site that has become trusted)

+ An authority within your industry, with lots of backlinks coming to it from related sites, as well as some links out to other authority websites

+ Focused on the same subject as your web page, even using some of the same keywords

+ Using meaningful anchor text that contains your keywords in the link to your page

Read more about the benefits and risks of link building in Book VI, Chapter 2.

You may have some "ideal" link candidates in mind already: sites that are well-respected and established authorities in your field. It's very likely, however, that you don't have nearly enough backlink candidates in mind yet. That's where looking at your top-ranking competitors comes in handy.

You can look at your competitors' links primarily to find good backlink candidates for your own site. The top-ranking competitors for your keywords probably have vetted worthwhile links that you could benefit from, too. After all, your competitor deals with the same type of information and customers that you do. If that third-party site finds it useful to link visitors to the competitor's site, it might find your site equally useful for its visitors to know about.

You can see a list of all the indexed backlinks that a competitor has by running a search engine query on Google. In the regular search box, type the query [**link:*domain.com***], substituting the competing page's URL for *domain.com,* and then click the Google Search button. (Don't include the brackets.)

The results come out in pretty much random order. You can go page by page and read through them, copying the ones that look promising as possible backlink candidates into another document for follow-up. Be picky here: You don't want any spammy links, and some may simply not be worth the time to pursue.

Suppose your competition has about 50 backlinks. How many do you really need to be competitive? In most cases, reasonably close is sufficient. Focus on developing links in a natural fashion — buying links or devoting huge amounts of time to obtaining reciprocal links is not a good way to gain links. The search engines have ways to detect unnatural links, and having them could cause your website to be penalized by the search engines. (You can read about search engine link penalties in Book I, Chapter 6.)

After you decide which websites you'd like backlinks from, you can begin your link-building campaign. Spend a little time looking at the candidate's web page. You want to know what it's about so that you can make sure your own web page has something of value to those users. Another thing you might find is something amiss on the third-party site, like a broken link or a missing image, which you can present to them. This could help you forge a mutually beneficial relationship. Connecting and developing relationships with these brands may eventually lead to natural links, especially if your site offers content (such as articles) that would be useful to their audience. Social media can be an excellent way to make these connections; you learn more about that in Book V, Chapter 7.

Never pay for a link to build your link equity. You can pay for advertising, if you want to attract more visitors or promote your site, but don't pay for links to increase your link equity. Buying links that look deceptively like regular links can get you in trouble with the search engines, especially Google. When Google detects a paid link, that link typically gets no value. Having too many paid links can trigger an algorithmic penalty (read more about penalties in Book I, Chapter 6). Selling links is also a gamble: If Google detects that you are selling links, it may drop your PageRank and you'll wind up nowhere in the search engine results. Webmasters have the right to put anything on their sites, but Google also reserves the right to take action so that the best results are delivered to its users.

Taking Cues from Your Competitors' Content Structure

You may have a lot of great content on your website, but if it's jumbled and disorganized, the search engines might not figure out what searches it relates to. This is why you should consider *content siloing,* which is a way of organizing your website into subject themes by linking related pages together. Content siloing lets you funnel link equity to your landing pages, which reinforces to the search engines how relevant those pages are for the keywords they contain. Linking is so important that it can override the actual content of the page. Siloing is comprised of two parts. One is internal linking and another relates to page and site architecture. Consider a good site map: one that, in a very detailed schematic, outlines the entire structure of a document. Siloing means that all the links on the website follow that outline exactly, without any straying from topic to topic. Literally, the anchor text links do more to inform Google than the content in those pages. Siloing is a big subject. See Book II, Chapter 4 and Book VI, Chapters 1 and 2 for more information.

Looking at the top-ranking competitors' websites, you can get some clues as to how they organize their content. This can benefit you in two basic ways:

✦ You can tell how well-organized the competitor's content is. If the site doesn't use siloing, your own use of siloing can give you an advantage over the competition.

✦ You can get ideas for beefing up your own content or for different ways of organizing your site.

Go to a competing web page from a search results page. What can you learn from this landing page about how it fits into the entire site and whether it uses siloing?

First, looking at the navigation structure may give clues. The following navigation example shows how a fairly clear directory structure would be organized by car make (Ford) and then by model (Mustang). This site may have its content siloed:

```
www.some-car-domain.com/ford/mustang/customize-your-mustang.
   htm
```

Now look at this URL, which contains codes and *parameters* (auto-generated URL characters that carry information to the receiving page about the user) that make it impossible to read:

```
www.another-car-domain.com/svcse/php?t=37481&_cthew=13%3A2
```

Obviously, sometimes the URL structure is informative and sometimes it isn't. Because the URL is another piece of communication that the search engines use to try to understand what a page is about, you want your pages to have meaningful keywords in your URLs. Although very little weight is placed on keywords in the URL, don't miss that opportunity. Human visitors appreciate the clarity even if the search engines don't. And if the sites you're competing against have gobbledygook in their URLs (like the second preceding example), you'll have another advantage.

Second, you can tell whether a site is well-organized into silos by looking at its internal links. We're not talking about the main navigation menu so much but about the related hyperlinks on the competitor's landing page. See whether there are links to pages full of supporting information on the same topic. Then as you click to view those supporting pages, look to see whether they contain links back to the landing page but not to other pages outside that topic. If so, that site is probably siloed.

If they don't have a siloed linking strategy, you might see

+ No links to related pages on the landing page

+ The same set of links on every page you look at

+ A haphazard assortment of links to various areas of the website, with no clear subject focus

Here are some questions you should answer about your competitors:

+ Does the competitor's site organize the main content categories in a clear, readable hierarchical and empirical structure with clear indexable (spiderable) navigation?

+ Does the competitor's site have quality content on each major category section?

+ How well does the site link to related articles and site guides?

If the competitor *isn't* siloing, and the vast majority of sites are not, that could give you an advantage as you create a theme for your site contents and implement linking within silos.

Detecting rel="nofollow" links

For the purposes of siloing, you need to look only at the links that are "followed" by the search engines. Links that have a rel="nofollow" attribute attached to them in the HTML code don't count for passing link equity. (By the way, the presence of a rel="nofollow" attribute on a website may itself provide a clue that there's an SEO expert on staff, and the site may be siloed.)

To see "nofollow" links more easily, you can install a free plug-in for the Mozilla Firefox browser called SearchStatus (http://www.quirk.biz/download-searchstatus). If you install this plug-in, links with a "nofollow" attribute automatically show up highlighted in pink on any web page.

After you figure out whether the competitor's site is organized into silos, take a look around and see what tips you can take from it. First of all, you might discover that it's covered something that you missed, like an article about how to preserve the original upholstery of a classic car so that it lasts for decades. Your site visitors probably want to know that, too, so make a note to write a new article to fill that hole.

A well-siloed website might also give you good ideas for organizing content. For instance, your silos might be set up by type of service (body work, reupholstering, complete restoration, and so on), whereas a competitor's silos might be set up by car make and model. The test of a good silo structure is how much traffic you're bringing in by being relevant to important keywords. If your structure is bringing in visitors and giving you enough *conversions* (sales, sign-ups, orders, or whatever action you want people to take on your site), you shouldn't tear it down.

You might still learn something from another site's silo structure, however, that you could apply as a horizontal silo within your current structure. A *horizontal silo* involves linking across silos very deliberately to create a secondary silo structure that can rank for other types of search queries. So if your silo structure is by services, you could consider linking your page titled Reupholstering a Ford Mustang to your pages for Restoring a Ford Mustang and Ford Mustang Body Work, and so on. That would create a set of horizontal silos that might help you rank higher for searches that include [Ford Mustang] as a keyword.

For more help with siloing and overlaying a horizontal silo, check out Book VI, Chapter 2.

**Book III
Chapter 3**

Applying Collected
Data

Book IV

SEO Web Design

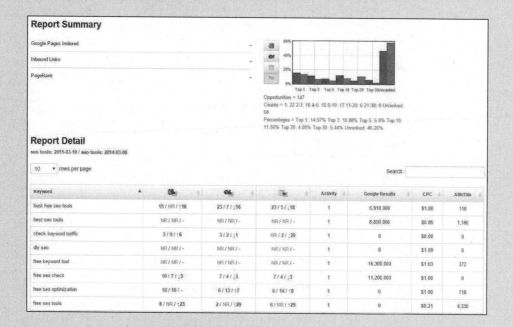

Contents at a Glance

Chapter 1: The Basics of SEO Web Design

In This Chapter

✔ **Deciding on your site content**

✔ **Choosing keywords**

✔ **Using H# tags for headings**

✔ **Cleaning up your page code**

✔ **Organizing your assets**

✔ **Naming files**

✔ **Making your site dynamic**

✔ **Developing a design procedure**

*I*n this chapter, you discover the basics of site design with search engine optimization in mind. Building a website is like baking a cake in a lot of ways; one of the first things you have to do is gather your ingredients.

In this chapter, we first guide you to deciding on the content and the types of keywords that you want. Then we discuss *H#* or *heading tags* (HTML code used to format headings), page headings, and the importance of using clean code for your site. You find out how to organize and name all the assets on your page, including images, videos, and podcasts. After you have everything organized, you discover how to actually construct your site.

We finish off the chapter by discussing keeping your page simple and neat, creating dynamic content for your site that is still seen as relevant by the search engines, and developing a design procedure so that everyone in the web development process is on the same page.

We talk a lot about HTML, Cascading Style Sheets (CSS), and JavaScript in the upcoming pages; however, we don't attempt to teach you to write code in this book. We strongly recommend that you learn at least the basics of HTML before you attempt SEO. Even if you aren't going to be the one doing the optimization on your website, it's a good idea to learn the basics. If you want to be good at search engine optimization (SEO), you need to understand both the marketing end *and* the technical end. If you know the basics of HTML, you can communicate with your IT guys in their own language, which prevents them from claiming something can't be done if it actually can. It also allows you to be able to catch mistakes others might miss, helps you research your competition's websites, and is just generally good to know.

Deciding on the Type of Content for Your Site

We have stated this time and time again throughout this book, and we'll continue to do so because it's important: You must know what your business is about. It colors how you choose your keywords and how you arrange your site. You need to know if you have a research or an e-commerce site, or if it's both. How can you tell? Here are a few ways:

✦ **Research:** A research site's keywords should lean toward how-to types of phrases. As in [How do you fix a lawnmower?] or [How do you say Where is the consulate, I lost my passport? in Spanish?]. Or even more specific keywords like [Mustang] or [John Wilkes Booth]. These are keywords that people use when they do research. If you have a site that provides information, such as recipes, lists of dead historians, or classic auto club newsletters, you want your keywords to be research-based. Research websites typically use keywords like [research], [reviews], [how to], [information], and so on.

✦ **E-commerce:** If you have an e-commerce site, your site is designed to sell things. Your keywords are geared more toward users who want to make purchases. That could include the keyword [free] because who wouldn't want free stuff? Also, you'd include much more specific keywords in an e-commerce site than in a strictly informational site, like [Ford Mustang convertible with leather interior], because people search for broader terms when doing research and more specific terms when they're ready to make a purchase. E-commerce sites have calls to actions in their content, using terms like [buy now], [purchase], [shopping cart], and so on.

✦ **Research and e-commerce:** Some sites provide both information and purchasing opportunities. You can have a site that provides tons of information and recipes for the best barbecuing techniques, and have things like grills and barbecue sauces available on your website for purchase.

Knowing what kind of a business you have (and what kind of website you want to build/redesign) helps you to pick out your keywords. Separate them into information-type keywords and transaction-type keywords. This means thinking about whether the keyword would draw someone doing research to your site or someone ready to buy something.

You have to do research and continue to do it. SEO is not like doing research for a tenth-grade English essay, where you do it once and then never have to do it again. The market changes constantly and you have to be able to keep up with it. See Book II, Chapter 1 for more information on keyword research.

Making a User-Focused Website

The process of building your website so that it functions in a way that caters to the specific needs of your customers is called building a *user-focused* website, or designing for *usability*.

A user-focused website is just as it sounds — a website that is created with a focus on users and their needs. (You can find out more about how to uncover your customer needs in Book V, Chapter 1.)

Designing a user-focused website means thinking about the preferences of your personas when you make decisions about your navigation, search functionality, visual elements, shopping cart flow, and any other elements of your website.

Whether you're building your website from scratch or making improvements to an existing website, always keep your user's preferences and needs in the front of your mind. Think:

✦ Will this placement confuse the user?

✦ Will this placement/font size/color/and other design aspects make my user happy?

✦ Can I alter this design in any way to improve my user's experience?

Keeping usability in mind keeps your end user happy, often resulting in more sales and conversions that in turn keep you and your boss happy, too.

Remember that SEO and usability are not mutually exclusive. Rather, they actually work hand in hand because many of the things that are good for human visitors are also helpful to search engines.

Usability may even make the search engine happy: Google lists "Focus on the user and all else will follow" as the number one item in its "Ten things we know to be true" company core values documentation. Keep in mind that you can never confirm the exact factors the search engines evaluate to determine rank, but you can look for clues and make educated guesses. Google's listing of "focus on the user" as the number one priority in its core values is a pretty good clue.

**Book IV
Chapter 1**

**The Basics of SEO
Web Design**

Choosing Keywords

After you decide what kind of site you're building and for whom, you have to choose what keywords will go where. You need to know what keywords to assign to each page in order to:

+ Focus the page content.

+ Make it faster for the viewer to understand the content.

+ Make it easier for a search engine *spider* (or *robot*, referring to the search engine programs that read your site and index its contents) to determine what each page is about.

Running a ranking monitor to discover what's already working

If you have an existing website, you have to first establish a *benchmark;* that is, you should find out what's currently working before you begin rearranging things. You need to find out which of your web pages already rank well in the search engines, and for which keywords. For instance, if you have a page on your site that's already ranking in the top five listings for one of your keywords, you should just designate that as the main page for that keyword and leave it alone. Check on which keywords are working for you and which aren't and don't fix something that's not broken. Conversely, if you have a page that is consistently not ranking for any keywords, it's time to fix that page.

To help you evaluate your keywords, you can take advantage of a useful tool called a ranking monitor. This tool is extremely helpful for keyword research and keeping track of how your pages are ranking, both now and further down the road as the market grows and changes.

A *ranking monitor* tells you without personalization bias where your pages rank in the search engines for each keyword, or whether they rank at all. (Remember from Book I, Chapter 3 that the search engine results each of us sees are often personalized based on search history, location, and other factors.)

At the time of this writing, we don't know of any ranking monitor available for free; however, subscribing to a paid monitor is worth the cost. At the risk of sounding self-promotional, the monitor available with our subscription SEOToolSet at www.seotoolset.com works and is fully integrated with many useful tools. The full suite of tools is available for $89 per month, but you can search online for others. No matter which you choose, you need to be looking for a ranking monitor that:

✦ Checks multiple search engines (domestic and international)

✦ Includes historical data, so you can see trends over time

✦ Is "polite" to the search engines by automatically spacing queries over time, or allows you to customize the crawl rates to use time delays

✦ Supports *proxy* (remote location) queries

✦ Offers multiple languages

✦ Is schedulable

✦ Runs from a server and not from your desktop computer

✦ Integrates with other tools to allow for analysis

Figure 1-1 shows a ranking report from the SEOToolSet. For every one of the site's keywords (which are pre-entered), the report shows if any page on the site ranks for that keyword, what number rank it has in each of the search engines, and the search activity (roughly the number of search queries per day). For each keyword, the specific URL of the ranking page is listed.

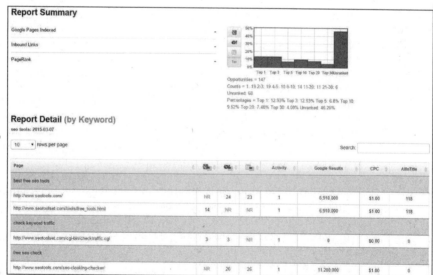

Figure 1-1: Ranking reports identify which pages rank well for your keywords.

Figure 1-2 is a ranking report that compares two periods of time, giving you a history of how your site ranked overall over time and a handy bar graph to go along with it. It's important for you to be able to track your rankings over time so that you know whether your search engine optimization efforts are working. Keep good records of all your changes so that you'll be able to relate them back to the rise and fall in your graph.

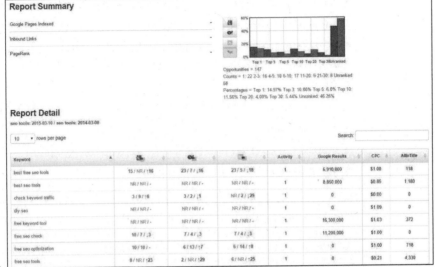

Figure 1-2:
This screenshot from the SEOToolSet shows overall keyword ranking over time.

Choose a ranking monitor that won't constantly hammer the search engines. (By "hammer," we mean that it won't constantly query the search engines. You don't want the search engines' spiders to crawl your site at full speed if it impacts your ability to do business by overloading your servers. We think it's just polite to return the same courtesy to the search engines.) We recommend you choose an online ranking monitor, rather than a software-based one, to be sure you don't get your personal IP banned: You don't want to limit your ability to do your own Google searches. If your monitor hits the engines with too many searches too fast, the search engine may identify your monitor as a machine and require you to prove you're a human user every time you try to run the application.

Choose a ranking monitor that either auto-spaces its queries or lets you request delays between searches because constantly calling on the search engine for rankings data can get you into trouble and will produce inconsistent data. The SEOToolSet ranking monitor waits several seconds between each query, just to be polite.

You should rerun a ranking monitor at regular intervals, storing up a history of biweekly or monthly ranking reports that you can compare to each other. There's no real benefit to running monitors more often as search engines change algorithms regularly, and less frequent monitors give better history and don't take up so much data. (Not to mention that you need to wait to see whether your SEO edits on your web pages were picked up by the engines in the first place.)

Having an archive of dated reports allows you to see your progress over time because each one is like a snapshot of your current SEO work. Especially as you begin implementing search engine optimization throughout your website, you want to run a ranking monitor regularly. You will definitely appreciate the trending reports in the long run.

Matching Meta tags and keywords to page content

After you run the ranking monitor, you can identify the pages that rank well for particular keywords. Consider those ranking keywords as being assigned to those pages. Remove other unrelated keywords so that your page stays focused very clearly on its main keyword. You want to follow some SEO best practices for how you assign keywords to a page. We go into depth on this throughout this book, but here's a brief intro to start with.

When assigning keywords to your web pages, select one to five main, related keywords (or keyword phrases) for each individual page. Allow two or three supporting keywords (or keyword phrases) per page. Supporting keywords may be suitable for developing pages around as well as for increasing your depth of content.

Make sure all keywords on the page relate to one another: Too many unrelated (but well-ranking) keywords can dilute the theme and bring your rankings down. If the page is about painting a classic Mustang, make sure the keywords all relate to painting a classic Mustang. Your page content should also include synonyms and clarifying words that a user would be looking for. Slang terms are excellent clarifying words because they mimic the way people actually speak: [stang] or [pony car] for Mustang wouldn't be considered secondary keywords, but they're important to proving your expertise to your visitors.

If you already have a website and need to tweak it for ranking, take a look at the page you have and think about where you can enhance it. Going back to the classic car customization example: If you have a page on your site that's mostly about tires but it also has a paragraph about rims and a line or two about wheel axels, that page is a little disjointed. Because the page is primarily about tires, make it *all* about tires and create a separate page for rims and another page for axels. Then pick two or three really good supporting keywords for your page about tires.

After you choose your main and supporting keywords for each page, you are going to arrange them strategically. You should put keywords in

+ The page's `Title` tag

+ The `Meta` description and `Meta` keywords tags (metadata appears in the `Head` section of the HTML code and defines the page content)

+ The headings on the page, especially in your `H1` tag

+ The page content

Search engines look at the `Title`, `Meta` description, and `Meta` keywords tags not only to understand what your page is about but also to grab text to display in your search results listing. Search engines pull the descriptive text that displays on their results pages from any of several different sources depending on the search query and the engine itself: from the `Meta` description tag, from the page content, occasionally from the Open Directory Project (DMOZ), and from Yahoo, which often uses the description from a site's listing in the Yahoo Directory.

See Book V, Chapter 3 for more help creating `Title` and `Meta` tags.

Using Keywords in the Heading Tags

When you're structuring the HTML coding for a web page, it can look a little like an outline, with main headings and subheadings. An important place to have keywords is in those headings, placed within heading tags.

Heading tags are part of the HTML coding for a web page. Headings are defined with `H1` to `H6` tags. The `H1` tag defines the most important heading on the page (usually the largest or boldest, too), whereas `H6` indicates the lowest-level heading. You want to avoid thinking of headings as simply formatting for your pages: Headings carry a lot of weight with the search engines because they're for categorization, not cosmetics. You can control what each heading looks like consistently through your site using a CSS style sheet that specifies the font, size, color, and other attributes for each heading tag. Here's an example of what various heading tags can look like:

```
<H1>This is a heading</H1>
<H2>This is subheading A</H2>
<H2>This is subheading B</H2>
<H3>This is a lower subheading</H3>
```

Search engines pay special attention to the words in your headings because they expect headings to include clues to the page's main topics. You definitely want to include the page's keywords inside heading tags.

Heading tags also provide your pages with an outline, with the heading defining the paragraph that follows. They outline how your page is structured and organize the information. The `H1` tag indicates your most important topic, and the other `H#` tags create subtopics.

You should follow several SEO best practices for applying heading tags. First, you want to have only one `H1` tag per page because it's basically the subject of your page. Think of your `H1` tag like the headline of a newspaper article: It wouldn't make sense to have more than one. You can have multiple lesser tags if the page covers several subsections. In feature articles in newsletters, you occasionally see sub-headlines that are styled differently than the headline: Those sub-headlines would be the equivalent of an H2.

Say that you have a page that describes how you can customize classic Mustang convertibles. Your very first heading for your page should be something like this:

```
<H1>Customizing Classic Mustang Convertibles</H1>
```

Your second paragraph is about customizing the paint job for the convertible. So it should have a heading that reads:

```
<H2>Customizing Paint for Mustang Convertibles</H2>
```

When you view the code of your page (which you should most definitely do, even if you have someone else create it for you), it should look something like this:

```
<H1> Customizing Classic Mustang Convertibles</H1>
<p>200 words of content about Customizing Classic Mustangs
    using the keywords.</p>
<H2> Customizing Paint for Mustangs </H2>
<p>200 words of content about Customizing Paint for Mustangs
    using the keywords.</p>

<H2> Customizing Upholstery for Mustangs </H2>
<p>200 words of content about Customizing Upholstery for
    Mustangs using the keywords.</p>
```

When assigning heading tags, keep them in sequence in the HTML, which is how the search engines can most easily read them. Heading tags should follow the outline structure you used in school for an outline or a technical paper. If you wanted to add an H3 tag, it would have to follow an H2 in the code. Similarly, if you had an H4 tag, it could only follow an H3 tag and not an H2.

Heading structure is a relatively simple concept, but you would be surprised at how many websites use the same type of heading for every paragraph or just use their heading tags to stuff keywords into the HTML code. In reality, many sites do not properly use heading tags, so it should be a quick win to place appropriate headings on your site. Absolutely avoid any headings that look like this:

```
<H1>Mustang Mustang Mustang Ford Mustang</H1>
```

This tag is unacceptable to search engines (to say nothing of your visitors), and is considered spam. See Book I, Chapter 6 for more on what may be considered spam.

The words in each heading tag should be unique and targeted to the page they're on. *Unique* and *targeted* means that your heading tag's content shouldn't be duplicated anywhere across the site. If the heading on your tires page is "Classic Mustang Tires," "Classic Mustang Tires" shouldn't be the H1 on any other page in your site.

Search engines look for uniqueness on your page. For example, if you have an H1 heading of "Ford Mustang Convertible" at the top of two different pages, the search engine might read one of the pages as redundant and not count it. Having unique heading tags allows the search engine to assign more weight to a heading, and headings are one of the most important things on the page besides the Title tag (which is discussed in Book V, Chapter 3).

If you want to have any of the elements on your website (Title tags, heading tags, and so on) help your pages rank in a search engine, they all need to be unique. It may take a little more time to go through your site and think up unique, relevant, keyword-rich tags for everything, but it's worth the effort. The little things count when it comes to SEO.

Keeping the Code Clean

Another part of building a search engine-friendly website is keeping your code clean and simple. When we talk about code, we're talking about languages like HTML, XHTML, AJAX, JavaScript, and the like. Coding supplies the building blocks of your website. If we were talking about building a house, the code would basically define the walls, floors, insulation, light fixtures, kitchen sink, and everything right down to the color of the paint in the bathroom.

We assume that you already know a little bit about HTML, CSS, and JavaScript code and what it all looks like. In this chapter, we assume that you're at the planning stage of your SEO campaign, gathering your assets and starting to visualize a big-picture plan for your website. In the next chapters, we cover how to apply what you've visualized to make an SEO-friendly site. But first, there are a few more concepts to grasp.

You want to streamline your site's code so that it's an easy read for the search engine spiders. Keeping the code as clean as possible, as it relates to SEO, means some specific things:

✦ Get to each page's content as soon as possible in the HTML view. You want your keywords to start showing up early in the search engine spider's crawl.

✦ Code by using as little on-the-page *markup* (formatting and other types of on-the-fly HTML codes, such as Font tags, which could be controlled in a CSS style sheet, instead) as possible. If you have useless tags in your code, get rid of them.

The preceding list gives you some great goals, but how can you achieve them? These best practices can slash the code clutter right out of your web pages:

✦ Use an external CSS file to define the look of your website, rather than relying on inline formatting.

✦ Move any JavaScript code into an external JS file when possible. Include simple calls to the JavaScript file from your pages, which keeps the on-page code short and sweet.

You may also have extraneous tags lying around in the HTML. Code gunk buildup can happen if you've cut and pasted content from another source (such as an old web page of yours or a document from Microsoft Word or other programs that add a ton of unnecessary HTML code to your text). Or you may have been working on a particular page for so long that it's acquired excess tags like barnacles on a ship's hull. Go through and remove all the extraneous tags and code from your pages, including extra carriage returns. Simplifying your code streamlines the site and makes it easier to read for the search engine spiders. If they read too much redundancy or if your page code appears too complex, they're less likely to assign a lot of weight or relevancy to your page. Just as two drops of dye in a small glass of water have a lot more impact than two drops of dye in a barrel of water, the messy code could "dilute" the strength of your keywords.

A couple of programs are available to clean up your code if you've got a bunch of gunk hanging out in the HTML. The cheapest is your friendly neighborhood text editor, Notepad. If you're used to reading HTML, just open your HTML file in Notepad and tidy up the raw code, one page at a time. If you're using a UNIX/Linux server, save your work in UNIX format.

For those who aren't able to read HTML easily, other tools are available for help. One free resource for tidying up cluttered code is aptly named Tidy (http://infohound.net/tidy), and it comes highly recommended by the W3C web standards consortium (we talk a lot more about the value of the W3C later, in Chapter 4 in this minibook). Another free and easy tool is Dirty Markup (http://www.dirtymarkup.com), an online tool that cleans up unruly HTML, CSS, or JavaScript with the push of a button, right in your web browser. See Figure 1-3.

Figure 1-3:
Dirty
Markup is
a free tool
that cleans
up HTML,
CSS, and
JavaScript
code right
in your web
browser.

Organizing Your Assets

Making a website is kind of like baking a cake. You have to have the recipe and all your ingredients together before you get started; otherwise, you could be in the middle of mixing only to find out that you have no eggs. Likewise, we have you go through all these steps first to make sure that you have everything ready before you begin constructing your website.

If you're just starting a website, it's important to organize your assets. What's going to go on your website? Sift through everything that you have. Remember, users love dynamic or engaging content (also known as *engagement objects*), so in addition to that must-have, readable, well-written text, include images and video to enhance user interest and engagement.

Go through all your print materials, if you have any, and choose images that you can use on your website. Do you have a commercial? How about an interview that you did for radio or television? Gather all these things and go through them. If you think something is useless, chuck it because clutter will always be clutter. But if you find an image or a video you think will work with your site, use it!

Besides text, you might want to consider putting the following types of engagement objects on your website:

✦ **Files:** First things first, organize your files into proper categories. And by files we mean everything: your pages, your data, your images, your videos, and your podcasts, if you have any. Main subjects go first, and the remaining subjects go down the line into subcategories.

✦ **Images:** If you have print materials, you probably have images. Use those images to enhance your website (and make sure you have the copyrights to use those images). Adding images can also help your page rank because of the ability to use keywords in the `Alt` attribute text (the HTML coding of the image), plus the ability to rank in image-centric *vertical search engines* (search engines that look for a specific type of file or location).

✦ **Videos:** If you have any commercials or videos lying around, consider uploading them and using them on your site. Search engines can't see a video, but videos can still enhance your rank by containing keywords in the text surrounding the video (such as if you put the video in a table cell with keyword-rich text above or below it) and by appearing in their own vertical results.

✦ **Podcasts:** If you have a radio show, it's not that hard to stream it online and create podcasts that are downloadable.

If you have any of these Engagement Objects, gather them and keep them organized. Engagement Objects don't stop there; also consider blogs, news, books, maps — anything that isn't just a standard text-based web page and that could catch the eye and engage a user with your site. You'll thank yourself later when you're actually building your website and have lots of content choices handy.

Naming Your Files

After you gather your assets and separate the wheat from the chaff, you need to name them as you're uploading them. How you name your files is important because a search engine looks at the filename as an indication of what's in the file, so this is another good place to have keywords.

Instead of naming your image of a red Ford Mustang like this:

```
*0035001.jpg
```

Rename the file as you're uploading it to describe it, using something like this:

```
*ford-mustang-1967.jpg
```

Not only is the file now easier for you to identify when building your pages down the line, but it also now contains three keywords that search engines can read and add to their algorithms for ranking.

Use filenames that make sense to both the search engine and the user. You might understand the gibberish you just used as a filename, but someone else who doesn't know you or your sense of humor might not. Also, use full words instead of abbreviations. Searchers generally don't use abbreviations in their search queries unless those abbreviations are very common.

The same advice is true for naming video and podcast files. Make sure that the filename is descriptive and simple: It helps you and the search engine in the long run.

When naming your files with phrases, don't leave spaces between words. Nor should you use an underscore (_) to separate words. Search engines interpret the underscore as its own character, so it's like naming your file `fordxmustang`, which misses an opportunity to use your keywords when a search engine spider crawls it. It's possible that search engines can figure it out, but you're better off naming your files properly in the first place.

Instead, if you have to use spaces (remember, search engines can parse words from web page filenames without any help), use hyphens. They won't be read as a separate character. That way, you can have files that look like this:

`ford-mustang-1967-good-condition.jpg`

Even without hyphens in your filenames, a search engine can actually parse out up to 500 words that are *concatenated* (run together without spaces). You might want to use a hyphen in places where there could be confusion in the parsing, either for a search engine or for a user. In those cases, you might want to throw in a dash in order to make it legible. For example, the distinction between `mensexchange.jpg` and `mens-exchange.jpg` is important, after all.

Eyetracking studies done by Mediative (formerly Enquiro) research have found that users are not likely to click on a long URL in the results page. They tend to click the result below the hideously long URL instead. So when you're naming the pages and files in your site, keep the length down to a reasonable level.

As descriptive as it is, you wouldn't want something like this as your base domain name:

`www.reallycoolclassiccustomcarsatareasonableprice.com`

Also follow a standard of using either all lowercase or all uppercase in naming files. Apache servers are case-sensitive: Lower- or uppercase makes a difference to them. The pages `/FordMustang.html` and `/fordmustang.html` are not considered the same to a case-sensitive server. Also, do not use more than two hyphens in a page URL, and avoid having more than one hyphen in the domain name. Filenames (like our `ford-mustang-1967-good-condition.jpg` example) are mostly exempt from this rule (we've found examples with 14 hyphens in the filename), but we still recommend economy in your naming conventions.

Keeping Design Simple

When it comes to designing your site, the old adage KISS is good advice: "Keep It Simple, Sweetie." Make your website as straightforward and easy to navigate as possible. Make sure the links and instructions are clear and not horribly complicated. Also, be aware of how much Flash you are using. Adobe Flash is a multimedia program that allows you to place animation on your website. There are many major companies out there with big, shiny websites that contain lots of complicated and cool-looking Flash. But here's a secret about those sites: A search engine can't read them.

A search engine is basically deaf, dumb, and blind. It can't see what the viewer sees; it can only read the code. It can't read a page like a person reads it (yet). The search engines are trying to emulate what a person can see and react to, but technology isn't there yet, so the search engine spiders have to make do with reading the code.

Websites built entirely in Flash generally don't have searchable content. A search engine, being blind, deaf, and dumb, can't see the Flash animations that describe all the cool things the website has to offer because all the search engine can see is the Flash plug-in in the HTML code. See Figure 1-4, for example. It's got some well-designed Flash, but a search spider can't see any of it, so the spider can't read any of the keywords or follow any of the links on the site. The capabilities of the search engines and of this technology are evolving rapidly. We may one day see Flash become as spiderable as text, but that day hasn't arrived yet.

That's not to say that your website can't contain Flash, but make sure there's readable content that goes along with it. Including a few Flash movies on the page is a good thing for user experience, provided they are relevant and are accompanied by a reasonable amount of companion text. Also, make sure that the Flash is not too complicated for the page, or for the user. Some sites create mini applications using Flash and include them on their websites. If that's your site, don't miss an opportunity to pull good text content out of the application to include on your pages, as well. For instance, if your Flash application contains instructions on how to use Flash, grab that text and make it part of the text on your page. Also, if you use Flash, place a description of the Flash content in the actual text of the page. That makes it easier for the user to understand, and a search engine spider can read it and use it in your ranking. It's a win/win situation.

Figure 1-4:
Although a human can read this page, a search engine robot can't.

Also, many websites include a Flash animation as the *splash page* (sort of like a site's welcome mat), and users have to sit and wait for it to load and play before going on to the actual site. In general, these pages are usually skipped. Most people want to go to the content right away instead of having to sit through a minute of pretty, but useless, animation. If you currently use this Flash animation on your site, you should probably remove it.

Here's another hint for your website. Some people out there think it's a cool idea to include music that plays when a user visits their website. We can tell you right now that many people do not enjoy this. There is nothing more annoying than visiting a site and being unable to find the music player to turn off the background music. The only people who enjoy having music playing on the page are the ones who put it there in the first place and the ones who pay to have it there. We would recommend that unless you have a site that actually sells music, don't include background music on your site. And if you really must, make sure it defaults to off.

Keeping the content on your page simple and easy to navigate not only helps you get better rankings, but it also means that your user has a much better experience and will return to your site again. Follow this general rule: If it looks cool but is a pain in the rear to use, users won't use it. Figure 1-5 is a great example of a simple, easy-to-use website.

Figure 1-5:
Google is committed to a clean, user-friendly design.

Google's home page is clean and simple, doesn't have any extraneous clutter, and is pretty self-explanatory when it comes to what the page does. The less you have to explain to your users, the better. Of course, Google doesn't have to worry about ranking for anything, but that doesn't mean its simple and clean design ethic can't work for you, too. Ask yourself if you are putting only what you need onto a page, and avoid the tendency to cram in just one more thing.

Making a Site Dynamic

A *dynamic* website is a site that is built using a template and a *CMS* (Content Management System) that gives you control of how to define your web page, pulling information from a database. This means that the pages don't exist until someone asks for them. If you have 10,000 products, you're not going to build 10,000 individual pages by hand. Instead, you use a CMS to build it dynamically on the fly. A CMS actually generates the page that a search engine spider crawls by taking the information in your database and plugging it into a template web page, so the CMS is responsible for creating all the tags, content, and code that search engines see.

The most important thing you need in order to have a dynamic site, and we really cannot stress this enough, is to have an SEO-friendly CMS. Any CMS that supports SEO completely allows you to access and edit these tags as well as to set rules for generating tags that are SEO-friendly. That means that you can focus on the content on your website. That content is what builds the page that the user sees. You need to be able to make changes to the H# tags and control the metadata on each page separately. Every element must be customizable.

If you cannot customize your current CMS, get a new one. End of story. If you can't write a Title tag individually, you're out of luck when it comes to SEO. If you can't control your H1 tag, you're out of luck. Chuck your inflexible CMS and get one that allows you to control page tags and content; otherwise, you can't do *any* of the SEO we've been talking about. Pixelsilk is a low-cost CMS that was designed from the ground up to be SEO-friendly. For simple websites, you could use blogging software like the highly customizable WordPress, which is free and open source.

Keep this list in mind when searching for a good CMS. It must be able to

+ Customize HTML templates
+ Produce unique Title tags
+ Produce unique Meta description/keywords tags
+ Produce unique heading tags (H#)
+ Categorize content by groups

Making Your Site Mobile Friendly

A *mobile-friendly* website is a site that looks and functions equally well on a mobile device, such as a smartphone or tablet, and a desktop computer. This is important because today more than a billion people worldwide are regularly using mobile devices to research and make purchases, and a good many of those people want to research and buy from *your* site. If your site doesn't look good on a mobile device, or if it's not easy to use, you are going to miss conversion opportunities left and right.

Having a mobile-friendly website is also important if you want your website to rank in mobile search results. Google takes the mobile user experience very seriously. There are some who also believe mobile optimization is on its way to becoming a desktop ranking factor, as well.

When optimizing your website to make it mobile friendly, you should take several factors into consideration, including the following:

✦ Choosing the right mobile design approach

✦ Designing for mobile user experience

✦ Understanding mobile's effect on SEO

✦ Testing for technical mobile-friendliness

You can learn more about those considerations in depth in Chapter 3 of this minibook. What's important to understand here is that mobile use is growing every year, and including mobile-friendly optimization as part of your strategy is essential — for the sake of both your SERP rank and your user experience.

Developing a Design Procedure

Developing a design procedure for your website is also important. Keeping a procedure the same through all parts of the design process helps you if something goes wrong. If your design procedure is a set procedure, you can more easily pinpoint where the goof-up happened and to fix it.

When developing a design procedure, create a style guide for your website conventions and best practices. If you use a template style guide, all images are named the same way, for example, using hyphens for spaces, and they are all saved under the same file folder. All videos are named in a standard way and go in their own folder, and so on. This prevents confusion down the line.

If you have a design team, make sure they're all on board with the style guide and that any newbies you bring in are trained to follow it. Also make sure it's a procedure that everyone can follow. Sure, it may all make sense in your head, but it needs to make sense to everyone else, too. (Besides, don't be too sure that what makes sense to you now will make sense to you in six months.) Document every last bit of your procedure, and if you have the resources, hire a technical writer to take it all down and rework it so that it's understandable for everyone else.

Here's a handy list of things you should be keeping in mind when you're coming up with the standard design procedure for your website:

✦ Know what your site is about.

✦ Know your page themes.

✦ Know the major categories/silos.

✦ Know the subcategories.

✦ Know your keywords and how you research and choose them.

✦ Know whether your site is e-commerce, research-oriented, or both.

✦ Know how you arrange your files.

✦ Have a set standard for naming files.

✦ Have a set standard for naming `Title` tags.

✦ Keep track of all your titles and headings in order to avoid redundancy.

✦ Know the color scheme, fonts used, and visual standard.

Having a set standard in place before you start also helps to keep the process moving as quickly as possible and results in the least amount of headaches for everyone involved. It also makes doing your SEO much easier because you don't have to waste time redefining your goal with every single page edit.

Chapter 2: Building an SEO-Friendly Site

In This Chapter

✔ Designing your website to be SEO-friendly

✔ Creating a style that attracts your targeted audience

✔ Planning your site navigation

✔ Implementing a search within your website

✔ Incorporating interactive media to enhance your search engine rankings

✔ Creating pages that convert

*I*n this chapter, you find out how to design websites with search engine marketing in mind. For many sites, search engine ranking is viewed as a part of the launch, but not as a part of the design. If you are fortunate enough to be newly building your website, you can construct it with search engine friendliness from the ground up. It's more likely, however, that your site already resides on the web. Search engine optimization (SEO) is a new phase of your site's development, but it's better late than never. This chapter contains many rules of thumb that can help you design — or retrofit — a site to be SEO-friendly.

Preplanning and Organizing Your Site

Start your SEO planning by inventorying your assets (which we cover in Chapter 1 of this minibook). What do you have that can possibly enhance your website? List all your potential assets, not just those that are already online. Be creative and very open-minded at this point. Take stock of all the following:

✦ Written materials you or your company has produced — such as brochures, catalogs, articles, user manuals, tutorials, online help, and customer correspondence

✦ Videos of interviews, television spots, commercials, award acceptances, speeches, and company events

✦ Audio recordings of radio interviews, and original music

✦ Photos of products, people, events, and buildings, properties

✦ Images that go along with your products and services, such as logos, statistical charts, diagrams, and illustrations

The items you gather may become site assets, but for now they're just ingredients waiting to be used. Looking to the materials your business produces outside your current website, you can probably find a lot of original content that, with a small amount of reformatting or updating, could enrich your online site.

To help you decide which elements to put on which pages, you need a combination of research and planning. The research half involves keyword research (covered in Book II) and competitor research (covered in Book III) — activities that give you lots of guidelines for your SEO work. The types of guidelines you may come up with through research include

✦ Your site's main purpose (research, e-commerce, or a mix of both)

✦ Your site's main keywords

✦ How much content you need to be competitive

✦ What kinds of content you need

✦ Which existing pages already rank well (you don't want to change them)

✦ How your site should be organized to best compete in your Internet market

Armed with this research, you are ready to enter the planning stage. Based on the guidelines you developed, you can determine what areas of your website need work. Or if you're building your site from scratch, you can lay out a big-picture site plan like a storyboard or a flow chart. Put your ideas for each page on paper. This organized approach lets you pair up items from your inventory of available content with your site's needs and move through the planning stage.

Designing Spider-Friendly Code

Whether you're writing your own HTML or hiring a webmaster to do it for you, you want to keep your site's underlying code spider-friendly. Basically, you need to streamline your site's code so that the search engine spiders have an easy time crawling your pages and figuring out what the pages are about. You do this by keeping the code as clean as possible. We cover cleaning your code in Chapter 1 of this minibook, but just as a reminder, for search engine optimization (SEO), here are some coding best practices:

✦ Use an external Cascading Style Sheet (CSS) file to define the look of your website.

✦ Use an external JS file to hold any JavaScript code you plan to use.

✦ Use as little inline *markup* (formatting and other types of on-the-fly HTML codes, such as `Font` tags to define the font style, and so on) as possible.

Creating a CSS file gives you a source from which to control the look of your entire website. In your CSS file, you can define, for instance, that all `H1` headings should be Arial font, size 3, bold, navy blue, and centered. Next week, if you change your mind and decide to make your headings purple instead, you can simply edit the definitions for your `H1` style in your CSS file and *voilà* — every `H1` heading throughout your entire site is now purple. That's a lot more efficient than going page by page through your site, manually updating every instance of an `H1` tag, and it eliminates the risk that you'll miss one.

Not only is an external CSS file efficient, but it also provides a few other big advantages. Having a CSS file allows you to remove inline formatting such as `Font` tags from your page content and instead insert a CSS tag identifying what style to apply. The result is much less HTML code cluttering your pages and significantly less page complexity. Less code means smaller file sizes. Smaller file sizes means your pages load faster for your site visitors and the search engine spiders have less junk to wade through as they read your text. It's a win/win/win for all involved!

If your site incorporates JavaScript, you want to externalize it as well, for similar reasons. Move the JavaScript off your individual web pages and into a separate JS file. Then your pages can include a single line of code that *calls* (that is, instructs the browser and spiders that the information in the file should be used in reference to the content on the page) the JavaScript file, rather than having tons of code on the page. Because JavaScript code can get really long and cumbersome, this decision alone may cut the size of a web page in half. Less code makes for spider-friendly pages with uncluttered text and clear themes.

One online business implemented just these two best practices on its website, creating external files for its JavaScript and using CSS, and the business reduced 20,000 lines of code to just 1,500. The keyword-rich content rose to the top of the page, and along with it the site's rankings rose for the keyword terms in search engine results.

Creating a Theme and Style

When it comes to design styles, people tend to have certain expectations about what's appropriate. Elegant restaurants don't seat people at tables with plastic chairs and red, yellow, and blue toy blocks for decoration.

Neither do preschools decorate their rooms with Persian rugs and neutral colors. A typical business designs for its intended audience, so assessing who makes up its target audience is one of the first things the business has to do. Online businesses should be no different, but many websites overlook this step in their creators' zeal to just "attract visitors, lots of visitors!"

Knowing what *kind* of visitor you want to attract influences many style decisions. It helps you make these types of design decisions:

✦ A color palette for the site

✦ The kinds of photos and graphics to include

✦ An appropriate reading level for your audience, including the complexity of the words and sentence structures

✦ The best tone to use when writing

✦ Font and layout choices that appeal to your target audience

✦ The complexity (or simplicity) of information to include

✦ The number of fun or interactive elements your site needs

✦ How "flashy" your site needs to be to attract and hold your audience

If you know the type of visitor you want, you can design your website to attract and hold those people's interest once they arrive. When we say *design,* we don't just mean the cosmetic look and feel, we also mean the site's voice and themes. Your site's main theme should be a focused idea of what your site is all about, using terms and keywords that match how your audience searches. For instance, if you have a business that customizes classic cars, your main site theme is classic car customization. We cover assigning keywords and themes more in Book II, Chapter 4, but basically, after you determine your main site theme, you can organize your content into categories and subcategories (that is, topics and sub-topics under the main site theme) and choose a specific primary keyword for each one. Every category-plus-keyword pair should have its own landing page within your website so that people searching for those keywords can click your listing and arrive at a page that's specifically relevant to their search query. (A *landing page* is the particular web page a user comes to when clicking a link.)

So far in this section, we've talked about theme in reference to the keywords and information your website provides. The site's theme is what the whole site is about; each page's theme is a subtopic and has content and keywords focused on that subtopic. Frequently, the word *theme* also applies to the design theme, or the look and feel of a website. Keep in mind that the design theme a web designer creates must integrate with the site's main content theme and be right for the target audience. They're all interrelated.

A design theme for a website needs to support the site's main theme. For example, if you have a website that offers dog kennel franchises, the design theme needs to include dog-related graphics in the same way the text talks about dogs. Similarly, the overall look needs to appeal to your target audience, just as the text should be tailored to dog-loving entrepreneurial adults. If you do market research to further narrow your target audience, you can make the site even better. Look at your current customers to determine what type of person tends to convert from a window-shopper to a customer. For instance, if it's usually women who become dog kennel franchisees, you can modify your site theme to appeal more to women. If it's usually married couples who go into the dog kennel business, by all means, include text references to marriage, as well as images of happy couples watching over lots of tail-wagging pooches.

Writing Rich Text Content

People do read, especially online. "Content is king" is a frequently stated maxim of Internet marketing experts because it's true. To have a successful website, you need lots and lots of content on your pages. How much content do you need? The answer depends somewhat on what is normal for your industry. When you research the sites that rank well for your keywords, some of the things you want to find out are how many indexed pages they have, as well as the quantity, quality, and structure of the keyword content on the high-ranking pages competing with yours. (Note that Book III explains how to do competitive research in detail.) When you know what level of content is currently succeeding in the search results pages for your keywords as an average, you get an idea of how many pages and words you need in order to play in their league.

We recommend that you have a minimum of 450 words of text content per page. That's a general rule, based on all our experience helping companies do SEO. If that sounds like a lot to write per page, think about it this way: The page that you're reading right now has about 450 words on it. Having fewer than 450 words on a page makes it hard to convince the engines that you're a subject-matter expert. In fact, depending on the industry and keyword, 450 words might still be too few. The SEO industry averages around 1,000 words per page, and this is true of other industries as well. Still, 450 is a good initial target number before you do competitive research.

Writing that much text for every page might sound like a daunting task, but keep in mind how it can help you:

✦ **Expertise goes up.** Search engines look for a site's expertise about a subject, and having a greater amount of relevant text signals that your web page is a subject-matter expert.

✦ **Trust factor goes up.** Users coming to your landing pages stay longer and trust it as more of an expert source if there's more content for them to read that matches their query.

✦ **Keyword relevancy goes up.** Long pages give you more opportunities to use your keywords without overusing them and creating spam.

✦ **Depth of content.** Multiple pages built around the same theme allow you to capitalize on niche and long-tail keywords that support your main keywords. For more on long-tail keywords, see Book I, Chapter 5.

The second main principle you should know about text content is this: In addition to needing lots of text on your site, you also want that text to be focused. Search engines (and users, for that matter) come to a web page seeking something specific. You want the content of each page to be focused on its keyword theme. This makes the page relevant to the user's search query.

Making each page's content relevant and focused helps the page rise in the search engine rankings. This concept ties into *siloing,* which is the process of organizing your site themes and content into categories and subcategories, each with its own main keyword. (You can read a full explanation of siloing in Book VI, Chapters 1 and 2.) For example, in your dog kennel franchise website, you might have a page focused on how much expected revenue a franchise can generate. In your more than 450 words of content, you wouldn't want to include a discussion of different dog food brands or grooming techniques. Including non-keyword-focused content like that would only dilute the information about your page's theme. Instead, you want to have lots of information about kennel rates, expected monthly revenues, and revenue-related content.

For many more in-depth recommendations, tips, and guidelines on writing good content, see Book V.

Planning Your Navigation Elements

Navigation elements make up the roads and highways of your website. They're the transportation system that can help people move smoothly from place to place, following clear signposts through well-marked paths. On the other hand, a website's navigation can make people frustrated and hopelessly lost, causing them to press the first Back button and get out of town.

If you create a good navigation plan right from the start, it's easy for site visitors and search engine spiders alike to move around your site. In fact, if your site doesn't have a good navigation system, it's unlikely that the search

engines can thoroughly index your site. Sites with a clear directory structure, siloed content, and easy-to-follow navigation are at an advantage over
sites without these foundational elements.

For maximum readability to the search engines, you want to format your
navigation elements as text links. That said, there are ways to help the
search engines read non-text navigation elements (such as Flash or image
mapping), which we get into in Chapter 5 of this minibook. Nevertheless,
you're going to get the cleanest, best read from simple text link navigation.

Figure 2-1 shows a sketch of a typical web page's navigation plan: It has three
basic areas for navigation links: top, bottom, and side (either right or left,
with left being more common than right). We explain what the differences
are at an initial design level, so you can evaluate what you're currently doing
for site navigation if your site is already in public use. If your site is still in
the design phase, you can start planning how you'll build your navigation.
(Note that we go into depth on navigation in Chapter 5 of this minibook.)

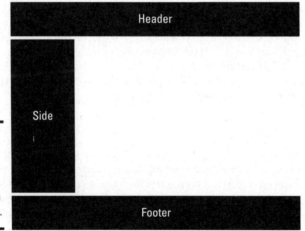

Figure 2-1:
The three
basic areas
for naviga-
tion links on
a web page.

Use frames only to create your navigation, unless you don't want the spiders
following those links. When you put content inside a frame, spiders see it as
its own separate page, so it can't be indexed as part of the current page's
content. For search engines, frames split up a page and remove all the associations of your navigation and the rest of your content.

Top navigation

Top navigation simply refers to the links at the top of the page. Usually
these are the "pretty" ones and the ones you want people to notice and use
to get to the main sections of your site. Also called *global navigation,* top

links often display site-wide, showing up conveniently on every page. A link to your home page is commonly found in your top navigation, as are links that give quick access to your main site categories. As appropriate for your user experience, you may also consider including usability links (sparingly, though), such as Check Out or Contact Us, in your top navigation.

Although the preceding list tells you common elements in the top navigation, they're not necessarily items that *you* want to have dominate your top navigation — it depends on your business strategy. For example, the About Us page and the Contact Us page don't necessarily do anything to enhance your overall site theme, so you may choose to include these elements in your bottom *(footer)* navigation.

Good labels are critical. Because your global navigation appears throughout your site, the *anchor text* of every link (which is the text label of the link, or what people click) carries a lot of weight.

Why shouldn't your home page simply be called Home? Because the search engines use the words in your anchor text to better understand what your website is about, using the word Home is a missed opportunity; the word does nothing to reinforce your site theme. (Learn more about theming and *siloing* in Book VI, Chapter 2.) We know of a window blinds company that radically improved its search engine ranking simply by changing its global navigation link from Home to Window Blinds. Within days, its web page jumped from the third to the first page of the search results for the keyword [window blinds] after this one simple change.

Footer navigation

Footer navigation refers to the navigational links at the bottom of a web page. Because search engines crawl all the way through a page, you can take advantage of another prime chance to show your keywords and increase your site's navigation and usability. Sites that have top navigation elements in Flash, Ajax, JavaScript, or images should see the footer navigation as a chance to restate all those links in search engine–friendly text at the bottom of the page. Footer navigation usually appears in a less conspicuous font, not trying to attract attention and simply offering a service to anyone who goes looking for more links to global topics. The footer is not the place for a link to every single page on your site, nor is it the place to excessively link to pages outside your site. The footer should include links to the pages linked in your top navigation as well as any additional user-friendly pages that weren't important enough to be in your main navigation, such as your privacy policy, your Contact Us page, your About Us page, and industry affiliations like the Better Business Bureau.

Your footer navigation generally should include:

✦ **Top navigation links (again):** You want to repeat all the links that are in your top, global navigation if your top navigation is in Flash or JavaScript which can prevent search engine spiders from reading it. Consider using anchor text that is more descriptive.

✦ **Contact Us:** You definitely want a link here to your contact information (especially if you left it out of your top navigation). This is good business practice so that people can contact you, but it also makes tons of sense for SEO. Local businesses that let spiders freely crawl all over their physical business address could wind up in local search results, too.

✦ **Physical address:** Include your physical address and local telephone number in your footer, especially if you're targeting local business. Both search engines and visitors use street addresses as a way to verify that you're a real business and not merely a scammer.

✦ **Legal stuff:** We recommend you include a privacy policy, copyright, and terms of use (if appropriate). These can be separate links in your footer even if they all go to the same legal-content page. You definitely want a privacy policy and copyright for your site — search engines look for these links because they help confirm that you are a legitimate company with accountability. Your trust factor increases, both with the public and the search engines, and because they can simply be inconspicuously placed at the bottom of each page, there's no reason not to do it.

✦ **Sitemap:** Include a link to your HTML sitemap to help the search engines and your users find their way to every bit of your content.

✦ **Link magnets:** If you have any piece of content that you're particularly known for or that people often come looking for on your site, providing a link to that content on every page of your site will satisfy users and ensure that search engines consider it a significant page.

Side navigation

Side navigation elements typically include category-specific links and are most commonly seen on e-commerce sites. Side navigation is context sensitive: The links vary from page to page. This helps with siloing because you can reinforce the landing page's theme by including links to supporting pages that help the user refine and dig deeper into the main category. For example, see in Figure 2-2 how the L.L.Bean website uses a side navigation with deeper, category-specific links to support its main top-navigation category?

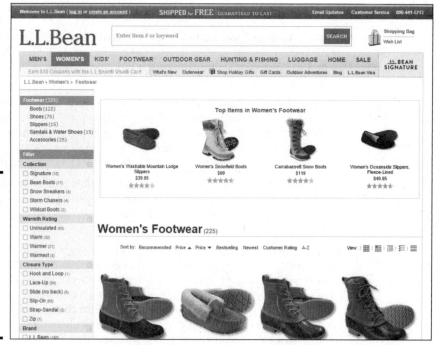

Figure 2-2: A side navigation with category-specific links that support the top navigation main category.

Implementing a Site Search

Many sites offer a Search text box right on their web pages that lets users search for information within the website (see the example below in Figure 2-3).

Site searches are essential if your website has tons of pages, such as for a magazine with years of archived issues, a large store with thousands of products, or a business with other extensive amounts of content. Smaller sites might also want a site search, but this decision should be made carefully. If you're thinking of adding a site search, consider the benefits and the potential drawbacks, and be sure to implement a site search that's effectively customized for your site.

The two major benefits of implementing a site search are:

✦ **Improving usability:** Ideally, a site search should improve usability and user retention. If your site search helps people find what they're looking for after coming to your site, it's doing good. For example, a site search is essential for a shopping site such as the Target website (www.target.com), which tries to keep users within the store after they

Search box

Figure 2-3:
A site
search text
box offers
a way to
search
within the
site.

arrive. Say a user comes to the Target site after running a Google search
for [snow shovels]. If the user next wants to find [tire chains], Target's
handy search function offers a quick way to find more products, add
them to the same cart, and check out one time. The user gets better convenience, and the website keeps a customer and increases its revenue.

✦ **Providing direct user feedback:** A site search provides you with a cache
of valuable information. Your visitors leave a trail that tells you what they
want in their own words. It's perfect as a feedback tool — users come
to you and type in exactly what they're looking for. By tracking all these
searches and the user experience following each one, you can identify
weaknesses in your site processes, keywords you may have overlooked,
pages of content you need to add, and also what's working successfully
or not working at all.

The main drawback of a site search occurs when it does not improve
usability. Many site searches fail to provide what the user is looking for and
become a side door where many visitors exit. You don't want to confuse and
lose your site visitors by giving them a technical tool that doesn't perform as
expected. So examine your website carefully in order to determine whether
the risk is worth it. If you have clear navigation and well-organized content,
you might be better off letting users find their way around rather than giving
them a shortcut to nowhere.

If you do decide to implement a site search, be sure to do it right. You want your site search to control the selection and presentation of results to make sure you've maximized the opportunity to give users what they need. When done well, an effective site search can prevent site abandonment and eliminate the multitude of brief, one-time visitors. It can guide users along the conversion path, getting them hooked along the way and encouraging them to explore. To make sure, watch your site analytics closely after you deploy a site search to see whether it's routing people well or causing them to take the nearest exit.

To be effective, your site search must be paired with good navigation and a well-siloed site. This combination is key to giving the user a good experience and developing the relationship between your brand and the customer. Here are some tips for maximizing your site search on an e-commerce site:

✦ List all major product categories and subcategories on your home page for easy navigation.

✦ Put a free-form site-search text box on every page with content that can lead to further searches. Like the Google search text box, this is a box where anything can be typed to get a potential answer.

✦ Implement guided search queries, where a user selects from a rigid pre-determined list to help narrow their search:

  • Provide site search for items by brand, price, color, sale, and so on.

  • Provide site search for featured products in every category.

  • Include every brand in every category in your site search database.

  • Include bestsellers in every category.

In some cases, your site may require separate search capabilities, or you may have to choose which kind of search to offer. The same underlying principles apply to non–e-commerce sites. Allow the site search to find your information in a variety of ways, broken down by lots of different categories, subcategories, and cross-categories. You want to give users many ways to get results, and you want to avoid search failure.

There are many free or inexpensive site-search kits you can use to incorporate a vertical search into your website. One reliable resource is the Google site-search option available at www.google.com/sitesearch. Paired with the free Google Analytics tool, any site search offers a good way to track user queries. Check out Book VIII for more on analytics in general. Book VIII, Chapter 3 covers Google Analytics in more detail.

Incorporating Engagement Objects into Your Site

It's a good practice to include Engagement Objects on your website. By *Engagement Objects,* we mean any type of interactive media object that gets users excited and offers them a way to connect to the content. The following sections specifically cover video and audio files. Including these types of rich media makes your website appear technically advanced to both users and search engines and engages your visitors.

Incorporating Engagement Objects into your website can also improve your search engine rankings. The reason is because of a concept called *blended search,* which is the mixing of different types of content in the search results. For instance, if you search on Google for [classic Ford Mustang], Google may include more than just web page links in your results. You might see photographs of restored Ford Mustangs at the top of your results page. Also mingled into the listings you might find a video link to a recent classic car show featuring Ford Mustangs. You might find a news article about a classic Ford Mustang that was the getaway car in a recent heist. Or you might find listings of classic car shops and other local businesses in your city that specialize in Ford Mustangs. Mixed in with these you would also see the top-ranked web pages for the keyword phrase that you entered. Now that there's blended search, the search engines show whatever types of files they determine to be the most relevant results. (As a side note, Google calls its blended search product *Universal Search,* and many in the search engine marketing community use that name to refer to all engines' blended search offerings.)

The concept of blending different types of files within a single search results set has raised the value of putting media on your website. In fact, some ranking factors have to do with what interactive media you have on your site. You want your site to get in on this action! You may find that just by adding some Engagement Objects to your website, your rank increases, especially if your competitors aren't currently using any on their sites. At the very least, you have an opportunity to satisfy your visitors better than your competition can.

Some sites offer video or audio files by displaying them in a separate pop-up window with no text. This has some value for visitors, but because search engines can't do much to understand the contents of a video or audio file, and because the pop-up window doesn't provide the spiders with any context that would help them understand the media's contents, the site has missed a valuable opportunity to enhance its keyword relevance with this great content.

TIP

A better way to handle video and audio files is to embed them right into your web pages. Let the video play right on the web page that also includes descriptive text about the video. Give users a hyperlink to let them hear an audio clip of a Ford Mustang engine on your Ford Mustang landing page, and let the anchor text and the sentences in the code surrounding the image help to support your page's keyword relevance. Some files, like a video transcript or an MP3 that contains clean narrative, can be indexed by the searches, but this process isn't perfect. The key to including video and audio files effectively is to place them in proximity to on-topic text that the search engines can read.

Video

You can include videos on your web pages if they're relevant to your topic. Basically, anything that can be shown in a short video that is relevant to your web page could be used: Just make sure it's ethical and within acceptable standards for your industry. If you can, you should always be hosting your videos on your site. You can upload them to YouTube as well, but it's your content and you should have it on your site. The possibilities are endless, but here are some examples of videos you might include, just to give you some ideas:

✦ **Product demo:** Include a small video demonstrating your product's or service's features and benefits. You can do this in a straightforward way or comically. For example, the Blendtec blender company uses video extremely effectively by showing videos of its product pulverizing things you'd never think to put in a blender (a shoe, an iPhone, and so on). The engaging videos alone have attracted thousands of interested buyers to the site (www.willitblend.com) and have become a viral Internet phenomenon in their own right.

✦ **Speech:** If you or someone notable from your company speaks in public, you could capture a digital video of an appropriate speech. Just a snippet might be enough.

✦ **Tour:** A video can be a tremendously effective tour guide. Show off your company building, impressive equipment, state-of-the-art facilities, or beautiful location — just pick something that can be well shown through a short video.

✦ **Interview:** You could interview one of your own personnel to give site visitors a "face-to-face" greeting, introduce one of your executives, or just give a video update of something newsworthy for your business. Alternatively, you could do a brief customer interview and post a live testimonial about your product or service.

Compression rates on the Internet mean that, to keep file sizes down, you often have to sacrifice video quality for speed. Put your money into making sure that the audio is crisp and clean. When it comes to quality, studies have shown that as long as the audio is decent, users will watch a video even if the picture quality is lacking. For more tips on the technical aspects of uploading videos to your site, see Book V, Chapter 2.

Audio

We confess that websites that greet their visitors with audio blaring really annoy us! From a usability perspective, making every person who comes to your site scramble to find their volume control buttons and do damage control with whomever may have heard their computer erupting in sound is a bad idea. You definitely want to avoid that. With that disclaimer made, we want to explain the *appropriate* use of sound files. Because in the world of SEO, embedding an audio file or offering a podcast carries weight with the search engines — not to mention users.

Consider what types of audio files you might offer on your site. Some ideas include:

✦ **Sounds:** If your site has anything to do with nature, consider offering nature sounds (a waterfall, mockingbird calls, hyenas whooping, and so on). You could demonstrate how quiet your product is by recording its noise compared to, say, a roomful of football fans after a touchdown play. Or, you could use on-topic recordings of bells ringing, trains whistling, tires screeching . . . . This list is going downhill fast, but you get the idea.

✦ **Music:** We suggest that you include music on your site only if your site is about music. (Background music for the sake of ambiance alone can be annoying, but as long as you default it to off and offer a volume control, it could be effective.)

✦ **Speaking:** You could include a recording of a presentation, speech, sermon, training event, poetry reading, or other public speaking event that's relevant to your page topic and keywords. Audio bits make for excellent SEO-friendly content.

✦ **Interviews:** A Q&A session with one of your own staff or a notable person in your industry could be recorded and offered on your website. If you hire a new executive, consider interviewing her talk-show format as an introduction that you can post on your website.

✦ **Podcasts:** To make your site even more advanced, host a podcast that site visitors can subscribe to. With a *podcast,* users can download digital audio recordings of a radio show or other type of regular program and listen to it on an iPod or other device. These are great for lessons, weekly recaps, radio shows, or even mixes of your favorite music with some commentary sprinkled in.

From an SEO perspective, there's a right way and a wrong way to add video and audio files to your website. You can read our specific recommendations for keeping your audio and video files SEO-compliant and user-friendly in Book V, Chapter 2.

Allowing for Expansion

When you're building your website, remember to allow for future expansion. A website is never "finished" any more than a business can ever set itself in stone. To be successful, especially in online marketing, you must stay flexible and allow room for growth — including on your website.

Database engineers have to think about future growth when they create a new database structure. They do not want to be in a position where the entire database needs to be torn apart and rebuilt simply because it cannot accommodate adding another layer of storage. Similarly, you don't want to box yourself in when it comes to your site design. To some extent, you can foresee future needs and plan ahead logically. Think about:

✦ **New products or services:** Try to predict what types of add-on product lines or services may come down the pike and need to be added to your site.

✦ **Expanded content:** You've read how important it is to have lots of content supporting your keyword themes, so try to identify where you have content holes that need to be filled with new pages of supporting information.

✦ **Enhanced features:** If you'd like to someday enrich your site by starting a blog or other interactive community feature, envision how this might fit into your site.

Despite your best efforts, however, you probably cannot predict all the changes coming in the future. For this reason, you want to keep your website design, navigation, structure, and even name somewhat open. For example, a business called George's Ford-Only Customization Shop has prevented itself right away from ever being able to expand to Chevrolets. Similarly, you wouldn't want your website's domain name to be restrictively specific. Today, your business might be all about repairing truck fenders, but if you choose the domain name www.truckfenderwork.com, you'd be stuck having to create a new URL if you want to expand your business to work on all-body work or on cars as well as trucks.

Because constant growth is the rule, you want to make your website structure modular. We cover the concept of *siloing* in Book VI, Chapters 1 and 2, which involves breaking your website content into categories based on a keyword theme. A proper silo structure allows you to add new silos without breaking your site's current linking architecture or navigation system. You can simply snap on another silo adjacent to the existing ones at the same structural level.

Developing an Update Procedure

You may be a one-person shop now or the only person in your company's web development department, like the Lone Ranger working to save the day. Or you might be part of a large team developing a voluminous website. Whatever your situation is today, the fact is that it will change. People may leave the company, you could be transferred, and new people could be hired. To survive the personnel changes that inevitably happen, your website must have a documented update procedure.

In Chapter 1 of this minibook, we cover creating a design procedure that functions as a style guide for your website. In this section, we want to help you expand that document to cover an update procedure, as well. You've done the research to know what your site needs in terms of SEO. If you don't write down guidelines related to search engine optimization and include them in a style guide that new webmasters, IT staff, marketing directors, and others can refer to, all your SEO progress could be lost. After all, without an education in SEO best practices, and without knowing how to do site analysis and competitive research (as you find out how to do in this book), people can make decisions about websites that drop the site right out of the search engine rankings. We've seen it happen.

Write down your update procedures, including your SEO do's and don'ts, to lay out the blueprint for others to follow. Make your list as exhaustive as possible. To get you started, here are some items to cover in your style guide and site update procedure:

✦ **File naming:** Specify how you name new pages, images, videos, audio files, and so on. You probably have developed syntax for these things, so you want to write down those standards. (We cover good file naming in Chapter 1 of this minibook.)

✦ **Directory structure:** How you name and structure your file folders should also be documented so that when someone creates a new silo or wants to add a new picture, he or she knows how to do it.

✦ **Redirects:** Document what your procedure is for redirecting traffic away from a no-longer-needed page. Because there are several types of HTML redirect codes, but only a 301 Redirect is good practice for SEO, instructions could help prevent a costly mistake. (For more information on redirects, see Book VII, Chapter 3.)

✦ **Linking:** You want to be sure to cover your procedure for adding new links. Explain why anchor text must contain relevant keywords (never just Click Here), and give guidelines for linking within silos, not between them, as a general rule. You may want to cover linking very thoroughly because it's so important to SEO — you can find lots more information on good linking strategies in Chapter 5 of this minibook, as well as in Book VI.

✦ **New pages:** Your procedure for adding a new page to your site should ask some critical questions, such as: What goal does this page meet? Does it fit into the silo? What are its main keywords? Whoever sets up the new page should be able to write down answers to these questions. In addition, because there are a number of things that must be carefully reviewed before a new page goes live, a checklist is helpful. Your new-page checklist should contain all the steps needed to make sure that the page is SEO-friendly and ready for the public. We suggest you start with the sample list we include in Book I, Chapter 1, and adapt it for your site.

Balancing Usability and Conversion

This chapter is all about building an SEO-friendly site. However, we aren't recommending that you design a website just for the search engines. Your SEO goal must be balanced with the need to create a user-friendly site. Unless you balance SEO-friendliness (to help people find your site) with user-friendliness (to make people want to stay there), you won't be able to achieve your true objective, which is conversion.

Conversion refers to whatever action you want your site visitors to take. That may be buying something, joining a group, signing up for a newsletter, registering for a seminar, filling out a survey, or just visiting more pages. Whatever your definition is for conversion, your real goal involves more than just generating traffic to your site's front door. When those people arrive, you want them to do something: That "something" is your point of conversion.

Usability and SEO working together

Usability refers to the way a person uses, or experiences, your website. Every now and then a familiar discussion resurfaces in the SEO community's forums, blogs, and newsgroups: When you are designing a website, whom should you be targeting, the search engines or the humans? Which should take precedence in your site design, and how do you serve both? Luckily, balancing these complementary needs is not as complicated as it seems. Search engine optimization and usability can work hand in hand. In fact, many of the things that are good for search engines benefit human visitors as well.

Some marketers are adamant that usability take priority over SEO, arguing that an unusable website can be at the top of the search engine results pages and still never make money. The reverse is pointed out as well — search engine optimization has to come first because the most perfectly usable site in the world still has to have visitors who use it before it is worth anything.

The confusion arises because people commonly mistake what the goal of each approach really is. This misconception leads them to make the assumption that the two are incompatible. In many people's minds, SEO advocates a complicated set of rules to follow, games to play, pages to write, links to attract, and hoops to jump through. Usability has also grown to complex proportions, incorporating the use of personas, *conversion funnels* (the path that a visitor takes to get to a conversion, most commonly a purchase), and psychology degrees in human factors.

But if you strip away all the methods used in both approaches, their goals are remarkably similar. *Search engine optimization* is the process of designing a web strategy that gives search engine spiders and human visitors the best picture of the website possible. *Usability* is the process of designing a web strategy that gives visitors the most satisfactory experience possible.

You need to focus first on the things that SEO and usability have in common and then put the rest into balance. SEO is about more than simply ranking well in the search engines. The key is to rank well in the search engines for the keywords that are most relevant. If your site is the most expert and the best choice for your human visitors, your SEO campaign should be working to demonstrate that fact to the search engines. Table 2-1 lists a few examples of how improving the usability of your site often benefits your SEO campaign, as well.

Table 2-1   Usability Improvements That Go Hand-in-Hand with SEO

Usability Improvement	*SEO Benefit*
Do research to find out where your target users are looking for you.	Combines with keyword research.
Develop each landing page so that it's well suited to help particular users based on their search queries.	Optimizes pages around specific keywords.
Build a larger network of links coming from external web pages so that more people can find your site.	Increases the perception to the search engines that your site is an expert and raises your link equity.
Discern where your target audience "lives" online when they aren't on your site.	Identifies where you need to be getting links because chances are, those sites are relevant.
Make your site navigation clear and easy to travel for users.	Allows search engine spiders to get around your site more easily.

(continued)

Table 2-1 *(continued)*

Usability Improvement	SEO Benefit
Write clean copy that states exactly what you offer visitors.	Helps search engines determine what each page is about.
Use clarifying words so that your terms make sense in context.	Helps search engines understand what queries are relevant to your pages.
Put your site on a fast, stable server to provide good site performance to users.	Speeds the search engine spiders along their way and helps improve SERP rank.
Create user-friendly error screens that explain the problem and give users links to other options when a page can't be displayed.	Optimizes the 404 Page Cannot Be Displayed error page and redirected pages so that search engines can move through them easily to functioning pages on your site.

So when you consider your visitors' needs in order to boost your site's usability, the nice part is that you're also supporting your SEO efforts. But what if there are conflicts? If the best way to serve your visitors seems to go against SEO best practices, there probably is a way to compensate.

We've found that there is nearly always a technical solution for achieving SEO, no matter what the site owner is trying to accomplish. Here are two scenarios where the site's usability objectives needed a technical solution for SEO:

✦ **Basic example:** A web designer wants to use a single image as the entire home page of a site. Knowing that search engines need to find content in order for that page to rank, you (as the SEO consultant) can use HTML to put content into the page, remove any words from the graphic and reset them as text, and use a CSS file to position the elements and give style to the page. The site's usability expert likes this solution because it offers accessible options for low-sighted visitors and provides flexibility for the layout.

✦ **A more complicated example:** To provide the kind of content its users need, a site uses query strings to dynamically build the page from a database rather than the page being static. To help optimize that site for search engines, a technical solution could involve renaming directories so that the URL of each page contains meaningful keywords and a link structure is implemented to assure crawlability; as a result, the human visitor sees the right content, and search engine spiders can see what the site is about based on its well-labeled physical directory structure. Everyone wins.

So between usability and SEO, which is more important to your website's success? The answer is that they're both equally necessary and, thankfully, can work hand in hand. Build your site for *all* your visitors, human and spider alike. Instead of taking the approach that one or the other is sufficient, realize that by doing them in tandem, your website can be stronger, easier to navigate, more accessible to your target audience, and more likely to generate conversions.

Go for conversions as your main target.

Here's why this tip makes sense. As you monitor your site traffic and conversions, you may notice a strange phenomenon: Sometimes being number three or four or five on the search results page is better than being number one. Sure, you get far more traffic in position one, but consider a typical scenario. Say a woman wants to buy a pair of designer shoes. She searches for the designer name and [shoes], and then begins clicking through the results. At the first website, she looks around and finds a pair she likes, but she doesn't purchase them because she isn't sure she's found the best style or the best price. She clicks the second, third, and fourth sites to continue her shopping and price comparisons. At the fourth site, she's done with price comparisons and has discovered that every site sells the shoes for the same price. She's now ready to buy and clicks Add to Cart on site number four: Because she's already on the site, it's the most convenient place for her to make her purchase. So site number four wins the conversion.

You have two choices in this particular situation: Be site number four, or be one of the first three sites that didn't secure the conversion and figure out why not. In this case, ranking number one might not get you the sale unless your site was a lean, mean, converting machine.

Creating pages that convert

Most people come to a web page and decide whether to stay there within the first couple seconds. That means that you have only three seconds to convince someone that your page offers what they're looking for. For each of your landing pages, ask yourself questions such as:

+ **Curb appeal:** Is the site able to satisfy the intent of the query, and is it appropriate to the visitor?

+ **Impressions:** At first glance, what does my page seem to be about?

+ **Focus:** Is it clear that this page is about the keyword?

+ **Ease of use:** How easy is it to achieve the desired task?

+ **More details:** Can a visitor easily access more detailed information if desired?

+ **Conversion:** Can a visitor easily navigate to where a conversion can take place?

You also want to consider your goal for each page and see if you're achieving it. This differs from deciding what the keyword is for each page. For instance, you may have a landing page on your classic car customization website centered on the keyword phrase [Chevrolet Camaros]; your text may be all about restoring classic Chevy Camaros; and your images might depict classic Chevy Camaros. So far, that's all good. But your goal for this page is a different issue. Your goal may be to get the user to click through to more pages on your website. Your goal may be to have the user download a coupon for a free tire rotation. Your goal may be to entice the user to set an appointment, make a phone call, order a service, make a purchase, or do something else. In short, the page's goal can be measured in terms of what you want visitors to do while on this page.

To help determine each page's conversion goal, ask yourself three questions about every page on your website that requires action (such as landing pages):

✦ **What:** What action is required?

✦ **Who:** Who must take that action?

✦ **How:** What information does the visitor need in order to know how to take the required action?

After you have each page's goal firmly in mind, usability really comes into play. Think of yourself as a professional usability expert for your website. You want to design your pages in a way that helps your site visitors successfully reach the goal. Don't just assume that you know what's best. Someone who knows the site and industry has a completely different opinion than a prospective user of the site. All the different needs and viewpoints of your potential audience should be explored. This is why if you have the budget for it, a professional usability expert can be worth her weight in gold.

For example, professional usability experts can help brick-and-mortar stores decide how to lay out their shelves for highest potential revenue. They can advise a bookstore owner that people tend to turn to the right when entering a store more often than they turn to the left, and the bookstore can apply this information by positioning a bestseller table to the right of the entry. Grocery stores are a great example of user psychology in action as well: You have to pass right through all the really tempting packaged goods, like doughnuts and chips, to get to the staple items, like milk and eggs, that are usually on your shopping list.

On your website, make each of your landing pages meet a particular goal. Often, you want the landing page to work as a funnel, collecting visitors and sending them through to some other page on your site. For instance, an Add to Cart link near the product information is a fairly standard way to turn a window-shopper into a customer, and if your site then displays a clear Proceed to Checkout or similar link, you can funnel the person to a page where she can make a purchase. If your site isn't about e-commerce, you still want to have clear signposts that lead visitors from each landing page to a conversion page. (***Note:*** We cover conversion funnels in Book VIII, Chapter 2.)

Engineering a website for human interaction does not always follow common sense. There's a whole usability science about how to design web pages for maximum return, but that's outside the scope of this book. If you want to research it, we recommend starting with the website Usability Effect (www.usabilityeffect.com). The site owner, Kim Krause Berg, began in the field of SEO and then moved to a career in usability consulting, so she understands both sides. You can discover a lot from the articles and other resources on her site.

Keep in mind that all usability theories remain just that — theories — until proven through user testing. You might add a button that says Free Tire Rotation Coupon on your website's home page, but until you analyze how many times people click the button to download the coupon, you don't really know if it's an effective conversion device. You would also want to know whether adding the coupon link draws more traffic to your site or alters your search engine ranking. To go a step further with your user testing, you might also try a few different versions of the button, varying its look or placement, and gather comparison data. However you approach it, you're going to want to prove your usability theories with some real-world testing.

Creating a strong call to action

Do your web pages have a clear "call to action," enticing people to do whatever action the web page requires? If not, this absence could explain a less-than-satisfactory conversion rate.

You need an effective call to action on any page where you want the user to do something. This goes back to knowing what your goal is for each page, whether it's to click through to another page, add an item to a shopping cart, or to take some other action. Because websites typically lose a percentage of people at every step along the way to conversion (known as *conversion drop-off*), you want your users' journey to be as direct and clear as possible. Don't confuse your users by offering them too many choices. Often, you end up paralyzing them with indecision or distracting them from their original goal. Either way, you lose your conversion.

The most effective calls to action make use of an imperative verb (like Add or Sign Up or Create) and a compelling benefit. Some of the very best calls to action are actually graphics or buttons that catch the visitor's eye but don't dilute your content with needless commercial language that could bias the search engines. If your site is research-oriented, you might want to obscure the words Buy Now by placing them in an image so that the search engines don't think that you're a retail site. This example could be from a business-to-business site. It's very motivating for an engineer seeking this type of solution:

```
Attend our Web cast "Process Excellence for Supply Chain
    Management" and learn how to reduce costs with our process-
    driven approach to align business practices within your
    organization.
```

Your call to action must tell visitors exactly what you want them to do. If you want them to buy your product, you could scatter multiple calls to action in strategic places within your copy, such as Buy Brand X now). If you want them to contact you by phone, list your phone number and provide instructions (Call us Monday–Friday from 8–5 PST at 1-866-517-1900). Repeat the number in bold text throughout your copy and again at the end. But be wary of spamming the page. Repeating your call to action works only if you don't annoy the visitor. For more on spam, see Book I, Chapter 6.

You should use meaningful words in the anchor text of any call to action in order to reinforce why the user would want to do it. The anchor text can incorporate keywords to clarify why a user would take an action. For example, if you have links in your web content that lead to a page where the user can sign up for your newsletter, include a brief description in every link like "Car Restoration Newsletter" rather than just "Sign up for our newsletter." Descriptive anchor text on your calls to action adds value for users and also helps search engines better understand what your web pages are about.

You want to make sure that you're not inadvertently thwarting anyone from getting to the point of conversion with confusing messages, broken links, or other weaknesses in your site. This is where micro-management is appropriate — gather lots of site analytics from your IT department and closely examine how effective your conversion path is every step of the way. You need this information to help you identify problems and then test and improve, test and improve again, and then again — it's an ongoing process.

A strong call to action is critical, but it's just one factor that helps you achieve conversions. In the end, your conversion rate reflects your ability to persuade visitors to complete their intended actions from A to Z. It is a measure of your effectiveness and of customer satisfaction overall.

Chapter 3: Building a Mobile-Friendly Site

In This Chapter

✔ **Choosing the right mobile approach**

✔ **Designing for a mobile user**

✔ **Optimizing a mobile site for search engines**

✔ **Testing for mobile-friendliness**

A *mobile-friendly* website is a site that functions and displays equally well on a mobile device — such as a smartphone or a tablet — and a desktop computer.

In this chapter, you learn how to build mobile-friendly websites that are optimized for search and optimal user experience. If you're still not convinced of the importance of mobile, consider these 2014 comScore statistics:

✦ The U.S. alone has 172 million smartphone owners and 93 million tablet owners.

✦ On average, 34 percent of monthly visitors come to top leading brands like Amazon.com, Google, Facebook, and CBS Interactive *exclusively* from mobile devices. That means that about 34 percent of all traffic to Amazon.com comes from users who use *only* a mobile device to access the site.

✦ As of June 2014, consumers say they spend 60 percent of their time interacting with digital media using mobile devices and 40 percent of the time interacting through desktop computers. These numbers represent a 13 percent decrease in desktop engagement with media over a 15-month period, and a 13 percent increase in media engagement via mobile devices.

✦ Approximately 60 percent of all Internet traffic comes from mobile devices and 40 percent comes from desktop computers. In other words: To access the Internet, people are using mobile devices — through apps and the mobile browser — 20 percent more than they are using their desktop computers.

The fact of the matter is that mobile use is growing every year, and access to mobile-friendly, user-focused websites is becoming more important to search engines and consumers. In April 2015, Google confirmed that it uses mobile friendliness as a ranking signal when delivering results to users searching on mobile devices. We mention elsewhere in the book that Google doesn't typically confirm or deny the signals that it looks at when ranking websites, so when Google tells you outright that something matters for search rankings, it's a big deal.

Not sure how to get started making your site look and function just as well on mobile as it does on desktop? Not to worry; this chapter contains many design, user experience, and optimization tips to get your site on the path to mobile friendliness.

Choosing the Right Mobile Approach

Because a desktop computer monitor and a smartphone are drastically different in size, designing for mobile means that you have to do one of three things:

+ Build a responsive web design that dynamically adjusts content from desktop format to mobile format

+ Use dynamic serving to make the mobile experience device specific and control how mobile content is delivered page by page

+ Create a separate mobile site designed specifically for mobile users

This section explores each of these three approaches to mobile-friendly website development. At the time of publication, responsive design is the mobile-friendly configuration recommended by both Google and Bing. That said, we recommend that you use the configuration that delivers the best user experience for your consumer's specific needs. Search engines will never penalize you for working extra hard to make your site visitors happy.

We talk about code and servers in this section. If you're a code person, you'll love it. If you'd rather not touch code or servers with a 10-foot pole, don't be alarmed. The idea here isn't to teach you how to become an IT guy or gal. The idea is to teach you how it all works so that you can communicate what you need and delegate the task of making it happen to the right person.

Option 1: Responsive design

Explained simply, *responsive design* is a web design technique that uses CSS and a series of coded rules to dynamically adjust the appearance of your desktop content so that it best fits within the screen-size parameters of different mobile devices. Responsive design uses JavaScript and *client-side serving* (also known as *front-end serving*) to alter the way pages appear in mobile or desktop browsers after the server has already loaded the page. See how responsive design works in Figure 3-1.

HOW RESPONSIVE DESIGN WORKS

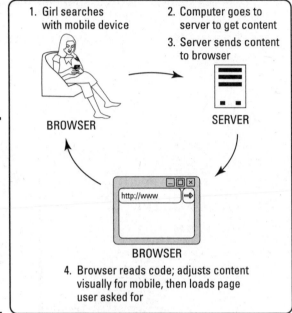

1. Girl searches with mobile device

2. Computer goes to server to get content

3. Server sends content to browser

BROWSER

SERVER

http://www

BROWSER

4. Browser reads code; adjusts content visually for mobile, then loads page user asked for

Figure 3-1: Websites that use responsive design to adjust the display of a website based on device type work in this way.

Websites using responsive design have one single set of URLs for all content regardless of whether that content is being delivered to a desktop computer or a mobile device. See the example in Figure 3-2.

When to use responsive design

Choosing responsive design makes sense in the following five circumstances:

✦ When you want a coherent desktop and mobile experience.

✦ When you have a strong desktop website that has built up years of link equity, trust, and industry authority. Responsive mobile sites benefit from *shared indexing* with desktop sites, which can result in improved mobile ranking. Although you can use special code if you go with other mobile design options for your website to make sure the search engine sees the mobile site as the same as your desktop site, this is a technical issue that can introduce complications. (Learn more about shared indexing in the "Optimizing to rank in mobile search results" section, later in this chapter.)

✦ When you want your desktop and mobile visitors to convert in the same way.

✦ When you have limited development resources, which can make maintaining a custom mobile experience with custom content seem out of the question.

✦ When you want to manage the maintenance and search engine indexing of just one site.

Figure 3-2:
BruceClay.
com is using
a respon-
sive web
design, so
the desktop
content
(left) and
the mobile
content
(right) have
the exact
same URL
but appear
differently
on different
devices.

Option 2: Dynamic serving

Dynamic serving is a *server-side* development approach that detects which type of device your visitor is using to deliver unique content that is optimized specifically for her device. As you can see in Figure 3-3, the user searches with a mobile device and the server responds accordingly.

Like responsive design, *dynamic serving* uses one single set of URLs for all content regardless of whether that content is being delivered to a desktop computer or a mobile device. But that's where the similarity ends.

See, responsive web designs dynamically adjust the *appearance* of content — but the URLs stay the same because the mobile content and desktop content are essentially the same, other than appearance. With dynamic serving, the URLs stay the same, but the content delivered to mobile devices is not always the same as the content delivered to desktop devices.

Figure 3-3:
What's happening behind the scenes when a website uses a dynamic serving approach to mobile design.

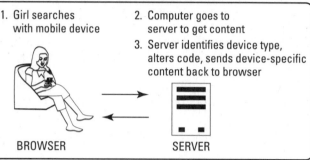

This difference in content is possible because dynamic serving is a *server-side* approach that alters content code (HTML, CSS, PHP) based on the device that is asking for it *before* the content is delivered to the browser (where the user sees it). This code allows the server to alter the content of the page without altering the URL of the page. You can find more on how to set up your server for dynamic serving in Book VII, Chapter 1.

When to use dynamic serving

Using dynamic serving makes particular sense in the following five circumstances:

✦ When your website needs to include complex mobile-friendly functionality, such as multipage forms or interactive tool dashboards. In this case, dynamic serving can be a great solution that allows you to serve the best experience based on user circumstances.

✦ When you find that your website needs to serve two different device markets very differently. Some examples are that your iPhone users take a very different path to conversion than your Android users, or you want your pages to render differently for smartphone users than for tablet users.

✦ When your visitors largely use different keywords to access your website via desktop search and mobile search. Dynamic serving lets you alter the way content is rendered on a page-by-page basis, so it is a great resource if you want to optimize specific pages for high-volume mobile keyword phrases without changing the desktop language.

✦ When you want your desktop visitors and mobile visitors to convert in different ways.

✦ When you have strong development resources that are comfortable with manually coding and maintaining complex, clean code.

Book IV
Chapter 3

Building a Mobile-
Friendly Site

Option 3: Building a separate mobile site

A *mobile site* is just what it sounds like: a separate website that has been created specifically for mobile device users. With a separate mobile site, rather than altering content for mobile upon request, when searchers navigate to your website from a mobile device, they are redirected to a mobile-only version of your website that lives on a unique domain, such as *m.domain.com* (as shown in Figure 3-4) or *mobile.domain.com*. If you go with this choice, you need to set up your server to detect the device and then send the user to the right site. Read about how to redirect users in Book VII, Chapter 3.

Mobile-specific URL

Figure 3-4:
Firestone uses an *m.domain. com* mobile site design.

An important technical implementation of a separate mobile site is the proper use of canonical tags. From your mobile pages, include a canonical tag that points to the correlated desktop page so that the trust, authority, and link equity of your desktop site will be associated with your mobile site as well. Read more about this in the Google Developers documentation (`https://developers.google.com/webmasters/mobile-sites/mobile-seo/configurations/separate-urls`).

When to build a separate mobile site

Here are a few circumstances in particular when it may make the most sense for your business to build a separate mobile site:

✦ When you need to prominently include elements on your desktop website that don't render well on mobile devices — Flash, for instance. Although we don't recommend using Flash or other high-bandwidth interactive elements on your website, we do recognize that sometimes you have to (say, if you are running a movie website and need to create image-based experiences and show movie trailers). If your boss says you have to to do this, you'll benefit from building a separate mobile site.

✦ When you need to build a mobile-specific conversion flow or your visitors use search terms on mobile that are very different from the search terms they use on a desktop.

✦ When you have a huge website with lots of pages and limited resources. Making a large website multi-device responsive can take a lot of resource time. A mobile site can be a solution that allows you to show your mobile users a smaller, refined, sampling of your website content.

✦ When your visitors use older — not "smart" — phones to access your website. Mobile sites tend to work better on these types of older, less dynamic phones.

✦ When you have the resources to build, update, and maintain a separate mobile site.

A note about mobile apps

A *mobile app* is a self-contained computer program, or *application*, built specifically to provide users with a tightly controlled way to access content outside the mobile browser. Although mobile apps are great for user experience, they are very different from mobile websites.

Because the scope of this book is limited to techniques that can help your mobile website rank in search engine results pages, we don't go into depth about when to build a mobile app, or how to optimize mobile apps for iTunes or the App Store. To learn more about that, we recommend that you dig deeper with a book specifically about mobile app marketing.

Designing for a Mobile User

Choosing a mobile development approach is all about directing your content to the user. Mobile design, on the other hand, is all about deciding what the user will see when the content arrives. How does the navigation look? Can users read the text? How do they contact you, or search for items?

To begin designing for mobile, you must wrap your head around what the "mobile experience" is.

First, mobile visitors are *mobile*. At least part of the time, your searchers use mobile devices to find you on the go from taxi cabs, dentists' waiting rooms, their backyards, and the aisles of your competitor's store. So when visitors access your site using a mobile device, their needs are inherently different than when they access your site from a desktop computer.

Second, remember that mobile devices are smaller than desktop computers, and that navigation and scrolling is done using touchscreens and *gestures* (swiping, tapping, and other physical interactions with the screen). See examples of gestures in Figure 3-5.

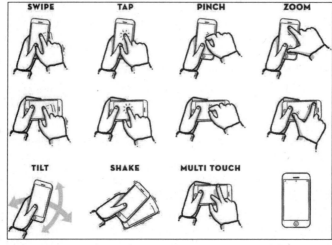

Figure 3-5: Some common mobile device gestures.

Courtesy of Julian Burford

Feeling mobile minded? Great! Next you can get started on learning how to design with the needs of mobile users in mind.

Prioritizing mobile content creation

Think of all the things your users see when they visit your website. From words, pictures, and video to your site's navigation, they see the *content* of your website.

Now, get in your mobile mindset and think about how your visitors will experience your website content when they are on mobile devices walking the streets of New York.

If you remember only one thing about designing for mobile friendliness, it needs to be this: Mobile-friendly websites need above all else to provide the best user experience possible.

Think of your user's needs first and you'll always end up with a better design. Plus, the search engines *love* a great user experience! So, by designing to make your human user happy, you are automatically designing to make the search engine happy. The following sections describe seven ways to design mobile websites that keep users happy.

Create single-tap calls to action

To make your content mobile friendly, you want to make it as easy as possible for your user to find what they need and take action. In the mobile environment, in which users are working with small screens and finger taps rather than mouse clicks, prominent click-to-call call-to-action buttons are a great way to help users easily accomplish common tasks. And completing a task means a *conversion* for you!

Click-to-call buttons are a great mobile-specific call to action because mobile users are often already holding a phone. This button helps users get what they need (a chat with you) and for you to get what you need (a conversion).

Figure 3-6 shows an example of a click-to-call button, placed strategically at the top of the Bruce Clay, Inc., mobile experience.

Also consider creating single-tap buttons that help mobile users find your store front or accomplish tasks on the go. You can see an example on the Progressive mobile site, shown in Figure 3-7, which has buttons to help users find local agents and make payments without having to scroll down the page.

Design for a small screen size

Mobile devices are smaller than desktop computers, so you have less room to fit content on the page and less room for white space. Some small-screen content optimization tricks include:

✦ Making your logo serve as a link that redirects back to your mobile home page.

✦ Minimizing white space and making sure that the majority of the page is filled with actual content.

✦ Building off-screen elements such as a *toggle menu,* which is a navigation element that can expand and close. (We discuss toggle menus in the "Designing mobile-friendly navigation" section, later in this chapter.)

✦ Shorten the text that appears on buttons when possible.

Click-to-call button

Figure 3-6:
Click-to-call
buttons
let mobile
users easily
take action
and get the
assistance
they need.

Be particular about what goes above the fold

Because mobile devices are smaller than desktop computers, they have less space to present content *above the fold* (in the space the user sees before scrolling down the page). Make sure to be thoughtful and user-focused when selecting your above-the-fold content. Also, make sure that the content you place above the fold loads quickly. Site speed and above-the-fold load time are important to user experience, and they're also important mobile ranking factors.

Choose a legible mobile font

Any time you put words on your website, the first priority needs to be user comprehension. Your user needs to be able to clearly see, and quickly read, your words on a variety of devices. Because no one-size-fits-all standard currently exists for mobile screen size or graphic quality, unfortunately we can't give you a one-size-fits-all recommendation for font selection. We do recommend that you keep it simple and user focused. Here are some rules of thumb to follow about fonts:

Get a Quote button

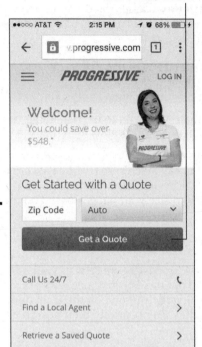

Figure 3-7:
One-click
buttons
above the
fold help
mobile
users
accomplish
tasks.

+ Whether you go with a Sans Serif or Serif font, consider the height of the characters in your font alphabet and the white space between the letters. Fonts with a moderately high individual character height and a little bit of space between letters can improve readability.

+ Know your demographic and remember that older folks may have a harder time reading smaller, more condensed fonts.

+ Make sure to provide enough contrast between the font and the background so that users can see your content, even outdoors or in other conditions where screen glare is a factor.

+ The safest route is to use a common font that mobile device manufacturers and users approve of, such as Arial, Helvetica, Courier, Georgia, Times New Roman, Trebuchet MS, or Verdana.

Optimize images

Not all images are created equal: Some are created in giant size for billboards, some are in high resolution for print; and some are compressed so that they load quickly on mobile devices. In this chapter, we're most concerned with the third type of image.

**Book IV
Chapter 3**

**Building a Mobile-
Friendly Site**

To make your website mobile-friendly, it's important to make sure your images are sized and saved in a way that allows them to load quickly on desktop and mobile devices. Optimized images that load quickly keep both the user and the search engine happy.

To optimize images for mobile, make sure to

◆ Save images in a compact file format, such as JPG, GIF, or PNG.

◆ Never size images larger than they need to be; remember that big images mean big file sizes, which in turn means slow load times.

◆ Optimize the size of images even if you're using responsive design. With responsive design, you can make sure that images are optimized for mobile by using CSS to write in a max-width clause — {max-width:100%} — which will resize your images based on the size of the detected screen.

Design for multiscreen

These days, it is not uncommon for customers to visit your site using multiple devices over a short period of time. For instance, visitors may start shopping your selection of boots using their phone on the train home from work and then, after they're home, they may continue their search using a desktop computer or tablet.

To optimize your mobile content for multiscreen use, make sure that the colors, fonts, and themes that you use closely imitate your desktop colors, fonts, and themes. Doing so helps your visitors feel confident that they've landed in the right place when they navigate to your website using a new device, and it can also help reinforce branding. Progressive Insurance does a good job of this, as shown in Figure 3-8.

Avoid using Flash

In general, designing with Flash is unreliable and not recommended for either desktop or mobile design. This includes relying on Flash to play video content. Some mobile devices, such as iPhones, can't render Flash at all, so any elements of your website that require Flash will render a poor user experience.

Flash is also bad for SEO because Google has been known to bump SERP rank and insert SERP warnings when mobile sites use Flash.

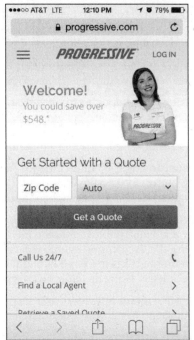

Figure 3-8:
Keep your
mobile and
desktop
designs
similar.

Designing mobile-friendly navigation

Your mobile-friendly navigation can take many shapes. The option that is
best for you depends on how complex your navigation needs to be, your
conversion goals, and your users' preferences.

Remember that your site's navigation needs to help visitors — and search spiders — navigate through your website. So your mobile navigation needs to be intuitive, functional, crawlable, and optimized for touch.

Keep these best practices in mind when designing your mobile-friendly navigation:

✦ **Keep it simple, sweetie.** Keep top-level navigation as simple as possible, especially if you want your navigation displayed across the top of your mobile page. Remember that you're designing for a small screen size. (An iPhone 6 is 750 pixels wide in portrait mode, whereas a 13-inch laptop computer is 1,280 pixels wide).

The point of a mobile site let your visitors easily browse your website with a mobile device. Your navigation should give them links to your main category pages and pages that improve usability (such as a "Call Now" option and a link to your shopping cart).

You don't have to link to every page in your website here. In fact, too many options can result in decision paralysis and confusion, which creates a poor user experience.

Including four to eight items in your top menu is usually a good rule of thumb. See the example of Bruce Clay, Inc.'s top menu in Figure 3-9.

✦ **List your most important pages first.** These are usually your conversion calls to action, such as "locate store," "shop," "subscribe," and "products," as shown in Figure 3-10. If your website is more content oriented than sales oriented, list your most important category first.

✦ **Consider losing the Home button.** To save space, you can leave off the Home button in your navigation and instead have your top-of-page logo navigate to the home page when tapped.

✦ **Design for touch and give enough space for a finger.** Because both your tablet and smartphone users are navigating your mobile site using touchscreens, it's very important to make sure that the tap sensitivity of your navigation buttons are large enough to use. The average finger requires a space at least 44 pixels large, left to right and up and down.

✦ **Make your menu intuitive.** Your visitors should know exactly where each of your menu items will take them.

✦ **Minimize multilevel navigation.** We encourage you to keep it simple, but if your navigation simply must have drop-down levels, never add more than two layers of drop-down functionality.

✦ **Make sure that drop-down menus are activated by touch.** Although mouse-hover activation works in the desktop experience, it leaves your user stuck in the mobile experience.

Figure 3-9:
Bruce Clay, Inc. simplifies its desktop navigation (top) significantly to improve mobile user experience. To help users with task completion, the mobile site navigation (bottom) also includes a click-to-call button.

Book IV
Chapter 3

Building a Mobile-
Friendly Site

✦ **Use visual menu indicators.** If you use an off-screen menu, use a three-line menu indicator so that your visitor can access your menu. We talk more about off-screen menus later in this chapter.

Figure 3-10: GameStop simplifies its desktop navigation (top) by including only user- and conversion-focused calls to action on its mobile home page (bottom).

If you have a multilevel navigation, use an intuitive symbol, such as a plus sign (+) to indicate that the menu item has further drop-down options. Also consider using a symbol to differentiate buttons that navigate to a new page from buttons that reveal more drop-down options. REI uses a right-pointing arrow (>) to indicate when a navigation item takes you to a new page, as shown in Figure 3-11.

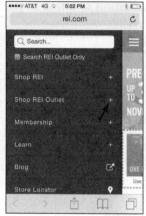

Figure 3-11: REI uses visual menu indicators to guide users through its multitiered navigation.

✦ **Add touch feedback.** When users tap an item in your navigation, something needs to happen to assure users that they tapped in the right place. This feedback can be a color change, a blink of color, or a font change. Figure 3-12 shows that Local, tapped by a user, is highlighted in blue (although you can't see the blue in the printed book).

Figure 3-12: Search Engine Land uses color-change touch feedback to let users know where they have tapped within the navigation.

✦ **Avoid horizontal scrolling.** In general, search engines aren't fond of excessive left to right scrolling, and neither are users. If your menu is too long to fit within the parameters of the screen from left to right, consider a vertical navigation.

Exploring mobile navigation styles

Because the space you have on a smartphone is so limited, the off-screen *toggle menu* (a navigation that can be expanded when tapped) is a common mobile navigation. With this option, the user sees three stacked lines in either the left or right corner of the mobile experience. The user must tap the lines to see the navigation. Figure 3-13 shows two examples of off-screen toggle menus.

Toggle menu   Toggle menu

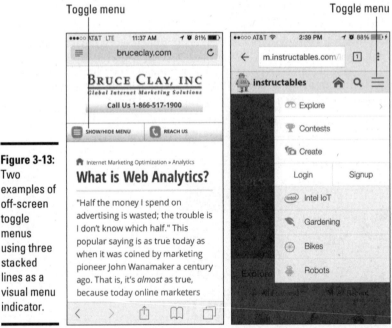

Figure 3-13: Two examples of off-screen toggle menus using three stacked lines as a visual menu indicator.

Another navigation option is to have a minimal static navigation that runs across the top of the mobile browser window. Figure 3-14 shows an example of the static navigation experience. In this example, GameStop has identified these five pages as being the most important to its mobile users' experience, so these navigation items are always present on the top of the mobile web page.

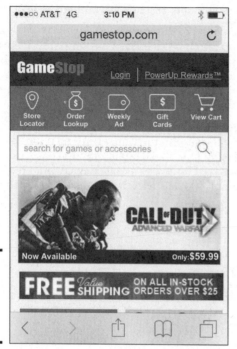

Figure 3-14:
An example
of static
mobile
navigation.

A third option is icon navigation. Figure 3-15 shows a mobile site that has created a series of graphic buttons as its home page navigation. Note that this approach is applied *in addition to* — not instead of — an off-screen toggle menu.

Optimizing forms

Forms are used on websites to collect information from users. Sites use this information to complete transactions and registrations, or to complete other tasks such as submitting an insurance claim online.

When approaching form design for mobile devices, keeping the physical mobile experience in mind is important. If you make your form slow to load or overly complicated, your visitors will likely abandon the form in the middle, or even before they begin.

Keep these best practices in mind when designing your mobile-friendly forms:

✦ **Keep forms short and sweet.** Make your forms easy to complete by minimizing the number of required fields. Having one field for "Name" rather than two fields for first and last name is a good example of an easy way to make your form one field shorter.

**Book IV
Chapter 3**

**Building a Mobile-
Friendly Site**

Ask for too much and you may end up with nothing at all.

✦ **When they can't be short, create multipage forms.** If you must have a long form, break it up into multiple pages, present only a few above-the-fold fields on each page ("above the fold" means before you have to start scrolling down the screen), and include clear Next buttons so that visitors don't have to scroll excessively. A progress bar can also help keep users committed to multipage mobile forms.

✦ **Make the Submit button and the form fields finger size.** Your mobile users are completing forms with their fingertips, so your fields and buttons need to be big enough to make tap interaction easy. No standard size exists that works best for every mobile device, but creating buttons and form fields that are 44 pixels wide by 44 pixels tall is generally a safe rule of thumb.

Toggle menu visual indicator

Figure 3-15: A mobile home page that uses a graphic navigation as well as text navigation that can be reached through a toggle menu.

Onscreen graphic navigation

✦ **Minimize typing by using drop-down menus, radio buttons, and auto-selected answers.** Anything you can do to limit the amount of typing required will help speed up the process and improve your customer satisfaction. For example, if your form asks for a state, let users select their state from a drop-down menu so that they don't have to type it.

✦ **Make what you're asking for clear.** Above each field, clearly specify exactly what you want the user to put in the form field. If you're asking for a birthday, for instance, clarify whether the form wants the birth year entered as two or four digits. See an example from Progressive in Figure 3-16.

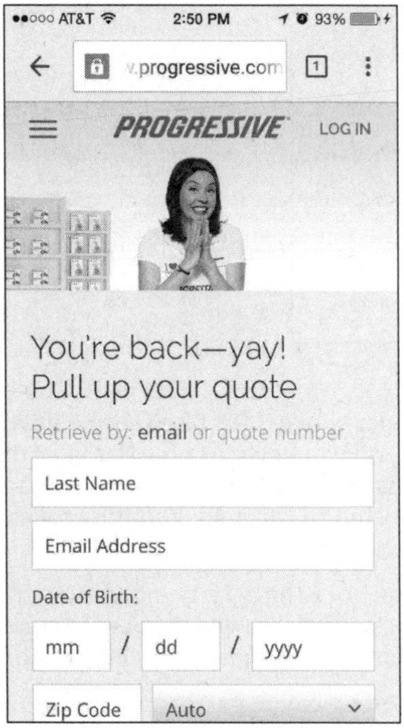

Figure 3-16:
Show users how they should enter birth date information.

Book IV
Chapter 3

Building a Mobile-Friendly Site

If you're asking for a piece of information that requires additional explanation, including a button that offers more information when tapped (often called a *tooltip*) can aid user experience. Figure 3-17 shows a form using a tooltip to explain what CCV means.

✦ **Clearly specify which fields are required.** If your form has more than one field, make sure that your users know exactly which fields are mandatory and which they can skip. Placing an asterisk (*) next to required form fields is a common convention. If all your form fields are required, place an asterisk next to all your fields. Don't assume that your visitors will understand that they are all required.

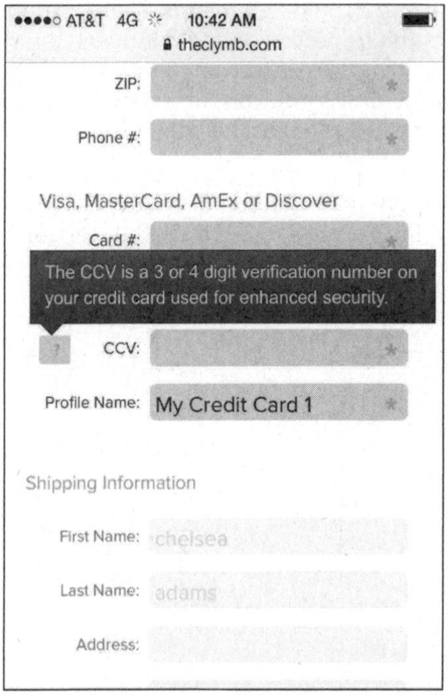

Figure 3-17:
A tooltip
button
explains the
form field
requirement.

✦ Allow log-in using a third-party provider like Google or Amazon.com.
Sometimes a registration form can become a barrier to entry for a first-time user. Allowing your customers to sign in using a third-party provider that they are already connected to can speed up the process and eliminate the registration barrier.

✦ Figure 3-18 shows an example of a third-party integration that allows first-time users to sign in using their Google account information. This is much easier for the user than typing registration information into a form.

Third-party log-in is also a great way to get customers through the purchasing form. By allowing users to log in and pay using a service for which they already have credit card information stored, such as Amazon.com, you allow your customer to skip a multifield credit card authorization form. See an example in Figure 3-19.

✦ Keep the focus on the form and minimize other content on the page.
When your visitors have landed on a web page with a form, they are on a *conversion* page, and you want the content of the page to do everything in its power to keep the conversion momentum going. You want to get your visitor interacting with the form and tapping the Submit button as soon as possible.

Figure 3-18: Because HubSpot Sidekick has optional third-party authentication, first-time mobile users can skip the form and register with their Google account information.

Figure 3-19: An example of third-party integration.

Adding a lot of content on top or next to your form can end up being a conversion distraction that can slow down or completely derail the form submission process. To minimize distraction, try to include only explanatory content that helps the user complete the form. If you do want to include content that isn't explanatory, keep it concise and directly related to the form — just like the example from BruceClay.com in Figure 3-20.

✦ **Visually validate when a form line is completed correctly.** Mobile users don't love filling out forms the first time, and they *really* don't love having to go back and fill them out a second time because the form has errors. Using visual cues to let your user know they have completed each line of the form correctly — or incorrectly — can save time and limit frustration (see Figure 3-21). A green check mark next to the field is a great way to clearly indicate that the field has been completed the right way, and a red X works well to communicate when something is wrong. If something is wrong with the line, make sure to clearly explain how the user can correct the error.

Figure 3-20: Keep language on forms to the point to increase conversion.

Figure 3-21:
Use visual and verbal cues to let users know whether they have completed each line of the form correctly.

Making Mobile a Part of Your SEO Strategy

To understand how mobile SEO and desktop SEO strategies work together, think of a successful SEO strategy as being like a large jigsaw puzzle with many pieces that rely on one another to create the big picture. *Mobile optimization* is just one piece of the puzzle. Without it, you have a large hole in your SEO big picture. On the other hand, get mobile optimization right and your website big picture becomes *less imperfect* over all. Get your site less imperfect than your competitors' sites, and now you're ranking above the fold on page one of the search engine results page — exactly where you want to be!

Read on to find out

✦ How mobile search results compare to desktop results

✦ How to use SEO to improve mobile search rank

✦ Whether Bing and Google consider mobile a ranking factor

Comparing mobile results to desktop results

Mobile search results are the results that users see when they search the web using mobile devices.

Sometimes mobile and desktop search results can look very similar. This is because Google uses one search algorithm to analyze and rank both desktop and mobile results.

Other times, mobile search results can look very different from desktop results. This is because Google and Bing use a number of *independently weighted ranking factors* within their algorithms, and because the search engines strongly consider mobile friendliness when determining the order of their mobile search engine results.

Despite the visual differences, the good news is that optimizing for mobile results doesn't have to feel like reinventing the wheel. In fact, it *shouldn't* feel like reinventing the wheel. Although you want to employ some mobile-specific optimization tactics to gain an edge over the search engines' weighted ranking factors, for the most part, your mobile site and your desktop site should be optimized using the same tactics — from keyword research to competitive analysis and technical SEO (which you learn more about in Book VI).

Optimizing to rank in mobile search results

Up to this point in Book IV, we discuss the principals of mobile-friendly website design. In this section, we tell you about the *mobile optimization* tactics that can help your mobile-friendly website rank higher in mobile search engine results. Yes; *mobile friendliness* and *mobile optimization* are not the same things. Making your site mobile friendly is the act of making sure that your site is designed to deliver an optimal user experience for your mobile searcher. Making your site *mobile optimized* means thinking about the factors that can help your site rank higher in search engine results pages — such as making sure that you're using keywords, optimizing for local search, and granting search engine spiders access to your content. To make matters just a tad more confusing, you should also know that making your site mobile friendly is actually a part of the mobile optimization process because the search engines consider user experience when they determine rank.

In addition to the SEO strategies that you learn throughout this book, the following sections describe several mobile-specific tactics that might improve your site's mobile search engine results rank.

Tag pages to combine mobile and desktop signals

Some optimization tactics, such as adding keyword phrases to your content, can be done in minutes. Others, such as earning industry authority, trust, and link equity, can take months or even years to build.

Regardless of the mobile design format you use (mobile-specific site, mobile-responsive site, or dynamically served pages), you have ways to tell the search engine that the desktop site and the mobile site should be considered the same. You want the search engines to understand your mobile site and your desktop site as one single entity sharing trust signals and link equity.

With proper tagging, a mobile-specific site gets to share the desktop site's strong link equity and trustworthy reputation, helping it rank.

If you've got a separate mobile site, getting tagging right is extremely important and can get pretty technical. We urge you to talk to your developer if you have any confusion or concern about the tags that search engines need to see. You actually have two tags to work with, `rel="canonical"` and `rel="alternate"`. In short, use `rel="canonical"` on your mobile page to point to the associated desktop page. From your desktop page, include the tag `<link rel="alternate" media="only screen and (max-width:640px)">` where max-width is the width of the mobile browser your mobile page supports. Google's got more reading for you on this topic in its Developers site at `https://developers.google.com/webmasters/mobile-sites/mobile-seo/configurations/separate-urls`.

Creating a superior user experience

According to the Google Developers website, "Mobile pages that provide a poor searcher experience can be demoted in rankings or displayed with a warning in mobile search results" (`https://developers.google.com/webmasters/mobile-sites/mobile-seo/overview/key-points`). In other words, search engines care about user experience, and a poor user experience is likely to cause a ranking drop.

To create an optimal mobile user experience, make sure that you

✦ **Make your website mobile friendly.** Check out the mobile design best practices that we discuss earlier in this chapter, in the "Designing for the Mobile User" section. For instance, make sure that your text is large enough to be read without zooming, your content is sized to fit the mobile device, and all your elements are designed for touch. In the section "Testing Mobile Friendliness", later in this chapter, we show you how to use the mobile-friendly test in Google Search Console.

✦ **Don't use Flash on your mobile site.** Many mobile devices cannot render Flash, which means that device users are out of luck if they run into a piece of content that relies on Flash. Even on devices that do support Flash, it significantly slows down load times, which can mean a major drop in rank. Instead of Flash, we recommend using HTML5 to build interactive elements.

✦ **Don't cross-link between your mobile site and your full desktop site, if possible.** Sending a mobile site user away from the mobile site and into your full desktop experience does not provide the best user experience. If at all possible, try to keep the links within your mobile site pointing to other mobile site pages.

If you have only a desktop-version of a page, never redirect your user to a 404 error page or a different mobile-optimized page instead of the page the user is asking for. Google considers this to be a faulty redirect, which creates a bad user experience and is grounds for a SERP rank demotion. Always think: *Will my users be happy with this experience? Am I giving them what they expect?* If the answer is yes, move forward. If it's no, think of a better way.

✦ **Don't include intervening pages that block access to content for any reason.** This includes any kind of page that asks for a login, a newsletter opt-in, or an app download. When searchers tap a link from a mobile search results page, both Google and Bing want the searchers to immediately be redirected to the content they are interested in, without any barriers. Pages that block the user from having immediate access to the content she wants creates a bad user experience and — because such pages can make your website *less imperfect* than your competitor's — often result in a rank drop.

Improving site speed

According to the PageSpeed Insights portion of the Google Developers help site, Google prefers above-the-fold content (what the user sees first) to render in under a second for a mobile user. Anything longer than a second, Google says, can result in a poor user experience. The search engines care a lot about user experience, so fast load times really matter when Google determines which of the least imperfect websites to rank the highest.

To improve your mobile site speed and ranking potential, try to eliminate redirect chains and loops, make sure that images are compressed and optimized (see the "Designing for a Mobile User" section earlier in this chapter), and always follow the page speed optimization recommendations outlined in the Mobile Analysis portion of the Google Developers PageSpeed Insights (`https://developers.google.com/speed/docs/insights/mobile`).

Optimizing for proximity

Search engines are always working to return results that give users exactly what they need, when they need it. For mobile users, this means returning local results that take location into consideration.

To learn more about optimizing your website for mobile proximity and local search, follow the best practices outlined in Book I, Chapter 4.

Making mobile content accessible and crawlable

Before your web pages can show up in search results, search engines need to be able to find, access, and index your content. To ensure that your mobile site can be found and crawled by search engines, be sure to grant search spiders access to all your CSS and JavaScript.

Many mobile sites render dynamically (or on the fly) using web development techniques like AJAX. These types of sites often do not alter the URL when displaying new content, and, as a result, are impossible for search engines to properly index.

If you build a separate mobile site, also make sure to have your web developer submit an XML Sitemap for your mobile site to the search engines. To learn more about XML Sitemaps, flip ahead to Book VI, Chapter 2.

Distinguishing mobile content from desktop content

You always want Google to lead searchers to the version of your website that offers the best user experience. This means that you never want Google to return your mobile site to a desktop user, and — unless no mobile alternative exists — you don't want the desktop version returned to a mobile user.

To help search engines discover, crawl, and index mobile-only web pages, be sure to specify in the HTML of your desktop website when you have an alternative (mobile) version of your web page by using the `rel="alternate"` HTML attribute, like this:

```
<link rel="alternate" media="only screen and (max-width:
    640px)" href="http://m.example.com/your-mobile-only-web-
    page">
```

You also need to include a `rel="canonical"` tag that points to the desktop version of your website in the HTML of your mobile page. Using this tag is like waving your hands in the air, telling the search engines "*Hey! I have two versions of this web page. The canonical is the original. The other one is the alternative. This is not duplicate content!*" To add the canonical tag, use code that looks something like this:

```
<link rel="canonical" href="http://www.example.com/desktop-
    version-of-your-page">
```

Optimizing on-page content with mobile keywords

Don't forget your keyword research and on-page SEO basics when optimizing for mobile! Use your favorite keyword research tool to research the language that your searchers commonly use when they are searching with mobile devices. These are called *mobile-specific keyword phrases,* and "near me" is a common modifier used by a mobile user. In some situations, you may find that your searchers use similar language to search on both desktop and mobile. Other times, you may find mobile search queries to be quite different from desktop queries. (Learn more about how to perform keyword research in Book II, Chapter 1.)

If you're using a responsive design, try to work mobile keywords into your content naturally as secondary keywords that support your primary desktop keywords. If you have built a separate mobile site, or are dynamically serving web pages, consider creating content specifically to target high-volume mobile keyword phrases.

Is mobile a ranking factor?

The search engines use hundreds of proprietary ranking factors to decide the order of search engine results pages. We know some of the factors for sure; for others, we have to make our best guesses.

But when it comes to mobile friendliness, we can say with 100 percent certainty that it is a ranking factor for both Bing and Google! In November 2014, Bing announced that it is officially taking into consideration a website's mobile friendliness to determine mobile search engine results rank. This means that the search engine will boost web pages identified as mobile friendly and demote the unfriendly results. "We know which pages are mobile-friendly so [we] automatically rank them higher with the new update," says the Bing blog (https://blogs.bing.com/webmaster/2014/11/20/bing-and-mobile-friends/).

In April 2015, Google confirmed the same in its Webmaster Central blog: "We will be expanding our use of mobile-friendliness as a ranking signal. [. . .] Consequently, users will find it easier to get relevant, high quality search results that are optimized for their devices" (http://googlewebmastercentral.blogspot.com/2015/02/finding-more-mobile-friendly-search.html).

It doesn't get much more straightforward than that. You must make your web pages mobile friendly in order to rank high in mobile search results.

Google has other ways besides higher rankings to show preference to mobile-friendly results:

✦ Google appends a "Mobile-friendly" label to mobile search results listings that are optimized for mobile user experience. You're safe to assume that not having the mobile-friendly label makes a site *less imperfect* — which often means a rank demotion.

✦ In recent years, Google put a lot of time into the development of mobile-friendly design documentation and tools to help website owners create improved mobile experiences for their users. Most notable among the list, perhaps, is the recent Mobile-Friendly Test tool that analyzes a website's mobile friendliness and offers feedback to help the site owner make improvements. Clearly, Google considers mobile friendliness *very* important.

Testing Mobile Friendliness

After you've selected a development approach, created mobile-friendly content, and optimized your website for user experience and SEO, you're done, right? Well, you've come a long way, but the truth is that an online marketer's job is never done. After you've built your mobile website to be just how you want it, it's time to start testing to make sure that everything is working how it should.

Never develop a "set it and forget it" mindset.

To test the mobile friendliness of your website, explore the following elements:

✦ **Does the website look and function correctly on multiple devices?** Your customers are using many types of mobile devices to access your content, so you must test to see whether your website works appropriately on all of them. To do this, use a device emulator that mimics the experience of tablets and smartphones, or test manually by using the actual devices if you have access to them.

✦ **Are all the usability features that you built into your web pages actually working for your users?** Have real people test your mobile site. This process is called *user testing,* and it should be a regular part of your website optimization strategy.

✦ **Does your site pass the "mobile friendly" test?** Navigate to `https://www.google.com/webmasters/tools/mobile-friendly/` and plug in your website URL to see whether your site passes the Google Mobile-Friendly Test (see Figure 3-22). This free tool gives you a pass or fail analysis of a specific website page's mobile friendliness. This is a great tool to determine whether your website is on the path to mobile optimization success.

You can also use the Google Mobile-Friendly Test tool to analyze your competitor's mobile website. Flip back to Book III for a refresher on competitive analysis.

Figure 3-22:
The Google
Mobile-
Friendly
Test.

✦ **How fast do your pages load?** Having a mobile site that loads quickly is important both for user experience and as a ranking factor. To test the site speed of individual pages on your mobile website, use the Google PageSpeed Insights tool, found at `https://developers.google.com/speed/pagespeed/insights` (see Figure 3-23). Enter a page URL into the free tool and you'll receive a 1–100 numerical Speed score, suggestions for fixes that could improve speed, and recognition for what you're doing right in the Rules Passed section.

✦ **Are Google crawlers seeing your site the way they should be seeing it?** This step is all about double-checking to see whether the search spider is understanding the elements of your mobile design in the same way your human visitors are. Webmaster Tools — a free Google resource that helps webmasters analyze how users and search spiders are interacting with their websites — is a great resource for performing this type of mobile testing.

Figure 3-23:
The Google
PageSpeed
Insights tool
rates Bing.
com 81 on
a 100-point
Speed
scale.

With Google Search Console open, find the Crawl portion of the dashboard and then find the Fetch as Google option. We explain more about this tool in the next chapter. But for now, know that using the fetch and render portion of Fetch as Google, you can ask Google to send the mobile crawler through your website (this is the *fetch* part) and show you exactly how the elements of your site appear to the spider (this is the *render* part).

The idea is to make sure that the Google mobile crawler recognizes your images and code without any hang-ups.

To get started with Google Search Console and the Fetch as Google tool, visit `https://www.google.com/webmasters/tools`.

✦ **How does your site look in mobile search results?** If your site has any elements that aren't ideal for the mobile environment, Google recognizes these less-than-friendly spots and warns users in mobile search results. Some warnings include "Uses Flash" and "May open the site's homepage" (see example in Figure 3-24). These warnings are clearly bad for search rank and bad for user experience. In the testing phase, be sure to look at your website in search results for these warnings.

Figure 3-24:
A home page redirect warning from Google.

Chapter 4: Making Your Page Search Engine Compatible

In This Chapter

✔ **Conquering HTML constructs**

✔ **Using clean code**

✔ **Designing with sIFR**

✔ **Externalizing code**

✔ **Validating HTML with W3C**

✔ **Choosing the right navigation**

*I*n this chapter, you get down to the nitty-gritty stuff that makes your page stand on its own. In addition to worrying about links or content, you have to get the nuts and bolts right. Your SEO strategy is only as strong as its weakest link, so make sure that every part of the chain is forged as tough as you can make it. Paying attention to the small stuff pays off big-time in the long run.

Success with *on-page optimization,* the changing of the underlying code of a web page for SEO reasons, isn't something that you can just guess at or just hope that you luck out. You need to understand every element of a web page and use it to its fullest potential. Knowing how spiders are going to see and react to your page is absolutely critical to your optimization efforts. For example mistakes with JavaScript can lead to a *spider trap,* where a spider gets caught in an endless loop and is forced to abandon the page because it has no other alternative. In this chapter, we cover the things that make your page search engine friendly and what the biggest pitfalls are. Getting these elements right is essential if you're going to obtain and retain traffic and rankings in the long term.

In this chapter, we show you how to create clean, attractive HTML pages that properly render in the browser and give search engines a clear path to index the page and understand its value to their users. You discover how to write every part of your page, from your HTML code to your JavaScript and CSS, in a way that supports your ranking goals.

Optimizing HTML Constructs for Search Engines

At first, the web was made up in great part by research papers posted by academics. They were formatted in a specific way, and most of them were heavily text-based. These days, the Internet contains document types of every shape and size. Images, videos, and Flash pages — you name it, someone's built it — all serve their purposes in the construction of a successful website. (You can find more about optimizing media content in the "Choosing the Right Navigation" section, later in this chapter and still more on video optimization in Book V, Chapter 2.) Nevertheless, when you get down to the basic structure for a web page, you're still looking at HTML.

HTML pages are the building blocks of your website, so it's worth it to take the time to construct them well. Unlike humans, search engines evaluate pages based on the code. Because search engines cannot understand images or similar content forms, that content is invisible to them, leaving them to only see the content in the text of an HTML page. You want to write your code so that it will be very easy for spiders to understand. You don't want to bury the content down in the code. This is intuitively obvious to web designers and seasoned search engine optimizers, but many people don't take the time to put it into practice. In the following sections, we break down, define, and explain how you can best optimize each of the so-called on-page elements of a successful web page.

The Head section

The task of optimizing every HTML page begins in the Head section. The Head section is where search engines are first introduced to your page and where they first discover what the page is all about. This section makes that infamous first impression that you only get one shot at. But the job of the Head section isn't only to impress the search engine. Search engines like to share the wealth when it comes to information, so parts of your Head section get starring roles on the search engine results page. Time to get those parts camera-ready!

The four important tags in the Head section are the `Title`, `Meta` description, `Meta` keywords, and `Meta` robots tags. *Metadata* is, quite simply, data about data. It is descriptive of the rest of the page. Each of these tags helps to define for the search engine what's coming up in the page and how it relates to other pages: the first three by defining the content, and the last by defining how the search engine should handle the information and links on the page. You can find out more about how these first three tags can affect your site's search engine rankings in the next few sections. For more on the `Meta` robots tag, jump to Book VII.

Optimizing `Title` tags for ranking and branding

The undisputed headliner of the Head section is the `Title` tag. Although the various search engines out there don't tell us how important any one element is in their algorithms, most industry experts agree that the `Title` tag is one of the most critical. Because the `Title` tag not only shows up in your browser window but also in the search engine results, it's easy to infer that this tag naturally has some impact in the search engine's ranking algorithms. The following code (and Figure 4-1) shows you how a `Title` tag appears in HTML.

```
<title>Good Titles Use Keywords like Ford Mustang 1967
    specs</title>
```

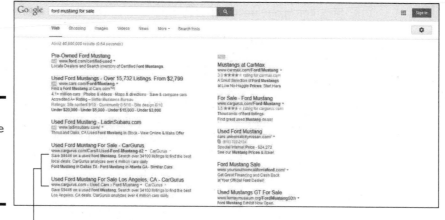

Figure 4-1: The `Title` tag in Google search results.

Title tags in Google search results

Getting this tag right has many benefits — increased ranking, branding, and click-throughs. Getting it wrong severely hinders your page's chances at ranking in the search engine — `Title` tags that appear on more than one page across a website *(duplicate `Title` tags)* are considered by search engines to be a signal of a low-value page and are filtered. Meanwhile, poorly written `Title` tags won't garner click-throughs or serve branding. Leaving out the keywords hurts your chances to rank for those words.

The `Title` tag, although short, tells the search engine what your page is about. The maximum number of characters allotted for the `Title` tag is approximately 45–70 characters, depending on character width. (Character width matters here because the `Title` tag length is actually based on a maximum width of 512 pixels, not an exact number of characters. Because each character has its own pixel width, the `Title` tag recommendation can't be based on an exact number of characters.) You have just a few words to inform, entice, and reinforce your brand to search engines and their users. In order to get your message through, you need to be specific with keywords. Entice searchers with calls to action and use "research" words like *how to* and *information.* Figure 4-1, shown previously, displays a `Title` tag as seen in Google's search engine results pages.

So what do you do about this short, yet critically important, piece of content? In order to maximize the effectiveness of your `Title` tag, you need to make some solid decisions first:

✦ **Focus:** Your page must have a single explicit subject. Put keywords related to that focus in the `Title`.

✦ **Silo:** Your page must support the theme of the page above that page, and it must be supported by the pages that link below that page. Theme-level keywords should appear in the `Title`.

✦ **Branding:** Some pages are critical to support branding; others are not. If branding is an issue, include branded keywords in the `Title`.

After you decide on your focus, theme, and brand emphasis, you're ready to start writing your tag. Even though the actual length of your `Title` tag varies depending on your industry standard, you can follow some basic guidelines to get started. The two most important terms to remember are *unique* and *keyword-rich.* You need to make sure that you're writing unique, keyword-rich titles for your pages. The title of your page should belong only to that page, and it should not be used anywhere else on your site. If you're following your focus, theme, and branding guidelines (see Book II, Chapter 4 for more on themes and siloing), you should already be using words in a combination that won't be repeated somewhere else. Your title should not be sensational or contain keywords that you don't expect to rank for. Be sure that you have only one `Title` tag per page. Duplicate `Title` tags are a severe issue that could lead to filtering of your pages by the search engines, denying them the ability to rank for key terms.

Your title should be fairly short. Google usually cuts your title off before 70 characters, so you need to get your message out right up front. Although Google indexes the whole tag, you want users to see your relevance immediately.

Put the keywords up front, and make them enticing for people to click through. Notice that in Figure 4-1, shown previously, the words *search engine optimization* and SEO are bolded wherever they appear in the `Title` tag. This is because Google sometimes bolds search query words, and query *concept synonyms,* that appear in the title, which may lead to higher click-throughs. Eye-tracking studies have shown that people are naturally drawn to boldfaced type. (Learn more about how Google connects information about various people, places, and things to generate concept synonyms in the Knowledge Graph portion of Book I, Chapter 3.)

If you're working to establish your brand, put your company name at the end, unless your brand name is a main keyword in your SEO strategy.

Be aware that there *is* a difference between being keyword-rich and being spammy. Spam by excessive repetition of keywords only hurts your `Title` tag. Always strive to play within the acceptable boundaries when it comes to SEO. The margin of safety changes all the time and without any warning at all.

Writing a Meta description

Working your way through the tags in a typical Head section, the next stop is the `Meta` description tag. Search engines use the `Meta` description tag to create the *snippets* you see beneath the page title in their results, so this is an important tag to get right. Write your `Meta` description like a sentence, describing what visitors can expect to find on the page after they click through from the search engine. If you fail to provide a `Meta` description, search engines often select text off the page that may or may not be a good representation of your page's real value. It is in your best interest to craft a unique, targeted `Meta` description tag for every page. The following code displays a sample `Meta` description tag as it would appear in the raw HTML of a web page:

```
<meta name="description" content="Your description tag should
    use keywords, describe the theme and purpose of the page,
    and be fairly short. It is structured as a sentence.">
```

The `Meta` description should be about twice as long as your `Title` tag. Like the title, words used in the search query that are also found in the description may be bolded, giving your listing another opportunity to catch the eye of the searcher. Google displays approximately 160 characters for the description, sometimes extracted from the page content. If the `Meta` description is used for search engine results, you must put your best information right up front. No one but the spider sees it if you don't. Figure 4-2 shows a `Meta` description tag appearing in Google's search results.

Your description should answer the question, "What is this page about?" Try not to repeat any word more than twice; any more than that may look unnatural to users and to the engines. Ask yourself what your target audience would be looking for when searching for what your web page offers, and write your metadata to address that person. Notice in Figure 4-2, shown previously, that descriptions are in sentence form and give you a very clear idea about the content on the linked page.

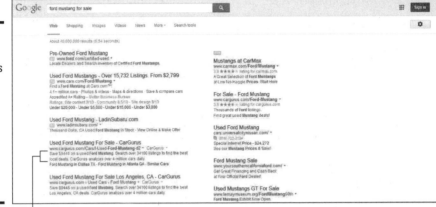

Figure 4-2:
Result
descriptions
in Google
search
results
are often
the page's
`Meta`
description
tag.

Result description

Like your `Title` tag, your `Meta` description tag must be unique; that is, it has to be unlike any other tag on your site and targeted to the content of the page it's on. If you repeat text in a tag, you run the risk of the search engines identifying the page as *duplicate content* (that is, content that appears elsewhere on your site or the web). Duplicate content is commonly filtered out of the search results by the engines because it's not in their users' best interest to show the same or similar pages more than once. Even if everything else on your page is unique and useful, a duplicate tag in the Head section can spell disaster for your rankings. Think of your metadata as the advertisement and the content as your product. Don't be guilty of false advertising!

Writing a useful Meta keywords tag

In the past, it used to be simple (well, okay, easier) to get ranked in the search engines. Use your keywords in the page's metadata (including `Title` and `Meta` description tags, as well as the keywords tag) and throughout the displayed body of the page, and within days or even hours, you could be on the top of any search engine you liked: Infoseek, AltaVista, Excite, or Yahoo. But times have changed, and search engines have developed algorithms that are much more sophisticated, containing many more variables. The `Meta` keywords tag, which is basically a place to list all the relevant keywords for your page, is very easy to abuse because it's not a user-visible tag and invites *keyword stuffing* — putting every word, not just relevant ones, into the content of the tag. As a result, the `Meta` keywords tag suffered a serious devaluation. To be frank, you are never, ever going to rank on the basis of your `Meta` keywords tag for any competitive term.

So why still use it? Although some engines claim that they don't even bother to index the `Meta` keywords tag, some still read and store it in the data portion. Although the `Meta` keywords tag is not a major factor in rankings, it's still better to sweat the small stuff and do everything right from the get-go. You can create a `Meta` keywords tag in only a few minutes, and search engines don't penalize you for having a `Meta` keywords tag on a page (unless you spam by keyword stuffing the tag). You can never go wrong by using a `Meta` keywords tag, and you only hurt yourself if you don't use this valid piece of HTML data. The following code shows you how to format a `Meta` keywords tag in HTML:

```
<meta name="keywords" content="First Keyword Phrase, Second
    Keyword Phrase, Repeated Keyword, Keyword">
```

Optimizing a `Meta` keywords tag is simple. Essentially, the only thing this tag requires is that you list all the keywords and keyword phrases that are important to your page. A general rule is that if a keyword was important enough to be included in your title and `Meta` description, it's important enough to include in your keywords tag. As a best practice, order your keyword phrases from longest to shortest (four-word phrases, and then three-word phrases, and then two-word phrases, and so on). This keeps you organized and gives the search engines the most targeted and usually the most valuable words right up front.

 Don't go overboard. Remember, excessive repetition could be considered spam. Try not to repeat any single keyword more than four times in the `Meta` keywords tag. If you stick to a keywords tag approximately twice the length of your `Meta` description tag, you're playing on safe ground.

The Body section

Other than the page title, which appears at the very top of your browser window in the page's tab, all the user-visible content is located in a page's Body section. As your site aims to satisfy the needs of users and search engines alike, dedicate ample time to producing high-quality body content.

After a search engine spider reads the summary-style information provided in a page's Head section, it should find that the content within the Body section also supports the established keywords. The vast majority of text content, links, and images are located in the Body section. Having a significant amount of keyword-rich text content in the Body section is absolutely necessary to achieving a web page optimized for search engines.

Headings

Within the Body section, the heading acts like the headline of a newspaper, identifying the topic of sections or paragraphs of a web page. As such, it plays an important role for search engines looking to classify the subject matter of the page. Because of this, search engines give heading text significant weight in their ranking algorithms; thus, it's very important that you optimize headings in line with your ranking goals.

As with a table of contents or outline, the heading is usually made up of short phrases, generally not complete sentences. Within the page, there are often sub-sections with their own subheading tag designations. Hence, an H1 tag may be followed by H2 tags. Figure 4-3 displays an H1 heading tag used in content.

Heading tag on page

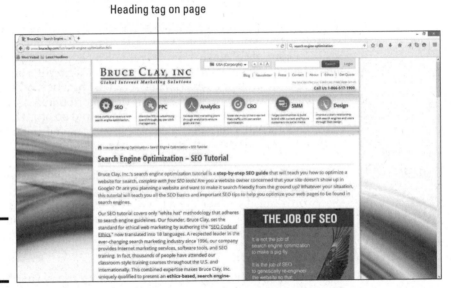

Figure 4-3:
A heading
on a page.

When you're writing an H1 tag, you must include the most important keywords of that web page, which are likely to be the keywords also used in the Title and Meta tags. When seen together with the other keyword-optimized page elements discussed in the following sections, all of your page's significant text works together to support the spiders' recognition of your keywords as your site's area of expertise. For this reason, we recommend that you always use at least one H# tag on every page of your site. You can use multiple headings as needed, but they should always be used in hierarchical order. An H1 tag is given more weight than an H2 tag. It's rare that there would be more than one H1 on a page because pages generally only have one major subject. (There are exceptions to this rule; for example, we have multiple H1 tags on our homepage at www.bruceclay.com because we have a very long page that is defining multiple top-level topics.)

All other subjects naturally fall below that top-level listing. Following an H1 tag, the next heading on the page can be represented by the H2 tag. In other words, heading tags should not be used out of order. The H1 tag should be followed by the H2 tag, which can be followed by the H3 tag, if needed.

Don't use excessive headings: Too many can actually dilute the theme of your page. Think of this structure as a table of contents, and you can't go wrong.

Each heading throughout the page should be unique. Because the purpose of the heading is to summarize the unique content of the page or section, each heading should naturally be unique as well. However, the content within a heading tag should be similar to the content in the Title tag because both share the task of summarizing the page content and including significant page keywords.

Try to keep headings from being too long. Because they are serving as a headline for the page, headings must be concise and to the point. Notice that the heading in Figure 4-3 acts as more of a title describing the subject of the page. A heading should usually be only a few targeted words and never more than a single sentence. Including an entire paragraph in a heading tag would likely be considered spam by the search engines. Here are a few points to remember about headings:

✦ Use heading tags as a headline for your page.

✦ Use heading tags in hierarchical order, following an H1 with an H2, an H2 with an H3, and so on.

✦ Keep headings short and unique.

✦ Don't use headings for styling text. Use CSS instead. For more on CSS, check out *HTML5 and CSS3 All-in-One For Dummies*, 3rd Edition, by Andy Harris (John Wiley & Sons, Inc.).

Content

Search marketers often say that content is king. Regardless of its relationship to royalty, tests show that content weighs heavily in search engine rankings. Although search engines are rapidly developing the capabilities to index other types of media, in most cases, you're dealing with a search engine spider that is deaf, dumb, and blind. Thus far, spiders cannot see images, watch videos, listen to podcasts, fill out forms, or use any other advanced features of your website, although they can detect that those engagement objects are present, and they're expanding their ability to index that content. For this reason, it's imperative that you have enough sentence-structured text content on your page for a search engine to adequately determine what your page is about. The amount of content necessary to be competitive varies by industry, but the trend is that the amount of content has steadily increased over time for all industries. Discover how much content is right for your industry by doing competitive research (as described in Book II, Chapter 1).

If you're just starting out and haven't done competitive research, plan for a minimum of 450 or more words of good, relevant, useful text content on your important pages. Your content should always be unique to the page it's on and should naturally incorporate the keywords found in your title, description, and headings. The reason for this is simple: The first three tags define what the page is about; therefore, it is only logical that those words are repeated again in the text content on your site. Don't fall into the trap of discussing something without ever naming what it is or relying on the images on the page to provide context. Remember that the search engines aren't able to look at the picture and understand what you're talking about. If your page is about Ford Mustangs, you need more than a picture of the car to let the search engines know that. Say what you mean.

Use synonyms and related words in order to reinforce your keywords. When discussing shoes, you should also be using words that help define what sort of shoes. Are the related words *heel, leather, instep, size,* and *designer?* Or are they *horse, anvil, iron,* and *mare?* You can see that many very different mental pictures are painted by placing the keyword *shoes* in context.

There's practically no maximum number of words you can put on a page: A search engine just keeps reading. (Your visitors might not, though! If you don't have anything interesting to say, stop talking.) You should have all the words discuss the same subject matter for SEO, but long pages are not frowned upon by search engines. There used to be upper limits on how large of a page the search engines would index, but those limits have gone out the window. (Note, however, that *page speed* — how fast your page renders in a browser — is a factor, and page sizes affect that speed. We discuss this in greater depth in Book VII, Chapter 1.)

And although the search engines might be happy to read your 50,000-word opus, keep user fatigue in mind. If you find yourself discussing several topics on a very long page, consider breaking that discussion up into multiple pages. This adds depth to your site by expanding the number of pages you have on a keyword phrase and also allows you to manage the site's themes.

When it comes to formatting the text on your page, remember, people tend to scan text on the Internet. Keep paragraphs short and direct. Give the facts as concisely as possible. Customers don't want to spend a long time reading if the web page isn't going to satisfy their requirements. Tell your customers who you are, what your product is, and why they should choose you over your competitors. Use lists, as well as **bold** and *italicized* text, to direct your visitors' eyes to important words and concepts. Bulleted lists are ideal for product pages, which users scan to pick up important information.

If you are writing content for your own website, your first response might be to feel frustrated. What on earth are you going to write about? Everyone knows everything that you could possibly tell her, and you're not a writer anyway. But that's just the thing: People *don't* know everything, and you *are* an expert on the topic even if you're not the world's best writer.

For most people, the hardest part of adding content to their websites is the writing of the content in the first place, but it doesn't have to be. There are lots of themes for you to write on and many topics available for you to write about. For e-commerce sites, this might include a well-written product description, user reviews, tips and tricks, or the inclusion of some frequently asked questions.

Remember that many people on the web are there to do research. You should address the concerns that your visitors may have and give them a reason to buy whatever you are selling (literally or figuratively). Search engines look for research words, like *how to* and *tips,* as markers that indicate that page will satisfy a user doing research.

Suppose, for example, that you're in the business of selling cowboy boots. You are an expert in your area. Brainstorm everything you can think of that relates to cowboy boots, even if it's only somewhat related. After you have all your ideas down, pick a few of the best. For example, you probably want to focus a section of your site on the keywords [buy cowboy boots]. Everyone, you think, knows about how to buy boots. It's just a matter of finding the right fit and style. You don't need to explain how to buy cowboy boots to your site's visitors. But it's one of your keywords, so you sit down and write all the obvious information.

Of course, you know how to check the fit of your boots and which styles work best for which people. It's obvious to you that your jeans should be tucked inside your boots if you're working outside and that you should take certain steps to care for your boots.

But most people don't know these things. That's why they're coming to your site in the first place. Your expertise is a valuable resource for the development of content. Explaining something that is obvious to you is probably the best way to introduce new customers to your products. If a visitor who is an expert comes into your site, having correct and informative content reinforces to him or her that your site is worthwhile.

Write your first draft with the page's keywords in mind. Use your keywords as a guide for the content. Tape them to the side of your monitor or put them at the very top of the document so they're on your mind as you write. Don't worry about keyword densities or forcing the words in. If it doesn't sound natural to use the keyword, don't use it. The first draft is just to get the information out.

Take a look at the tone of your piece:

✦ **Match your audience.** Are you writing to the right audience? Baby boomers and teenagers have very different ways of expressing themselves, not to mention widely different cultural touchstones, and writing the same way to each of them is probably not going to work. You have to speak their language.

✦ **Engage the reader.** Your content should get users involved and offer them ways to connect to the material.

✦ **Solve a problem.** Does your content solve a problem or help the customer make a decision? Fighting fear, doubt, and uncertainty increases your conversions as visitors learn to trust you.

✦ **Educate.** If your website deals with a highly technical area that your customers probably don't know enough about to ask intelligent questions, have you educated them enough to feel comfortable in making their decision?

Revise your draft with these ideas in mind. Knowing your audience means putting in the kinds of words that they will be looking for: the same kinds of words that help them understand what the best choice of products is for them.

After your next draft, ask someone else to read it over for you. The best person for this task is someone who fits the profile of a site visitor. Have that person read it aloud to see if it is easily readable and answers his or her questions in an easy to understand way. If not, revise the content to meet that person's understanding. You might even find that you're going to need another page of content in order to answer the questions.

After you have a final draft, incorporate your final product into the destination page, and use a page-rating tool to determine the validity and strength of the document. Tweak it if necessary. Keep in mind how the content supports the website theme as a whole. This ties into the linking strategies discussed throughout Book VI.

The final thing to remember about writing for search engines is that there is no magical formula for writing the perfect copy. You're going to have to put in hard work and pay attention to detail to meet the needs of both the search engines and your human visitors. Start writing and go from there.

Links

Links within the Body section of a web page provide *anchor text,* which is the text that the user clicks on in order to follow the link to a new page (see the following code). When they are measuring the relevance of the web page, search engine spiders consider the anchor text of links pointing to that page.

The keyword used within the anchor text of the hyperlink is not added to the *keyword frequency* of your website (how many times a keyword is used and how far apart in the text it appears), but it does add to the relevance of the target web page in the search engine.

```
<a href="http://www.mydomain.com/bikerboots.html">Motorcycle
    Boots</a>
```

Links have a lot of power when it comes to a website appearing high in the search engine results page. How many links a particular page or site has is part of the algorithms search engines use, simply because it's saying that your page or site has meaning and carries a certain amount of expertise. It's like being the most popular kid in school because everyone says you have all the answers.

With anchor text, you're basically describing to the search engine what the page you're linking to is about. So if you provided a link with the words *Pink Cowboy Boots* as the anchor text, the engine reads that and adds it to the relevance of the page. So if all the hyperlinks to that page within your website say the same thing — that it's a page about pink cowboy boots — the engine's going to pick up on that like a giant blinking neon arrow and say that your page is about pink cowboy boots when someone enters that search query.

Two types of links can be used in the Body section: relative links and absolute links. An *absolute link* is a link that contains the whole file path, so when it appears in code, it begins with `http://`, as shown here:

```
<a href="http://www.classiccarcustomization.com/fords/
    mustangs/tireoptions.html">
```

That's the whole file directory in the link itself. A *relative* link references a file located in a physical directory relative to the current page or the root of all directories, so it can simply start with the page name and leave off the `http://` and domain. If you're on the page `www.classiccarcustomization.com/mustangs/paintoptions.html`, you could use `<a href="tireoptions.html">` to reach `http://www.classiccarcustomization.com/mustangs/tireoptions.html`.

You can use two periods before the filename to indicate that the page is located one directory up (closer to the root) from the directory the page is located in. For example, the HTML on the same page — `<a href="../tireoptions.html">` — indicates that the link goes to a page located at `www.classiccarcustomization.com/tireoptions.html`.

Relative links are a bit of a shortcut, and on the whole, we recommend that you don't use them, especially if you're building your site from the ground up. When you use a relative link, it works only in relation to the page that the link is contained on. So `tireoptions.html` is only going to work if there's a `mustangs/tireoptions.html` for it to link to.

If the directories were to get switched around or taken out for whatever reason, the relative link would no longer work: Where it linked to no longer exists. So if the page with the link on it (in this case, `paintoptions.html`) was moved to the `/mustangconvertible` directory, the relative link of `<a href="tireoptions">` would not work anymore because there's no `tireoptions.html` page located in the `/mustangconvertible` directory. A link to `/tireoptions.html` and an absolute link would still work. Without the leading slash (/), the link goes to the current directory only.

An absolute link is easier to maintain than a relative one because it is very clear what you're linking to and why, and there will be no confusion if the location of a page changes. Although fixing one or two broken links isn't a big deal, if every link on your site is relative, you'll have a huge repair project every time you decide to reorganize your page. And forget about reusing snippets of code from page to page. Relative links, unlike absolute links, rarely still take you to the page you intended if you happen to reuse the code on another page.

Bottom line: The absolute link `<a href="http://www.classiccar customization.com/mustangs/tireoptions.html">` always gets you to the Tire Options page. A relative link like `<a href="tireoptions.html">` gets you there only if you're starting from the same directory. In the long run, absolute links are less of a hassle.

Images

Images in the body of your site are also pretty important. Not only do they add to the overall aesthetic of your website and provide a visual of the product if you're trying to sell something, they also add weight and relevance to your ranking. Images aid users and they provide search engines with additional clues about the page. Images can also appear in *vertical search engines* (search engines that look for a specific file type only).

Images should contain keywords in their filenames (when they're named properly; see Chapter 1 of this minibook for more info). A search engine can read the filename and add it to the overall relevancy of the page. Also, although search engines cannot see images, they can read `Alt` attribute text. *Alt attribute text* is the HTML code that describes the image. The `Alt` attribute is designed to be an alternative text description for an image. The `Alt` attribute displays before the image is loaded (if it's loaded at all) in the major browsers; the `Alt` attribute also displays instead of the image in text-based browsers, such as Lynx. `Alt` is a required element for images in order to help vision-impaired people, and it can only be used for image tags because its specific purpose is to describe images. Stuffing many keywords into the `Alt` attribute text is considered spam and will pull your site from a search engine's *index* (list of websites they crawl during a search). Instead, `Alt` attribute text should be a short descriptive phrase that clearly describes the content of the image. In the sample code, `"1967 Ford Mustang with dented rear fender"` is the `Alt` text for the image named `ford.dented.fender.jpg`:

```
<img src="ford.dented.fender.jpg" alt="1967 Ford Mustang with
    dented rear fender">
```

Make your images relevant to the overall content of the page. You can't have a picture of a duck on a page about classic cars, for instance — not unless the duck is driving a classic car. Another way a search engine can "see" an image is by the descriptive text around the image, so the image had better be relevant to the text describing it. As we mentioned previously, the image name, if it contains keywords, also helps to identify the image to the search engines. The identification of the image related to the keywords of the page it's on allows the image to contribute to the page as content. This helps your relevancy.

Enriching Your Site with Rich Snippets

Earlier in this chapter, we tell you that *snippets* are the sentence or two that search engines show in the search results below the page title. Usually pulled from the `Meta` description tag, the point of the snippet is to describe to visitors what they can expect to find on the page after they click through from the search engine.

As with traditional snippets, *rich snippets* also appear in the search engine results pages (SERPs) under the page title. The main difference is that traditional snippets pull in text that describes your content, whereas rich snippets can actually add a visual — and sometimes interactive — element to your SERP result listing.

Although this list is ever evolving, at the time of publication, both Bing and Google support rich snippet markup for seven categories:

✦ People

✦ Products

✦ Reviews and ratings

✦ Businesses and organizations (including name, address, telephone number, geo location, and logo)

✦ Recipes

✦ Events

✦ Music

Bing also supports a Breadcrumbs snippet, and Google also supports markup for video content, TV episodes, and software applications.

Figure 4-4 shows two rich snippets, Ratings and Recipes, displayed in a Google search listing.

Figure 4-4:
A SERP listing showing rich snippets for recipes, which can include an image, ratings and reviews, cook time, and calories.

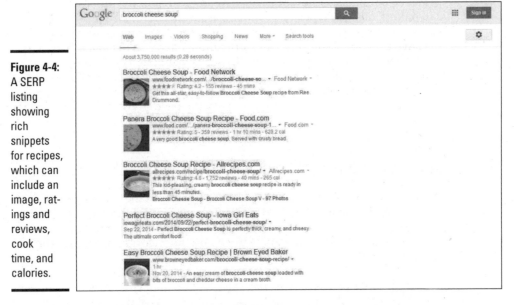

A good way to wrap your head around snippets and rich snippets is to think of them as a preview of your content that is created to set expectations and naturally encourage users to click through to your site.

Marking up content for rich snippets

Rich snippets are created by adding special lines of code called *structured data markup* to your website. Essentially, adding structured data markup to your HTML is like adding big neon arrows that make it clear to search engines what the people, places, or things (known in the search world as *entities*) are on your website.

To make sure all the sites are using a common vocabulary to describe the entities on their web pages, structured data languages like microdata (including Schema.org), microformats, and RDFa exist.

If you are a web developer, we encourage you to choose a structured data format and write your own rich snippet code. If you are not a code person, fear not. Thanks to the Google Structured Data Markup Helper, you don't need to be a microdata or Schema.org expert to add rich snippets to your web pages. All you need is a basic knowledge of HTML and the ability to copy and paste code into the HTML of your web pages.

Here's how to automatically generate your rich snippet markup using the Structured Data Markup Helper:

1. **Decide which web page you want to create a rich snippet for.**

The Structured Data Markup Helper tool can generate snippet code for only one web page at a time.

2. **In your web browser, navigate to the tool at** `www.google.com/webmasters/markup-helper/u/0/` (see Figure 4-5).

3. **With the Website tab selected (not the Email tab), choose a content type that best represents your web page (Google calls it a "data type").**

Google provides ten options; if you're not sure what type of content you're working with, it's probably an article.

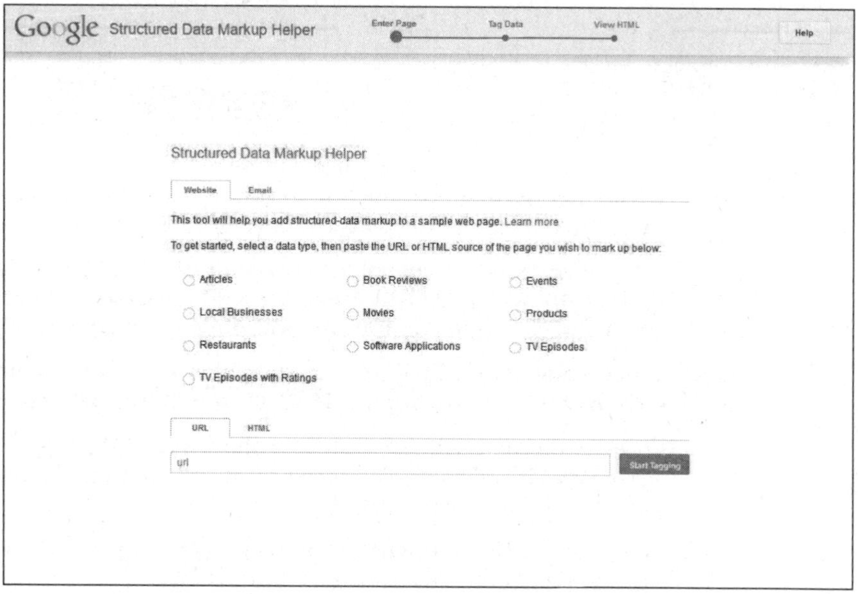

Book IV Chapter 4

Making Your Page Search Engine Compatible

Figure 4-5: The Structured Data Markup Helper asks you to choose a content type.

4. **Enter the URL of the web page you want to mark up.**

5. **Click the Start Tagging button.**

   The Structured Data Markup Helper will load two columns. In the left column, you see a page that looks just like your web page; in the right column, you see a list titled My Data Items.

   To generate rich snippet markup, use the mouse to highlight the items listed in the right column within your website in the left column. With the item highlighted, use the drop-down menu that appears to identify the item. (Is it the brand name? The logo? The price?)

   For example, if you click the logo image in the left column, choose Brand and then Logo from the drop-down menu, as shown in Figure 4-6. (We know that Logo is under Brand in the drop-down menu because that is the way it is listed in the My Data Items column to the right.)

Figure 4-6: Using the Structured Data Markup Helper to identify your logo as an entity.

6. **If you highlight the product price in the left column, choose Offer and then Price from the drop-down, as seen in Figure 4-7.**

7. **If there are any data elements you can't highlight in the left column, such as the web page URL, click the Add Missing Tags button at the bottom of the right column and add the tags, as seen in Figure 4-8.**

8. **When you've identified all your data items, generate your rich-snippet code by clicking the Create HTML button in the right column.**

   You see the right column expand to show the HTML of your web page. Within that HTML view, you see several code phrases highlighted; this is your rich-snippet markup code!

9. **Using the HTML view as a reference, copy and paste the highlighted lines of code into your own web page HTML.**

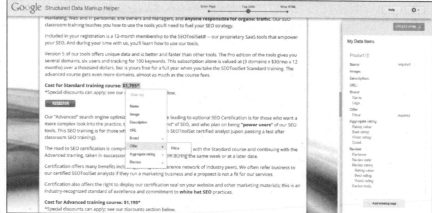

Figure 4-7:
Using the Structured Data Markup Helper to identify your product price.

Figure 4-8:
Add missing tags manually if there are elements you can't highlight in the Structured Data Markup Helper.

10. **After you've added rich snippet markup to your web page, use the Structured Data Testing Tool (**`www.google.com/webmasters/tools/richsnippets`**) to test that your code snippets have been added correctly.**

Always be careful when altering your website code. Something as small as a period in the wrong place can cause errors to appear on the live website. Although the Structured Data Markup tool lets noncode writers easily generate rich snippet code, we recommend as a best practice that you not make any permanent changes to your website code unless you feel confident that you know what you're doing. If you *think* you know but you're not sure, ask your web developer for help.

Understanding how rich snippets affect rankings

To help you grasp how rich-snippet markup can potentially improve SERP rank, we need to revisit the *semantic search* topic that we cover in Book I, Chapter 3.

In a semantic search world, the search engine begins with user intent and tries to understand the query itself, not just the keywords in the query. In other words, the search engine wants to understand the meaning and context of the query's intent, just as a human would. To do this, semantic search technology seeks to extract *entities* (people, places, and things) from its database as answers and display personalized search results that are just right for the individual user.

When you are adding rich snippet markup to your pages, essentially you are using a special kind of code *(structured data markup)* to give your content more meaning and context. Optimizing your content with rich-snippet markup can also help the search engine better understand your content as an *entity* (person, place, or thing).

In other words, rich snippets can help Google more thoroughly understand your content, the context of your content, and the relevance of your content in relation to specific search queries.

So, although Google says that rich snippet markup on its own does not directly boost your rank, the added context provided by rich snippets very well may.

The context your rich snippet markup gives Google can also help your SERP rank by helping the search engine populate the *Knowledge Graph* database (read more about the Knowledge Graph in Book 1, Chapter 3). By helping to inform and expand the Knowledge Graph, your semantic markup also helps Google more thoroughly understand and index your content. This can lead to improved rank because added contextual understanding may help Google see your web pages as more relevant to the search query.

Google and Bing never promise to use the `Meta` description text or the rich-snippet markup you supply; sometimes they use it and sometimes they don't. Even without a 100 percent guarantee, including rich-snippet markup whenever possible is still worthwhile because SERP listings with rich snippets tend to see a significant increase in click-through rate.

Plus, even when your rich snippets don't show up in SERP results, they still supply search engines with structured data that helps them better understand (and rank!) your content.

Using Clean Code

When designing or building your website, keep the code as clean as possible. If you have useless tags in your code, get rid of them, and code in as little markup as possible. That means no extraneous tags lying around in the HTML. You want to streamline your site's code so it's an easy read for the search engine spiders. If you can define something in 200 tags instead of 400, cut out all the tags you don't need.

Code gunk buildup can happen if you've cut and pasted code from another source (like an outdated web page of yours) or if you've been working on a particular page for so long that it's acquired excess tags. Go through and remove all of the extraneous tags and code from your page. Simplifying your code streamlines the site and makes it easier for the search engine spiders to read. If spiders read too much redundant stuff, they're less likely to assign a lot of weight or relevancy to your page and are more likely to throw out the page.

With clean code, the goal is to have a high amount of content with the least amount of markup. This means there's more content going on than HTML coding. Figure 4-9 shows two different pages' HTML code side by side. On the left is a messily coded image of a table, and on the right is the clean version of the same table. Note the difference between the messy code and the

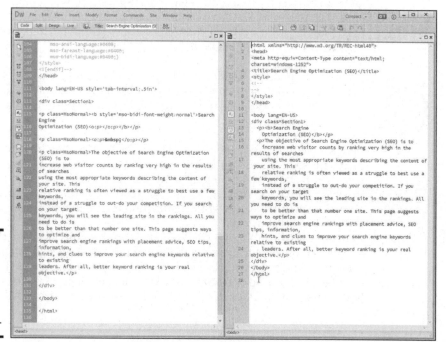

Figure 4-9: Note how the clean code has more content in it.

clean code: The clean code has a higher content-to-code ratio. The less code a search engine spider has to read, the faster it can crawl your page. And the sooner it gets to the content of your website, the better. The first 200 words of a page carry the most weight, so it's important to get the spider to the actual content as soon as you can.

Making Your Site W3C-Compliant

One of the ways to get your code nice and clean is to validate it. *Validating* code means making your website W3C-compliant. The *World Wide Web Consortium* (W3C) is an international consortium where member organizations, a full-time staff, and the public work together to develop web standards. The W3C's mission statement is "to lead the World Wide Web to its full potential by developing protocols and guidelines that ensure long-term growth for the Web."

W3C goes about achieving this mission by creating web standards and guidelines. It's basically like health code guidelines for a restaurant. A website needs to meet certain standards in order to be as least imperfect as possible. Since 1994, W3C has published more than 110 such standards, called W3C Recommendations.

A compliant page is known to be spiderable and to have links that are crawlable, so although the search engines do not require W3C compliance, it's not a bad idea. If you have complex or just plain ugly web page code, or if you're having issues getting your pages crawled and indexed, validating your code to W3C standards might help.

On the front page of the W3C's website (www.w3.org) is a sidebar called W3C A to Z, which contains all sorts of links. Bookmark this page: These links are a great reference to help you understand the standards that the web is built on.

Here's something about search engines: The harder they have to work to read your site, the less often and less thoroughly the search engines index your site. Because more content tends to mean more authority, you are less likely to receive top ranking. In fact, if a search engine has to work too long at reading your page, it might just abandon it all together.

So it's a good idea to follow the W3C standards, simply because they make for a faster, more efficient page that is set up the way a search engine expects to find things. It's like having your house swept, cleaned up, and in order when the spiders come to visit: It makes them like what they see. (Internet spiders, that is. It doesn't work that way for the arachnid variety.)

If your site doesn't comply with the W3C standards, the search engines might not crawl all your pages on your site. Because you can't rank pages the search engines don't know about, that's a big problem.

To comply with W3C, every page should declare a *doc type* (document type) and validate itself. To declare your doc type, include a line at the very top of your HTML code, which declares the document as an HTML document and identifies the type of HTML you are following. Because HTML has changed since the early days, some versions are different from others. Declaring a doc type is telling the search engine what it's going to be reading. It's important to comply with your declared doc type. If you don't, you confuse the search engine spider, and it takes longer for the spider to crawl your pages.

To validate your page, go to the W3C's Developer Tools page (`http://www.w3.org/developers/tools`) and use the free tools on that page, as shown in Figure 4-10.

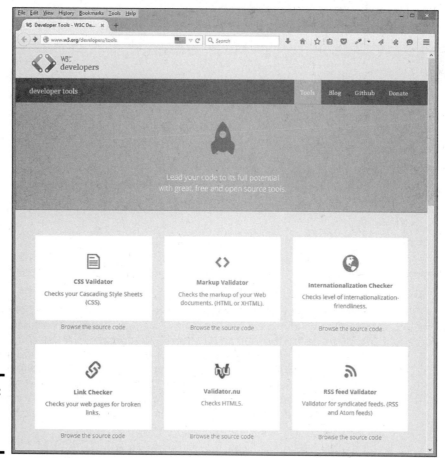

**Book IV
Chapter 4**

**Making Your Page
Search Engine
Compatible**

Figure 4-10:
The W3C
Developer
Tools.

These are tools that you can use to basically "proofread" your site in order to make sure they comply with the W3C standards.

Access the Markup Validation Service, shown in Figure 4-11, by clicking the MarkUp Validator link on the W3C Quality Assurance Tools page. Also known as the HTML validator, it helps check web documents in formats like HTML, XHTML, SVG, or MathML. If you plug your site's URL into the text box and click the Check button, the tool checks your website to see whether the code matches the declared doc type.

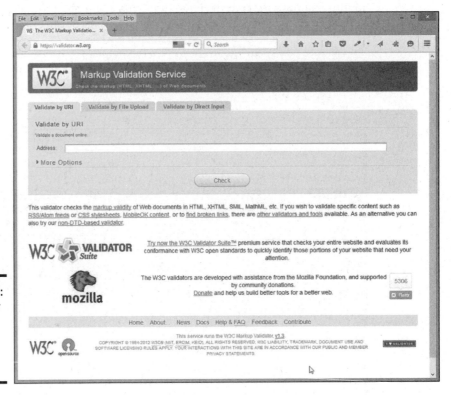

Figure 4-11: Check your website's code with a markup validator.

The link for the Link Checker tool (see Figure 4-12) appears below the MarkUp Validator link on the main Quality Assurance Tools page. It checks *anchors* (hyperlinks) in an HTML/XHTML document. It's useful for finding broken links, redirected pages, server errors, and so on. There are some options for your search — like ignoring redirects and the ability to check the links on the pages linked to from the original page — and you can also save the options you set in a cookie to make it quick to run it again in the future. If you don't select the Summary Only check box, you can watch it go through each link on the page. Most of the time, you just need to run the tools without making any adjustments, so don't stress about the options. Many other link checkers are also available out there. The W3C's tool is great for checking one page (if you were putting up a single new page with a lot of links, for example), but for checking the links in a whole site, we prefer Xenu's Link Sleuth, which is a great (and free!) link-checking tool that makes sure all your links work. It's available at `http://home.snafu.de/tilman/xenulink.html`.

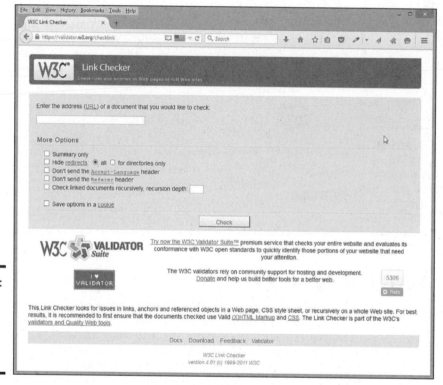

Figure 4-12:
The Link Checker validator from the W3C.

Click the CSS Validator link on W3C's Quality Assurance Tools page to access the CSS Validation Service, which validates CSS style sheets or documents using CSS style sheets. As shown in Figure 4-13, it works a lot like the Markup Validation Service. Just put in the URL of the site you wish to validate, and then click the Check button.

Validating your CSS ensures that your site looks picture perfect whenever a standards-compliant browser (like Firefox) or spider (like Google) comes by and checks it out.

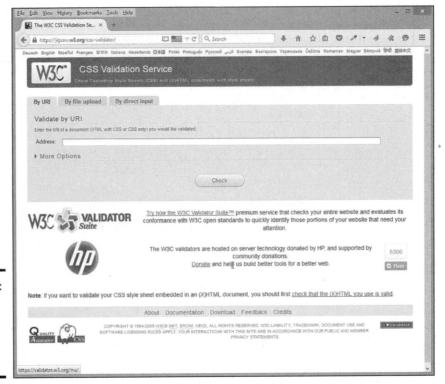

Figure 4-13:
The CSS
Validation
Service
from the
W3C.

Externalizing the Code

When you're working with CSS and JavaScript, it's important to externalize the code. *Externalizing the code* is basically putting all your definitions in a file, putting that file on your site, and using a single line of code within your actual pages to tell the browser (and search engines) where to find it. Because the code represents the building blocks of your website, there's going to be a lot of it. Just the JavaScript for your analytics alone can take up dozens of lines of code, maybe even hundreds. Externalizing your code is streamlining your page-designing process.

Not only does it reduce the size of your page to externalize CSS and JavaScript, giving your browser less to load, but if you want to go in and change all your headings to blue, all you need to do is go to the glossary page where all the terms are defined and change that particular code to `blue`; the change then appears throughout your website. You don't have to go through every single page and do it by hand. The advantage for SEO is that externalizing your code makes the page code much cleaner, thus making the content-to-code ratio much higher overall.

Choosing the Right Navigation

You can allow a user to navigate your site in several different ways. There's text-based navigation, which means all the *navigation info* (links, information about those links, any cool little widgets you have, and so on) is listed in the text. There's image-based navigation, which means you click an image linked to another page or a section of an *image map* (the image is on a layer that allows for attaching links and other goodies) and navigate via that link. Then there's navigation using scripts such as JavaScript or technology such as Flash to build your navigation. For search engine optimization, we recommend that you use text-based navigation. This ensures that the search engine spiders can read and understand it. You can, if you really want to, use any of the other ways to build a navigation system for your site, but they all have significant drawbacks when it comes to search engine optimization.

Image maps

Using an image map for your site navigation doesn't help with SEO because you don't have any anchor text to take advantage of. Your anchor text is important because it tells the search engine what that page you are linking to is about. When a page is linked to the anchor text *classic cars,* search engines tend to think, "Hmm, this page must be about classic cars." The more links you have with that anchor text pointing to that page from other pages, the more it's like a giant blinking neon sign telling the search engine that this page is about classic cars. The search engine then assigns more weight to the link and increases the perceived relevance of the linked page.

Because an image map does not contain any readable text, any text that is contained within the image is not going to be seen by a search engine spider. A spider is deaf, dumb, and blind and can only understand the code on the page; spiders do not see what a human user sees. Any text within the image-map navigation is not counted toward your overall page rank. The search engine can read only the Alt attribute text. And because you have one image for the navigation, that's only going to be one Alt attribute tag. Some designers break up a big image into several smaller images so that they can use multiple Alt attribute tags, but Alt attribute tags still do not carry as much weight as hyperlinked text, especially because those trying to game the system may be able to deceive a search engine with spam in the Alt attribute tags.

When deciding which type of navigation to build, you also want to consider your mobile users and how images load on different devices. (Find out more about designing mobile-friendly navigation in Chapter 3 of this minibook.)

You will also want to consider the possibility that desktop users do not have images turned on in their browsers, usually because they're still on a dial-up connection and they want pages to load sometime this century. (They are still out there.)

Flash

Another type of navigation system is Flash. Navigation that utilizes nonanimated Flash-file text may be readable by a search engine, but this is only for the latest versions, and search engines still won't be able to read any of the links or anchor text.

Also, some search engines see Flash files as files separate from the page they're attached to, and they do not count the Flash content toward that overall web page. Flash can also be annoying because it can break, slow down load time, or start playing unwanted music or videos. On many Apple devices, such as the iPhone and the iPad, Flash doesn't work at all. In addition, many people choose to turn off Flash in their browsers in order to avoid Flash-based advertisements, and they wind up stranded on your page if your navigation is Flash-based because they won't even be able to see it.

JavaScript

JavaScript is a program that the search engine spiders attempt to crawl. Both JavaScript and AJAX, which stands for "asynchronous JavaScript and XML," may be indexed by the search engines. To determine whether your JavaScript is being seen by a search engine, use Fetch and Render (found in Google Search Console), as described in Chapter 5 of this minibook.

Text-based navigation

Text-based navigation is the navigation you should rely on when designing your page. Search engines can read the content of your text and can use the anchor text in the links to assign weight and relevance to those pages. Text is also clean, simple, and easy to use, and you don't run the risk of users being unable to see it in their browsers because all browsers can read text.

Not only is text easy (search engines and users can easily read it), but it's also highly controllable and customizable. You can add JavaScript to the text using CSS for increased interactivity or styling and still have it be understandable to a search engine.

A word about using frames

Frames have fallen by the wayside as site design has advanced in the past several years, but a few sites out there still choose to use them. Our advice is to not be one of them. Search engines read a frame as a completely separate page, so if your navigation is in a different frame than your page content, they're being read as two separate pages. Splitting up the relationship between your content is a bad idea. Just don't do it.

If you decide to use images, Flash, or JavaScript for your navigation, at least use a text-based footer on the page that offers alternative text links to your pages and to your site map so that search engines can follow that and can do a read-through of your site.

Chapter 5: Perfecting Navigation and Linking Techniques

In This Chapter

✔ Formulating a category structure

✔ Building landing pages for silos

✔ Absolute versus relative linking

✔ Types of navigation

✔ Tools to ensure that your navigation is search engine friendly

✔ Naming links

*I*n this chapter, we talk about how to physically structure your site in the most efficient way possible with siloing. Siloing is the process of categorizing your web pages into subject themes in order to group related content. In this way, you present clear and straightforward subject relevancy that increases your site's perceived expertise to the search engines.

Search engines award keyword rankings to the site that proves that it is least "imperfect" for the relevancy of a subject or theme. That means that the more clearly on-topic a site is for a user's search query, the more relevant it is, and the more likely it is to appear near the top of search results. Search engines try to dissect a site into distinct subjects that add up to an overall theme that represents a straightforward subject relevancy. If a search engine can clearly understand what you're talking about, it's going to consider you more of an expert on the subject and award you a higher rank than the other guy who's diluted his theme and cluttered his page with junk that's not relevant to his site. More often than not, a website is a disjointed array of unrelated information with no central theme, and it suffers in search engines for keyword rankings. If you visit a website and you wind up not being exactly sure whether it's about electric shavers or rubber pants, odds are a search engine isn't going to know either. Siloing a website helps to clarify your website's subject relevance.

In this chapter, we discuss how to physically arrange a site for siloing. We go into much more depth on siloing in Book VI, but this chapter gets you started. The first thing we talk about is formulating a linking structure and landing pages: what they are and why they're important. Next we revisit absolute versus relative linking. Finally, we discuss the types of navigation to use when building a silo, and we finish off with the naming of links.

Formulating a Category Structure

Formulating a category structure is basically grouping your site content to put all your categories together into related directories. In Chapters 1 and 2 of this minibook, we talk about picking major categories and smaller subcategories to go with them. If you've already done this, formulating a category structure shouldn't be so bad.

First, you need to figure out which page is the most important, and then have all your other pages point to it. What page do you think represents your website best? What page do you want your visitors to first see when they visit your website? After you determine your most important page, you can figure out your linking structure. You need to decide what your categories are and what you want to link where so that you can keep from diluting your theme.

Going back to the jar of marbles analogy we discuss in previous chapters: If you have black, gray, and white marbles all bunched together in a jar, it's hard to figure out what the "subject" of the jar is. Is it a jar of black marbles with some white and gray mixed in, or a jar of white marbles with black and gray marbles mixed in, or a jar of gray marbles, or something else? Search engines function much the same way when they index a page or a site. Search engines can only decipher the meaning of a page when the subjects are clear and distinct. Take a look at the picture of the jar of marbles in Figure 5-1. How would search engines classify it?

In the jar, you can see black marbles, gray marbles, and white marbles all mixed together with seemingly no order or emphasis. It would be reasonable to assume that search engines would classify the subject as a jar of marbles.

If we then separate each group of colored marbles into separate jars (or websites) as in Figure 5-2, they would be classified as a jar of black marbles, a jar of white marbles, and a jar of gray marbles.

However, if you wanted to put all three marbles (categories) into a single jar (website) as in Figure 5-3, you would create distinct silos or categories within the site that would allow the subject themes to be black marbles, white marbles, gray marbles, and finally the generic term marbles. Most websites never clarify the main subjects they want their site to become relevant for. Instead, they try to be all things to all people.

Categorizing your website makes it easier for a search engine to read and understand the page's content, and it also helps the user navigate the page.

Figure 5-1:
A mixed jar of marbles — how would a search engine classify it?

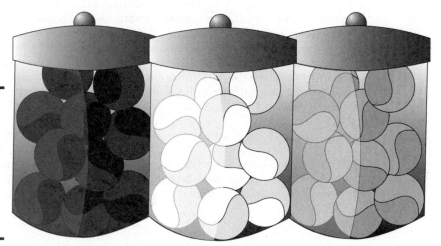

Figure 5-2:
In separate jars (or on separate sites), notice how easy it is to categorize by color.

Figure 5-3:
This jar
has three
distinct
themes, or
silos.

After you have your categories and subcategories picked out, now it's time
to upload them and set up your site's directories for easy navigation and
siloing. When building a directory structure, it's important to not go too
deep. The directory structure refers to where your files physically exist
within the folders on the site. For example, take a look at the following URL
of a web page. The full web address identifies the directory where the page
physically resides:

```
http://www.customclassics.com/ford/mustangs/index.html
```

The URL lets you know where the page is. Notice that there are only two
subdirectories under the main domain. Having too many levels of subdirectories does the following things:

✦ The farther the file is from the root directory, the less important it seems to the search engines.

✦ Long directory paths make long URLs. Studies have proven that users avoid clicking long URLs on a search results page.

✦ Long URLs are more apt to cause typos. This could cause broken links within your website (if the webmaster uses absolute linking); also, users could make mistakes typing in your URL.

Therefore, don't get category happy. Making your directory structure ten directories deep is bad; having five deep is bad too. Having three levels of directories is not as bad, but it's not great either. We recommend going no more than two directories deep.

For example, our classic car website has only one main category (the car's make) and two subcategories (model and year). If you have enough content to support multiple sublevels (substantial pages for each category), you could set up the directory structure with two levels. The top-level folders would be labeled with the make; the subfolders would be named by the model. Each page within the subfolder could represent a particular year. So the directory structure would look something like this:

```
http://www.customclassics.com/ford/delrio/1957.html
http://www.customclassics.com/ford/fairlane/1958.html
http://www.customclassics.com/ford/mustang/1965.html
```

Note that the directory structure is only two levels deep.

The grouping of content on the site is very significant. One of the ways to think about it is to think of a website as compared with a book: The table of contents describes the overall subject at the beginning of the book, and then the book breaks down into different chapters that support that major subject. The different chapters are the different top-level folders, whereas each chapter (each folder) contains pages (the individual HTML-page files).

The folder or directory is the physical organization of the files (pages) in that root directory. Because a spider cannot physically read the files on the server or in a database (it takes a Content Management System to format pages), you can use several strategies for dynamically organizing data, making even the most ornery Content Management Systems (CMSes) flexible for implementing directory structures. There are two separate ways to understand how a directory structure looks visually — by the URL structure and by folder view:

```
http://www.classiccars.org/index.shtml
http://www.classiccars.org/Ford/index.shtml
```

**Book IV
Chapter 5**

**Perfecting
Navigation and
Linking Techniques**

```
http://www.classiccars.org/Business_Partnerships/
    Support_Other_Businesses.shtml
http://www.classiccars.org/Business_Partnerships/
    Value-Added_Partnerships.shtml
http://www.classiccars.org/Chevy/index.shtml
http://www.classiccars.org/Chevy/Comet.shtml
```

Notice how none of the preceding URLs are longer than one main category and two subjects. Knowing how to group related subject files on your website provides greater primary- and supporting-subject relevancy while also lending a strategy for identifying which sections of your site require greater amounts of content.

Three major subjects define what impact link structure has on implementing silos on your site:

✦ Internal site linking is how the pages are linked within the span of your site, whether it be linking between major silos or cross-linking related subject pages.

✦ Outbound, or external, linking represents the offsite links to other sites that are subject-relevant and that provide resources to users that your site can't offer.

✦ Backlinks are the format by which other websites link to the pages on your website. You should understand the difference between links from sites that support your theme and links from sites that have no subject matter relevance. The first are good, but the second kind may dilute your subject relevancy.

Having sites with unrelated subject matter link to your site causes the relevancy to be diluted. The purpose of inbound links is to reinforce subject relevance. This is a major issue for sites that purchase links because the links often originate from a completely irrelevant site.

Selecting Landing Pages

When you're ready to choose your subject categories, go through and pick what you think would be the most important pages for each category, the ones you want the users to see in the search results and ultimately land on. These are the aptly named landing pages. A landing page can be any or all of three things:

✦ The first page where users land when clicking the link to your site during their search query

✦ The page where a user lands after clicking a paid ad

✦ The page at the top level of a silo

When choosing a page on your site to be a landing page, keep in mind that it should be a big topic with links to a lot of pages that support the topic. If you have less than five pages of support for this page, it's probably not a landing page. See Figure 5-4 for an example of a landing page with its supporting pages.

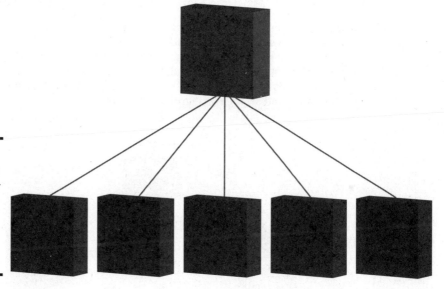

Figure 5-4:
The landing page is supported by at least five subpages of related content.

Figuring out your landing page depends on what keywords you choose for the page. You want it to be a gateway page to the rest of your site. It should contain the broad keywords you need to draw in the query, and it should funnel users to the other pages with the more specific information they need.

You should be thinking about these questions when deciding which page to use as your landing page: Does the landing page content answer the search query? Does it contain enough information on that page or on its subpages that provide information for a search query? If users don't find what they're looking for on your website's landing page, they're not going to stick around and explore the rest of your site. Remember, you want people to explore your site, and having a well-crafted silo not only helps your search engine rankings but also enhances the user experience.

One thing to keep in mind is that every page on your website has the potential to be a landing page. One of your subpages could be drawing all the traffic because it contains more relevant information than the actual landing page. This is not a bad thing; it just means one page ended up being a better landing page than the one you thought of. So it's important to optimize every page just in case. Make sure it reads naturally and is not too forced or obvious; a human user knows when things on a page seem stilted or forced. When linking your pages, you can link as much as you like within a silo (to any related page, whether a landing page or subpage), but if you have to change the subject, always try to link to the landing page of the other subject, not to any subpage. If you must link to a non-theme-related, non-landing page, you need to use a `rel="nofollow"` parameter on the link.

Linking predominantly to landing pages in the silo is also important. A normal silo looks like Figure 5-5, where the subpages link either to other subpages in the same silo or to the landing page. Notice that they don't link across silos to other subpages in different silos. A good comparison of siloing is to think of it like a pyramid, where the top tier is supported by the level below it, and so on, throughout the pyramid.

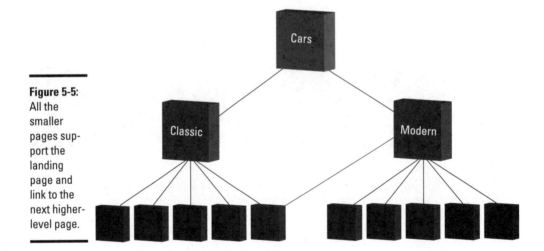

Figure 5-5:
All the smaller pages support the landing page and link to the next higher-level page.

Absolute versus Relative Linking

In a web page's HTML code, you have two ways to include a link: relative links and absolute links. An absolute link is a link that contains the whole URL of the file you're linking to. When it appears in code, it looks the same as when it appears in the browser's address bar:

```
<a href="http://www.classiccars.com/fords/mustangs/
    tireoptions.html">Anchor Text</a>
```

That's the whole file directory in the link itself. A relative link looks like only part of a full-path URL:

```
<a href="tireoptions.html"> Anchor Text</a>
<a href="../tireoptions.html"> Anchor Text</a>
```

When designing your website, we recommend that you don't use relative links, especially if you're building your site from the ground up, so you won't have the added headache of verifying page and media final placement. When you use a relative link, it works only in relation to the next directory up. For example, a link from `mustangs/paintoptions.html` to `<a href="tireoptions.html">` takes you to the intended page only if your site has a `mustangs/tireoptions.html` for it to link to.

If the pages that were linking out were to get moved somewhere else, the relative link would no longer work because where it linked to would no longer be valid. So if the page was moved from the `/mustangs` directory to the `/mustangconvertible` directory, the relative link of `<a href="tireoptions,html">` would break because there is no `tireoptions.html` page in the `/mustangconvertible` directory.

An absolute link is easier to maintain in situations like this because it's very clear what you're linking to. With absolute links, the links still work, even if the pages move.

Use the fully qualified URL (that is, the link target that begins `http://domain.com`) every time you create a link. Not only is it easier for the engines to understand, but there are also fewer mistakes in the coding of the website, and any mistakes can easily be caught and corrected.

Dealing with Less-than-Ideal Types of Navigation

In Chapter 4 of this minibook, we describe the various types of navigation used in building websites and recommend what is best to use and what is best to avoid. For SEO, it's important to use text-based navigation because it's clean, simple, and can be seen by both the search engine and the user.

Unfortunately, you can't always use text as your navigation system. Sometimes you have a boss who wants the bells and whistles, and you can't convince her that text links work best. Sometimes your CMS won't allow you to use only text. And sometimes competing in your industry demands those bells and whistles, and users won't trust your site without them. For example, a movie site may require a more image-based site that includes Flash animation and navigation to showcase movie trailers; a user would think something was terribly wrong with a movie site that's entirely text-based.

Fear not, for there is a way around these problems in your navigation. You can work around the problems caused by image-, JavaScript-, and Flash-based navigations in order to still rank in the search engines. There is a technical way of working around every problem. It may require a little more work, but if the bells and whistles are something you have to have, the tips in the following sections can help, especially in terms of keeping your silos neat and clean.

Images

As we advise in more depth in Chapter 4 of this minibook, don't use images for your site navigation unless you have to. Because an image map does not contain any readable text, any text that is contained within the image is not going to be seen by a search engine spider. A spider can only understand the code on the page, not what a human user sees. So any text within the navigation is not counted toward your overall page rank. The only text it is going to read is the Alt attribute text. If you have only one image for the navigation, that's only going to be one Alt attribute tag. Alt attribute tags do not hold a lot of weight with a search engine because they are easily stuffed with keywords and are spammable.

When you're building a silo, however, using image-based navigation can be useful. If you need to remove keywords that otherwise dilute your page's target, you can place them in an image, rendering them unseen by a search engine, but still visible to a user.

For example, say you have a page you want to rank in the search engines for research-type search queries. To make this happen, you need to remove any call-to-action keywords such as [purchase] or [buy now] from your web page. Having those keywords on your page enters it into ranking against e-commerce sites, and you run the risk of diluting your page theme and losing the rankings you really want, which are the ones for a research site.

The simple solution is to place all the call-to-action keywords within an image, which renders them invisible to a search engine but still visible to the user. It's important to keep keywords that do not pertain to your particular silo (remember, they run along a common theme, like a certain model of car or colors of paint) invisible to a search engine.

JavaScript

The problem with JavaScript when used in site navigation is that it can confuse the search engine with too much or too little information, especially if the JavaScript navigation is the primary way of getting into a silo. Using JavaScript in the form of a drop-down menu as your site navigation might look pretty and keep navigation convenient, but the search engine reads all this information in each page and attributes it to every single page, as Figure 5-6 shows. Every page on the site would have the unrelated link to the Contact and About pages, which don't need a global link.

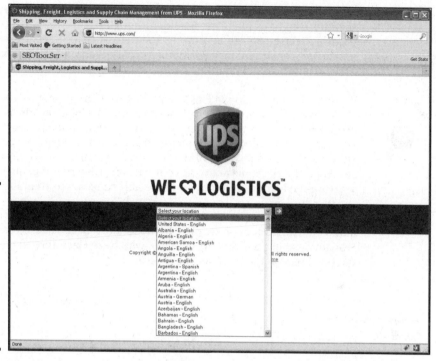

Figure 5-6:
The search engine reads all the information in a drop-down menu and attributes it to that page.

If your drop-down menu links to other unrelated pages, the search engine is going to read all the unrelated keywords in that menu and include them when weighing relevancy of that page. For example, your page is about black marbles, but the JavaScript navigation also links to all your pages on white marbles, blue marbles, green marbles, and pink marbles. When every page on the site links to every other page on the site, it dilutes the page content and weakens the silo.

The solution is to externalize the navigation into its own separate JavaScript file that is loaded with JavaScript or in an iFrame. (An iFrame, or inline frame, is an HTML element that lets you embed another HTML document inside the main document.) By externalizing this way, the navigation isn't read as part of the page but rather as its own separate page, so the navigation doesn't dilute your landing pages and silos.

Flash

Flash content is generally not advisable when doing search engine optimization, simply because a search engine can't read it. There have been some advances with the latest version of Flash that make the text created in Flash readable by spiders, but because it's so easily spammable, it does not carry as much weight as plain text would. Although some companies' websites require the use of Flash in order to compete or to look reliable — such as the movie website we mention earlier in this chapter — we recommend not using Flash to create your navigation whenever possible.

Putting your navigation in Flash can be a problem for people who have Flash turned off in their browsers in order to avoid Flash-based ads or to keep their browsers from crashing because of a slow-loading modem. Some people will also have trouble accessing your site from a mobile device (especially from an Apple device, such as an iPhone or iPad) because Flash isn't supported at all. When these people arrive at your website, they're not going to be able to see your navigation, and they won't be able to navigate your site.

The easy way to fix this problem is to have a text-based version of the information at the bottom of the page in the footer that the search engines can read and use in their rankings. People who have Flash turned off can also see the text links on the page, as in Figure 5-7.

Figure 5-7: Repeating Flash content in text in a website's footer makes the page accessible for users without Flash and allows search engines to "see" the page.

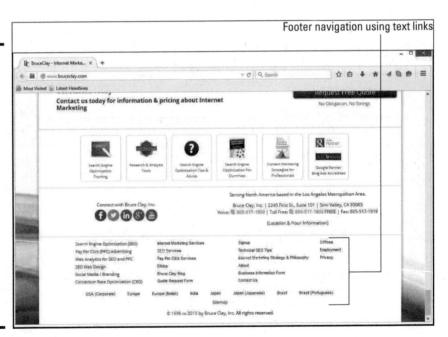

Checking to see what Google sees

If you think you're dealing with a less-than-ideal type of navigation, a handy tool called Fetch as Google lets you see whether your site's images, JavaScript, or Flash are obstacles to search engine bots. The Fetch as Google tool simulates what Googlebot does when it arrives at your web page. Found within the Crawl reports in Google Search Console (free for all site owners at `www.google.com/webmasters/tools/`), you use Fetch and Render to see your site as Google sees it.

Both Google and Bing have multiple crawlers to replicate different browsing experiences. For instance, the search engines have a standard crawler, which acts like a desktop browser, and a mobile crawler, which replicates how a mobile browser interacts with a web page. When you use Fetch as Google, you can choose to see how Googlebot views your page in desktop mode, smartphone mode, or feature phone mode. (A feature phone is a phone that can access the Internet but doesn't have the advanced functionality of a smartphone).

In Figure 5-8, you can see a Fetch as Google report. On the left, you can see "how Googlebot saw the page," and the image on the right is how a user saw the page on his or her desktop browser. Below that, the report lists any resources on the page that the crawler couldn't get to, along with a reason.

Figure 5-8:
The Fetch as Google report in Google Search Console shows you how Google sees your page and lists any resources on the page that it can't reach.

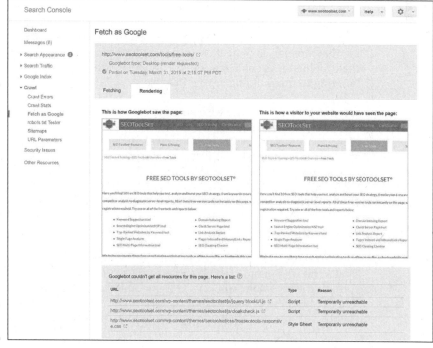

Book IV
Chapter 5

Perfecting Navigation and Linking Techniques

When you're using Fetch as Google to identify problems with your website's navigation, look for big gaps where your navigation should be in the side-by-side images displayed in the fetch-and-render report. If the image that Googlebot sees and what your visitors see is vastly different, or if Googlebot can't see something your visitor can see, you may need to give the search engine bots a different way to reach that content on the page. This kind of content gap analysis is a good idea for not only your navigation but also your whole website. Use Fetch as Google to see whether you're inadvertently blocking chunks of a page from Google's view.

Naming Links

The naming of links, or writing the anchor text (the words that make up the actual links someone clicks), is one of the most important aspects of siloing. Providing anchor text for a link tells the search engine what the page that's being linked to is about. If the page content talks about tires, and the anchor text says it's about tires, and any other links to that page all contain the word tires, that's a giant neon arrow to the search engine that that particular page is about tires.

When linking to your own content internally, make sure that the anchor text matches the heading of the page you're linking to. It's positive reinforcement for the search engines. If the sign that says Pancakes is pointing to a building that advertises pancakes in the window, it's a pretty safe assumption that the business sells pancakes. That goes double if there are multiple signs pointing to the building saying Pancakes.

Another way of working with anchor text is to vary the actual anchor text. In the case of the signs, it would be something like "Let's go eat at the pancake place," "This place makes great pancakes," and "Let's go here for pancakes." You can expand this as well and say the page is about all types of pancakes, so you'd want to link back using synonyms for pancakes like flapjacks, hotcakes, and other types of pancakes. Using synonyms creates good varying anchor text, assuming there were no pages about those synonyms on your site. They all mean the same thing, but the different wording allows for the anchor text to match a greater variety of search queries.

Slight variations in your anchor text wording also sound more natural. That's the way people talk. It's important to keep your link names as natural-sounding as possible. Not only is it uncomfortable for users to read things that seem stilted or forced, but the search engines expect to find text that sounds natural, and they may suspect spam otherwise.

Book V
Creating Content

Get some tips for bringing some life to content about topics that might seem too boring for words at www.dummies.com/extras/searchengine optimizationaio.

Contents at a Glance

Chapter 1: Selecting a Style for Your Audience

In This Chapter

✔ **Knowing your target audience**

✔ **Looking at your current customers to understand their demographics**

✔ **Interviewing and researching to analyze your target audience**

✔ **Choosing the right tone to engage your audience**

✔ **Using a blog to build a relationship with your audience**

✔ **Using personas to define your audience**

✔ **Understanding the benefits and drawbacks of using personas**

The slogan "Content is king!" has been stated and restated in every blog, forum, conference, and seminar that has anything to do with search engine optimization (SEO) or Internet marketing. Content includes all the stuff inside your website: everything from the words you read, to the pictures and videos you view, to the audio you listen to. In this chapter, we teach you all about the most important content element for SEO — the words on the page. The text content draws people to your site, starting with the brief title that shows up on a search results page. Content holds a visitor's interest long enough to read your page and, hopefully, move on to do more. Content is what gives your website credibility with both your visitors and other sites so that they want to endorse you with a link or purchase. Content tells the search engines what you're all about. Content proves (or disproves) that you know what you're talking about.

And content takes hours and hours and even laborious days to create. If you feel overwhelmed by the need to write tons of new content, we understand. The prospect of writing page after page of content may make you want to crawl under the nearest desk, but the truth is, your website really cannot do without it. Good content and plenty of it is needed if you want to rank well with the search engines and attract users who convert into customers (however you define that conversion). For this reason, Book V, which deals with content creation, may contain the most valuable pages in this book.

Good, relevant content is your single most potent SEO tool. It allows you to do the following:

+ Differentiate your site from the masses

+ Attract expert links to your site

+ Develop a loyal site following and brand

+ Launch your site higher in the search engine rankings

In this chapter, you think through how to create the best content for your site's purposes and target audience. You first need to understand whom your site needs to appeal to, so we begin by discussing what demographic information you need to know about your target audience and how you can find it out. Next, you discover how to choose a dynamic tone and style that can effectively communicate with your audience and yield conversions. Last, you find out how to create a *persona* (a profile that represents your target audience based on calculated averages of their buying processes and demographics) so that you can design appropriate content that satisfies a specific, highly targeted group.

Knowing Your Demographic

Before you communicate anything, asking "Who is my audience?" is a great first step. You might be an expert in your field, but unless you can explain what you know in a way that your target audience understands, you can't communicate your expertise. With your website, your job is not only to communicate but also to persuade, because you want *conversions* (visitors who make a purchase, sign up for a newsletter, or take whatever action your website requires). Understanding who your audience is becomes even more essential in order to better target your conversions.

Many new web marketers make the mistake of thinking they don't have a target audience: They see the Internet as a vast crowd of people and just want them to come to their sites. But attracting visitors to your site who then convert requires specific targeted marketing. The Internet population includes many types of people, and the more precisely you can figure out who your target visitors are, the more effective you can be at attracting and holding their interest and making conversions.

Finding out customer goals

Beyond knowing who your target audience is, you also want to find out what they need. You know what your website offers. Now turn your chair around and look at your site from the other direction. Why would people come to your site? What goal would they be trying to meet?

You want to be sure to meet your visitors' needs first before trying to motivate them to do anything else. Imagine you've spent two hours working and sweating in the hot sun to fix a broken sprinkler in your yard. You finally get it under control and walk toward the house for a cold drink. You have only one thing on your mind: your thirst. If another family member meets you at the door to show you something, how attentive will you be? You're probably not going to give her much attention until your need for a cold refreshment is satisfied.

Similarly, your website visitors come to your site with a need in mind, and your first priority should be to meet that need. It may be to get information. It may be to research a product to buy. It may be to find a better price, free shipping, or some other special deal on a product they've already decided to buy. When you figure out what your site visitors' goals are, you can make sure your web pages deliver.

Meet each visitor's goal in the easiest, quickest way possible. If your site sells choir robes, help your visitor pick out the right styles, fabrics, sizes, and quantities as smoothly as possible. You can present lots of textual information to help him make the best choices, but be careful not to distract him with cute videos of choir performances, or clutter up your shopping cart page with Flash animations. His goal is to purchase choir robes. Your goal is to help him do it as directly and pleasantly as possible. Do this by leaving clues in your web content for your visitors. Tell them how to accomplish their goal. Remember that the trigger words for shopping and research differ: *buy, free,* and *sale* appeal to different visitors than *how-to, step-by-step instructions,* and *more information.*

A visitor who's using a smartphone, tablet, or other device to come to your site may have different goals than someone using a desktop computer. Consider tailoring the options you provide to the user's device type. Check out Book IV, Chapter 3 for help with designing for mobile versus desktop users.

The more you know about your target audience — who they are and what their goals are — the more effective your website can be.

Looking at current customer data

The best way to begin researching your target audience is to look at your existing customers. (We call them "customers" for ease of writing, but depending on your business model, you might call them subscribers, members, clients, or another term.) What do you know about the people already on your customer list? You probably won't succeed in gathering all this information in the following list, but here are a few types of demographics to look for. These facts are helpful in profiling your target audience:

✦ **Gender:** Are most of your customers male or female, or are they evenly split?

✦ **Age:** Maybe your customers fall into a single age group; for example, tweens, teenagers, college students, young adults, 30-somethings, and so on.

✦ **Location:** Do you know where your customers live? They may be concentrated within a given geographic area, in which case being included in local search engines and utilizing local ads might be part of your strategy. Geo-targeting is becoming an important factor to ranking. A study by Chitika found that as much as 43 percent of all Google search queries are meant for local businesses, products, or services (`http://www.reviewtrackers.com/43-percent-google-searches-local-business-listed-sites-find-you/`).

✦ **Marital status:** Do you know whether your customers tend to be single, married, or divorced? You can cater differently to married couples than you would to singles by using certain elements in site design and style.

✦ **Education:** What level of education do your customers have? This ties into the age category, too, but if your audience is made up of adults, knowing whether they never attended college or hold master's degrees definitely impacts how you can communicate with them.

✦ **Occupation:** Do you know what field your customers are in specifically? If your website offers an industry-specific product, it's obviously an important factor for your target audience. But even if you offer products to the general public, knowing customer occupations can help you with more targeted web marketing. If you know, for instance, that a lot of nurses like your product, one place you might want to develop links to your site (or run ads, and so on) could be on sites that are popular with nurses.

✦ **Beliefs:** What do you know about their religious, political, or philosophical beliefs? For instance, if your site collects signatures for various petitions, knowing how your typical petition signer leans politically helps you target the right audience for your site.

✦ **Lifestyle/situational:** What do you know about their lifestyles? You may find a trend among your customers to be single parents or married couples with children; apartment renters or homeowners; city dwellers, suburbanites, or farmers; boat owners or horse owners; or other. Whatever extra information like this you can gather gives you useful clues about your target audience.

✦ **Much more:** Customize this list with other types of pertinent information for your website marketing. You probably won't be able to get all the information you want, but having a wish list is a good start. Income level, ethnicity, and hobbies are all excellent things to know about your customers. Much of this information is easily obtained just by asking for it. The registration process on many sites often asks for these facts. If your registration process includes the capability to do so, turn it on and see what you learn.

Researching to find out more

In addition to examining the customer data you have, you can look at industry statistics. Find out what data is available out there. Do some homework online and track down information sources. If there's a trade association for your industry, see if it can provide statistics, member rosters, and other types of information. You might find news articles, court cases, studies, or who knows what else, but see what's out there that gives you more information about your typical customer.

Interviewing customers

Consider interviewing past and current members of your target audience to find out more about them. A typical method is to ask users to complete a form on your website. It might be a sign-up form at the beginning of your conversion process or a feedback form you pop up on the screen at the end of a process. Or you might prefer to interview the old-fashioned way and directly contact people by mail, phone, or email. A survey can work great, although you may need to offer some incentive to the user for filling it out (a discount, a coupon, or some other prize).

You can ask people to complete a survey online. Sites like QuestionPro (www.questionpro.com) make setting up an online survey very easy to do; you just need to plan the questions you want to ask (see Figure 1-1). The costs can be nominal, depending on what services you use.

When interviewing people, try to gather some personal demographic information (such as the items in the section "Looking at current customer data," earlier in this chapter) as well as some feedback about their experience on your website. It's a golden opportunity for valuable feedback from past customers. Here are some good things to learn during your interview:

✦ How they found your website

✦ What their impressions were of the site

✦ Whether they had any difficulty getting around your site, or whether they found it easy to use

✦ Whether they were pleased with the service or response they received (if applicable)

✦ What type of product or service they were looking for

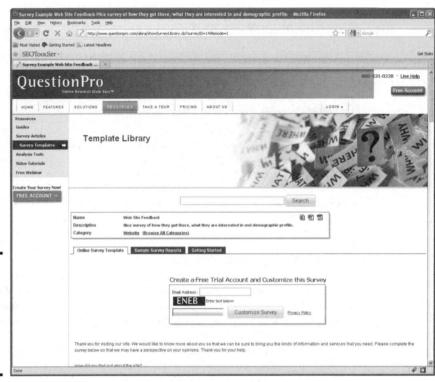

Figure 1-1:
Online surveys are easy to set up and can be inexpensive, too.

Include these two questions in your survey to get a technical picture of your customers' awareness:

✦ How often do you go online, and how long do you spend there?

✦ Which of this website's competitors' sites do you visit?

You can also use surveys in conjunction with the data your analytics tool gathers (for more on analytics tools, read on) to discover information about your customers' browsing habits. You can easily get the following data:

✦ The type of computer they use

✦ The ISP (Internet service provider) they use to access the Internet

✦ The type of Internet connection and device they use

✦ What Internet browser they prefer

The answers to these questions can give you an idea of how tech-savvy your customer base is. For instance, website if your users get to the Internet through an AOL interface and stay there throughout their web session, you know you're probably dealing with a less-technical user base.

If you have any professional associations in your industry (the SEO community has the Search Engine Marketing Professional Organization, or SEMPO, for example), check with them to see if they've done any demographic research, which is likely more cost-effective than conducting your own research. This is a particularly good idea for a new site that might not yet have a large user base to interview.

Using server logs and analytics

Your website's server logs contain valuable data about your visitor counts and their behavior. It's also a good idea to have *analytics* embedded in your web pages, which are program routines a website can use to track user behavior on the website. Talk to your IT department or webmaster and see what they can tell you about your web traffic and the user behavior on each page.

If you would like more analytics operating on your website or want to know all the choices out there, we cover web analytics in detail in Book VIII. We also recommend you check out the following resources:

✦ **Google Analytics** (www.google.com/analytics): This is free analytics software and resources from Google that we recommend you take advantage of.

✦ **Adobe Marketing Cloud** (www.adobe.com/solutions/digital-marketing.html): Adobe is one of the top vendors for analytics programs.

✦ **The Digital Analytics Association** (www.digitalanalytics association.org): The trade association for web analytics professionals is a good source for information.

Analytics tools can look at your recent website traffic and tell you where visitors came from. Further, demographics reports inside Google Analytics can give you statistics about your web audience such as percentages by gender, age, and so on. And reports in your free Google Search Console account (www.google.com/webmasters/tools/) can even tell you what search terms people have used in Google searches to find your website.

Analytics tools are extremely valuable for SEO. Knowing where your users come from can give you clues to their goals. For instance, if your site sells shoes and you find a lot of visitors coming from youth soccer sites, they're likely looking for children's soccer shoes and cleats. This information can help you style your site to help those visitors find exactly what they need.

Creating a Dynamic Tone

The way your content comes across to your potential customers is as important as the services and actions you have to offer visitors. When you write content for your website, your text should

✦ **Engage your target audience with an appropriate style and tone.** For example, this book uses a conversational tone that wouldn't be appropriate in a scholarly journal. A site targeting teens might rely more heavily on modern slang than a site targeting baby boomers. As a general rule, effective website copy should be *dynamic,* meaning always changing, purposeful, and energetic.

✦ **Lead visitors to the goal you have for each web page.** As we discuss in the section "Finding out customer goals," earlier in this chapter, each of your web pages should have a goal that matches the visitor's perceived goal, which may be to gather information, clarify a question, sign up for something, make a purchase, or do something else.

✦ **Meet the visitors' needs with relevant content as directly and quickly as possible.** The text on each page should immediately engage the readers' attention and interest and lead them to fulfill the goal. Proper design can help the content create conversions, but the content must be engaging on its own.

The tone of a written piece can make or break it. *Tone* refers to the writer's attitude toward the subject matter and toward the reader. Tone creates an emotional response in readers. The wrong tone can turn off an audience within the first sentence or two.

When people talk about the way a piece "comes across," they're talking about its tone. In speaking, people call it the "tone of voice," and it affects communication powerfully. Dogs, for example, can tell a lot by the sound of their master's voice: They might come running or hide their tails based solely on their master's tone. In written communication, an author's tone comes through in more subtle ways. Word choice, sentence length, punctuation, grammar, sentence structure — all these and more convey the tone.

Your writing tone should support your site goal and be appropriate for your target audience. For example, if you're a heavy-metal band promoter, you wouldn't want to greet your visitors with rainbows and ponies and a jaunty message like, "You've arrived! Mr. Ponypants wants you to have a super fun day!" The bouncy, enthusiastic tone is all wrong for the target audience and would probably have visitors heading straight for their Back button. There's nothing wrong with heavy metal or ponies, but typically fans of each aren't found in the same audience. Instead, you'd want the tone to come across as rebellious or rowdy, meeting your target audience in the same spirit they're showing. Only then would you be able to achieve your site's conversion goal, which is to engage people and interest them in becoming clients.

Look at your current website and ask yourself how you feel when you read it, but don't just stop there. Read it out loud to yourself or someone else to see if it flows nicely to the ear. This is usually an enlightening experience. Ask someone you know to read it with fresh eyes to give you this feedback. Ask her to tell you what attitude comes through the writing. How does it make her feel: happy, lighthearted, positive, hopeful, enlightened, or wanting more? Or does it make her feel uncomfortable, belittled, creepy, angry, annoyed, or frustrated?

Think about what response you would want your target audience to have when they read your website. The emotional response your tone evokes in your readers can make them want to stay or run away, so choose it carefully.

Choosing a Content Style

After you know who your target audience is, you can adjust your website to be appropriate for them. We talk in Book IV, Chapter 1 about tailoring your website design to your target audience. In Book V, we focus on tailoring the content style to your target audience.

Listen to your customers. The words they use to talk about your industry and your products and services could be very different from how you describe the same things. Jargon that may be commonplace in your offices won't necessarily be familiar to your potential clients. You want to incorporate their words into your website. Not only does this ensure that people understand what they're reading on your site, but it also adds keywords that people search for when they to try to find you.

You also must listen to the way in which your customers talk — not just the words they're using, but how they're using them. If your target audience is children, you don't want your website to read like a dry academic text, or you'll just bore them. If your target audience is medical researchers, your website can be written in a more academic style with longer words and sentences. You want to make visitors feel that they've come to the right place. You can do this when you support relevant content with a style and tone that feel natural and appropriate. So use a style that reaches your target audience and feels natural for the content.

Developing a Blog

A *blog* (originally short for "web log") on your website can provide a platform to let your voice be heard and interact with your target audience. Content marketers often consider their site's blog to be the axis of their community outreach. The blog connects people to your website and pulls them in with a regular supply of fresh, timely content that can be linked to and shared across various social media channels.

Blog posts can be published more quickly and easily than static web pages. Blog posts can cover anything related to your business or industry. If new legislation is passed, write a timely article explaining the new law's impact on your customers. If you attend an industry event, you can use your blog to share ten takeaways you learned that might help others. The possibilities are endless; the point is, blog software makes creating a post fairly painless.

Your tone in a blog post can usually be quite conversational and more personal than on your main website. On the Bruce Clay, Inc. blog, for example, writers often inject their own thoughts ("Seriously?") and reactions ("That's awesome!") into their posts. Have a conversation with your reader, as if he or she were sitting across from you asking questions about your subject. If you think about what your reader needs to know, you can break down any topic into useful information that's friendly and interesting.

The blog environment is perfect for showing personality and helping people feel like they can relate to your company or organization. Far more than static web pages can, a blog lets you "put a face" on your brand. It's not just the company owner or CEO who can create this kind of genuine human interaction for a brand. The best brands encourage trusted employees to use their own names and faces, representing the company but also becoming known as recognizable individuals in the industry. As an example, the writers' names and faces appear alongside the articles on the Bruce Clay, Inc. blog, as shown in Figure 1-2. When a brand empowers its blog writers (and social media writers) to be themselves as they work, the audience sees the people behind the logo. Suddenly, your brand becomes more human and more trustworthy. And people feel like they know you.

Most blog software is fairly simple to set up. We cover more of the benefits and how-tos of blogging in Chapter 7 of this minibook.

Figure 1-2:
Readers get to know blog writers if their names and faces are visible, such as in the Bruce Clay, Inc. Blog sidebar.

Using Personas to Define Your Audience

To help you evaluate your website from your target customer's perspective, you can create a fictional web persona based on all the customer data you accumulated.

A *persona* is like a role, and it includes how a person acts, talks, thinks, believes, and so on. The customer web persona you create is a profile that represents your target audience based on calculated averages of your customers' buying processes, goals, and demographics.

Companies use personas as user "archetypes." These *archetypes* are a compilation of general personality traits, behaviors, wants, and needs attributed to a type of target customer, which can be applied to a larger category of customer types. This helps guide their decisions concerning product launches, new features, customer interaction, and site design. It's easier to evaluate your website from a particular Jane Doe's or John Doe's perspective than just imagining a vague customer group. By understanding the goals and patterns of your audience, your company can create archetypes to help create services to satisfy a specific, highly targeted group.

Your goal is to create a persona that encompasses the most complete picture of your target audience. In fact, you may want to create several personas, depending on your website's various goals and how varied your customers are. Linda, the mother of two, has different motivations for being on your site than Debbie, the high-powered sales exec, or Fred, the college student. Creating more than one persona allows you to produce the maximum amount of appeal to your real-life customers. Creating effective personas helps you

+ Understand (and keep in mind) your target audience's goals and beliefs.

+ Develop the most effective voice (your brand's representation in its web content) for your company's website.

+ Determine what products/features are and are not accepted by your audience.

+ Get to know your audience on a more personal level.

+ Build a shared vocabulary between you and your audience to avoid confusion.

+ Enable your company to make informed decisions.

Creating personas

Creating personas helps you identify your customers' buying decision processes to allow you to maximize your conversion rate. Acquiring and analyzing the type of data listed in the sections, "Looking at current customer data" and "Interviewing customers," earlier in this chapter, can help you develop a more complete picture of who your audience really is, how they spend their time, and what they value as being important. After looking at this information, you can start to see patterns emerge. These patterns are the basis for the personas you create.

In looking for patterns, notice the similarities and differences between your customers through your research. Keep in mind that personas represent your audience's behavior patterns, not job descriptions, locations, or occupations. Although it's important to be aware of this information, these details should not be the basis of your archetypes. A properly defined persona gives you a well-rounded picture of your customers' attitudes, skills, and goals; it's not just a résumé that only offers a surface view.

After you have your data, group the information in a way that makes the most complete picture of a person. This includes assembling key traits (such as behavior patterns and similar buying processes) to try to form a cohesive "person." You should be able to use the collected information to form a small group of "people" that you feel represent your audience. Each persona (like your real audience) should be different, wanting and looking for different things.

When you are creating your personas, *do not* model them after someone you know. Creating personas based on familiar people in your life alters how you work with those personas. A persona should be a purely fictional character that you feel best represents some segment of your audience.

After you have your persona, don't keep her (or him) to yourself. Share it with the other members of your company to get their insights. They may have valuable opinions that help you narrow or fill out the personality of your customer. Use this time to fill in any blanks. Name your persona to differentiate her from the others: Don't just call her *Jane Doe.* Choose a name that you can believe in, not one that's just a stand-in.

Using personas

You now have your persona: You've named her, you know where she comes from, and you know what she's looking for. But you're not done. It is now time to put your persona into action. Use your persona to role-play the following:

✦ **Case studies:** Imagine your persona coming to your website for various purposes. Walk through the types of steps any given persona would go through.

✦ **User testing:** Using your persona, try out a feature of your website. You can also use your persona when running different keyword searches, starting at a search engine, and find out how quickly that persona can find relevant information on your site.

✦ **New feature evaluation:** Try out any new pages or features of your website from your various personas' points of view and see how easy they are to use.

✦ **Product decisions:** Coming from each of your personas' perspectives, think through how useful a new product would be. You may be able to identify whether the product meets a typical user's need as is, or needs some value-add to have better marketability.

✦ **Design decisions:** See your website design through a persona's eyes to determine whether the colors, placement, layout, bells and whistles, and other design elements make it easier or harder for visitors to achieve their goals.

✦ **Customer service:** Use your personas to find out how easy it is to get help when using your website. Remember, your web persona doesn't know that you have an exhaustive help system linked from the site map or that clicking a tiny link somewhere in the footer launches a live chat window. The persona only knows what it can easily see during the user-engagement process, so this is a valuable way to find weaknesses in your website.

Persona type scenarios

Here is an example of a persona and how you can put it to use. Alice is a competitive personality. Social status is very important to her, and she appreciates it in others. She tends to be impulsive and doesn't mind the impersonality of doing things online as long as she is able to get what she needs quickly and efficiently. She is looking for verifiable results and quantifiable bottom lines. Social interaction is not important to her. She is willing to pay more to get a little extra. She is unmarried and does not see marriage in her near future.

Alice is very Internet-savvy and uses the Internet for ten or more hours per day. She has multiple email accounts from various service providers and does all her shopping and banking online. Alice works for an Internet company and has just purchased a modest condo in the suburbs outside a large metropolitan city.

By analyzing the profile of Alice, you can better target her needs. Based on this, you can see that her primary concern is for quick, expert information. Alice is an impulsive buyer; the key to acquiring her conversion is to give her information in a quick, easy-to-read format while touching on her desire for prestige and quality. She considers convenience, as well as easy access, important. You can guess that when she first visits your site, her eye quickly scans the content for keywords. If you lose her interest for a moment, she's gone.

The profile also gives you an idea of Alice's experience level with your product. This information can help you decide how to target her. Here are two example scenarios:

✦ **Scenario A: Alice at a technology-related website:** If you're a technology company, you know that Alice has a certain experience level with your breed of product. You can assume that Alice likely understands the basic workings of your merchandise without you having to break things down step by step. Based on her Internet savvy, you know she likely has little or no problem navigating through your site, but if she doesn't find what she's looking for immediately, she will likely take off and visit one of your competitors' sites. For Alice, brand loyalty comes second to quick service.

✦ **Scenario B: Alice at a non-technical website:** If your product is home- or garden-related, you know that Alice needs a lot of detailed information to better understand how your product or service could benefit her. You need to make sure your information is presented upfront so that Alice doesn't wander away from your site. You know that Alice just purchased her first home. It's likely she is looking for easy ways to spruce it up. How can you gear your marketing campaign to address this goal? Perhaps there's a way to market your product as a "timesaver" so that she can focus on other things. Is Alice likely to have a pet? Maybe your product can do a better job of keeping her pet safe. By understanding Alice, it allows you to target her more efficiently.

Using Alice's persona helps you identify the language that most likely appeals to her and satisfies her motivations and needs. When you're testing out new features or campaign plans, make sure to keep Alice in mind. Ask yourself these types of questions for each of your personas:

✦ **Benefits:** Does this feature offer a clear benefit to this persona?

✦ **Level of explanation:** What, if anything, do I need to provide this persona with to help her understand this benefit?

✦ **Wording:** What kind of language should I use? Does this persona understand industry jargon, or do I need to define terms in the page content for her?

✦ **Style:** How can my writing style fit this persona and give her what she's looking for most naturally and directly?

✦ **Tone:** What tone would seem most natural to this persona? Would a tone that's friendly, professional, enthusiastic, subdued, energetic, calm, or other best suit her goals and influence her to stay on the site and move toward my web page's goal?

✦ **Clarity:** Does this persona realize the problem this feature is supposed to address? How much do I need to spell out?

Benefits of using personas

Personas provide many benefits. First, by speaking with your customers directly while gathering the data to create your personas, you have taken the first important steps to creating brand loyalty. Taking time to ask them about their needs and their interests shows them that you are interested in who they are, not just that you are out to make a sale. You want to learn about them, their goals, and what is important to them so that you can make your product better for them. Customers are likely to remember such a move and are more likely to do business with you in the future. By investing in them, you have made it easier for them to invest in you.

Secondly, your personas can alert you to problems you might not have known about. For example, while doing your research, you may discover that your customer base is larger and wider than you imagined. Knowing this shows you that there are two or more very different audiences that you must address. This could lead to creating a whole new product or set of instructions to fit more advanced users, while still catering to your more inexperienced ones. It could also lead to adding more pages to your website or incorporating more appropriate text on each page.

Drawbacks of using personas

Many companies resist the idea of personas because they don't understand how they work. They may design personas that are too vague to be efficient in helping with the direction of their company. If not done correctly, personas may cause companies to pigeonhole their audience, negating the basic purpose of creating personas.

Another drawback of using personas is that no matter how much research you do or how deeply you analyze it, you can never know for sure that your customers feel exactly the way that your fictional personas do. If you tailor your campaigns too closely to a persona, you risk alienating some of your other customers. This is why it's important to create multiple personas: You have a better chance at targeting the largest number of users.

At the end of the day, despite your best efforts at analyzing your customers' personalities, all you are left with is a best guess about what they're looking for and who they really are. Using web personas allows your guess to be an educated one and provides your company with an invaluable tool to help keep users' interests in mind.

Chapter 2: Establishing Content Depth and Page Length

In This Chapter

✔ **Writing for maximum readability**

✔ **Varying content to increase user interest and search engine ranking**

✔ **Optimizing images and video**

✔ **Enabling user-generated content**

✔ **Writing an effective call to action**

Search engines find out what your web pages are about by reading them. They read everything they can find on your site — the text on your pages, the text in your HTML code, the names of your files and directories, and the *anchor text* in all your links (which is the text someone clicks to follow the link). They also read the anchor text of any inbound links to your site from other people's websites to find out what those sites have written about you. Using all this textual information along with a few other factors like links and Engagement Objects (described in Book III, Chapter 3), search engines determine what your site is about, what search terms your web pages are relevant for, and how much of a trusted authority you are on your topics — and then rank you accordingly.

Because of this focus on written words, a successfully optimized website must have a lot of content. A home page with a single graphic and no textual content can't rank well with the search engines, no matter how cool it looks. On the other hand, a page with a lot of words but no cohesive theme also won't rank well, and for the same reason: The search engines can't figure out what the page is about. The right balance is to have enough content *and* to have it focused on a theme. Then the search engines can index your site and know exactly what it's about.

In this chapter, you find out how to develop content ideas, how to integrate various types of content for a blended approach, and all about the rules for optimizing images and video. You also discover the importance of formatting text so that it's readable and how you can allow user input to build a stronger site. Finally, you find out how to create user engagement by writing effective calls to action.

uilding Enough Content to Rank Well

How much content do you need in terms of words per page and pages per subject? Before we tell you our SEO best practices, we want to stress that the answer greatly depends on what is normal for your industry and keywords. When you research your competitors' sites that rank well for your keywords, some of the things you want to find out are how many indexed pages they have and how many words are on the pages that outrank yours. (Note that Book III explains how to do competitive research in detail.) Analyzing these figures among your competitors gives you an indication of what level of content is currently succeeding in the search engines for your keywords. This helps you know how many pages and words you need to play in their league.

Now for the best practices. Depending on the type of web page it is, the general length recommendation varies. First, for research pages (where a visitor's goal would be to get information), we recommend that you have a minimum of 500 words of text content per page. That's a general rule, based on our experience across multiple niches, for research-type pages. If all the top-ranking pages for your keywords have more than 1,000 words each, you may want to consider 1,100 words on your page in order to compete. (Remember that the search engines' algorithms include many factors, and amount of content is only one of them.) But if your research hasn't indicated that you need an unusually high number of words for your industry, 500 words gives the search engines enough content to work with and gives users a satisfying amount of information, as well. It's about one page of typed copy using a 12-point font and single line spacing. In fact, the page that you're reading right now has a little more than 500 words on it, so you can get an idea of what that amount of content looks like. Also, the number of words you need on a page has been steadily increasing over the years. When we first started recommending adding content back in 1997, we set our minimum at merely 75 words per page. Today, the number of words on top-ranked pages in competitive markets is actually closer to 1,000. This variance is why analyzing your competitors is so crucial.

Other types of web pages don't need quite as many words. Blog posts, for example, can range in length based on their purpose, but a best-practice guideline would be at least 200 words per post. E-commerce or shopping pages, which tend to have lots of product pictures, have a recommended minimum of 300 words of content. Just be sure that some of it, at least, is original. If all you include are manufacturer-provided descriptions, what will distinguish your product page from all the other retail sites selling the same product with the same text? Not only will your page not rank, but also you could suffer a search engine penalty for having "thin content," something that Google's Panda algorithm update is particularly sensitive to. See the "Google's Panda: Enforcer of quality content" sidebar for more information on avoiding a Panda penalty.

As a general rule, you need at least five pages to support each theme, meaning at least five supporting pages for every theme landing page on your website. (A *landing page* is your primary page of information on a particular topic or subtopic, so it's the page where you want users to land when they search for those keywords and click your listing.) Keep in mind that the required minimum number of pages varies depending on what your competitors have. The search engines want to return the most relevant results to a user's search query, and they want their users to be satisfied. It makes sense that the search engines would rank most highly the sites that seem to be the experts, or authorities, in the subject the user is interested in.

For instance, if you're trying to rank for the keyword phrase [Ford Mustang], you're going up against sites that have dozens of related pages about Ford Mustangs including facts, forums, customer reviews, multimedia, and so on. That kind of competitive environment would require you to have a lot more than five pages of content on Ford Mustangs to be considered as much of an authority as the other sites are. You'd need to really beef up your site to make it into the top 10 to 20 search results.

If you've already worked on categorizing your website into subject themes, as we explain in Book II, Chapter 4 and elsewhere, you should have a good idea of what "holes" you need to fill in your website. As you go through this chapter, keep in mind your list of landing-page topics and what you need in terms of new content either on those pages or on supporting pages. Figure 2-1 shows a sample website in the construction stage. As you can see, it looks like Topic A needs more pages.

Google's Panda: Enforcer of quality content

Google introduced the Panda update in February 2011 as a filter to remove low-quality content from search results. Since then, many sites have suffered a Panda "penalty," or a ranking demotion, and have been forced to remove or rewrite large portions of their web content. It is possible to recover from a Panda penalty, but not without first cleaning up the low-quality content that caught Panda's attention in the first place.

Panda goes after sites whose content is "thin" (in other words, generally lacking) or does not provide any unique value for users. Too much duplicated content can cause a Panda penalty. An example is a site with many copies of the same page, each with just one or two words changed (as through a find-and-replace operation). Pages with no content or no original content can also be penalized, such as product pages that show only the manufacturer-provided picture and description with no extra text. Panda also targets machine-generated, or "spun," content.

To prevent Panda from hurting your rankings, be sure that you have unique content on every page that gets indexed. For instance, does your in-site search function create category pages with unique URLs but nothing except links on the page? Add a short paragraph of text about the category above the linked results. The best you can do to stay clear of Panda is to give each page at least some unique and valuable content.

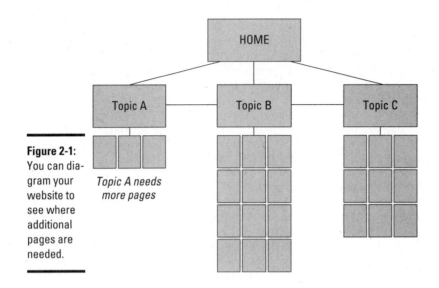

Figure 2-1:
You can dia-
gram your
website to
see where
additional
pages are
needed.

*Topic A needs
more pages*

Developing Ideas for Content

You may feel overwhelmed at the thought of writing pages and pages of content for your website that have at least 500 words each, but take heart. There are lots of ways to get ideas for content, and even some shortcuts for creating it.

In the following sections, we help get you started with four ways to find content ideas:

+ **Brainstorming:** You want to tap into your own creative juices first. Get input from your employees and coworkers, too.

+ **Looking at competitors:** Don't copy them, but you can definitely get ideas from them.

+ **Utilizing your offline materials:** Repurpose what you've already written.

+ **Listening to customers:** Find out what they want to know.

Brainstorming to get ideas

The best source of original content for your website may be yourself. You and the other people in your website business are authorities in one thing: your own business. You know the most about your website's goals, products, services, clientele, methods, expertise, history, personnel, and so forth. You might discover that a lot of that information would be interesting and useful for your site visitors. For example, you could ask the founder to write a three-paragraph history of how the company got started (or have someone interview him and write it up). Or you might write about your operations or your facilities like a tour guide, complete with pictures. When you write about your company, industry, and products, it's easy and natural to include lots of keywords, which benefits your SEO efforts. You probably have a wealth of interesting information about your company and its products and services that could be turned into website content.

Brainstorm other kinds of content ideas, too — at this stage, accept any idea that could be useful and engaging to your target audience. Make a list of all possible articles, stories, topics, tidbits, quotes, and so on. Don't stop at just what you're able to create. Consider things that you could write about as well as subjects you could find someone else to create content about. You're just idea-gathering now, so be as creative as you can.

Looking at competitors for content ideas

One of the best ways to fill content holes on your website is to do some competitive research to see what others in your industry are writing about. You want to see what they're doing right, where they're missing the mark, and what you could add to your site that they haven't even thought of yet.

Travel your competitors' websites like a user and discover what they have to offer. In particular, look at the landing page that is competing with your own for the same keyword. Notice its content, as well as the various supporting pages linked from it. (***Note:*** You also can do some serious analysis of these pages by using the procedures we describe in Book III, Chapter 2, but right now you're just trying to get some ideas for new content.)

When you go through your competitors' sites, you're essentially looking for anything they have that gives them an advantage — any special content that appeals only to a certain sector or that is attracting links. You are not using their site as a blueprint to copy. You can get ideas for original content that are just as good as, or better than, your competitors'.

What you're looking for depends on your content needs. If you're looking to beef up the number of pages on your site, look at what your competitors offer and how they're marketing themselves, and then find ways to differentiate yourself. You want to make yourself equal to the competition before you can set yourself apart. Make sure you match what they offer in your own way, and then provide content that explains why you're unique, more trustworthy, and overall just better-suited to fit a visitor's needs.

One thing you can notice is how they structure their information compared to how your site does it. For instance, if the two websites sell competing products, compare how they're each presented. Your page might offer a description in paragraph form only, whereas your competitor may include a complete bullet list of features with links to view a schematic diagram, product dimensions, installation instructions, and consumer reviews. In that situation, you know you have some writing to do to boost your content about that product.

You also could get ideas for how to present similar information more effectively than the competition. For example, say your product is cowboy boots. A brief mention on a competitor's site about the importance of breaking in your boots before the beginning of rodeo season could spark the idea to write a whole article about this topic on your site. Or your competitor's site might have a chart showing boot sizes compared to normal shoe sizes. That's useful information that could help the consumer make a purchase decision, so you want to add this feature to your website — but do it better. You might add a third column with the corresponding sock sizes. Or make it a neat, interactive tool rather than a static chart. Or enhance it with illustrations of different-sized feet . . . you get the idea. Develop a page debating the eternal question: to tuck your jeans into your boots or not to tuck? Have customers respond and send in pictures with their explanations.

By looking at competitors, you can identify holes in your own site as well as ideas to set your site apart. You want to be continuously looking for creative ways to make yourself more interesting and more useful to your visitors. As much content as there is on the web, a lot of it can be improved. It can be written to be clearer, updated to be more relevant, or tweaked to allow users to interact with it in a fresh way. Be on the lookout for these types of opportunities to make your site stand out.

Utilizing your offline materials

One shortcut to creating website content is to pull material from what you already have. Review everything your business has ever written to see if it can be repurposed for your website or blog. Brochures, flyers, catalogs, articles, manuals, tutorials, online help resources, and even customer correspondence may contain volumes of helpful content. Do you have a user manual or instructions to go with one of your products? Consider replicating it online in HTML. The same goes for marketing materials, text on packaging, or other printed collateral. The writing may need to be updated, but starting with content makes your job much easier than starting from a blank page.

Frequently asked questions (FAQs) can be a popular website feature, and they're very useful in helping site visitors find the information they need. If your company maintains a support staff for customer assistance, that staff may already have an FAQ list started. If you work for a company, ask around to find out what your various departments already have documented that could be polished a bit and used on the web.

Listening to customers

You want your website to serve your customers and target prospects, so try to address what they'd like to know. Talk to your customers. Ask some questions. Also talk to your support people to find out what customers ask about frequently. You may find great ideas for articles to add to the website (and help out your support department as a bonus). If you have a site search, you can mine those queries as well. What is of interest to one customer might be valuable to more customers, particularly if variations on the same keyword phrase keep popping up.

You might also check blogs and social media sites for your industry, your area, or your target demographic (whichever of those apply) to see what people are talking about related to your keywords. Search for your keyword phrases, your company name, and other pertinent search terms. You can get some excellent ideas for website content by listening to what's being talked about. Just make sure that the ideas relate closely to your web business so you don't dilute your themes with unrelated content.

Using Various Types of Content

Search engines may be deaf, dumb, and blind, but users aren't, and search engines understand that. So far in this chapter, we've focused on writing text that not only gives the readers content to consume but gives the search engines additional reasons to rank your site. In this section, we want to turn to the other side of the equation: creating content to engage your users.

Pictures, movie clips, sounds — all these things help hold a visitor's interest on your website. Including other types of content besides text is a good idea for many reasons. The advent of blended search made these files important for search engine rankings, as well. (*Blended search* is the search engines' method of combining different types of listings in a search results page, such as web pages, news articles, pictures, videos, blog posts, and so on.) Google and the other search engines consider these *Engagement Objects* (images, video, audio, interactive technology, and so on) among the factors that help a web page rank well. If two pages are otherwise equal, it makes sense that the search engine would prefer to send its users to a page that has pictures, videos, or other types of content to make the experience more engaging.

Optimizing Images

When you include pictures, video, or other non-text elements in your website, you need to describe them in the surrounding text. This is the key to optimizing your multimedia elements so that search engines know what they're about. Search engine spiders can't watch a video or see a picture accurately yet, though they are working on it. So you must explain the image, video, or any other non-text element using words.

For images (including JPEG, GIF, and other types of picture files), you have several places where you can put descriptive text that the search engines can read. You can refer to what the image is about in the following locations:

✦ **Text surrounding the element:** Include descriptive text either above, below, or next to the picture, video, or other non-text element. A caption or a lead-in sentence that explains what the image shows works well. This gives search engine spiders text they can read and index, but it also helps communicate your intended meaning to users.

✦ **Filename:** The filenames of your image, video, and other types of multi-media files should contain actual words.

✦ `Alt` **attribute:** You can also put brief descriptive text into the `Alt` attribute attached to any image. For example, `alt="1968 Ford Mustang California Special Gas Cap"`. Find out more about `Alt` attributes in the Images section of Book I, Chapter 4.

Naming images

Because both people and search engines are going to read your filenames, make sure to use good, descriptive words when naming your image, video, and other types of multimedia files. Here is another opportunity to provide readable content (with keywords, if appropriate) to the spiders. Instead of naming your image `A1234.jpg`, call that photo of a skier falling on his face `skier-faceplant.jpg` so that the search engines know what it is, too.

To separate words, don't use a space or an underscore (underscores are seen as an alpha character, rather than as punctuation). Instead, use a hyphen or a period to separate words in your filenames. But try not to over-use them either — just because you can have many dashes in a URL doesn't mean that you should.

Also, keep filenames brief. Remember that long filenames cause URLs to get longer, too (such as if one of your images gets returned in an image search). Because people generally avoid clicking long URLs, keep your names to a reasonable length. Six words in a filename would generally be too much. Keep it simple: A picture of a Ford Mustang with a dented fender shouldn't be called `ford-mustang-with-a-dented-fender.jpg`, just call it `dented-ford-mustang.jpg` or `mustang-dented-fender.jpg`. You'll have on-page text and `Alt` attributes to explain to the engines what the content of the image is.

Alt attributes and the law

You want to help all types of visitors access your website, including people with disabilities. It turns out that there's an easy thing you can do to make your site easier to use for people with vision impairments, and that is to use Alt attributes on your images. Not only does that improve your site for visitors, but the law also requires you to use them.

The Americans with Disabilities Act (ADA) states that persons with disabilities may not be denied equal access to goods and services. In 2006, a court ruled that this applied to websites as well as physical retail establishments. The case, which was between the National Federation of the Blind and Target.com,

resulted in a ruling that websites must accommodate vision-impaired users by putting Alt attributes on every image. Vision-impaired people navigate the web using screen-reading software. The software vocalizes the text and describes the graphics by reading their Alt attributes. If an image doesn't have an Alt attribute, the screen reader actually says the image's URL out loud! This doesn't help anyone, and not getting a description of the image is definitely user-unfriendly!

Put Alt attributes in your image tags to communicate what the image is about and include your keywords. It's a win-win for you, the search engines, and your users.

Handling image size

Size matters, especially when it comes to images. In this section, you learn guidelines and some recommendations for resizing your images and their Alt attributes.

Alt attribute length

We've already said that you want to write descriptive text around images and in their Alt attributes. But how much text you use depends on the size of your image. For example, if you have a 50-x-70-pixel photo of a writer's face next to an article, it's enough to just put the person's name in the caption. You could include a longer description of her credentials in the byline copy, but you wouldn't need an entire paragraph of text captioning a small image like this. On the other hand, larger pictures should have longer text descriptions. If the image is important enough to take up a lot of screen space, it's important enough to tell the search engines about. Explain the picture with at least a sentence of text.

Image dimensions

If pictures help engage your users, big pictures can satisfy them even more. If you're offering very large images, you might want to put them on a separate page so that only users who really want to see the full-size view have to wait for them to display. However, you don't want the search engines to miss the fact that that picture is part of your page's content, and not some separate, unrelated page. To keep it related, you can show a *thumbnail* or small version of the image on your original page, with a text description, Alt attributes, and the works. Then if a user clicks to view the full-size image in a separate window, consider including a text description there, too — but definitely give it an Alt attribute and filename that describes what's in the image.

When writing Alt attributes for images, make the length proportionate to the image's size on-screen. Create a brief Alt attribute for a small image, and longer ones for large images. As a general guideline, we believe the Alt content should not exceed 12 words.

Image size for mobile

Someone visiting your website on a smartphone doesn't want to wait long for your page to display. One second is about all the time you have to show at least the top of the page before a user decides your site is not mobile friendly.

Slow site speed can be caused by many things, but fat image files are a common culprit. You want to make an image's dimensions shrink so that it fits on a smartphone screen, and webmasters have several tricks up their sleeves to do that (by including responsive design; using JavaScript, which is a coding language; and specifying height and width attributes in the image tag). However, simply squeezing a big image to fit a smaller layout can cause your page to load too slowly, which may be compounded by an image-heavy web page. That's because changing the viewing size doesn't reduce the size of the image file that's being sent, sometimes across low-bandwidth connections, to a person's mobile device. So not only do you want your images to look good, you also them to download quickly.

Image optimization for mobile should involve reducing the amount of data by reducing the picture's file size, not just its dimensions. This can be done with various web design techniques including *image compression* (a method of reducing file size by simplifying the image data), JavaScript, and/or the HTML5 <picture> element. How to implement these technically goes beyond the scope of this book, but at least you have a starting place for a conversation with your web designer. You learn more ways to improve mobile optimization in Book IV, Chapter 3.

Mixing in Video

Video enriches your website by offering media content that search engines and users are increasingly looking for. For quick reference, here's a summary of the best practices for mixing in video, which we explain in the following sections:

+ **Placement:** Embed the video on the page it relates to, rather than in a separate window.

+ **Descriptive text:** Include an explanation of the video in the surrounding text on the page where it is played.

+ **Saving:** Save the video file inside the current silo directory, rather than in a central video directory. (*Note:* You can find out more about silos in Book VI.)

+ **Play:** Use the HTML5 player to ensure that your video is compatible with different browsers and devices. Don't set up your page so that a video starts playing automatically. Let users start it themselves.

+ **Size:** Choose a viewing size that fits your audience, and make sure that your video player can adjust the size automatically as a viewer's screen size shrinks. There are various ways to handle this. For more on this type of responsive design, see Book IV, Chapter 3.

+ **Quality:** Render your video in a file size that fits your audience. Tech-savvy or urban audiences generally have faster connections and can handle larger file sizes. However, files need to be smaller for smooth mobile viewing. Find the balance between good quality and fast download speed.

+ **Length:** Shorter videos obviously are easier to download and more convenient to watch. Although the content largely determines the length, short is better than long on the web. Plan to make videos no more than two or three minutes long, if possible. Five minutes is an extremely long time on the web (though certain types of videos are expected to run longer, such as live event footage or recorded video conferences).

+ **Posting:** In addition to posting your video on your site, to help your video get noticed, you can upload it to a video-sharing site like YouTube (`www.youtube.com`), Vimeo (`www.vimeo.com`) or Metacafe (`www.metacafe.com`), and link it back to your website. Or you can upload your video directly to one of these sites and use the provided embed code to show it on your site. Both methods have pros and cons, so read on.

✦ **Schema markup:** Wherever a video is embedded on your site, adding a bit of *Schema markup* in your HTML code can help search engine spiders recognize and index your video more fully. We cover Schema markup more in Book IV, Chapter 4.

✦ **XML Sitemap:** Tell the search engines where to find your video with a *video XML Sitemap* (a text file listing the URLs of all videos on your site). See Book VI, Chapter 2 for more on creating and submitting XML Sitemaps.

Placing videos where they count most

To include a video on your website, the SEO best practice is to embed it within the applicable page. Don't show it in a pop-up window where it's isolated from the text describing it, because you want the spiders to see the video as part of the current page. Many sites move videos into separate windows with no title or text, but this is a lost opportunity from an SEO perspective. Unless you describe the video in words the spiders can read, more than likely it won't be ranked with your content because the search engine cannot tell what it's about. Figure 2-2 shows an embedded video with related text near it on the page.

If you're worried that your page may load too slowly if you embed the video, here's one possible solution. The video can be collapsed when the web page initially loads, displaying only a link to it. Then if the user clicks the link to watch the video, it can expand and play within the page. This technique uses an expandable `Div` tag that works like a toggle switch, expanding or collapsing the video at the user's choice. You may find that this improves the usability of your page because the user stays in control.

Saving videos, plus a word about formats

If you upload videos you produce and save them on your own website, the search engine optimization benefit is that click-throughs go to your site directly, not to a third-party hosting site. You can do a big push to get it noticed, such as promoting your new video with a press release, a blog post, social media links, word of mouth, and so on. With any luck, your video will get talked about and linked to. Search engines following these links will understand that your site gets the credit for originating and owning that video; then optionally, you can later upload the whole video or an excerpt to a sharing site like YouTube, as well. That's one strategy to maximize the SEO value of a video.

If you upload a video to your site, where you save the video file matters. For example, if your video shows the inside of a Ford Mustang and plays from your Ford Mustang page, save the file inside a directory in your Ford Mustang silo rather than, say, in a video directory within the site. That way, the search engines know for certain that it's a video about Ford Mustangs.

Figure 2-2:
Embed a
video on a
page that
has closely
related text.

For videos hosted on your own site, you'll want to use HTML5 as the player.
The previous standard was to save videos in SWF format for viewing in the
Adobe Flash Player. However, Flash content can be hidden from spiders and
does not work on mobile (for instance, Apple does not support Flash on iOS
devices such as the iPad or iPhone). HTML5 is compatible with most browsers, plays well on mobile screens, and enables native video embedding. As
for the video file format, there are many acceptable types; MPEG, MP4, and
WebM are just a few standard ones. Your choice should be based on your
needs.

Another best practice for SEO is to use Schema.org markup to label various
pieces of information about your video on the page where it's embedded.
This helps search engine spiders better understand that it's a video with
various properties (such as length, title, and so on) so that it can be indexed.

Finally, you want to create a *video XML Sitemap* (a text file listing the URLs
of all videos on your site) and submit it to Google Search Console and Bing
Webmaster Tools. This step helps ensure that the spiders find and index
your video content quickly.

Hosting your own videos may not be the best course of action, especially
if your site has limited server resources (such as shared hosting, which
many WordPress and smaller sites have). A limited amount of *bandwidth*
(amount of Internet space available for data to flow) can cause a problem
because videos can be very large files. If you lack the server resources to
allow many people to download videos from your site, playback may be very

slow or, worse, your site could crash. In addition, you need a little technical know-how to make your hosted video viewable on any screen size and easily downloadable for smooth play. For these reasons, you might prefer uploading videos to a third-party video-hosting site and simply pasting the provided embed code on your site where you want the videos to be viewed. Read on for more about posting videos.

Sizing videos appropriately for your audience

When you're deciding how big to make your video, consider your audience first. If they tend to have the latest technology and fast Internet connections, you can upload large-display, good-quality videos without too much concern for their big file size. But if your audience is varied, or not technically savvy, you may want to stick with smaller files that can easily stream over lower Internet connection speeds.

Video dimensions should equate to either a 4:3 aspect ratio (standard view) or 16:9 aspect ratio (widescreen), but size varies. Save your video at the largest viewing size needed (such as for a desktop user) and then enable it to reduce in size as the user's window or screen size shrinks. The embed code provided by a video-hosting site accounts for that automatically, or your webmaster can include some JavaScript that makes a video resize responsively.

Choosing the best video quality

Quality in this sense refers to the resolution of the video image (how clear it looks compared to the original) and how clean the audio sounds. The higher the quality, the bigger the file. You might be tempted to put a full-size, full-quality video on your site because it looks and sounds great on your desktop, but after it's online, it may be too large for anyone to download. Weigh what's best for your audience. Studies have been done on video quality, and if you have to pick between decent picture quality and decent audio quality, go with audio quality. Most people are willing to put up with reduced picture quality as long as they can hear the audio clearly, but not the other way around. That said, you can probably keep the audio quality at 128 Kbps (kilobytes per second) maximum and meet the dual objectives of good audio quality and good download speed.

Choosing the right video length

Shorter videos are easier to watch than longer ones, download faster, and don't get "stuck" in the middle as often. People also prefer to watch a video that they know will take only a few minutes of their time. They may be reluctant to start a video that requires a lot of time to watch. A software company began creating Flash tutorials that were 15 to 20 minutes long for users to view online (modeling them after the step-by-step approach that had always worked in live trainings). The tutorials seemed like a big success until some-one examined the server logs. Of all the people who started watching the tutorials, only 3 percent watched them all the way through, with 90 percent exiting within the first two minutes. Needless to say, the next tutorials were two minutes or under in length.

Posting your videos to increase traffic

Videos can attract users who wouldn't otherwise find your website or hear about your brand. One strategy for attracting a bigger video audience is to upload your videos to a video-sharing site such as YouTube (www. youtube.com), Vimeo (www.vimeo.com), or Metacafe (www.metacafe. com). YouTube is owned by Google and also happens to be the second larg-est search engine, though every one of these hosting sites provides free hosting that's easy to use.

You may want to upload a video only on your site, at first, and give it time to gain some links that can be spidered. Then, after you've established ownership of the video, perhaps after a couple of months, you can post it on a video-sharing site to expose it to a bigger audience.

When you post a video on YouTube or another site, follow these best practices to optimize the video for searchers:

✦ **Upload to your channel:** Uploading self-produced videos to your *brand channel* (a customizable page with links to all the videos you've uploaded that interested viewers can subscribe to) lets viewers easily browse your other videos and also reinforces your branding because your company name appears prominently. Figure 2-3 shows an example of a brand channel on YouTube.

✦ **Link to your site:** Entice people watching your video to visit your site by linking to your site from the video description. Also show your logo, a call to action, and your web address somewhere in the actual video.

✦ **Use keywords appropriately:** Video is another form of content, so before you post it, do some keyword research and pick the keyword phrase that best represents the video subject matter. Then include the keyword in the video title, tags, and description.

✦ **Upload a transcript:** Search engines can read text, so upload your written script or a transcript with your video. If you don't have one, in YouTube you can use the *closed captioning* feature to automatically generate text captions.

Figure 2-3:
Increase
brand vis-
ibility and
your video's
viewing
audience
by upload-
ing your
videos to
your brand's
YouTube (or
other video-
hosting site)
channel.

Making the Text Readable

Your text content needs to be plentiful and focused for the search engines, but it also needs to be readable for your users. Here are some tips for improving your text's readability:

✦ **Use a spelling checker.** When your writing includes spelling errors and typos, what does that say about your company? It may communicate that you are unprofessional, that you have no quality control, or that you simply don't care — none of which are good impressions to give your site visitors. Spelling checkers don't catch everything, but they can point out things that aren't even words. Then have someone proofread to catch any remaining problems.

✦ **Break your writing into smaller chunks.** When we recommend a minimum of 500 words per page, we aren't suggesting you put it all into one gargantuan paragraph. It's difficult to read large blocks of text on a screen. Short paragraphs of three to five lines are easier to track with your eyes. It's also easier to hold your readers' interest and keep them moving to the next thought when you separate a piece into short sections. You can use bullets, a Q&A (question and answer) format, lists, subheadings, and other techniques to make your text more digestible.

✦ **Use bullets.** Bullet points make for easy reading. They visually parse the text into small, digestible bits. Readers can see at a glance how many there are, what they relate to, and how long it's going to take to read through the list. You don't have to stick to the standard black-dot style bullet, either, but keep in mind that some bullets created in text (rather than using a graphic bullet) also signal to search engines that these are bullet points, which helps them decipher what your content is about.

For a good example of how this works, look at a news story on CNN's website (www.cnn.com), which summarizes the main "story highlights" of the article in bullet points next to the full text, making the article easy to skim while offering more information to an interested reader.

✦ **Choose the most appropriate reading level for your audience.** One of the metrics you should look for when you're analyzing your competitors' pages is the average reading level of those reading the pages. One scale known as the Flesch-Kincaid readability score measures the corresponding U.S. grade level of written text. So, for instance, a Flesch-Kincaid score of 8.0 would indicate an eighth-grade reading level; a score of 16.2 would mean it's appropriate for people with four years of college education. The Single Page Analyzer in the free Lite version of the SEOToolSet returns this number, as does Microsoft Word. To turn on the advanced page statistics in Word, choose File⇨Options⇨Proofing, and then in the dialog box that appears, select the Show readability statistics check box. (See Figure 2-4.) Run a spelling check on your document. After the check is complete, a dialog box pops up, containing information related to the general ease of readability of your text.

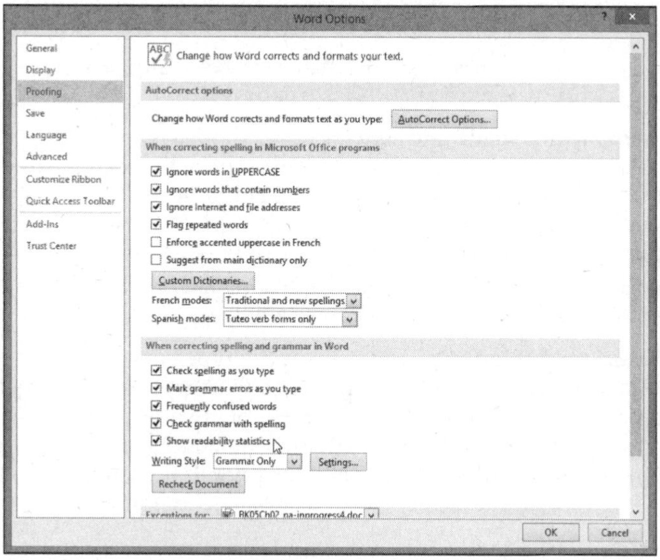

Figure 2-4:
Turning on readability statistics in Word gives you the grade level and Flesch-Kincaid score of the document's text.

To come up with a number, both the Single Page Analyzer and Word analyze the average number of syllables per word, words per sentence, and sentences per paragraph. For the Flesch-Kincaid grade-level score, a higher number is more difficult to read; lower is easier. The Flesch grade level corresponds roughly to the American school system. A grade of 9.6 would be about the reading level of a high school freshman midway through the year. If you find your pages scoring way too high or too low for what's natural in your market, you should adjust your word length and sentence structure.

✦ **Name your nouns.** Don't write about "*the thing*"; call your product or keyword by name every time you mention it. Don't overuse pronouns like "it," "them," "that," or "those"; instead, spell out what you're talking about. When you clarify what you're writing about each time, you prevent reader confusion and give the search engines more uses of your keywords.

✦ **Be careful with acronyms.** Jargon alphabet soup — those three-letter acronyms that separate "us" from "them" and identify who's in the know from outsiders who haven't got a clue what everyone is talking about — doesn't belong on your website without being clearly defined. Not only do you risk ostracizing site visitors who don't know your acronyms, but also you risk keeping search engine spiders in the dark. Instead, use the good journalistic practice of writing out the phrase the first time it occurs on every page, followed by the acronym in parentheses. You might also consider spelling out your phrase in every usage if it improves your keyword density. If you must use acronyms exclusively, you can use the Acronym HTML tag — this helps users by allowing them to hover the mouse over the word to get the full definition. There's no SEO value in the tag because search engines ignore the tag as it can be spammed.

```
Example: <acronym title="Search Engine
    Optimization">SEO</acronym>
```

✦ **Allow white space and margins.** Empty space around text makes it easier to read, so don't think of white space as wasted screen real estate. Use margins and spacing to avoid a cluttered look. Edge-to-edge text looks like too much to read, so people won't try. Also consider indenting paragraphs by wrapping the left or right edge of your text nicely alongside a graphic. This can add visual appeal as well as reduce the width of your paragraph and increase readability.

✦ **Select readable fonts.** You can specify typefaces that are *serif fonts* (fonts that include little strokes at the ends of characters, such as the feet on a capital A) or *sans-serif fonts* (fonts without serifs, such as Arial, Verdana, and others) for your body text. Although users may have their own opinions on this, sans-serif fonts are considered the king of web text because serifs often make small letters less readable on a computer monitor or smartphone screen. And to keep from cluttering your HTML with inline font tags, be sure to specify what typefaces to use on headings, captions, body text, and so on, using an external CSS (Cascading Style Sheet). (For more on that, see Book IV, Chapter 1.)

It's important to note that even if you specify what typeface you want to use, the font cannot show up if users do not have that typeface installed on their computers. For this reason, specify multiple fonts or end your font command with a generic command, such as `serif`. This way, if a user's browser can't find the exact font you wanted, it can at least substitute a similar font.

✦ **Choose backgrounds and colors for readability.** The most readable text is black type on a white background. You can vary from that, but do so carefully. For your main body copy, do use dark fonts against a light background for maximum contrast and readability. Using *reverse copy* (light text against a dark background) should never be applied to an entire website. Not only is it harder to read, but also you risk letting your users print out blank pages when they choose File⇨Print (white text tends to not show up on white paper).

Also be careful of having too little contrast between your background and type colors. You've probably watched presentations where the slides were illegible because they had peach text on a beige background, or some similar combination. It's the same principle on your website. Make the words stand out. In addition to usability, adequate contrast between text and background is an extremely important point for search engines: Text that is too similar in color to the background could be considered hidden text and marked as spam.

✦ **Keep mobile users in mind.** Make sure that your website text is legible on mobile screens of all sizes and shapes. In general, that means using large, clean, sans-serif fonts, high-contrast colors (such as black text on a white background), and properly implemented images. Good readability in a mobile environment depends on more than content, however. For more on mobile-friendly web design, see Book IV, Chapter 3.

✦ **Plan for printing.** People may want to print your web pages, so be sure to create a print style sheet that defines how all your site fonts should translate for printing and how to lay out the content on an 8½-x-11-inch piece of paper. You should also specify the images to print, removing unnecessary ones in order to save your users time, ink, and paper. Neglecting to create a print style sheet can cause printing nightmares, and people can waste tree-loads of paper in the process.

Allowing User Input

Letting users contribute content directly to your website meets at least two goals simultaneously: It adds more content to your site and stimulates higher user engagement. Although you might feel nervous about letting other people write text that appears on your website, the advantages make it definitely worth considering. And you can still hold the reins to make sure your site contains accurate and constructive information. The primary SEO motivation for allowing user-generated content (UGC) is to add unique content to pages that would otherwise contain only duplicate content.

One of the best applications of user-generated content is reviews. Letting users write their own reviews of your products and services is a fantastic way to get content on your site. Users write about your products in their own words, which become natural-language search terms. Including user reviews might help you capture *long-tail queries* (search queries for long, specific phrases that indicate a serious, conversion-ready searcher) if you make sure those pages can be crawled by the search engines.

It's great for business, too. Facilitating online user reviews of your products or services can help you sell them. Consumers also trust user-generated content more than traditional sales copy. After reading reviews, people are often more likely to purchase because they have more faith in what they will receive. Educated consumers also make better customers, with less potential for returned merchandise.

Website owners often fear that people will write bad things about their product or service and negatively impact their brand. However, statistics show that the majority of user reviews are positive. For instance, the online-reviews website Yelp (www.yelp.com) says that 85 percent of reviews are positive. Similarly, the site Bazaarvoice (www.bazaarvoice.com) claims that 80 percent of all reviewers award four or five stars.

That being said, you can always expect a few people (or spambots) to write defaming, nonsensical, or offensive comments that don't belong on your website. To take care of unwanted reviews, you should

+ Monitor your user-generated content, either automatically using a service, or manually, so that you can remove the offending entries.

+ Consider tracking the IP addresses of reviewers so that you can identify someone who leaves a truly malicious comment.

+ Consider requiring a *CAPTCHA* (an interface that asks the user to type the characters displayed) or an account login for anyone who submits a review. The drawback is that your security gate may dissuade people from participating, but it would give you assurance that you're dealing with real people only. (*Note:* Too much UGC spam on a page can actually cause search engines to consider the page low quality and demote it in the search engine results pages [SERPs], so this is worth policing.)

✦ Allow users to comment on other people's reviews (with a link such as "Was This Review Helpful?"). Then the reviews can become self-regulating to a certain extent.

Negative feedback can often help a business, so don't shun it entirely. Negative reviews help people understand the product's limitations and further build trust. ("It didn't work for them, but their situation is different than mine.") Online reviews can also alert you to cases where your products or services truly did fall short so that you can address the problems. When a disgruntled user has a legitimate issue that you read about in the user-generated content, you can immediately contact the person to resolve it. After the person's issue is resolved, she might be so happy that you end up getting another, completely positive review of your customer service.

Another interesting thing to note about negative reviews is that they can actually help build trust. Many people say that they don't trust a product that doesn't have anything but positive reviews. Negative reviews actually validate the user's sense that nobody's perfect.

Besides reviews, you might consider adding these other types of user-generated content to your website:

✦ **User forums online:** These discussions can become free-for-alls, but they also allow significant user interaction and provide you with excellent feedback from your user group. You can decide whether to participate with "official" responses or not. Depending on how they're handled, responses from a company representative can either hurt or help the brand.

✦ **Comments:** News sites do this all the time. After an article, they put a Comments link and let people respond. The number of comments can even make the article appear more popular, relevant, or interesting.

✦ **Social media timelines:** You can display a live social media feed right on your website, in a sidebar or elsewhere, to show what people are saying related to your brand or subject. By adding just a bit of HTML code, you can embed live-streamed views of Twitter tweets or Instagram posts that mention your brand or a particular *hashtag* (a word or phrase beginning with a pound sign (#) that people include in a post to identify the topic). This content would not be spiderable but could nevertheless provide social proof to site visitors that your brand is worth talking about, and it could also build engagement with your social media community.

Creating User Engagement

A lot of what you learned in high school English class can help with your website writing and make it more engaging to read:

✦ **Choose strong verbs that convey action.** Avoid overusing the forms of "to be" verbs (*is, are, was, were,* and so on) because they stick a sentence together with all the excitement of white glue. Instead, generate interest with active verbs like *drive, soar, infuse, create,* and so on.

Also avoid using the passive voice, which dulls down your writing and makes it sound like a dry treatise or a political science textbook. English teachers suggest asking, "Who kicked whom?" in order to find out what a passive-voice sentence really means. Here's a passive sentence that lacks excitement: "Up to 20 pairs of skis can be stored in the MegaRack ski hauler." You can rewrite it by identifying a subject ("you") and making it active: "You can pack skis for a 20-person ski party into this trunk-top MegaRack ski hauler."

✦ **Show, don't tell.** Your website needs to persuade people, interest them, and draw them in with good content. For this reason, you should write as if they're there, not just reading about an event after the fact. Newspaper reporting tells what happened: "On Friday night, Racer Rick won the Indy 100 driving a bumper car." But to engage your readers, you want to show them what you're talking about. Describe the scene when the race began; what Racer Rick looked like; how his bumper car looked compared to all the Formula Ones on the track; what people said before, during, and after the race; the blow-by-blow of the race action; and the spectacular finish. Don't just tell people about your product or service; make them feel it.

✦ **Use sensory words.** Your text needs to make readers feel, taste, touch, hear, and see what you're talking about — to experience it themselves — rather than to just read a report about it. You achieve this using sensory words and good descriptors. For instance, "The XJ-7 ski pole improves your downhill speed" tells the facts. But "Wrap your fingers around the XJ-7's form-fitted grips and hold on tight as you zip around curves, adjusting your descent with light touches of your diamond-tipped poles to the snow-packed ground racing beneath you" makes your readers experience it. Not to mention that you can integrate your keywords more easily into a descriptive paragraph.

✦ **Be specific and give details.** As we suggest in the section "Making the Text Readable," earlier in this chapter, your writing needs to call things by name. Don't be vague — it leads to ambiguity and confusion for your readers. Because *you* know exactly what you mean, you may generalize or put together phrases that don't make sense to someone unfamiliar with your business. To help you improve your text, you might ask someone who's a complete novice to review your copy and point out anything that's unclear.

✦ Also, try not to use pronouns like *it* and *that* or generic words like *stuff* or *thing* when you can use words packed with meaning instead. As a bonus, restating the proper name of the thing you're talking about helps the search engine understand better that your page is about that thing, whether it be ski poles, cowboy boots, or search engine optimization.

Keep in mind that your website is never "done." Good writing, if you remember your high school or college composition courses, involves continuous revision. When you think you are finished and that the writing is good enough, you should put the pages away for a few days, do something else, and then come back and look at them again. More than likely you can find a few more things that can be made better. And as always, try to have fresh eyes look at what you've written. Someone who has not seen it before can usually see shortcomings that you could not see because of your familiarity with the subject.

Writing a Call to Action

You know the goal that you have for your web page visitors — to make a purchase, sign up for your newsletter, subscribe to your RSS feed, sign a petition, become a member, or something else. *Calls to action* are the words that clearly give users that opportunity. "Buy your XJ-7 poles now," and "Try out the new XJ-7 ski poles," and "See the XJ-7's new colors" all represent calls to action that can help convert a website visitor into a customer.

For search engine optimization, include descriptive words in your calls to action. Notice that every example in the preceding paragraph mentions the name of the product (XJ-7) and something meaningful about it. If your call to action says only "Buy now" or "Add to cart," you're missing an opportunity to clearly specify (to the search engines) that this is the page where the XJ-7 can be purchased. Your website design may have a standard interface that includes generic options under every product listing, but you could consider also including a more specific text link under the product description. Or for another example, if you have links in your copy to sign up for your newsletter, include a brief description in every link like "Get the Car Restoration Newsletter" rather than just "Sign up for our newsletter." Contextual links that include specific versus generic words clarify things for users and add SEO value, if the anchor text is a natural description of the destination page and not keyword stuffed.

With internal links, be careful not to make your pages appear "over optimized" for a particular keyword. That can happen if a page's primary keyword phrase is used through the page's head and body sections, in the site navigation, and also in anchor text from pages all over the site — each time, exactly the same. See Book VI, Chapter 1 for a full description of internal linking best practices.

To be most effective, a call to action should use an imperative verb (like *see, try,* or *buy*) and a compelling benefit. The following example could be from a business-to-business site. A call to action like this would be very motivating for an engineer seeking this type of solution:

```
Attend our webcast "Process Excellence for Supply Chain
    Management" and learn how to reduce costs with our
    process-driven approach to aligning business processes
    within the supply chain.
```

Your call to action should tell visitors exactly what you want them to do:

✦ If you want them to buy your product, you could scatter multiple calls to action in strategic places within your copy, telling them how to do it (such as a button or text link with "Click here to buy Brand X now").

✦ If you want them to contact you by phone, state your phone number and instructions ("Call us Monday–Friday from 8–5 EST at 1-800-999-9999"). You could repeat the number in bold text throughout your copy and again at the end.

Be wary of spamming the page. Repeating your call to action works only if you don't annoy the visitor. From an SEO perspective, you can configure a page for a user, for a search engine, and for your conversion objective.

An effective call to action entices users to click. It motivates users to move further into the conversion process (leading them to whatever your goal is, whether a purchase, signup, or other). Often, you won't be able to know conclusively what phrasing works best until you've tried them. So if you're debating between three different calls to action, you could set up a test alternating between versions, tracking how many people clicked on each version, as well as the eventual conversion rate (how many of those clicks resulted in the desired goal). Then you would know which call to action is most effective for your current audience and website.

Chapter 3: Adding Keyword-Specific Content

In This Chapter

✔ **Creating your keyword list**

✔ **Developing content using your keywords**

✔ **Including synonyms to widen your appeal**

✔ **Deepening your content for semantic search**

✔ **Optimizing your content for search engine rankings**

✔ **Finding the best tools for keyword integration**

You may have a website already up and running, or you may be in the planning stages of a brand-new site. Either way, you should be ready to identify where you have content holes that need to be filled. In this chapter, you hone your skills at creating content that can rank well with the search engines.

First, ask yourself: What is my website about? The answers to this question give you a foundation for all your content planning and writing. Some sites try to be everything to everybody, but those sites don't rank well in searches. When a site's content is unfocused and too general, search engines can't figure out what the site is about. The site doesn't demonstrate expertise in any one thing, so the search engines don't know what search queries the site is relevant for. The result? The site doesn't rank well in search results.

You must clearly know your site's main subject *themes,* or the primary categories of information in your site, as a first step to planning and writing effective content. In a nutshell, you need to identify your themes, categorize them into pages, and then create focused content on those subjects. This is what we cover in this chapter. (For more on how to choose a theme for a website, see Book II, Chapter 1.)

Creating Your Keyword List

After you know your website's main subject themes, you can begin building a keyword list. A *keyword* is any word used as a search query. Search engines try to give users what they're looking for by searching for those keywords among their indexes of websites and then displaying the most relevant, trustworthy results. You want your website to be considered the most relevant for the keywords that match what your site is about. You need to choose your keywords so that you can proactively create focused content that can be considered most relevant.

Your first step in building a keyword list should be to brainstorm. At the brainstorming stage, write down every keyword or keyword phrase that comes to mind for your themes. You can filter them later; for now, you just want to amass the longest list you can of one-word, two-word, three-word, and longer potential keyword phrases that relate to your website. (Note that the multi-word phrases are important to plan for because people tend to search for more specific keyword phrases when they're ready to make a decision, but they search for shorter keyword phrases when they're just doing research.) To get more input, ask other people what they would call the information, products, or services you offer. Ask people involved in your business or industry, but also ask your neighbor, your niece, or others who are unfamiliar with your industry. You're trying to find all the ways someone might try to find what you have to offer.

After you've brainstormed, the next step is to organize your long list of potential keywords into subject categories, broken down from the broadest to the most specific. If your website is about customized classic cars, an outline might look something like this:

```
Classic Cars
Classic Cars 1950s
Classic Cars 1960s
Classic Cars 1970s
Classic Cars American
Classic Cars Ford
Classic Cars Ford Mustang
Classic Cars Ford Mustang Convertibles
Classic Cars Ford Mustang Hard Tops
Classic Cars Ford Comet
Classic Cars Ford GTO
Classic Cars Chevrolet
Classic Cars Chevrolet Sedans
Classic Cars Chevrolet Trucks
Classic Cars Customization
Classic Cars Customization Paint
Classic Cars Customization Upholstery
Classic Cars Customization Upholstery Leather
Classic Cars Customization Upholstery Vinyl
```

These are all terms people might search for when they are looking up classic cars, or customization, or both, and all of them can be used as keywords on your website. You can go into even more breakdowns and come up with specific keywords into the hundreds or thousands, as appropriate for your site.

After you have your initial keyword list, you need to evaluate the keywords and identify which ones are your main subjects. Then organize the more specific subtopic keywords below them. You want to structure your website to assign each of your main keywords to a specific *landing page* (the page you want users to come to because it's the best source of information for that topic on your site). For instance, you'd want to build a landing page for the keyword phrase [classic cars Ford Mustang] that has focused content on Ford Mustangs and that links to subpages of supporting information about Ford Mustangs. Doing this makes it easier for search engines to know that the page is relevant to searches for [Ford Mustangs] or [classic Ford Mustangs] or [classic Mustang cars], and so on. We recommend that you include a minimum of five subpages supporting each of your landing pages to present depth of content to the search engines. Organizing your site into categories like this is part of *siloing* (subject theming), and it's covered at length in Book VI, Chapter 1.

Weed out keywords that don't support your subject themes: Unrelated words that show up too frequently on a page dilute the page's subject relevance. For instance, if your Ford Mustangs page lists all the possible tire and wheel options and mentions "tires" too many times, the search engines might think it's a page about Ford Mustang tires, and then they might lower its ranking for the keyword [Ford Mustang].

For more help selecting good keywords, see Book II, Chapter 2.

Developing Content Using Your Keywords

After you have your categories and subcategories mapped out, look at your website content and choose (or plan) a landing page devoted to each one. For every landing page, you also want to assign a primary keyword or keyword phrase. In other words, your site needs to have a focused page on each of your important keywords.

Your goal is to have the search engines recognize what each one of your landing pages is most relevant for so that it can show up in search results for its keywords. And the better you can focus your content on those targeted keywords, the higher your URL is likely to be in the list.

Your website's landing pages present the all-important first impression to site visitors. You want to make sure your landing pages not only put your best foot forward but also interest visitors enough to entice them to go further, and hopefully convert. The pages have to look good to users *and* search engines.

As a general guideline, the pages at the top of each silo (your landing or index pages) should have at least 500 words of text content and be supported by at least five subpages (each with at least 500 words) within the same theme. (*Note:* The minimum word count guideline for a product page containing lots of pictures is lower; see the previous chapter for more details on length.) Writing that much content may sound overwhelming, but you can tackle it as you would any big project. Develop a strategy for adding original text to each page. Setting a schedule and producing X number of pages every week eventually builds up a site that can serve as a subject matter expert in the areas that are important to your business. Focus not on gimmick pages, *link bait* (short-lived attention-getters), Top Ten lists, or other flash-in-the-pan strategies, but on developing content that will satisfy researchers and convert them to buyers. (For more on link bait, see Book VI, Chapter 1.)

Your landing pages need to have enough content so that people reaching them from a search engine feel satisfied that they've come to the right place. You want the content to engage visitors enough so that they want to stay. You also need your landing pages to link to other pages that offer more detailed information within the subject category and lead to opportunities to buy, sign up, or take whatever action your site considers a conversion.

Beginning to write

When writing your web content, it's best to use simple, everyday language that people are likely to understand and possibly search for. As a general rule, we recommend including a keyword or keyword phrase often enough to be prominent so that someone who reads the page will be able to pick out what the most important word is. Don't force your keywords into your content. Let it sound natural.

Additionally, you should avoid using only general phrases; be sure to include detailed descriptive words as well. If your keywords are too general, they are likely to be up against too much competition from others targeting the same keywords. However, fewer people search for very specific terms, resulting in fewer potential visitors. It's a balancing act, and the rules aren't hard and fast. You need to find the right mix for your site by finding the keywords that bring traffic that actually converts: In other words, you want to put out the bait that brings in the right catch. Also keep in mind that the broader keywords go on the upper landing pages and more specific keywords go on the subpages, so you might need to focus on several more specific variations of a keyword phrase to rank for the broader term. For example, targeting a general keyword phrase like "used cars" could have supporting long-tail keyword variations such as "used cars in New York City" and "used 2014 Mustangs" and more.

When you start to write a new page, stay focused on the page's theme. Write as much as you can about that subject theme, even if the information seems totally obvious to you. What seems obvious to you probably would be new information to someone unfamiliar with your subject. After all, that's why someone would come to your site: to read what a subject expert has to say. Begin by stating the obvious; it establishes your credibility when your visitors find information they already know to be true on your pages, and they'll be more likely to trust your site to give them further information.

As you write your first draft, don't worry so much about keyword placement. Do include your keywords, but let the language flow naturally around the topic. Later you can analyze what you've written and refine things like keyword density and distribution (more on that under "Optimizing the Content," later in this chapter).

To test whether your writing comes across as natural, try reading it out loud. Text that sounds like conversational language engages readers.

Keeping it relevant

Make sure that you don't dilute the subject theme by including irrelevant information. Some pruning might be necessary if you're working on an existing page rather than starting one from scratch. If the page is all about Chevrolet Camaros, keep the discussion focused on that car model, without a lengthy discussion of how it compared to the competing Pontiac Firebird back in the 1970s. Too many mentions of another type of car can dilute your Camaro theme and confuse the search engines, thereby reducing your subject relevance to [Chevrolet Camaros].

Including clarifying words

You want to include secondary words that help clarify what your keywords are about. For example, if you have the keyword [apple] for one of your pages, the search engines are going to look at all the text near the word *apple* to figure out whether your page is about the fruit or the technology company. If this was your web page, you could use words like *software, iPad,* or other related terms to clarify that you mean Apple as in tech company.

You want to put your clarifying words close to your keywords in the text. The closer the proximity, the stronger the correlation.

Another reason to include clarifying words is to match more search queries, especially long-tail queries. *Long-tail queries* are longer, targeted search phrases that aren't frequently used, but they generally have a high conversion rate because searchers entering these queries know exactly what they're looking for. Search engine users are becoming savvier as time goes on, and they know that a single keyword is probably going to be too broad. A good example is what happens when you do a search for [security]. You might be in need of a security guard service, but doing a quick search on Google with the keyword [security] gives you the Wikipedia article on security, the Department of Homeland Security, the Social Security Administration, and many listings for computer security software. Using a long-tail search query like [security guard service Poughkeepsie], on the other hand, turns up map results listing local businesses, two local business sites for hiring security guards, and a couple of news articles about security services in Poughkeepsie.

You can see why it's a good idea to include supplemental words and phrases on your web pages. Search engines can match queries to words that can be found in proximity to each other on your page, even if they never appear as a phrase. So for instance, if your web page has the heading "Oldsmobile 98s Make the Coolest Convertibles," and the body copy contains all these words in close proximity as well, your page would be found relevant to the search query [Oldsmobile 98 convertible], even though you never used the exact phrase.

Including synonyms to widen your appeal

Synonyms of your keywords also need to show up on your web pages, in your HTML tags, and in the anchor text of links to your pages. People don't use the exact same words to describe things, so it appears more natural to search engines to find backlinks to your pages using a variety of different terms that all mean roughly the same thing.

Including keyword synonyms also helps you match more search queries. People search for things in their own words, not yours. For instance, if you have a page on your classic cars site all about Oldsmobile 98s, you should make sure your keywords include both [Ninety-Eight] spelled out and the numeric [98], because people could search either way. In another example, a web page that sells ski boots would optimize that page for the keyword phrase [ski boots]. But they'd also want their listing to display when people search for [ski footwear], [snow boots], or [winter apparel]. Unless they have synonyms like these within the page, the search engine won't find it relevant and won't include it in the search results.

Also, don't forget nicknames! If your main subjects have common nicknames, these are important to include — possibly as keywords, but at least in your body content. For instance, on your classic cars site, your Chevrolet Camaro page should include the word [Chevy], your Ford Mustang page should include the nickname [Stang], and so forth.

Of course, your hunt for good synonyms could begin in a thesaurus. Even better, find out what words Google thinks are synonymous with your keywords. Do this by searching for a keyword and then noticing the other words that Google formats in bold on the results page besides the words you typed.

Dealing with stop words

Stop words are small, common like *a, the, at, to, will, this, and, with* and others. Because they typically add little meaning to a query, the search engines used to ignore them almost entirely. Today, however, search engine algorithms are intelligent enough to recognize phrases that contain stop words, rather than discard them completely. For example, a search for [holiday on ice], which is the name of a touring ice show, brings back entirely different results from a search for [holiday ice], even though the preposition "on" is a stop word. Further, queries that are made up completely of stop words, such as [The Who], can be understood and processed as is. In today's world, in which search engines increasingly understand the semantics of spoken or written language, you can feel free to include stop words in your keyword phrases as appropriate.

Freshness of the content

Content freshness can affect a web page's rankings, depending on the topic. Google likes to show current information, especially for queries on trends, celebrities, technology, and other quickly evolving subjects. With our Bruce Clay, Inc. blog, we have noticed that posts about competitive keywords show up higher in Google search results when they are newer and decline in ranking over time. We have a few notable exceptions, but overall, newer blog posts have a ranking advantage over older ones, all else being equal.

Another benefit is that the more often your site has fresh content, the more often the search engines want to index it. News sites, for example, have to be crawled constantly because of how frequently they post new stories. On a lesser scale, if you have a blog on your website that has new activity every day, the spiders crawl your site more often than a site that updates once a month.

If your site content gets indexed in news searches, you definitely need fresh content to stay near the top. Without frequent posts, news articles may fade into the oblivion of the search results' back pages. For a blog, you want to post often enough to merit frequent return visits from readers as well as spiders. Set your posting schedule based on your own and your target audience's needs, but try to make fresh, original content available on a regular basis.

Your site's ranking in normal search results does not change based on how frequently the search engine spiders crawl your site. Where you might suffer as a result of infrequent search engine indexing, however, is if you've made SEO-related changes to your site since the last time the search engine spiders crawled the site, and those changes have not yet been indexed. If that's the case, you can bring them to the search engine's attention by manually submitting the changed page URLs. See Book VII, Chapter 6 to learn about direct submission.

Periodically, you should review your site content to make sure it stays fresh. See if anything has changed, and either update or add to the text that's there. This is pretty much common sense, but it has the added benefit of providing fresh content to keep the spiders coming back to your site.

Deepening your content

The engines look for depth and breadth of content on a subject to confirm that a web page really knows what it's talking about and deserves to be a search result. This is even more true since the birth of Google's Knowledge Graph, which seeks to understand not just the meaning of words but also the connections between entities on the web (see Book I, Chapter 3).

When you include supplemental words and phrases beyond your keywords, you help search engines map your web page content to their Knowledge Graph data. They increasingly understand the relationships between various people, places and things (that is, entities). So when they index a web page about a subject, they expect to find words that relate to it. For example, a page about John Wayne would be expected to include supplemental words like "actor," "western" and "movies"; a page lacking these semantically connected words probably wouldn't be considered much of an expert on the subject of John Wayne. In order to be found most relevant to searches for your subjects, consider increasing your pages' depth of content.

Dynamically adding content to a page

You may use a Content Management System (CMS) that takes your content and automatically builds your web pages from it. If so, you'll want to make sure it's dynamically adding content properly, taking into consideration everything you know about SEO and good content writing. For instance, the text should sound natural, use your keywords in the appropriate amount and distribution, and make sense. Also, make sure that the `Title` and `Meta` tags in the page's Head section are being created properly, emphasizing appropriate keywords, with every page unique.

You don't want to ever lose control of your website by using a poor-quality CMS that is not configurable. Because search engines decide whether your pages are relevant for search queries based on having keyword-rich, focused content and unique headings and tags, you can't afford to let an inflexible CMS limit how much you can customize each page.

Another thing to avoid is auto-generated text. Generally, machine-written content sounds unnatural and won't do a good job representing you either to users or to the search engines. (For more discussion of content management systems, see Book VII, Chapter 5.)

Optimizing the Content

When you have pages of content to work with, you can refine them for search engine optimization (SEO). If you haven't already set up the text content in an HTML document, do so now because part of what you need to optimize is the HTML code behind the page.

Setting up the HTML

Looking at your page in the HTML code view, your first step is to do what we call "getting the red out." (In the Single Page Analyzer tool, things that need to be corrected are displayed in red text, so it's easy to figure out where to start.) You want to fix the blatant SEO issues, the ones that are the most obvious and often the easiest to fix. Here's what to look for:

+ `Title` **tag:** The `Title` tag should appear at the top of your HTML code's `Head` section. It should be unique and contain your page's main keyword (with no word repeated). Normally the `Title` tag should be between 6 and 12 words in length (brief).

+ `Meta` **description tag:** The `Meta` description tag should appear after the `Title` tag in your HTML Head section. It needs to contain all the keywords used in the `Title` tag, and it should be written like a sentence because this is often what search engines display within a result listing. Any word should not appear more than twice. The length guideline is 12 to 24 words.

+ `Meta` **keywords tag:** The `Meta` keywords tag should appear after the `Meta` description tag in your HTML `Head` section and should contain all the words used in the `Title` and `Description` tags. It can be written as a list separated by commas, starting with the long phrases and ending with single words. No single word should be used more than four times, and the total length should not exceed 48 words.

✦ **Heading tags:** Heading tags (H# tags) set apart your on-page titles and subheadings, and search engines analyze them to determine your page's main ideas, so make them meaningful. You want to use an H1 for the first and most important heading on the page only. Second-level headings should be given H2, third-level headings H3, and so forth; also, they should never be placed out of order. Just think back to school term papers, outlines . . . . When the search engines were built, their main purpose was to index educational, technical, and professional papers, and very little else. The engines still rely on the same basic information architecture that they started out with.

A good heading length is from one to five words, but how many headings you should have on a page depends on the content. Only use an H# tag when it defines a change in the content structure, much like a table of contents outlines the structure of a book. You will almost never have multiple H1 tags (not many pages have more than one main topic, after all), but you could have multiple H2, H3, and so on, if the content supports it.

For example:

```
<h1>Ford Reviews</h1>
    Content about Ford Reviews (200 words)
    <h2>Mustang Reviews</h2>
    Content about Ford Mustang Reviews (200+ words)
    <h2>F-150 Reviews</h2>
    Content about Ford F-150 reviews (200+ words again)
```

In the preceding example, the H1 and H2 tags are used properly. Think about it as a school or technical paper. It has to follow an outline format completely. You can have an H3 heading, but only if it's below an H2 tag. If you had a section for the engine specs of the Ford Mustang, for example, that could be considered an H3.

The usage of H4 and H5 tags would have to be, again, related sub-content to the H3 tag, and so on.

Digging deeper by running Single Page Analyzer

After you have your document all cleaned up, and the Single Page Analyzer tool doesn't report any more red items to edit, you can work on optimizing the body content you wrote. We suggest you run the page through the Single Page Analyzer by following these steps:

1. **Go to** `www.seotoolset.com/tools/free-tools/`.

2. **Locate the Single Page Analyzer on this page and enter the page's URL (such as** `www.yourdomain.com/pageinprogress.html`**) in the Page URL text box.**

3. **Click the Run Page Analyzer button and wait until the report appears.**

The Single Page Analyzer report compiles lots of useful information for you to analyze your page content and plan improvements, as we explain in a moment. We suggest you look at the following six areas to diagnose issues and improve your page: the Heading section, frequently used words, reading level, keyword density, keyword frequency, and keyword distribution.

✦ **Head section problems:** You can see at a glance if you've overlooked any of the problems that need fixing; the report shows exceptions in bright red text. For instance, if you used a word in your Meta description tag but forgot to include it in the Meta keywords tag as well, under the Meta keywords tag heading, you would see this message:

> META Keywords is **MISSING** a word that is in either the TITLE or META Description.

✦ **Frequently used words:** Figure 3-1 shows a portion of tables from the report listing one-word and two-word phrases that are used at least twice in the page.

Figure 3-1: A portion of a Single Page Analyzer report showing one-word and two-word phrases repeated in a web page.

Word Phrase Usage

Keyword	Title	Meta Desc	Meta Keywords	Headings	ALT Tags	First Words	Body Words	All Words
1 Word Phrases								
Used Words	5	27	57	27	3	200	243	362
butter	1	4	15	3	1	8	12	36
peanut	1	5	15	2	1	6	9	33
soy	0	0	4	2	0	3	4	10
2 Word Phrases								
Used Words	5	27	57	27	3	200	243	362
peanut butter	1	4	13	2	1	6	9	30
soy butter	0	0	1	1	0	2	3	5
butter ville	0	1	0	1	1	1	1	4
butter peanut	0	1	3	0	0	0	0	4
carbs then	0	0	0	1	0	1	1	2
butter substitutes	0	0	2	0	0	0	0	2

Looking across the rows, you can also see what section of the page each phrase appears in, whether it's in the title, description, keywords, headings, image Alt codes, or something else. Because search engines look for repeated words to ascertain what your page is all about, look carefully at these tables. The most frequently used words appear at the top: These should be your keywords. You also want to make sure you don't have frequently repeated words that might distract the search engines from understanding your main page theme. You can see how this report can save you hours of manual work counting instances and trying to make sure your keywords, synonyms, clarifying words, and so on are adequately used.

✦ **Reading level:** In the Text Metrics section, the report shows you details about your text's reading level. Because you want your site to be appropriate for your target audience, this is important. The row (not shown in the figure) labeled "Kincaid Grade Level" identifies the U.S. school grade level that your writing matches. If it says 16.0, that means your text is appropriate for someone with four years of college education. The Kincaid score is based on the average number of syllables per word and words per sentence. If you find your pages scoring way too high or too low for your target audience's education level, you should adjust your word length and sentence structure. For instance, a website directed at tweens needs to have a low Kincaid score (around 5.0 to 8.0), but that reading level would not be appropriate for a site targeting doctoral candidates.

You can also check your document's Flesch-Kincaid score and Flesch grade level in Microsoft Word. Check out Chapter 2 in this minibook for instructions on how to turn on your readability statistics in Word.

✦ **Keyword frequency:** Because the use of keywords is so crucial to your search engine optimization, examine your *keyword frequency* (the number of times the keyword appears on the page). This number shows in the All Words column of the Single Page Analyzer report. And as with keyword density, you need to size up your competitors to find out what number to shoot for.

✦ **Keyword distribution:** One last measurement that affects your search engine ranking for a particular keyword is the *distribution,* or placement throughout the page. Your site might use the keyword phrase [classic cars] the right number of times (frequency) and in the right proportion to the total amount of text (density), but it also needs to distribute the phrase *regularly* throughout the page. If you use it only in the top quarter of the page, the search engines assume that your page, as a whole, isn't as relevant to classic cars as it would be if the phrase appears throughout the copy evenly.

You can find out the typical keyword usage for your competition by running the Single Page Analyzer on your competition's web pages. You can also subscribe to tools that produce this comparison data in one step, such as the Multi Page Analyzer from the SEOToolSet Pro tools suite, which you find at www.seotoolset.com. (For more help doing competitive research, see Book III. Detailed instructions on how to approximate the results of the Multi Page Analyzer are available in Book III, Chapter 2.)

Finding Tools for Keyword Integration

In this section, we give you a handy list of optimization tools for your reference. These tools can help you analyze your web page content to make sure you've set up your keywords effectively. They are shortcuts that show you some key factors that the search engines look for to determine relevance. Remember, in almost every case, the search engines themselves are going to be your best asset in terms of analyzing your market. The following are some useful optimization tools for your site:

✦ **Single Page Analyzer** (`www.seotoolset.com/tools/free-tools/`): The Single Page Analyzer is your primary keyword analysis tool. See the previous section for more detail.

✦ **Copyscape** (`www.copyscape.com`): This free tool lets you check for duplicates of your web page text elsewhere on the web. You want to make sure you have original content on your site because duplications can cause your page to be filtered out of the search engine's index. (We cover avoiding duplicate content in Chapter 5 of this minibook.)

✦ **Keyword Activity** (`http://www.bruceclay.com/seo/keyword-research.htm`): Part of analyzing keywords is finding out how often people search for them. The free Keyword Suggestion tool lets you see suggested keywords and check their search activity (and do many other search-engine-optimization–related tasks). You can also do keyword research using the free Search Engine Optimization/KSP tool, available at `www.bruceclay.com/seo/combining-keywords.htm`. Alternative recommended tools that give you robust reporting (for a fee) include

- **Wordtracker** (`www.wordtracker.com`): Measures keyword traffic. Wordtracker offers both annual plans and monthly plans. The annual subscription starts at $449, and the monthly plan costs from $27 to $99 per month. You also can try it out for free.

- **Keyword Discovery** (`www.keyworddiscovery.com`): Offers a free trial for its subscription service, which runs from $30 to $200 a month, depending on your subscription level.

✦ **Mozilla Firefox** (`www.mozilla.com`) **and Google Chrome** (`www.google.com/chrome`): Available as a free download, Mozilla's Firefox browser is one of the most powerful SEO tools out there, with multiple add-ons that allow power users to slice and dice almost any aspect of a website. Right out of the box, Firefox lets you do a rough keyword distribution search on a page. Ctrl+F brings up a search text box: Just type your keyword, and then select Highlight All to see where the words fall on the page you have open in the browser.

Also available as a free download, Google's Chrome browser has some nifty features. One of its best features is the ability to see how a word or phrase is distributed throughout a page visually. With any web page open, simply press Ctrl+F to activate a drop-down search box. Then type the word or phrase you want to find. Though this book is in black and white, every instance of the word searched for in Figure 3-2, "search engine optimization," is automatically highlighted in yellow. And colored bands appear in the vertical scroll bar, representing each time the selected word or phrase is used in the page content. Seeing a keyword's distribution at a glance like this can help you distribute it evenly throughout your page.

Figure 3-2:
Google
Chrome lets
you see
a word's
linear
distribution
using col-
ored band-
ing in the
scroll bar.

Competitive Analysis Tools

It's a competitive world, and ranking well has everything to do with what your keyword competitors are doing. The optimal keyword frequency and distribution are determined by analyzing the top-ranked sites. The search engines are clearly accepting the keyword usage of the top sites, so being better than these competitors is often simply a matter of careful page editing.

✦ **Single Page Analyzer:** The tool we cover in the section "Digging deeper by running Single Page Analyzer," earlier in this chapter, can also help you analyze the keywords and content of the top-ranked web pages.

✦ **Multi Page Analyzer** (www.seotoolset.com): A tool that looks at multiple competitors' web pages and analyzes them in one fell swoop for you is ideal for competitor research. There are several products on the market, so check your existing SEO tools subscription to see if you already have access to a similar report. If not, a subscription to our SEOToolSet Pro costs $89 per month, or you can do the comparisons by hand (see Book III, Chapter 2 for instructions).

Chapter 4: Adapting Your Content for Local Search

In This Chapter

✔ **Exploring the formats of local results**

✔ **Maximizing your visibility in organic local results**

✔ **Understanding the need for local SEO**

✔ **Meeting Google's Pigeon algorithm**

✔ **Optimizing content to be found in local searches**

✔ **Creating local landing pages the right way**

✔ **Answering common questions for the mobile searcher**

Do you have a brick-and-mortar storefront and want to make sure the locals can find you in online searches? Or maybe you have a service business and you serve all the towns and cities within driving distance. Perhaps your business has multiple locations around the region or country, or maybe just a national headquarters. Regardless, you still want to show up in location-based searches and compete against local businesses for your keywords.

How can you make your business visible to local searchers? For each of these business scenarios, the answer varies a bit. In this chapter, you learn how to create and optimize content to help secure a local presence in the search engines. We also cover some factors besides on-page content optimization that can help strengthen your local visibility. Getting your business to appear for relevant searches that have local or geotargeted intent is what this chapter is all about.

Taking Advantage of Local Search

The search engines logically interpret some types of search queries as local, or location-based, searches. For example, you might search for any of the following:

✦ [dog groomers]

✦ [dry cleaners]

✦ [tires near me]

The search engines know that these search queries most likely mean you are looking for someone in your local area who can provide a service. If you live in Poughkeepsie, New York, you're unlikely to be looking for a dry cleaner in Miami. You're also unlikely to be interested in dry cleaning techniques, or the history of dry cleaning, or any other research-type information. Because the search engines want to satisfy you with relevant results (they want you to keep coming back to them), they assume that your intent is to find a local business, and they give you a list of dry cleaners in and around Poughkeepsie.

The search engines know where you're located. If you're searching on a desktop computer, they have two ways of figuring this out: First, you might have specified a city in your profile (if you're logged in to your account for the search engine you're using) or in a previous web search. Second, your computer's *IP address* (the numeric "Internet Protocol" code assigned to your computer) identifies your approximate location. If you're using a web-enabled mobile device or tablet, your exact current location can be pinpointed.

You can do local searches in three ways:

✦ **Logical local searches:** Sometimes search queries just logically bring up local businesses or services (such as [dry cleaners] and so on). This is especially true for mobile searches, because search engines expect that if you're out and about, you're likely to be searching for some place nearby.

✦ **Geographic search terms:** Search queries can include a city or ZIP code, such as [dry cleaners Miami], [dog groomers in Sacramento CA], or [new tires 90210].

✦ **Map searches:** People can search directly on a physical map (using a map interface) to find local businesses in a selected area.

Understanding local search results

If you run a local search in Google, you usually see a handful of local business listings pinpointed on a handy map, as shown in Figure 4-1.

Search engines use a variety of layouts for displaying local business results, depending on the query. These *local-pack results,* any of the formats that Google uses to display local results, come in a variety of forms. Google may show local results in a sidebar or box, or, as in Figure 4-1, within a map next to local listings.

Google may also display local business listings at the top of the page in a carousel formation, as shown in Figure 4-2. Another arrangement for serving local results is an expanded three-pack, as shown in Figure 4-3.

Figure 4-1:
Business
listings
display at
the top of a
local Google
search
results
page.

Local results carousel

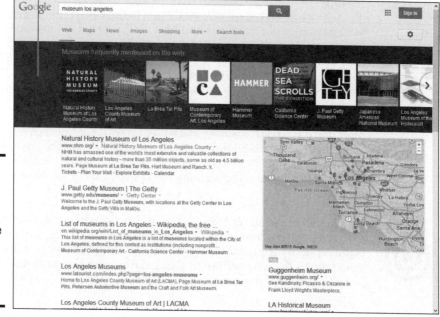

Figure 4-2:
For some
location-
based que-
ries, Google
displays
results in
carousel
display.

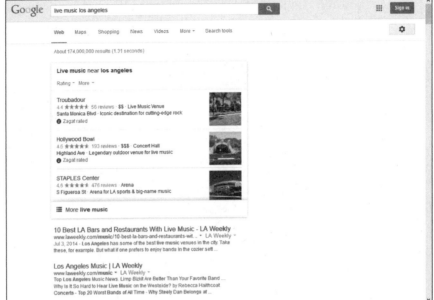

Figure 4-3:
Google may
display local
business
listings in an
expanded
three-pack.

Local pack

All these local pack display formats pull listings from the search engine's local database, not from its web index. To be included in these local pack listings, the business owners of these sites at some point completed a business listing form with Google. If you haven't done this yet, take a little time now and register your business with the local directories for all the major search engines (Google, Yahoo, and Bing). For detailed instructions, see Book I, Chapter 4.

After you have your business listing set up with each search engine, you can enter the race. All the relevant businesses then jockey for position. While different areas and industries vary in competitiveness, having content that's locally optimized and high quality helps you gain one of those coveted local pack spots.

To qualify for a local profile with Google My Business, you need to have a physical presence where in-person contact with customers during stated business hours is available. Google allows certain exceptions that change from time to time, so be sure to check the current Google Guidelines here: https://support.google.com/business/answer/3038177.

Organic geotargeted results

If your business doesn't have a physical location in a community and can't have a Google My Business profile there, it will not be able to appear in local pack listings. However, your web pages can still show up in the regular organic results for local and geotargeted queries. Search engines display organic results below the local pack results, and often one or more organic results appear above the local pack as well.

In a nutshell, the way to show up for geotargeted organic results is by creating content relevant to the search query *that's also optimized for the geographic location.* This is a large part of what we call local SEO.

Introducing local SEO

Local SEO is the process of optimizing a business to be found when some-one searches for a specific geographic location. Local SEO is often over-looked in a company's marketing strategy because it's a step beyond the usual SEO goal of optimizing for products or a service category. Local SEO can also be pretty complex, requiring attention to things like maintaining consistent business information in search engine databases and local direc-tories, obtaining local citations, amassing positive customer reviews online, and more.

Local SEO is worth the effort for many marketers for two main reasons:

✦ **Demand:** A huge percentage of searches have *local intent* (that is, people want to find businesses near them or in a certain geographic area). On mobile, that percentage is about half. So if your business can meet a nearby searcher's need, make sure that it can be found in local search.

✦ **Supply:** Search engines give local listings the lion's share of space on Page 1 of search results when they detect local intent. Why not take your rightful place?

Of all the factors influencing local search engine rankings, a survey of digital marketers conducted annually by David Mihm of Moz continues to find that the largest single piece of the pie goes to on-page signals — elements of the web page itself, such as its title, body length, and so forth, rather than exter-nal factors such as links. The way you build your web pages and the content you put in them matters most. (The complete survey results are worth reading: `http://moz.com/local-search-ranking-factors`.)

Google's Pigeon: Local search algorithm

Google's update, dubbed "Pigeon," has radically impacted the way local search results are ranked since its release in the U.S. in July 2014. Pigeon affects Google's web and map searches, with the goal of making the local ranking algorithm align more closely with the way Google's core search algorithm works. In effect, it rewards sites for following traditional SEO best practices as well as using local optimization techniques.

Pigeon also boosted some third-party review sites and directories in results for geotargeted queries. Yelp, Zagat, TripAdvisor, Kayak, Urbanspoon and others began getting higher visibility in search results after Pigeon was launched. That's why a search for [manhattan deli] returns not just local delicatessens but also Yelp and other review sites' pages showing lists of different delis with customer reviews. This is good news for the deli owner who has lots of happy customers.

Google's local results format became more flexible under Pigeon. Previous to Pigeon, local results always showed a "seven-pack" of listings on a map; now, Google seems to prefer smaller local packs as well as other formats, some of which are pictured in this chapter (for example, the "three-pack" shown in Figure 4-3).

Google's plans for Pigeon are unclear. Several months after the U.S.-only release, Google released Pigeon to the United Kingdom, Canada, and Australia. Although future rollouts are unknown, we can be sure that local search will continue to evolve.

Optimizing Content for Local Searches

To reinforce your business's actual location and help your website appear in local searches, showing your physical address on your website is important. Your physical address is part of a trio of information about your business that's such a major signal for local search ranking that the SEO community has given it an acronym: *NAP* (name, address, and phone number). If you have a brick-and-mortar location, be sure to include the address and local telephone number where users can easily find it. Even if your business is an online-only service, you increase trust by displaying an actual address and phone number. Note that your NAP information should be consistent on your site *and* across the World Wide Web. If on your website you go by the name Classic Car Customization, don't register a Google My Business profile under the name Classic Car Customization Co.

Show your NAP information preferably on the home page as well as your contact page. Make sure that whatever page contains this information is linked from your sitemap, to make sure that search engines can easily find your address. (A *sitemap* is a page containing links to the pages in your site, like a table of contents.) Showing your name, address, and contact information to users also makes them feel more comfortable doing business with you because you're not just a virtual company being operated from some post office box.

You could put your address information in the footer that's visible at the bottom of every page. This is recommended for businesses with one or a small number of locations because a user can view your location(s) from anywhere in the site. However, if you have a long list of locations, you don't want to list their addresses on every page. Always keep in mind what makes sense for the user; that's who the search engines want to serve, too. Showing a massive block of tiny addresses probably wouldn't be good for anyone, and from an SEO perspective, you'd be better off separating geographic terms. Consider putting a single link in the footer instead for "Locations" or something intuitive that leads to more information.

Creating region-specific content

Wherever you have a physical business location, you now know that you need to claim your local profile with the search engines. But that's not the only thing you can do to reinforce your business's relevance for geotargeted and local searches. In your website content, reinforce your community connection by talking about the place where you do business.

Businesses such as a plumber, roofing contractor, or other type of service area business might be located in one town but serve all areas within a 30-mile radius. Other businesses may be quite remote but still want to target a particular local area because it makes sense — for instance, if you do classic car customization nationwide, and you know that Detroit, Michigan, has a huge concentration of classic car buffs, you want to be visible in Detroit-based searches. In all these cases, you can increase your chances of being found in these other local area searches if you create region-specific content.

Creating content around geotargeted *keywords* (search terms relevant to your website) helps you optimize your site for local search. So as you read the following sections, consider that there may be several "local" areas that you want to optimize for, not just your own physical location.

In general, you need to create content pages that tie together your business offerings (by keywords) with that city. Obviously, for cities outside your own business location, you have no local address or business listing to pin down your connection. So to show up in searches for [classic car customization in Detroit], for example, you need to create location-specific content, as described in the upcoming section.

In addition to creating content, you have other creative ways to attract business in a remote location. You can take out geotargeted ads on Facebook or other sites, which would appear only to someone in that local area. You can get involved in the local community by sponsoring events or helping with fundraising. Best of all is having local customers write about you in glowing terms on their websites or in review sites for that area.

Create local landing pages

There's a right way and a wrong way to create content for local searches. One wrong approach is to just list a bunch of city names or ZIP codes in a text block, hoping to rank for those terms. But users won't like it, and the search engines might suspect spam and hit you with a ranking penalty.

Another wrong method is to generate a hundred copies of a web page and then use a find-and-replace method to substitute a different city name on each page. That approach creates thin, mostly duplicated content that's likely to attract a penalty from Google's Panda algorithm and damage your site's rankings. (See Chapter 2 in this minibook for more on Panda and the need for unique, quality content.) This type of find-and-replace approach also doesn't convince your users or the search engines that you really can do business in those locations.

So what should you do? The right way is to create unique, original content for each location where you want to do business. It depends on your site structure and goals, but consider devoting specific pages to locations and then talking about what you do in that location throughout the text. For each local *landing page* (the page where you want a searcher to land when clicking through to your site), do the following:

+ **Mention the location.** In your landing page `Title` tag, body text, and possibly also in a heading tag on the page, mention the name(s) of the local city or cities this page focuses on. You might have one page about your classic car services for Poughkeepsie, another for Detroit, and so on.

+ **Include conversational local modifiers.** Beyond the place name itself, searchers may indicate that they're looking for something local using words such as "near me," "nearby," and "neighborhood." These words that signal interest in location-specific results are becoming increasingly common as searchers speak queries into mobile phones. Sprinkling in conversational local modifiers near your keywords may make sense, with phrases like "Looking for car customization near your Brooklyn neighborhood?"

+ **Talk about things related to the location.** Don't just give the city name; instead, also mention geographic terms related to it, as you would naturally in conversation. For instance, if you're establishing that you do business in Los Angeles on a given page, you can also include "Hollywood" or "sunny Southern California" in the text.

✦ **Make it unique.** Think creatively about ways to vary the content on each local landing page. Here are a few ideas to get your brainstorming started:

- Show local customer testimonials.

- Include descriptions and pictures of work you have completed in that city.

- Talk about local events your company attended or sponsored.

- Offer a city-specific special (could rotate between cities).

- Publish photos you took in the city or a video you created there.

- Talk about information that's specific to that city, such as local regulations, data, weather, statistics, history, events, people, places, or other facts relevant to your business.

If you have a blog, use the preceding list of ideas to stimulate geotargeted blog posts as well. For instance, you can write a blog post about an auto show in Detroit that showcased lots of great classic cars. Link from the blog post to the appropriate local landing page to give it added support.

Answer common questions

Put yourself in local people's shoes who might be looking for a business such as yours. What do they need? Local searches are often performed by people using a smartphone or other mobile device. What kind of questions would mobile users be asking?

For example, if you have a restaurant, a person living nearby who looks up your restaurant might want to know your address, directions, payment types that you accept, hours you serve lunch and dinner, and your menu options. Design your site to provide all that information, and make it easy to see and navigate through for mobile users. Further, consider personalizing your content with scenarios a local person might relate to. For instance, if a theater is down the block from your restaurant, you might talk about theatergoers coming to your restaurant before a show, or the ease of making a reservation for a relaxing dinner after the show, just half a block up beautiful downtown Main Street. Think of scenarios you can write that connect questions users have (for example, Do you take reservations? Where can we go eat after a show?) with local geographic terms (such as the theater and Main Street) in an engaging way.

Make sure that your website answers the questions local searchers ask. Doing so makes your site relevant for local search results and attracts more satisfied customers. Remember that people are searching more and more using mobile devices, and the majority of mobile searches have local intent. For that reason, mobile and local are inescapably linked. If you want to rank in local search, make your site mobile-friendly, by all means. For help making your site mobile-friendly, see Book IV, Chapter 3.

Chapter 5: Dealing with Duplicate Content

In This Chapter

✔ Understanding duplicate content so that you can avoid it

✔ Recognizing how content can become duplicated

✔ Resolving duplicate content issues

✔ Understanding how a federal copyright can protect your site

✔ Handling your content

*I*n this chapter, you find out how to avoid having duplicate content on your own website and why that's important. We also explain how your content can become duplicated (copied) on other websites and the variety of causes for it, ranging from accidental to downright malicious. Because you want to protect your original website content and prevent duplication as much as possible, we list various sources of duplicate content and give you recommendations for how to deal with each type of situation.

Duplicate content refers to text that is repeated on more than one web page either on your site or on other sites. Some duplication is natural and not a problem. For example, if you write about someone's article, you naturally include quotes from that piece; if you revise your terms of service, you may need to keep both the old and new versions alive on your site; and so forth. But beyond those kinds of minor duplications, you need to vigilantly avoid duplicate content — not only because you want your pages to each provide unique value to users and be competitive in the search engines, but also because too much duplication can get your site filtered out of results or even penalized.

When search engine spiders crawl and index sites into a searchable database, they can detect that a page on any website is a copy of another page — on another site or even your own. The spider then determines which page is the original or most authoritative version to show in search results. The grouping of duplicate content could hurt your rankings because duplicate pages won't make the cut. It's not that the copycat page is penalized in the search engine's *index* (the searchable database of website content). The search engines just cluster similar results together and filter duplicates out of search results pages, because the engines don't want to give users redundant listings. When your own site has duplicated pages, other websites link indiscriminately to whichever form of the content they like best, which dilutes your *link equity* (the value of all the inbound links pointing to your web page) by splitting links across several duplicated pages.

Being filtered out of search results as a duplicate is bad for your SEO, but getting a penalty is worse. Sites with widespread duplication may earn a search engine penalty for having thin, low-quality content — something Google's Panda update tries to remove from search results. (See Chapter 2 of this minibook for more on Panda's penalties.) Worse yet, a site with mostly duplicated content could be seen as spam and even removed from the index. So although a little duplication might not hurt you, too much could sink your SEO ship.

Sources of Duplicate Content and How to Resolve Them

Content can become duplicated either intentionally or by accident. There's a saying that "Imitation is the sincerest form of flattery." Well, you can do without this kind of flattery when it comes to your website. Whatever the copycat's motivation is, you don't want people copying your original content and having it indexed as theirs if you can help it.

There are two basic types of duplicate content:

+ **Outside-your-domain duplicate content.** This type happens when two different websites have the same text indexed in the search engines.

+ **Within-your-domain duplicate content.** This second type refers to websites that create duplicate content within their own *domain* (the root of the site's unique URL, such as www.domain.com).

Sites can end up having within-your-domain duplicate content due to their own faulty internal linking procedures, and often webmasters don't even realize they have a problem. (We explain some of these in the following sections.) If two or more pages within your own site duplicate each other, you inadvertently diminish the ability for one or the other to be included in search results. In some cases, a webmaster inadvertently causes half or more of a site's pages to be completely ignored by the search engines because of duplicate content issues.

You can end up with duplicate content within your own site for a variety of reasons, such as having multiple URLs all containing the same content; printer-friendly pages; pages that get built on the fly with session IDs in the

URL; using or providing syndicated or third-party content; problems caused by using localization, minor content variations, or an unfriendly Content Management System; and archives.

Multiple URLs with the same content

Even with websites under your own control, you may have duplicate content resulting from any of the following sources:

+ Similar pages in the same website (www.*yourdomain.com*)

+ Similar pages in different domains that you own (www.*yourdomain.com* and www.*yourotherdomain.com*)

+ Similar pages in your www-prefixed site and the non-www version (www.*yourdomain.com* and *yourdomain.com*)

When search engines find two pages with nearly the same content, they may include both pages in their index. However, they take only one of these pages into consideration for search results. The search engines do this because they want to show users a variety of listings — not several that are the same. To make the entire body of your website count, you want to ensure that each of your web pages is unique.

But here's the rub: The search engines may consider two pages the same even if only part of the page is duplicated. Just the headings, the first paragraph, the Title tag, or any other portion being the same can trigger "duplicate" status. For instance, if you use the same Title tag on multiple pages, the search engines might see them as duplicate pages just because they share that single, but important, line of HTML code.

To avoid issues with duplicate content, you always need to write unique headings, tags, and content for each page in your website (see Chapter 3 of this minibook for more).

Finding out how many duplicates the search engine thinks you have

A good place to start looking at duplicate content is to find out how many of your web pages are currently indexed, versus how many the search engines consider to be duplicates. Here's how:

1. **On Google's website (**http://www.google.com**), type [site:*domain.com*] in the search text box (leaving out the square brackets and using your domain), and then press Enter.**

2. **When the results page comes up, scroll to the bottom and click the highest page number that shows (usually 10).**

   Notice the total number of results shown in "Page 1 of about ### results" at the top of the page.

   The "of about ###" number represents the approximate total number of indexed pages in the site.

3. **Now navigate to the very last page of the results.**

   The count shown there represents the filtered results. The difference between these two numbers represents the number of duplicates as well as pages the search engine considers low-quality. Typical examples are outdated product pages or those with parameters in the URL.

For performance reasons, Google doesn't display all the indexed pages and omits the ones that seem most like duplicates. If you truly want to see *all* the listings for a site, you can navigate to the very last results page of your [site:] query and click the option to "repeat the search with the omitted results included" at the bottom of the page. (Even then, Google only shows up to a maximum of 1,000 listings.)

Google Search Console (the free communication hub and toolset that Google makes available to every website owner) can give you a hand discovering duplicate content on your site. Just run the Duplicate title tags or Duplicate meta descriptions reports (located under Search Appearance ⇨ HTML Improvements) to identify any pages indexed with the same tags. (More tips on using Search Console can be found in Book VIII.)

Avoiding duplicate content on your own site

When it comes to cleaning up duplicate pages on your own website, which you have control over, after all, don't spend time wondering, "How similar can they be?" As much as possible, just make the content different, and you'll follow the best practice of having unique, original content throughout your site. In some situations, duplication may be unavoidable, so read on for recommendations. But stay away from the edges of what might be all right with the search engines.

To keep your site in the safe harbor, here are some ways you can avoid or handle duplicate content within your own website:

✦ `Title` **tags, and** `Meta` **description and keywords tags:** Make sure that every page has a unique `Title` tag, `Meta` description tag, and `Meta` keywords tag in the HTML code.

✦ **Heading tags:** Make sure the heading tags (labeled `H#`) within the body copy differ from other pages' headings. Keeping in mind that your headings should all use meaningful, non-generic words makes this a bit easier.

✦ **Repeated text, such as a slogan:** If you have to show a repeated sentence or paragraph throughout your site, such as a company slogan, you should consider putting the slogan into an image on most pages. Pick the one web page that you think should rank for that repeated content and leave it as text on that page so that the search engine spiders can crawl it. If anyone tries to search for that content, the search engines can find that unique content on the page you selected.

For example, if your classic car customization website has the slogan, "We restore the rumble to your classic car," you probably want to display that throughout your site. But you should prevent the search engines from seeing the repetition. Leave it as HTML text on just one page, like your home page or the About Us page. Then everywhere else, just create a nifty graphic that lets users, but not search engines, see the slogan.

✦ **Sitemap:** Be sure that your HTML *sitemap* (a page containing links to the pages in your site, like a table of contents) includes links to your preferred page's URL, for example, `http://www.sitename.com/silo1/` versus `http://www.sitename.com/silo1/index.html` (in cases where you have similar versions). The sitemap helps the search engines understand which page is your best or preferred version.

✦ **Product pages:** Make sure to include unique text content on all product pages, not just the manufacturer-supplied descriptions. It creates a lot of extra work to write original descriptive text and/or incorporate user-generated text such as reviews on each product page. But if you want to rank for "Acme X19," you have to differentiate your Acme X19 page from all the other retail sites carrying that product.

On the other end of the sales spectrum, if you produce a product that is sold on other people's sites, determine whether you want your own page to rank for that product. If so, you need to keep your page unique. Consider distributing different descriptive text to your resellers than what you show on your site.

Product variations, such as different colors or sizes, ideally should not be on separate pages (though you may have a highly sought-after variation that merits its own page). Use drop-down lists or other web design elements to let users choose the size, color, and other options so that you can keep a product consolidated on one page.

✦ **Canonical tag:** For situations in which duplicate pages are unavoidable, you can use the *canonical tag*. This is an HTML link element (`rel="canonical"`) that can be inserted in the head section of each duplicate page to indicate which URL should be considered the *canonical* (best or original) version of that page's content. Back in 2009, Google, Yahoo, and Microsoft got together and created the canonical tag to give webmasters a last-resort solution. The search engines take the tag as a suggestion, not a directive, but it can often resolve duplicate content and prevent search engine penalties. Currently, Google seems to acknowledge canonical link elements most of the time, whereas Bing only sometimes observes them.

Applying canonical tags is tricky; it should be handled only by an experienced webmaster who understands both how to use them and the risks involved. For that reason, we don't give specific instructions in this book. If you want more information, search for [canonical tag] in Google Search Console Help (https://support.google.com/webmasters/).

✦ **Block indexing:** You may have duplicate pages that you need to keep on your site. For example, a site may need to retain previous years' terms of service pages for legal reasons, even though they've been superseded by a slightly altered current version. In cases like that, you could block the search engines from indexing the page either by specifying it in your site's robots.txt file or by inserting the following tag into the Head section of a particular page: <meta name="robots" content="noindex"> Read more on blocking pages from indexing in Book VII, Chapter 1.

✦ **Consolidate similar pages:** If you have whole pages that contain similar or identical text, you may be able to combine them and edit the content as needed. Ask why the duplication occurred, and choose the correct remedy. You may have a legitimate need for the additional version of the page (in which case, canonical tags may be your answer, as mentioned earlier in this list). But if that additional page isn't needed, trimming the extra page is recommended.

If you do need to consolidate pages to a single page, a few precautions are in order (see the following numbered list for details). You don't want to accidentally wipe out any link equity you may have accumulated. *Link equity* refers to the perceived-expertise value of all the inbound links pointing to a web page. You also don't want to cause people's links and bookmarks suddenly to break, which causes an error message if they try to open your old page.

When consolidating two pages to make one your main version, follow these steps to take some precautions:

1. **Check for inbound links.**

   Do a [**link:*domain.com/yourpage*.html**] search in Google or use a third-party backlink checker to find out who's already linked to your different URLs for a page. If one version has 15 links and the other version has 4,000, you know which one to keep: the one that 4,000 people linked to.

2. **Update your internal links.**

   Make sure that your site map and all other pages in your site no longer link to the page you decided to remove.

3. **Set up a 301 Redirect.**

   When you take down the removed page's content, put in its place a *301 Redirect,* which is a type of HTML command that automatically reroutes any incoming link to the URL with the content that you want to retain. (***Note:*** For help on using 301 Redirects, see Book VII, Chapter 4.)

Avoiding duplications between your different domains

Most websites today operate both the domain that begins with www and the domain without this prefix (such as www.*yourdomain.com* and *yourdomain.com*). You do not want to duplicate your site content between these two domains. Instead, set up a 301 Redirect from one root domain to the other and keep only one set of your web documents in production. (***Note:*** It doesn't matter whether you redirect the www or the non-www version, although it may be more common to make the www version the main site.) Users coming to either URL can get to the same content.

If you own multiple domains with the same content, you can solve the problem of duplicate content with the same technique. Decide which domain you want to rank well for your keywords and redirect the other domains to that one. Or if you truly need separate sites with duplicate content, know that you're going to pay a price when the search engines pick one page version that they decide is the authoritative one and ignore your others. (You can learn technical solutions to get around some of these issues, as well. See Book VII for more details.)

Printer-friendly pages

A common practice that inadvertently creates duplicate content within a website involves printer-friendly pages. *Printer-friendly pages* are separate pages designed for printing, without the heavy images, navigation elements, and advertisements that eat up a lot of printer ink. Recipe sites are notorious for these pages, but many sites offer both an HTML version and a simplified version of each page that their users can easily print. The printer-friendly page has its own URL, so it's actually a twin of the HTML page.

You don't need to have separate text-only pages for printing. The best way to allow easy printing, keep your users happy, and follow SEO best practices is to use *CSS* (Cascading Style Sheets, an efficient way to control the look of your site by defining styles in one place). A print style sheet within your CSS can reformat your HTML pages on the fly so that they can be easily printed. Inside your CSS file, you can specify how a page should automatically change when a user chooses to print it. Your CSS can control print formatting such as page width, margins, font substitutions, and which images to print and which to omit. Creating a print style sheet within your CSS file is a much easier and search-friendly solution than duplicating your pages with printer-friendly versions.

If you do not want to use CSS for printable pages, you have to find ways to avoid several problems if you have twin versions of each content page, one for viewing and one for printing:

✦ **Link equity gets reduced.** This problem is common to all forms of duplicate content. People are going to link to both versions, so the link-equity value for your content is effectively split between the two pages. Because link equity helps search engines determine how much authority a web page has for a relevant search query, a diminished link-equity value means that your page won't rank as well in search results.

✦ **If you decide to consolidate the pages down the line, inbound links could break.** Because people link to both versions, when you're ready to do away with printer-friendly pages, existing links may break. (*Note:* You want to create 301 Redirects for those pages, which fixes the links but costs you some initial work and ongoing vigilance to keep those codes in place forever.)

✦ **Double the maintenance is a hassle.** If you have printer-friendly duplicate pages on your site, you already know that anytime you want to make a change to one, you have to remember to make the same change on the other. (We thought we'd mention that this is a pain, in case you didn't know already.)

✦ **Search engines pick just one page.** Having two versions of a page on your site forces the search engines to pick the one they think is the original and filter out the other one from their search results. And because the simplified version is probably much easier to crawl than your beautiful HTML version, they may choose the printer-friendly page particularly if your printer-friendly page has received more backlinks than your HTML version. So basically, you lose control over which version greets first-time visitors coming from a search results page.

If you currently have printer-friendly versions of your pages as separate URLs, we suggest you convert to a print style sheet in an external CSS file. You won't need the Printer Friendly Version hyperlinks on your pages anymore (unless you want to leave them for usability, maybe changing the wording) because whenever a user prints a page by choosing File ➪ Print or pressing Ctrl+P, your CSS automatically takes charge and delivers a printable version.

When getting rid of printer-friendly pages that you no longer need, be careful. Check for inbound links, update any internal links you may have to those pages, and set up a 301 Redirect on the removed page. You want to make sure not to hurt your link equity or cause your users any problems when you remove a page.

If you decide you still want to keep your printer-friendly text versions, circumvent the duplicate content problem by putting a `noindex` command in the HTML code to prevent search engines from crawling these pages. You'd probably lose some links, but at least the search engines wouldn't confuse these pages with your main content.

Dynamic pages with session IDs

Many websites track the user's *session* — the current time period the user is active on the website since logging on. Sometimes these sites add a session ID code to each page's URL as the user travels the site. This is a really bad way to handle passing a session ID from page to page because it creates what looks like duplicate content. Even though the page itself has not changed, the varying parameters showing at the end of each URL causes search engines to think they are separate pages.

In fact, you don't want to put any type of variables directly into your URL strings except for ones that actually correspond with changed page content. You need unique content for every URL. If your site passes session IDs through the URL string, here are three ways to fix it:

✦ **Stop appending session IDs.** Ideally, you should correct your Content Management System (CMS) or server application so that it no longer creates URLs with session IDs. Instead, use *cookies. Cookies* are small bits of code that the server assigns to a user's browser that tracks and stores the user's behavior or information the user provides from page to page in order to serve up a customized browsing experience.

✦ **Tell search engines how to handle parameters.** In Google Search Console, you can use the URL Parameters tool to specify what parameters are used on your site, what they refer to, and whether Google should crawl them. Bing has a similar webmaster tool. However, it's better if you can stop adding codes to a user's URL. (For more information, read Google's support article here: `https://support.google.com/webmasters/answer/6080550?hl=en`.)

✦ **Show spiders friendly URLs.** This is a more advanced solution, but you could consider using "user agent sniffing" to detect search engine spiders. User agent sniffing occurs when websites show different content to different users depending on the browser. If the page detects it's a search engine spider, it could deliver parameter-free URLs to that spider. This sniffing is invisible to the spider and, with a 301 Redirect on the old URL pointing to the rewritten URL, the spiders have a URL that they can index. For more information on 301 Redirects, visit Book VII, Chapter 3.

Delivering *exactly* the same content to a search engine as to a user is very important; delivering different content is considered a form of spam.

Content syndication

Content syndication simply means sending out your website content to others. The big upside of syndicating your content is having more people read your stuff, which in turn can lead to increased traffic coming back to your website. The potential downside of syndication is duplicating your content. In essence, you are trading potential search engine ranking for direct links and the traffic that your content syndication brings in.

Blog index pages

Blog posts are not isolated articles; they exist among many other posts accumulating over time in a blog. Although each post has a distinct page URL to identify it, the blog as a whole also has an index page and usually category pages that list multiple blog posts. When a blogger publishes a new post, the blog software automatically adds the new post's title and an excerpt to these index and category pages, which is super convenient for readers and bloggers alike. But blog index and category pages can inadvertently create duplicate content issues for a website if too much of the article is reused. To avoid this problem, include only a portion, not the full text of the article, in the excerpt. Even better, if bloggers manually edit the excerpt slightly, they can ensure that it isn't duplicated as well as word it to stimulate someone who's reading the excerpt to click through for the full story.

Press releases

Then there is the problem of press releases. Press releases are posted on wire services for the express purpose of being picked up and duplicated on as many sites as possible. If your company puts out press releases, don't stop. Even though they do become duplicate content that may not bring any unique ranking to your website, you distribute a press release for other reasons than search engine ranking, such as for branding, public relations, investor relations, and so on. These are legitimate goals, too.

Be sure to make the text content of your press release unique. In other words, don't copy your announcement word for word from your website's static pages. And include a brief "About" section for the press release that doesn't exactly match company information found on your website.

Also be careful not to load your press release with backlinks to your website. Links from press releases are considered "unnatural" links (because you paid for them) and could get you in trouble with Google's Penguin algorithm. A single link from your brand name to your home page should be okay. (For more about Penguin and avoiding link penalties, see Book VI, Chapter 3.)

Syndicates

You might also use more traditional ways of syndicating your content, which means to create the content and receive a fee from other sites that want to use it. For example, newspaper artists draw their cartoons and then use a syndicate to make them available to any news organization that cares to run them, in exchange for a fee. However, if you syndicate your website content, you are very likely to run into duplicate-content problems. If an expert-level website takes your content, chances are *that* site will become the canonical source for that information. For instance, if a big city news organization decides to fill one of its columns with your articles, chances are that the search engines will determine that the big-city news site takes precedence over yours (because it's the 800-pound gorilla), and that site would outrank you for that content if someone searched for it. If the sites are equal in every other way, however, the search engines look through their indexes to determine the original, or earliest, source of the content and filter out the copies that came later as duplicates. If you weigh the advantages of getting your content (and brand name) in front of a bigger audience through syndication, the sacrifice of not being the ranking source may be worth it.

Social media sharing

Bloggers and other content producers routinely turn to social media to share any new content they publish. The best way to do this depends on your target audience, whose preferences should influence how you share — which social media sites you use, how long your posts are, what types of media to include with your post, and so forth. Whatever method you choose, you want to spread news of any new blog post or website content you create using social media. We cover more about social media in Chapter 7 of this minibook.

To avoid creating duplicate content with your social shares, post a snippet or summary, not the entire text of your website content or blog post, into Google+, Facebook, LinkedIn, Tumblr, or other social media site. Or, rewrite the content enough so that you're posting a new version of it in social media, linked back to the original on your site, if appropriate.

Curation

Because we're talking about avoiding duplicate content, it seems fitting to mention curation, which can be a highly effective form of content generation when done right. When you *curate* content, you pull together several existing articles or other types of content from various sources and then create a new article that presents that content to readers with your own added commentary. Top Ten lists are a good example. The curated article gives a short description of each item with a link to the source. When curating content, you can quote small bits, but be careful not to duplicate the original sources. And always include your own fresh text to add value.

Localization

Many websites repurpose the same content for various locations. For example, a large real estate company with brokerage offices throughout the state offers the same template to all their brokers, customized only with a different city name and local property listings. Or a national cosmetics company gives local representatives their "own" sites, but all of them have the same standard template and content.

For local searching, a template site may do all right. For instance, if a person located in Poughkeepsie searches for [real estate for sale], or if anyone searches with a specific geographic term such as [real estate listings Poughkeepsie], that searcher will probably find brokerage sites that are located in Poughkeepsie, including the sites built within a national company's template for that location, which may include duplicated content. However, if the Poughkeepsie broker himself would like to rank for a broader search query like [New York properties], he's probably out of luck. His website won't have enough unique content about that keyword phrase to rank in the search results. Doing a quick find-and-replace search for a keyword to create "new" targeted pages (such as changing Poughkeepsie to Albany) is not enough to create unique content and is in fact considered spam by the search engines. You must have truly unique content on unique pages in order to survive and thrive in the search engines.

You can use a template to create many web pages or sites, but here's how to do it without creating duplicate content. You need to do more than just a find-and-replace search for a few terms. Customize the content for each location, including the headings, Title tags, Meta tags, body content, and so on. Unless you're located in a highly competitive demographic market area such as Chicago or New York City, your template-based site may be sufficient if you're only after local search business.

If you want to rank for non-local search queries, you absolutely need to customize your site content and make it unique. Add information that shows you know about that local area. Depending on what kind of traffic you hope to attract through the search engines, you probably need to make changes to your content focused on improving both the quality and quantity.

Mirrors

On the web, a *mirror* refers to a full copy of a web page or site. The mirrored version is an exact replica of the original page. Yes, this is blatantly duplicate content, but there are a few legitimate reasons to mirror a web page.

✦ You may need to mirror a web page for user convenience, such as when multiple websites offer copies of a downloadable file so that users can access it at each location.

✦ You may be testing different versions of a page. A common type of web test, known as a *split test* or *A/B test*, involves directing half of the visitors coming to a page to the normal page, while the other half sees a slightly different version of the page. The server splits the traffic randomly, and data collected over time shows whether Page A or Page B performs better. We recommend that you run limited tests on specific variables (that is, minor variations between pages A and B). Use the Google Analytics Content Experiments tool (part of the free Google Analytics software) so that the search engine understands you are just testing.

✦ You may want to display a backup version of a page that's temporarily down.

✦ Many websites have a separate mobile site (usually set up as a subdomain m.*yourdomain*.com) that contains nearly the same content as the desktop site. This is not really a problem, but use canonical tags to ensure that the search engines know which is which. Set up the tags to indicate that the desktop (www.*yourdomain*.com) version of each page should be indexed as canonical. For more tips on setting up a mobile SEO-friendly site, see Book IV, Chapter 1.

Mirroring should never be done deceptively. Hackers and pornography sites are notorious for mirroring sites, having content in 20, 30, 40, or more locations because of how frequently their sites are discovered and taken down. You want to ensure that search engines consider you a legitimate company with original content. Unless you have a need to put up a temporary page such as the ones mentioned above, try to avoid using mirrors on the web.

CMS duplication

Many sites use a *content management system* (CMS), an automated online shopping platform, or both. These types of software programs help create and maintain web pages on a site. Some CMSs, however, have a problem: They generate duplicate content. It's just the way they're programmed. Or is it?

Your CMS should allow you to customize all parts of your web pages, from the body text to the `Title` tags to the anchor text of links. If your CMS currently doesn't allow this, talk to your IT department and ask them to revise the settings. If you're a small business without an IT department, we recommend scrapping your inflexible system and starting over with a CMS that allows you to make these changes. Seriously, it's that important.

According to a September 2008 Google Webmaster Blog post, most site owners who ask about duplicate content are worried about issues like having multiple URLs on the same domain point to the same content. This is a situation that many CMSs create naturally. The example given in the blog post featured these two addresses:

```
www.example.com/skates.asp?color=black&brand=riedell
www.example.com/skates.asp?brand=riedell&color=black
```

Both of these URLs bring up the same web page, but they're different URLs because the CMS put the parameters for color and brand in a different order.

If that example looks like your site, you should realize that this can be prevented. Your CMS needs to facilitate control of your site's URLs. If the page has unique content, don't change the URL.

Similarly, if your website lets users navigate to a page from various categories, be sure that your site contains only one copy of each file, not multiple copies. For instance, an e-commerce site selling ladies shoes might have separate navigation choices for dress, casual, sandals, pumps, open-toe, closed-toe, and so forth. One shoe could fall into many different categories, but no matter how the user navigates to find it, that unique shoe should have only one page at only one URL address.

If your site does have category-type pages with their own URLs, try to add at least a sentence or two of unique content about the category. For instance, a clothing site with a category page for women's shoes could contain a little text above the list of results (which are inevitably duplicated from other pages on the website), such as "Find a large selection of women's shoes including sandals, athletic shoes, casual and professional footwear, boots, slippers and high-fashion shoes. Our shoes can take you anywhere, from the beach to the mall to the classroom, boardroom, or ballroom!" Original, descriptive text can help you avoid a search engine penalty for thin content, and it can also make your page more engaging to readers.

Archives

After your website has been up for a while, you eventually need to trim some older content to keep the current information uncluttered. If the older pages are still useful, you can put them into an *archive* (storage area where older content is out of the way, but still accessible). Just be careful that your archive doesn't create duplicate content problems with current information on your site. (Without correction, duplicate-content issues are almost always the case with blogging software and with news content.)

Keep one best practice in mind when you set up an archive: Do *not* change the archived page's URL. It's best to let pages stay at their original web addresses when you set up an archive so that the URL stays golden through time. If you must change a URL, remember to do a 301 Redirect to the new name.

Active blog sites tend to need archiving sooner than other content pages because they fill up with text and comments so quickly. Blog software programs generally include prior posts at the bottom of new posts and create copies of blog posts for appropriate categories or time periods, so duplicate content is sort of built-in. They also automatically move older posts into archive directories. If your blog is updated regularly and actively commented on, you don't really have to worry about duplicate content because the search engines are used to seeing this behavior. However, if you don't publish a lot of new content to your blog, the search engines filter out pages that seem to duplicate each other.

Duplication by Outsiders

In this section, we address the more serious issue of people taking your content on purpose. If you've got loads of useful and engaging information, there is a good chance that someday it will wind up being intentionally copied and republished on someone else's site. Sometimes the external site courteously blocks the duplicate content from being indexed (such as by putting a *noindex Meta tag* in the page's Head section to tell search engine spiders to ignore the page), in which case you don't have a problem. But the more usual situation is that your page is simply copied as indexable content. This kind of duplicate content happens frequently, and it can damage your site's reputation and authority with the search engines.

There is no excuse for taking someone else's page intact, adding a different façade, making a few top-of-page cosmetic changes, and then uploading it to another site for indexing with the search engines. Sometimes it even still contains the original displayed text and links! Unfortunately, there is no foolproof defense against someone taking your content from the web.

To deter others from copying your content, we recommend that you take the following steps:

✦ Display a copyright notice on your website.

✦ Register for a federal copyright.

These two proactive steps can help you defend your website against intentional spam. It's a good idea for you to register for a federal copyright of your website as software. This is a low-cost and important step in your anti-theft effort. Even though all content carries copyright naturally, you want to actually file for a copyright registration because only a federal copyright has enough teeth in it to help you fight violations of your copyrights in court, if it ever comes down to that. (See Chapter 6 of this minibook for instructions on how to go about filing for a federal copyright.)

With a federal copyright on file, you have legal recourse if things get ugly. You also carry a lot more weight when you tell people your work is copyrighted with the U.S. government and then ask them to remove it from their site. The federal copyright can be enforced throughout the United States and internationally.

In the following sections, we list different types of intentional spam, with tips for what you can do to protect your website.

Scrapers

Scrapers are people who send a robot to your website to copy (or "scrape") the entire site and then republish it as their own. Sometimes they don't even bother to replace your company name throughout the content. Scraping a site is a copyright violation, but it's also more than that: It is theft, and if the content is protected by a federal copyright, the thief can be sued in federal court.

If your website has been scraped, you need to decide what your objective is. Will you be satisfied simply to get the content pulled down? Or do you feel that the other party's actions are so serious and malicious that you want to sue for damages? You need to decide how much money and effort you're willing to spend and what outcome you're really after.

If your site is scraped, your first step can be a simple email requesting that the site stop using your content. Often this is enough to get it removed. You can also report the site to the search engines or the *ISP* (Internet service provider) that hosts the site domain. If you notify the ISP that the site has been scraped and provide some proof, that ISP may shut the site down.

Because scraping is a crime, you may choose to file a police report for theft. You should have printouts and other evidence that the text is yours and that it has been stolen to back you up. You can even hire a lawyer and serve the scrapers with a cease-and-desist order, demanding that they take down the offending web pages or face legal action. As a last resort, you can file a lawsuit and fight it out in court.

Clueless newbies

Clueless newbies are what we call people who take someone else's website content but don't realize they've done anything wrong. They may be under the mistaken impression that everything on the Internet is fair game and free for the taking. They may not realize that intellectual property laws apply to the Internet just as they do everywhere else.

If your content has been stolen by one or more clueless newbies, we suggest you email them. Tell them that it's copyrighted material and kindly ask them to take it down. If you're feeling generous, as an alternative, you might suggest that they only include an excerpt or summary of your content, link to your site instead, and put a `Meta` robots `"noindex"` tag on their page so that the search engine spiders won't crawl it. The newbie site owner may comply, and you have taught him or her a lesson in Internet etiquette. But even if they don't comply, the duplicated page is probably a low risk to you. A new site generally doesn't have much authority in the search engine's eyes, so their site may not hurt your rankings. They have no right to your content for their own commercial use, however, so you don't have to let them use it.

Stolen content

When you work hard to create unique, engaging content for your own website, it can be frustrating for you or even damaging to your search engine rankings when that content gets stolen and duplicated on some other site.

We suggest that you regularly check to see if your website content has been copied and used somewhere else. You have two ways to check this:

✦ **Exact-match search:** Copy a long snippet of text (a sentence or two) from one of your web pages. Then paste it within quotation marks (" ") in a search box to find any indexed web pages containing that exact text.

✦ **Copyscape:** Another method uses the free service at Copyscape (`www.copyscape.com/`). Figure 5-1 shows how straightforward Copyscape is to use; you just type in your page's URL in the text box and click Go. If the page has been scraped, you see the offending URL in the results.

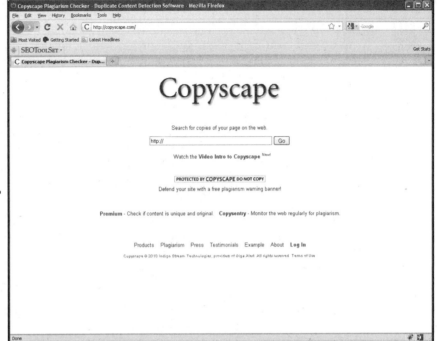

Figure 5-1:
Copyscape lets you find copies of your website content anywhere on the Internet.

When your content is stolen, you may see it appearing everywhere. Like playing the Whack-A-Mole arcade game, you might succeed in getting one site to remove your stolen content, only to find it popping up on another.

If you're in the Whack-A-Mole situation and lots of other sites now have your content, hopefully you have a federal copyright and can follow some of the recommendations we give in the section "Duplication by Outsiders," earlier in this chapter. If you don't have a federal copyright, you may have only one recourse: changing your content. It's unfair, it's a pain, but if you don't have a registered copyright, you can't do much to stop people from stealing your stuff. Being unique on the web is more important to your search engine rankings than playing Whack-a-Mole, trying to stop thieves from taking your content; so rewrite your own text to be different from theirs. Enforce your copyright when you find people ripping you off, but don't think that it will solve your stolen content problem.

Chapter 6: Crediting Your Content

*I*f you've applied the ideas laid out in Chapters 1 to 5 of this minibook, you are well on your way to a successful website. Your website hopefully contains lots of engaging content that your users love, with pages focused on your *keywords* (specific words or phrases entered in a search query) so that search engines can clearly establish your site's subject relevance.

In Chapter 5 of this minibook, we cover the evils of duplicate content in many of its forms (site scraping, duplicate pages within the same domain, printer-friendly pages, dynamic pages with session IDs in the URLs, content syndication, localization, mirrors, archives, spam, and stolen content). In this chapter, we want to provide the remedy. Here, you discover what to do if your content is stolen by some other website. By the time you finish reading this chapter, you'll be well-armed to deal with this inevitable problem.

We also explain how you can incorporate content from other sites, if you should ever want to do that. Because Chapter 5 of this minibook is an entire chapter on how to avoid creating duplicate content, we figured it's time to balance the subject with information on how to use content from another site the *right* way: Sometimes, as with news sites, you'll need to do it.

Factoring in Intellectual Property Considerations

Not everyone realizes that websites are the intellectual property of their owners. Your website content is your intellectual property, just as much as a book is the intellectual property of its author and publisher. And as intellectual property, your website is governed by copyright laws that protect it, especially if you've obtained a federal copyright. (We talk about that process in the section "Filing for copyright," later in this chapter.)

Nevertheless, website content is often stolen and republished. If you've created lots of great content for your site, we almost guarantee that sometime, somewhere, you'll see your content pop up on someone else's site.

This book is not intended to replace legal advice. You should seek a copyright lawyer in order to get the full picture regarding your legal rights and options.

What to do when your content is stolen

You can expect some duplication of your content, especially if it's good quality and attracting visitors and links. After all, imitation is the sincerest form of flattery, as the saying goes. Still, you might feel hopping mad to find out that your carefully crafted and possibly expensive content has been ripped off by a website, giving you no citation or link and acting as if it is that site's own work.

In the "Stolen content" section of Chapter 5 in this minibook, you learn ways to discover other websites that are using your own content. But how can you respond when your website content is copied and posted on some other website? You can do a number of things if your content or entire site is stolen:

+ **Email a request.** A good first step can be a simple email request to the site's webmaster or contact person. Ask nicely to stop using your content. Often, this message is enough to get the stolen content removed.

+ **Report it to the search engines.** You can file a report of copyright infringement with the search engines to have the offending web pages removed from their index. This procedure is allowed under the Digital Millennium Copyright Act. For instructions for Google, see www. google.com/dmca.html. Google's support has a Legal Troubleshooter section where you can file a legal removal request to eliminate web pages that contain your stolen content from the search engine's results pages (see Figure 6-1). For Yahoo's procedure, check out http:// info.yahoo.com/copyright/us/details.html. To make a similar request on Bing, go to https://support.discoverbing.com/ eform.aspx?productKey=bingcontentremoval&ct=eformts& scrx=1&st=1&wfxredirect=1.

+ **Report it to the offending site's ISP.** You can find out which *Internet service provider* (ISP) is hosting the site and contact the ISP. If you notify the ISP that your site has been scraped and provide some proof, it may shut down the site. (You can use the WHOIS Lookup at www.whois.net to identify information about a site's registered owners, including the domain servers that host the site, which is the same as the ISP.)

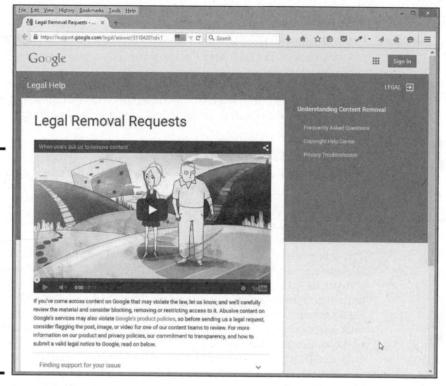

Figure 6-1:
Google gives site owners a way to request removal of search results that contain stolen copies of their website's contents.

✦ **File a police report.** Because theft is a crime, you can file a report with your local police or sheriff's department. Make sure you have undisputed evidence that the text is yours and that it has been stolen. Print the offending page as it appears in your browser, and then print the HTML code for that page so that you have it. Call a friend to have him verify that the theft has taken place, as well.

See if the offending site contains a References or Clients page. If so, you can consider writing down the names and URLs of these sites so that you can notify them of the theft a little later. You might also run a search to discover the list of sites that link to the offending pages ([**link:*offendingdomain.com***]), and later send the emails informing them of inadvertently supporting a scraped site and inviting them to link to the "source" of the content — your website — instead.

✦ **Send a cease-and-desist order.** You can have a lawyer draft a cease-and-desist order, demanding that the website take down the offending web pages or face legal action. The downsides with this approach are that it's costly and it gives the other party advance warning if you plan to file a lawsuit later. So before you do this, be sure to put together all the evidence recommended in the preceding paragraph.

✦ **File a lawsuit:** In serious cases in which your business has been materially damaged, you can hire a lawyer and sue the other party. But make sure that you have lots of evidence. Follow the recommended ideas for evidence gathering under the previous "File a police report" bullet.

The preceding list is not meant to be a step-by-step procedure. You can pick and choose from these suggestions based on your situation. But remember that you have options in case someone does steal your content.

Filing for copyright

To protect your website content, we recommend that you do two things:

✦ Display a copyright notice on your website.

✦ Register for a federal copyright.

These are two proactive, low-cost steps that can help you defend your website against theft. When you've registered for a federal copyright of your website as software, you have legal recourse if you need to file suit. Only a federal copyright allows you to successfully fight violations of your copyrights legally. Your words also carry a lot more weight when you tell people your work is copyrighted with the U.S. government when you are asking them to remove your content from their sites. The federal copyright can be enforced throughout the United States and internationally.

The U.S. Library of Congress manages the U.S. Copyright Office. The U.S. Copyright Office considers Internet pages to be software programs. To have a copyright simply requires that the work contain a valid copyright notice as follows: © *year author name* (such as © 2015 John Wiley & Sons, Inc.).

Registering a copyright is not mandatory, but this is a time-proven and effective step. After you register your site, the copyright stays in effect. Unless you completely replace your site with a new one, because it is "software," your future website updates continue to be protected by your initial registration.

To register, you should refer to the filing procedures required by the U.S. Copyright Office. You can handle the registration online — see the website at www.copyright.gov.

On an international level, the U.S. government became a member of the Berne Convention in 1989 and fully supports the Universal Copyright Convention. Under this Convention, any work of an author who is a citizen of a Convention country automatically receives protection in *all* countries that are also members, provided that the work makes use of a proper copyright symbol (©). The degree of protection may vary, but some minimal protection is defined and guaranteed in that agreement. Jurisdiction for prosecuting violations lies exclusively with the federal government.

Using content from other sites

Now, what if you want to use *other* people's content on your site? Perhaps you've seen a chart or image online that is relevant, useful, and perfect for your site's users; or maybe you read an article in a magazine that says exactly what you want to tell your users. You also realize that reusing something that's already written is undoubtedly the fastest way to add bulk to your site. So you believe your site simply *must* have these things. Can you — should you — use them?

Be careful! You don't want to have duplicate content on your site, because that won't help and could even harm your site rankings (as we cover in length in Chapter 5 of this minibook). You also don't want to be deceptive and make it look as if it's your original creation — that's called plagiarism. Deceiving your users or the search engines usually backfires. For instance, your pages could be filtered out of search results, you could damage your reputation with customers, you could be sued, and so on.

But say that you've found something you know would add tremendous value for your users that's also right on topic for your website. Here are some best practices for the times you need to use external content on your website:

✦ **Read the site.** Often sites will have a copyright or legal page that details their use permissions. Starting with the legal page gives you guidelines on what you'll be able to reasonably expect to be allowed to use.

✦ **Get permission.** If you want to republish something you saw on someone else's site, ask for permission. Not every website owner will agree, but you can still ask. When you make your request, be sure to say you'll give a link back to their site and give them credit.

✦ **Do not use the whole thing.** Whether it's a full article, a full poem, a full page, or something else, do not republish someone else's content in its entirety (unless you have an agreement with the owner).

✦ **Excerpt or summarize it.** You can write a brief summary or review in your own words, rather than displaying the original text (give a link instead). Don't use more than an excerpt if you're posting the original words. For instance, if it's a magazine article you wanted, you could write a review, rebuttal, or summary and give a link to read the article on the original site. The most you should copy directly is a short excerpt in a quote.

Excerpting and summarizing are writing methods used in *content curation*. This popular technique pulls from related resources to create a new article that cites and contains links to the sources with original, added-value text. For more on curating content, see Chapter 5 of this minibook.

✦ **Set the other source's content apart by using quotation marks or a block quote.** The idea is to make it clear to users that the excerpted content is quoted, not original to you. You can also make that clear to search engines by indenting the text with a `Blockquote` HTML tag.

Some people claim "fair use" when reusing other people's content. The doctrine of fair use says that under some circumstances, it's not a copyright violation to quote another's work. This is a confusing part of copyright law, and the line between fair use and infringement is very fuzzy. One clear guideline is that you can't use the borrowed content for profit in any way. If you have an ad or sell things anywhere on your site, it's considered a for-profit website. Basically, no business qualifies for fair use. In the area of copyright infringement, it's best to keep your website in the safe harbor and follow the best practices listed here.

Crediting original authors

When you do use someone else's content, be it text or other types of content such as images or video, give credit where credit is due. Attribute the work to its author or to the originating website. In addition to setting text apart with quotation marks or as a block quote, you can include a line that says something like: "Used by permission of . . ." or "Courtesy of . . ." or "Provided by . . ." and identify the name of the author. If you weren't able to get permission, you still can mention where the information comes from. You may also want to include the `cite` attribute in a quote or `Blockquote` tag. The `cite` attribute is used in the `Quote` `Q` and `Blockquote` tags to reference the source for material that originally appeared elsewhere.

The `Q` tag is used for short, inline quotes, such as

```
<P>According to a World Research Foundation article, <I><Q
    CITE="http://www.wrf.org/news/news0017.htm">In nine
    double-blind studies comparing placebos to aspirin,
    placebos proved to be 54 percent as effective as the
    actual analgesic</Q></I></P>
```

Note that you may want to include the quoted text in italics — as in the preceding example — or in quotes, because most browsers do not render the `Q` tag correctly (they don't place it in quotes or format it correctly to distinguish it).

The Blockquote tag is used for longer quotes, usually where an entire paragraph or more is referenced. For example:

```
<BLOCKQUOTE CITE="http://www.wrf.org/news/news0017.htm ">
   <P>I don't believe that the use of placebos is immoral
   or unethical. In reality, it seems that the medical
   profession's lack of understanding and utilization of the
   mechanism of the placebo in the healing process is tragic,
   shortsighted and cowardly. Cowardly in the aspect that
   it has been far easier for doctors to simply say that
   the placebo response is worthless, and nothing more than
   someone's wishful thinking or trickery of the mind. The
   bottom line is the response; for whatever reason, placebos
   seem to work... patients get better.</P>
<P>An interesting statistic has shown that virtually all
   newly introduced surgical techniques show a decrease in
   success over time. Is this also a placebo response?</P></
   BLOCKQUOTE>
```

Some browsers indent blockquote text on both the left and right sides, but you should not count on this formatting to occur. Also note that Blockquote may contain block-level elements such as P (paragraphs) and Table (tables), but the quoted materials may not be contained within inline elements (such as A, B, I, U, or Strong tags).

Also, be sure to link to the source. Give your users a link back to view the original content in context. This keeps your "borrowing" above board, boosts your credibility, and improves the users' experience. Plus, by treating the originating author respectfully, you may just build a business relationship that yields long-term benefits.

Sourcing and protecting images

Images require special mention in a chapter on intellectual property considerations. Content with images satisfies and attracts readers far more than plain text does, so you want your website and social media content to include photos, diagrams, and other types of images. However, you can't just grab any photos you like and use them. You need to take care choosing, creating, and protecting your images online.

Image sources

Most website owners and content creators do not create their own original images. When looking for images online, you ideally want to find photos and illustrations that can be used without *attribution* (naming the source) in your website or blog. Many stock photo sites let you search for an image, pick the image size you need, and then pay a small license fee to download each image. Examples include Dreamstime (www.dreamstime.com) and iStock (www.istockphoto.com). You can also find sites that let you download images that are completely *royalty free* (don't require payment or attribution to use someone else's intellectual property), but those sites are harder to confirm and may have limited inventory. One example of a free photo site we have used is Pixabay (www.pixabay.com).

Unfortunately, not everyone realizes that images are protected by copyright. As a website owner or blogger, you need to protect yourself from liability by knowing how to incorporate third-party images legally.

Be careful to read the license terms of each image you want to use. For example, if you do an image search in a photo-sharing site such as Flickr (www.flickr.com) or in a general Google Image search (images.google.com), you must dig a little to see what restrictions the owner of that image requires.

Even if you filter your image search to find Creative Commons (CC) images only, you need to research what a photo's requirements are because there are many levels of permissions within CC. (*Creative Commons* is a license classification for sharable creative works.) For instance, if you find an image on Flickr, notice below the photo whether it has "All rights reserved" or "Some rights reserved." If all rights are reserved, you're out of luck; you need to find a different image. If only some rights are reserved, you must click the "Some rights reserved" link (shown in Figure 6-2) to find out what the owner requires you to do. Depending on the license, you may need to caption your image with a link to the source page, the license page, or both; you may need to "share alike" by uploading your modified version back to Flickr; or you may be free to use the image without any attribution.

Using someone's image without the proper permission to do so breaks the law. We know of lawsuits that cost ignorant website owners thousands of dollars in damages for posting images that were restricted by copyright. Although the owners complied by taking the images down right away when they were notified, a court still found them guilty. With a little due diligence, you can avoid becoming liable for a copyright lawsuit and keep your images, and your brand's reputation, clean.

Figure 6-2:
Be sure to
check the
copyright
holder's
"rights
reserved"
and abide
by them
when using
someone
else's
image.

Rights reserved

Original images

When you take the time to create a unique image such as an infographic,
consider including a copyright and/or logo somewhere on it in order to
brand the image. If anyone reuses it, you have a good chance of preserv-
ing your branding visibly. For example, we created the infographic shown
in Figure 6-3 for our online SEO tutorial. Notice the small text line near the
bottom of the image that identifies who owns the copyright.

Protecting images that you create (even if they do not have a visible
copyright or logo) may be a bit easier than protecting text content. You
can prove that an image has been stolen because the evidence is visual.
Discovering who has stolen your images is the real trick.

Figure 6-3:
When possible, include your own logo or copyright statement on images you create.

Copyright line

To locate places where your image may be used, we recommend that you do a *reverse image search,* which lets you find images that are like another image. If you have the actual image file, you can upload it into a reverse search engine. If not, such as if the image you want to search for is on another website, you need to copy its URL. To do this on a PC, right-click the image and choose "Copy image URL"; on a Mac, move your mouse pointer over the image and Control-click the link; next, select "Copy Image Location." Now you can search based on that URL using either of these two sites:

✦ **Google Reverse Image Search** (`http://images.google.com`): Click the camera icon to open Search by image. Then paste the image's URL into the box and click the Search by Image button.

✦ **TinEye** (`https://www.tineye.com`): You can use this free site to upload an image or simply enter the URL for an image into the search bar, as shown in Figure 6-4. TinEye compares your image pixel-by-pixel to find similar images on the web.

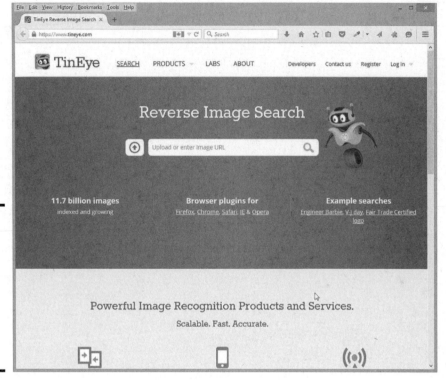

Figure 6-4:
Reverse
search
engines let
you locate
where a
specific
image
appears on
the web.

Chapter 7: Using SEO to Build Your Brand

In This Chapter

✔ Selecting keywords that help build your brand

✔ Using search to maximize brand awareness

✔ Distributing press releases effectively on the web

✔ Increasing your chances of showing up through blended search

✔ Creating Engagement Objects

✔ Building an online community

✔ Using social share buttons to promote your brand

*T*raditional marketing just isn't enough to build a *brand name* (company or product name) these days. You can't just have a good product and decent service, take out a Yellow Pages ad, print some business cards, and set up shop. Your marketing plan now needs to be bigger, more engaged, and more interactive. To build a successful brand name, you need to be where people will see you, hear what others say about you, and join in the conversation — and that's on the web. A good marketing plan today needs to consider that "word of mouth" has gone digital, and somehow tap into that online buzz.

Search engine optimization (SEO) gives you the skills you need to make sure your website can be seen where people search. That's crucial because the majority of people coming to any website get there through a search engine. But to really grow your brand, you have to stretch beyond pure SEO and do some broader Internet marketing, which means delving deeper into understanding your target audience and interacting with them, especially through social media. In this chapter, we discuss how you can raise brand awareness among your target audience. We also cover how you can give your audience a voice and form an online "community" that supports your business goals. These are the branding activities that help you thrive in the world of Internet marketing.

In this chapter, you discover how to do online brand building from A to Z. We begin with the meat-and-potatoes of SEO, keyword selection, but approach it from a brand-building perspective. Then we move on to creating press releases, videos, images, and other objects that help engage the audience members you need to attract. Last but not least, we take you into the world of *social media* (Internet sites that enable people to share and discuss information and build relationships, like Facebook, Twitter, and Reddit). You find out how you can use blogging, content marketing, and the many available social media outlets to build your reputation and a community at the same time.

Selecting Keywords for Branding Purposes

If the goal of branding is to make your name known and respected, you want your name to be visible when people go looking for it in the search engines. To get started, for each of your notable brand names (your company name, your product name(s), and your own name, if you're trying to become an authority in your industry), run some name searches and see whether your website ranks for your brand in the search engines.

If your company name is a unique brand, like Nike, Bruce Clay, Inc., or John Wiley & Sons, Inc., you definitely want your own website to come up in searches for your brand. However, you may have chosen a brand name containing *keywords* (the terms people search for) instead. Examples are Classic Car Customization and RunningShoes.com. If you have a brand name like that, you'll be competing against lots of other sites to rank for your brand because those are their keywords, too. It takes time and a lot of SEO know-how to get your brand to the top of the search engine results pages (SERPs). However, moving your brand up in the search results should be a goal for any company that wants to build a long-term clientele. The payoff comes when past customers or people who've heard about you through word of mouth go looking for you by name in a search engine and can find your site.

Brick-and-mortar and local businesses should try to show up in mobile and geographically targeted searches for their brand name, business category, or keywords. Showing up in local and map searches requires dotting a few *i*'s and jumping through a few hoops. Read Chapter 4 of this minibook for help setting up your business for local search.

How to Build Your Brand through Search

You have a great opportunity to increase your brand's online presence through the many different search avenues available today. Once upon a time, there was only your website to represent your company online. Like a solitary island in a sea, you just had to hope searchers would know enough about your company to notice the blip of your website on their online radar. Today, you can use search marketing to connect your website to the world. Through SEO, you can enable your site to show up when people search for your keywords. But there's also much more you can do to make your brand visible.

The goal is to increase awareness of your company and to make your brand something people recognize and even talk about; the big win is to have your brand searched for. Search marketing gives you lots of channels to accomplish this, from search engines to social networking to video sharing to press releases to blogs to news to *wikis* (information sites containing all user-generated content, such as Wikipedia [www.wikipedia.org]) to bulletin boards . . . and the list goes on. When you make your brand name show up in many of these, it builds an online presence that raises your brand awareness. You can think of it as *halo media* — a variety of media channels that surround your company like a halo, giving it presence and making your brand known, as shown in Figure 7-1.

The flip side of using search marketing to build your brand has to do with managing your brand's reputation. It's all well and good to get your name out there, but what happens when someone misrepresents you or posts something awful about your company? And when the buzz about your company starts to turn negative, it can turn into a firestorm fast. Once again, search comes to your aid! You can monitor the online conversations and decide when to jump in and do some damage control.

Figure 7-1:
Halo media happens when your brand is visible through many online channels, not just through your own website.

The following sections cover the practical steps you can take to create halo media around your brand. We begin the discussion with press releases, and then we move on to discuss videos and other Engagement Objects and tips for effectively using social media for your business goals. Throughout the chapter, you build the skills you need to manage your brand and make it thrive in the online world.

Writing press releases

Distributing Internet press releases is an effective and not-too-costly way to increase public awareness of your company. To do this, write and send your press release to a third-party distribution company such as PRWeb (www. prweb.com) or one of the others we mention later in this section. That company publishes it on its site and pushes it to other news sites that may pick it up and republish all or a part of it, so for a short time, your news continues to circulate on the web and get exposure. For the long term, the distribution company archives the press release on its website, and you should also archive your press releases in a News or Press section of your site.

When writing press releases (as with any content), keep in mind your keywords. Use your keywords throughout the text, and especially use them within the first 200 words on each page because that's the part the search engines count more heavily when calculating a page's relevance to a user's search. Don't repeat the keywords over and over again — that's called *keyword stuffing* and should be avoided — but use them within the natural flow of your writing.

Also include a link to your site in your press release. This ensures that readers can easily find your website. Press releases used to be a good place to put additional *inbound links* (hyperlinks on an external site that take users to your site) that contained optimized *anchor text* (the link text that can be clicked) linking ideally to high-priority *landing pages* (the pages where users arrive at your site because they're the ones most focused on particular keywords) for your most profitable and most searched services. However, Google now considers multiple links from a press release to be a type of link buying and may penalize your site's rankings as a result.

To keep buzz circulating about your company, distribute press releases regularly — at least once every two to three months, but more frequently if possible. Our schedule is semi-monthly based on announcement-worthy content, so your mileage may vary. Your press release should announce some achievement or event about your company, so always be thinking of good topics that could be publicized. An effective press release should contain factual information that doesn't sound too much like marketing copy. (It's a good idea to put opinion-type statements like "Our super-fantastic new buffing tool is going to revolutionize the car customization industry!" in quotes.)

Newsworthy ideas for press releases include

✦ New service or product being launched

✦ Special deal announcement

✦ News about the website or company in general

✦ Employee promotion or new hire (especially of a company executive or notable person)

✦ Contest being offered through your website

✦ Launch of a cool interactive feature on your website

✦ Award given to your company

✦ Other significant event or announcement

We recommend you check out the following press release distribution services. Compare their coverage, options, and prices to find the one that suits you best. Also, different services feed different news outlets, so if there's a particular news outlet that you definitely want your news appearing in, that could be a deciding factor:

✦ **PRWeb (**www.prweb.com**):** Besides being a very reliable distribution service, it offers helpful tips on how to write an effective press release (see www.prweb.com/pressreleasetips.php).

✦ **Marketwired (**www.marketwired.com**):** Marketwired news stories pop up nicely at the top of Google search results and elsewhere, so they're another good one to consider.

✦ **PR Newswire (**www.prnewswire.com**):** This is one of the biggest press release operations in the United States, so it's another good choice.

Optimizing for blended search

All the major search engines can display a mix of different types of results in the SERPs, a presentation known as *blended search*. (Google calls it Universal Search, but it's the same concept.)

Before the advent of blended search, when you went to a search engine and looked for something, your search results only contained web page links. You had to choose Images in order to search for photos, News if you wanted to find news articles, Video if you were looking for videos, and so forth. With blended search, your results may contain these types of links in addition to website listings, all presented together in a single SERP.

You can run a search for a specific well-known person or thing to see blended search in action. For instance, if you search on Google for [classic cars on display], you might get back a variety of different images, web pages, and news results all blended together, as shown in Figure 7-2.

What does blended search mean to you as a website owner? It means that you can't afford to have a website full of text alone anymore. A website that includes videos, images, and other types of media has more chances to be shown in search results than a text-only site does. In fact, sites that include videos and other media elements now outrank those that do not, all other factors being equal. To develop and strengthen your brand, add video elements to your site and post your videos on YouTube.

You might wonder why a site with a video should outrank a site without one. We know that Google and the other search engines' goal is to present the most relevant content based on a user's search query. That in itself doesn't explain it. However, search engines also want people to like using them and to be satisfied with the websites they go to. The search engines want the experience of searching to be as engaging as possible. A SERP with a mix of photos, videos, news articles, and book links increases user engagement. In addition, users are better satisfied with the results if the sites themselves are more engaging.

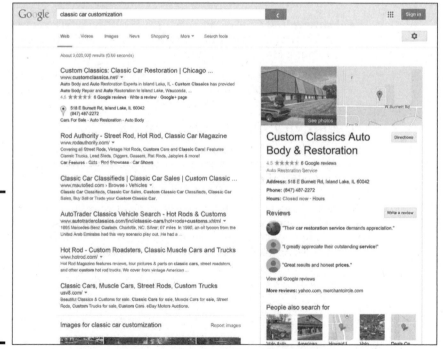

Figure 7-2:
Blended
search
gives users
various
types of
results
mixed
together.

Using Engagement Objects to Promote Your Brand

The lesson of blended search is clear: Enhance your website with Engagement Objects, and you will be rewarded for it. *Engagement Objects* are nontext elements, such as images, videos, audio, games, and applications, that help engage your website visitors' interest. When people first come to a website, they tend to decide whether to stay or leave within the first two to five seconds.

Say people are searching for [classic Mustang colors] and find your classic car customization website. If they see just a headline and several paragraphs of information, they probably head for the Back button. To grab their interest, your page needs photos of Mustangs, hopefully showing the various paint colors. You might also have a video link showing how to prep a classic car for repainting. Or you could have an interactive wheel created in Flash that shows all the manufacturer's color choices for the model year that a user selects. The more engaging you make the landing page, the more likely it is to satisfy your visitor, and, all other things being equal, the more likely Google and other search engines are to list your landing page among their top search results.

Engagement Objects are expected to play more and more heavily in search ranking as time goes on. The search engines have been working hard to "read" non-text content and understand what it's about. They're getting better at converting the various types of non-text-based files into words that they can *index* (include in the search engine's database of web page content for search results). Google, in particular, made great strides in 2008, beginning to convert the soundtracks from video and audio files into text. Search engines can now read non-moving text created in Adobe Flash, as well. (*Flash* is a software program used to create animated and interactive objects for websites.) As search engine technology advances, you can expect Engagement Objects to continue to gain importance as a ranking factor.

You can consider including several different types of Engagement Objects to optimize your website for blended search. We've listed the most common ones in the following list:

✦ **Images:** Search engines scan websites to find large photos, infographics, diagrams, illustrations, or other types of image files. To help the search engine understand what your image is about, include a brief description in the surrounding text, in the image's `Alt` *attribute* (HTML description), and in the filename. Many websites use infographics and charts right now because those images provide easy visualization of complex topics. (***Note:*** You learn how to source and protect your images in Chapter 6 of this minibook.)

✦ **Video:** Embed your video right in your web page for maximum benefit (so people can visit and possibly link directly to your site).

✦ **Audio:** Include audio files embedded in your pages and be sure to explain what they're about in the surrounding text. Also, don't annoy your users — be sure to set the default audio file to "off."

✦ **Flash:** It's against SEO best practices to create much of your website in Flash because the search engines can't index moving text or images. In addition, Flash is generally not mobile friendly (as described in Book IV). However, if you can make your website more interactive by including Flash objects, consider using Flash to build useful or entertaining animated elements (or *widgets*) for your site that engage your visitors, and be sure to describe those widgets well in the surrounding text.

✦ **News articles:** If your press release gets picked up by a news organization, it could become a search engine news result. Plus, archiving your press releases on your site gives you more content and possibly search traffic if people go looking for the information later.

✦ **Blog posts:** Search engines scan blogs that are updated regularly, especially if many people contribute to them. Recent posts to a blog sometimes come up in related search results, so an active blog on your website can increase traffic. (More on blogging in the section "Blogging to build community," later in this chapter.)

✦ **Games:** Games are a great way to build user loyalty and increase engagement. High score tables, badges of achievement, and bragging rights are all ways to keep a user excited about your game and your brand.

✦ **Interactive applications:** This is sort of an "everything else" category. Financial calculators, AJAX apps that let someone design their own car, fun quizzes, and anything else that you could put on your page that a user can engage with and respond to all make great content for fixing the message of your brand in people's minds. HTML5 is rapidly developing as a search-friendly method of designing interactive web features.

Building a Community

Who are the people your brand appeals to? What other products, services, sports, hobbies, and things interest them, besides your brand? When you can identify their other common interests, you can work to associate your brand with those interests. If your car-customizing enthusiasts also tend to be into wine-tasting, you can research to find where wine tasters hang out online. Wherever it is, you want to be there, too! As your target audience starts to see your brand and your voice popping up around the Internet, not just when you're selling to them but particularly when you're just part of the conversation, they find out who you are and start to trust you. They begin to feel like you're one of them. That's community building.

To build a community online, you need to use blogs and the various types of social media sites. Think of these sites as channels for communication — channels that go in both directions. You can get your message out to your prospects and develop a voice in your industry, but you can also listen. Probably never before has there been more opportunity to hear what people think about your products, your services, your ideas, and your company. Social media provides that channel. So use social media first and foremost as a way to research what people like and don't like about your brand and your industry. Approached with a willing ear and an open mind, these online conversations can give you an unlimited flow of ideas for improving your business.

Being who you are online

Before diving into the various places that you can be social online, take a moment to think about who you want to be when you get there. Most importantly, you want to be genuine online. Don't claim to be someone you're not, or you'll get burned. The Internet population at large doesn't take kindly to imposters, and when the discovery is made, your brand could be damaged permanently.

You need to be transparent about your identity online. Many CEOs and other company executives now write blogs online, such as Tony Hsieh, CEO of Zappos; Bill Marriott, chairman and CEO of Marriott International; and George Colony, CEO of Forrester Research. Writing as themselves is the key, and this allows them a platform where they can spread a message but also become a real person that customers can get to know. You don't want to *claim* to be the CEO if you're really writing the blog as a freelancer in another state.

The perils of posing as someone else

An infamous example of a company getting caught misrepresenting itself online is Walmart. In mid-2006, a blog called *Wal-Marting Across America* featured the travels of two "regular people" driving across the country, independently interviewing Walmart employees. When it was discovered that the two people were actually being supported by Walmart and that the blog had been concocted by Walmart's PR firm, bloggers across the Internet retaliated with angry posts. Both Walmart and its PR firm were seriously embarrassed by the flap, although the impact was not seen in traffic statistics.

Some companies choose to set up an alias to blog under, which is fine, as long as you make it clear that it's an alias. The *Chicago Tribune,* for instance, set up Colonel Tribune as its social media ambassador. "He" has a profile in lots of social media sites, where he posts interesting bits of news with links back to *Tribune* articles and blogs, as well as other sites. His picture is an illustration rather than a photo (see Figure 7-3).

Whoever you choose to be in the social media realm, make sure you do it authentically. After all, you're trying to build customer and industry relationships that will last. You're trying to create trust. You have the opportunity to become a voice. You first need to know who you are and be true to that.

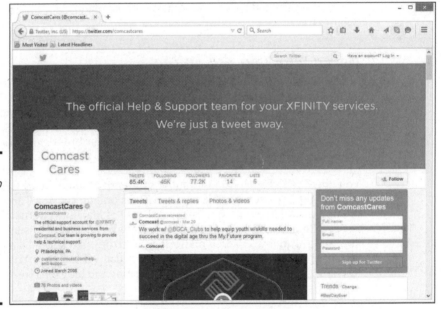

Figure 7-3: The *Chicago Tribune's* Colonel Tribune doesn't claim to be someone he's not.

Blogging to build community

Blogging is arguably the oldest and most mature type of social media on the web. It also can be important for your company website and SEO efforts. The search engines each have a *vertical engine* (a specialized search that finds one type of result only) devoted just to blogs, and blog posts are now being linked in blended search results when they closely match a search query.

Adding a blog to your company website has many benefits beyond providing additional pages for possible search results. First of all, it's a great way to add content to your site that's fresh and original. It also invites visitors to have a conversation with you, which builds valuable relationships with your target audience. Through your blog posts, you can express your ideas and let your personality come through. You can start conversations, guide those conversations, and establish yourself as a leader. When people post comments to your blog, you get user-generated content that other people trust and want to read. You get feedback that can help you see opportunities and put out fires. With an active blog on your site, you have a community in the making.

If you're just starting a blog, you might check out the various blog software programs available either for free or for purchase/license. Blog software is a specialized type of *content management system* (software that automates web page production) designed just for maintaining a blog, such as WordPress (http://wordpress.org) and Movable Type (www.movabletype.com). There are a wide variety of choices out there, though. We suggest you consult with your webmaster (if you have one where you work) and research to find the best option for your site.

For a corporate blog, you should consider hosting your blog on your domain (for example, you can find our blog at www.bruceclay.com/blog), but if you're just blogging as yourself, a hosted blog at a site like Blogger (www.blogger.com) could be just fine although using a host site doesn't look quite as professional as hosting it yourself. Spend the money on a domain and host it yourself. (Alternatively, if you're a really big company, you can buy the hosting company and put all your official blogs there. That's what Google did. Its official blog is http://googleblog.blogspot.com. However, most of us don't have that option.)

You can use some tips and tricks to help you use blogging effectively to build an online community. Here are some blogging do's and don'ts:

✦ **Do** write in your blog regularly and often. Set a minimum goal of one new post per week, but write more frequently as ideas come to you.

✦ **Do** write in a conversational tone that's informative and entertaining to read.

✦ **Don't** use much profanity or vulgarity in your writing. You'll want to write appropriately for your target audience, but keep it a cut above to encourage readers to feel comfortable in your space.

✦ **Do** take the time to run your posts through a spelling checker (by copying them into a word processor if your blog software doesn't offer this feature) and proofread them before posting them. Keeping typos and mistakes to a minimum helps you look professional and makes people take your comments more seriously.

✦ **Do** include links to other people's blog posts and articles, and let the anchor text be meaningful words, not just a URL. Things you read on other blogs within your industry can be great topic starters, so feel free to summarize in your own words, and then rebut or expand on their posts in your own blog (including a link to the original post). This is another way to form industry connections and build community.

✦ **Don't** be afraid to raise controversial topics related to your industry. Stating a contrary opinion can generate lots of interest and comments. People are more likely to talk about what you wrote in other social media sites as well, and even if they disagree with you, they often link back to your site.

✦ **Do** use your blog to show you care about your industry. Talk about issues and develop a strong industry voice. This generates respect for yourself as a thought leader (people look up to you as a person that thinks and leads in innovative and competent ways), and you also may find yourself helping to steer your industry.

✦ **Do** encourage conversation by approving people's comments promptly (but not the ones that are obviously spam). Also, write your own comments in reply when appropriate.

✦ **Do** comment on other people's blogs, too, especially other thought leaders in your industry. You can use your brand name with a link back to your blog or home page as your signature line, but other than that, be careful not to be overtly selling/pushing anything. Done with tact, posting on other people's blogs can help build community and a name for yourself within the industry.

Try to avoid responding to unfounded attacks. Many people try to engage others on the Internet for the wrong reasons. Lowering yourself to their level is seldom a good move: That way lies madness.

Here's one more idea for you: Be on the lookout for other people's blogs that are popular with your target audience. When you find one that's highly read, get in touch with the blogger and let him or her know about your company and product. If you can encourage the blogger to give your product a try, you can suggest that he reviews it in his blog and give an independent opinion. People are highly influenced by a trusted reviewer's opinion, so this could generate a lot of traffic to your website and help boost your brand.

Using other social media to build community

The good news is, you have lots of ways to talk to people online. The bad news is, there are *lots* of ways to talk to people online! Because your time is probably limited, it's important to figure out which websites and methods most effectively help you connect with your target audience on the web. We give you some tips throughout this section on how to go about making that decision.

The important thing is to be where people are talking about your company and products — or, if your business isn't very well-known yet, to be involved in related conversations where you can help to make it known. Social media sites give you a way to do that.

Being connected through social media can also help you deal with a public relations crisis. If a customer slams you online, it can become a PR nightmare. Although it might be tempting to think of the offending customer as evil and clearly attacking you, try to think of it as an opportunity to demonstrate your care and interest, resolve the issue, and then thank that person. Try to turn a problem into a positive statement that you care about people's comments.

There are a few ways social media can help you deal with bad publicity:

✦ You hear about the complaint quickly, while it's still a small flare-up, because you're monitoring conversations about your brand name.

✦ You can analyze the complaint and determine its validity (or lack thereof). Self-analysis before jumping into a crisis is always wise.

✦ You can contact the person directly to resolve the issue, if you choose. You might turn a disgruntled customer into a loyal one through your fast response and excellent customer service.

✦ You can publicly post an explanation and apology, if appropriate. But do not attack the attackers! They are your clients, or should be.

✦ You can monitor and "control" the conversation, as needed.

✦ You can enlist the help of your *brand evangelists* (people who've supported your brand online in the past) to stick up for you, if you decide a response would be better coming from an impartial third-party source not directly related to your company.

✦ You can use social media profiles to help push down the offending sites in the search engine results pages so they do not get as many views from potential customers.

As of January 2015, nearly 1.7 billion people worldwide have active social media accounts (according to `www.JeffBullas.com`). Brands and businesses stand to gain — or lose — a lot by connecting with consumers on social media. Being approachable and accessible can make all the difference in your brand perception. According to `www.Business.com`, 39 percent of social media users expect a response from a brand *within an hour* when they take to a social network to communicate with the brand. And when it comes to complaints, customers demand a response. Responding to a complaint made via social media increases brand advocacy by 20 percent, but failing to respond decreases brand advocacy by 43 percent. So there's a real opportunity for business owners here to connect with people online, but there's also a need to do it in order to protect their brand's reputation.

Connecting to your audience with social networking

Social networking involves "meeting" people online through a website designed for this. Popular social networking (or *social media*) sites in the United States include Google+ (`http://plus.google.com`), Facebook (`www.facebook.com`), LinkedIn (`www.linkedin.com`), Instagram (`www.instagram.com`), and Twitter (`www.twitter.com`), although the list is very long and constantly evolving.

To participate in a social networking site, people first set up their profile page, which contains a variety of basic or trivial information about themselves such as name, age, favorite books, favorite music, or whatever they choose to enter, as well as photos and links and a customizable background. Many social media sites (including Facebook, LinkedIn, Google+, and Twitter) have a way for a business to set up a business profile instead of a personal one and assign more than one person to have access.

Before jumping into a social networking site for your brand, do a little homework first. Research the demographics of the various social networking sites. About.com provides a short list of the top social networking sites (`http://webtrends.about.com/od/socialnetworkingreviews/tp/Social-Networking-Sites.htm`) and provides a few facts about each, including the types of content it's most popular for and some basic facts about each site's focus and purpose. We also suggest the direct approach — talk to your current customers and ask them where they "hang out" on the web. You're looking for the social media sites that are the most popular with the people you're trying to reach.

After your profile is set up, you can connect with other users. On Facebook, you send a "friend request" or in the case of a business you "like" the page; on Twitter, you choose to "follow" another user; on Google+, you "circle" a person or brand in order to see that brand's content on your home page. Another good method is to invite people to "Join our community" or "Follow us" by including links on the bottom of emails and e-newsletters you send out. You could include links to your profile pages on various social networking sites, giving people a choice. If they also have a profile on that site, they can easily request you as a friend/follower.

You have some measure of control over who you network with. After a friend request is made on Facebook, the recipient can either approve or deny it. Most other social media sites, such as Instagram and Google+, enable people to follow another user without getting permission first. However, users can choose overall privacy settings, and you can set each post to either "public" or "private." You also have the ability to block someone in every network. To build your network even faster, look at the suggested friends-of-friends that you might know or want to follow. So after you start to build your network, use the technology to help it grow. You can also use search functions within these social networking sites to find people talking about issues that matter to you (that is, your keywords). These let you dive right in to the middle of conversations where you want to have a voice. Often, you form new connections and grow your network the best by commenting and interacting on topics of common interest, whether you originated the post or not. Communication lets people get to know you or your brand, and two-way conversation is the most authentic kind.

How you choose to interact with your network depends a lot on your strategic goals. Maybe you're trying to

✦ Build closer relationships with your best customers.

✦ Generate awareness about your brand and products.

✦ Build trust with potential customers.

✦ Find people for a long-term focus group.

✦ Gather ideas for new products and services.

✦ Locate disgruntled customers and address their satisfaction issues before it becomes social news.

✦ Assist with Customer Service inquiries or general information.

You could have any number of different objectives for getting involved in social networking, so make sure you're starting off with your goal clearly in mind so that your time and efforts are well spent.

Many brands have a Twitter account dedicated to customer service and community building. Operated by real people who constantly monitor for any mention of their company, these accounts are useful for responding and resolving issues quickly. As an example, the airline company JetBlue Airways (Twitter account @JetBlue) is known for enhancing its customer service and company image through Twitter. Figure 7-4 shows its profile page on Twitter; notice the follower count of 1.95 million, tweet count of 286K, and the prominently displayed J.D. Power customer satisfaction award.

Figure 7-4: Through a Twitter profile, JetBlue Airways reaches out to its customers.

How to stay on top of your keywords on Twitter

Using the search function at `http://search.twitter.com`, you can search for a specific keyword or phrase on Twitter to find all the recent entries that contain the keyword. To keep a continuous stream of those mentions flowing, we recommend that you use TweetDeck (`http://tweetdeck.twitter.com`). Search for a keyword and then click "Add Column" at the bottom of the search results. The new column is dedicated to showing you any tweets with that keyword. You can monitor in real time and know instantly when someone mentions that keyword so that you can engage with the person, if desired. Also, you can respond to people talking about what's important to you online, interacting in a helpful and real way that builds your online community reach.

Spreading the word with social share buttons

Social media sites can help you generate interest in your brand and specifically in your website. Links from blog pages, social media sites, wikis, or forums help your link equity only for a short time and should not be relied on in the long term. However, many of those people who find your site through such a referral may end up liking what they see and bookmarking it or linking to it themselves. Plus, you're bringing in more traffic and building more awareness of your brand.

Social share buttons, also called social media buttons or just share buttons, let users recommend a web page to others through a social media site. There, they can also write a review, comment on it, start a discussion about it, and so on. Say someone reads your article "Making a Chrome Bumper Shine without Elbow Grease" and loves it. The reader can recommend it by sharing it on Reddit (`www.reddit.com`), Facebook (`facebook.com`), Twitter (`twitter.com`), LinkedIn (`linkedin.com`), Google+ (`plus.google.com`), or any number of other social networking sites.

Your goal is to get your website visitors to see something on your site and then post about it elsewhere. Social media buttons make it easy for your readers to share your articles with the rest of the world because they can post a link to your page on their social account without ever leaving your website. Somewhere on your article or web page, you can offer social share buttons, which are small icons that let the reader recommend the article to a social media site. Figure 7-5 shows a typical set of social share buttons on a web page.

Figure 7-5:
The Hollywood Reporter includes share buttons for Facebook and Twitter on its articles.

You can add social share buttons to your web pages rather easily via free tools available on the Internet. Two popular free options are ShareThis (www.sharethis.com) and AddThis (www.addthis.com), the latter of which has a Pro upgrade option that offers share buttons that are *mobile responsive* (a web design technique that adjusts how a web page displays when it is viewed on a mobile device. Read about the importance of designing a website that looks good to visitors on mobile devices in Book IV, Chapter 3.) Many share button generators let you pick and choose which social networking sites you want to offer, in case you want to channel the conversation (although we don't see any problem with being all-inclusive and offering a social share button for many popular social networks).

Book VI

Linking

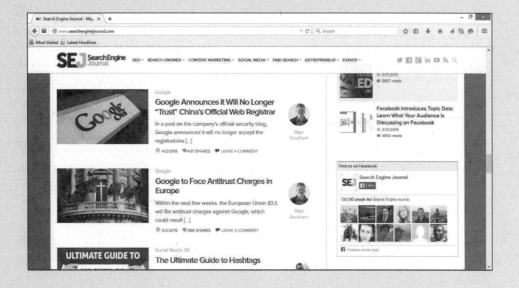

Go to www.dummies.com/extras/searchengineoptimizationaio to see how to use the Free Link Analysis Report tool.

Contents at a Glance

Chapter 1: Employing Linking Strategies

In This Chapter

✓ Theming your site by subject

✓ Implementing clear subject themes

✓ Organizing your content with silos

✓ Making the most of outbound linking

✓ Tackling link building

*I*n Book II, Chapter 4, we briefly discuss *siloing,* which is a way of arranging your website according to themes that allows for prime search engine optimization. In this chapter, we go into the meat and bones of siloing.

Siloing your site is one of the most important things you can do for search engine optimization. It organizes your website so that a search engine (and a user) can get a good, clear picture of who you are and what you're about. A non-siloed site versus a siloed one is like the difference between having a bookcase with books and DVDs and CDs and knickknacks all crammed onto the same shelf versus a bookcase with books on one shelf, CDs on another, DVDs on a third, and knickknacks on the fourth. It's easier to figure out where things are on the organized bookcase versus the messy bookcase.

In this chapter, we discuss how to build categories and themes for your website and how to incorporate those into your silos. We also discuss how links to your site from others support your site's relevance in the eyes of search engines.

Theming Your Site by Subject

You can do many things to your website to provide evidence of subject relevance. One of these things is understanding what it means to theme a website. *Theming* is grouping website content in a manner that matches the way people search. One site can have many themes. Each theme can have sub-themes. In our example classic-car customization site, the main theme is customizing classic cars; a sub-theme is restoration of classic Mustangs.

In order to rank for your keywords within Google, Yahoo, and Bing, your website has to provide information that is organized in clear language that the search engines can understand. When your information has had all its design and layout stripped away, is it still the most relevant information when compared to other sites? If so, you have a pretty good chance of achieving high rankings and, in turn, attracting users looking for those products and services. In order to do so, you have to be thinking about the following things:

✦ The subject themes your website is currently ranking for in the search engines.

✦ The subject themes your website can *legitimately* rank for. False advertising is *always* a bad idea.

✦ How to go about properly implementing those subject themes.

As you see throughout this book, we often explain the importance of creating silos for your subject themes by using the analogy that most websites are like a jar of marbles. Search engines can only decipher the meaning of a website when the subjects are clear and distinct. Take a look at the picture of the jar of marbles in Figure 1-1 and think about how search engines would classify the theme(s) of the jar.

In the jar, you can see black marbles, gray marbles, and white marbles all mixed together with seemingly no order or emphasis. You can reasonably assume that search engines would classify the only theme as "marbles."

If you then separate each group of colored marbles into separate jars (or sites) as in Figure 1-2, they would be classified as a jar of black marbles, a jar of white marbles, and a jar of gray marbles. Now your site could rank for the narrow terms [black marbles], [white marbles], and [gray marbles], but you would be lucky to rank for the generic term [marbles].

If you wanted to keep all three types of marbles together in a single jar (or keep various topics on your website) and go after the very important generic term, you would go about creating distinct silos or categories within the jar (or site) that would allow the subject themes to be [black marbles], [white marbles], [gray marbles], and finally the generic term [marbles], as in Figure 1-3.

Most websites never clarify the main subjects they want their site to be relevant for. Instead, they try to be all things to all people and wind up with a jumbled mess.

Figure 1-1:
Our jar
of mixed
black, white,
and gray
marbles.

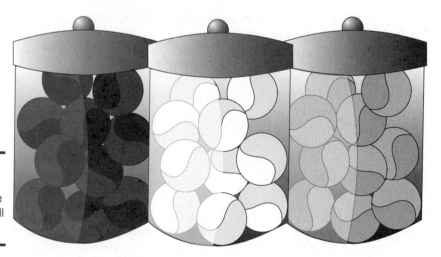

Figure 1-2:
Now your
marbles are
easier to tell
apart.

Figure 1-3:
Arranging
the marbles
by theme
allows you
to keep
them in the
same jar
and still be
able to tell
them apart.

The goal for your site, if you want to rank for more than a single generic term, is to *selectively* decide what your site is and is not about. Rankings often are damaged in two major ways: by including irrelevant content or by having too little content for a subject on a website.

So what subject themes are you currently ranking for?

The best places to start to identify which themes are your most relevant are your keyword research and the data from your website. You can start by examining the data from the following sources:

✦ **Web analytics:** These are program routines embedded in your web pages that are designed to track user behavior.

✦ **Pay per click (PPC) programs:** You can use traffic from any paid advertisements you run in search engine results to estimate whether a keyword is worth targeting in your SEO campaign.

✦ **Tracked keyword phrases:** All the phrases you are tracking in your monitors are valuable sources of information when you apply competitive research tactics.

Each of these sources of information can provide the history of who visits the website and why. They won't tell you why the site isn't ranked for desired keywords directly, but they help you understand what keyword phrases your site currently ranks for organically and which visitors find your site relevant.

Web analytics evaluation

You have several ways to obtain the data or logs for the search engine spider history and the footprints of visitors to your site. First off, you may go right to the source and download the actual log files from your server using FTP. If your server comes with a free log file analyzer, you can use that, or you can use a program like Webtrends (`www.webtrends.com`) or dozens of other desktop applications that help decipher Internet traffic data. Many businesses also use on-demand services that use cookies and JavaScript to pull live data on the patterns of search engines and visitors. These businesses do so through online services like the exceptionally powerful Google Analytics (`www.google.com/analytics`), which is a free service. However you access the data history, you are looking for information on how users came to your site. Book VIII focuses on web analytics and guides you through many of your options.

PPC programs

You can also find clues to the words that your current site is relevant for by evaluating the words that you bid on with pay per click programs offered by all major search engines. Often, companies bid on words that they would *like* to be relevant for within the organic search arena, but that for one reason or another they have not yet achieved ranking success.

Tracked keyword phrases

The last and most accessible method of discovering your website's most important subject themes is to find out which keyword phrases rank the pages within the site best. What phrases are pulling people to your website? Running a keyword monitor and checking your web analytics program reports and server logs for the most-trafficked pages on your site, and using the search engines' webmaster tools are ways to discover which queries are already bringing you traffic. The Search Queries report under Search Traffic in Google Search Console (`https://www.google.com/webmasters/tools/home`) lists the top queries bringing traffic to your site from Google searches, along with stats for *impressions* (how often your result is seen by a searcher), clicks to your site from that query, and your site's average ranking on a results page for that keyword. In Bing Webmaster Tools, you find a comparable report in the Reports & Data section under Search Keywords.

Obviously these aren't the only terms that you'll want to focus on in your SEO campaign, but they are important to optimize for so that you don't lose the traffic they're already bringing you. Pair them with your new keyword list when you do your organization. See Book V, Chapter 3 for more on creating keyword lists.

After you identify your keywords and implement them in your campaign, you want to continue to track them, paying close attention to which keywords are bringing traffic and, of that traffic, what percentage of visitors are converting.

Keyword research

After creating a starter list of 10 to 100 keyword terms that appear to be most relevant to your company's product or services, it's time to begin keyword research. During the process of keyword research, the first goal is to grow that keyword list as large as possible. Cover as many relevant subjects that can be remotely connected to the website's subject themes as you can. Use Trellian's Keyword Discovery tool (www.keyworddiscovery.com) or Wordtracker (www.wordtracker.com) to identify keywords and synonyms that are related to the site's subject matter. Another excellent tool is the Google AdWords Keyword Planner tool (https://adwords.google.com/KeywordPlanner). Refer to Book II for the nitty-gritty on keyword research techniques.

After you answer the question of where the site currently ranks by running your keyword monitor or analytics tool, you know two major factors: the phrases for which your site ranks and the phrases for which it doesn't rank in the search engines. The next challenge is to understand what subjects your site is legitimately relevant to and why you are ranked as you are currently.

Many site owners get incensed that their sites don't rank higher for terms they feel they are relevant for. These owners feel that engines misjudge the value of their sites. But a poor mechanic always blames his tools. There *are* rare exceptions where the tools are at fault, but 99 percent of the time, the problem is that the site is not focused enough on its dominant topics. Owners try to cram in too many things at once, and the search engine has a hard time figuring out what the site actually is supposed to be about. Your task is to figure out what your site is about after stripping away all the visual hoo-ha and getting down to the actual content.

Page Analyzer

A great place to begin is to run Page Analyzer within the SEOToolSet. SEOToolSet Lite includes the full-featured Page Analyzer tool and is free for sign up at SEOToolSet.com. Page Analyzer reveals the density, distribution, and frequency of keyword phrases used throughout the page (for more information on measuring keywords, see Book III, Chapter 2). By running the main pages of your site through this tool, you can begin to identify whether the major themes are used throughout the titles, Meta tags, headings, Alt attributes, and body content. If your terms are absent, make a note that the keyword densities seem low. Evaluate how often a phrase is repeated in each major category element and take note of the commonly repeated phrases and infrequently repeated phrases. Are all the terms concentrated only near the top of the pages? If so, make a note that the distribution of the keywords could stand to be more spread out. Don't bunch them all together.

Multi-Page Analyzer

SEOToolSet Pro subscribers can use the Multi-Page Analyzer to further help their siloing efforts. After evaluating, if the pages throughout your site contain keyword rich densities, compare your pages to that of the top ten competitors for your major keyword terms. Using Multi-Page Analyzer, you are given a report that summarizes why the competitors' sites ranked highly and recommends how to adjust your own pages to have keyword densities similar to those of the top-ranked sites.

Implementing Clear Subject Themes

As we describe in the preceding sections of this chapter, you need to know what you are ranked for and what you're considered to be relevant for, and hopefully you will have performed some analysis on the data you gathered so you can determine why your competition ranks the way they do. But even if you've taken care of all that, you're still not done. For each keyword phrase you've identified, you need to make a decision: Is it worth the work to write dozens of pages of content to rank for a subject you don't *already* rank for? To make this decision, consider whether your site is really about that theme and whether adding more content about the subject could make your site become *less* relevant for more important terms. You do not want to dilute your site. You need to sit down and figure out whether you're willing to make the commitment to establish a theme and do the work required.

There are many ways to establish a clear theme: Begin by visualizing the primary and secondary categories that you would prefer for your site. If you don't have a clear idea of the primary theme of your website, search engines and users are going to be confused as well. You can start figuring out your primary theme by creating a simple outline. Think of this chart like a business's organization chart, except for themes. Define the major theme or primary subject that you want to become relevant for and create an organization chart or linear outline to cement your ideas in place. Often, it's not until you actually put pen to paper that major subject complications or contradictions surface. Look at Figure 1-4 and note how one main topic is supported by several smaller subtopics.

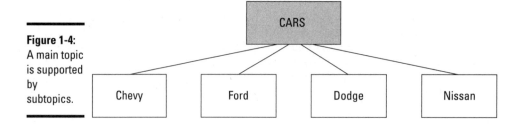

Figure 1-4:
A main topic is supported by subtopics.

Or you can use a simple bulleted list, like this:

✦ Major theme

- Subtopic 1

- Subtopic 2

- Subtopic 3

- Subtopic 4

Creating an organization flow chart is a third way to lay out your subject themes visually. The Organization Chart is an easily accessible tool that can be found within Microsoft Visio, or you can use another organization chart–creation software program. Using one of these visual representations of your themes and subtopics (outline, bulleted list, or organization chart) provides the opportunity to visually explain to others involved in the website what the focus of the website should be and what subjects actually serve to distract the search engines from the main subjects.

After completing this exercise, ask yourself what keyword phrases users actually type into the search engines when looking for this information. This helps in organizing your broad phrases for the large, traffic-heavy pages for your site and the smaller, more specialized phrases that go on your sub-pages.

Siloing

After you have your main themes and subtopics laid out on paper (or on the computer screen), you can start organizing and laying out your website content into subject silos. You may have a good *landing page* (a page that users come to from clicking a search result or an outbound link from another site) for each main topic; if you don't, put creating landing pages at the top of your list. Next, you want to make sure you have enough subtopic content, or sub-pages, to support each main topic. You also want to make sure that every page's content is focused on its particular theme. In other words, it's time to start arranging your website into silos.

One way to visualize a silo is to think of a pyramid structure. Look at Figure 1-5 and notice the top tier. That's a landing page, which has the big broad terms you want to be ranking for. The pages underneath it are the supporting pages, which are the smaller subcategories you came up with to support the main term.

Figure 1-5:
A silo looks
a lot like
a pyramid
in that the
main topic
is supported
by the
smaller
subtopics.

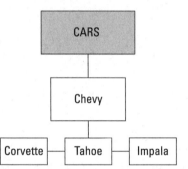

The top page receives the most support (and hopefully the most traffic) because it's the most relevant and focused page about its particular subject. Your site proves that it's the most important by the way it's structured, with supporting pages under the top page, and by the way its links are set up. The way you set up your site should tell the search engines exactly what each page is about and which is the most important page for each keyword theme.

There are two ways of doing siloing. One way is *physical* (or *directory-based*) *siloing,* which involves building the directory structure to reflect your site themes and constructing your links to follow the structure of your directory, where sub-pages in a directory are also sub-pages for a particular theme. The other way is through *virtual siloing,* which establishes what your main subject themes are based entirely on links without the reinforcement of your directory structure.

Doing physical siloing

One way you can do your siloing is to link in the same pattern as your directory structure. (The *directory structure* refers to the arrangement of the folders where your website files physically reside.) When you upload files to your site, you place them in a directory. A siloed directory structure has a top-level folder for each main topic, subfolders within each main-topic folder for its related subtopics, and individual pages inside each subfolder (as shown in Figure 1-6). Linking then naturally follows this structure, effectively reinforcing your directories through links.

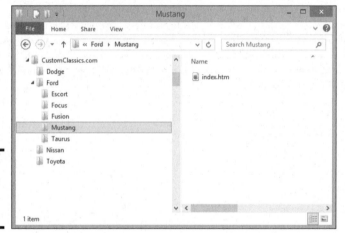

Figure 1-6:
A siloed file directory structure.

When building a directory structure, be sure not to go too deep. For example, take a look at the URL of the page. The full address is the directory of where the page is. Observe:

```
http://www.customclassics.com/ford/mustang/index.html
```

The URL lets you know where the page is. Notice how the page named `index.html` is saved within the folder named `mustang`, which is a subfolder of the main directory `ford`. This page is only two levels deep in the site structure, which is good.

Too many levels of subdirectories can have the following negative effects:

✦ The more clicks it takes to get from the home page to the target page, the less important it is deemed by the search engines.

✦ Long directory paths make long URLs, and studies have proven that users avoid clicking long URLs on a search results page.

✦ Long URLs are more prone to typos. This can discourage deep linking or even cause broken links to your web pages from other sites. Also, users can make mistakes typing in your URL.

So don't get category-happy. Making your directory structure ten directories deep is bad, having five levels is probably too much, and even having three levels of subdirectories is still not great. Although there's no hard-and-fast rule, you should try to keep your directory structure quite shallow: One or two levels deep is usually sufficient. The closer the page is to the root of the directory, the more important your page looks to the search engine.

For example, our classic car website only has one main directory level (the car's make) and two directory levels of subcategories (model and year). The directory could look something like this:

```
http://www.customclassics.com/ford/delrio/index.html
http://www.customclassics.com/ford/delrio/1957.html
http://www.customclassics.com/ford/delrio/1956.html
http://www.customclassics.com/ford/fairlane/index.html
http://www.customclassics.com/ford/fairlane/1958.html
http://www.customclassics.com/ford/fairlane/1959.html
http://www.customclassics.com/ford/mustang/index.html
http://www.customclassics.com/ford/mustang/1965.html
http://www.customclassics.com/ford/mustang/1966.html
```

Note how shallow the directory structure is: No page is more than three directory levels away from the root.

The other thing to keep in mind when working with physical siloing is the difference between absolute and relative linking. A *fully qualified link* provides the entire URL within the link, and a *relative link* is only linked to a file within the current directory. A fully qualified link looks like this:

```
<a href="http://www.classiccars.com/ford/mustang/tireoptions.
html">
```

A root-relative link looks like this:

```
<a href="/ford/mustang/tireoptions.html">
```

And a directory-relative link looks like this:

```
<a href="tireoptions.html">
```

When you use a relative link, it's only going to work in relation to the current directory (or the next directory up, if you use slash characters relative to the root of the site). So a link to `tireoptions.html` works only if there's a file called `tireoptions.html` for it to link to in the same directory as the file you are linking from.

With fully qualified linking, there is no confusion about where the file is located and what it is about. A fully qualified link has the added bonus of being very clear for the search engine to follow. Fully qualified links allow the search engine spider to have the full address when it follows a link and ensures that the pages being linked to can be found and indexed when the spider returns in the future. Using relative links, or using links that are not fully qualified, can send the spider to a wrong page. Fully qualified links make links easier to maintain and ensure that the search engine spider can always follow them.

Whenever you move files, links need to be updated. Absolute links break absolutely if you rearrange folders, whereas if you picked up an entire subdirectory and moved it somewhere else, relative links actually still work. The disadvantage of relative linking is not being able to see at a glance the complete path where a file exists, which may make it tougher to maintain.

Doing virtual siloing

You may have your website directories currently set up in a non-siloed structure, with thousands of files and hundreds of folders already in place. Or, you may need to maintain a directory structure that does not reflect your site theme for some other reason. Never fear: As with most difficulties, you can use a technical solution that still lets you silo your site and achieve better search engine optimization.

You can make the theme of your web pages clear to the search engines even if you do not follow your directory structure, so long as you connect your pages on the same theme through internal linking. This is *virtual siloing.*

Here's how to think about it in the simplest terms possible: The Internet is a series of web pages connected by hyperlinks. A website is a part of the great Internet soup, being both a member of the whole vast network and an individual group of pages unique unto itself. What search engines attempt to do is collect information from individual sites into content groups: "This site means this, and that other site means that, and so forth." They try to determine every site's content and give the content a category. Search engines award the websites that have the most complete subject relevance with high rankings for those keywords.

The difference between physical siloing and virtual siloing is that in physical siloing, it's about how you set up your directory structure and links. Virtual siloing is about setting up your links regardless of your directory structure. In virtual siloing, the following are your tools:

✦ **Anchor text:** The hyperlinked text that describes what the hyperlink actually links to

✦ **Internal links:** The links within your site

Anchor text

The anchor text for a link tells the search engine what the page that's being linked to is about. Clicking a link that says "tires" should take you to a page about tires. Because if the page is about tires, and the anchor text says it's about tires, and any other links to that page all contain the word *tires* (or synonyms of *tires*), that creates a giant blinking neon arrow to tell the search engine that that particular page is about tires. *Anchor text* is the hyperlinked text that explains what the link is and what the page it is linking to is about. It sometimes helps to think of anchor text as your ability to vote for what keyword phrase the target page should rank for.

Book VI
Chapter 1

Employing
Linking Strategies

Internal linking structure

The last part of virtual siloing is building subject relevance using the navigation and on-page elements of your website. This means arranging the main subjects in the most straightforward way possible in order to build subject relevance, and organizing your navigation menus to categorize the content of your site. Remember the pyramid that we tell you about at the beginning of the chapter? The broader terms are supported by the lesser terms, and the lesser terms are supported by the even lesser terms, and so forth.

Every silo needs to be assigned a main landing page focused on that silo's primary subject theme. The landing page should have a substantial amount of supporting pages. Supporting pages can also have supporting pages. Linking should stay within the silos or point to other important landing pages. Look at Figure 1-7, which shows a graph of a silo with one big broad page and five smaller subcategory pages, each with its own attached supporting pages.

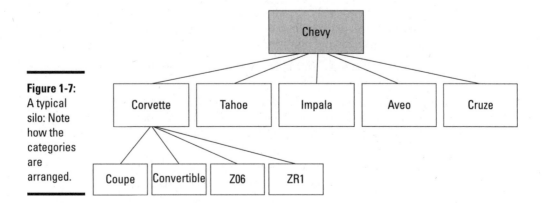

Figure 1-7:
A typical silo: Note how the categories are arranged.

When you're building your silo, the smaller pages should not link cross-category. Your page on Ford tires should not link to a page about Chevy tires, for instance. Instead, have both pages link to a separate landing page about tires. Too much cross-linking between unrelated subjects dilutes the silo and confuses the search engine.

You can also use a couple of tricks with cross-linking in order to keep the links streamlined, but they should be used sparingly. If you must cross-link theme-supporting pages (not landing pages), you may want to add the `rel="nofollow"` attribute to a link to keep the search engine from following the link. This allows unrelated pages to link to each other without confusing the subject relevance. Alternatively, you can use one of the methods we talk about in the following section on excessive cross-linking.

The `nofollow` attribute is not a substitute for having a good linking strategy, and every page on your site must be linked to from at least two perfectly normal, followable links on perfectly normal, indexable pages.

Making the Most of Outbound Links

Your outbound links are the links that you have going out of your site. Having outbound links to resources and experts in your industry that help your visitors is important. Also, such links show the search engines that you recognize who the other experts in your industry are and helps the search engines define your site by association. Here are some aspects to keep in mind for your outbound links:

+ **Link to other experts.** Pick noncompetitive sites that you feel are relevant to your own site and are experts in their subjects. Having these links not only increases your standing with the search engines (experts linking to experts), but also makes you appear more trustworthy to users.

+ **Make sure that the link is useful to your users.** Having a bunch of irrelevant links on your site damages your expertise in the eyes of the search engines. It also makes you look bad to your users. They're coming to your site for research, and if you can't give them any useful links to follow, they're probably won't come back.

+ **Relevancy is key.** Your links have to be relevant to your site, for you and for the search engines.

+ **Validate links.** Make sure that your links are legitimate and won't get you in trouble with the search engines. (For more on how to avoid getting into trouble with search engines due to links, reference Chapter 3 of this minibook.)

+ **Be selective.** If you're associating with another website, make sure that it's a good one — no bad neighborhoods, no irrelevant links.

Obtaining Inbound Links

Inbound linking (also called backlinks) is perhaps the most well known and often discussed of the link structure elements in search engine optimization. These *backlinks* are the links that point into your site from an outside website. You might be saying to yourself, "Hold up, I can't control what people say about me." That is true, to an extent. However, you can encourage supporters and people interested in spreading the word about you to add a mention of your site to their personal or even company websites by generally being an awesome resource.

Link building, the process of attracting inbound links, is covered in depth in Chapter 3 of this minibook, but here are a few different ways to solicit links to your site:

+ Link magnets
+ Link baiting
+ Link buying

Link magnets

When we say *link magnets,* we mean elements on your site that you build in such a way that people naturally want to link to them. Much like a magnet attracts iron filings, these site-content elements simply attract links. People happen upon your site, find the link magnet, and decide that it's relevant and worthy of a link, so they stick a link to your content on their site. This happens because someone finds your page both useful and interesting — and it's a process that happens over time. But it means that the link is generally going to be from someone who is actually interested in your industry, not just in your gimmick. Remember, search engines judge you based on your expertise, and good quality links from relevant sites add to that.

The Search Engine Relationship Chart available at Bruce Clay's site (`www.bruceclay.com/serc`) is a good example of a link magnet. People in the search engine optimization industry find it relevant to their sites and useful for reference, so they link to it. We continue to keep the chart updated, so it always reflects the current state of the ever-changing search engine landscape. For this reason, the chart maintains its relevance over time, as opposed to something brief and flashy that has no long-term value.

Link bait

Link bait is an accelerated version of a link magnet. *Link bait* is anything that is deliberately provocative in order to get someone to link to you. Examples would be a cartoon that someone did of your boss, or a video depicting wacky hi-jinks in your office that was linked to by a few well-read blogs.

Link bait, unlike link magnets, is usually more broadly appealing in scope and probably won't appeal solely to your core market. Like any other non-relevant link, a link generated from link bait is often not one that would be considered a high quality link in general. But it does have the bonus of bringing a lot of traffic to your site, and hopefully a few of those visitors may poke around your site and decide to give you a permanent link.

An excellent example of link bait is any kind of viral marketing. Blendtec, a blender company, gets tons of links and traffic from its videos on its Will It Blend? site, where spokespeople put all manner of strange and surprising things into Blendtec blenders (like rakes, marbles, and iPhones) and post the videos on the Internet. Most sites linking to Will It Blend? are not directly related to blenders, commercial or retail, and certainly can't be considered blender "experts" by the search engines, so those links count for less. However, the sheer volume of links that include the relevant keyword [blend] in the anchor text helps the Will It Blend? site rank.

Link buying

By ad link buying, we don't mean going out and selling or buying links to your own site for SEO link-building purposes. There are two loose groupings of link buying: buying advertising for traffic purposes but not for SEO, which is acceptable, and buying a link for SEO purposes that is not a qualified testimonial, which is considered deceptive and if detected could result in a spam penalty.

Acceptable link buying is paying for a link on someone's advertising site. You *must* do it strictly for advertising and traffic purposes only, and not for link popularity. Google doesn't like to consider paid links and does not assign weight to a paid link. Paid links may pass some value until detected, but after they're detected, you lose all SEO value and could incur a penalty. If you do have a paid link on someone else's site, ask that person to place a rel="nofollow" attribute on it. This attribute alerts the search engines that link equity should not be passed via that link. This is also important because if Google discovers a sold link on the site, it might stop passing link equity to all the links on the site. Read Chapter 3 of this minibook for the important technical requirements you'll want to do to make sure your paid advertising links are search engine approved.

If you decide the traffic and advertising is worth the effort, it's perfectly acceptable to pay a site to have it run your banner or text-link ad. Be aware, however, that part of the whole "paid links" issue is that you have to pay for them.

Chapter 2: Structuring Internal Links

In This Chapter

✔ **Theming your website by subject**

✔ **Optimizing link equity**

✔ **Creating and maintaining silos**

✔ **Understanding sitemaps**

✔ **Figuring out sitemaps**

Siloing is a way of arranging your website according to themes, allowing for prime search engine optimization. We discuss siloing in Chapter 1 of this minibook, but in this chapter, we go into how to actually build and structure your site in order to have the best silos possible.

First, we review the subject theming of your site, and then we discuss link equity. From there, we cover actually creating and maintaining your silos. This means we walk you through the setup, construction, and maintenance work necessary for good silos.

Another thing you read about in this chapter is a sitemap. There are two different kinds: the traditional HTML sitemap (two words) and the XML Sitemap (one word — and yes, that's confusing). A traditional *sitemap* is a web page that is designed to guide users to all the pages on your site. It's a little like an index page in the back of a text book where every page is listed and linked to, usually grouped by subject theme. An *XML Sitemap* is a document designed specifically to be readable by a search engine. You can tell a search engine all about your site using this kind of document. Despite their confusingly similar names, the two types of documents aren't interchangeable, and they both have their uses. In this chapter, we show you how to use both to your advantage.

Subject Theming Structure

We talk about *subject theming,* which is picking out your themes in order to better arrange your silos, in Chapter 1 of this minibook. This section tells you how to actually implement your themes into a silo structure. Look at Figure 2-1, which is a silo pyramid.

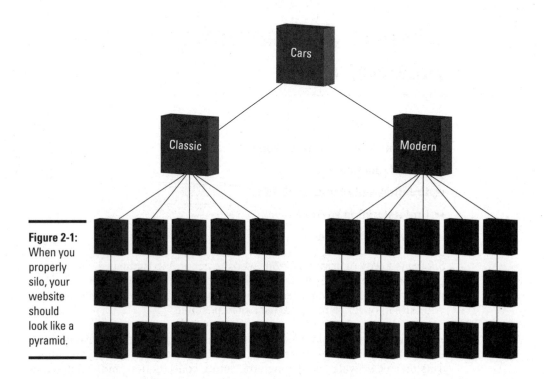

Figure 2-1:
When you properly silo, your website should look like a pyramid.

The example we're using is a classic car website. The very top of the page represents one of the broadest themes, which are the makes of cars.

You can accomplish siloing by setting up either directory-based silos, where the linking structure follows the physical setup of the site (physical siloing), or non-directory-based silos, where the linking structure alone defines the theme (virtual siloing). These types of silos both create themes through linking, but they do so in different ways. Virtual silos create content and subject relationships through cross-linking alone to create a theme, whereas physical siloing creates relationships by utilizing directory structure and links to group like content. They can both be used in the same site, depending on organizational structure.

In a physical silo, relationships between pages are created by grouping pages with like content in a single directory and linking those pages together. The names of the pages help to focus the subject matter of the directory. The theme of the directory is tied into the directory structure itself.

Directory structures require at least five pages of textual content that support whatever topic the directory is addressing. Physical (directory) silos must be very structured and highly organized.

In a virtual (non-directory) silo, the theme is created through linking. The physical location of each page is not important because the pages in the relationship are not necessarily in the same directory. The silo is instead defined by what pages are linked together. Thus, you are creating a theme based solely on links rather than hanging the linking framework on the directory structure. You have the landing page, or the main page, at the top of the silo, and, underneath, you have pages that support the main landing page's theme.

The difference between a primary and a sub-silo is like the difference between a main theme and a secondary theme. A primary silo should be on the main subject you're wishing to attract to your site. The sub-silos branch off from the primary silo, covering their own smaller sub-themes. These sub-silos should both clarify and support the primary silo.

Optimizing Link Equity

Part of the *search engine algorithm* (how search engines rank your site) is measuring your *link equity* to see whether you're an expert on your subject. In broad terms, more links equals greater expertise, especially when the links are from expert sites that are relevant to your site. The more outside websites that link to you, the more expert your site appears to the search engines.

Say you're a member of the Better Business Bureau (BBB). Being a member of the BBB is a good practice for a business. It's a trust issue for your visitors who feel better knowing that you're a member. Naturally, you want to tell people this affiliation, so you place a link to the BBB on your website. Unfortunately, if you're like a lot of webmasters out there, you were so proud of joining the BBB that you stuck a badge and link to its site on every page of your entire site. In doing this, you just gave a huge amount of link equity to a site that is not your own. Having the BBB badge is a good trust signal for the consumer, but perhaps you should consider linking to it only once, from your About Us page, instead of at every appearance of the badge.

Link equity is something Google measures when reading your site to determine whether a site is an "expert" in that field. If many people are linking to you from relevant quality sites, obviously you must know something, or so the logic goes. Obviously you can create spammy links to fool the engines, but that won't last long. Valid links from other sites, on the other hand, contribute to search engines recognizing your site as an expert.

It's not a bad idea to link out to other sites. You *want* to link to other sites. It gives you an air of respectability when you point to other sites (through your links) and say, "This person is also an expert in the field, and you should check him out." It makes you look like you know what you are talking about. Also the person you link to may turn around and link back to you, thus proclaiming you to be an expert, as well.

On the other hand, you have to be picky about whom you link to and where you place those links on your site. (Check out Chapter 3 of this minibook for details on dangers to avoid with outbound linking.)

Creating and Maintaining Silos

If you're like most businesses, you probably already have a website, and you can't exactly chuck the whole thing out the window and start over from scratch. But there is a way to streamline and tweak your site to build better silos. Just follow these steps:

1. **Identify your main themes.**

   These will become your main silos.

2. **Identify the smaller sub-themes.**

   These sub-themes become your sub-pages or support pages for your silos.

3. **Identify the keywords for each page.**

   We go over choosing keywords more in depth in Book II. You should choose the broader keywords for the main themes and the more specialized keywords for the sub-pages.

4. **After you have your pages organized, you can start linking them.**

Silos contain three basic types of pages:

✦ **Landing pages:** The pages that you want to direct your users to. These are the main subjects that are supported by the smaller sub-pages.

✦ **Sub-pages:** The supporting information for your main subjects or landing pages. All landing pages need at least five sub-pages of information to support them, as a general rule. As it happens, these sub-pages may evolve into landing pages themselves if they have enough supporting material of their own.

✦ **Article pages:** Classified as sub-pages. These are pages that contain articles, history, or any sort of information about your theme. These pages usually contain lots of text and are a good place to have concise keywords.

To correctly implement a directory silo, you would group like content into separate directories. Take Ford and Chevy, for example. You would create a directory for each theme, one for Ford and one for Chevrolet. Within these directories, you would have subsequent content-rich pages to support the overall theme of the directories. If you have two models of Ford you want to use, Mustang and Explorer, these would fall underneath the Ford page. You'd need further information about Mustang and Explorer, and all the information regarding each model type would fall underneath its respective directory.

So, what if you want to link between the Ford directory and the Chevy directory? You have a page underneath the Ford directory that discusses a model of Chevy that is very similar to a model of Ford, and you want to do a link between these two pages. Rather than linking from that model of Ford to the similar model of Chevy that complements it, you would only link from the model of the Ford page to the Chevy landing page. Although you could link to the specific Chevy model page, you would need to add a `rel="nofollow"` attribute to that link because the model page is not a landing page for the silo. The reason for this is that if you have multiple links that connect models of Ford with models of Chevy (the supporting pages underneath the landing pages), you're diluting your themes (Ford and Chevy). This makes it difficult for your keywords to stand out and tell the search engines what your pages are about. If you have two distinct categories, or silos, one for Ford and one for Chevy, it's much easier for your keywords to stand out and, consequently, be ranked by the search engines.

In your classic car website, you have your site split into two main categories, Ford and Chevy. The Ford page would be one of your main landing pages, and the Chevy page would be another. Say also that you have additional pages that discuss the specific years of cars, but they are located in different silos. These pages all link separately to your main landing page, and they also link to each other, thus helping to build the theme of that silo. See Figure 2-2 as an example of siloing.

You must decide what you want to be ranked for: Do you want to be ranked for Ford as a general keyword, or for specific types of Fords? Siloing too tightly would mean that you would not be supporting your general term with your specific terms. In this respect, cross-linking sub-silos within a main silo would be okay. It all depends on which keywords you want to be ranked for. You definitely should target the more specific keywords that are relevant to your site, but you may also want to try to rank for more general keywords, which tend to be more competitive and harder to optimize your site for. To rank for general terms, you need to have some general content pages at the top of your site that link down into your category silos (picture an extra row above your pyramid of silos) but that don't receive links back up from the pages below them.

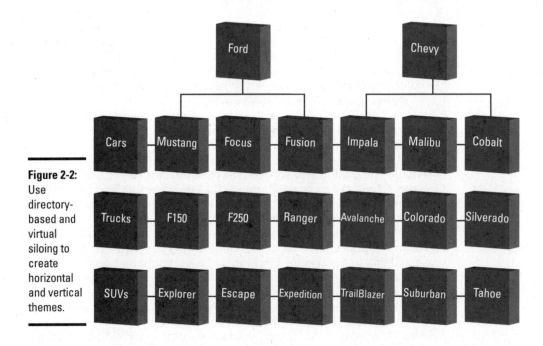

Figure 2-2:
Use directory-based and virtual siloing to create horizontal and vertical themes.

Cross-linking between subjects dilutes your theme. The point of linking within your website is to group similar subjects in order to tell the search engine what this section of your site is about. You want a giant neon arrow pointing to your subjects on your site, and keeping them free of other unnecessary links and keywords helps to do that.

Say that you want to discuss Chevy as well as Ford. The Chevy page would have its own silo design. The landing page would be the Chevy page, and, as in the Ford silo, any pages that discuss varieties of Chevy would be the subsequent pages that would all link to the Chevy landing page but not to each other.

In your Ford page, which discusses a particular year of Ford, you might also want to discuss a Chevy model manufactured in the same year. Rather than directly linking from the 1962 Ford page to the 1962 Chevy page, you would link from the 1962 Ford page to the Chevy landing page. The reason for this is that if you have multiple links linking different Ford years and Chevy years, you dilute your theme, which makes it difficult for your keywords to stand out and tell the search engines what your pages are about. Again, it is possible to link from one unrelated page to another directly if you use a `rel="nofollow"` attribute to block the passage of link equity.

Still confused? Not to worry. Siloing is a tricky process, so we've put together a handy illustrated guide in order to walk you through it.

Building a Silo: An Illustrated Guide

Start each silo with an index page. This is the main landing page, which is the big enchilada for your silo. This is where all the big broad keywords go within the silo's theme, and it's where you introduce yourself to the world as an expert on this subject. In your directory, you would call this the `index.html` page. So, the URL would read `www.classiccarcustomization.com/index.htm`, as shown in Figure 2-3.

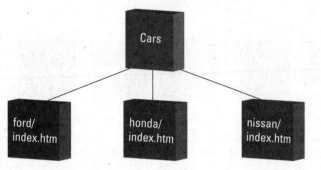

Figure 2-3:
The landing pages of a silo, usually named `index.htm`.

Branching off the silo's landing page, you would have several sub-pages that support the theme. If your silo theme is Ford, you would have sub-pages about the history of Ford, the different types of Ford models, pictures of Fords, some Ford videos, and maybe some articles discussing Fords. Each of these subjects would get its own separate page and would be named in the Ford directory as follows:

```
www.classiccarcustomization.com/Ford/index.html
www.classiccarcustomization.com/Ford/articles.html
www.classiccarcustomization.com/Ford/models.html
www.classiccarcustomization.com/Ford/pictures.html
www.classiccarcustomization.com/Ford/video.html
www.classiccarcustomization.com/Ford/history.html
```

Each sub-page would link back up to the index page but not to each other. When siloing, the rule of thumb is to link up. See Figure 2-4.

Any one of these sub-pages can become its own landing page as well. If you intend to make a sub-page a landing page — for example, if you want to rank for the keyword phrase [Ford history] — make sure that it has its own sub-pages to go along with it. You need at least five sub-pages of support for each landing page. Making the Ford History sub-page into a new landing page creates a smaller silo below the Ford silo, with just one overlapping page in common.

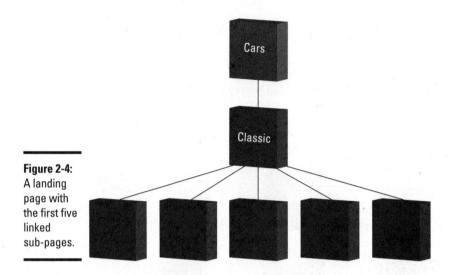

Figure 2-4:
A landing page with the first five linked sub-pages.

Next, build a sub-silo for the Ford Mustang content that you have. Mustang falls under Ford, so you would want a page devoted to the keyword [Ford Mustang] in the Ford silo, with a link from the Mustang page going to the Ford page, as in Figure 2-5.

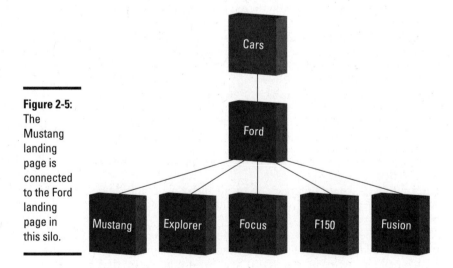

Figure 2-5:
The Mustang landing page is connected to the Ford landing page in this silo.

That Mustang page simultaneously functions as a sub-page within the Ford silo above it and as the landing page for the Mustang silo. In addition to this index page, the Mustang silo needs at least five sub-pages linking to the index page (they could be its own history, articles, years, pictures, and video sub-pages). The directory structure would look something like this:

```
www.classiccarcustomization.com/Ford/mustang/index.html
www.classiccarcustomization.com/Ford/mustang/history.html
www.classiccarcustomization.com/Ford/mustang/articles.html
www.classiccarcustomization.com/Ford/mustang/years.html
www.classiccarcustomization.com/Ford/mustang/pictures.html
www.classiccarcustomization.com/Ford/mustang/videos.html
```

The silo now resembles Figure 2-6, which goes down another level to show the Mustang silo.

Figure 2-6:
The sub-silo increases the relevance of the site for both [Ford Mustang] and the more general term [Ford].

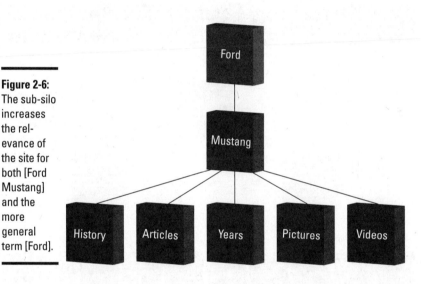

Now, if you want to have a link from one of the smaller Ford sub-pages to the Chevy sub-pages, you would not link directly between them. Instead, you would link the Ford sub-page to the Chevy landing page, as in Figure 2-7. Remember, this method of linking is to avoid dilution of the silo themes.

But if you really want to have links between the sub-pages (usually to enhance the user experience), you can. All you need to do is use a non-spiderable method to link: Create the links in an *iFrame* (an iFrame, on inline frame, is an HTML element that lets you embed another HTML document inside the main document) and then block that content from the spiders in your *robots.txt file* (the document on your website that tells the spiders how you want them to crawl your site), or add a `rel="nofollow"` tag to the link in order to keep the search engine spiders from seeing that link as a part of the page, as in Figure 2-8. This way, your silo still reads like you don't have any links between the sub-pages, but the user can follow the link with no problem.

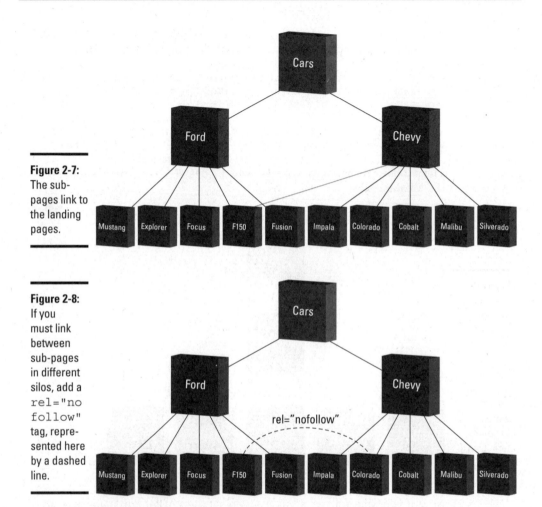

Figure 2-7:
The sub-pages link to the landing pages.

Figure 2-8:
If you must link between sub-pages in different silos, add a `rel="no follow"` tag, represented here by a dashed line.

Maintaining Your Silos

Whenever you make content changes to an existing site, you run a risk of losing ground in the search engine rankings for a while. If your changes are well-planned and SEO-smart, your long-term gains are worth the risk. However, you need to know how to maintain your site with care.

It's pretty common for people to ask, "How can we modify our site to better focus our silos without losing our existing rankings?" Well, think of your site as a work that's constantly in progress. In order not to alienate visitors and keep your traffic consistent, consider expanding or growing your site one or two silos at a time and then carefully analyzing how each change you made affects your rankings. Also, don't change the site in one giant update and just hope everything is re-indexed properly. Hundreds of different configurations of silos may end up being a better fit; all it takes is constant tweaking in order to figure out what is working best for your site.

It is our experience that you can update an entire site all at once without any loss of ranking, but it's not something that we would recommend doing without our help or the help of an SEO professional. It's very easy to make a mistake. We doubt that any improvement to a site will result in a loss of rankings, but because these modifications are extensive and often involve other changes with less-certain benefit, we strongly suggest that you exercise caution in your updates.

Part of the maintenance aspect of your site is watching your silos to see if they're considered a strong silo or a weak silo in the search engine rankings. One example of a weak silo is a silo without enough content in it. If you're not ranking for your theme, your silo probably needs more content, more links, or more pages added to it to strengthen it.

A critical part of maintaining any site is cutting back or pruning parts of the site that are diluting your theme. It is simply getting rid of clutter on your site. Keywords or pages that do not fit your silos and no longer belong on the site should be removed in most cases. Silo pruning also helps if you are doing a targeted promotion, like offering a coupon. You don't want the search engines to index the promotion because it'll dilute your site, so you use a piece of code (an iFrame, pop-up window, JavaScript link) to prune it out of the silo and insert the `noindex` command in the `Meta` robots tag of the Head section of the page. It's linked so the users can find it if you want them to, but the link and the content aren't indexed. Your users can see it, but the search engines can't. Make it a routine part of site maintenance to remove links that decrease subject relevance.

If you prune a page that has backlinks, include a 301 Redirect that sends someone who has entered that page's URL to another page on your site so that you don't break those links and lose that link equity.

Including Traditional Sitemaps

Traditional sitemaps are static HTML files that outline the first- and second-level structure of a website. The original purpose of a sitemap was to enable users to easily find items on the website. Over time, sitemaps also became useful as a shortcut method to help search engines find and index all the parts of a site. Today, we recommend that you have an XML Sitemap, which effectively provides an easy-to-read link dump for the spiders to index. Although certain web browsers can display an XML Sitemap for users to read as well, you should offer both kinds of sitemaps (HTML sitemaps and XML Sitemaps; see this chapter's introduction for the difference between these two) if you want to be sure to cover both the search engines and your users. However you implement them, sitemaps play an important role in your siloed web design.

A sitemap displays the inner framework and organization of your site's content to the search engines. Your sitemap reflects the way visitors intuitively work through your site. Years ago, sitemaps existed only as a boring series of links in list form. Today, they are thought of as an extension of your site. You should use your sitemap as a tool to lead your visitors and the search engines to more content. Create details for each section and subsection through descriptive text placed under the sitemap link. This description helps your visitors understand and navigate through your site and also gives you more food for the search engines. You can even go crazy and add Flash to your sitemap! Of course, if you do include a Flash sitemap for your visitors, you must include a text-based sitemap as well because sitemaps must also aid users who aren't using advanced technology like Flash or JavaScript.

A good sitemap does the following:

+ Shows a quick, easy-to-follow overview of your site
+ Provides a pathway for the search engine robots to follow
+ Provides text links to every page of your site
+ Quickly shows visitors how to get where they need to go
+ Utilizes important keyword phrases

When it comes right down to it, the purpose of a sitemap is to spell out the central content themes and to offer a cohesive representation of where to find information on your site. At its best, a sitemap is your table of contents; at its worst, it's just an index.

Now what do sitemaps have to do with content siloing? A well-planned sitemap can help improve the organization of a site and focus its theme, which may in turn influence rankings. The reality is that few site owners make any real effort when creating outlines of the content on their sites. They add content arbitrarily, either as brochure marketing or as a sales tool, or because they are told they need it to qualify for keyword ranking. Instead, the sitemap should be the *first* document created in a website construction project, laying out all the structure and content to follow.

We can already hear dissenting voices arguing that you can engineer a site to qualify for high keyword relevance without tailoring the entire site by subject relevance. The reality, though, is that most organizations forget what their focus is, and the site often devolves into a mish-mash of competing subjects or is forced to remain stagnant, without any clear plan on how to expand content. Adding a well-designed site outline in the form of a traditional sitemap encourages organization without restricting creativity. A good site outline shows where the site is trying to go by offering a clear purpose. Since when is offering clarity a bad marketing or sales tool? Get everyone in your company on the same page with a well-conceived and well-rendered sitemap.

Sitemaps are very important for two main reasons. First, your sitemap provides food for the search engine spiders that crawl your site. The sitemap gives the spider links to all the major pages of your site, allowing every page included on your sitemap to be indexed by the spider. This is a very good thing! Having all your major pages included in the search engine database makes your site more likely to come up in the search engine results when a user performs a query. Your sitemap pushes the search engine toward the individual pages of your site instead of making the spider hunt around for links. A well-planned sitemap can ensure your website is fully indexed by search engines.

Sitemaps are also very valuable for your human visitors. They help them to understand your site structure and layout, while giving them quick access to your entire site. They're also helpful for lost users in need of a lifeline. Often, if a visitor finds himself lost or stuck inside your site, he looks for a way to find what he's looking for. Having a detailed sitemap shows him how to get back on track and find what he was looking for. Without it, your visitor may just close the browser or head back over to the search engines. Conversion lost.

Here are some sitemap do's and don'ts:

+ **Your sitemap should be linked from your home page.** Linking it this way gives the search engines an easy way to find it and then follow it all the way through the site. If it's linked from other pages, the spider might find a dead end along the way and just quit.

+ **Small sites can place every page on their sitemaps, but larger sites should not.** You do not want the search engines to see a never-ending list of links and assume you are a link farm. Use nested sitemaps if you have many pages to cover. A *nested sitemap* contains only your top-level pages on the main sitemap and includes links to more specific sitemaps. A search engine sees more than 99 links on a page as suspicious, and you don't want to make your visitors wade through hundreds of links to find what they want.

+ **Some SEO experts believe you should have no more than 25 to 40 links on your sitemap.** This also makes it easier to read for your human visitors. Remember, your sitemap is there to assist your visitors, not confuse them.

✦ **The *anchor text* (words that can be clicked) of each link should contain a keyword whenever possible.** Also, make sure the anchor text links to the appropriate page.

✦ **After you create a sitemap, go back and make sure that all your links are correct.** A broken link on a sitemap is a terrible user experience.

✦ **All the pages shown on your sitemap should also contain a link back to the sitemap.**

✦ **If you have a very extensive website, you should create a separate sitemap for each silo.** Each silo's sitemap links up to the sitemap of the silos above and below it, which would further reinforce your silo organization to the search engines. You would also create one master sitemap at the top level of your site — this would be the one linked from your home page — which contained links to all the other top-level sitemap pages. The master sitemap would not contain all pages in your website, but would lead search engines and users to the appropriate sitemap for their area of interest. In essence, you need to silo your sitemap just like the rest of your site.

Just as you can't leave your website to fend for itself, the same applies to your sitemap. When your site changes, make sure your sitemap is updated to reflect that. What good are directions to a place that's been torn down? Keeping your sitemap current helps make your site a visitor and search engine favorite.

Using an XML Sitemap

Your XML Sitemap should be constructed according to the current Sitemap Protocol format (which is regulated by Sitemaps.org). Sitemap Protocol allows you to tell search engines about the URLs on your website that should be crawled. An *XML Sitemap* is a document that uses the Sitemap Protocol and contains a list of the URLs for a site. The Protocol was written by the major search engines (Google, Yahoo, and Bing) to be highly scalable so that it can accommodate sites of any size. It also enables webmasters to include additional information about each URL (when it was last updated, how often it changes, and how important it is in relation to other URLs in the site) so that search engines can more intelligently crawl the site. Note that even though its name is similar to the traditional HTML sitemap, an XML Sitemap is a totally different kind of document, and the two are not interchangeable. You shouldn't rely on an XML Sitemap alone for your site.

XML Sitemaps define for the spider the importance and priority of the site, better enabling the search engine to index the entire site and to quickly re-index any site changes, site expansions, or site reductions. This XML format offers excellent site indexing and spider access. Additionally, many sitemapping tools can diagnose your XML Sitemap, informing you of duplicate content, broken links, and areas that the spider can't access. Sitemaps.org has a tool that constructs an XML file for you: This is a great place to start.

Google adheres to Sitemap Protocol 0.9 as dictated by Sitemaps.org. Sitemaps created for Google by using Sitemap Protocol 0.9 are therefore compatible with other search engines that adopt the standards of Sitemaps.org.

A normal version of the XML code looks something like this:

```
<?xml version="1.0" encoding="UTF-8"?>
<urlset xmlns="http://www.sitemaps.org/schemas/sitemap/0.9">
<url>
<loc>http://www.example.com/</loc>
<lastmod>2005-01-01</lastmod>
<changefreq>monthly</changefreq>
<priority>0.8</priority>
</url>
</urlset>
```

Table 2-1 shows both the required and optional tags in XML Sitemaps.

Table 2-1	Sitemap Tags in XML	
Tag	*Required or Optional*	*Explanation*
`<urlset>`	Required	Encapsulates the file and references the current protocol standard.
`<url>`	Required	Parent tag for each URL entry. The remaining tags are children of this tag.
`<loc>`	Required	URL of the page. This URL must begin with the protocol (such as http://) and end with a trailing slash, if your web server requires it. This value must be less than 2,048 characters.
`<lastmod>`	Optional	The date of last modification of the file. This date should be in W3C Datetime format. This format allows you to omit the time portion, if desired, and use the YYYY-MM-DD format.

Table 2-1 *(continued)*

Tag	Required or Optional	Explanation
`<changefreq>`	Optional	How frequently the page is likely to change. This value provides general information to search engines and may not correlate exactly to how often they crawl the page.
`<priority>`	Optional	The priority of this URL relative to other URLs on your site. Valid values range from 0.0 to 1.0. This value has no effect on your pages compared to pages on other sites and only lets the search engines know which of your pages you deem most important so that they can order the crawl of your pages in the way you prefer. The default priority of a page is 0.5. We recommend setting your landing pages at a higher priority and your nonlanding pages at a lower one.

The XML Sitemap also must

✦ Begin with an opening `urlset` tag and end with a closing `urlset` tag.

✦ Include a `url` entry for each URL as a parent XML tag.

✦ Include a `loc` child entry for each `url` parent tag.

As we explain earlier in this chapter, content siloing can be strengthened by both traditional sitemaps and XML Sitemaps. A lot of evidence supports the adoption of complete site transparency in search engine optimization. That means that all the elements of your site should consistently offer subject relevancy. You can always work on different projects and use different methods, but a clear and concise method of building and maintaining your site is the best way to go. You are helped by using traditional sitemaps and XML Sitemaps, which ensure that everyone (visitors and search engines alike) is on the same page. Not only will your IT and marketing departments agree, but even the site users will be able to tell what your site is trying to say.

Chapter 3: Obtaining Links

In This Chapter

✔ Understanding the benefits and risks of link building

✔ Identifying quality links

✔ Attracting links naturally

✔ Creating link magnets

✔ Fostering relationships with industry influencers

✔ How not to obtain links

*W*hen people to link to you, it affects your overall ranking within the search engines. Having links from good reputable websites lends to your site's overall credibility and is used in the search engine's *algorithm* (formula that measures a web page's overall relevancy to the search query) to determine whether you can be considered an "expert" in your field. Remember, the search engines want to give their users the best results possible, because if they give the users what they want, users come back and continue to use the search engine.

In this chapter, you learn the benefits and risks of link building. You also find out how to research and attract links to your site as well as how *not* to obtain links.

Understanding the Benefits and Risks of Link Building

When it comes to link building, there are benefits and risks. Here we explain why links matter to Google and what the hallmarks of a high-quality link are. You also discover what constitutes a bad link and find out the consequences you face if you have them.

Why links are important

One of the key factors Google and other search engines use to determine whether your site ranks is the presence of links pointing to it. An abundance of high-quality, trustworthy external links that are relevant to your site are evidence to Google that visitors find your site useful. It is, therefore, in your best interest to earn and attract links to your site.

A brief explanation of PageRank

PageRank is a term that is unique to Google. Google considers a hyperlink to a page to be a vote of confidence for that page. Every site on the web has a certain PageRank, or PR, based on these votes and how much PageRank the linking pages have. PageRank is distributed within a site based on links: those coming from third-party sites and from the site's internal linking. Usually, the home page of every site has the most PageRank because it has the most direct links from other sites and because it is commonly linked to from every page internally. The terms *link popularity* or *link equity* are often used synonymously with PageRank. They refer to the same concept, but are more generic and can thus be used when discussing any search engine.

High-quality links are relevant to your own website. Google expects to see links that are natural; for example, if your site is about hair care products, it would be natural for hair styling sites to link to yours, but it would not be natural for a tractor company to link to you — see the difference?

In addition to relevance, reputation also matters. The more reputable a site is, the better. For example, a respected news site like CNN will provide a stronger link than the average personal blog. In other words, CNN has a higher PageRank than the blog. You can read more about how to identify quality links in Chapter 4 of this minibook.

Why links are dangerous

Not all links are created equally — and bad links, in fact, can do more harm than good. While good links increase your PageRank, bad links (links that are reciprocal, incestuous, or come from link farms, web rings, and bad neighborhoods) do quite the opposite. (Read more about all these types of dangerous links in Chapter 4 of this minibook).

Google can detect when you have bad links. Google can take away the link's PageRank as well as the link and domain equity/authority, and won't pass on any link value to your page. Google won't count the bad incoming link, and if it suspects that you're doing something sneaky and devious with it, it even penalizes you for it. The penalty could be as simple as removing all the link equity of your site, or you could have your rankings reduced on the results page. Google may even remove your page or your entire site from its index. Ouch! We've stated this before, but dishonesty (like crime) never pays.

Bad or spammy links are links that exist solely to manipulate ranking and PageRank — and if it appears your site has them, Google will lower your rankings.

What is a Penguin penalty?

In April 2012, Google launched an algorithmic penalty called Penguin. Penguin was designed to crack down on spammy links. When Penguin detects that inbound links are "unnatural," or intended to manipulate search rankings, the site the unnatural link points to will drop in the rankings. Google sees the following as signs of link manipulation:

✔ Gaining too many links too quickly

✔ Having a significant presence of links from irrelevant markets

✔ Having too many links with exact-match anchor text

Getting hit with a Penguin penalty is serious business, and it will take a lot of effort to clean up your backlink profile by link pruning (read more on link pruning in Chapter 4 of this minibook) — and even then, you have no guarantees that the penalty will be lifted. So if you're considering in engaging in spammy link-building techniques, don't. It's not worth running afoul of Google's angry bird.

It's best to play on the safe side and never do anything to confuse or deceive the search engines. The easiest way for a search engine to catch you doing something wrong is to look like you are doing something wrong.

Identifying Quality Links

So we've talked about the benefits of good links and the dangers of bad links, but how can you tell what links you want to attract? *Quality links* are links that contribute to your perceived expertness and your overall link equity. These are the links that point to you and declare that you know what it is you're doing. Your classic car customization site would want the kind of links that shout, "These people are good at what they do, and we think you should check them out." Those kinds of links establish you as an expert.

Here are the three different types of quality links that you want to attract:

✦ Complementary subject relevance links

✦ Expert relevance reinforcement links

✦ Quality testimonial links

Complementary subject relevance

Complementary subject relevance links come from a site that has similar content to yours. The site's content might not relate exactly to your site's content, but its subjects and themes are close enough to be complementary.

If you have a classic car customization site and you receive a link from a website devoted to classic car enthusiasts, this is a complementary link. Your site discusses something that the other site also discusses, and that site has declared your site to be worth reading. This kind of link is worth more than a link from, say, Harry's House of Hamsters.

It doesn't matter whether the link from the hamster site has great anchor text (the text that is the outgoing link). The search engine will read the surrounding text around the link on the hamster site, the overall content of the page, and the content of the site itself, and the search engine will figure out that this is a site about hamsters, and hamsters don't really have anything to do with classic cars (unless, of course, instead of horsepower, your car runs on "hamster" power).

When the search engine notes that the site linking to yours doesn't have a whole lot of relevance to your subject, it will say that the link is not a quality link, and the link is not going to add anything to your overall link equity. It also doesn't matter whether the page linking to your site has relevance. If the linking site has a page devoted to mesothelioma (the cancer caused by asbestos) but the rest of the site is about peanut butter, the mesothelioma page just looks crammed in there. It dilutes that site's theme and might raise a red flag with the search engines.

Figure 3-1 illustrates the power of sites that link to your site. The numbers are on a scale of 1 to 10, with 1 being the least relevant and 10 being the most — and the higher the number, the more that link adds to your link equity.

Figure 3-1:
Link equity is passed depending on how much relevance the link has.

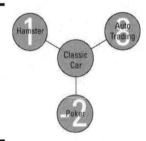

The circle in the middle is your classic car site. The circle with the 1 is Harry's House of Hamsters: It bears very little relevance to your site, so it carries very little weight. The circle with the 8 is a link to a large, official auto-trading website. Because it is a large, official website with a lot of expertise on its own and it has relevance to your site, the worth of the link goes up. (***Note:*** We use these numbers simply to represent varying weights given by relevance — we're not referring to PageRank at all here.)

Then there's the −2 poker site that has linked to you. The poker site comes from a spammy, spammy industry, used to shady doings and basically being a headache for the search engines. Having a link from one of those sites not only gives you no link equity but also might actually cause your site to get flagged for review if you have a lot of these kinds of shady backlinks. By associating with one of these sites, you make it easy for the search engines to assume that you are doing something shady, too. Although Google says that almost nothing someone else does can harm your site, that doesn't mean that there's *absolutely* nothing at all. Don't sweat a few bad links coming to you, but do your best to work on acquiring links from quality sites only.

The links you need to be attracting are the kind that have relevance to your industry. Remember, link equity comes from how much of an "expert" in your subject you are, and the more people with similar content link to your site, the more of an expert you are.

Expert relevance reinforcement

Experts naturally link to other experts. If you are an expert in your field, you are naturally going to be linking to other experts in your field. It's like a Nobel Prize–winning physicist name-dropping another Nobel laureate in economics, as opposed to a kid who won his school science fair.

Experts require validation from their peers. When scientists publish a science paper in a journal, they expect other scientists to go out and test the published theory on their own, in order to receive validation from these other scientists. The same is true for websites. If an expert website discusses you on its own site and then provides a link to you, claiming you as another expert, that just reinforces what you say on your own site.

To put it another way, if the biggest, baddest, classic car customization site on the whole Internet has a link and a section describing you and linking to your site, that means a lot more than your brother's very small classic car site giving you a link.

Quality testimonial links

In the preceding sections, we discuss three kinds of linking sites in this chapter — the good, the bad, and the really ugly:

+ **The good:** The expert industry site; a big-name classic-auto trading site that links to your classic-car customization site, for instance

+ **The bad:** A site that really has no overall relevance to your subject (such as the hamster site linking to the classic car site)

+ **The ugly:** The spammy, spammy poker site that offers nothing of value and only makes you look bad

But there is one type of link that is considered the best of them all: the testimonial link.

A *testimonial link* is a link that appears in a paragraph in the context of a lot of relevant information and then points to you as another resource of information. The topic of the linking site as a whole needs to relevant to your site. Say that a site that sells parts for car restoration has a post describing how to properly customize classic cars. The site then provides a link to your site, as in the following example. Note that the text *classic car customization business* serves as the anchor for a link back to www. classiccarcustomization.com.

```
There are many classic car customization businesses out
    there, but for the best, you have to check out Bob's
    Classic Car Customization, which has tons of resources
    for restoring and customizing every kind of classic Ford,
    Chevy, and '50s hot rod on the planet. Check out its
    gallery of restorations for some cool, classic autos.
```

A testimonial link is worth a whole lot of link equity and is one of the best kinds of links you can receive when it's from a related site. Just be sure that it doesn't come from any sites that practice the worst practices for linking that we outline in the "How Not to Obtain Links" section at the end of this chapter.

Link equity is always important to keep in mind when you're vetting external links. One good testimonial-grade link is worth a lot more than a hundred decent links or a thousand bad links. Link equity through a testimonial link is the highest grade of link equity possible.

Attracting Links

You can acquire new *backlinks,* or inbound links to your site, in a number of ways. Examples include writing articles, creating new widgets for your site, and so on to make people want to link to your site. Each technique can produce results, but the amount of time and effort that goes into them can be costly. So it makes sense to consider attracting high-quality links to your site with content people find valuable — especially if you have limited time, energy, and money to pursue new links. You can read more about what makes valuable content in Book V.

The benefit of quality content is that it can attract quality links on its own (and those links are likely to stay there), as well as help you build your business reputation. The idea is to attract long-term expert testimonial links to your site. It makes you seem more authentic and trustworthy to the users and search engines alike. Although developing quality content also takes time and effort, the added benefit of building your reputation as an authority in your industry has lasting value and allows you to compete more successfully on the Internet.

If you've already got that exciting and interesting content all ready to go (lucky you), and you want to be more proactive about obtaining links, you can go about it in several ways. First, you need to think about what kind of sites you want to link to you. Brainstorm about places that might link to you, and vice versa. Think about your competition and who's linking to them and especially why. Take note of whether your competition uses paid advertising (such as banner ads) or hosts banner ads on their own sites.

After you have a working list of possible sites, you have a long list of points to consider when you start thinking about attracting links from different websites. If you're going to spend money, the cost of advertisements has to be justified based on the potential increase in traffic and brand awareness, not the potential ranking benefit. Pages that are visited often on your site are better targets for purchased links or advertisements.

The quality and reputation of the site that links to you is crucial. Although Google states that there is almost nothing another site can do to harm yours, *almost nothing* is not the same as *absolutely nothing*. Links from unethical sites, such as sites involved in spam or unethical search engine results page (SERP) manipulation, can seriously damage your reputation and rankings with the search engines if they show up in large quantities, and you could even wind up pulled from the search engines' *indexes* (the database of websites that search engines maintain for all queries). Never solicit links from any site that you suspect may be engaged in spam or unethical practices.

The terms *natural* and *unnatural* are used to categorize links. Natural links come from sites that are strongly related to the industry or overall themes of your website, and at a number and frequency that indicate organic growth (that is, growth without some obvious effort). Unnatural links, by contrast, are links received for the sake of the link itself, usually from a desire to gain a ranking boost. Unnatural links are detectable by search engines in a number of ways: by coming from sites with unrelated themes; by occurring in big batches at one time; and by coming from a site or group of sites already suspected by the search engines of link manipulation. Paid links are also considered unnatural because some effort was made by the linked-to site to obtain that link, rather than having been unsolicited. (See the sidebar later in this chapter on using rel="nofollow" so that you can tell the search engines about your paid links and not get penalized for them.)

Bear in mind that a link from a newer site can have just as much value as (or more than) an established site if the new site has a lot of link popularity or authority within the search engines. Also consider that a newer site could potentially drive much more traffic than an older site with stale content, an old design, and little or no maintenance. It's a matter of trial and error.

A natural inbound link profile has links from sites with varying PageRank values. A natural distribution of links to any given page includes a majority of links from PR3 or lower pages. Generally, there should be fewer links from PR4 pages than from PR3 and lower pages, even fewer from PR5 pages, and so on. With that said, do not avoid getting a link from a higher PR page if you are obtaining it in an ethical way.

A natural link will give your site the most value if it does not include a `rel="nofollow"` attribute or otherwise block the spiders from following and indexing links. Links using JavaScript, AJAX (Asynchronous JavaScript and XML), or Flash (with rare exceptions) are not ideal because in many cases search engine spiders can't crawl them. Each link should also directly connect to the designated page in the target site. Links acquired should point to different landing pages within the site, as well as the home page. They should be based on topic relevance of the anchor text and the page they are being referred from.

Make sure linking sites are not part of a *link farm* (sites that exist only as thousands of links for the sole purpose of fooling the search engines) or another search engine spam network.

Reciprocal links (an "I'll link to your site if you link to mine" swap) should be avoided as a general solicitation practice. However, this doesn't mean that you should *never* have reciprocal links. Remember, the search engines want to do what's best for your users. If your users would find value in a site that links to you, by all means, link back.

Ads or other bartered links should only be obtained from relevant sites. Linking to a spam network puts you in danger of getting pulled from the search engine index, so be very careful and review all sites accordingly.

Develop a list of the preferred anchor text you would like to see on each URL from which you are seeking inbound links. Your anchor text describes to the search engine the subject of the page linked to. It's like a sign that you point to yourself. Ideally, all links should use the preferred anchor text you provide to the site. If any "tailoring" occurs, be sure that the anchor text still contains your main keywords (meaning, no one has removed them). Realistically, you do not control the site linking to you, so in the end, it's up to the linking sites to use whatever anchor text they feel is best. Suggested link text is just that: a suggestion.

Links should remain on the original URL from the date placed and should not move around. The goal is to achieve link stability and longevity. Check back occasionally on solicited links to find out if they're still there.

Use social media sites (social networking sites like Facebook, communication sites like Twitter, and social news sites like Reddit) to generate interest in your site. The goal is to get others to see the post and then post about the article elsewhere. However, be aware that links from non-related blog pages, social media sites, wikis, or forums only help your link popularity in a limited fashion. (See the section "Generating link magnets," later in this chapter, for more details.)

Linked pages should ideally have unique content, and not content used on other domains. The `Title` and `Meta` tags on linked pages should also be unique.

In some cases, attracting an inbound link from a high-quality education (`.edu`, but not student accounts) site should be considered. Inbound links from an `.edu` site can hold increased authority value when the link is relevant (for example, the `.edu` links to your page discussing research in which that educational institution is involved).

Although obtaining links from directories is a good way to build the link popularity of a new website, your long-term link-building strategy cannot consist solely of directory links. The vast majority of your links should be from non-directory-based sites.

It's natural for sites with a top-level country domain (for example, `.co.uk` for the United Kingdom, `.co.nz` for New Zealand, and so on) to obtain links from other sites that have the same country code top-level domain (ccTLD) designation and are hosted in the country associated with that top-level domain. Links from other top-level domains are fine as well, but without links from other sites in the same ccTLD as your domain, your site may not rank well in search engines specific to your country.

Linking sites should reside on different IP address ranges than your site. Additionally, there should not be a large number of links from the same C-block of IP addresses. (The *C-block* is the third set of numbers in an IP address. In the sample IP address, 255.168.219.32, 219 is the C-block.) If all of your links are from the same C-block, it looks unnatural and spammy. Excessive linking between sites on the same IP ranges might be seen by search engines as a link-farm community.

Links should be obtained gradually over time, not in the span of a few days or weeks. This is the footprint of natural link growth that avoids the risk of having search engines flag your website for forced or artificial increases. This guideline is more important in regards to advertisements, as they can be obtained at a much faster rate.

Now that we've gone over the hallmarks of good natural links, the following section covers appropriate ways to attract inbound links to your site that search engines approve and visitors benefit from, too.

Generating link magnets

Remember playing with magnets as a kid and marveling at how the one magnet pulled the other to it by some invisible force? That law of natural attraction is the Holy Grail of link building — an ideal link is obtained when Internet users can't help but link to your page because it's worth sharing. This is the driving concept behind the link magnet. *Link magnets* are typically creative web applications, tools, how-to guides, reference materials, or any information that is unique and valuable to users. In a similar vein, *link bait* is content created for the purpose of attracting attention and links. The difference between the two is that a link magnet is for the purpose of attracting relevant links, whereas link bait is mostly good for short-term traffic. Rarely, link bait can translate into long-term links, but that's only if you have good content to go along with the video or blog or other tantalizing things you've just released.

Generating information, applications, tools, or ideas that people talk about is a surefire way to generate links: This is the benefit of a link magnet. Developing an idea for a link magnet takes some dedicated brainstorming and creative thought, as well as a good understanding of your target audience and what they might find useful or even humorous. For example, research that generates data or insights into the differences between competing services might be highly valued by a technology audience.

Creative insight that grabs everyone's attention and generates discussion is what you're after. When you come up with an idea, actual construction of the link magnet may also require hard work, although some link magnets can be developed with little effort. Articles and videos are two types of content that can perform well as link magnets.

Articles

Adding an article section to your site or posting articles on a blog can be a valuable source of links. Not only are articles a good way of adding keyword-rich content to your site, but they can also be a good way of attracting links. Other sites frequently link to articles that provide useful advice or information in order to share it with others.

There is a difference between articles that you write to provide information about your products or company and articles that can be deemed link worthy. The latter tends to be noncommercial, informative, and entertaining, whereas the former tends to be more marketing oriented, such as a page describing your product or service that is not designed to garner links and draw traffic but merely to give more information to people already interested in your business or product.

The key to writing articles that generate links is to make sure that the article is something that viewers want to read and share with others. Think of it as an article you would read in a print magazine, not just something written strictly for SEO value.

Many different types of content can be used as link magnets:

✦ **Top ten lists:** These have nearly become cliché online, but they can still be effective if they are new and fresh.

✦ **How-to guides:** Explain how to do something in a clear and easy way. Visuals, like images or videos, can be helpful.

✦ **Articles about hot-button issues:** Debate a controversial, industry-related topic.

✦ **Resources:** Offer new research, information, tools, charts, or graphs.

✦ **Humorous and off-beat material:** Include funny stories and topics.

✦ **Games:** They can be developed for fun, and they may or may not be related to your industry.

Videos

Using Engagement Objects such as images and other rich media can be an integral part of link building. Some people online are looking for more than just static web pages. You can utilize video, Flash animations and videos, and podcasts to reach this audience. Not only does this help your overall Internet marketing campaign and raise brand awareness, it can also help generate quality links.

Videos can be used as link magnets and link bait and can be a great way of increasing awareness of your website. The key to a good video link magnet is to make your video unique and link-worthy. The video should incorporate branding and advertising strategies, but above all, it should be entertaining.

Videos from YouTube (www.youtube.com) currently rank high in Google video results. Although videos on YouTube can increase exposure for your company, they do not necessarily build link popularity for your website. However, YouTube can be used to raise awareness for the video link magnets that are hosted on your site. You can do so by posting shortened video clips on YouTube that link back to additional or higher-quality videos posted on your website.

To effectively build link popularity by using a video link magnet, embed the video into a web page on your site. This way, anyone linking to the video is directly linking to your site, which is of course the primary reason for creating a link magnet. However, showing up on a search results page as a blended result might be a secondary goal as well. You can increase the likelihood of meeting that goal by adding links from your site to the videos you have put on YouTube. Google is doing an increasingly good job of ranking videos from websites that aren't solely devoted to videos, but you might be able to rank more easily from a major video site such as YouTube or Metacafe (`www.metacafe.com`) than from your own site.

One famous example of a video link magnet is the "Will It Blend?" series of videos done by Blendtec, a company that manufactures blenders. Blenders may seem like a boring product for a video, but Blendtec makes its videos entertaining by obliterating all sorts of items in its blenders and styling the demos like a 1960s game show. Blendtec posts its videos on YouTube as well as integrates them into its website.

After you create a video link magnet, you need to promote it. Issuing a press release is one way to do this. (See the following section for more on how to do this.) You can also bring awareness to your video by encouraging social sharing on Twitter (`http://twitter.com`) and Facebook (`www.facebook.com`), which also offer great ways to build a community and put out information as well. We cover working with social networking in much greater detail in Chapter 5 of this minibook.

Spreading the word through social media and press releases

If you've created a link magnet or posted valuable content to your site, you need to let people know about it. The saying "If you build it, they will come" doesn't necessarily apply to your link magnets. Get your article, resource, video, or interactive application in front of people.

Of course, you should link to your article on your website, but you also need to spread the word to other websites. Social media is a great way to do that. One way to spread the word is by using *social share buttons* on your articles that allow people who view the content to share the page to their social media profile, — whether Twitter, Facebook, LinkedIn, or Google+ — by simply clicking a button on your page (read about adding social share buttons to your site in Book V, Chapter 7).

The purpose of attracting links to your content from social media sites is not just to get the link popularity from the links. After all, the benefit of these types of links is short-lived because news changes constantly. The real reward is that social media sites help generate traffic and awareness. Your goal is to spread the word about your article and get people to read it and want to share it with others by linking to it and discussing it. With luck, permanent and valuable links are built as a result.

Internet press releases are an effective and economical solution for distributing information to the public. After a press release is sent out through a third-party company, the information it contains is usually archived on that company's website. Most of the companies that offer this service allow you to write your own content, including links to your site. This ensures that you acquire an inbound link that a reader can follow to learn more about you.

Press releases should be written once every couple months (minimum), discussing new services that are being offered, the latest deals available, and what is happening on your site in general. You can generate press releases for significant announcements or events worthy of a press release. A press release can also be used to help promote and bring awareness to your link magnet. For example, if you have created a chart or checklist as a link magnet, write an article that shows how helpful your chart, widget, illustration, or checklist can be and send out a press release announcing its launch and covering the main advantages.

You can do all your press release writing yourself, or you can hire a writing service to generate your release for you. It all depends on how confident you are in your ability to write for journalists. Good companies to use when distributing press releases include PR Newswire, eReleases, and Business Wire.

As with guest posting and paid advertising links (which you can read about later in this chapter), Google asks that links from press releases include a `rel="nofollow"` attribute. In July 2013, Google said that it treats links in press releases like paid links, and the search engine publicly discourages the practice of using press releases to build links for a search engine ranking boost. Google also suggests including only one link in a press release that points to a domain home page or About page to avoid being viewed as manipulative.

Here are some other tips for writing an article or press release:

✦ **Avoid sounding like an ad.** No one likes to read a press release that offers nothing more than a commercial. Gather quotes from relevant parties to support your assertions and work them into your text.

✦ **Avoid promoting your company or product too much in articles.** If your article seems too much like a sales pitch, people are less likely to read or link to it.

✦ **Offer something new.** Provide something new in your article. Avoid repeating the same information that may be online elsewhere.

✦ **Use keywords in the title.** The article should have a catchy headline that makes people want to read it but that also includes the keyword phrase you are targeting. Others will likely link to the article with the title, so including the main keyword phrases in the title can help you incorporate keyword-rich anchor text into the links.

✦ **Avoid keyword stuffing.** Use a natural writing style that appeals to your audience, and avoid overusing or "stuffing" keywords.

✦ **Be truthful.** Don't use articles or link bait to lie to your visitors, because they will never return to your site if you can't deliver something you promise.

✦ **Tackle controversy.** Don't be afraid to tackle a controversial subject. Articles that cause people to think or want to debate the topic can make them more apt to want to post a link about it elsewhere.

✦ **Always opt to use the exact phrase you are trying to optimize in your articles.** If your keyword phrase is *SEO training,* it should appear right up front, not just in the title, but also in the first sentence and then throughout your text. Just as you do when optimizing a web page, you need to emphasize what you want people to consider to be the point of your article.

For more tips on writing effective press releases, visit `www.bruceclay.com/blog/how-to-write-a-press-release/`.

Guest posting

Guest posting refers to writing an article or blog for a website other than your own. As the name suggests, you're writing as a guest. Guest posting should be done on sites that are within your industry or niche. If you have a digital marketing agency, for example, guest posting on a PPC or web design blog would make sense. Guest posting for a cooking blog, on the other hand, would not make sense.

You benefit from guest posting, by getting in front of a new audience: You're providing high-quality content that potential customers will find useful. The next time they need your service, you will come to mind and earn business. Guest posting, then, is about expanding your audience and creating relationships with new readers. When a new audience sees your article, they may follow the link back to your site and engage with you further.

Guest posting should not be used as a tactic for increasing PageRank. In fact, any link that you include in a guest post should include `rel="nofollow"`. In January 2014, Google cracked down on links in guest posts because many people were writing guests posts that offered no value and existed solely as a link to point back to their own site. Because of this, Google has taken a strong stance against guest posting for links. A single suspicious link in a guest post can lead to a fall in rankings, and in some cases it can even trigger a Penguin penalty. Your best bet is to include the `rel="nofollow"` attribute to any links in a guest post — better safe than sorry. (You'll learn more about using the `rel="nofollow"` attribute later in this chapter!)

Fostering relationships

Guest posting is actually one way to go about employing a larger strategy for building backlinks to your site, with that strategy being focused on fostering relationships. Think about this. The search engines' continual goal to wipe out deceptive practices and shortcuts is really aimed at giving credit where it's due. Search engines want to count links that happen because someone's saying, "Hey, look at this! I really like it and you might, too!" Now consider something else: Who in the offline world is most likely to vouch for you? Your family, friends, and partners, of course! We're talking about people who know you and have a relationship with you. The same principle holds true online. If you invest in your relationships with businesses, organizations, and individuals online, links will naturally follow as a result. Seek to create a network of supportive connections: You support what others do, and they return in kind. When you've created some valuable article or resource to share, give your online network a heads-up, and they may post links and happily share that content.

True relationship building is a very laborious process, so it makes sense to choose the right fit when you're identifying whom to network with. The right fit will be enormously beneficial to both you and the other site because you'll have similar goals, audiences, and topics of expertise in common.

As you look for people and websites to foster relationships with, you need to determine which sites are the best candidates. You may know of some off the top of your head; if so, great. If you don't have a go-to list of networking targets and you want to get scientific about relationship building, you have a couple ways to go about it. One way is to use tools to identify *influencers* in your industry. An influencer is someone who has a good following and is respected online in a particular niche. Every industry has influencers, including yours, even if you aren't already aware of them.

Many tools are available to help you discover who your industry's influencers are. By the same token, your own industry may have forums, discussion boards, and private groups that tools won't find and only true insiders will know about. But you can generally get started by looking at some of the most popular social watering holes, like Facebook, Twitter, and YouTube. Traffic Spy (www.trafficspyapp.com) is a desktop application for Windows and Mac that lets you enter your industry or keywords so that it can report back to you with the top content and people for those terms across Facebook, Twitter, LinkedIn, YouTube, and Pinterest.

A tool that has in-depth analysis of Twitter influencers is Followerwonk (www.followerwonk.com). Figure 3-2 shows the results of a search for Twitter users with "classic cars" in the profile, arranged by number of followers. The tool also gives it a "Social Authority" score, a relative indicator of how influential that account is.

Figure 3-2:
Use Follower-wonk to search for influential Twitter users in your niche.

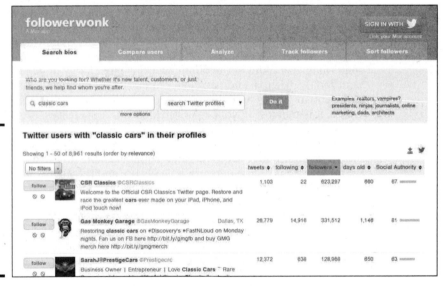

The other way to identify a business or person you want to build a relationship with is to research sites that link to the web pages that already rank for your keywords. Chances are that if the website has linked to your competitor, it might be a good candidate to start building a relationship with.

To discover what sites link to your competitors, follow these steps:

1. **Identify your competition: Run a search on Google (or Yahoo or Bing) for your search terms, the keywords you're trying to rank higher for.**

2. **Go through the results one at a time, opening the pages if you have to, to understand what kind of sites they are.**

   If the page is a direct competitor or is not likely to link to your site, move on to the next URL in the results. (If the page isn't a direct competitor, search for information on how to contact the site's webmaster. These sites could be good backlink candidates, too.)

3. **Make a list of the web pages (URLs) that rank well in your keyword search results page.**

   These are your competitors.

4. **After you identify your competition, find out who links to them by running your competitors' URLs through the Link Analysis Report that's available as a free tool on our SEOToolSet website (**`www.seotoolset.com/tools/free-tools/`**) or through another comparable tool.**

   The paid version of the SEOToolSet has a competitive link analysis tool that compares six sites and their linking schemas that is also useful for this.

Look over the report, which shows external pages with backlinks to your competitor. Figure 3-3 shows a Link Analysis Report from the SEOToolSet free tools page that shows you sites that link to the sample page.

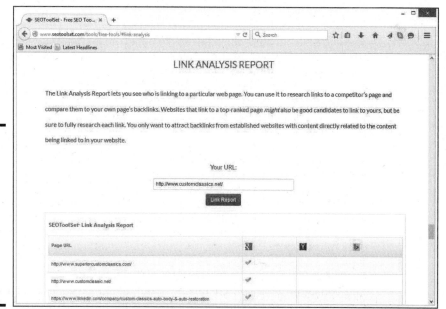

Figure 3-3:
A portion
of a Link
Analysis
Report
showing
web pages
that link
back to a
particular
page.

Here's what you should look for as you review the various URLs shown on the report:

✦ **Newness:** If a page that appears on the report already links to your web page, examine the anchor text and see if it would be better to change it or even to point to a more relevant page on your site. If it's already a good link, ignore it. You want to find *new* candidates for backlinks.

✦ **Relevancy:** Make sure the content on the web page relates to your page content. You don't want to obtain irrelevant links that won't pass any link equity. Also, the page should not have dozens of links to non-related sites.

✦ **Appropriateness:** We get into this more in Chapter 4 of this minibook, but you don't want links from bad neighborhoods. If the page is nothing more than a list of 100 random links with no content or theme, or full of paid ads, or looks spammy, or smells fishy . . . you don't want any part of it.

When you've determined good websites and individuals to network with, you want to start interacting with them. Interactions can happen in many places, including in the comment section of that website's blog and on social media networks. If you can subscribe to the blog RSS feed, do so, and read new blog posts and add your comments. The blog author will make note of you if she sees you in the comments section from time to time. You also want to search for that brand or individual on the popular social media sites. Follow the brand or person on Twitter, Facebook, Google+, or LinkedIn (wherever the person is most active) and then like and favorite his posts, answer his questions, start discussions, and reshare his posts.

The end game in all of this is to strike up a true and mutually beneficial relationship for you and the other person or website. Then, when you have a link magnet of some sort that you think is relevant to the website or influencer, suggest that she consider visiting your cool chart, table, interactive tool, or other widget to see if she believes it would add value for her site visitors. You don't have to ask for the link or share; if she likes your link magnet, she'll make that decision on her own.

A share or link request should come only after a relationship is established. This may take a time, but there is no shortcut to a relationship and the value it can bring, whether in the form of links or otherwise. After all, you're trying to start a business relationship that could have value in itself. In the best-case scenario, the other site's webmaster gives you a backlink that lasts for a long time to come and may end up passing quality traffic to your site that goes beyond better rankings.

In all your interactions, you should seek to be genuine and human, show that you know what you are talking about, illustrate your expertise, and demonstrate your commitment to success for both parties. If you have a link magnet or valuable resource that you hope your network will share, consider how each website or individual in your network would react to a request and adjust your approach accordingly. In some cases, it might be appropriate to pick up the phone and call the webmaster or even visit the website's offices in person. (Visit them in person *after* you've made phone or email contact, please: We don't want to encourage cyber-stalking!) It all depends.

Soliciting paid links for advertising

Obtaining a free link is not always possible. In those situations, you may want to come up with a plan to approach websites' webmasters about direct advertising on their sites. In that case, you have to determine a price point that is acceptable to you and to the other site as well. In some instances, a partnership may be developed that benefits both parties. If an agreement for a paid link is secured, in whatever form that link takes — a text link or a link on a banner or display ad — you want to be sure that you include a `rel="nofollow"` attribute on the link.

When soliciting paid links, remember to do it *only* for the traffic or the advertising. Obtaining a paid link gives you no direct SEO benefit and soliciting a paid link in order to increase your ranking is definitely not recommended. Google hates that. A lot. But if you've decided to try to solicit some paid links for the advertising traffic, you need to properly evaluate the websites you are looking at in order to make sure that you get a quality link and don't get ripped off.

First, check out the site and see how much traffic it gets. Also, take a good, hard look and determine whether the site uses spam techniques. If you think that it's a good legitimate site, send that site's webmaster a solicitation letter. Suggest a trial run for your ad; for example, you could pay the site for a month's worth of advertising, and then you can check to see whether your site's traffic has increased.

Using rel="nofollow"

You don't want the search engines to suspect your website of soliciting manipulative links and bring down an unnatural link penalty, such as from Penguin, on you. Because advertising links have an important purpose for users but not for search engines, the search engines recognize a piece of HTML code that webmasters can append to a link to tell them when a link is paid for or is in some way unnatural.

The `rel="nofollow"` attribute should be placed within the anchor tag (a) of a paid link. This attribute tells the search engine not to index the link or pass link equity through it. Users can still access the link, but the search engines won't follow it.

Here's an example of how to format a link with `rel="nofollow"`:

```
<a href="http://www.
    domain.com/page.html"
    rel="nofollow">Link Text</
    a>
```

You'll steer clear of manipulative link penalties if you tell search engines about any advertising links on your site and any advertising links that you obtain on others' sites using this little piece of code.

You have other methods of gauging or estimating traffic to a site before you purchase advertising. Most sites that are serious about selling ads have demographical and traffic data available. Sites such as Experian Hitwise (`www.hitwise.com`), comScore (`www.comscore.com`), Compete (`www.compete.com`), and Alexa (`www.alexa.com`) can give you some idea of what they can do for you.

One thing to monitor is the quality of the traffic that your advertisement is bringing you. Is it bringing you conversions or just a lot of traffic? Your ad might not be worth the money you spend on it if the traffic doesn't bring you any conversions. Instead, you can wind up just paying for the ad and the extra fees when your server gets hammered by all the new traffic.

How Not to Obtain Links

As with many things in life, there is a right way and there is a wrong way to go about obtaining links. We've put together a handy list of what *not* to do when trying to get links to your site:

✦ **Do not spam.** This means no sending of mass emails like, "Dear Webmaster, can you please link to me? Here is the anchor text I want to use. XOXO. Me." If you are soliciting links from a website, make sure to customize each and every email you send.

✦ **Avoid incestuous linking.** If you build a vast network of websites that only links back to itself, it's considered incestuous linking. This is a huge no-no for Google, and there are actual penalties involved: Your site could be removed from the index or be subjected to heavy ranking penalties instead of just having your links disregarded as part of the PageRank.

✦ **Do not buy links for ranking.** You can buy links in terms of traffic and for advertising, but buying a link for ranking is a definite no-no for Google, which disregards the weight of paid links and possibly any and all links on a page that contains paid links. Be safe by asking that any links bought for advertising include a `rel="nofollow"` attribute or be placed in a non-spiderable format.

✦ **Do not use run-of-site links.** *Run-of-site links* happen when a site has links to your site on every single one of its pages. These kinds of links are heavily discounted and are usually immediately flagged as paid links at best and spam at worst.

✦ **Do not use link farms.** There's more about link farms in Book I, Chapter 6. Link farms are spam, and you incur penalties for using them. You could get your site yanked from the index; if this happens, you need to clean it up and grovel to the search engines to get back in.

✦ **Do not solicit links from irrelevant sites.** It does not matter if the site is very, very popular: It won't help you if your content is in no way related to its content — like, say, your dog-grooming business soliciting a link from a gossip site like Gawker (`http://gawker.com`). (Unless, of course, you're grooming a celebrity pup! That may be great link bait.)

✦ **Do not set up several different sites all with the purpose of linking to yourself.** This is spam. Spamming is bad.

In general, think about how you would want people to try to obtain links from you. Treat others as you want to be treated. Also, always avoid sneaky, underhanded, or devious techniques. You will be caught and will have to do it the right way anyway. It saves you the time and effort of cleaning up your page and the hassle of begging Google to consider resubmitting your site into the index. We go deeper into the inbound links to avoid and how to remove bad incoming links in the next chapter of this minibook.

Chapter 4: Vetting Inbound Links

In This Chapter

✔ **Identifying inbound links**

✔ **Avoiding poor-quality links**

✔ **Dealing with link spam issues**

✔ **Cleaning up spammy inbound links**

*I*n the previous chapter, we discuss how inbound links can help and hurt your website, and how to tell good links from bad ones. *Inbound links* are the links pointing to your site. If you are Bob's Classic Car Customization, and you get a link from Motormouth Mabel's Classic Car Boutique, that's an inbound link. In addition to rankings by content, part of how search engines rank pages is based on inbound links. Google's description of its *PageRank* system (a part of Google's link algorithm) for instance, notes that Google interprets a link from page A to page B as a vote of confidence, by page A, for page B. That means that it reads an inbound link from another page as a testimonial link in your page, as if it means, "Hey, this guy knows what he's talking about!" Unfortunately, as is true of a lot of things in life, there are good inbound links and bad inbound links.

The previous chapter, looks at how to attract good links; now, in this chapter, we help you identify any bad inbound links and then tell you how to get rid of them (at least as far as the search engines are concerned).

Identifying Inbound Links

So how do you know who's linking to you? Well, in Chapter 3 of this mini-book, we explain how to attract links from other sites. You may publish link magnets or invest in your online relationships. Sometimes a site stumbles upon you and decides you'll be excellent to link to, and it just gives you a link. You can achieve this favorable treatment just by being awesome (or, more clearly, by having good design, a lot of relevant information, and interesting and dynamic content that the other site thinks its users would find interesting).

One way to find out who is linking to you is to view the inbound links reported in your free Google Search Console (`https://www.google.com/webmasters/tools/`) and Bing Webmaster Tools (`http://www.bing.com/toolbox/webmaster`) accounts. These free inbound links reports give you a good idea of your incoming links, but not a complete view. For a more comprehensive reporting of your website's inbound links, link reports from Majestic (`https://majestic.com`) show the most complete, historic view of inbound links of any available tool, making it worth the cost of a monthly subscription for any webmaster who suspects possible spam links in his site's inbound link profile.

If you are a smaller site, you need to be checking on your links constantly. If you have 50 incoming links, all those count toward your *link equity* (how much weight Google assigns your links). If you are a large, fairly well-known site, it's typically not going to matter much when one or two sites start or stop linking to you — but it can if they are major sites. Regardless of the size of your website, inbound link monitoring and maintenance has become an important part of online marketing since Google began cracking down on link spam with the first Penguin algorithm update in 2012. Get acquainted with the Penguin algorithm update and link-derived penalties in Chapter 3 of this minibook.

Avoiding Poor-Quality Links

Receiving inbound links is generally a good thing — it tells the search engines that you have a vote of confidence in your "expertness" level — but some inbound links out there only hurt you in the long run. There are several kinds you should be on the lookout for: from non-harmful reciprocal links to the riskier incestuous links, web rings, link farms, and bad neighborhoods.

Reciprocal links

If a site links to you, and you give it a link back, that's a *reciprocal link*. Doing this may limit the value of the link in either direction. Google usually, but not always, rates those links as having no value. The reasoning is that Google can't possibly judge the intent of every reciprocal relationship. Google doesn't know whether your intent is good or if you're trying to trick its search engine. Reciprocal links are bartered exchanges, so they might be treated just like an ad from a search engine perspective.

If you have a reciprocal link, don't expect it to carry any value, especially if you have a small site. If you are linking out, link to a noncompetitive relative expert. However, if you want to provide some reciprocal links that would be valuable to your visitors, by all means do so. Just be aware that they may not count toward your link equity.

Incestuous links

Incestuous links occur when people link to their own properties or among a group of friends' sites and then try to pass the links off as legitimate links from outside sources. If you have several sites, and they all link to each other, and you're trying to pretend that you don't own half of those sites, that's some incestuous linking going on.

Some large networks exist that do link between their properties, such as the Gawker Media Network, which has links between all its sites (www.gawker.com, www.jezebel.com, www.io9.com, www.lifehacker.com, www.gizmodo.com, among many others). This is not incestuous linking by definition. The company is linking within its network, yes. But it is, first, a large company and, second, not trying to hide the fact that it owns the sites in the networks. Generally, linking within networks happens for user experience or for branding purposes. Large companies know that linking within their own networks doesn't mean that they gain any link equity from it. In most cases, these links are for commercial value and perhaps credibility, but not for link equity or PageRank. And most important, they're not trying to hide the fact that they do it. It's a general rule of thumb: If people are trying to hide something that they did, they're probably doing something wrong.

**Book VI
Chapter 4**

Vetting Inbound Links

We call these types of links *incestuous links* because they are no good and should make you feel icky. Smaller sites caught using them are punished. When you are caught using incestuous links, not only do you run the risk of having those links devalued, but your site could also be marked as spam, and you may have *all* your links devalued. And that's not even the worst that can happen.

When you get penalized for this type of spam, your site can vanish from the index altogether. We know of one site (that shall remain nameless) using incestuous links and ranking really, really well, with a ton of link equity. Then Google made some tweaks to its algorithm and discovered that this particular site was using incestuous links. So Google punished that site. The site's rankings dropped down to the thousandth place on every one of its keywords, and it couldn't even rank for its own name. Trust us when we say dishonesty doesn't pay.

Link farms

We discuss link farms in Book I, Chapter 6 when we talk about search engine spam. *Spam* includes any sneaky, devious, or underhanded technique used to trick search engines into giving websites higher rankings. *Link farms* are literally pages of hundreds (or even thousands) of links on many sites that all link together. This is slightly different than incestuous linking because you might not own the properties involved. In general, you should be very suspicious if someone asks for a link from your site and offers you a link from a totally different site in exchange. That's a classic warning sign for a link farm.

Link farms are sites that have many different links to multiple different sites, all for the express purpose of passing link equity and giving those sites a higher rating in the search engines. Sometimes, you can't help it if a link farm links to you. If you discover that your site is part of one, politely ask for it to be removed as soon as possible. Being caught as part of a link farm could lead to all your links losing their link equity or even harsher penalties.

Web rings

Web rings are not necessarily spam. *Web rings* are any collection of websites from around the Internet that join together through interlinking in a circular structure. When you join a web ring, you become part of a circle of related websites. One way to get caught up in a web ring is by including a third-party *widget* (an interactive piece of HTML coding) on your site or by making a widget available for others to include on their sites. Figure 4-1 shows an example of a web ring widget.

We don't recommend joining a web ring, because all those links do not give you any link equity. On top of that, it probably isn't worth the traffic you'll be receiving.

Figure 4-1: This is a web ring for fans of a TV show; they were especially popular before search engines became ubiquitous.

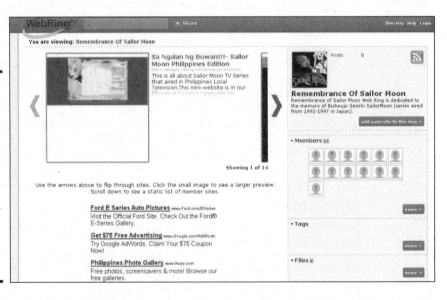

You want *natural* links. You want people to link to you because they feel that your site is worthwhile. Web rings aren't natural links. And although they've fallen out of favor in recent years, they do still exist. But quite honestly, they're not worth the trouble.

Bad neighborhoods

Say you have a site that wants to link to you. You take a quick look at the site and check to see whether it's in the search engine's index by entering it into Google. But this site does not show up anywhere in the search results. Do you want a link from this site? Chances are, probably not.

Sometimes, a website isn't part of a search engine's index. It could be that the website is too newly created. But it's more likely that the website comes from a *bad neighborhood.* This is a website that got yanked from a search engine index, and probably for a good reason. Either it was spamming or it was using other sneaky methods to try and fool the search engines, and it got caught.

Being part of a bad neighborhood or accepting links from a site that has been banished from the index is about the same as if you had suddenly associated with the bad kids at your high school. Your site gets flagged, and you come under suspicion of using spam techniques yourself.

You can't help it if someone chooses to link to your site. But it's a good idea to avoid actively attracting unsavory attention. Try to avoid poor links whenever you can, and focus on attracting quality links that will add to your PageRank and grant you link equity. If you do get an unsavory link, the search engines give you a way to publicly distance yourself from it, as we explain later in this chapter.

Book VI
Chapter 4

Vetting Inbound
Links

Dealing with Search Engine Spam

As we discuss in Book I, Chapter 6, people can use several different ways to *spam* (deceive or trick) the search engine into giving their pages higher rankings than they deserve or allowing them to rank for keywords that have nothing to do with their sites. Search engine spammers also use links to practice their sneaky ways. Here are some of them:

✦ **Link farms:** We've warned you against getting involved in a *link farm,* any website that links to a large, random assortment of different websites which all link back to each other, because search engines see these as spam. Most link farms are created through automated programs and services. Search engines have combated link farms by identifying specific attributes that link farms use and filtering them from the index and search results, including removing entire domains to keep them from influencing the results page.

✦ **White text/links on a white background:** Putting white text and links on a white background (or black text on a black background, and so on) renders the text invisible to a user unless it is selected with the mouse. Spammers can then insert text that is merely keywords or hyperlinks that the spiders read and mistakenly count as relevant.

✦ **Hidden text or links:** Spammers sometimes hide content by covering it with an image or other layered element so it is not visible. People also specify a negative page position so that the page technically stretches up higher or wider than the browser window. Or they hide spiderable content under the page content (layer) so that can't be seen with the naked eye.

The problem with link spam is that you cannot always help who is linking to you. What you *can* do is disassociate yourself from them as quickly as possible.

You might drop a line to Google and report any link farms or any other unsavory links to its spam department (www.google.com/webmasters/tools/spamreport).

Identifying inbound link spam

This minibook tells you how to find out all the pages and sites linking to you. It also familiarizes you with the characteristics of a link that can harm you if the search engines recognize it as spam. So how can you find out whether any of your inbound links are seen as spam by the search engines?

Webmasters with all the best intentions may find themselves suffering from a link spam penalty as a result of Google's having suddenly changed its guidelines. For instance, you may have used guest posting or press releases as an inbound link strategy, but then found yourself at risk of a penalty when Google announced in 2013 that links from press releases are unnatural, and then, in 2014, that guest post links are unnatural (read Chapter 3 of this minibook for the types of links that Google considers unnatural). Whether inbound link spam happened before you managed the website, or because the search engines changed their rules, or because you trusted someone to do SEO on your website and that person went about it in a risky way, you can deal with it — don't lose hope.

The first thing to know about how search engines handle inbound link spam is that a website can be penalized for spam in two ways. An *algorithmic penalty* is built into the search engines' ranking algorithms. The search engines have identified attributes unique to link spam and can match that pattern to any site's inbound links in order to filter them from the results. The other approach that a search engine may take to combat spam is a *manual penalty.* True to its name, a manual penalty can happen when a site gets a serious search by a human instead of by using the search engine's normal algorithms. When a human investigates the site, anything hidden from the search engines in images or with any other kind of technology is visible. It's a little bit like being audited. If the person doing the inspection catches you doing something against the search engine guidelines, you are penalized. A penalty can range in severity from having your whole site removed from the search index altogether to keeping individual pages on your site from ranking for key terms.

Manual action penalties

Determining whether Google has placed a manual penalty against you is as easy as checking your free Google Search Console account. When you're signed in to Google Search Console, go to Search Traffic and then Manual Actions. Figure 4-2 shows an example of a manual action notification for unnatural links reported in Google Search Console. Here are the types of spam Google will alert webmasters of:

Figure 4-2:
Check Google Search Console for reported manual actions against your website, such as this report of detected unnatural links.

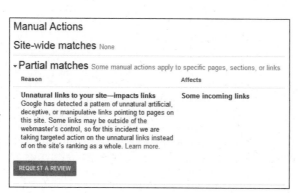

Manual Actions

Site-wide matches None

▾**Partial matches** Some manual actions apply to specific pages, sections, or links

Reason	Affects
Unnatural links to your site—impacts links Google has detected a pattern of unnatural artificial, deceptive, or manipulative links pointing to pages on this site. Some links may be outside of the webmaster's control, so for this incident we are taking targeted action on the unnatural links instead of on the site's ranking as a whole. Learn more.	Some incoming links

REQUEST A REVIEW

+ Unnatural links to your site

+ Unnatural links from your site

+ Hacked site

+ User-generated spam

+ Thin content with little or no added value

✦ Hidden text or keyword stuffing

✦ Cloaking or sneaky redirects

✦ Spammy freehosts

✦ Pure spam (defined by Google as "aggressive spam techniques such as automatically generated gibberish, cloaking, scraping content from other websites, and/or other repeated or egregious violations of Google's quality guidelines")

The Bing Webmaster Tools site also has an area that's used to alert webmasters of suspected spam, but in our experience, Bing is not as forthcoming with its messages to webmasters. You can check the Index Summary chart in the Bing Webmaster Tools Dashboard for how many pages of your site are indexed, and if the number of pages indexed is zero, then it's safe to assume your site has been severely penalized.

Algorithmic penalties

Determining whether your site got caught in an algorithmic update targeting link spam requires a little more legwork than simply checking Webmaster Tools for a message. Basically, you check to see whether your search traffic dropped on the same day as any known algorithm updates.

In Chapter 3 of this minibook, we introduce you to Google's Penguin penalty targeting link spam. This algorithmic penalty was first released in April 2012, but a number of updates have refined Penguin since then. Google doesn't always announce or confirm changes to its algorithm, so the search engine marketing community has attempted to record the dates of all Penguin updates in order to help webmasters in their efforts to pinpoint any negative effects by Penguin on their websites. Visit `https://moz.com/google-algorithm-change` for the most complete list of Penguin (and all other) updates. Then, compare your search traffic reported in your analytics tool and see whether traffic drops align with any of the Penguin updates.

A tool can do this comparison for you if you use Google Analytics (`www.google.com/analytics/`) as your analytics software. Digital marketing agency Barracuda released a free tool called Panguin (`http://www.barracuda-digital.co.uk/panguin-tool/`) that marks up your search traffic graph with the known dates of algorithmic penalty updates, including for Penguin and Panda (see Book V, Chapter 2 for more on how Google Panda penalizes websites for content-based spam). The example of the Panguin tool in action in Figure 4-3 shows that this site probably benefitted from the January 2013 Panda update, gaining a significant spike in traffic following the update.

Figure 4-3:
A tool like Panguin helps web-masters compare known search engine algorithm updates against their website traffic to identify spam penalties.

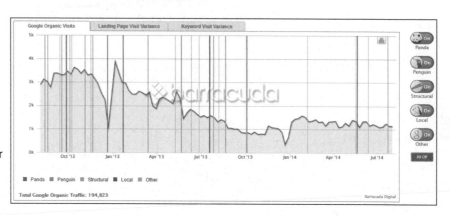

Removing unwanted links

With luck, your research will show that you aren't being penalized for unnatural links. But if you think you are, you have recourse! Unfortunately, the process for cleaning up spammy inbound links is laborious and time intensive. On the upside, it has been shown to work! The process of inbound link cleanup has three parts: Link pruning to get spam links removed; link disavowal to tell the search engines that you know a link is spam but you can't get it removed; and then (in the case of manual penalties) asking the search engine to reevaluate your site and lift any penalties.

Figure 4-4 shows a flowchart for removing unwanted links. Apply this flowchart to every one of your inbound links. We discuss getting a listing of your inbound links in Bing Webmaster Tools, Google Search Console, and Majestic earlier in this chapter, in the "Identifying Inbound Links" section. If you suspect that you have a link penalty against you, you should get the full, historic link report available from Majestic so that you can vet all your links as the flowchart describes.

Keep meticulous records of your inbound link cleanup process because in the end, you'll ask the search engine to reconsider your site in its newly cleaned form and explain what you did to get there. The last step in getting an unnatural link penalty lifted is to tell the search engine everything you did, or even tried to do, to get rid of bad inbound links. Google expects you to tell it if you asked for changed anchor text, added nofollows, and performed link removal. Google doesn't make the process easy, and that's intentional. The search engines hate spam and will make a site pay for a chance at forgiveness.

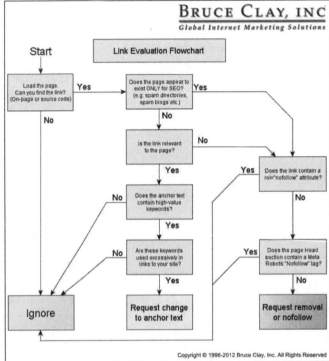

Figure 4-4:
Use this flowchart to tell whether an inbound link qualifies as spam and needs to be removed.

Link pruning

To remove unwanted links, identify links that are unwanted and then request that the linking site change or remove it. This is the process of *link pruning*. Create a template email to send to the websites you're asking for a link removal, nofollow, or anchor text change. The request you send should politely explain that you are a webmaster trying to recover from an unnatural link penalty. Be agreeable and appeal to the person's sense of generosity in taking the time to help you out with your request. Include all the details about the link she needs to easily find it on her site and change or remove it.

We've developed a spreadsheet to keep track of a link pruning project. Import your complete list of inbound links into a spreadsheet with the following column headings. Before each group of column headings, we explain what the information is and where to get it.

Link information

This information is about the link itself, such as the page it's on and the anchor text it uses. Include these column headings in your link removal spreadsheet:

✦ **Target URL:** The page on your site the link points to.

✦ **Source URL:** The origin point of the inbound link,

✦ **Source rank:** A designation of quality of the link based on the authority of the linking page and the relevance to your site. If you're using Majestic, you can record the Citation Flow and Trust Flow scores that Majestic calculates here.

✦ **Source crawl date:** The date the information was collected.

✦ **Anchor text:** The text used as an anchor for the link.

✦ **Image link:** Check whether the link is an image.

✦ `ALT` **Text:** Descriptive text if the link is an image.

✦ `nofollow`: Check whether a `nofollow` attribute is on the link.

✦ **Redirect:** Check whether a redirect occurs as part of the link.

✦ **Frame:** Check whether the link is contained in a frame.

Book VI
Chapter 4

Vetting Inbound
Links

Contact information

To ask for a change to or removal of a link, you need a contact to reach out to. Get this information from contact info on the site or from a whois directory that lets you look up site owner information. Include these column headings in your link removal spreadsheet:

✦ **Owner name**

✦ **IP address**

✦ **Owner address**

✦ **Owner email**

✦ **Owner phone number**

✦ **Registrar name**

✦ **Name servers**

✦ **Net name**

✦ **Data source:** The website or whois registry where you got the site information. This is needed in case you need to refer back to the source.

Correspondence record

Record your attempts to get in contact with the site owner as well as any response you receive. Include these column headings in your link removal spreadsheet:

✦ **Date of initial contact**

✦ **Date of received response**

+ **Removal verified:** Put the date of confirmed removal in this column.

+ **Other response requests**

+ **Date(s) of follow-up contact**

After you send out a link removal request, any one of the following things might happen:

+ **The site owner removes the link and tells you.** If you get a reply saying that the action you requested was taken, check to make sure it did and then mark your spreadsheet with the date that the removal is verified.

+ **The site owner removes the link and doesn't tell you.** If you don't get a response, check to see whether the link was removed without you being notified. If it was removed, mark your spreadsheet with the date that the removal is verified.

+ **The site owner tells you something is keeping him from making the change.** You may receive a response outside of simple compliance to your request. Record any response you get, including requests for payment to remove the link.

+ **You get no response and no action.** If you can't reach the site owner and the link is still there in its original form, follow up a couple weeks later with another request. The standard due diligence for link removal is three requests. If you've asked three times with no success, move on to the next step — link disavowal.

Disavowals

Because you can't control whether another site removes a link, search engines have given webmasters a way to tell them that you don't want to be associated with that link anymore. The search engines call this disavow- ing the link, and both Google and Bing have a disavow links tool in their Webmaster Tools. In Bing Webmaster Tools, go to Configure My Site in the navigation and then Disavow Links in the resulting subnavigation. To disavow links with Google, go to the disavow links tool page while logged in to Google Search Console (`https://www.google.com/webmasters/tools/disavow-links-main`).

Google has issued a warning for those considering using this tool (`https://support.google.com/webmasters/answer/2648487?hl=en`):

First and foremost, we recommend that you remove as many spammy or low-quality links from the web as possible.

If you've done as much work as you can to remove spammy or low-quality links from the web, and are unable to make further progress on getting the links taken down, you can disavow the remaining links. In other words, you can ask Google not to take certain links into account when assessing your site.

This is an advanced feature and should only be used with caution. If used incorrectly, this feature can potentially harm your site's performance in Google's search results. We recommend that you disavow backlinks only if you believe you have a considerable number of spammy, artificial, or low-quality links pointing to your site, and if you are confident that the links are causing issues for you. In most cases, Google can assess which links to trust without additional guidance, so most normal or typical sites will not need to use this tool.

If you use the tool with knowledge and after much determined effort to remove unnatural links, the disavow tool is a powerful aid in helping you get a link penalty lifted. The full extent of using the disavow tools isn't covered in these pages, and we urge you to educate yourself by reading the search engines' help and support documentation before using this powerful tool. As an example of the nuance you need to familiarize yourself with, there's a difference between a domain-level disavow and a page-level disavow. Disavowing a domain is like using a machete, cutting off all links from a domain. Page-level disavow, meanwhile, has the precision of a surgeon's knife, slicing out individual offending pages from your inbound link profile. Instructions for submitting a link disavow file to Google are available in the Google Support article found here: `https://support.google.com/webmasters/answer/2648487`. Instructions for disavowing links with Bing are given in this Bing Webmaster Help article: `http://www.bing.com/webmaster/help/how-to-disavow-links-0c56a26f`.

Book VI Chapter 4

Vetting Inbound Links

We created a tool that gives us a fast track for flagging inbound links that have been disavowed by others, and we've made this tool available for free to everyone. Use DisavowFiles (`www.disavowfiles.com`) to compare your inbound links against a database of known disavowed pages and sites. This helps you zero in on possible known spam link offenders so that you can determine whether you want to disavow the URL or domain for yourself.

The next step for you to take after link removal and disavowal depends on whether you're addressing a manual penalty or an algorithmic one like Penguin. If your efforts at link cleanup were related to a Penguin update, all you can do is sit tight and wait for Google to update Penguin again, taking into account your cleaned-up backlinks and link disavowals. If you've removed links in response to a manual penalty, your next step is a reconsideration request.

Reconsideration requests

After you've pruned and disavowed unnatural inbound links, you're ready to run your site by Google for reconsideration. We say Google here and not the search engines because the reconsideration process is unique to Google. We can only assume that your link cleanup project is ultimately accounted for algorithmically as Bing factors in your disavowed links and, as it crawls the web, sees that unnatural links no longer exist.

So for Google, at least, the final step in getting a manual penalty lifted is submitting your site for reconsideration. Log in to Google Search Console and go to Search Traffic and then Manual Actions. Next to the manual action that Google reports is the Request a Review button (refer to Figure 4-2). Google wants you to do three things in your reconsideration request:

1. Explain the exact quality issue on your site.

2. Describe the steps you took to fix the issue.

3. Document the outcome of your efforts.

You can link to any documents that describe your cleanup efforts, and that's where your link-pruning spreadsheet shines. In the Google Support article on reconsideration requests (`https://support.google.com/webmasters/answer/35843`), you see some common pitfalls that will cause your reconsideration to be denied. These include disavowing all your backlinks without even trying to get them removed, and using the disavow tool wrong, such as on a domain-level disavowal when a page-level disavowal is more appropriate.

You may have to wait a few days before you get a response from Google about your reconsideration request. First you get notice of receipt of your request, and you may hear that your request is being processed. Within a few days, you receive a message in Google Search Console that the manual penalty was revoked (in which case, congrats!) or that your site is still violating Google Guidelines. If Google still sees unnatural links pointing to your site that qualify your site for a manual penalty, examples of these unnatural links will be listed in the message. At this point, you pick back up with unwanted link identification, removal, and disavowal, allowing at least a few weeks before submitting your next reconsideration request.

Removing spammy inbound links will alleviate the negative effect of a penalty, but it won't return your search rankings to where they were before you were caught manipulating PageRank signals. If you succeed in getting a manual link penalty removed or can shake off Penguin during the next update, follow this up with the lessons in Chapter 3 of this minibook — attracting true quality links that your stellar content deserves.

Google's site quality guidelines

The following is Google's policy when it comes to quality for the sites in its index. This was taken from the Google Webmaster Guidelines at `www.google.com/support/webmasters/bin/answer.py?hl=en&answer=35769#3`. We include it here in its entirety as a handy guide. Be aware that Google does occasionally update its guidelines, so you should monitor the website (or search for [Google Webmaster Guidelines] in Google) so that you're always playing within the rules:

> These quality guidelines cover the most common forms of deceptive or manipulative behavior, but Google may respond negatively to other misleading practices not listed here. It's not safe to assume that just because a specific deceptive technique isn't included on this page, Google approves of it. Webmasters who spend their energies upholding the spirit of the basic principles will provide a much better user experience and subsequently enjoy better ranking than those who spend their time looking for loopholes they can exploit.

> If you believe that another site is abusing Google's quality guidelines, please let us know by filing a spam report. Google prefers developing scalable and automated solutions to problems, so we attempt to minimize hand-to-hand spam fighting. While we may not take manual action in response to every report, spam reports are prioritized based on user impact, and in some cases may lead to complete removal of a spammy site from Google's search results. Not all

manual actions result in removal, however. Even in cases where we take action on a reported site, the effects of these actions may not be obvious.

Quality guidelines — basic principles

- Make pages primarily for users, not for search engines.
- Don't deceive your users.
- Avoid tricks intended to improve search engine rankings. A good rule of thumb is whether you'd feel comfortable explaining what you've done to a website that competes with you, or to a Google employee. Another useful test is to ask, "Does this help my users? Would I do this if search engines didn't exist?"
- Think about what makes your website unique, valuable, or engaging. Make your website stand out from others in your field.

Quality guidelines — specific guidelines

Avoid the following techniques:

- Automatically generated content
- Participating in link schemes
- Creating pages with little or no original content
- Cloaking
- Sneaky redirects
- Hidden text or links
- Doorway pages

(continued)

(continued)

✔ Scraped content

✔ Participating in affiliate programs without adding sufficient value

✔ Loading pages with irrelevant keywords

✔ Creating pages with malicious behavior, such as phishing or installing viruses, trojans, or other badware

✔ Abusing rich snippets markup

✔ Sending automated queries to Google

Engage in good practices like the following:

✔ Monitoring your site for hacking and removing hacked content as soon as it appears

✔ Preventing and removing user-generated spam on your site

If your site violates one or more of these guidelines, then Google may take manual action against it. Once you have remedied the problem, you can submit your site for reconsideration.

Chapter 5: Connecting with Social Networks

In This Chapter

✔ **Attracting links with blogs**

✔ **Leveraging social news sites**

✔ **Defining media optimization**

✔ **Implementing social media optimization**

✔ **Gaining search visibility through social activity**

✔ **Building a community**

✔ **Adding interactivity to your website**

*I*n recent years, the world of *online social networking* (sites where people can meet and interact with one another online) has exploded in popularity. You may have heard of sites like Facebook, Twitter, and LinkedIn, which allow users to create their own web pages, publish content, and connect with other users all over the globe. This kind of social networking has expanded to include news sites, entertainment media, and beyond.

Social networking is another way to find and attract links. The majority of links from *link magnets* (media or articles created to attract links by offering something unique or engaging) comes from social networking sites. Social networking can also help you build your brand and a name for yourself. This is where true grassroots marketing begins — and if you're creative and smart enough, you can use social networks to your advantage.

In this chapter, we discuss what you need to do to take advantage of: blogging, social news sites, social media optimization, community building, and interactive applications.

Making Use of Blogs

Blogs (short for web logs) are primarily an online conversation medium. Blogs can be anything — from people's personal journals, in which they talk about their day, their trip to the hair salon, and the rude guy who cut them off on the way to the grocery store, to media and corporate blogs that describe new products and services. Blogs cover entertainment, politics, fashion, lifestyles, and technology. If you name it, you can probably find somebody out there blogging about it. Although the exact recommendations for a blog will vary by industry, blogs should be updated at least a few times per week.

One way to use blogs is to set up a blog on your own website. A blog can increase the amount of *content* (the text and media offered) on your site that relates to your subject matter because an actively used blog site builds content rapidly. A blog also helps you by improving user engagement on your site and strengthening your customer service: Blogs provide a place for you to hear from your users and to interact with them. (For more information on setting up a blog, see Book V, Chapter 7.) In general, blogs take a lot of attention and time, and although they may get links very quickly, they lose those links just as fast. Blogs, like all social media links, are high-maintenance and require consistent care.

Blogs can also benefit you when someone writes about your website or company and then links back to your site from an on-topic website. (Read about natural versus unnatural links in Chapter 3 of this minibook.) The worth of a link from a blog varies, however. If an authoritative blog — such as the political gossip blog Wonkette (www.wonkette.com) or the car enthusiast blog Jalopnik (www.jalopnik.com) — links to your website, that link could equal a whole lot of traffic for you, plus the prestige that comes along with such a link. On the other hand, most links from blogs are actually pretty worthless. You see an increase in traffic only within the first day or maybe just a few minutes; after that, the link cycles off the page, the blogger updates with new content, and your link is yesterday's news. Links from most blogs are good for passing around link magnets, but not a whole lot else.

Most blogs allow users to comment on them. You can click a button at the end of the blog post and leave your thoughts, criticisms, or links of your own. Other users can reply to your comment, as can the author of the blog. Blog comments usually don't pass any *link equity* (the worth of a link as defined by the search engines). The `rel="nofollow"` attribute (an HTML code that tells search engines not to follow a link) was actually invented for blog comments to stop spammers from crashing blogs and cluttering up the Comments page with useless, unrelated information. Most blog software programs apply a `rel="nofollow"` attribute to every link by default, so anything in the comments is not counted by a search engine.

However, don't let the lack of link equity stop you from using the comments option and interacting with other readers on a blog. Like other forms of business networking, the comments section of a blog can be a great place to network with other people and find out what the guy on the street is saying about products or services in your industry. People interact with you in the comments section; they might decide to check out your site and wind up giving you a link from their websites.

This type of link building by relationship building is a much slower process than the normal heavy traffic that you would receive if you were linked through the blog, but these kinds of links (and the traffic gained from them) based on a relationship formed through a blog stick around longer. Don't be afraid to interact in the comments section on a blog. Just be sure to practice good etiquette. Be who you are, not some fictitious persona. Also, don't go around trolling on other blogs. *Trolling* is the act of deliberately being rude and offensive just to make people angry on blogs and other web forums, and it most definitely gets you banned from the blog or site.

If you are publishing a blog on your website, take care to make sure that the topics of your posts are always hyper-relevant to the main themes and don't dilute the overall focus of your website. The Google penalty that demotes a site's search rankings for low-quality content, known as Panda, may trigger if a blog looks like a sprawling collection of unrelated, unorganized articles. Read about the Panda algorithm and how the search engines penalize low-quality content in Book V, Chapter 2.

Discovering Social News Sites

Today, the Internet puts the news right at your fingertips, and you can find hundreds of sources for news out there. You can go to a site such as CNN.com or any newspaper site and read articles at their source. But the Internet has turned news-reading into a social activity, too. A *social news site* is a site where users can vote on news stories and articles from anywhere on the web, and the audience — rather than the editors of the site or source — determines the importance of a story or article. Digg (digg.com) and StumbleUpon (www.stumbleupon.com) are social news sites, but far and away the most popular social news site out there is Reddit (www.reddit.com), which has dubbed itself with the slogan "The front page of the Internet." With a social news network, users decide what stories are most important and entertaining. The stories and articles posted to Reddit are organized by thousands of categories called subreddits. There's a subreddit for nearly every interest and topic under the sun, and users can vote and comment on stories, with the most popular stories rising to the top of the category page. If a link to your web page gets a lot of attention on Reddit, expect a sharp, temporary spike in traffic.

You can make your articles and web pages easy to post to Reddit and other social news sites by including *social share buttons* on the page. A share button is a graphic icon that readers can click to post the page they are reading to their favorite social website. When you read an article on a news site, a blog, or an Internet-savvy company's website, near the top or bottom of an article, you can usually find share buttons to social news sites and other social media sites such as the ones shown in Figure 5-1.

Figure 5-1:
Social share buttons let readers post and comment on an article on popular social websites.

When you find a story or article that you find interesting, you can click the share button for your preferred social networking site, which brings you to the social website where you can write a short description of the news item or article and then post it to the network. The most common networks with share buttons these days are the social news site Reddit and social media networks Facebook, Twitter, LinkedIn, and Google+, which we talk about more in the next section.

With time, effort, and good luck, a site or article could make it to the first page. If it's your site or article, congratulations! But sorry about the server crash. Reddit alone has 174 *million* unique visits a month. The higher you appear on its news pages, the more traffic you get. Success with a social news site can be both a blessing and a curse: It has the possibility of generating more permanent links, but your server might not be able to handle the traffic.

An article's popularity varies from network to network because each network has its own unique appeal to different kinds of users. Reddit's network tends to be generally young, male, liberal, and technology-savvy. You also can find smaller, more niche-oriented social news networks that focus on a particular interest, such as the technology-oriented Hacker News (`www.news.ycombinator.com`) and the politically leaning Newsvine (`www.newsvine.com`).

Promoting Media on Social Networking Sites

Social media sites are another way to get links via relationship building. Posts that promote your Engagement Objects are good forms of link magnets that can pay off with huge amounts of traffic and short term links. Taking advantage of the social media sites requires some advanced planning. After you identify which site would be best for your subject and audience, you still need to make some decisions about how, when, and what. If you plan to submit different forms of media to social networking sites, consider optimizing the content for those sites first. The media in question includes videos, podcasts, and images.

If you have videos, put them on your website, as well as on video-sharing sites such as YouTube. People who view them on the other video-sharing site read your description and hopefully follow the link back to your site that you include in the description, as shown in Figure 5-2.

Figure 5-2: Within your video descriptions on YouTube, include a link back to your site for viewers who want to visit and learn more.

Hyperlink in the video description

Your media has to be engaging. Make it funny, creative, educational, and engaging or, if all else fails, controversial. You want to get people talking about it. Don't be afraid to make people angry, if it comes right down to it. One of the fastest ways to get links to a blog is to write something that's sure to make people angry — but turn the comments off. People go running back to their own blogs and newsfeeds to write what they think about you, including a link back to your site. This benefits you in terms of link equity. The thing about link equity is that Google doesn't care if a link is positive or derogatory. Google still passes link equity.

Another thing to keep in mind about your content is not to be stingy with it. Share it! A comparison has been made about media and the card game Canasta. In Canasta, a good strategy to win is to give away all your best cards in the beginning so that you get them back at the end. Similarly, if you freely give away your media, people come to your website.

For example, you can put your images on the photo-sharing site Flickr (`www.flickr.com`) under the Creative Commons license, which allows you either to retain some rights over your image or to make it free for use in the public domain. (You can find out more about the Creative Commons license options at `http://creativecommons.org`.) You can make the images free for public use as long as they provide a link back to your site, which people generally more than happily provide. In any kind of photo-sharing network, you also have the option of tagging your photos with relevant keywords, as well as providing links to your site.

As with most links you want to attract, you want to attract media links naturally. You want links to come to you on their own because people find and enjoy the media you put out there and think your site is a relevant and entertaining place that they would recommend to other users to check out. You have to have a vested interest in creating quality content. Give the people out there something of value. For example, musician Jonathan Coulton makes all his songs available for public use on his website under the Creative Commons license (an alternative form of the traditional copyright that specifies the conditions under which a person may use copyrighted content). He allows others to use his songs for their videos and media projects, which allows him to introduce his music to a much wider audience. Go to YouTube and check out how many people are using his music for their own projects, and you'll get an idea.

If you have a classic-car customization website, for example, you can give away useful information by making a video about how to properly repair chipped paint on a classic car or fix a dented fender (or get a little silly and teach them to properly hang dice from a rearview mirror). But you want to do so in a way that is clever and entertaining. For instance, you might dress up as ninjas while repairing the chipped paint. The easiest way to draw people to your website is to be clever and entertaining. (This is why it's a good idea to watch those social news networks, so you can see what is funny versus something that is definitely *not* funny.)

You can also allow people to take your content that is under the Creative Commons license and post it on their own sites, as long as they give you a link back. People are usually more than glad to give you a link.

Optimizing Social Media

Social media is any sort of online environment that allows social interaction, including blogs, social news sites such as Reddit and Digg, social networking sites such as Facebook (www.facebook.com), and others. Social media sites have become great for branding. Not only can they bring you inbound links, but they also provide great opportunities for reputation management because you can read and respond to what's being said about your brand. Developing a strong following on Facebook is extremely useful for building a connection with your brand's supporters.

Twitter (https://twitter.com) is a popular microblogging site that allows you to update your status via the web or through text messaging. (*Microblogs* are like blogs, but they allow you to update only a few words at time.) Because of how frequently Twitter is updated, Google and Bing rely on a direct feed straight from Twitter to keep their search indexes updated with the constant stream of content. This means that Twitter posts can rank in search results. But beyond the possible SEO opportunity, Twitter is a great way to control your branding because it allows you to go out and engage other users.

The important thing to remember is to snap up your brand name right away on each of the major social media sites. Go out and register your name and every variation that you can think of as fast as you can. You want to keep others from taking them and potentially using them to pretend to be you, damaging your online reputation (we go over this problem in the section "Building Community," later in this chapter). This has happened many times, and when someone does take your name before you can register it, there's not much you can do about it. So make sure you grab your own brand name.

There is an online service called KnowEm (http://knowem.com) that will register your name on hundreds of blogging, microblogging, bookmarking, photo and video hosting, and community sites. The basic plan (for a one-time fee of $85) gets your name registered and profile filled out on the 25 most popular social media profiles. There are also business and enterprise packages covering between 100 and 300 profiles, plus a program for ongoing registration on new social sites every month. Currently, KnowEm tracks and registers names on more than 500 social media sites.

One thing to think about when it comes to social media optimization is what your web pages look like when someone shares a link to your site on a social network. Facebook shows a preview of an article when a user shares a link. This preview might show up with a large image or a small image, plus a headline and a description. How do you think Facebook comes up with the image and text to put in the preview? The website can tell Facebook through some simple code on each page, or it tries to guess at the best image and text to use. Figure 5-3 shows how a link shows up with an image and descriptive text when it's shared on Facebook.

Figure 5-3: You can pick the image, headline, and description that show up in a preview of your articles when they're shared on Facebook.

No surprise here, but you should definitely take the opportunity to specify the image and text you want to show up in a Facebook preview and customize it to attract viewers to click through to your page. Twitter also has special code that you can add to your pages to customize the appearance of your content when it's shared in a tweet. Learn about Facebook Open Graph tags in the Facebook Developers site (`https://developers.facebook.com/docs/sharing/best-practices#tags`) and Twitter Cards from Twitter's Developers documentation (`https://dev.twitter.com/cards/overview`).

Social Signals as Search-Ranking Factors

Social media optimization aims to improve how a piece of content performs on a social media network. For content posted to YouTube, taking care in crafting the video, the description, and your user profile are all things you might do to optimize a piece of media for discoverability and engagement on YouTube. Another way social media contributes to online marketing is through its influence on search engine results. When search engines use social media activity as part of their SERP ranking, those algorithm factors are called *social signals.*

Because search engines tend not to publish or confirm any individual ranking signals in their algorithms as a protection against spam, we don't have a definitive list of social signals that affect search engine rankings. But we *can* draw some conclusions from tests and observations that point to a correlation effect of social activity on search rankings.

It's generally believed that a page will tend to rank better over time if it goes *viral* — which means that a page suddenly gets a lot of mentions and links. The majority of links to viral content will come from social media networks, and the search engines may use *buzz* as a social signal, the sudden but temporary effect caused by a velocity of social media links. Buzz as a social signal likely has a temporary effect on search engine rankings. Viral content will also generate links from static pages, like news websites and blogs sharing that story with readers, and these are the links that have a more lasting benefit on a page's search engine rankings.

One of the viral campaigns of 2014 was the Ice Bucket Challenge benefitting research to cure ALS, also known as Lou Gehrig's disease. Celebrities and normal folks alike posted videos of themselves pouring buckets of ice water over their head and pledging donations in the name of ALS awareness. Along with the plentiful links from social media, major news organizations and other authoritative websites linked to the ALS Association website while reporting on the phenomenon that had swept the country. The links generated on social media caused a buzz effect, making the Ice Bucket Challenge a hot topic of discussion at the time it was happening and increasing Google searches for ALS-related terms by 90 percent, as shown in Figure 5-4. The links from static pages on authoritative websites brought the ALS Association website lasting SEO benefit.

Figure 5-4:
Viral
content
can cause
a spike
in search
volume, as
shown in
this Google
Trends
graph of
search
volume
during the
ALS Ice
Bucket
Challenge.

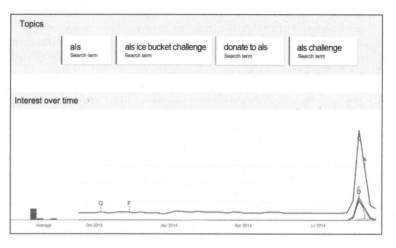

Building Community

Community building involves managing how you build your reputation and brand via the social networks. Social networks are not traditional networks, and traditional advertising (such as "Our product is great, please buy it!") generally doesn't fly with the Internet audience. Companies that try to use the same types of traditional marketing messages that work in print and TV advertising do not do very well with Internet marketing. On the whole, Internet users are turned off by traditional marketing methods.

So what do you do in this situation? The solution is to give away control. That's right: There is only so much you can do for your brand, and, at a certain point, you must allow it to work for itself. When you're engaging others in a conversation on the Internet about your brand, you cannot control the conversation. You can only be a *participant* in it.

A website for a large car manufacturing company was able to find out about problems with its vehicles through its Internet *forums* (a message board where users can log on and post about topics on a related subject). If you are willing to use social networks and actually listen to what your users say, you can get some great feedback on your products and services, and on your competition as well. People are honest in their online comments (often, brutally so). Don't disregard the positive or negative feedback. This is good, usable information. You can see what you are doing right and what your competition is doing right. On the flip side, you can also pinpoint your weaker areas, as well as where your competition is messing up.

Twitter is also a great resource for this. You can pay attention to what people are saying about you, and you have the ability to search and listen in. With Twitter, you can *follow* people (that is, read all their posts) and, in return, people follow you and read your posts. Figure 5-5 shows an example of a customized Twitter home page. Being a microblogging site, Twitter consists of nothing but short posts (the maximum you can type in one post is 140 characters, including spaces).

Figure 5-5: When you're logged in, your Twitter home page has a profile box, a list of trending topics, and a timeline of updates from people you're following.

Companies can search for their names in public posts. A colleague *tweeted* (that's what Twitter calls "posting") about Southwest Airlines when his flight was late, and six minutes later, a Southwest Airlines representative was following him on Twitter.

Another example is a cable TV company that has used Twitter to help improve its reputation. The company does not have a great reputation when it comes to customer service. However, the organization assigned an employee to do nothing but manage a Twitter account for the company. His job is to sit on Twitter and catch tweets about problems with the company, respond, and then fix the problems. And he does. He offers technical solutions through Twitter, and then he calls and arranges for a service technician to come out to fix problems he cannot fix himself. This is an example of a company using social networks to the fullest. The company is using

Twitter to fix problems and expand its reputation as a company that cares about its customers.

Another example is Zappos (www.zappos.com), an online shoe retailer. Every employee is on Twitter, and they are encouraged to talk. This is community building for the company. Even the CEO has his own Twitter account. For Zappos, it's not just a product that the company is selling: It's selling customer satisfaction. It's selling its employees. With its products, the company provides free overnight shipping. It doesn't advertise this, but when a user makes a purchase, Zappos emails the customer and informs him that it has free overnight shipping. Plus, it has a very easy return policy. Simply call it, and you are sent a box with a label, for no charge, and you are given a refund. The point of Zappos is not how much money a customer spends, but whether its customer is satisfied. This is a grassroots marketing campaign that works not only because the company's satisfied customers want to do business with it again, but also because those customers tell others about their experiences and bring in new customers to Zappos.

On the Internet, people are going to care more about a company that seems to be listening to them and engaging them. That is why it is important to always be genuine with your customers and with people on the social media sites. You have to be out there, talking to your customers. But be honest. People — on the Internet, and everywhere else — hate being lied to. If they find out you are not being genuine about yourself or your intentions, woe to you. As Shakespeare once (sort of) said, "Hell hath no fury like an Internet scorned."

Astro-turfing is a term used for a fake grassroots market campaign (a term based on AstroTurf, which is artificial grass). For example, it was discovered that several blogs praising Walmart were fake. Supposedly these blogs were written by "real" customers, but they were actually written by Walmart's public relations firm. This was uncovered because the bloggers sloppily provided links to their PR firm. Needless to say, that did not go over well with the Internet audience. Be warned: As soon as people find out they're being deceived, they turn on you.

Lonelygirl15 was a popular video blog series on YouTube, until it was discovered that the girl was an actress, and the blogs were scripted. Lonelygirl15's popularity dropped off sharply after that, and the video blog series is now defunct. If you are going to create something along these lines, be up front right away that it is not real. Don't hide the fact that something is a marketing campaign. Users do not like feeling tricked.

You also have to be concerned about the problem of people taking your brand and then using it to harm you. In one case on Twitter, a company supposedly had two IT guys, both with account names that included the brand name, giving out advice on how to fix problems. The trouble was that one of these IT guys was a fake; he did not work for the company and was giving out particularly bad advice. Unfortunately, the company couldn't do much beyond letting people know that the person was not employed by that company. (This is also why it is important to keep track of your employees and what they're supposed to be doing.)

If someone illegitimate does get hold of your brand name, you can't do a whole lot other than distance yourself from him and make sure that your customers know that the guy who stole your name or who is pretending to be you is not affiliated with you in any way.

The Internet is still like the Wild West. No law exists to deter someone who registers your brand name, and there are no punishments for people who pretend to be you. To protect your brand, the most you can do is proactively register your brand name and variations across social networks, like the service KnowEm helps with, and register your website under a federal copyright and hope that gives you enough teeth to take out someone who steals your name. (See Book V, Chapter 5 for more on copyright infringement.)

Incorporating Interactivity

One of the hallmarks of the Internet in its modern form is its interactivity. Society uses technology today to bring people together, enhance creativity, and stimulate conversation. The early Internet was made up of static pages without any means of interaction, but now users expect living sites that react to them and give visitors a way to affect the status of the page. Social networking sites, where you can upload your profile, talk to friends, and make new connections, are the most well-known aspect of the interactive web. There are also tools that can be incorporated onto all kinds of websites that let visitors interact with pages. A *widget* is a piece of HTML code that you can embed in a page and that a user can interact with. One social media professional likes to say that a widget is what's left of a page if you get rid of all the junk like the navigation, the template, and the footer, leaving only the content. That's pretty accurate.

Toward the goal of community building, the major social media networks have created widgets that can be embedded on a web page to encourage visitors to like or join the business's social media community. If you decide that your customers use Twitter and you'd like to build your community on that social network, you can add the HTML code for the Twitter Follow button into your website design. Facebook has a similar widget that lets your website visitors follow your business's Facebook page right from your website, as shown in Figure 5-6.

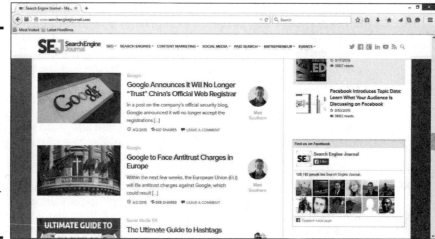

Figure 5-6:
The Search Engine Journal home page has a widget that allows visitors to follow and like the publication on Facebook.

But you can use other kinds of custom widgets, as well. Many personal blogs include links to online quizzes. These quizzes can be about anything — personality, astrology, which TV show character you most resemble, or how long you can survive chained to a bunk bed with a velociraptor. For the most part, these quizzes are for entertainment purposes only. But all these widgets feature a link for other users who see these quizzes and want to take them themselves, bringing other users into that website. The results of the quiz come with a line of HTML code that you can use to post your results on your personal blog or on a social networking page such as Facebook. The HTML coding presents an image that shows your results and a link back to the site that features the quiz.

A clever and entertaining widget can generate lots of traffic for your site and bring you plenty of links because all the widgets feature a link back to your site. These can be both fun and functional. For your classic car site, you could create a quiz that tells a person which classic car matches his or her personality most, along with an image and link back to your site.

It's very important to prominently display your link and not try to hide it. If you are hiding something, the search engines might think you are doing something wrong. The link must also be relevant to the widget and to your website. Don't hide links to other sites in the widget; otherwise, the links from the widget are discounted. Also, beware of using widgets for spam. Don't use the widget for any sneaky, devious, or underhanded techniques. You will be caught and punished.

You can use other types of widgets for your site. Again, just make sure they're relevant. You might have a widget on your site that can tell your

users what time it is in Tokyo, but if it's for your American classic car customization site, it wouldn't be relevant. What might be better is a quiz that
determines whether your driving skills enable you to outrun a herd of ram-
paging wildebeests (because people respond to cleverness and creativity,
and, when all else fails, wildebeests are always entertaining).

Another type of widget that might be worthwhile is a poll. Polls ask questions and publish counts of people's answers, like in Figure 5-7.

Figure 5-7:
Even a very
simple poll
invites user
engage-
ment.

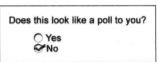

A poll is a way of engaging your audience and finding out what it is that
they're actually thinking. Your audience also checks back to see how the
poll is doing, and, if you leave a comments section with the poll, your audience can interact with one another and discuss the poll. Even if the poll
doesn't actually mean anything, if you make it fun, it can help build community and bring you traffic. Another example of widgets includes a sports
statistics ticker that constantly gives updates. It could include scores, who's
won, who's on first, and so on. These are useful for sites that are related to
sports in some way.

Stock market tickers are another excellent example of a widget. They give
constant updates on how the stock market is doing that day — although
these days, you might prefer to remain in the dark. These are useful for
sites having to do with finances or brokerage firms. Pretty much anything
you think of can be a widget. In most cases, if you have an idea for a widget,
you need to build it yourself or hire a clever programmer to build it for you.
Some companies do have widgets of their own that you can customize (like
for a poll), but that's not always the case.

The primary results of widgets are traffic and engagement, and the secondary results are branding and linking. An effective and clever widget can be
associated with your website and ultimately boost your brand.

Book VII

Optimizing the Foundations

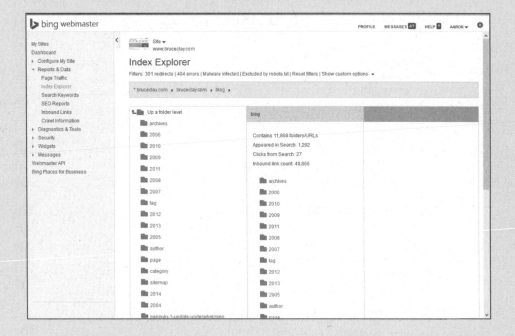

You have other options for domains than just .com and .net! Find out more at www.dummies.com/extras/searchengineoptimizationaio.

Contents at a Glance

Chapter 1: Server Issues: Why Your Server Matters

In This Chapter

✔ Getting to know the servers

✔ Making sure your server is healthy and fast

✔ Excluding pages or sites from the search engines

✔ Passing instructions to search engines with a robots text file

✔ Using `Meta` robots tags

✔ Building a customized 404 Error page

✔ Avoiding dirty IPs and bad neighborhoods

✔ Serving your site to different devices

Your *web server* is the software application or service that runs your website. (The term *web server* can be used to refer to both the hardware and the software that runs a website, but in this chapter, we talk about the software.) Anytime a user does something on your site, such as loads a page or views an image, your web server receives the request and serves up what the user wants. Like a good waiter in a restaurant, you want your site's server to be as fast and efficient as possible so that your site visitors feel happy and well satisfied. This is especially important when it comes to Google as page speed is a factor in its algorithm.

Server issues impact search engine ranking, from the type of server you use to how well it performs. Search engines don't want to present sites that frustrate users by being slow or unavailable in their results. A slow server, or a server that fails often, can cause a site to drop out of the search engine's *index* (the databases of website content that Google, Yahoo, or Bing pull from when delivering search results) or prevent a site from ever being indexed in the first place. A key and yet often overlooked point of failure for a website is the server environment where it resides.

If your site is up and running, you're either operating your own server equipment or using a hosting facility. Either way, you need to know what type of server you use. You also need to know something about the IP address that your site occupies. An *IP (Internet Protocol) address* is the numeric code that identifies the logical address where your site resides on the web — as well as other server-level factors that can have a big impact on your success with your search engine optimization (SEO) efforts.

In this chapter, we discuss the importance of choosing the right server and keeping your server in optimal health. You also discover ways to identify server problems that can have a negative impact upon your search engine ranking so that you can address them.

Meeting the Servers

In the world of web servers, two competitors hold more than 65 percent of the market share: Apache and Microsoft IIS. In this section, we give you some basic information on each server to introduce you to these two reigning heavyweights.

Using the Apache server

The most popular web server on the market, the Apache HTTP Server is an *open-source software application* (a computer program whose source code is available for free to the public) maintained by the Apache Software Foundation. Currently in version 2.4.12, the Apache web server supports approximately 40 percent of all sites on the World Wide Web. The fact that it's free may contribute to its popularity, but the Foundation people in charge say it also contributes to its strength because the entire Internet community can participate in identifying and fixing bugs, and in improving the software.

For search engine optimization purposes, Apache is the best server available. Its configuration options make it the most flexible server, which is important because SEO requires constant monitoring and tweaking. Apache also gives you direct access to the server even if a third-party hosting provider runs your site. This access offers a crucial advantage over the Microsoft IIS server environment.

Using the Microsoft IIS server

The main competitor to the Apache server is Microsoft Internet Information Services (IIS). This *proprietary software* (meaning that you must purchase it from Microsoft) provides a platform for running a website. IIS is currently in version 8.5 and comes included with the Windows Server 2012 R2 operating system for data centers. IIS is primarily used for sites that are written on a Microsoft stack (.NET, ASP, and others — technical stuff that you don't really need to know other than whether your site is set up on IIS). If your website is programmed in .NET, your only option is to use an IIS server.

Microsoft IIS has the second-most market share after Apache. The main disadvantage with IIS occurs if your site resides on a shared server operated by a third-party hosting provider. With an IIS server, only the administrator can access the server directly — so anytime you need to look at or make changes to your server files, you have to go through the hosting provider, which can cause delays and end up being a little frustrating. However, if you have a *dedicated server* (a server not shared with any other sites) that you can access directly, the IIS server can accommodate your SEO needs if you have administrator-level access rights.

You can overcome some of the administrator-rights requirements and get Apache-like, flexible functionality out of your IIS web server. To do this, you need to install an ISAPI_Rewrite plug-in into IIS. *ISAPI* stands for Internet Server Application Program Interface; you can get ISAPI_Rewrite software from several vendors. If you're using IIS 7.0 or higher, we suggest that you download the software directly from Microsoft. Another version that's excellent and that works well on IIS 5.0, 6.0, or 7.0 comes from Helicon Tech (www.isapirewrite.com). (For more information on ISAPI_Rewrite, see Chapter 4 of this minibook.)

Using other server options

NGINX is currently the third most popular web server, with just over 14 percent of the market, and developers call it a strong choice because it's speedy and secure. As with Microsoft IIS, you need administrative access to the server, or at least to the place where NGINX configuration files are allowed, to make changes. A bunch of other little guys out there also offer web servers with intriguing names like Appweb, Barracuda, Cherokee, Yaws, and IceWarp. Red Hat makes an *enterprise* (large-scale) edition of the Apache server that targets large clients with high-traffic demands. All of these have different limitations that you won't find with the Big Two (Apache and Microsoft IIS).

For your SEO efforts, we generally recommend using an Apache, NGINX, or Microsoft IIS server to ensure you have the flexibility and performance you need.

Making Sure That Your Server Is Healthy, Happy, and Fast

A slow server can spell disaster for your site. If the search engines keep trying to visit your site to no avail, eventually they may stop trying. They don't want to index a site that isn't going to load when users try to access it — search engines don't want to give their users unreliable, slow information. That kind of thing makes the search engine look bad.

If your website takes forever to load a new page, or links end in error messages, you also won't have happy site visitors. And you may lose their business for good.

To succeed with search engines and users, you need a fast, clean server. You should check your server's health regularly to ensure it's performing well. Here are three things you should look for:

✦ **Malfunctions:** You need to make sure that your site remains free of server problems such as improper *redirects* (server directives that detour a request to a different page), script errors, or malfunctions that could cause a page not to display.

✦ **Fast processing speed:** Speed counts a lot with the search engines. Kind of like the postal service through rain, sleet, or snow, the search engine spiders have a lot of ground to cover as they roam the Internet. If your site bogs down their progress due to a slow server, they're less likely to crawl it completely and won't re-index it as often.

Servers, in the overall scheme of things, are pretty cheap. If you take the cost divided by the number of visitors per year, you are talking about pennies. You should therefore address speed issues head-on, buying servers any time performance is slow.

✦ **Clean and uncrowded IP:** Your IP address also matters and should be monitored because your site can be adversely affected if another site on your IP is caught *spamming* (intentionally trying to deceive or manipulate the search engines) or doing other dirty deeds.

Running a Check Server tool

One way to check the status of your server is to run a quick diagnostic utility called a *Check Server tool.* This utility attempts to crawl your site the same way that a search engine spider does. If the Check Server tool runs into any obstacles that could prevent the spider from indexing your site, it tells you about them on a report that the utility creates. Even if your content is perfect, a poorly functioning server can keep your site from reaching its full potential in the search engine rankings. It's a good idea to run this diagnostic tool on a regular basis.

You can use any Check Server tool you have access to. We offer a free Check Server tool located on our website. To run our Check Server, follow these steps:

1. **Go to** www.seotoolset.com/tools/free-tools/.

2. **Go to the Check Server Page tool and enter your website's domain (such as** www.yourdomain.com**) in the Your URL text box.**

3. **Click the Check Response Headers button and wait until the report appears.**

A Check Server tool performs several different page requests and checks the returned status codes and the content. If they don't match up, by showing error codes or inconsistent page content, it may be that your server is showing the search engines an error, even though there's no real problem. Having this information lets you fix issues quickly, which is important because search engines often reduce website rankings because of web server errors that they encounter. At the very least, even if you encounter a common error that would not cause a search engine to drop you from its index, a cleaner site likely ranks higher in the search engine results.

In the first row of the table on the report, you'll notice a number — in Figure 1-1, it's *200*. This represents the web page's status as a search engine would see it. The server code that you see in the figure, *200,* means the page is normal.

Your URL:

http://www.nytimes.com|

Check Response Headers

SEOToolSet® Server Header Check Report

Header	Value
Status	200 - OK (http://www.nytimes.com/)
x-api-version	5-5
x-varnish	827204781 827172217
x-cache	HIT
x-app-name	homepage
set-cookie	RMID=007f010119af5526c03b0000;Path=/; Domain=.nytimes.com;Expires=Fri, 08 Apr 2016 18
age	323
vary	Host
server	Apache
transfer-encoding	chunked
connection	close
via	1.1 varnish
cache-control	no-cache
date	Thu, 09 Apr 2015 18
content-type	text/html; charset=utf-8
x-pagetype	homepage

Other Info

Original URL	http://www.nytimes.com/
DNS IP	**Address:** 170.149.168.130
Ping	Successful (Average Ping Time: **7ms**)

Figure 1-1:
Our Check Server report identifies the server status code for a web page.

Table 1-1 explains the most common server status codes. These server statuses are standardized by the *World Wide Web Consortium* (W3C), an independent governance organization that oversees Internet standards, so they mean the same thing to everyone. We've boiled down the technical language into understandable English to show you what each server status code means about your web page. You can find the official definitions on the W3C site at `www.w3.org/protocols/rfc2616/rfc2616-sec10.html`, in case you want to research further.

Table 1-1   Server Status Codes and What They Indicate

Code	Description	Definition	What it Means
200	OK	The web page appears as expected.	This is what you want to see. Your server and web page have the welcome mat out for the search engine spiders (and users, too).
301	Moved Permanently	The web page has been redirected permanently to another web page URL.	When a search engine spider sees this status code, it moves easily to the appropriate new page. A 301 Redirect status *isn't* a problem for your search engine optimization.
302	Found (Moved Temporarily)	The web page has been moved temporarily to a different URL.	This status should raise a red flag if you find it on your web server. Even though there are supposed to be legitimate uses for a 302 Redirect code, they can cause serious problems for your optimization efforts. Spammers frequently use 302 Redirects maliciously, so if you don't want a search engine mistaking your site for a spam site, avoid these redirects.
400	Bad Request	The server couldn't understand the request because of bad syntax.	This code could appear because of a typo in the URL. Whatever the cause, you don't want a search engine spider blocked from reaching your content pages, so investigate this if you see this status code on your site.
401	Unauthorized	The request requires user authentication.	Usually, this code means that you need to log in before you can view the page content. Not a good error for spiders to hit.

Code	Description	Definition	What it Means
403	Forbidden	The server understands the request but refuses to fulfill it.	If you find this status code on your website, find out why. If you want to block the spiders from entering, there ought to be a good reason.
404	Not Found	The web page isn't available.	You've seen this error code; it's the Page Can Not Be Displayed page that appears when a website is down or nonexistent. You definitely don't want a spider following a link to your website only to be greeted by a 404 Error! That's like visiting a house and finding the lights off and the doors locked. If your server check shows you have a 404 Error for one of your landing pages, you definitely want to fix it ASAP.
500 and up	Miscellaneous Server Errors	The 500–505 status codes indicate that something's wrong with your server.	Check out what's causing the problem.

From the Check Server report, you can also glean whether the page is cloaked. *Cloaking* (showing one version of a page's content to users but a different version to the spiders) is a big no-no with the search engines, so if your page appears to be cloaked, you need to know about it. If the page uses cloaking, the Check Server report says so.

Indulging the need for speed

You also want to monitor your site's *performance,* which is computer-speak for speed. The faster your server can deliver a page after it has been requested, the better. You want your human visitors to have a smooth, pleasant experience using your site because that leads to more *conversions* for you (which could be sales, sign-ups, subscriptions, votes, or whatever action that you want people to take on your site). More importantly for your search engine rankings, you want the search engine spiders to be able to move fast and freely through your site. The quicker they can get to your pages, the more pages they'll index and the more often they'll come back.

You can tell how long it takes a search engine spider to retrieve your web pages. This information shows up as a call in your server log (a *server log* is a complete record of requests sent to the web server and the server's actions in response). You should be able to check your server logs and establish a benchmark, and then regularly check it again for comparison. If checking your server logs sounds too complicated, try this easier way: Use the Web Page Analyzer free tool offered at www.websiteoptimization.com/services/analyze, instead. Either way, one factor that influences your search results ranking is your page response time, so this is a good thing to keep tabs on.

Many factors influence your website's performance. The user's Internet connection speed, location, and computer have a big impact on how fast your site is, and these factors are frustratingly out of your control. When a search engine spider comes to crawl your site, you can rest assured that on *its* end, things are humming. On *your* end, though, many things can affect site speed. These include server computing power (also known as *chip speed*) and setup, the amount of Internet bandwidth available compared to the amount of traffic, the efficiency of your HTML code and programming, contention with other sites sharing your IP, and whether you're the only site on your IP address, to name a few.

Testing your page speed with Google

As mentioned earlier in this chapter, Google considers page speed in its algorithm. Google representatives have said that Google's search engine has more than 200 variables in its algorithm. Remember, an *algorithm* is the search engine's formula for calculating what sites it presents to a user for any given *query* (a word or phrase searched for). Google isn't always forthcoming about what those variables are because if everyone knew, some people might use that information to try to cheat the system.

But every now and again, we are given clues and verification about what those variables are, such as when Google announced in spring 2010 that site speed is a factor in its algorithm for ranking sites.

Site speed is so important to Google because Google wants everyone to help make its search engine and the web faster for its users. So, how do you improve your site speed? Let's look at some of the ways.

Many factors impact the speed of your site, including anything on the user's end such as connection speeds and location. What are some of the things that can improve the speed of your site? One way is to compress the information between your web server and the search engine browser. This can be done using what's called gzip compression. Gzip compression can be enabled through the server configuration. The Google Developers site has more tips on how to start using gzip on your site (https://developers.google.com/speed/docs/insights/EnableCompression).

Other ways to improve your site speed include things like minifying JavaScript, cleaning up your Cascading Style Sheets (CSS) code, and compressing and choosing the best file extension for your images (for example, GIF) throughout the page, just to name a few.

As we said before, many factors impact the speed of your site. This includes anything on the user's end, such as connection speeds and location, and on your end, including server computing power, sharing IP addresses with other sites, and much more.

Google offers a variety of tools to test and improve site speed in its official resource site for developers, aptly named Google Developers and found at `https://developers.google.com`. To get a good idea of how fast your page is, you can check out Google's PageSpeed Insights tools at `https://developers.google.com/speed/pagespeed/`.

PageSpeed Insights is actually a collection of tools aimed at speeding up your site. You can simply enter a page URL into the online version of the tool, or install an extension to the Chrome browser to get suggestions for making components of a page load faster. Google has stated that it uses the PageSpeed extension to introduce new performance best practices. This helps keep you updated about what Google deems important. Google also offers add-ons for Apache and NGINX web servers that automatically optimize web pages at serving time. You can also get to PageSpeed Insights while signed in to Google Search Console (it's under Other Resources), and here you'll see your site as it's experienced by users on both desktop and mobile devices. Google designed this tool to emulate how a browser displays your page to visitors using a desktop or a mobile device, and as it loads, it takes note of the resources that are slowing down load time and offers suggestions for speeding it up.

Excluding Pages and Sites from the Search Engines

Sometimes, you need to block a spider from crawling a web page or site. For instance, you may have a development version of your website where you work on changes and additions to test them before they become part of your live website. You don't want search engines to index this in-progress copy of your website because that would cause a duplicate-content conflict with your actual website. You also don't want users to find your in-progress pages. So, you need to block the search engines from seeing those pages.

Using a robots text file

The best way to exclude pages from the search engines' view is with a robots text (.txt) file. The *robots text* file's job is to give the search engines instructions on what *not* to spider within your website. This is a simple text file that you can create using a program like Notepad, and then save with the filename `robots.txt`. Place the file at the root of your website (`www.yourdomain.com/robots.txt`), which is where the spiders expect to find it. In fact, whenever the search engine spiders come to your site, the first thing they look for is your robots text file. This is why you should *always* have a robots text file on your site, even if it's blank. You don't want the spiders' first impression of your site to be a *404 Error* (the error that comes up when a file cannot be located).

With a robots text file, you can selectively exclude particular pages, directories, or the entire site. You have to write the HTML code just so, or the spiders ignore it. The command syntax you need to use comes from the Robots Exclusion Protocol (REP), which is a standard protocol for all websites. And it's very exact; only specific commands are allowed, and they must be written correctly with specific placement, uppercase/lowercase letters, punctuation, and spacing. This file is one place where you don't want your webmaster getting creative.

A very simple robots text file could look like this:

```
User-agent: *
Disallow: /personal/
```

This robots text file tells all search engine robots that they're welcome to crawl anywhere on your website *except* for the directory named `/personal/`.

Before writing a command line (such as `Disallow: /personal/`), you first have to identify which robot(s) you're addressing. In this case, the line `User-agent: *` addresses all robots because it uses an asterisk, which is known as the *wild card* character because it represents any character. If you want to give different instructions to different search engines, as many sites do, write separate `User-agent` lines followed by their specific command lines. In each `User-agent:` line, you replace the asterisk (*) character with the name of a specific robot:

✦ `User-agent: Googlebot` gets Google's attention.

✦ `User-agent: Bingbot` targets Bing.

The search engines have a number of crawlers tasked with specific jobs, including bots that look for news, video, images, and mobile content. You can further control how the search engines crawl your site by blocking any of many specific user agents. Google's common user agents are listed at `https://developers.google.com/webmasters/control-crawl-index/docs/crawlers`. Meet the Bing crawlers here: `http://www.bing.com/webmaster/help/which-crawlers-does-bing-use-8c184ec0`. Remember that at this time, Yahoo contracts to use Bing's crawlers and index for its search results, so anything you block from Bing, you also block from Yahoo.

Note that if your robots text file has `User-agent:  *` instructions, as well as another `User-agent:` line specifying a specific robot, the specific robot follows the commands you gave it individually, rather than the more general instructions.

You can type just a few different commands into a `robots.txt` file:

✦ **Excluding the whole site:** To exclude the robot from the entire server, you use the command:

```
Disallow: /
```

This command actually removes all your site's web pages from the search index, so be careful *not* to do this unless that is what you really want.

✦ **Excluding a directory:** A word of caution — usually, you want to be much more selective than excluding a whole directory. But if you really want to, you can exclude a directory (including all its contents and subdirectories), by putting it inside slashes:

```
Disallow: /personal/
```

✦ **Excluding a page:** You can write a command to exclude just a particular page. You use only a slash at the beginning and must include the file extension at the end. Here's an example:

```
Disallow: /private-file.htm
```

✦ **Directing the spiders to your sitemap:** In addition to `Disallow:`, another useful command for your SEO efforts specifies where the robot can find your *sitemap* — the page that contains links throughout your site organization, like a table of contents:

```
Sitemap: http://www.yourdomain.com/sitemap.xml
```

We should point out that in addition to the commands discussed in the preceding list, Google recognizes `Allow`, as well. Only Google uses this command, and it may confuse other engines, so we don't recommend using it.

We recommend that you always include at the end of your robots text file a `Sitemap:` command line. This line ensures that the robots find your sitemap, which helps them navigate more fully through your site so that more of your site gets indexed.

Here are a few notes about the robots text file syntax:

✦ The commands are case sensitive, so you need a capital D in `Disallow`.

✦ Always include a space following the colon after the command.

✦ To exclude an entire directory, put a forward slash after, as well as before, the directory name.

✦ If you're running your website on a UNIX machine, *everything* is case sensitive.

✦ All files not specifically excluded are available for spidering and indexing.

To see a complete list of the commands, robot names, and instructions about writing robots text files, go to www.robotstxt.org.

Always be aware of your robots text tag. Mistakes here can absolutely destroy your site's rankings in the search engine. Here's a story that's unfortunately all too common about a business that learned about this the hard way. The company had a huge website and multiple development environments in which staff made changes and tested new pages before those pages went live. Of course, they set up a robots text file set to Disallow: / all pages on the test site because they didn't want the search engines to index an in-progress copy of their website.

After a major revision, the company moved the finished test site into place, replacing the old site files entirely — including the robots text file. Unfortunately, the company neglected to take out the Disallow: / command. Soon, the search engines stopped crawling its pages. The site started to drop like a boulder in the rankings, and no one knew why. It took the company three days to figure out that the cause was its robots text file! By simply changing one line of code in that file, the company fixed the problem, but it was a costly lesson. Its estimated revenue loss topped $150,000 per day. The moral of the story: *Don't forget to update your robots.txt when you upload a new site!*

As a further safeguard, make it part of your regular site maintenance to check your robots text file. It's such a powerful on/off switch for your site's SEO efforts that it merits a regular peek to make sure it's still functioning properly.

Using Meta robots tags

Besides the robots text file, there is also another way you can prevent search engines from seeing something on your site. On an individual web page, you can include a special tag in the HTML code to tell robots not to index that page or not to follow the links on that page. You would place this tag after the other Meta *tags,* which are part of the HTML code located in the Head section of a web page.

Using Meta robots tags is less efficient than using a site-wide robots text file for two reasons. First, robots sometimes ignore Meta robots tags, and second, these tags slow down the robots reading your pages, which may decrease the number of pages they're willing to crawl. Also, this method can give your webmaster headaches because the tags have to be maintained on the individual pages, rather than in a central file.

Removing content from an index

If you discover that a search engine has indexed content from your website that you wanted to exclude, there is something you can do about it. The search engines offer ways to request that a particular URL be removed from their index. Here are links to get the instructions (or you can search for current info):

✔ **Google:** `https://www.google.com/webmasters/tools/removals`

✔ **Bing and Yahoo:** `http://www.bing.com/webmaster/help/block-urls-from-bing-264e560a`

This `Meta` robots tag tells the search engine robot not to index the page and not to follow any of the links on the page:

```
<meta name="robots" content="noindex, nofollow">
```

You can use this tag to tell the robot to read and index the page's content, but not to follow any of the links:

```
<meta name="robots" content="index, nofollow">
```

This tag instructs the robot to ignore the page's content, but follow the links:

```
<meta name="robots" content="noindex, follow">
```

Being wise to different search engine robots

Not all search engines are created equal. We focus on the crawlers for Google and Bing because they account for nearly all search-generated traffic on the web. Note that Yahoo has contracted with Bing to use its crawler. Even among these, however, you find a few slightly different options for your `robots.txt` file and `Meta` robots tags.

For example, you can use a different `Meta` robots tag per search engine to partially control where the two-line description appears that accompanies your page's link on a search engine results page (SERP). To see what we're talking about, look at Figure 1-2, which shows a typical SERP result with its two-line description.

The search engines pull SERP descriptions from varying places, depending on which seems most relevant to the user's search query. They sometimes pull information from a *directory* that they either manage or contract with,

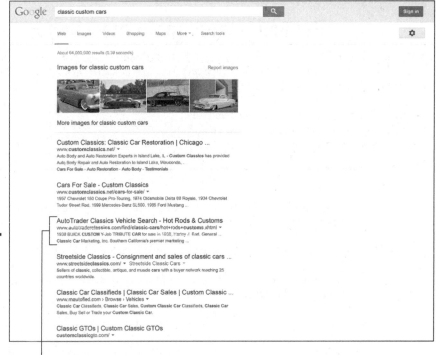

Figure 1-2:
Search engines display a brief description with each link.

Each link gets a description

which is a hand-assembled set of website data arranged like a list. Different search engines work with different directories:

✦ **Google:** Uses one of three sources for its search engine results descriptions: the *Open Directory Project* (historically known as ODP and today known as DMOZ), which is a hand-assembled, human-edited directory of website data (go to `www.dmoz.org` if you want more information about this ambitious project); the `Meta` description tag on the web page itself; or a snippet Google chooses from the on-page content that contains the searched-for keywords and some surrounding text (also referred to as an *auto-snippet*).

✦ **Yahoo:** Displays a description pulled from the `Meta` description tag, or the on-page content.

✦ **Bing:** Pulls descriptions from either the `Meta` description tag or the on-page content.

You can prevent the search engines from using the directories, if you feel the manually edited description there is either out of date or inaccurate for some reason. For SEO purposes, you're always better off to avoid showing someone else's description for your pages. If you like that description's wording, use it on your web page, but we recommend that you exclude the directories. By using the proper `Meta` robots tag, you can force search engines to pull descriptions from your `Meta` description tag or your web page.

This tag instructs Google not to pull the description from the Open Directory Project:

```
<meta name="robots" content="noodp">
```

Within a `Meta` robots tag, you can include multiple commands by separating them with a comma. To tell all robots not to pull descriptions from the DMOZ directory and not to follow the links on the page, you write the tag like this:

```
<meta name="robots" content="noodp, nofollow">
```

Creating Custom 404 Error Pages

You've seen it probably a hundred times — File 404: Page Can Not Be Displayed. It's the error page that means, "Sorry, you're out of luck. The web page you wanted is broken or missing, and you can't see it right now. So go away!" A user will probably do only one thing when presented with this 404 Error page, and that's hit the Back button.

You can give your website visitors and search engines a much better experience than getting the generic 404 Error page if your website has a problem displaying a page. You can present them with a customized 404 Error page that's actually helpful and friendly, rather than the standard browser-issued version.

This issue matters to your SEO efforts, too. If the spiders find a default 404 Error page on your site, you've thrown a roadblock in front of them that they have no way to get over. Search engines can't hit the Back button or use the other advanced features of your website. All they can do is follow links. If they come across a bad link and you don't give them anywhere else to go, they leave your site. This may result in entire sections of your site not being indexed. Creating a custom 404 Error page that includes links to other pages on your site helps prevent this from happening. You have to give the engines something to follow.

Designing a 404 Error page

Here are tips for creating a user- and SEO-friendly 404 Error page for your website:

✦ **Design the page to look like your website.** Let your users know that they're still on your site and everything's under control.

✦ **Apologize and tell them what happened (include a message such as "Sorry, the page you requested is unavailable").** Your message should match the tone of your site, but consider making it humorous to keep your readers engaged, such as, "The well-armed monkeys normally operating this web page are engaged in full-scale warfare at the moment. To avoid the flying fur, try one of the escape routes suggested below."

✦ **Offer suggestions that include links to other pages that the user might want to go to.** Include helpful descriptions in the links. ("Read about our <u>car customization services</u>." "See pictures of <u>'new' classic cars</u>." "Hear <u>what our customers say</u> about us.")

✦ **Include a link back to your home page, including meaningful keywords in the *anchor text* (the visible link text that a user can click).** Don't call this link just Home.

✦ **Include a link to your sitemap.** This is especially important for search engine robots because they can follow that map to get around your entire site. Providing access to your sitemap becomes even more beneficial because the engines continually return to your site to see if those non-existent pages have returned. If they have, the search engines re-index them. If they haven't, the robots still find your 404 Error page and all your relevant links.

✦ **If you have a good programmer, customize the page contents based on where the user had a problem.** For instance, if the page was supposed to show Ford Mustang steering wheel options, the message and links could dynamically change to offer the user a way to get to another Ford Mustang page in your site, instead of just showing him a generic error message.

✦ **If you're running a sale, put images linked to your current ads on the page.**

✦ **Put a search text box on your error page, front and center.** Let users type in what they're looking for and go to that exact page on your site.

✦ **Put a `Meta` robots tag on your custom 404 Error page.** Tell the search engines to follow the links on the page but not to index it:

```
<meta name="robots" content="noindex, follow">
```

✦ **Don't redirect your 404 Error page.** For more on handling redirects properly, see Chapters 3 and 4 of this minibook.

✦ **Be sure that your 404 Error page passes a 404 Error code, which prevents search engines from indexing it.** Many sites forget this step, and their error pages can show up in search results (see Figure 1-3).

Error pages can accidentally show up in search results

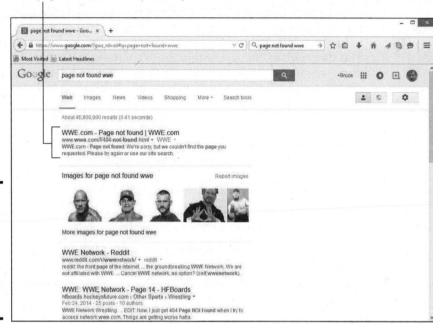

Customizing your 404 Error page for your server

After you've created your 404 Error page, you need to customize it for your server. The instructions vary depending on which server you use, so we provide a list of options in the next few sections.

Apache

For an Apache server, you need to add some code into your .htaccess file that instructs the server to present a custom page (in this case, 404.php), instead of the standard error, in the event of a particular error occurring (in this case, ErrorDocument 404):

```
ErrorDocument 404 /error-pages/404.php
```

If you like, you can enhance the user-friendliness of your site even more by creating custom pages for other types of errors, as well. In the following code snippet, the server is told to display five different custom pages that have been built for different kinds of errors that could occur on the site:

```
ErrorDocument 404 /error-pages/404.php
ErrorDocument 403 /error-pages/403.php
ErrorDocument 401 /error-pages/401.php
ErrorDocument 500 /error-pages/500.php
ErrorDocument 501 /error-pages/501.php
```

Microsoft IIS

Configuring a custom 404 Error page in the Microsoft IIS server environment is easy if you have the administrator rights to access the server. (If you have to beg your ISP staff to do it, the task may take longer but can still be done.) You simply make changes within the Properties dialog box to point the 404 error type to the customized error page you created. You can also assign custom pages to other error statuses (401, 500, and so forth, as shown in Table 1-1) if desired, but 404 is the most important one to set up for your site visitors. To get ready, you need to have your site up on your IIS server (at least one page, anyway) and have already created a custom 404 Error page. (We call the page `404error.aspx` in the following steps.) To create a 404 Error page in IIS, please follow these steps:

1. **Open the Internet Services Manager.**

   Typically, you can find the Internet Services Manager in your Programs list below Administrative Tools.

2. **Click the plus sign (+) next to your server name to expand the list.**

3. **Right-click the Default Web Server (or, if you've renamed it, whatever the new name is) and choose Properties from the pop-up menu that appears.**

4. **Click the Custom Errors tab.**

5. **Select the error 404 from the list, and then click the Edit button.**

6. **Browse and select your custom error page.**

   Figure 1-4 shows `400.htm`, but you should name yours `404error.aspx` or something similar.

7. **Click OK to exit the dialog box.**

NGINX

NGINX also provides an easy way to present a custom 404 Error page (in this case, `404.html`). Inside your NGINX configuration file and inside the settings for your site, simply put in the following lines:

```
error_page 404 = /404.html;
location /404.html {
    internal;
}
```

Monitoring your 404 Error logs to spot problems

You can find out a lot by monitoring your *404 Error logs* (the server record of every time a page could not be displayed on your site). The error log can alert you of problems with your web pages so that you can fix them.

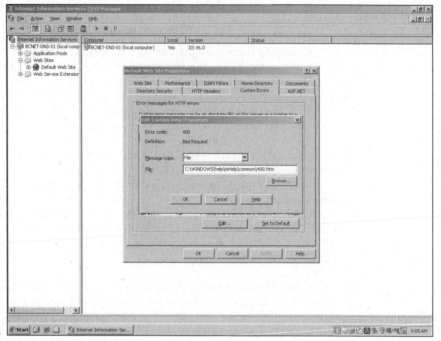

Figure 1-4:
You can
edit your IIS
server prop-
erties to set
up a custom
404 Error
page.

**Book VII
Chapter 1**

Server Issues: Why
Your Server Matters

You may also notice people linking to your site with an incorrect URL, in
which case you could redirect those bad links (by using a 301 Redirect) to
another page that's valid. Because 404 errors are a major reason why people
abandon a site, tracking where your site gets 404 Errors can help you capture and hold visitors, improving your traffic and your bottom line.

Fixing Dirty IPs and Other
"Bad Neighborhood" Issues

Knowing the IP address of your site and monitoring it to make sure that it
remains clean are good ideas. It's like renting an apartment: Just because the
neighborhood was quiet and peaceful when you first moved in doesn't mean
that it won't change over time and become an undesirable place to live.

IP addresses come in two flavors: virtual and dedicated. If you're using a
virtual IP address, it means that multiple websites (as many as your server
allows) use the same IP address as you. If you're using a *dedicated IP address,*
you're the only site on that IP.

We recommend that you use a dedicated IP for your site, if possible, to provide maximum site performance. Even so, you still need to monitor it to make sure it stays clean because you can also be affected by bad behavior of other IPs within the same *C block*. (The second-to-last set of digits in an IP address, such as the *179* in the IP address 208.215.179.146, identifies the C block, which is similar to an area code for a telephone number, except that unlike your area code, you can change C blocks. You can move your site to a new IP address and C block if you have trouble with the one you're in. Call your hosting company and tell it you want to be moved.)

If you do share a virtual IP with other sites, which is often the case with small or brand-new websites, it's like being in an apartment building. Similar to living in an apartment building, it's important that the IP isn't full of bad neighbors, even though that's pretty much out of your control. If the search engines find out you're next door to a spam site, for example, your site could be tainted by association. Google has indicated that it is difficult to be tainted by surrounding sites, but why take a chance? We recommend being in clean IP blocks whenever possible.

The other drawback of using a virtual IP is that, occasionally, a search engine or a user navigates to your website by your IP address, rather than your URL (usually, only if your server is configured incorrectly). If you're on a virtual IP, they may not be able to find your site. Any of the various sites located on that IP could come up; it'd be the luck of the draw. And do not forget that shared IPs may mean that your server performance will slow down based on the traffic load of your neighbors.

To find out your website's IP address, look no further than our free Check Server Page tool, which we cover in the section "Running a Check Server tool," earlier in this chapter. The report identifies your DNS IP address (refer to Figure 1-1).

After you have an IP address, you can find many tools on the web that can evaluate whether it's clean. By "clean," we mean that the IP is not on any *IP blacklists,* which are lists of sites suspected of illegal acts such as child pornography, *email spam* (sending unsolicited email indiscriminately to tons of people), or *hacking* (attempting to break into computer networks and bypass their security). You may have never done anything unethical on your website, but your IP's history with previous sites (or other current sites, if you're on a shared IP) could still haunt you.

Being blacklisted is bad news. Most major email services (Hotmail, Yahoo, AOL, Gmail, and so on) block any email coming from a blacklisted IP address, so being blacklisted seriously affects your ability to communicate with the outside world. For instance, it harms your ability to reply to sales inquiries and thus can cost you money.

Being blacklisted also puts you in hot water with the search engines. Search engines refer to these IP blacklists for purposes of website crawling, indexing, and ranking. We don't know how much the IP blacklists influence the individual search engines, and Google indicates that it should not, except in severe cases, impact your rankings. However, the search engines do flag your site and watch it closely because they assume that a site involved in email spam has a high likelihood of being involved in other types of spam. Simply put, you become guilty by association.

To find an IP checker tool, do a search on Google for ["ip blacklist" check]. We found several free options this way — one you might try is MX Lookup (www.mxtoolbox.com). Alternatively, we recommend the monitoring reports at DNSstuff (www.dnsstuff.com), which are available for a paid subscription only.

When you run an IP check, it shows you the status of your IP with many different blacklists. If you see any red flags, you need to take steps to get off of that blacklist ASAP by following these steps:

1. **Contact your ISP (Internet service provider) and request a change to a clean IP.**

   Better yet, try to move to an entirely new C block. You want to get as far away as possible.

   Alternatively, ask your hosting provider to clean up the neighborhood, and then to petition the search engines to have the IP marked as clean. They can do that.

2. **If your hosting provider won't cooperate, then cut your losses and change hosting providers.**

   However, this problem should never occur. There is no excuse for an ISP operating blacklisted IP ranges.

3. **Run an IP check on your new IP address when you get it.**

   Confirm for yourself that you're moving into a good neighborhood. If you can, try to check the target IP before you're moved to it.

The diagnostics available through Google Search Console (www.google.com/webmasters/tools/) are extremely helpful. After you sign up your website (which is free), Google verifies your site and then sends a spider to check it out. You receive a report that quickly tells you if it found anything wrong. Hearing in Google's own words that your site is A-OK is reason enough to celebrate, but you get the added bonus of lots of cool tools to try. (See Book VIII if you want more coverage of analytics and webmaster tools.)

Serving Your Site to Different Devices

In Book IV, Chapter 3, we outline your options for a website that satisfies your customers using mobile devices. You can create your mobile website to be one or a combination of the following types:

1. A *responsive website:* Your single website looks different depending on the visitor's device.

2. A *dynamic-serving site:* You can give a mobile visitor different content from what a desktop visitor sees.

3. A *separate mobile site:* This type of site is designed specifically for mobile users.

We list the preceding options for handling your mobile website in order of preference. The search engines prefer that webmasters use responsive design because of its advantages over the other options: You have to maintain and optimize only one code base and one server architecture to serve your site to any device and have it look and behave correctly. But different websites have different needs, and you can find in-depth coverage of when you use each mobile development technique, as well as how to decide the right one to use for your business, in Book IV, Chapter 3.

The following sections describe the basic server setup for each type of mobile website implementation, giving you background so that you know where to start when speaking with your developer.

Server setup for a responsive website

Actually, with the exception of how JavaScript is handled (you have some options here), no special server setup is required for a responsive website. Remember that a responsive site responds to a visitor's mobile or desktop device by adjusting appearance and function, and everything a browser and a search engine need to know about serving a page to a device, small or large, is contained on the page. There are, of course, technical elements that need to be in place on the page to signal to a browser and search engine that your website is responsive.

In its mobile guide for developers, Google explains that a search engine spider will automatically detect a responsive site if you do the following:

✦ Allow search engine user agents to crawl the page and its assets (CSS, JavaScript, and images)

✦ Use the viewport `Meta` tag in the Head section of the page, a signal to browsers that your page will adapt to all devices

In order to allow the search engine to crawl all the assets of the page, you need to make sure that those files are not blocked in your `robots.txt` directive, explained earlier in this chapter in "Using a robots text file."

The viewport `Meta` tag that you want to include on the page looks like this:

```
<meta name="viewport" content="width=device-width, initial-
    scale=1.0">
```

Read the Google Developers guide to responsive websites for more, including methods for serving JavaScript on the page: `https://developers.google.com/webmasters/mobile-sites/mobile-seo/configurations/responsive-design`.

Server setup for a dynamic website

In this design, depending on the user agent requesting the page, the server gives different HTML, CSS, and so on for the same URL. If Google's standard desktop user agent comes across the page, it won't be apparent that different content is available for a mobile agent unless you give Google a hint to send its mobile agent by to pick up the mobile content. If you've got a dynamic-serving site, make sure that your server is set up to do both of the following:

✦ Detect user-agents correctly (sometimes called user-agent sniffing)

✦ Use the Vary HTTP header in your server response

The Vary HTTP header looks like this within your server's response to a request:

```
HTTP/1.1 200 OK
Content-Type: text/html
Vary: User-Agent
```

User-agent detection can be tricky and requires constant updating of user-agent strings to match new user agents. We recommend you read more about the technical requirements of dynamically serving your website in the Google Developers guide to dynamic serving: `https://developers.google.com/webmasters/mobile-sites/mobile-seo/configurations/dynamic-serving`.

Server setup for a separate mobile site

If you have a separate website designed for mobile browsers, you need to set up your server to detect the device and redirect to a mobile site, or vice versa. You have a few ways to detect whether the visitor is on a mobile device, including the use of plug-ins for content management systems like

WordPress and Joomla and the use of JavaScript to see whether the browser window is smaller than a certain width. You and your developer can decide the best way to handle device detection and serving for your site.

Along with the server-side setup, you also need to put in place some code that tells the search engine that the two URLs (the mobile version and the desktop version) for each page should essentially be treated as the same page and should have all their link and ranking signals combined. For the benefit of search engines and your search rankings, you need to

✦ Detect user agents correctly (requiring a constant updating of user-agent strings, as explained in "Server setup for a dynamic website")

✦ Use `rel="canonical"` and `rel="alternate"` attributes to indicate the relationship between corresponding desktop and mobile URLs

You place the `rel="canonical"` attribute on the mobile page pointing to the corresponding desktop URL. You place `rel="alternate"` on the desktop page pointing to the corresponding mobile URL. You should place this annotation in the HTML of the pages themselves, and you may also include it in each website's XML sitemap.

You can find more details, including the exact implementation of the `rel="canonical"` and `rel="alternate"` link attributes, in the Google Developers mobile guide to using separate URLs: `https://developers.google.com/webmasters/mobile-sites/mobile-seo/configurations/separate-urls`.

Chapter 2: Domain Names: What Your URL Says about You

In This Chapter

✔ Choosing your domain name

✔ Registering your domain name

✔ Understanding country codes and top-level domains

✔ Securing domains for common misspellings of your name

✔ Considering domains with alternate extensions

✔ Choosing the right hosting solution

✔ Knowing how search engines view subdomains

Shakespeare once said, "A rose by any other name would smell as sweet," implying that a name doesn't affect an object's essential makeup. That may be true, but a website isn't a rose — your site's name is critical to its success. Your *domain name* (the root of your site's URL address, such as `yourdomain.com`) must be chosen strategically, based on your business goals. Pick a good domain name, and you've got a foundation for a successful online presence.

In this chapter, we explain some guidelines for selecting an appropriate domain name for your website. You discover the basics, like how to register for a domain name and how to pick a hosting service to get your site up and running. You also find out about securing variations of your domain name in order to protect your *brand* (company name) in the long term.

Selecting Your Domain Name

Picking the right domain name for your website depends on your business strategy. You need to decide how you want people to find you on the web. You have basically two ways to approach choosing a domain name — by brand or by *keywords* (search terms that people might enter to find what your site offers).

If you have a unique brand name and want people to be able to find your website by searching for your brand, secure your brand as your domain.

Having a brand for your domain name makes sense if any of the following is true:

✦ Your brand is already established and recognized (Nike, Xerox, and so on).

✦ You've advertised or you plan to advertise to promote your brand.

✦ Your brand is your own name (such as Bruce Clay, Inc.) or very unique.

✦ You want your site to rank well in search results for your brand name.

As an alternative, you can choose a domain name that contains keywords that identify what your business does. For instance, if your business is called Marty's Auto but your website is focused on your classic-car customization business, you might choose `classiccarcustomization.com` as a domain name rather than `martysauto.com`. Search engines can parse the domain name to recognize the distinct words *classic car customization,* and your keyword-laden domain name could make your site more relevant to searches for those terms. *Exact-match domains,* which are domains that have the exact query as their URL, used to be rewarded with higher search rankings in the past. However, you don't want to stuff or repeat keywords in a domain name today, as that's the kind of thing Google and other search engines see as a red flag (as the sidebar "Beware keyword-stuffed domain names!" later in this chapter explains). Although the business name Marty's Auto doesn't identify what services you really offer — it could be auto sales, auto repair, or something else auto-related — it is a unique brand name that you can build over time and achieve reputation and rankings for, at least in local search. (You learn about ranking in the local search results in Book V, Chapter 4.)

You may run into problems getting your first choice of domain name because someone has already registered it. People often buy domain names that they don't intend to use, just so they can turn around and sell them later. Your desired domain may fall into that category, in which case you can try to contact the domain owner and negotiate to buy it. However, that isn't always possible, especially when the domain is legitimately operating as a thriving website. So in this case, you need to be creative and start thinking of alternative domain names that would work for your website.

Here are a few points to keep in mind when you try to come up with a good domain name:

✦ **Length:** A short domain name is better than a long one. There are three reasons why: The URL string for your files can be shorter, and people tend to avoid clicking long URL links on search results pages; a short URL is easier to remember than a long one; and there are fewer opportunities for typos when someone enters your URL in a browser window or sets it up as a link.

✦ **Multiple words:** Search engines have no trouble parsing words that are *concatenated* (run together without spaces). Most website domains for businesses with multiple-word brand names run the words together, such as `bankofamerica.com`, `bestwestern.com`, and so on. Concatenating domain names is the best practice. However, sometimes, you may need to separate words visually to make them easier for users to understand. When you must separate words, use a hyphen. The search engines interpret hyphens as word spaces; underscores (_) don't work well because they count as alphanumeric characters. Imagine that you own a tailoring business called the Mens Exchange and that you're interested in branding exactly that name. But wait a second: The domain `mensexchange.com` could be parsed two ways. To make sure the site name isn't misunderstood, a hyphen is needed; `mens-exchange.com` prevents any misunderstandings.

We recommend that you use no more than one hyphen (or two, at the most) in a domain name — more than that can make your site look suspicious to the search engines, like *spam* (deliberately using deceptive methods to gain ranking for irrelevant keywords). Although none of the engines ban you for having a multihyphenated domain name, they may still think that your domain `buy-cheap-pills-and-try-free-poker-here.com` looks a little suspicious. What's more, your visitors do, too.

✦ **Articles:** Part-of-speech articles such as *a, an,* and *the* may help you create a unique domain if they make sense within your name. For instance, Hershey's has a website at `hersheys.com` that's consumer-targeted and all about chocolate. But for its investors, the company has a separate domain at `thehersheycompany.com` that's full of company-related news and information. In most cases, however, you won't need the article, so don't worry about it.

You also want to consider your future plans as much as possible. It might be hard to foresee how your business may change and expand, but try to avoid boxing yourself in. For example, Marty's Auto might decide to branch out and also do classic car brokering and resale, or possibly include current-model car customization, bicycle customization, or another type of expanded service. In those cases, the domain name `classiccarcustomization.com` may become too restrictive in the long run.

As a general rule, you want to choose a domain name that will last. This makes sense from a usability point of view because you want your customers to rely on your website, bookmark it, and come back often. It's also important from a search engine optimization (SEO) perspective. The search engines consider domain age as a factor when ranking sites. The longer your domain has been continuously registered and active on the web, the higher your score is for the age factor. Granted, this is only one of more than 200 different ranking factors Google considers, but that doesn't make it insignificant.

Because competition can be so tight on the web, you want every advantage you can legitimately get.

Remember in the 2008 Summer Olympics, when Michael Phelps won a swimming relay by ¹/₁₀₀th of a second? That was in a field of only eight swimmers. When you consider how many thousands of competitors you could face on the web, you see why every little advantage can make such a big difference. In SEO, you need to sweat the small stuff. Having a domain that endures is a small thing that can pay off big with long-term customers and search engine rankings.

Registering Your Domain Name

To find out whether a domain has already been taken, start by just typing it into the address bar of your web browser and seeing what comes up. If you see an error message saying Address Not Found or something similar, you might think you're in luck and have located an available domain. But sometimes a domain may be taken even though no site displays, or it may look taken when in fact the domain holder would like to transfer it to someone else.

A more foolproof way to check for available domains is to go to a *domain name registrar* (a company accredited and authorized to register Internet domain names) and use its domain name search tool. A domain name search tells you whether the name is available and then quotes prices to register it to you if it is. Domain name registrars we recommend are

✦ Register.com (www.register.com)

✦ Moniker (www.moniker.com)

✦ GoDaddy.com (www.godaddy.com)

✦ Namecheap (www.namecheap.com)

✦ Whois.Net (http://whois.net)

✦ Domain.com (www.domain.com)

✦ Network Solutions (www.networksolutions.com)

Also check with your website hosting company to see what it can do for you. Many provide all the same services as a domain name registrar.

If a domain is available, you can claim it on the registrar's website. The standard price to register a .com domain name is $9.95 a year or greater (international domains can cost much more), although you may be able to secure it for two or more years up front at a discount.

In the future, you'll need to renew your domain name registration. You don't *buy* a domain name; they're only licensed for a period of time. So when your current registration is near its expiration date, you need to re-register it and then repeat this process throughout the life of your website.

If a domain name you really want is already taken, according to a domain name search, look at the website that uses the domain name. See if it looks like a real site doing business or just a placeholder site or, better yet, if it just brings up an error. All these could indicate that people have registered the domain name but haven't gotten around to creating a site yet — or that they don't intend to. Domains are often purchased on speculation and sold later. In these cases, you may be able to negotiate with the domain holder to obtain the domain. There's no telling what the initial price might be that the domain holder would require, but it may be worth it to you to negotiate a deal. Some sites, such as Moniker (`www.moniker.com`), also operate periodic auctions where domains are auctioned by their holders.

You can find out the name and contact information of the registered domain holder by using the WHOIS Lookup tool on the home page at `http://whois.net`. Then try your best persuasive techniques and see what happens.

Covering All Your Bases

**Book VII
Chapter 2**

**Domain Names:
What Your URL
Says about You**

You may want to register other domains, in addition to your main URL. Often companies try to cover all their bases — not just to attract more *traffic* (visitors) to their sites, but to protect their brand and their future online business, as well. Securing other domain names besides your primary domain can be a proactive step for your website, but you want to do it strategically. This section covers why you might want to have more than one URL. We also help you understand the variety of choices beyond the .com domains, so you can make informed decisions.

Country-code TLDs

You may be wondering what to do about all the other types of domains besides .com. There are many domain name extensions other than the familiar .com extension, such as .net, .org, .me, and so forth. Known as *top-level domains,* or *TLDs,* they represent the topmost part of a domain name under which all domain names within that TLD are registered. So, .com is a TLD, and all domain names that use the .com extension (`wiley.com`, `amazon.com`, and so on) fall within that TLD.

Who's in charge of the domain system, you ask? The Internet's domain name system is managed by the Internet Corporation for Assigned Names and Numbers, or *ICANN* for short. This not-for-profit international organization coordinates the Internet globally, creating technical naming and numbering standards to ensure that every website and computer on the Internet can be identified uniquely, which is a technical necessity. You can read more about ICANN on its site (www.icann.org).

There are two main types of TLDs within the Internet's domain name system: country-code TLDs and generic TLDs.

Country-code TLDs have a dot followed by two letters. Here are a few examples of country-code TLDs:

.au	Australia
.ca	Canada
.de	Germany
.eu	European Union
.fr	France
.il	Israel
.mx	Mexico
.us	United States

When a country-code TLD is established, the country can issue domain registrations for that TLD as it sees fit, according to its own local policies, so the rules vary from country to country. We recommend that you obtain a domain within the country's TLD for any country where you might do business. Secure your domain name if you can. You need to research the rules for establishing a domain in each country, however. Here are some specific examples:

✦ .de: If you want to do business through a German domain (.de, for Deutschland), you are required to either live in Germany or have a physical business located there.

✦ .ca: Canada has less stringent requirements; if you have a relative who lives in Canada, you can obtain a .ca domain.

✦ .us: If you're located in the United States, by all means, pick up a .us domain name. The .us domains aren't very common yet because most American companies use .com, but some notable examples are Delicious (www.delicious.com, a popular social bookmarking site), which started life at the much more complicated http://del.icio.us, and directory pages for each U.S. ZIP code that contain information about that locality (such as www.93065.us).

✦ `.co.uk`: Sometimes, a country-code TLD looks more complicated than a simple two-letter code. The United Kingdom, for example, chooses to register domains with an additional second-level domain specified in its extensions. So, a business website in England typically ends with `.co.uk`; an English non-profit group would have a site ending in `.org.uk`; and so forth.

✦ `.fm`: The Federated States of Micronesia has reserved the TLDs `.com.fm`, `.net.fm`, `.org.fm`, and others, but makes money by allowing anyone in the world to register a `.fm` domain. Although this scheme is unconventional, `.fm` has become popular with sites related to FM radio and Internet radio (such as the social music site `www.last.fm` or the Internet-marketing industry site `www.webmasterradio.fm`).

✦ `.tv`, `.me`: Occasionally, a country goes so far as to sell the rights to operate its TLD, such as the `.tv` country code (for Tuvalu) and the `.me` country code (for Montenegro).

Generic TLDs

Generic TLDs (gTLDs) are usually three or more letters long. The most common are `.com`, `.net`, and `.org`, but hundreds of TLDs exist at this time, with hundreds more going through the ICANN approval process at any given time. Some can be registered by anyone who's interested, but others require that you meet certain eligibility requirements. Table 2-1 shows many common generic TLDs and offers details about who can obtain their domains. (*Note:* The *sponsor* of a gTLD is responsible for administering the policies and ensuring that all domain registrants meet the eligibility requirements.)

Book VII Chapter 2

Domain Names: What Your URL Says about You

Table 2-1	Popular Generic Top-Level Domains (TLDs)	
TLD	**Purpose**	**Our Comments**
`.biz`	Restricted to businesses. Sponsored by Neustar, Inc. of Sterling, Virginia.	Theoretically restricted, `.biz` has a reputation for being home to less-than-sterling web businesses and spammers.
`.com`	Generic use (unrestricted).	Originally intended for commercial sites, this is the most popular TLD (with more than 60 percent of all sites). People think of this extension by default, so we recommend that you have a `.com` domain. Some browsers even have a keyboard shortcut (Ctrl+Enter) for adding `www.` and `.com` around a domain name in a browser to make these URLs easier to type.

(continued)

Table 2-1 *(continued)*

TLD	Purpose	Our Comments
.edu	Reserved for post-secondary institutions accredited by an agency on the U.S. Department of Education's list of Nationally Recognized Accrediting Agencies (in other words, American colleges). Sponsored by EDUCAUSE in Louisville, Colorado.	.edu domains used to hold a lot of weight in the search engine's eyes. For example, if your site had a link from an .edu, that link could elevate your site's PageRank. This is because .edu used to be heavily viewed as an authority site. Today, other factors come into play that make the influence of the .edu less important.
.gov	Reserved exclusively for the U.S. government. Sponsored by the General Services Administration in Washington, D.C.	
.info	Generic use (unrestricted).	Originally intended for informative sites, this TLD has really taken hold with millions of registered, active domains.
.mil	Reserved exclusively for the U.S. military. Sponsored by the DoD Network Information Center of Columbus, Ohio.	
.net	Generic use (unrestricted).	Originally intended for networks, anyone can now register for a .net domain.
.org	Generic use (unrestricted).	Originally designed for organizations such as non-profits, this TLD can now be used for any type of site.

In 2011, ICANN announced that it was open to applications for new gTLDs, changing the system of 22 generic top-level domains that had stood for decades. Today, websites can end with all sorts of words, and businesses are experimenting with using these creative options for branding. Some of the gTLDs that are available now include .accountant, .tickets, .tours, .golf, .tech, .fan, .yoga, .photography, .auction, and even .ninja! ICANN expects thousands more to be released in the next few years, so for a complete and ever-updating list of gTLDs, see ICANN's official list of "Root Zones" at http://www.iana.org/domains/root/db.

For most businesses, the standard .com may be the most timeless and the easiest for your customers to remember. Also, the risk with the fancy gTLDs is that certain ones will become overrun with spammers in time, as happened to .biz. You may consider whether a special gTLD provides advantages for your business strategies — but just don't assume that using a gTLD that's specific to your industry will help you rank.

After you've chosen your domain name, you may want to register a few of the common variations. Pick up the .com, .net, and .org if they're available. Remember, this is your future business reputation you're protecting. If you set up your website at www.classiccarcustomization.com but don't secure the other most common TLDs for that domain name, down the road, someone may build a competing site at www.classiccarcus tomization.org. Potentially they could confuse your customers, take away some of your traffic, or even damage your reputation by using your brand name for different purposes. By locking up those other domains now, you could be safe, not sorry.

Vanity domains

A *vanity domain* is an easy-to-remember web address used to market a specific product, person, or service. You would obtain a vanity domain with your users, not search engines, in mind. Movies often register a vanity domain, in addition to their primary location on the studio's website. For example, the 2008 movie *The Dark Knight* snatched up the vanity URL www.thedarkknight.com to capture all the *direct type-in traffic* (users who type a URL directly into their browser's address bar) of people looking for the movie by name. However, www.thedarkknight.com redirected you automatically to http://thedarkknight.warnerbros.com/dvdsite/, a subdomain on the Warner Brothers studio site containing the movie's web pages.

Obtain a vanity domain if you want to market your product or service with a simple website address. A long, complicated URL doesn't look good in ads and isn't easy for people to remember. You might also want to register relevant, really good vanity domains just to keep your competition from getting to them first.

Misspellings

Another good idea is to register domains that are commonly misspelled versions of your main domain name. Not only might this help you rank better for your misspelled brand name in the search engines, it also helps you capture the *direct type-in traffic,* or the people who type a URL directly into the address bar of a web browser. Figure 2-1 shows a typed-in URL, which bypasses the search engines and takes the user straight to a website (assuming the URL is entered correctly).

Beware keyword-stuffed domain names!

Something to keep in mind when choosing a domain name is the filter in Google's ranking algorithm that's set to catch keyword-stuffing spam in the domain name itself. This filter was called the EMD (Exact-Match Domain) Update when it was released in 2012. Before the EMD Update, spammers could register domain names with the exact keyword strings they wanted to rank for — and it was effective! Google noticed that low-quality websites could rank well just by having keywords in the domain name, so it released the EMD Update as a corrective measure. When this update was announced, Google said that it was targeting low-quality sites with exact-match domains. Having keywords in your domain isn't bad by itself, so don't fear a penalty if you have a high-quality website offering rich content and a pleasant user experience. As usual, don't try to deceive the search engines or shortcut rankings by way of a few primely placed keywords.

Figure 2-1:
You can type a URL directly into the address bar to open a website.

Google, for example, has covered its bases by securing close misspellings of its domain name. If you type www.gogle.com into your browser's address bar and press Enter, you instantly get redirected to www.google.com. This also works with www.googlee.com because Google has registered it, too.

To support your www.classiccarcustomization.com website, you might want to pick up the misspelled versions (such as www.classicarcustomization.com), as well as the hyphenated versions www.classic-car-customization.com and www.classiccar-customization.com, and then redirect them all to your primary site. For ideas on the common misspellings of your brand name, look no further than your customer correspondence (such as letters and emails).

Consider all the ways that people might try to find you, and make all paths lead to your site. Secure all the different variations of your actual domain name that are available and make sense.

Pointing Multiple Domains to a Single Site Correctly

After you've registered a bunch of domains, you need to know what to do with them. Having multiple domains all point to a single website is usually bad for search engine optimization because the search engines think you're trying to index multiple websites using the same content. They can tell that it's duplicate content (by matching long text strings, file sizes, and so on), and they usually use only one site and throw the others out of their search results.

You can correct this problem by using an *IP funnel*. This is a method for funneling many domains to a single *canonical site* (your primary, main website) correctly, so that search engines won't view your multiple sites as deceptive or misleading.

With an IP funnel, you don't have to host all your different domains and set up redirects on them. (*Redirects* are HTML code that automatically forwards links to a different page.) Instead, you only have to host two domains — your canonical site plus one other domain, and then "funnel" the other domains to the canonical site domain. You save money and effort and prevent duplicate content.

An IP funnel corrects the problem of multiple domains pointing to the same content. Figure 2-2 shows how you could set up an IP funnel to reroute many different domains to your canonical site domain.

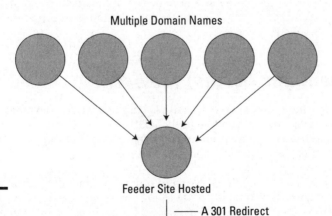

Figure 2-2:
Using an
IP funnel
to reroute
multiple
domains.

Most domain name registrars provide the ability to "point" or "forward" domains to another site. If you had six extraneous domains in addition to your main site domain, you would first choose one of the six to be your "feeder site" because it "feeds" all traffic to your canonical site. All the other five domains should point to the feeder site (not to your canonical site). These five extra domains do not need to be hosted on a server; you can just have all requests for those URLs forwarded automatically to your feeder site.

The feeder site (we call it www.feeder.com for our example) should be hosted, but it doesn't need to have a visible user interface. The feeder site only needs to have two files:

```
www.feeder.com/index.htm
www.feeder.com/robots.txt
```

The index.htm file has an optimized Title tag, Meta description tag, and Meta keywords tag. It also includes a Meta refresh statement and a Meta robots "noindex" command.

You can leave the robots text file blank. It just needs to exist so that when the search engine spiders go looking for it, they aren't met with an error. For more on creating a robots text file, see Chapter 1 of this minibook.

The last thing you need to add is a *301 Redirect command* (server code that indicates where the site has permanently moved) to the feeder site. You want to redirect the feeder site domain to your main site so that any links are passed automatically. The feeder site can then correctly redirect traffic to your "real" site.

Choosing the Right Hosting Provider

Deciding where to host your website is very important. Pick a reliable host, and managing your site can be fairly headache-free. Choose a bad one, and you could have a nightmarish experience with unreturned calls, unanswered emails, and a website that visitors can't access.

Unless you have your own server and other equipment in-house, and the technical know-how or staff to run them, you're going to need a website hosting provider. *Hosting providers* are third-party companies that lease out web space by month or by year, similar to office space. In addition to space on their servers, they offer varying degrees of additional services.

The following list explains the key things you should ask about when you research hosting providers. Keep in mind, however, that what works for your friend's site won't necessarily work for yours. Factors include the amount of traffic your site receives, how complex your site or application is, how much storage space you need, and so on. The best hosting provider is the one that meets your needs and provides the right balance between quality and value.

✦ **Customer service:** One of the most important elements of a good hosting provider is its level of service, which can range widely. How easy is it to contact the provider for support, and how quick and helpful is its response? You can get a feel for this by asking a few questions of different providers in advance. Don't let them intimidate you with technical-speak. They should be willing to answer your questions promptly and in an understandable way, or they aren't the people you want to work with.

✦ **Server:** The type of server software the provider uses is critical. To ensure enough flexibility for SEO, make sure you go with either an Apache server or a Microsoft IIS server. (Chapter 1 of this minibook explains more about the servers.)

✦ **Dedicated versus shared IP:** If you have a small site that's just getting started, you might initially share an IP address with other sites. (An *IP [Internet Protocol] address* is the numeric code that identifies the logical address of a server or a computer on the web.) Having an IP that hosts only your website, however, is preferred for many SEO-related reasons. This is called a *dedicated IP.* Here are good things to find out from a prospective hosting provider:

  • If you have to share the IP, ask how many sites share it (the fewer, the better).

  • Ask whether it offers dedicated IPs and find out how you can get one.

✦ **Uptime:** The percentage of time the site is up and running, not including scheduled maintenance periods. A guaranteed uptime of 99 percent is not uncommon, so make sure you're contractually covered.

✦ **Bandwidth:** The amount of bandwidth available to your site determines how much traffic your site can comfortably handle. *Bandwidth* refers to the flow of data transferring over an Internet connection. You can think of it like a pipe — the pipe's diameter determines how many gallons of water can flow through it at the same time. The bigger the pipe, the more water it can transfer. The higher the bandwidth, the greater the number of consecutive visitors your website can handle. You need more bandwidth in any of the following situations:

  • Your site has a large number of pages.

  • Your site has a lot of regular traffic at peak periods.

  • Your site serves many Flash and sound files or has large images, audio, video, or other elements that require a lot of bandwidth to display.

Very large or application-intensive websites that need maximum connectivity should find a hosting provider that's physically located on what's known as the *Internet backbone*. This refers to the main hub connections of the Internet, which are primarily located in major cities around the world (Los Angeles, Denver, New York, and so on). A site right on a hub means that data can transfer to and from the site faster than if it had to travel through multiple spokes to reach the server.

✦ **Storage:** File storage space is cheap, and most hosting providers give out a generous amount, even to the smallest sites. However, more storage space is needed if you plan to have a ton of image, audio, or video files on your site. If you're going to operate a *social media site* (a website that enables user participation and consists of user-generated content) where people can upload their own videos, for an example, you want to be prepared with lots of storage space to hold them.

✦ **Server capacity:** The processing power of the server. You know how a new computer always seems to work faster than the old one did? That's because the new computer has a much more powerful processor. Similarly, server capacity affects the performance speed and capacity of your website. If your site application requires a lot of processing power, ask about how the host providers allocate server capacity and strongly consider requiring a dedicated IP.

✦ **Scalability:** The ability to expand your server resources, as needed. If and when your website business grows, you want to be able to scale your server resources up to deliver the same or better site performance. You also may want to add storage space, bandwidth, or server capacity to your site at peak times, or all the time. Make sure you have a flexible hosting environment that is easy to adjust as your site needs change.

✦ **Clean IPs:** You don't want to move into a bad neighborhood, so you make sure that your site isn't on a dirty *IP address* (the Internet Protocol numeric code that identifies the logical address of a server or a computer on the web). Because you have no way to know in advance what IP address you'll get, make sure your service level agreement includes that you require a clean IP that's not *blacklisted* (listed on anti-spam databases).

When researching hosting providers, look up online reviews written by current or former customers. These can be very insightful. Just remember that each website has different needs, so you have to take others' comments with a grain of salt.

One last recommendation about choosing a hosting provider: Don't consider it a permanent arrangement. You hold the rights to the domain and the site assets, and you can host them wherever you think best. Move to a new hosting provider if your current provider isn't cutting it.

Understanding Subdomains

In the domain name system (DNS), a *subdomain* is a dependent domain set up within the primary domain. Here's an example: The following code shows the URL if you set up a subdomain called `events` in your classic-car customization business domain:

```
http://events.classiccarcustomization.com
```

`events` is the subdomain, `.classiccarcustomization` is the domain, and `.com` is the TLD.

Why people set up subdomains

Websites often create subdomains in order to segregate sections of web pages to create a virtual site within a site. In the example in the previous section, an events subdomain could be used to hold information about classic car shows, car industry conventions, company-sponsored events, or other types of event-related information that you decided not to include within your main site navigation scheme.

Some social media sites automatically create a subdomain for each person who signs up (such as *myname.socialmediasite.com*). Similarly, some companies choose to create subdomains for their different employees. So, you could have

```
http://bob.classiccarcustomization.com
http://katie.classiccarcustomization.com
http://susan.classiccarcustomization.com
```

Other sites set up subdomains as a way of separating all their website content into different categories:

```
http://remodels.classiccarcustomization.com
http://paint.classiccarcustomization.com
http://parts.classiccarcustomization.com
```

In other parts of this book, we recommend *siloing* your website, which basically means organizing your website content into a hierarchy of subject themes, with each silo focused on its own particular theme, including keywords and relevant links. Although the example subdomains in the preceding list appear to be organized by subject theme (remodels, paint, parts), this is *not* siloing. (For more on siloing, see Book VI.) We don't recommend organizing the bulk of your site content by subdomains for several reasons, which we discuss in the following section.

How search engines view subdomains

Search engines consider subdomains to be entirely separate sites. Subdomains can endanger your search engine optimization if you want content on your subdomain to be considered as part of your main site. Search engines don't see the subdomain as part of your main site and they also don't see any connection between your various subdomains. By using subdomains, you effectively put up walls between your different sets of content. In essence, you're taking all the benefit of your inbound links and all your well-thought-out content, and dividing them across several separate web properties. Unless you have a lot of both, dividing them up is a really bad idea. But if you did it, you would need to optimize each subdomain for the search engines separately, if you wanted them to rank.

You benefit from using subdomains on your website only in the following cases:

✦ **Totally unrelated content:** If you wanted to start a side business selling bicycles, you wouldn't want to dilute your classic car customization website by including pages about frame sizes, bicycle brands, and prices. You could register an entirely different domain for this, or you could handle this new business as a subdomain of your main website.

Blog sites (initially short for *web log* sites, though now far removed from that origin) provide another great example of subdomains. If you sign up for a blog account on WordPress.com (`www.wordpress.com`), for example, your blog receives the `yourname.wordpress.com` subdomain. Your blog contains your writing and thoughts, and has no relation to other people's blogs. Subdomains work well in this situation because each blog contains legitimately different content.

✦ **Large brands:** Huge companies with highly branded names can successfully use subdomains to separate their content. Why? First, they have *tons* of pages about each division or product, enough so that each subdomain ranks well with the search engines on its own. Second, it benefits users to have the well-known brand name in every URL because it confirms that the pages legitimately belong to that company. Third, having multiple subdomains could yield multiple results on a search engine results page (SERP), if several come up for the same keyword.

Companies that use subdomains include Google (`news.google.com`, `images.google.com`, `maps.google.com`, and so on) and National Geographic (`kids.nationalgeographic.com`, `video.nationalgeographic.com`, `animals.nationalgeographic.com`, and so on). Large education institutions (`.edu` sites) also use subdomains because each institution may only have one `.edu` domain name, leaving only subdomains to separate the different schools within it.

✦ **International sites:** Targeting different countries can very effectively be done through the use of subdomains. If you don't have the resources to buy www.*mybusiness*.co.uk, or if that domain is already taken (not all domains are available around the world), you can target the United Kingdom by using uk.*mybusiness*.com, instead. We discuss more about international SEO in Book IX.

✦ **Secure content:** If part of your website can only be accessed through a logon, it could be set up effectively as a subdomain. Search engines don't spider content that's behind a logon anyway, so having it in a separate subdomain doesn't matter to your SEO efforts.

Your site needs a lot of subject-relevant content to reach the front pages of the search results. Most people struggle to have enough site content to support their keyword themes and get the rankings they're after. If you're like them, splitting up what content you have into separate subdomains is self-defeating. And if you're currently using subdomains as a way of organizing your site content, stop it. Use siloing, instead. (For more on siloing, see Book VI.)

Chapter 3: Using Redirects for SEO

In This Chapter

✔ **Understanding when to use a redirect command**

✔ **Discriminating between the different types of redirects**

✔ **Understanding 301 and 302 Redirects**

✔ **Knowing when to use** Meta **refreshes**

✔ **Considering JavaScript redirects**

✔ **Dovetailing your www and non-www domains properly**

*I*n your toolbox of search engine optimization (SEO) techniques, the redirect tool is an important one to master. *Redirects* are HTML or server commands that automatically forward incoming links to another page. With this tool, you can trim outdated pages off your site without losing the visitors who still go to those pages. You can also organize many *domains* (root names of website URLs) into one site, so that they won't be competing with each other. With redirects, you can avoid creating *duplicate content* (web pages that search engines see as duplicates of each other) that could damage your rankings on search engine results pages (SERPs). And the best part is that redirects are not at all hard to learn.

This chapter covers the four main types of redirects. We explain what each type is for, although for SEO purposes, only one type of redirect is safe to use — a 301 Redirect. In Chapter 4 of this minibook, you can discover the how-to's of placing 301 Redirects in your website.

Discovering the Types of Redirects

There are several different types of redirects in the world of the Internet. These commands give you a way to redirect your site visitors from one *URL* (the web address of a page, such as www.wiley.com) to another (like www.wiley.com/index.htm). Often, you need to use a redirect to reroute people linking to an old page to its replacement page, especially if your website undergoes reorganization so that files and directories have to be renamed and moved around. You also need to use redirects in the normal course of site maintenance, to help visitors coming to alternative *URLs* (such as the non-www version of your domain instead of the www version, and so on) to get to the URLs that contain the content they're looking for.

Short for *redirection status codes,* the various redirects are defined by the World Wide Web Consortium (W3C), an organization that oversees Internet practices and creates standards that enable websites all over the world to work smoothly together as one giant network. Webmasters have a bunch of tricks that they can use, but not all of them benefit you, your site, your users, or your search engine rankings. In the case of redirects, although the available redirect methods are intended to have different functions, only one is thoroughly search engine friendly.

In the following sections, you can find out about the four most common ways to handle automatically redirecting one URL to a different URL: 301 Redirects, 302 Redirects, Meta refreshes, and JavaScript redirects.

301 (permanent) Redirects

The *301 Redirect* is the preferred and most SEO-friendly form of redirect. Also known as a *permanent redirect,* the 301 Redirect informs a search engine that the page has been permanently moved to a new location. This is the cleanest redirect because there's no ambiguity — the search engines get a clear message that one page is history and some other URL has now taken its place.

To put it in perspective, say that your favorite barbeque restaurant closes without your knowledge. Fortunately for you, the next time you head over for its mouth-watering ribs, you see a sign in the window: We've Moved to a New Location: 123 Yummy Drive. This sign enables you to get back in the car and head to the restaurant's new location without too much inconvenience.

A 301 Redirect is kind of like a We've Moved sign, but better. On the web, visitors don't even have to realize you've moved. Your website automatically redirects them to the new URL and displays the new page.

If you've registered a *vanity URL* (an easy-to-remember domain that isn't your main business domain name), you should put a 301 Redirect on the vanity URL so that when users go to it, they end up at your real site, instead. For example, people interested in a currently playing movie often type the movie title directly into their browser's address bar, so movie studios try to register those URLs in advance. For the 2008 movie *The Dark Knight,* if you type in www.thedarkknight.com, you're automatically redirected to http://thedarkknight.warnerbros.com/dvdsite/, which is a subdomain on the Warner Brothers studio site. That's because the studio wisely secured the movie title URL and then redirected it to the actual site by using a 301 Redirect, thereby capturing more website traffic.

For site maintenance, you could use 301 Redirects when physically reorganizing your pages and directories. For instance, you might redirect a page with a ghastly long URL (such as www.classiccarcustomization.com/extras/dashboard/gauges-chevrolet-impala/speed-or-tach/139348w9d.htm) to a new and cleaner URL address (like www.classiccarcustomization.com/chevrolet/gauges/impala-tachometer.htm). You wouldn't want to keep the old page location active on your website, but there are *backlinks* (incoming links from other websites) to the old page that you don't want to break. So you can't bring in the wreaking ball and just demolish the page — you need to redirect the old URL to the new one instead. The right way to do this is to set up a 301 Redirect from the old URL to the new one. Then, users who click to come to the old page automatically find themselves looking at the new one; also, search engines get the message loud and clear.

When a search engine encounters a 301 Redirect, it does three things:

✦ Drops the now defunct page from its *index* (database of web pages from which the search engine pulls search results) so that that page won't be included in future search results.

✦ Includes the new page in the index, available for listing on search results pages.

✦ Transfers link equity from the old page to the new. (*Link equity* refers to the value of all incoming links to a page, which the search engines use to help determine a web page's authority, or expertise, in its subject matter.)

The 301 Redirect is the SEO-recommended form of redirect because it reduces duplicate content within the search engine index. Duplicate content hurts your search engine rankings because search engines don't want to show their users results that are essentially the same. Therefore, if a search engine detects that two pages it has indexed are the same, it filters out the less authoritative page so that only one of the pages can appear in search engine results pages (SERPs). Because a search engine responds to a 301 Redirect by dropping the old page entirely from its index, the chance of having two pages in the index with the same content is nil. (See Chapter 4 of this minibook for details on implementing 301 Redirects.)

302 (temporary) Redirects

Another commonly used form of redirect is the *302 Redirect,* which signifies Document Found Elsewhere. You use this redirect for temporary relocations of a web page. Search engines see the new page as only temporary and continue to crawl and index the original location, instead.

Although the search engines claim to be able to interpret a 302 Redirect correctly, 302 Redirects can cause search engines to index duplicate content. Because duplicate content can cause search engines to filter pages from SERPs or assign pages to a supplemental index, for the sake of your SEO efforts, avoid using 302 Redirects. (***Note:*** We cover duplicate content in depth in Book V, Chapter 5.)

Remember, 301 and 302 Redirects are server (not HTML) commands, whereas you use the types of redirects in the following sections within an HTML page.

Meta refreshes

A `Meta` *refresh* is a type of `Meta` *tag* (a command located in the *Head section,* or top section, of a web page's HTML code) that tells the page to refresh automatically after a given time interval. When you *refresh* a page (by clicking the browser's Refresh button, for example), it causes the page to reload and redisplay its contents. A `Meta` refresh command can be written in several ways:

✦ Refresh the page instantly (time delay = 0).

✦ Refresh the page after an interval (time delay = 1 or more seconds).

✦ Refresh the page repeatedly every *X* number of seconds.

✦ Refresh to another page (with or without a time delay).

Officially, search engines say that they handle `Meta` refreshes as follows:

✦ A `Meta` refresh that has a time delay of zero (0) or one second (1) is treated like a 301 Redirect.

✦ A `Meta` refresh that has a time delay of two (2) or more seconds is treated like a 302 Redirect.

However, we've observed that this isn't usually the case. The search engines sometimes follow the link (as they would with a 301 or 302), but sometimes they don't. Sometimes they index the new content, but sometimes they ignore it. The search engines don't handle `Meta` refreshes reliably, and that's one reason to avoid using them in your website.

Another reason to steer clear of `Meta` refreshes is that they look suspicious to the search engines. Because `Meta` refreshes can be used to show different content to a search engine than to a user, they have traditionally been used by *spam sites* (websites that intentionally deceive search engines about their real content). In one case, a site put up pages about baby blankets, but it was just a cover for a pornography site. The search engines didn't see the porn content because the `Meta` refreshes delayed the change.

A grandmother searching for baby blankets discovered the truth and reported the site. The search engine's spam team went to work, and soon that site was banned from the index. (For more about spam, see Book I, Chapter 6.)

Many sites use `Meta` refreshes for legitimate reasons, as well. For example, the *Los Angeles Times* (`www.latimes.com`) uses a `Meta` refresh to refresh its front page every 600 seconds (ten minutes). It refreshes its front page to make sure that online readers always see the most up-to-date news because its stories change frequently. However, search engine spiders don't stay on the page for ten minutes to read the new content. The spider sees only what's on the page at the outset.

With a typical site (less well known than the *L.A. Times*), you don't want the search engines to miss reading all your rich content, so you can have the maximum chance of ranking in search results. Even worse, using a `Meta` refresh may get your site flagged as suspected spam. Search engines especially suspect sites that use a `Meta` refresh to fetch another page. Bottom line: If you need to redirect users and search engines to a new URL for a page, do it with a 301 Redirect.

JavaScript redirects

The search engines have a hard time following and indexing your pages properly if you program a redirect by using *JavaScript* (a scripting language that can add functionality to websites). JavaScript redirects give you the ability to customize the user experience, so the benefit is all on the usability end of the spectrum. (*Usability* refers to the user-friendliness of the site, which in this case runs counter to search engine–friendliness.) A JavaScript redirect is also not recommended from an SEO perspective. The problem is that search engines cannot execute JavaScript and therefore cannot follow the redirect to a new page.

With JavaScript, you can redirect users to particular versions of a page based on settings that can be detected by JavaScript. You can detect the user's browser type, Flash capability, cookies settings, and so forth. So you could deliver a page that has Flash animations to users who have the Flash plug-in installed, but show a non-Flash-enhanced page to others — in other words, personalize it somewhat. That's a useful application, but sites can also use JavaScript deceptively to create a "bait-and-switch" type of effect.

The search engines usually flag instances of JavaScript redirects for human review. Flagged sites are then dependent on the discretion of the human reviewer, who determines if the redirect benefits the user — in which case it's usually allowed — or if it is a tactic for delivering a different page to a spider than it delivers to a user — in which case the site could be penalized for spam (that is, thrown out of the index or buried way down in the results page). And because the search engines continuously improve their spam-detection efforts, you want to make sure to keep your website practices in the safe harbor.

We recommend that you *never* implement JavaScript redirects, except for personalization. Even if you're not doing something wrong, you don't want to attract negative attention from the search engines. It's similar to driving when there's a police car present. You watch your speedometer to make sure you don't go over the speed limit even a little because that could catch the officer's attention. And if the police officer notices you, she might also notice that you're not wearing a seatbelt or that your right taillight is out. You're better off just not attracting attention in the first place.

Reconciling Your www and Non-www URLs

How can you use redirects on a practical level? One common situation solved by a 301 Redirect involves how to reconcile your www and non-www domains.

If you're like most website owners today, you probably have two versions of your site URL, one with and one without the www. in front of the domain name, such as

```
www.yourdomain.com
yourdomain.com
```

Having both versions is recommended because users have a tendency to type either of the versions into their browser, and you want to receive all that traffic. However, because these are treated as two different websites, you have to make it clear to them which address is the main, or *canonical,* site. Otherwise, you may end up competing against yourself for search engine rankings.

Unfortunately, many websites don't handle the dual-version URL issue correctly. They end up with pages from both the www and the non-www URL versions indexed by the search engines. This is a problem because if both the www and the non-www versions of a URL are indexed, your pages look like duplicates in the index — this causes the search engines to filter some of your pages out of their search results. Similarly, if there are links pointing to both versions (either internal links on your own site or *external links* originating on other websites), your link equity is diluted because it's split between the two URLs. (*Link equity* refers to the value of all your incoming links, which search engines use to determine your page's authority and expertise on its subject matter.)

We always recommend that sites use a 301 Redirect on the non-www version of any URL to the www version. Doing so prevents the search engines from indexing duplicate content and protects your link equity from being diluted.

It doesn't matter which way you go — you could point the www version to the non-www version just as effectively as you could point the non-www version to the URL starting with www. However, it's more usual to make your www version the main site.

To ensure that www.*yourdomain*.*com* is indexed as your canonical site, you need to do one of two things. The best way to make sure that the search engines index your site in the way you want is to set up a 301 Redirect (a permanent redirect, not any other kind) that points the entire *yourdomain*.*com* site to www.*yourdomain*.*com*. Using a 301 Redirect ensures that any kind of spider or browser that comes to your site gets the version of the domain that you want it to see, with no mistakes. (Remember, you can find all the nitty-gritty details on doing this in Chapter 4 of this minibook.)

However, if you can't set up 301 Redirects and don't want to dump your web host, you have another option. You can submit www.*yourdomain*.*com* to Google as your preferred domain. (This works for Google only, so you might still have issues with Bing and thus Yahoo by proxy.) Google allows you to submit your preferred domain to it in its webmaster tools. This allows you to decide which versions of your URLs you want Google to index, which can help prevent any potential problems from the non-www issue. Please see www.google.com/support/webmasters/bin/answer.py?answer=44231 for more information about this particular feature.

Specify your canonical pages

In February 2009, a rare collaboration by Google, Yahoo, and Bing resulted in a new Head section tag called `link rel=canonical`. If you have a single website domain that has identical or nearly identical pages that have different URLs (such as pages with session IDs or tracking codes), there's now a way you can specify which page you prefer to have indexed and treated as the original.

Identical but separate pages within a site can be the result of poor site design, but more often than not it's the result of a content management system (CMS) spitting out long URL strings full of parameters, categories, or ses-

sion IDs. This causes search engines to find lots of different URLs that all contain the same page content. That kind of duplicate content is bad for your search engine optimization.

The big three search engines say that this feature is not something that should take the place of proper redirects or any of the other best practices we cover for avoiding duplicate content (in Book V, Chapter 4, for example). However, if your site has duplicate content issues that you cannot solve in one of the preferred ways, you should use this to hint to the engines which page they should treat as the original.

(continued)

(continued)

You add `link rel=canonical` tags to your HTML pages to tell the search engines which of your pages to consider the canonical versions and which ones to consider duplicates. You could do this for every instance of duplicate content on your site. Here's how:

Say that the following is your preferred (canonical) page for Ford Mustang hubcaps:

```
http://www.classiccars.
    com/product.php?item=
    MustangHubcaps
```

But your CMS sometimes creates URLs such as these for the same page:

```
http://www.classiccars.com/
    product.php?item=MustangHub
    caps&category=accessories
http://www.classiccars.com/
    product.php?item=MustangHub
    caps&trackingid=1234&sessio
    nid=5678
```

You can now add the following tag in the Head section of these duplicate content URLs to tell the search engines where to find the canonical version of that page:

```
<link rel="canonical"
    href="http://www.
    classiccars.com/product.
    php?item=MustangHubcaps" />
```

Resmember that this Head section tag works only for pages within the same domain, but that includes subdomains. So, it works for `your domain.com` and `www.yourdomain.com`, but you can't use this feature to clarify things between `yourdomain.com` and `otherdomain.com`.

An especially important use for the canonical tag is for websites with separate desktop and mobile-specific sites. In this case, point to the desktop version of a page from the canonical tag on the mobile version of a page and the search engine will be able to see the two pages (and all their off-page signals) as one and the same. Read about handling your mobile site right for search engines in Book IV, Chapter 3.

For more info on how to use this tag, you can read about it in Google Support (`https://support.google.com/webmasters/answer/139066?hl=en`) or Bing's announcement and implementation guide (`http://www.bing.com/community/site_blogs/b/webmaster/archive/2009/02/12/partnering-to-help-solve-duplicate-content-issues.aspx`).

Chapter 4: Implementing 301 Redirects

In This Chapter

- ✔ Redirecting a page to a new URL
- ✔ Creating 301 Redirects on an Apache server
- ✔ Doing 301 Redirects on a NGINX server
- ✔ Implementing 301 Redirects in Microsoft IIS
- ✔ Setting up 301 Redirects in ISAPI_Rewrite
- ✔ Accomplishing 301 Redirects using header inserts
- ✔ Setting up 301 Redirects with a WordPress plug-in
- ✔ Moving a site to a new host

*R*edirects are HTML or server commands that automatically forward incoming links and users from one page's URL to another URL, so redirects provide you with an extremely useful website–maintenance technique.

Of the four types of redirects we cover in Chapter 3 of this minibook (301 Redirect, 302 Redirect, Meta refresh, and JavaScript redirect), only the 301 Redirect passes the test for search engine optimization (SEO)–friendliness. In this chapter, we cover how to set up 301 Redirects and show you some specific situations that call for them. Because a lot of this explanation involves step-by-step instructions, we give a set of instructions for each kind of server. Your *server* is the software that runs your website. The server receives and "serves up" user requests to display pages or perform other site tasks.

If you don't know what type of server your site runs on, ask your webmaster or your *hosting provider* (the service that physically hosts your website).

Getting the Details on How 301 Redirects Work

A 301 Redirect tells the search engine that the page at Location A has permanently moved to Location B. The 301 Redirect gives a very clear-cut, unambiguous message that one URL is forever replaced by another URL, such as "`www.shoe-site.com/oldpage.htm` has moved to `www.shoe-site.com/newpage.htm`." The search engine responds by doing three things:

✦ **Dropping the now defunct page from its *index* (the database of web pages from which the search engine pulls search results).** Dropping the old page ensures that the old page doesn't appear in search engine results pages (SERPs).

✦ **Including the new page in the index so that it's available for searching.**

✦ **Transferring the old page's link equity to the new URL.** (*Link equity* refers to the value of all incoming links to a page, which the search engines use to determine a web page's authority and expertise in its subject.)

In the following sections, you can find instructions for creating 301 Redirects on the following types of servers:

✦ Apache server

✦ NGINX server

✦ Microsoft IIS server

✦ ISAPI_Rewrite for the Microsoft IIS server

Don't forget to test. After you put your redirect in place, be sure to test to make sure you did it properly. Just type the old URL into your browser's address bar and press Enter. If you implemented your 301 Redirects correctly, you'll immediately see the new page (and the new page's URL in your address bar).

When setting up redirects, you must be careful. The server programs require a strict syntax to be followed, similar to a programming language. If you change a server configuration file (such as .htaccess) and your changes are just one character off, it can literally take your site offline until the mistake is corrected. Reading this book alone cannot prepare you to work at the server level. Make sure that whoever makes the types of modifications that we discuss in this chapter really knows what she's doing.

Implementing a 301 Redirect in Apache .htaccess Files

Redirecting pages or sites on an Apache web server is very easy. You do it by modifying a file on your website called the `.htaccess` file (note that the actual file name begins with a period). The *.htaccess file* is a control file that allows server configuration changes on a per-directory basis. The file controls that directory and all the subdirectories contained within it. Usually, this file is placed in the root folder of your website. It is very important, when you edit Apache files, that your editor saves the file in UNIX format; otherwise, errors may occur.

TIP

The .htaccess file should be set up by default, but if your root folder doesn't contain the file, have someone who understands how to build an .htaccess file create it. Be careful here. Some upload (FTP) programs hide the .htaccess. You don't want to overwrite an existing .htaccess with your update.

Here's an example of an .htaccess file for a site that moves from ASP to PHP and redirects the non-www version to the www version (note that where it says *mydomain*, you should put in your own domain):

```
# BEGIN
    <IfModule mod_rewrite.c>
    RewriteEngine On
    RewriteCond %{HTTP_HOST} !^www\.mydomain\.com$
    RewriteRule ^(.*) http://www.mydomain.com/$1 [R=301,L]
    RedirectMatch 301 (.*)\.asp$ http://www.mydomain.com$1.php
    </IfModule>
    # END
```

Note that the preceding example redirects anything that is not www.mydomain.com. In other words, it also redirects subdomains, such as subdomain.mydomain.com and test.mydomain.com. This could create confusion if you're using subdomains for test environments or other uses.

Before you start, you should make sure that you can access your .htaccess file. If you have access to your server so that you can upload and modify files, you should have no problem. (With the Apache server, modifying the .htaccess file does not require administrator-level access rights.) If you cannot access files in your web folders, call your hosting provider and request this ability (or contact the person who can access these files for you).

To edit the .htaccess file to redirect page(s) on your website, you must first know the URL(s) of each web page/site you want to redirect and the URL(s) of the new page/site where each will be redirected to. Then follow these steps:

1. **Log on to your website and, in the root web folder, locate the file called** .htaccess.

If there is no .htaccess file present, you need to create one. Again, be careful that there really is no .htaccess present and that you aren't overwriting one.

.htaccess is a hidden file, so you need to enable your FTP program to view hidden files to be able to see it.

2. **Open the** `.htaccess` **file by using a text editor with UNIX-style line endings such as Notepad++.**

   A code editor such as Adobe Dreamweaver also handles the `.htaccess` file perfectly because it opens the file as text, but a simple text editor can do the job.

3. **Edit the file, as needed, being careful to follow the exact syntax required.**

   See the examples in the following sections.

To add a 301 Redirect to a specific page in Apache

Add a line to the `.htaccess` file that tells the server what to do. The two ways to do this follow, and they both accomplish the same thing. (**Note:** You would substitute your own file URLs and *domain name* [the root part of your site's URL] when using the examples given here.)

```
RedirectPermanent /old-file.html http://www.mydomain.com/new-
    file.html
```

or

```
Redirect 301 /old-file.html http://www.mydomain.com/new-
    file.html
```

To 301 Redirect an entire domain in Apache

To redirect an entire domain, you add a line to the `.htaccess` file that gives the server your instructions. A redirection from one domain to another would be written like this:

```
RedirectPermanent / http://www.new-domain.com/
```

To break these down, each 301 Redirect command contains three parts:

✦ The first part tells the server what to do, and you can type this in two ways, either **RedirectPermanent** or **Redirect 301.**

✦ The second part shows the old file's *relative path* (its file location in relation to the current directory where the `.htaccess` file is located). If your `.htaccess` file is in your root web directory, you can use the file's URL without the domain name, such as `/old-file.html`.

✦ The third section is the *full path* to the new file. Starting with the `http://`, you want to include the complete URL (such as `http://www.mydomain.com/new-file.html`).

After you insert the 301 Redirect commands to redirect your pages, you need to put a blank line at the end of the file. Your server reads the `.htaccess` file line by line, so you have to include line advance (carriage return) character at some point to let the server know you're finished.

Implementing a 301 Redirect on an NGINX Server

Redirecting pages or sites on an NGINX web server is easy and quite similar to doing a redirect on an Apache server, but with slightly different syntax. You do it by modifying the configuration file, so you need administrative privileges on the server to edit this file. By default, the configuration file is named `nginx.conf` and is placed in the directory `/usr/local/nginx/conf`, `/etc/nginx`, or `/usr/local/etc/nginx`. In your NGINX configuration file, you add the following line into the block that defines your site's configuration:

```
rewrite ^/category/something/(.*)$ http://site.com/
    something/$1 permanent;
```

Implementing a 301 Redirect on a Microsoft IIS Server

Whereas an Apache server is comparatively easy to deal with, IIS is much more complex. Our recommendation is to consult with your ISP to validate all IIS changes before you make them live. If your website resides on a Microsoft IIS server, you must have administrator-level access rights in order to set up a 301 Redirect. You can add greater flexibility to your IIS server by installing a plug-in called ISAPI_Rewrite. With this plug-in, you can access your web files without needing administrator access rights to the server. (We recommend that you request the ISAPI_Rewrite for your IIS server because with it you can work with the files hands-on rather than relying on a third party to make the changes you need.)

To redirect page(s) on your website, you must first know the URL(s) of each web page or site you want to redirect and the URL(s) of the new page or site where each will be directed to. Then, follow the steps in one of the following sections, depending on which version of IIS you're running.

To 301 Redirect pages in IIS 5.0 and 6.0

To redirect pages in either IIS 5.0 or 6.0, follow these steps:

1. **Start the Internet Services Manager (Start ⇨ Programs ⇨ Administrative Tools ⇨ Internet Information Services Manager) and select the website from which you want to redirect.**

2. **Right-click the file or folder you wish to redirect and choose Properties.**

3. **Click the Home Directory tab and select the option at the top labeled A Redirection to a URL.**

4. **Enter the full URL of the page or site to which you want to redirect.**

5. **Make sure that A Permanent Redirection for This Resource and The Exact URL Entered Above are selected.**

6. **Click Apply.**

You may also want to pass a *control variable* to the new URL (the one you're redirecting to), which is a code that communicates additional instructions to the server. Control variables can make your job a lot easier, giving you shortcuts for applying changes. Table 4-1 shows the various options.

Table 4-1   Control-Variable Options for a Microsoft IIS Server (Version 5.0 or 6.0)

Variable	Function	Example
$P	Passes parameters that were passed to the URL to the new URL	If the request contains parameters such as www.mydomain.com/mypage.asp?Param1=1, $P represents all the values after the question mark in the URL (for example, $P would equal Param1=1).
$Q	Passes the parameters, including the question mark	This is identical to $P but includes the question mark (so $Q would equal ?Param1=1).
$S	Passes the matching suffix of the URL to the new URL	If the request is for www.mydomain.com/mydir/mypage.asp, $S represents /mypage.asp. If the request is for www.mydomain.com/mydir, the value of $S would be /mydir.
$V	Removes the server name from the original request	If the request is for www.mydomain.com/mydir/mypage.asp, $V would contain everything after the server name (such as /mydir/mypage.asp).
*	Wildcard symbol used to take the place of any character	If you want to redirect all requests for HTML pages to a single .asp page, you could do so using *;*.htm;myasp.asp.

To 301 Redirect an entire domain in IIS 5.0 and 6.0

When redirecting an entire domain, the control variable $V is the most useful. If you're preserving the directory structures and page names completely and only want to change the domain name, you can simply type the new URL (such as the one below) with the variable in the Redirect To text box:

```
http://www.new-domain.com$V
```

Putting the $V control variable at the end of the new site URL redirects all directories and pages from the old site to the new one, as long as they have not changed. For example, www.oldsite.com/directory1/page1.html would redirect to www.newsite.com/directory1/page1.html. For comparison, without the $V variable, you would only redirect the home page. When you have pages that rank well with the search engines in your site, it's especially helpful to redirect those pages using these variables as well.

To implement a 301 Redirect in IIS 7.0 and higher

This section tells how to implement a 301 Redirect within a Microsoft IIS 7.0 or 8.0 server. Note that in many cases, *rewriting* a URL would be more appropriate. Rewriting a URL means just changing the displayed URL, rather than sending a user to a new page. (We talk about rewrites in Chapter 5 of this minibook.)

You set up a redirect in IIS 7.0 or 8.0 when you need to physically move files or directories or when you need to relocate your physical site contents from one domain to another. In order to set up a 301 Redirect on a Microsoft IIS server version 7.0 or higher, you must have administrator access to the IIS Manager. To have this access, your site must use a *dedicated server* (meaning that yours is the only site on the server), and you must have administrator-level access rights.

If you can take care of those preparation issues, you're ready to set up your 301 Redirect by following these steps:

1. **Open the Internet Services Manager (Start ➪ Programs ➪ Administrative Tools ➪ Internet Information Services [IIS] Manager).**

2. **In the left column, select the site, directory, or page from which you want to redirect.**

3. **Using the Features View in the main window, locate the icon labeled HTTP Redirect and double-click it.**

4. **Select the box labeled Redirect Requests to This Destination and type the URL to which you want to redirect.**

   These examples show the proper syntax for different types of destinations:

   - *Redirecting to a single page:* www.mydomain.com/newpage.htm

   - *Redirecting to a directory:* www.mydomain.com/newdirectory

   - *Redirecting to a domain:* www.mydomain.com/

5. **If you're keeping the directory structures and page names the same, make sure that the two check boxes below Redirect Options remain unselected.**

   - **Redirect All Requests to Exact Destination:** Select this option only if you want every file within the directory or domain you're redirecting from to be rerouted to a single page.

   - **Only Redirect Requests to Content in This Directory:** Select this option if you want to redirect only the files located in the selected directory, not any subdirectories.

6. **For the Status Code, choose the Permanent (301) option.**

7. **From the menu in the right column, choose Apply.**

To implement a 301 Redirect with ISAPI_Rewrite on an IIS server

The ISAPI_Rewrite plug-in can make your life much easier if your site runs on a Microsoft IIS server. It allows you to upload, download, and modify your website files yourself, without administrator access to the server. It also lets you handle 301 Redirects without having to get your hosting provider involved.

You can obtain ISAPI_Rewrite from a number of software vendors, but here are the ones we recommend you check out:

✦ **Helicon Tech:** The ISAPI_Rewrite plug-in from Helicon Tech (www. isapirewrite.com) is excellent; this is the one we usually use in-house. Helicon has a free and a paid version. If you are on a shared hosting server, you need the paid version to apply the changes to only your site as the free version makes changes globally (to all sites on the web server). This software works with all IIS versions.

✦ **Microsoft:** If you're using IIS version 7.0 or 8.0, you can use the Helicon Tech tool or the Microsoft URL Rewrite module, which you can download and install into IIS. The download is available in two versions, so download the appropriate one for your server, either 32-bit or 64-bit (`www.iis.net/downloads/microsoft/url-rewrite`). Two exciting features of this product are its ability to import Apache `.htaccess` files and convert them into the rule set for IIS and its helpful interface for writing rules that's an improvement over simply editing configuration files.

Because there are different flavors of the ISAPI_Rewrite software, your actual code syntax may be different. You need to follow the specific rules for your software. However, for your reference, we give you two samples of redirects created in ISAPI_Rewrite in the next two sections.

To 301 Redirect an old page to a new page in ISAPI_Rewrite

Follow these steps:

1. **Open the file named** `httpd.ini` **located at the root of your website.**

2. **Type the appropriate code into the file.**

   Follow this example, but substitute your own *oldpage* filename and *newpage* URL:

   ```
   RewriteRule /oldpage.htm http://www.mydomain.com/
       newpage.htm [I,O,RP,L]
   ```

To 301 Redirect a non-www domain to the www domain in ISAPI_Rewrite

Follow these steps:

1. **Open the file named** `httpd.ini` **located at the root of the non-www version of your website (the site from which you're redirecting).**

2. **Type the appropriate code into the file.**

   Follow this example, which redirects `http://domain.com` to `www.domain.com` (be sure to substitute your domain name):

   ```
   RewriteCond Host: ^mydomain\.com
   RewriteRule (.*) http\://www\.mydomain\.com$1 [I,RP]
   ```

How to move a site to a new host

Occasionally, you may need to change hosting providers or move your site to a new IP address. Your domain name stays the same, but you must communicate your new *IP address* (the numeric code that identifies the logical address where your site resides on the web) to the Internet at large. There can be a delay before all computers see your new location because of the way DNS servers *cache* (store) domain information. (A *domain name system [DNS] server* is an authoritative database that publishes information about the various domains assigned to it, which the rest of the Internet can see.)

The following procedure can help you minimize the downtime and confusion that your site may experience while your new DNS information is being propagated. Refer to the following figure and follow the path numbers as you read the corresponding numbered steps.

To move a site to a new hosting provider, follow these steps:

1. **Modify the DNS on your new host to point to your existing (old host) site first.**

   Don't skip this important first step.

2. **Change the *TLD* (top-level domain) information at your *domain registrar* (the company where you registered your domain name) to point to your new site DNS.**

   Your old site should still show by either IP or domain name. This step starts propagating your new DNS information to DNS servers worldwide.

   Although the actual length of time varies, depending on when each server next grabs its update, it's a safe bet that the whole process will take up to 72 hours to complete. Therefore, you shouldn't proceed with the next steps until waiting about four days.

3. **Copy your existing site to your new site and then validate that all files have transferred and that the links work.**

4. **After waiting the four days for your new DNS information to be propagated, point your new DNS to your new site.**

5. **Check to confirm that your old site's mailboxes have been emptied before you change any DNS information.**

   After this DNS change occurs, you won't be able to retrieve your old mail.

6. **After everything has been validated, point the old DNS to your new site.**

   This is for safety, just in case you run into a propagation problem.

Using Alternate Ways to Redirect a Page

If you're just skimming through this chapter because you don't have access to your server configuration files (the .htaccess file on Apache, the nginx.conf file on NGINX, or your Windows IIS Manager), fear not! There are other solutions that enable you to redirect web pages. One easy solution is available only to sites built in the WordPress content management system. The other solution can be implemented on any site. These are a bit more tedious than the other methods described in this chapter, but they work.

Implementing a 301 Redirect with header inserts

An alternative way to implement 301 Redirects is by adding code directly into the page you want to redirect. Yes, it means opening and modifying each page individually, but sometimes that kind of granular control is a good thing — especially if you only need to redirect a few pages. Called a *header insert,* this method involves placing a small amount of server code into the HTML of each page you want to permanently redirect to another URL.

Most web programming languages allow you to add a header insert on a page. Note that all these languages are *server side,* meaning that they're compiled or interpreted on the server into a page and then the compiled version is sent back to the user's browser. This type of 301 Redirect involves modifying the *response header* information on a page (extra information that's passed from the server to the browser, which helps the browser display the page properly but which is not visible to users). So you must insert the code at the very top of your page's HTML code (on line #1) for the 301 to work. This ensures that the server sees this code first before sending the page back to the user.

Book VII Chapter 4

Implementing 301 Redirects

For your reference, we've compiled a list of the most common programming languages and given sample code for each. Note that the examples are case sensitive, so you want to follow their use of uppercase and lowercase characters exactly. Based on which programming language your website uses, you can refer to the correct example in the upcoming sections to see a header insert that accomplishes a 301 Redirect in your programming language.

PHP 301 Redirect

The PHP scripting language is widely used for creating web pages. (PHP originally stood for Personal Home Page, but it's grown a lot since its infancy in the mid-1990s.) Some attributes of PHP are that it

✦ Is usually used with Apache web servers, but can also work with IIS

✦ Has really good community support and several plug-ins/frameworks that make it pretty easy to use

✦ Is fairly fast

Here's the sample 301 Redirect code for PHP:

```
<?php
header("HTTP/1.1 301 Moved Permanently");
header("Location: http://www.mydomain.com/newpage.php");
exit();
?>
```

ASP 301 Redirect

ASP stands for Active Server Pages, which is Microsoft's original server-side script environment. Developed to run with Microsoft's Internet Information Server (IIS) version 3.0 Web server software, it's admittedly an old program, but many websites still use it. (Note that Microsoft is currently vending IIS Version 8.) Some attributes of ASP include the following:

✦ Works with IIS servers. With the advent of ASP.NET development, most ASP scripts are being upgraded to ASP.NET.

✦ Is backed by Microsoft, so the support is pretty good. There are a lot of good examples and scripts to use and customize.

✦ Is fairly fast.

Here's sample 301 Redirect code for ASP:

```
<%
Response.Status = "301 Moved Permanently"
Response.AddHeader "Location", "http://www.mydomain.com/
   newpage.asp"%>
```

ASP.NET 301 Redirect

ASP.NET is a free website-building technology available from Microsoft. Some attributes of ASP .NET are that it

✦ Is almost always used with IIS servers. This technology also works with Apache servers that have the MONO extension installed.

✦ Has great support from Microsoft.

✦ Has good speed, overall. The initial request may take a little longer while the application puts everything together, but after that's done, it's fast.

The following sample 301 Redirect code for ASP.NET must be inserted in the .aspx file:

```
<script runat="server"
private void Page_Load(object sender, System.EventArgs e)
```

```
{
Response.Status = "301 Moved Permanently";
Response.AddHeader("Location","http://www.mydomain.com/
    newpage.aspx");
}
</script>
```

JSP 301 Redirect

JSP stands for JavaServer Pages, which is a Java-based web development technology. Here are some attributes of JSP:

✦ Usually used on the Apache Tomcat web server.

✦ Supported by Sun and an open-source community. It has excellent documentation.

✦ Is pretty fast, with the initial request taking a little longer while the application puts everything together.

Here's some sample code for a 301 Redirect on JSP:

```
<%
response.setStatus(301);
response.setHeader("Location","http://www.mydomain.com/
    newpage.jsp");
response.setHeader("Connection","close");
%>
```

ColdFusion 301 Redirect

Now an Adobe product, ColdFusion is another programming language frequently used for web pages. Here are some attributes of ColdFusion:

✦ Usually hosted through a Microsoft IIS web server, but can also be run in Apache.

✦ Made and supported by Adobe. You can find adequate documentation for it.

✦ Has okay, but not great, speed.

ColdFusion 8 or later versions require 301 Redirects to be written like this:

```
<cflocation url="http://www.mydomain.com/newpage.cfm"
    addToken="no" statusCode="301">
```

ColdFusion 7 or earlier versions require 301 Redirects to be written like this:

```
<cfheader statuscode="301" statusnext="Moved Permanently"
<cfheader name="Location" value="http://www.mydomain.com/
    newpage.cfm">
```

CGI Perl 301 Redirect

Some websites are built by using CGI (Common Gateway Interface) scripting in the Perl programming language. Some attributes of CGI Perl are

✦ Perl can be run on anything, but it is usually run through an Apache web server.

✦ Perl has been around for a very long time, which makes finding examples and documentation easy. There are a lot of modules that you can use to help with specific tasks.

✦ The speed isn't as good as some of the other, newer languages, but it still delivers fast enough web responses.

Here's sample 301 Redirect code for CGI Perl:

```
$q = new CGI;
print $q->redirect( -uri =>

"http://www.mydomain.com/newpage.cgi", -nph => 1, -status =>
    301);
```

Ruby on Rails 301 Redirect

The Ruby on Rails web development tool is specifically designed for building database-backed web applications. Attributes of Ruby on Rails include

✦ Fast application development. It can run through the IIS and Apache web servers but requires a back-end server such as Mongrel, as well.

✦ Ruby on Rails is a relatively new language. You can find reliable documentation and community support.

✦ The speed isn't as fast as some other scripting languages.

Here's sample 301 Redirect code for Ruby on Rails:

```
headers["Status"] = "301 Moved Permanently"
redirect_to "http://www.mydomain.com/newpage/"
```

Implementing a 301 Redirect on a WordPress site

If your site uses WordPress as a *content management system* (software that lets you publish and maintain a website from a central location), your life is good! Although 301 Redirects can be put in place through a WordPress site's server configuration files, if you don't have access to your server configuration files (or if you don't want to mess with code — thanks, WordPress!), there's a plug-in for that. One of the nice things about websites built on the WordPress platform is the vast library of modules, called *plug-ins,* that modify the way the website works. With the click of a button, you can install a plug-in to handle the redirects for you.

Many excellent plug-ins are available for handling redirects. You simply need to search the WordPress Plugin Directory (`https://wordpress.org/plugins/`) for a redirection plug-in that will handle 301 Redirects. Look for one that has a high star rating and a high number of sites actively using it; these are good signs that the plug-in is trustworthy and easy to use. One such plug-in, named Simple 301 Redirects, has more than 100,000 active installs and a rating of 4.5 out of 5 stars.

Be sure to keep any plug-ins that are installed on your WordPress site updated. A plug-in that is not maintained can leave your site open to hacking and malware. If any of your plug-ins require updating, you see a little red number next to Plugins in the navigation when you're signed in to WordPress.

**Book VII
Chapter 4**

**Implementing
301 Redirects**

Chapter 5: Watching Your Backend: Content Management System Troubles

In This Chapter

✔ **Meeting the content management system (CMS)**

✔ **Avoiding the problems caused by dynamic URLs and session IDs**

✔ **Selecting a good CMS**

✔ **Making your CMS work with your search engine optimization (SEO) efforts**

✔ **Using hosted e-commerce solutions effectively**

✔ **Helping search engines read a website built completely in JavaScript**

*B*ehind every web page viewed in a browser is a host of technologies and services known as the *backend* that work to make the star performers look good. Just as a Hollywood blockbuster has a crew of people supporting the actors, your website has servers, code, shopping carts, and, most important, your content management system, which all must perform at their best to turn out a superior experience for your customers. A web *content management system* (CMS) is a software program that helps simplify website creation. A CMS uses a database (such as your database of products, if you have a store) and publishes web pages in an orderly, consistent fashion. One thing a CMS can do is pull information from your database and build pages *dynamically,* which means the pages don't actually exist until someone asks for them. If you have 10,000 products, you don't want to build 10,000 individual pages by hand. Instead, you can use a CMS to build them dynamically on the fly.

In this chapter, you discover some common problems that may occur when using a CMS to build your website. For all their advantages, content management systems demand some attention to get in line with your search engine optimization (SEO) efforts. You also can discover some technical solutions that can help you overcome these CMS issues, such as rewriting URLs to have names that are more search engine–friendly. We also give you tips for picking a good CMS and how to modify its settings to work better for SEO. For those of you who use a hosted e-commerce solution for your website, like the Yahoo Store, we tackle how to optimize those product pages. Last, we warn you about the JavaScript website framework that is growing in popularity but risky for search indexing and rankings — along with what you can do to improve a JavaScript site's SEO friendliness.

Avoiding SEO Problems Caused by Content Management Systems

Content management systems can be a website owner's best friend. A CMS gets a website operational fast and keeps it running smoothly. It can manage data, image files, audio files, documents, and other types of content, and it puts them together into web pages. A CMS creates the pages based on *templates,* which are standard layouts that you design, so that your website has a consistent and cohesive look. Large sites that manage thousands of items use a CMS because it keeps everything organized and systematic. Small-site owners benefit because if they use a CMS, they don't even have to know *HTML* (HyperText Markup Language, the predominant markup language used on the web): The CMS can do the technical work for them.

There is a catch, however. With automation comes a loss of control. When an airline pilot puts his plane on autopilot, the computer takes over completely and flies the plane according to a set course, adjusting things like altitude and speed based on its preprogrammed settings. If the plane needs to land unexpectedly, the pilot first has to take it out of autopilot mode. Otherwise, the autopilot stubbornly keeps the plane on its predetermined course.

Similarly, you don't want to run a CMS on autopilot. In order to optimize your website for the search engines, you must be able to customize your pages down to the smallest detail, and catch and manage any machine-generated issues that work against your SEO efforts.

Understanding why dynamically generated pages can be friend or foe

If you have a store with several thousand products for sale, you don't want to create a page for each item by hand. Instead, you're going to use a CMS to assemble web pages with product descriptions, pictures, prices, and other content pulled directly out of your product database. These dynamic pages look unique to the end user, but behind the scenes, they're usually not.

For your pages to rank well in search engines, they must be unique. Search engines want to give their users a selection of relevant results. The search engine isn't doing a very good job if half of the first ten search results all point to the same content. Instead, search engines try to give users a choice by offering results, each dealing uniquely with the *keywords* (the word or phrase the user searched for). So, the search engines are always on the lookout for *duplicate content* (web pages that contain some or all of the same text). When they identify duplicate content, they keep what they think is the most authoritative version and throw out the rest. Because of this, pages that are too similar run the risk of being excluded from search engine results pages (SERPs) altogether.

CMSs may create all kinds of duplicate content problems. If not looked after, they may build *nontargeted content,* or generic text that isn't customized for your various subject themes and keywords. You want to make sure *each and every one* of your web pages has *unique* text for all parts of your web pages, including

✦ **Title tags:** The `Title` *tag* is part of the HTML code behind each web page, and the search engines pay a lot of attention to it. The `Title` tag usually gets displayed as the bold heading in a SERP result, so it should specifically contain that page's keywords.

   If you don't specify otherwise, CMSs often put the same `Title` tag on every page. It might be the company name, the *domain name* (the root part of the website URL, such as `wiley.com`), or the company name plus a few keywords applied as one-size-fits-all.

✦ **Meta tags:** Your `Meta` description and `Meta` keywords HTML tags also need to be different on every page. The `Meta` description is often what shows in your SERP result as the two-line description. The `Meta` keywords tag needs to contain the keywords that are specific to that page. Out of the box, your CMS can't be trusted to build these `Meta` tags in an SEO-friendly way.

✦ **Headings:** Your H# heading tags are HTML-style codes applied to your page's headings and subheadings to make them stand out. The search engines look at these heading tags as clues to what a page's main points are. They need to be keyword-rich and unique.

   A CMS may create heading tags that are generic (such as Features Overview or More Details) rather than specific and full of your targeted keywords.

Dealing with dynamic URLs and session IDs

Content management systems create pages that search engines may consider duplicates in another way, and that's through dynamic *URLs* (the web addresses of pages, usually starting with `http://` or `https://`).

There are ways to set up a CMS to build the URL string dynamically for every page request. Dynamic URLs created by a CMS often contain *variables* (characters that vary). When variables are added to the end of a URL, it forms a

Book VII
Chapter 5

Watching Your
Backend: Content
Management
System Troubles

new URL. If the search engines think each URL is a distinct page, duplicate content issues may arise when the same content shows up under many different URLs.

Here are two common types of variables that CMSs often add to URLs, but there are many others:

✦ **Session IDs:** Many CMSs add a session ID code to the end of URLs as a user travels through the site. The purpose is to track the user's *session* (the time period the user has been active on the website), but appending the session ID to the URL causes every view of every page to have a different URL.

✦ **Categories:** Products can be classified in many ways. For instance, an online shoe store could let users search by style, color, size, price, and so forth. Giving users many different paths to get to the same pair of shoes is good for your business and your users, but your CMS needs to handle it correctly. You don't want the same product page to end up displaying under multiple URLs. For example, the two following URLs would both point to the same content, but the URLs differ because the CMS put the parameters for color and brand in a different order based on the user's selection path:

```
www.shoe-site.com/pumps.asp?color=red&brand=myers
www.shoe-site.com/pumps.asp?brand=myers&color=red
```

There are many good reasons not to like dynamic URLs:

✦ **They can cause duplicate content.** As we mention in the preceding list, you can end up with different URLs having the same page content because their parameters vary.

✦ **They aren't user friendly.** Dynamic URLs usually include *query strings,* which are the parts of a URL that pass data to a page. Query strings aren't readable because they contain symbols (such as ?, &, and +) as well as codes, session IDs, and so on. They look messy or, worse, intimidating to your human visitors.

✦ **They're long.** Dynamic URLs with query strings end up being really long and cumbersome. These URLs are impossible to remember and difficult to type. Studies have shown that long URLs on search results pages aren't clicked as often as shorter, understandable URLs, so your long URLs could actually be driving business away from your site.

✦ **They can confuse search engines.** *Static URLs* (URLs that don't change) are easy to crawl and index, and thus are preferred by the search engines. If a URL has a long string of parameters, the spider may just stop right there and not even crawl the page. (***Note:*** The big three search engines have given webmasters a way to suggest what parameters to ignore.) So, if you're using dynamic URLs, make the search engine spider's job as easy as possible by setting up URL parameters to ignore in Google and Bing Webmaster Tools. We tell you about ways to set up URL parameters in the upcoming sections.

✦ **They could be bad for your SEO.** If the search engines give up on an overly complex URL and don't crawl your page, that page doesn't end up in their *indexes* (databases of web pages that search engines maintain), which means that searchers won't be able to find it.

The best condition for search engine optimization is to *have one static URL per unique page.* Where the page content remains unchanged, there should be no change to the URL. You don't want to put any variables directly into your URL strings except for ones that actually correspond with changed page content. You need unique content for every URL.

Now that we've made a case against the use of dynamic URLs, we want to explain how you can compensate for them on your website.

Specify parameters to ignore in webmaster tools

One way to address the search engine indexing issues that result from parameters in dynamic URLs is to tell search engines any and all parameters to ignore. The major search engines have made it possible for you to tell them when parameters caused by dynamically loaded pages should be ignored for crawling and indexing purposes. This trick works in Google, Bing, and Yahoo by way of Bing. (As of 2009, Bing and Yahoo share the same crawlers and index.)

Know that the search engines already try to detect duplicate content caused by URL parameters. They group detected duplicate pages into a cluster and do some fancy detective work to pick the best URL to represent the cluster in search results. They also consolidate ranking and relevance signals to that page. If your parameters are kept to a minimum, the search engine is likely to pick the right version of the URL as the *canonical,* or preferred, version of a page. But the search engines are just machines, and they can get things wrong. It's much better for you, the wise human webmaster, to tell the robots what URL is the canonical version of a page and which dynamically generated URLs are none of their business.

Bing's Ignore URL Parameters tool is in the Configure My Site section of the free Bing Webmaster Tools (`http://www.bing.com/toolbox/webmaster`). From here, you can submit the exact parameters that are causing multiple variations of a URL pointing to the same page. Here you also find parameters that Bingbot has come across while crawling your site

Book VII
Chapter 5

Watching Your
Backend: Content
Management
System Troubles

and that it thinks may be safe to ignore. Just click the suggested parameter to add it to your list of URL parameters to ignore.

Google's URL Parameters tool is also free to use as part of Google Search Console (`https://www.google.com/webmasters/tools/crawl-url-parameters`). From your site dashboard, go to Crawl and then URL Parameters in the navigation. From here, click Add parameter or select from the parameters listed. Google asks for a little more information here than Bing does. The next step is to indicate whether that parameter is active or passive. An *active* parameter changes the actual content displayed on the page, for example, by narrowing the page content the way a pagination parameter does. A *passive* parameter, which is commonly a session ID or affiliate ID, doesn't impact the page. If the parameter you're adding is passive, you click Save. If you're adding an active parameter, next pick an option for how you want Google to treat the parameter. These are your options:

✦ **Let Googlebot decide:** If you pick this, Google will do its best to decide whether to crawl and index the URL.

✦ **Every URL:** This setting tells Google that you want every URL with this parameter to be counted as a separate page. So rather than eliminating duplicates, you tell Google that a page with this parameter is unique and worth indexing.

✦ **Only URLs with specified value:** Choose this if you want Google to crawl only one value of a parameter with multiple value options. An example is if you want Google to crawl a page sorted by pricing from low to high and ignore the same page sorted by pricing from high to low.

✦ **No URLs:** With this setting, Google won't crawl any page if this parameter is in the URL.

Your last step in using the Google URL Parameters tool is to tell Google which version of a page with parameters is the canonical, your preferred version for serving in results and consolidating ranking signals. (***Note:*** If the canonical page you specify has significantly different content than a URL with parameters, Google reserves the right to ignore your indications and keep the page indexed. Oh, that know-it-all Google.)

Rewriting URLs

Another option you have if your CMS insists on building URLs that are long and ugly, is to go over its head and rewrite the URLs at the web server layer. (The *web server* is the software application that runs your website, which receives each user request and serves back the requested pages to the user's browser.) An advantage of this solution is that the search engines will never see the URLs with parameters and have the chance to crawl and index them (provided that redirects are in place and your URLs with parameters aren't linked to anywhere).

At the *server layer* (the viewable layer, or how the URL appears to the user and to search engines), you can rewrite complex URLs as clean, concise, static-looking URLs. Rewriting doesn't change the name of a physical file on your web server or create new directories that don't physically exist. But rewriting changes the page's URL on the server layer and appears on the presentation layer. So, for example, if you have a shoe website and your CMS spits out product pages that have long, parameter-laden URLs, like this:

```
http://www.shoe-site.com/product.cfm?product_id=1234&line=wom
    ens&style=pumps&color=navyblue&size=7
```

you could rewrite them to something simpler, like this:

```
http://www.shoe-site.com/womens/pumps/productname.cfm
```

Notice how much more readable the rewritten URL is. This directory structure shown is just an example, but it illustrates how you can potentially have the domain name, directories, and the filename give information about the web page. In this case, not only have you gotten rid of the ugly query string, but also the directories "women's" and "pumps" are short, understandable labels. People seeing this URL have a good idea what the web page contains before they even click to view it. Presenting a concise, informative URL like this to search engines can increase your web page's ranking — you've basically got the makings of a keyword phrase right in the URL. Additionally, presenting this type of short, readable URL to users can also make them more likely to click to your page from a SERP, which increases traffic to your site.

The process of rewriting a URL is often called a *mod_rewrite,* which stands for module rewrite because that's what it was originally called on the Apache server. Today, that term is used generally to refer to any URL rewrite, regardless of which server brand is involved. You need someone who's trained to work with your server software to create mod_rewrites. If you're determined to try it out yourself, we list a few websites that you can look at for reference, based on your server:

Book VII
Chapter 5

Watching Your
Backend: Content
Management
System Troubles

✦ **Apache server:** The Apache website has full documentation on how to do mod_rewrites (`http://httpd.apache.org/docs/2.0/mod/mod_rewrite.html`).

✦ **NGINX server:** The NGINX rewrite documentation is available online (`http://nginx.org/en/docs/http/ngx_http_rewrite_module.html`).

✦ **Microsoft IIS server version 6.0 or earlier:** You need to install an ISAPI_ Rewrite plug-in in order to rewrite your URLs. We recommend the one from Helicon Tech (`www.isapirewrite.com`). From the same site, you can access extensive documentation that includes a lot of examples.

✦ **Microsoft IIS server version 7.0 and later:** You can install the Microsoft URL Rewrite Module that can be downloaded and installed into IIS 7.0 or 8.0 (`http://www.iis.net/download/URLRewrite`).

When you rewrite web pages to new URLs, you also need to redirect the old URLs if they are already indexed with the search engines. (A *redirect* is a server directive that automatically forwards incoming links to a different page.) One SEO rule of thumb is that whenever you remove a page that's been indexed, you must redirect it with a 301 (permanent) Redirect to another page. That way, the search engines and any visitors linking to the old page are automatically sent somewhere new. You also don't lose the *link equity* (value of the incoming links, which the search engines count toward your page's authority) from whatever links may exist on external websites that point to your old URLs. (We cover redirects in Chapters 3 and 4 of this minibook, so check those chapters if you want more information.)

Managing URL parameters for search engines in other ways

Here are some other solutions for dynamic URLs:

✦ **Remove session IDs.** If your site passes session IDs through the URL string, you may be able to correct your CMS or server application so that it no longer does this (using cookies or some other technology). If that's not possible, consider using user-agent sniffing to detect search engine spiders, or try the link `rel=canonical` tag that we discuss in Chapter 4 of this minibook. When the page detects a search engine spider, the exact same content could be displayed, but in a parameter-free URL instead.

✦ **Control the parameter order.** Make sure your CMS allows for ordering logic. You need to specify the sequence of parameters in URLs. One product could fall into many different categories on your website, but no matter how the user navigates to find it, that unique product should have only one page at only one URL address.

✦ **Limit the number of parameters.** If possible, keep the number of parameters being passed to a minimum. If you can limit it to one parameter in a URL, the search engines should be able to spider your pages and accurately detect a canonical version to show in search results. Plus users won't find them too intimidating. Here's a sample URL with one parameter:

    http://www.yourdomain.com/product.cfm?product_id=xyz

Choosing the Right Content Management System

Despite the extra maintenance a content management system may require to keep your site SEO-friendly, many websites simply can't do without one. For large stores, social media sites, forums, and other sites that have a large amount of page content that changes frequently, a CMS that can produce a site dynamically is a practical necessity.

To ensure that a CMS won't *impede* your SEO efforts, the main thing you want to find is a customizable system. You need to be able to change anything and everything on a per-page basis and not have your hands tied. SEO requires a lot of tweaking as you monitor each page's performance, your competitors' pages, the user experience on your site, and so forth. You must be able to modify a `Title` tag here, a `Meta` keywords tag there.

Here are some attributes to look for when you're shopping for a CMS:

✦ **Customizable look and feel:** This isn't SEO really, but it's important nevertheless — you want to be able to choose a "look" for your site that fits your subject matter and appeals to your audience. We've already discussed minimizing bounce rates and increasing conversions. If the design turns off your target visitors, or if it looks like a bunch of other sites, you're sabotaged from the start. Be sure that you can modify the HTML *templates* (page layouts) and *CSS styles* (formatting of fonts and so on, using Cascading Style Sheets) so that you can ensure an appropriate look and feel that's consistent throughout your site.

✦ **Mobile-friendly:** If you plan to use a theme that the CMS offers to stylize the look of the site, make sure that it's mobile-friendly. You likely want a

Book VII
Chapter 5

**Watching Your
Backend: Content
Management
System Troubles**

Which CMS is best for SEO?

We wish that we could come right out and tell you which CMS we recommend. But we can't. The CMS that's right for one site doesn't necessarily work for another. They have different features and capabilities, and you have to choose one based on what your site needs. Thankfully, SEO friendliness is a feature of most CMSs today. The basic abilities to customize titles and descriptions, customize directory structure and URLs, and add analytics tracking codes are even available in free hosted solutions. Many options are available to businesses today when it comes to SEO-friendly CMSs, so as you're doing your homework to pick the content management system for your website, look at all the features and functions a CMS provides (including SEO-minded customization, of course).

responsive design that adjusts the navigation and layout of pages when visitors are on a mobile device. Book IV, Chapter 3 is dedicated to how to build a mobile-friendly site.

✦ **Ability to externalize CSS and JavaScript:** Your CMS must be able to set up external JS and CSS files. You need to externalize it to keep your code nice and tidy and keep your pages running fast. Plus, if your CSS is externalized, you have to make changes to only one file instead of hand-editing every single page each and every time you want to tweak the look of your site.

✦ **Customizable directory structure:** You want to be able to control how your files and directories are organized. Ideally, when you categorize your website into subject themes (which we call *siloing*), it's reflected in the physical file structure, as well as in your internal linking scheme. Deciding how to categorize your website is an SEO activity, based on how people search and what brings in the most traffic. You don't want your CMS dictating, for example, that your files should be organized by brand and then by product type, if your SEO research tells you that you'll get more search traffic organizing by product type and then by brand. (For more on how to silo your site, see Book VI.)

✦ **Customizable page elements:** Your CMS must allow you to customize the Title tag, Meta description tag, Meta keywords tag, H# heading tags, link *anchor text,* image Alt attributes, and every other element on your pages. You need this flexibility for every page, whenever you see fit.

✦ **Customizable HTML output:** You need to be able to control the HTML output of pages on your site. How the HTML is structured matters because that's where the search engine spiders crawl. You want to control, for example, the order of tags in the Head section (Title at the top, followed by description, keywords, and then any other Meta tags you need). You may also need to do *content stacking,* which moves large blocks of HTML coding down to the bottom of the page so that the spiders can get to your rich text content as soon as possible. You want to ensure the other SEO-friendly guidelines are followed, such as using an external CSS file to control formatting and an external JS file to house JavaScript if that's used on your site.

✦ **Ability to include analytics tracking codes:** You need to know what's happening to your site, where your visitors are from, where they're going, and how they behave. You also need to follow each visitor through a conversion.

✦ **Customizable rules:** Your CMS should let you specify rules that can be applied across lots of pages at once, especially if you have a site with thousands of products. You don't want any factory presets spitting out the same Title tag on every page, for example. Instead, you should be able to write a rule for how each product page's Title tag should be created to ensure each tag is unique and SEO-friendly (for example, Item Category Brand or Category Item), and you should have the ability to change any element by hand if deemed necessary.

Customization is crucial for your search engine optimization. You *need* a CMS that allows for customization of every single element on your website. Period. You also want a website that loads fast, provides a good mobile experience, and lets your pages be easily spidered — also issues that can come down to your CMS. Google has created a guide to help site owners ensure SEO and mobile friendliness for the most popular CMSs, including WordPress, Drupal, Magento, and Joomla! (`https://developers.google.com/webmasters/mobile-sites/website-software/`).

Customizing Your CMS for SEO

The shopping list we just laid out can help you pick out a good CMS if you plan to purchase one. Or, if you already have a website that runs on a CMS, the preceding section should help you figure out the strengths or weaknesses of that purchase. Better yet, if your site doesn't have lots of changing content, you can avoid the CMS issue altogether and code the whole website from scratch! But for those websites that need a content management system, this section gives you tips for making your CMS work for you.

The two main principles are

✦ Set up rules that make every page have the ability to exist with unique SEO elements.

✦ Customize these individual page elements as needed to optimize them against the competition for the search engines.

**Book VII
Chapter 5**

Watching Your
Backend: Content
Management
System Troubles

Creating rules for each of your important SEO elements is a key part of making a CMS work for you. You should be able to define how the CMS puts together the `Title` tags, `Meta` description and keywords tags, heading tags, hyperlink anchor text, image `Alt` attributes, and everything else on your pages.

For instance, if you have an e-commerce store, you have many fields in your database that pertain to each product, such as the product name, product ID, and product description. You've also done some categorization work and probably have each product assigned to a product category, style, type, size, color, flavor . . . you get the idea.

Often, manufacturers require that all retailers use their predefined product descriptions. You might be struggling with this very same problem because obviously it's hard to rank well for product searches if your page just duplicates the same text shown on countless other sites. Here's what we suggest you can do to make your product pages stand above the rest:

✦ In addition to the mandatory product description, include more descriptive text on the product page itself. How-to instructions, useful historical information, even just a paragraph about a hands-on viewpoint are all options for adding keyword-rich content.

✦ Make sure that you fully optimize the other on-page factors and use these to help increase keyword effectiveness on the page.

✦ Make sure that the image `Alt` attribute is unique and contains keywords.

✦ Customize the `Title`, `Meta` description, and `Meta` keywords tags on the page.

✦ Enable users to write product reviews on your site. User-generated content (UGC) adds text about the product in the users' own words, which can potentially match more search queries and adds more unique content to a page.

Create rules that define how the `Title` tag, `Meta` description tag, and `Meta` keywords tag should be put together on each product page. These rules should produce tags that meet the best practice guidelines for SEO, including the proper length, capitalization, ordering, and so on. (You can find best practice details in Book V, Chapter 3.)

Also, create rules that apply `H#` heading tags appropriately throughout your page. Headings should be hierarchical, with an `H1` at the top of the page and other heading tags (`H2`, `H3`, and so on) throughout the page. Search engines look at the heading tags to confirm that the keywords shown in the `Title` and `Meta` tags at the top are accurate, so make sure that they contain the page's main keywords and are unique to that page.

You should specify rules for every output element possible. You want to take advantage of the CMS's ability to automate your site, but you also want to control that efficiency. Make sure that your resulting site is search engine–friendly and user-friendly, full of pages that are each unique.

After you have rules set up for how the CMS should construct your pages, the second part is customization. You should be able to tweak individual pages, applying all the SEO principles covered throughout this book as needed. Here are a few scenarios to consider:

✦ **Single-page tweaking:** Your online shoe store might carry a shoe that's a hot seller in brick-and-mortar stores, but for some reason, you aren't getting much traffic for it online. You might want to do some competitive research and keyword research, and then manually modify the keywords in the tags and body copy of that particular product page to see if you can improve sales through that page. (You could also consider creative marketing options to attract more business for that product, such as adding supporting pages with articles, video, images, reviews, links, and so on.)

✦ **Long-tail keyword targeting:** If your tags and headings contain specific product information, this information helps you rank well for *long-tail* *queries* (search queries that contain multiple specific terms, rather than generic words). For instance, someone who searches for a particular shoe by using a specific search such as [Rockport Navigation Point brown] tends to be a serious shopper ready to make a purchase. You want to optimize your pages for long-tail queries because the low amount of traffic they generate is offset by the high potential for conversion. Make sure that your CMS doesn't build only generic tags and headings.

✦ **Generic word targeting:** To balance out the preceding scenario, you also may want to bring in more traffic to your site by optimizing for generic words and phrases. For instance, the pages on your shoe store site that have Rockports could also be optimized for the phrases [Rockport shoes] or [mens shoes] or [leather shoes]. In those cases, you want the ability to tweak certain things on the individual pages in order to rank for generic keywords as well and to capture more traffic to your site.

SEO is often a balancing act. Those last two bullet points illustrate this — these two scenarios explain why you want to optimize the same shoe product page for specific (long-tail) keywords and for generic keywords simultaneously. To practice effective SEO, you must be able to override the default output created by the CMS and modify individual pages as needed.

Optimizing Your Hosted E-Commerce Site

Book VII
Chapter 5

Watching Your
Backend: Content
Management
System Troubles

Many service providers make it easy for people use to set up an e-commerce storefront quickly. Online options for proprietors range from joining an online marketplace (like Etsy for retailers and Fiverr for those offering creative services) to building your own website. You can run your online storefront on your own domain; some e-commerce platforms offer store owners design templates, easy wizards for inputting products, and functionality to accept credit card, debit card, and PayPal payments. These e-commerce content management systems come in two flavors: hosted and self-hosted. With a *self-hosted* e-commerce platform, you get software to build and manage your site, but you have to get your own web host. One popular self-hosted e-commerce CMS is Magento. The SEO concerns and considerations for such websites are covered throughout this chapter.

What you should know about SEO considerations of a *hosted* e-commerce solution (which means that the same company that you use to create and manage your website also hosts it) is a little different. The biggest difference affecting your SEO campaign if you're using what's sometimes called an e-commerce service system is a loss of flexibility — you're limited to the constraints of the shopping cart software and the provided hosting. On the upside, a hosted e-commerce platform is an attractive solution for small and mid-sized retailers because it gives you just one vendor to turn to for all website support. Hosted e-commerce platforms include Yahoo Small Business (`https://smallbusiness.yahoo.com/ecommerce`), Shopify (`www.shopify.com/`), Squarespace (`www.squarespace.com`), and Wix (`www.wix.com`).

If you've got a site built with a hosted e-commerce service, read on: This section shows you how to get the most SEO value out of your hosted online store.

It *is* possible to make a hosted store rank highly for certain keywords. You can modify things, such as the look of the site, the domain name, and some of the important page elements. When you're researching hosted e-commerce solutions, check to see whether you have control over as many of the following as possible:

✦ **Domain name:** If you want your store to rank in the search engines, you should use your own domain. Register a good domain name (see Chapter 2 of this minibook for some guidelines) and then set up your store using the platform's provided domain settings.

✦ `Title` **tags:** Because the `Title` tag is a key indicator to the search engines of what your page is about, you want the ability to customize what shows up in your `Title` tags so that they are each unique, have an appropriate length, and contain the keywords you're trying to rank for in the search engines. A good hosted e-commerce solution lets you edit your `Title` tags individually and manually.

✦ `Meta` **tags:** A hosted platform may create `Meta` description and `Meta` keywords tags by default. You'll want the ability to modify them as needed.

For guidelines on how to write effective `Title`, `Meta` description, and `Meta` keywords tags that help your pages rank with the search engines, see Book IV, Chapter 4.

✦ **Custom URLs:** Being able to control the URLs to include keywords, make sure that they're not too long, and support your themed architecture is important for SEO.

✦ **Organization of products by category:** For *siloing* (a way of organizing your content into themes through site architecture and linking, covered in Book VI), you want to be able to separate products into categories.

✦ **301 Redirects:** You want to be able to put in place 301 Redirects, the best way to tell search engines that a page has been removed and replaced by a new page.

✦ **Robots text (`robots.txt`) file:** Your `robots.txt` file instructs the search engine spiders which pages not to index and where to find your *sitemap* (a file that lists the pages in your website, linked so that spiders can easily navigate). An SEO-friendly hosted store will let you customize your `robots.txt` file.

✦ **Sitemap:** An XML sitemap page that's invisible to users but available to the search engines is critical to getting your site crawled and indexed by search engines. Check that your hosted e-commerce platform generates and links a proper `sitemap.xml`, listing every single URL on your site. If you choose to use a JavaScript-heavy template, the XML sitemap should allow for complete indexing of all pages. See what a sitemap should do in Book VI, Chapter 3.

✦ **Custom 404 Error page:** Understand how your hosted store handles the 404 server status (the error code that means the page isn't found) when a user tries to access a page that doesn't exist. You want control over the content of the 404 Error page and where error pages may redirect. (For help building a custom 404 Error page, see Chapter 1 of this minibook.)

An SEO checklist for hosted stores

To optimize your hosted store, you should approach it like any website optimization project. Go through this checklist of items we explain throughout this minibook:

✔ Know clearly what your site is about, who your target audience is, and what your site's goals are.

✔ Inventory your site and your off-site resources (such as printed material) to see what kind of content you can add to enhance your site's subject relevance.

✔ Do keyword brainstorming and research to determine for what words and phrases you want to optimize.

✔ Do competitor research for those keywords, looking for opportunities to move your pages up in the search engine rankings.

✔ Silo your site by establishing clear subject themes between related pages through linking.

✔ Examine your pages (using tools) and then work to improve the on-page elements like text content, headings, and `Meta` tags, optimizing for your keywords.

✔ Make sure every page, heading, and tag is unique.

✔ Create a keyword-rich sitemap.

✔ Implement good navigation links throughout the site that pass link equity to the main pages that you want to rank well and give users an easy way to move through the site.

✔ Consolidate different domains into one (such as the non-www and www versions of your domain) to avoid having duplicate content.

✔ Monitor, analyze, and continue to go through this checklist, refining and adjusting your site. (Remember, SEO is never finished.)

**Book VII
Chapter 5**

Watching Your
Backend: Content
Management
System Troubles

Avoiding Problems with JavaScript Frameworks

JavaScript frameworks are the new kid on the block in the web development world and are growing in popularity among developers. This method of building a website or application is attractive because JavaScript is a programing language that allows for interactive effects that can look cool and impress your visitors. In the last few years, advancements in modern browsers like Mozilla Firefox and Google Chrome make processing and rendering JavaScript faster than ever. That's why today it's possible to build a whole website or application in JavaScript. But hold your horses! Possible is not the same as recommended, and a website built in a JavaScript framework is problematic from a search engine ranking and visibility standpoint.

To understand the problem, you need to understand that JavaScript frameworks are rendered in the browser only. This is different from traditional web frameworks and content management systems, in which every page load is a separate request to the server. When a website is built in a JavaScript framework, the HTML and content are fetched via JavaScript and put together by the browser. This causes problems for search engine bots.

For one thing, search engine bots don't get the HTML with all the data and content in it. Instead, search engines may see an empty shell of HTML. Among all the search engines, Google has made strides in the area of rendering JavaScript, but even Google crawlers can't execute it the same way a browser does. If your site is rendered in JavaScript, search engines could miss your content and index your pages with as little as an empty HTML template. To see how much of your JavaScript site is lost to Google, use the handy Fetch and Render tool found within the Crawl reports in Google Search Console. Free for all site owners at `www.google.com/webmasters/tools/`, the tool simulates what Googlebot does when it arrives at your web page. (Checking to see your site as Google sees it is covered more in Book IV, Chapter 5.) But don't forget that there are more search engines than Google, and a website built in a JavaScript framework is definitely not friendly to them.

Another issue for your site's search engine rankings is that URLs in this scenario are either not unique or are absent altogether in the case of single-page websites. When a JavaScript application needs to get more data, it uses an AJAX request, which doesn't require a reload of the page to get the data from the server. This means that links to other "pages" and other general assumptions about navigation are thrown out the window! When an entire website's content is essentially contained on one URL, you can't organize content into themed silos with landing pages and support pages. You can't create pages with keyword-specific optimization. You're basically losing the ability to do all the SEO best practices. Ouch.

If your website falls into the category of a JavaScript framework, all is not lost. You have some ways to help make your website more search engine friendly.

✦ **The best way by far is to *pre-render* your content.** Pre-rendering means to give a static, fully rendered HTML copy of your page to the search engines. You can either pre-render your content manually or use a service like Prerender.io (`https://prerender.io/`). Basically, you create a copy of your page as JavaScript renders it in a browser by taking HTML "snapshots" and then make those snapshots available to search engines in a specific way. You can find more info in the Google Developers guide to making AJAX applications crawlable: `https://developers.google.com/webmasters/ajax-crawling/`.

✦ **Make sure that links go to unique URLs.** Make an initial static copy of your content or a pre-rendered version of that content available at those URLs.

✦ **Put initial content into the pages.** This way the search engine will get something — even if it's not everything.

We generally counsel you to stay away from JavaScript frameworks if you want to rank well. But if you have a JavaScript site and are sticking with it, take the steps to help get your content indexed and make ranking possible.

**Book VII
Chapter 5**

**Watching Your
Backend: Content
Management
System Troubles**

Chapter 6: Solving SEO Roadblocks

In This Chapter

✔ **Ensuring that search engines see your site**

✔ **Creating effective sitemaps**

✔ **Avoiding page hijacking from 302 Redirects**

✔ **Handling SEO problems connected with secure sites**

You know the part of an instruction manual that's just labeled Troubleshooting? It's sort of a catchall for problems you might have that don't fit anywhere else in the manual, with tips for what you can do about them. This chapter is sort of like that Troubleshooting section — a place for us to address miscellaneous problems you might run into and give some advice on how to resolve them.

You should look at your search engine optimization (SEO) project as an ongoing process. It's not a journey with a fixed end point. There's no "destination" that you can reach and then hang up your keyboard and mouse and declare, "Ahh . . . we've made it!" Even if you reach the number one spot on the search results, you can't relax; you must continually monitor and fine-tune your site to stay ahead of the competition.

Occasionally, you will hit roadblocks to your SEO progress. Don't confuse these roadblocks with the time lag that normally occurs before results become apparent. Usually, it takes an SEO project three to six months to see a website rise considerably in ranking and traffic, after you put the initial site optimization in place. Of course, results are always based on the keywords and condition of your site when the project starts. Your mileage is going to vary based on the competition. Sometimes, it happens within a few weeks or even a few days, but that's very unusual — normally, results take several months. Some keywords actually take years to rank well.

However, you can run into obstacles with SEO. You might find out that a search engine doesn't have any of your pages in its *index* (database of web pages that a search engine pulls results from). Or you might find your site plummeting down the search engine results for no apparent reason. Or you might have difficulties related to setting up a secure *server* (the software and hardware that runs a website) for parts of your website. In this chapter, you find out what to do when you run into these kinds of roadblocks.

Inviting Spiders to Your Site

You may have pages that are missing from one or more of the search engines, which causes lower or non-existent search engine rankings. If you suspect a specific page is missing, find out for sure by entering a long snippet of text from that page in a search query, enclosed in quotation marks like this: ["Here's a long snippet of text taken directly from the page"]. The quotation marks force the search engine to look for an exact match, so your page should come up in the results if it's in the index at all. (By the way, this is also a great way to find duplicate content from your site.)

You can also check to see how extensively the search engines have indexed your entire website in a single search. To check for this at Google or Bing, enter the search query [site:*yourdomain.com*], replacing *yourdomain.com* with your actual domain (and removing the brackets). You can also gain intelligence about how the search engines have indexed your site using Index Explorer in the free Bing Webmaster Tools (`http://bing.com/toolbox/webmaster`). If you've verified your site in Bing Webmaster Tools, you can navigate to Index Explorer in the Reports & Data section. Here you'll see how Bing sees your site. As shown in Figure 6-1, Index Explorer takes the pages of your site in Bing's index and organizes them based on directories. Select a folder and drill down to see how many pages and folders are contained within, how many times pages in that directory have shown up in search, how many clicks they got from a Bing search page, and how many links point to it.

Figure 6-1: Bing Index Explorer reveals how many of your site pages are indexed.

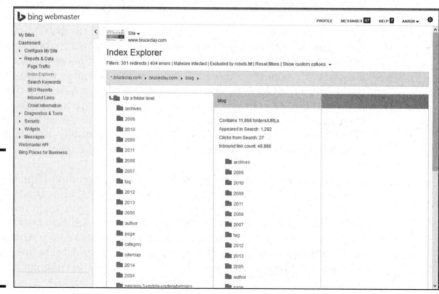

So if, for example, you had an indexing problem with Bing, you could use this tool to see all the pages Bing knows about and compare it to an independent crawl of your site to see whether

+ Bing is ignoring an entire directory

+ One of your directories is getting a lot more search visibility than others

+ A disparity exists between search visibility and inbound links

+ One of your folders has more indexed pages than you got from your crawl, in which case you've probably got some problems

If you discover important pages that haven't been indexed, you need to invite the spiders to your site. You want them to travel all your internal links and index your site contents. What follows are several effective ways you can deliver an invitation to the search engine spiders:

+ **External links:** Have a link to your missing page added to a web page that gets crawled regularly. Make sure that the link's anchor text relates to your page's subject matter. Ideally, the anchor text should contain your page's keywords. Also, the linking page should relate to your page's topic in some way so the search engines see it as a relevant site. After the link is in place, the next time the spiders come crawling, they follow that link right to your page. This sort of "natural discovery" process can be the quickest, most effective way to get a page noticed by the search engines.

+ **Direct submission:** Each search engine provides a way for you to submit a URL, which then goes into a queue waiting for a spider to go check it out. A direct submission isn't a fast or even reliable method to get your page noticed, but it doesn't hurt to do it.

+ **Internal links:** You should have at least two links pointing to every page in your site. This helps ensure that search engine spiders can find every page.

+ **Sitemap:** You should provide a sitemap (a list of the pages in your site that includes keyword-rich links) for your users, but for the search engines you want to create another sitemap in XML (Extensible Markup Language) format. Make sure that your XML Sitemap contains the URL links to the missing pages, as well as every other page that you want indexed. When a search engine spider crawls your XML Sitemap, it follows the links and is more likely to thoroughly index your site.

**Book VII
Chapter 6**

**Solving SEO
Roadblocks**

The two versions of your sitemap provide direct links to your pages, which is helpful for users and important for spiders. Search engines use the XML Sitemap file as a central hub for finding all your pages. But the user's sitemap is also crawled by the search engines. If the sitemap provides valuable anchor text for each link (for example, Frequently Asked Classic Car

Questions, rather than just FAQs), it gives search engines a better idea of what your pages are about. Google specifically states in its guidelines that every site should have a sitemap (`www.google.com/support/webmasters/bin/answer.py?answer=35769#design`).

The number of links you should have on the user-viewable sitemap is limited. Small sites can place every page on their sitemap, but larger sites shouldn't. Having more than 99 links on a page just doesn't provide a very user-friendly experience — no user wants to wade through hundreds of links to find what he's looking for. So just include the important pages, or split it into several sitemaps, one for each main subject category. (For more tips on creating an effective sitemap, see Book VI, Chapter 2.)

However, unlike a traditional sitemap, XML Sitemaps don't have a 99-link limit. There are still some limitations, but the file(s) is meant to act as a feed directly to the search engines. For full details on how to create an XML Sitemap, visit `www.sitemaps.org`, the official XML Sitemap guideline site run by the search engines.

In addition to having the search engine spiders come crawl your site, which is the first goal, you also want to direct them to where you want them to go within your site. For comparison, when people come over to your house, you don't just let them roam around and look anywhere they want, right? You lead them around, showing them what you want them to see — probably skipping the disorganized garage and messy utility room.

With search engine spiders, you don't want them to see every page or follow every link, either. The two reasons you want them to crawl around are

✦ **Indexing:** You want the search engines to index your pages so that they can find those pages relevant to people's searches and return them in search results.

✦ **Better ranking:** When the spiders follow your links, they pass *link equity* (the perceived-expertise value of all the inbound links pointing to a web page, which is a search engine ranking factor) to your *landing pages* (the pages you set up to be the most relevant for a primary keyword). Concentrating link equity on your landing pages makes those pages move higher up in the search engine rankings and bring in more traffic.

Some pages, like your Privacy Policy or Terms of Use, need to be in your global navigation but they don't need to rank well in the search engine's index. You don't want to rank for those pages or to dilute the link equity being passed to your landing pages. Instead, you should "herd" the spiders where you want them to go. To keep spiders away from certain pages, here are a couple of techniques you should know:

✦ **`nofollow`:** You can put a `rel="nofollow"` attribute on any link that you don't want the spiders to pass link equity to. Using this technique on links to unimportant pages, you could concentrate link equity onto your landing pages.

✦ **Robots text file (`.txt`) exclusion:** Be consistent. If you add `rel="nofollow"` to a link to prevent spiders from crawling to your privacy policy page, for instance, do it everywhere. Put the `nofollow` attribute on every link to that page. Also instruct the spiders not to index the page by excluding it in your robots text file (a central file that gives instructions to spiders of where *not* to go; check out Chapter 1 of this minibook for more on editing your `robots.txt` file).

✦ **`Meta` Robots exclusion:** Another way to put up a Do Not Enter sign for search engines is with a `noindex` `Meta` robots tag on a specific page. (A *Meta robots tag* is an HTML command in the Head section [top part] of a web page's HTML code that gives instructions to search engine spiders whether to index the page and whether to follow its links.) This tag is not needed if you've excluded the page in your `robots.txt` file. But to put the exclusion directly into the page code, you can add a tag such as this:

```
<meta name="robots" content="noindex">
```

In Chapters 1 through 5 of this minibook, we talk only about the good search engine spiders — the ones you want coming to your site. However, bad spiders are also out there, ones that come only to harm you.

Supplementing siloing with `rel="nofollow"`

The `rel="nofollow"` attribute may help with *siloing* your site, which is a method of organizing the site into subject themes. Because the search engines look for the most relevant pages for any search query, you can strengthen your site's subject relevance by linking related pages together into themed silos. Each silo should have a main landing page and at least five supporting pages linked to it, all centered on a particular keyword theme. To reinforce your landing pages' relevance to certain keywords, you can apply `rel="nofollow"` *sparingly* to only those cross-silo links that your users might need but which would only confuse the spiders' understanding of what the page is about. No link equity is preserved using the `rel="nofollow"` attribute. This was a popular technique a couple of years ago, but remember, there is no substitute for a good site architecture built in right from the start. (For more on siloing, see Book VI, Chapter 2.)

Spiders called *scrapers* come to steal your site content so that they can republish it on their own sites. Sometimes they grab entire pages, including the links back to your site and everything. One problem with scraping is that it creates *duplicate content* (the same or very similar text on two or more different pages) on the web, which can cause your page to drop in ranking or even drop out of the search results if the search engines don't correctly figure out which page is the original. Another problem is that scraped content may end up ranking above your page/site and grab traffic that should have been yours. Scraping is a copyright violation, and it's also a crime punishable by law, if you choose to pursue that. Unfortunately, the more good text content you have on your site, the more likely you are to attract scrapers. So as your site expands and your SEO project raises your rankings, you're probably going to run into this issue.

Webmasters have tried to prevent site scraping in various ways. Some have gone so far as to build a *white list* (a list of approved sites or agents) that contains only the known good spiders, and then exclude all non-white-listed spiders from entering their sites. Webmasters don't often use that extreme measure because they can't easily maintain a current white list without potentially excluding legitimate traffic to their sites.

A more typical defensive move is to sniff out a bad spider by using a server-level process known as *user-agent sniffing.* This process identifies spiders coming to your site, kind of like a security guard at your front door. If you know who a bad spider is, you can detect its arrival and keep it out. Or, some webmasters choose to do more than just block them; they redirect them to a page with massive quantities of data in hopes of crashing the bad spider's site. Block them or punish them, you choose, but unfortunately you can only do this *after* you've identified a spider as a scraper — not before you know who it is.

To deter others from copying your content, we recommend that you display a copyright notice on your website and register for a federal copyright. To register for a federal copyright, visit `http://www.copyright.gov/`, where you also find helpful information about the entire federal copyright process. For more suggestions on handling scrapers, see Book V, Chapter 5.

Avoiding 302 Hijacks

Here's a scenario that we hope never happens to you: Your website is running smoothly and ranking well with the search engines for your keywords. One day, you find that your search engine traffic is dropping dramatically. Then you notice that your pages have disappeared from the search engine results pages.

This nightmare scenario could mean that your site was a victim of a 302 hijack. A *302 Redirect* is a type of *redirect* (an HTML command that reroutes a user from one page to another automatically) used to indicate that one web page has temporarily moved to another URL. The search engine retains the original page in its index and attributes the content and link equity of the new page to the original page.

An unethical way to use 302 Redirects is called *302 hijacking*. This technique exploits the way search engines read 302 Redirects in order to cause a web page's traffic and SERP rankings to be drained away and given to some other page (the "hijacker"). The hijacker is basically stealing your website, rankings, and search traffic.

Here's how it works: The hijacker sets up a dummy page, often containing a scraped copy of your web page's content and a 302 Redirect to your ranking page. The search engines see the 302 Redirect and think that the hijacker's page is the *real* version that's temporarily using your page's URL. So, the 302 Redirect tricks the search engines into thinking that your ranking page is the temporary version of the hijacker's virtual page. The search engine therefore gives all your link equity and rankings away to the hijacker's URL. Figure 6-2 shows how a hijacked page's listing might appear in a SERP. Notice that the URL on the bottom line doesn't match the company name shown in the listing; clicking this link takes the user to some other page off the company's site.

Hijacker's domain   Hijacked result

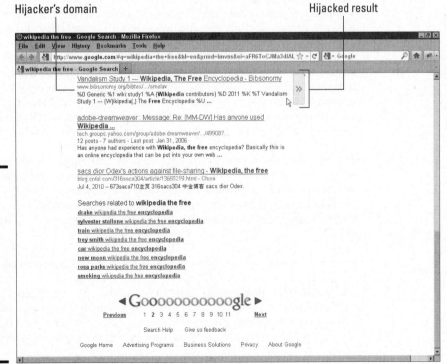

Figure 6-2:
A page hijacking transfers existing search engine rankings to another URL of the hijacker's choice.

A 302 hijacking can devastate a site, causing duplicate content penalties and loss of ranking. The search engines are aware of this issue and have tried to put preventive measures in place. They've had some success combating this crime, but it still happens.

Be on the lookout for page hijacking by regularly searching for snippets of your page text (do a search using quotation marks to find an exact match) to identify copycat pages; you'll know for certain that it's happening when you see someone else's URL showing up on your SERP listings. If you have this problem, contact the third-party site and ask it to cooperate with you to fix the situation. Page hijacking is often accidental (through improper use of 302 Redirects), so you may be able to resolve it with the site easily. If you discover that the site's intentions are malicious, however, you should report the site to the search engines immediately for investigation. If you're ever in this situation, you need to contact the search engine directly. Unfortunately, there's not much you can do to fix it on your own — the search engines have to remedy the situation for you.

Handling Secure Server Problems

You may have pages on your site where users provide sensitive data, such as a credit card number or other type of account information. The Internet solution for protecting sensitive information is to put those web pages on a *secure server*. Technically, this means that the web page is on a secure port on the server, where all data is *encrypted* (converted into a form that cannot be understood except by knowing one or more secret decryption keys). You can tell when you're looking at a web page on a secure server because `http://` changes to `https://` in the URL address. In 2014, Google announced that page security was a ranking factor and that pages hosted on a secure server got a minor ranking boost. So, especially for pages that handle sensitive data, an https:// URL is highly recommended.

Secure servers can cause duplicate content problems if a site has both a secure and nonsecure version of a web page and hasn't told the search engines which of the two is the preferred, or canonical, version. Two versions of the same page end up competing against each other for search engine rankings, and the search engines pick which one to show in search results.

Here are some SEO-minded best practices for handling secure servers:

+ **Don't make duplicates:** Many times, people just duplicate their entire website to make an `https://` version. This is a very bad practice because it creates instant duplicate content. Never create two versions of your site or of any page on your site. Even if you exclude your secure pages from being indexed, people link to them at some point and the search engines find the secure versions through those links.

✦ **If you have cases of duplication caused by http:// and https://, indicate a canonical version:** Any time you have pages with similar or duplicate content, you can tell the search engine which page you prefer to show up in a search result and which page to give all the link equity to by using a canonical tag. Read all about using the canonical tag in Chapter 2 of this minibook.

✦ **Secure the pages that need to be secure:** If the page doesn't receive sensitive account-type information from users, it doesn't need to be secured. However, if it isn't cost prohibitive to do so, you may choose to secure many pages across your site for the marginal ranking benefit.

✦ **Spiders *shouldn't* be blocked from crawling secure pages if those pages are important for rankings:** Search engines do index secure pages, if they can get to them. Banks usually have secure pages indexed because they often put their entire site on an https://. Because of the nature of their business, it makes sense that banks want to give their users the utmost level of confidence by securing their whole site. It's a good user experience for a page to show up when a user's searching for it, for example, if a user is looking for her online banking login page.

If your website has secure pages that violate these best practices, here's how to fix them:

1. **Identify which pages on your site need to be secure.**

   Always secure the pages on which users need to enter account information.

2. **Make sure that your secure pages are not duplicated.**

   Your secure pages should have only an https:// version. Don't offer a non-secured duplicate version. If you do have a duplicate-page situation, include a canonical tag that tells search engines which page is the best one to use. All links to and from secure pages should be *full path links,* meaning they begin http:// or https://. Using relative links to secure pages is just asking for trouble.

3. **Clean up duplicate pages by using 301 Redirects.**

   If you currently have secure pages that don't need to be secured, redirect them to the http:// version by using a 301 (permanent) Redirect. That way, any links going to the secure pages are automatically redirected to the right pages. The same goes for non-secure pages that should be secured, only vice versa.

Book VIII
Analyzing Results

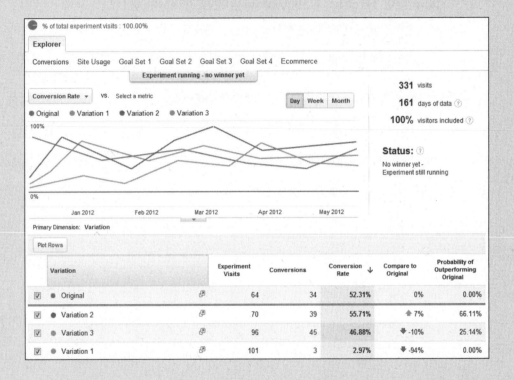

Find out how to set goals in Google Analytics at www.dummies.com/extras/
searchengineoptimizationaio.

Contents at a Glance

Chapter 1: Employing Site Analytics

In This Chapter

✔ Discovering web analytics basics

✔ Measuring success

✔ Identifying what you're tracking

✔ Deciding on your key performance indicators

✔ Examining analytics packages

✔ Analyzing log files

*W*eb analytics are two words that can strike terror into the heart of any unsuspecting practitioner of search engine optimization (SEO). You've been monitoring your *pay per click (PPC) campaigns* (advertising campaigns in which you pay every time someone clicks your link), and you're watching to see how well your pages rank within the search engines. So you should be able to do web analytics, right?

Well, web analytics can be a little more complicated than that. For a lot of people, web analytics seems to consist of wild guessing and reading tea leaves. It can be pretty complex, but we walk you through it so it hopefully makes a little more sense. In this chapter, we give you a basic overview of web analytics, before we dive into the nitty-gritty later on in this minibook. We go over how to measure your success in the search engines, identify what numbers you need to be tracking, point out key indicators to be watching when measuring your performance, and cover tools and software that help you with web analytics and what a log file analysis is.

Discovering Web Analytics Basics

Web analytics involves taking the information you glean from all your research and sitting down, looking at it, and figuring out what it all means. Bear with us: This can get a little tricky because the terms are so similar. In order to figure out web analytics, you need to know the two different sets of numbers you're looking at — web metrics numbers and web analytics numbers.

Web metrics

Web metrics is the measurement of what's happening on the Internet itself. It's focusing on the number and types of people online, the number of broadband versus dial-up connections, advertisers, advertisements (shapes, sizes, level of annoyance), and all things related to the Internet as a whole. Web metrics asks: How many websites exist? How many searches? How many emails? How many of those emails are spam? Does it make sense to promote items online for sale to certain countries or to seniors? How many people search at Google versus Yahoo versus Bing?

There are four ways of tracking web metrics data, and several kinds of companies that fall into a particular niche. These firms study the Internet as a whole. Think of them as Internet archeologists. They take all the raw data they get and interpret it in their own way, using information from many, many sites and sources out there on the Internet:

+ **People:** The first kind of company that tracks web metrics data does so by using large panels of people whom the companies follow while they surf the Internet as part of their daily routine. These companies report which sites are the most popular and can have their panels check out your competitors and do a comparative analysis. These kinds of companies include Nielsen Online (`www.nielsen-online.com`) and comScore (`www.comscore.com`).

+ **Hits:** The second type of web metrics firm checks out the hits on the ISPs (Internet service providers). These firms are watching the masses out there surfing on the Internet. They report on how these unidentified (and sometimes unwashed) users research cars, read the latest celebrity gossip, and watch news stories. Hitwise (`www.hitwise.com`) is one such firm that tracks ISP hits.

+ **Responsiveness:** A third type of web metrics firm watches the responsiveness of popular websites. They track how well a popular entertainment site holds up during the Oscars or the Emmys or if sports sites can handle the traffic during the Super Bowl, and which ones run the fastest and which ones drown under the increased demand. Two firms that do this kind of web metrics are Keynote (`www.keynote.com`) and Tealeaf (`www.tealeaf.com`).

+ **Commerce:** The final group tracks online commerce. They watch how much these commerce companies are spending on advertising and what percentage the consumer is spending on the Internet. They also track the growth rate of companies, as compared to their competition. One of the big tracking companies in this niche is eMarketer (`www.emarketer.com`).

Web analytics

On a smaller but no less important scale is web analytics, which concerns itself with the particulars of a single website, instead of the entire web.

The people who do web analytics are looking at how successful your site is in attracting the kind of visitors who bring you *conversions.* Visitors who convert do whatever your website is asking of them: make a purchase, sign up for a newsletter, watch your videos, and so on. Using web analytics means looking beyond just finding out where you rank or how many people clicked over from the search engine listing and actually checking to see how many visitors came to your site and provided you a conversion.

Your first step with web analytics should be to determine what your visitors do and what they should be doing when they arrive on your website. Where do they go on your site? Do your visitors drill down to the product information? Do they put things in their shopping carts? Are they less costly customers because they use the online customer care tools and services? Do they leave your site right away or do they stay a while?

Hopefully they're able to easily accomplish what they came to your website to do. But if you have a website, you need to be able to measure whether your website design and development are worth the effort you've put into them.

This site-level arena in web analytics is governed by software and tracking systems that gather, crunch, and report on data from server logs, cookie data, JavaScript, e-commerce information, and so on.

Without web analytics, search marketers are obsessed only with achieving a high ranking. If they're a little more on the ball, they focus instead on generating as much traffic as they can. Unfortunately, high ranking and high traffic are only part of running a successful site. If you're getting high volumes of traffic but your visitors aren't doing what you want them to do (for instance, people aren't asking you to customize their classic cars), all that high traffic is just going to cost you money. Your server is now handling more non-converting traffic, your PPC campaigns are being clicked on with no return on investment (ROI), and even the time you spent on optimizing your site to rank organically is time that you could have spent making money. Traffic is worth the effort only if it provides ROI.

This is why targeted traffic is so important. *Targeted traffic* is traffic that is interested in your product or service and provides you conversions. Your success is determined not by the volume of visitors you receive but by the quality. First, however, you need to figure out what it is you want that targeted traffic to be doing. That's what we cover in the next section.

Measuring Your Success

The first thing you need to figure out before you get started with web analytics is to figure out your goals for your site. Say that you have a website that specializes in classic-car customization services. The first thing you want to do is measure the amount of sales generated on your site. That's easy enough — but other activities need recording as well. Other activities you can record include email newsletter signups, file downloads, *RSS subscriptions* (news feeds that automatically show updates to a site that offers one), and user account creation.

There is no one-size-fits-all approach to measuring success. Goals differ based on what your website does and what you want users to do once they reach your site. For example, your custom car site would be tracking different user actions than a political site that wants people to sign up for a newsletter. Many advancements have been made in analytics, so if you have something you need to track, you can do it with an analytics program.

You're probably like most people building commercial sites: A website is a key component of your business, and you need to be making money from your site in order to be successful. The common adage is true: You have to spend money to make money; however, you need to be spending money in the right places or you might as well be setting the cash on fire. So, what is it that you want your website to do? This should be a fairly obvious question, but in order to accurately do web analytics for your site, you need to know what it is that gets you conversions. It's extremely important to define your business objectives.

There are four basic classifications for commercial websites: e-commerce sites, content sites, lead-generation sites, and self-service sites. In this list, we provide some basic goals for the four types of commercial websites, and you can use this information when you define your own business objectives:

✦ **E-commerce site:** The objective with e-commerce is to increase your sales and decrease your marketing expenses. Basic measures include sales, returns and allowances, sales per visitor, cost per visitor, and conversion rate. Advanced measures include inventory mix, trend reporting, satisfaction, and RFM (recency, frequency, monetary) analysis.

✦ **Content site:** The objective here is to increase your readership-level of interest and time the user spends on the site. The things you measure are visit length, page views, and number of subscriptions and cancelled subscriptions.

✦ **Lead-generation site:** The objective is to increase and segment lead generation (things like newsletters). Basic measures include downloads, time spent on the site, newsletter opt-ins, reject rates on contact pages, and the leads-to-close ratio.

✦ **Self-service site:** Finally, the objective here is to increase customer satisfaction and decrease customer support inquiries. Basic measures include a decrease in visitor length or fewer calls to a call center, as these are measures of customer satisfaction.

With clearly defined objectives and a good analytics tool, measuring your website's success becomes a whole lot easier. Your objectives state what you want to do with your website or your marketing campaigns.

Identifying what you're tracking

In order to start analyzing whether your website is doing what it needs to be doing, you have to acquire a sample of data. This sample allows you to extract a baseline report of data on your users.

Types of data vary from site to site. A data sample from an e-commerce site reads differently than a sample from a political newsletter. For websites that aren't impacted by *seasonal trends* (meaning they see a spike in business around a certain time of year), a three-month sample is a great baseline range to work with. After you've determined what your baseline sample is (if you have seasonal trends, take a sample from your busy and slow periods), start recording numerical and trended data for analysis.

As someone who is going to be doing web analytics from an SEO perspective, you have to be looking at the information that makes your life easier in the long run. You can do that by focusing on the elements that are most relevant to search engine referrals — information such as

✦ Percentage of traffic from search

✦ Conversions (leads, sales, and subscriptions) from search

✦ Average time a user spends on your site (or *visit duration*)

✦ Share of search traffic (Google versus Yahoo versus Bing, and so on)

✦ Pages that visitors click

The information that you use in your baseline should be unique to your business goals and ambitions.

It's also critical to separate your paid search results from your organic search results. Paid search results come from pay per click (PPC) programs, where you can buy an advertising link on Google or any of the other search engines and pay a sum every time a user clicks on your ad. You need to separate these two types of results because it can skew your data and throw off proper analysis. You have to understand how subtleties in an SEO program, like descriptions in a listing or movement in a *SERP* (search engine results page), can impact your traffic and productivity.

This is also true with all your PPC paid search programs when you need to calculate your return on investment (ROI) on specific engines, *keywords* (search terms), or ad campaigns. Many PPC programs include the ability to tag your pages and track visitors from click to purchase. For more on PPC analytics, please refer to Book II, Chapter 3.

With analytics, you can use different types of reports from any number of analytics packages as long as you know what to look for. But even without the analytics part, you need to think about a quality search experience. Regardless of how users search, you have to get them the information they want while also trying to get them to perform your desired actions.

To help get you started, here are a few tips on items that you can track and measure:

+ **Top search queries:** You would be surprised how many businesses lose out on those desired conversions simply because they're targeting the wrong keywords. This is why keyword research is so very necessary. Sometimes what you think would be a good keyword search term turns out to be quite the opposite. This is why it's so important to be thorough in keyword research. You can read more on how to properly research keywords in Book II. This can be a tricky thing to measure because it's a self-fulfilling prophecy. Targeting terms that already are bringing you traffic could mean missing out on a better term that would bring you even more traffic. Watch this metric, but don't put all your eggs in this basket.

+ **Top landing pages:** A *landing page* is a page that someone uses to get onto your site. It might not always be your main page, but generally that would be the one you want to be your big landing page. When dealing with top landing pages, your concern should be the source of referrals. Because we're talking about search engine optimization, we recommend looking at search engine results. This is your first contact with a potential visitor, so make sure that elements of your landing page speak to the search terms and the type of user you want to bring to your site. Changes in page titles, listing descriptions, and URLs can have an impact on a user's desire to click on your page.

+ **Top exit pages:** Something you also have to monitor are the exit pages. If users are consistently leaving your site on a common page, it's a good idea to figure out why. The process of *pathing* is reviewing the flow, page by page, that a user takes while visiting your site. If you begin to see that quality search referrals come into your site but are always leaving at a particular point, you need to work on the content or user experience you provide to keep those users from leaving. To figure out your exit pages, you need to perform a reverse path analysis to determine why so many people are leaving at this one particular page. If the top exit page is the Thanks for Ordering page, you have nothing to worry about. However, these situations are rare. The most common top exit page is usually your home page.

✦ **Bounce rate:** The *bounce rate* measures the percentage of people who leave your site right after entering a page, usually within seconds and without visiting any other page on the site. This stat goes hand-in-hand with measuring exit pages. If you have specific pages designated for SEO purposes, be sure to measure and track the bounce rate on a regular basis. You don't get desired conversions if no one wants to stay on your page. Maybe you're targeting the wrong people with that landing page — after all, just because you rank well for a particular keyword doesn't mean the page that ranks is saying the right things to the people who come to that page. You need to dig in deeper and figure out what the mismatch is. Are your images loading too slowly? Is the page layout confusing? Does the content of the page not meet the visitor's expectations?

Experimenting with web analytics is key, especially because all sites and report suites differ. So find out as much as you can about your visitors and don't be afraid to experiment with your reports and theories. There is always more information to know, and, like everything else in life, we often don't even know what it is that we don't know. The only way to shed light on the activities going on with your site is to start investing in web analytics.

Choosing key performance indicators

Key performance indicators help organizations achieve organizational goals through the definition and measurement of progress. Key performance indicators (KPIs) are the yardstick by which you measure your website's success. In order to properly do web analytics, you need to know what your goals are in order to know what it is you need to be watching.

Your KPIs should be based on your overall business goals and the role your website plays in achieving those goals. KPIs should be specific to your company, they should not be influenced by the industry averages or your competitors' KPIs, and they should be specific, significant, and measurable:

✦ **Organizational goals:** It is important to establish KPIs based on your own business goals rather than standard goals for your industry. For instance, a company whose goal is "to be most profitable" has different KPIs than a company that defines its goal as "to increase customer retention 50 percent." The first company has KPIs that relate to finance and profit and loss, whereas the second focuses on customer satisfaction and response time.

✦ **Measurement purpose:** It's important to analyze KPIs over time, allowing you to make changes to improve website performance and then periodically reevaluate performance to verify your progress. So KPIs must be measurable. The goal of "increase customer retention" is useless because there is no real goal; the goal of "increase customer retention by 50 percent" has a definite number that can be tracked.

✦ **Managerial consensus:** Having all managers on the same page is important because personnel from different functions within your company help create the KPIs. If your KPIs truly reflect your organizational goals, all levels of your company have to get with the program. Encourage company unity and enthusiasm for the project, and make sure that everyone knows what the KPIs are. People have to be on board, and they have to know what it is that they're doing. A crew can't steer a ship if one half of the crew thinks they're sailing to Zanzibar and the other half thinks they're supposed to be Saskatchewan pirates.

✦ **Goal continuity:** KPIs are *long-term* considerations designed to help with your strategic planning. Although having targeted goals is important, those goals should also lead to an overall success. Just because something is measurable does not mean that it is significant enough to be a key performance indicator. You must define your KPIs and weigh them the same way from year to year. It's not that you can't adjust your goals, but you should use the same unit to measure those goals. For example, your website goal should be to increase the number of conversions by the same amount year in and year out.

Although you should be creating very specific KPIs for your business, a few metrics qualify as regular key performance indicators all across the board. These include the KPIs for measuring reach, acquisition, metrics, conversions, and retention.

Measuring reach

Every business that promotes products and services needs to measure its reach on an ongoing basis. Basically, *reach* is how you reach your customers. The following metrics are useful for understanding the effects of marketing programs designed to reach new customers:

✦ **Overall traffic volumes:** Tracks large spikes or dips in the requested page views.

✦ **Number of visits:** Indicates how well you reach and acquire your visitors.

✦ **Number of new visitors:** Gives you the number of first-time users. This number is the first part of two numbers that you need to calculate ratios that determine the quality of new visitors. Are they giving you your needed conversions? Overall conversion rate is calculated by dividing the total number of transactions (conversions) by the total number of visitors. Obviously, higher is better.

✦ **Ratio of new to returning visitors:** Identifying changes in overall audience makeup. In general, keeping an existing customer is cheaper than bringing in a new one. Are you retaining your customer base? Have you made changes that alienated your core demographic? Was your core demographic converting as well as the new demographic?

✦ **Percentage of new visitors:** Helps track the changes in your traffic due to marketing reach and acquisition efforts.

✦ **Visitor geographic data:** Identify your traffic spikes from unexpected locations. Where is your traffic coming from? This can give you information you can use to better reach your customers.

✦ **Your top five to ten error pages:** Helps you identify and resolve visitor experience problems.

✦ **Impressions served:** The number of times the page loaded and a user viewed the content. You can use this metric to calculate your reach and the overall success of your marketing campaigns.

Acquisition

Measuring acquisition is easier than measuring reach. *Acquisition* is the measure of users that you bring to your site. The difference is that reach metrics depend on information from various sources, whereas acquisition metrics come from your own web analytics data.

Acquisition measurement focuses on the number of visitors your website acquires and where they all come from. The following list gives you the metrics that can help gauge the success of your website and marketing initiatives in acquiring prospects and customers. The metrics you should be watching for acquisition are

✦ **Percent of new visitors:** You can use this number to flag big changes in new visitor acquisition and their effect on overall web traffic. You use this number in conjunction with your total conversions to help you determine whether they are giving you conversions or just slowing down your servers.

✦ **Average number of visits per visitor:** This stat can help you ensure that content consumption remains stable, which is an indirect measure of user experience.

✦ **Average number of page views per visit:** This metric allows you to understand the changing nature of visitors attracted to your website. Do they peruse the whole site or escape after one or two pages?

✦ **Page stick and slip (time on page and bounce rates):** View big changes in stickiness (how long a user stays on a page) or slip (how quickly visitors leave a page) on your home page and key entry pages, including PPC campaign landing pages.

✦ **Average pages viewed per visitor:** This is a short-term measure of how well you direct visitors beyond your home page or landing page.

✦ **Cost per visitor:** This is a rise/fall metric that shows fluctuation of visitor acquisition costs due to an increase or decrease in your marketing spending.

Response metrics

Response metrics are what your users are responding to on your website, be it an image or a newsletter or an email. These are the key items you need to be watching for:

+ **Responses and respondents:** These are important indicators of campaign success.

+ **Cost per acquisition or cost per click:** Measuring these keeps you within your campaign budget.

+ **Referring domains/URLs:** These help you watch your visitors based on needs and origin. Where are they coming from and what can you glean about their needs from the site they originated from?

+ **Search engines:** Check to see who's coming in from the search engines to ensure that the money you spend on SEO and PPC is justified.

+ **Search keywords and phrases:** Track what keywords are bringing visitors to your site. You can use this info from search queries to refine your marketing message and materials to include these keywords.

Note that the raw data for the preceding metrics is not useful by itself: Your most important metric is the relationship between your current data measurements and your previous data measurements. As indicators of change, the preceding KPIs can alert you to the ever-changing quality and quantity of your visiting traffic, and this may call for additional research.

Conversions

Conversion metrics are among the most important indicators to measure and monitor. Conversion rates are easy to measure and can be improved by fine-tuning your website; every online business should watch these numbers and have Plan B ready in case key conversion rates suddenly plunge.

When you measure conversions, you also look at abandonment — the ones who got away. Maybe they intended to complete an action but were frustrated during the process and bailed out. Industry-neutral average conversion rates hover around 3 percent. This means that only 3 out of 100 visitors across all industries complete an intended action.

What conversion rates should you measure? There are three basic processes that can be measured for conversion versus abandonment and each depends largely on what your ultimate goal for your site is.

✦ **Activities that lead to an acquisition or conversion:** The user makes a purchase or requests a service. This one is probably the easiest to measure because you know when it's done and you have the money in hand. You can see the actual impact in your bottom line.

✦ **Activities that lead to gathering important data:** The user fills out a form, signs up for a newsletter, or contacts you. You haven't actually made a sale yet but you have more information about that user and probably also her permission to continue the business relationship. This might be the end in itself or just a step along your conversion process.

✦ **Activities that direct visitors to information that reduces your operational costs:** This one is trickier to measure because you have to track multiple data points — how often someone accesses your FAQ or Help section, how many calls to your customer support group you're receiving, how much those calls diminish after implementing a change aimed at giving greater support up front, or any other operational changes aimed at reducing overall cost.

Retention

Retention is how many customers you keep after they come to your website. Customer retention is important to websites for various reasons. For instance, research shows that keeping existing customers costs less than attracting new customers. Studies have shown that the cost for acquisition on a per-customer basis is much more than that of customer retention. Research also says there is a small chance of converting a prospect to first-time customer status and a low percent chance of reacquiring a lost customer. So customer retention is key.

The following metrics and ratios can help you determine how you rate at customer retention:

✦ The number of returning visitors

✦ The average frequency of your returning visitors

✦ The ratio of returning visitors to all visitors

✦ The frequency of the visit

✦ How recent the visit was

✦ The activity of retained visitors

✦ The views of key pages and contents

✦ Your retained visitor conversion rate

✦ The customer retention rate

✦ The average frequency of return for retained visitors

Although some business models do not expect customers to make a second purchase right away (for example, auto, housing, or travel), very few websites are designed for a single visit from a visitor without a return. The KPIs listed here should be tracked regardless of your business model or industry:

+ The ratio of daily to monthly returning visitors — a quick measure of the average frequency of return for all visitors.

+ The percent of returning visitors and the frequency of those returns.

+ The loyalty measurements for groups of returning visitors — this monitors big changes in visitor loyalty. How many are you losing?

+ Your retained visitor conversion rate; this helps in determining website or campaign success.

+ Your customer retention rate; this helps you determine your website success.

Examining Analytics Packages

Analytics takes a long time, several in-depth volumes, and possibly a college course or two to really properly do on your own. Fortunately for you, several analytics packages out there do the number-crunching for you and make sense of all the metrics you're watching out for. Analytics packages are governed by software for sale and systems for use that gather, crunch, and report data from server logs, cookie data, JavaScript, e-commerce information, and so on. The free Google Analytics has the lion's share of the market. In addition to being free, Google Analytics is full of advanced functionality and is familiar to every online marketing professional. Most website owners need look no further than Google Analytics (GA) to procure information about visitors' activity on your site. We tell you more about GA in the upcoming section, but first we say a bit about your other options.

Adobe Analytics (`http://www.adobe.com/marketing-cloud/web-analytics/marketing-analytics-capabilities.html`) is considered one of the best analytics packages, with a price tag that only the biggest enterprises can consider. Adobe Analytics is a high-end analysis tool that can perform multidimensional queries. If you have a smaller website, knowing who showed up when, from where, and what they did would probably be enough data for you. But if you're a much larger company, you need these more sophisticated tools to help you find more prospective customers and better assess the competition. Be prepared to spend $1,500 or more for this monthly subscription service if you purchase it directly from Adobe. Installation is also expensive: Setup fees are usually around $5,000.

StatCounter (www.statcounter.com) is a free analytics package. It offers custom summary stats based on all your visitors and a detailed analysis of your last 500 page loads. StatCounter is pretty good for a free service, but the free Google Analytics has the advantage of integration with other Google products, including AdWords and Search Console, that StatCounter can't match.

Webtrends (www.webtrends.com) is a popular analytics company. It offers tools tailored specifically to your business model, such as retail, travel, technology, and so on. It has programs for international websites as well, including programs for Germany and France. Pricing is available upon request because the company tailors specifically to your needs. Contact it via its website for more info.

Other analytics software packages are available, but for the vast majority of businesses today, GA is a must.

Google

The most well-known web analytics offering is Google Analytics (www.google.com/analytics). Google is putting everything it can think of in this tool in order to show you just how important it is for you to keep buying more keywords. Google Analytics also generates detailed statistics about the visitors to a website. The main highlight of this program is that it's aimed at *marketers* as opposed to webmasters and technologists from which the industry of web analytics originally grew, which means it's geared specifically toward business types, not tech types.

Google Analytics can track visitors from all referrers, including search engines, display advertising, pay per click networks, email marketing, social networks, and even digital collateral such as links within PDF documents. Google Analytics also allows you to track your landing page quality and monitors your conversions. Remember, conversions don't always mean sales. This program can track whether users are viewing the page you want them to view. Figure 1-1 shows you the overview from Google Analytics, a listing of all verified sites in your account.

You can also use Google Analytics to determine which of your ads are performing (when you use it in conjunction with Google AdWords, Google's pay per click advertising program, which we talk about in Book II). Google Analytics also provides shorthand information for the casual user and much more in-depth info for those who are a little more versed in web analytics.

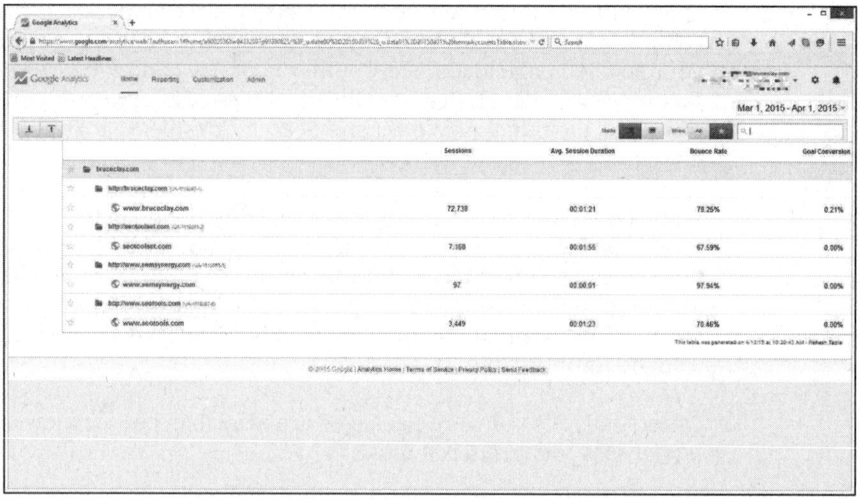

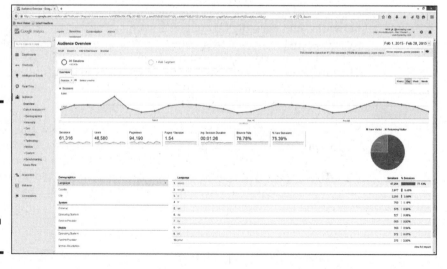

Figure 1-1:
Google
Analytics
is a free
analytics
program.

Google Analytics works through the *Google Analytics Tracking Code* (GATC). The GATC is a snippet of JavaScript code that users add onto every page of their website. This code acts as a beacon, collecting anonymous visitor data and sending it back to Google data collection *servers* for processing. Data processing takes place hourly, although it can be three to four hours before you can get your data back. The Google Analytics Dashboard (shown in Figure 1-2) can give you information at a glance about traffic, site usage, and traffic sources, among much more.

Figure 1-2:
The dash-
board for
Google
Analytics
provides
at-a-glance
reporting on
your site.

The Google Analytics Tracking Code also sets first-party cookies on each visitor's computer. *Cookies* are parcels of text that are used to track, authenticate, and maintain specific information about users. The cookies are used to store anonymous information such as whether the user has been to the site before (new or returning visitor), what the timestamp of the current visit is, and where the user came from.

Google Analytics is very easy to install on your website and can be done in one of two ways. One approach is to add the code with Google Tag Manager. Google recommends this way if you want to manage all special tracking tags on your site, including AdWords conversion tracking and remarketing tags, from one place. The alternative method is copying and pasting Google's provided code snippet into your site's Global element, which means that the code snippet applies to every page across your site and you won't have to go in and add it by hand, unless you're using goal tracking or conversion tracking code. If the only tagging you plan to add to your site is for Google Analytics, this method is the easier of the two.

Log Files Analysis

Even if you never implement a full analytics software suite, you have other ways to get useful data about your site's traffic. Your website generates a lot of information. All you need to do is check out your server logs to see that. Your *server log* is something your server automatically creates showing a record of all the activity it performs. It's a record of everything that happens during a given time period, be it hours, days, or minutes. More than just recording page loads, the server log includes every image loaded, every script run, and so on. It is a moment-by-moment map of site activity that involves your server. So it should be really easy to just pull up your server logs and read who's coming into your site, what they did, and where they came from, right?

Well, not really. Figure 1-3 illustrates what your server log looks like. It doesn't make for light afternoon reading.

A server log is filled with incredibly dense information because the computer records that information in its own language, which isn't exactly readable for someone who doesn't speak server-ese.

When a user connects to your server, the server records a line of data that looks a little like this:

```
72.173.901.16 - - [06/Oct/2008:19:46:42 -0800] "GET /
   Mustang67red.html HTTP:1.1" 200 22832 "-" "Mozilla/4.7
   (compatible; Firefox)"
```

Figure 1-3:
A server log is extremely informative after you've learned how to read it.

Here's what the data means:

✦ `72.173.901.16:` The numbers at the beginning of the line tell you who asked for the file. A *reverse DNS lookup* (which finds the server the visitor is coming from) will tell you that the visitor came from `www.mabelsmotors.com`.

✦ `19:46:42 -0800:` The server log displays time in the Greenwich mean time (GMT). In this case, 19:46:42 (7:46 p.m. on the 12-hour clock); the `-0800` means the visitor is eight hours behind GMT and therefore in the Pacific time zone.

✦ `Mustang67red.html:` The data after `GET` indicates that the visitor came to your site and looked up a file named `Mustang67red.html`.

✦ `HTTP:1.1" 200:` The request was from the 1.1 Hypertext Transport Protocol, and your server returned a 200, which means it happily showed the file. A 404 or any other *error code* (a message the server sends when something goes wrong) means that the server couldn't find the file or that something went awry on your site. Errors are usually found in a separate error log.

Next, the log file shows that the server sent back 22,832 bytes of data, and the hyphen in quotes (" - ") lets you know the referral link. (The hyphen indicates that the website link was entered manually rather than clicked. A visitor coming from a link would have a referring URL in place of the hyphen.) The end line lets you know that the user is using the Mozilla Firefox browser.

If your head is spinning, that's completely understandable. And here's what's worse: The preceding code is (comparatively) simple to understand and analyze. But a big website generates something in the neighborhood of more than 80 gigabytes of server logs *a day*. So it could get pretty tedious, extremely time-consuming, and definitely frustrating to try to do this all by yourself. Fortunately, that's why you have a computer.

If you have a large site, you definitely want to host your log-file analysis on a different server than the one you use to serve up the web pages on your site. Major companies such as Google have numerous rooms full of servers because they serve millions of pages a day, but they have entire server farms dedicated to log-file analysis. Serving data is one thing; actually analyzing it is another bag of cookies altogether.

If you serve a million pages, and each page is made up of ten files, and each file is about 20 kilobytes, your server has to find, read, and send 200 gigabytes of data. To analyze the data, the software needs to categorize it, hold it in memory, compare it, and report on the findings. Sifting through a gigabyte of data is not something you want to do on the same machine that is serving those pages. The amount of work the machine has to do makes viewing your site incredibly slow, never mind making the server keel over and catch fire. So having a separate server (or servers) for your log file analysis is a good thing.

There's the human factor, as well. It takes much more than a few IT guys on entirely too much caffeine to do a log file analysis. You're going to need some tools to help you as well. But choosing the right one is a little tricky and there are some things you need to be thinking of when choosing a log file analysis tool:

✦ **Target audience:** You need a log analysis tool that you can tailor specifically to your website's needs. Some tools are meant for large, robust sites that have to crunch huge numbers daily; others are made for only basic use. Some tools are very user friendly, and others expect a certain level of expertise on your part. You have to take into consideration your industry, your website's ins and outs, and your promotional campaign.

✦ **Flexibility:** The more powerful the tool, the more flexible it can be. Generic reports can be useful, but if you want to make your log file analysis really work for you, you need a tool that you can customize to your website's goals. It's not likely you'll be able to do this with a log file report.

✦ **Archiving:** Log file analysis becomes more successful over time, but storing the data can become unwieldy. You need a tool that offers file compression and archiving that shrinks the files and stores them for future use.

✦ **Output:** Some tools just spit out numbers. Others arrange them neatly into graphs. A really good tool allows you to manipulate the data much easier than a bad tool in order to compare and contrast from outside sources.

✦ **Scalability:** The larger the site, the more likely it is that a low-end tool (or even a free one) is not going to cut it.

✦ **Speed:** The difference between getting your log reports right away versus getting them the next week depends on how powerful your machine is. Faster reporting gives you an edge, and the better tools use special indexing techniques to allow them to perform much faster.

Be aware that there is no such thing as an overnight success; you get no guarantees and no instant gratification. Log-file analysis, like all of SEO, is something that takes time and concentrated effort to do properly. Remember, the cheaper you want it, the cheaper you get it. High-performance, accurate tools that don't crash because of large amounts of data are worth what they cost you.

Log-file analysis tools

Several log-file analysis programs are available (usually, running a quick search on Google turns up several), but here are a few so that you know what to expect:

✦ **WebLog Expert** (http://weblogexpert.com)**:** The website says, "WebLog Expert will give you information about your site's visitors: activity statistics, accessed files, paths through the site, information about referring pages, search engines, browsers, operating systems, and more. The program produces easy-to-read HTML reports that include both text information (tables) and charts." WebLog Expert offers a free demo version, and commercial versions start at $99 up to $399.

✦ **Sawmill** (www.sawmill.net)**:** Three different versions are available. Sawmill Lite is the cheapest of the bunch and does the basics of log-file analysis. Sawmill Professional, the next step up, is highly customizable. Sawmill Enterprise is the most expensive and has the most gadgets, including multi-processors and e-commerce options. You can test a trial version, and the commercial versions run from $99 to $35,000. Enterprise versions for extremely large sites are also available.

✦ **AWStats** (www.awstats.org)**:** The free AWStats log-file analyzer can do graphical reports by browsers used, countries of visitors, screen size, and most viewed, entry and exit pages, plus other useful stats for understanding the activity of visitors and bots on your site.

Check out traffic numbers

Here is a list of things to look out for in your log files to make sure your numbers are correct. Not every visitor to your site is a human, and it's the humans you want the data on — not the robots:

✦ **Search engine spiders:** Search engines use programs (commonly called *spiders* or *robots*) that come to your site and "read" it to help the search engine analyze your site. You can check and see if the `robots.txt` file was requested (this is how you figure out if your site was spidered or not). When you recognize a spider, grab the IP address and let the analytics software know to ignore hits from that address. Most good log analyzers use reverse IP lookup to find spiders and ignore them for you.

✦ **Masked IP addresses:** Not every IP address represents an individual user. Corporations, universities, and even users from AOL can show your server a single IP address when in fact many people have visited your site. Watch for high traffic from a single IP address to see if you have more visitors than your log file suggests.

✦ **Cookies:** Don't expect accurate visitor counts from cookies. Many people set their browsers not to accept cookies. Cookies also can't distinguish multiple users on the same computer (like a library or school computer). Log files, however, do not contain cookie info.

✦ **Busting caches:** *Caching* is what happens when there is a saved copy of your website. It throws off your analytics numbers because you can be accidentally working off of an old copy of your page. (JavaScript doesn't cache, so you do not have to worry about this if you are running JavaScript tags.) One way to solve this problem is to create a dynamic page. A *dynamic* page is a page that is built on the fly from the database using scripts. You can also set your server to prevent caching if you have enough bandwidth.

✦ **Know your audience:** Some sites track only users who are logging on from home or work while filtering out users coming in from libraries and schools using public terminals. In general, this means they require a login or a persistent cookie, which public terminals are not likely to allow.

Here's the bottom line with log-file analysis as an analytics solution: It's tedious and not as useful as installing an analytics package. However, it is a way to get hard numbers about your site. If you're willing to dive into it, it can be rewarding.

Analytics is not just about gathering data. It's all about knowing what you want from your website and then being able to read the pile of data you've acquired in order to see whether those goals are being reached, and to determine what else you need to be doing differently to get a higher rate of conversion.

Chapter 2: Tracking Behavior with Web Analytics

In This Chapter

✔ **Measuring website usability**

✔ **Getting a handle on conversion tracking**

✔ **Tracking the success of your SEO project**

✔ **Analyzing rankings**

To properly do web analytics, you need to gather your data. But web analytics is not just about collecting data. It's about collecting your data in such a way that you can read it, understand it, and use it to make the necessary changes to your website. In this chapter, you discover several ways to gather analytics data.

You have to measure your website's usability in order to figure out whether your web design works for your users and brings you those conversions. Next we talk about conversion tracking. Is your site getting the number of *conversions* you want? Conversion tracking helps you measure not just the final number of conversions, but where people drop off before they make the final conversion.

To track the success of your SEO project, you need to monitor your keywords and your search engine rankings, whether they're at the place they need to be, and whether your traffic is increasing due to those rankings. Finally, we discuss how to analyze your rankings by putting them in the context of your business. Do your rankings in the search engine mean anything to your ROI (return on investment)? Read on to find out!

Measuring Website Usability

One of the first things you should do is to gather data in order to measure your website's usability. This means going through your site to test how your users see your site and measure whether the users are interacting with your site the way you want them to. A few different ways are available to do this: by using personas, A/B and multivariate testing, and cookies and session IDs. We discuss all these methods in the following sections.

Personas

You create *personas* to measure certain statistics for your website. To create a typical persona, profile a user who fits the demographic information of your target audience, but customize the profile to fit a real person.

Here are a couple of sample personas: Jill is a 20-something female from New York. She's a professional with a fairly large disposable income, but she doesn't drive. She reads through your website, and because it's about classic-car customization, she doesn't find anything of interest to her, so she clicks away. Doug is in his mid-thirties, works for a real-estate firm, and has three cars of his own already. He wants to stop and take a look at your site and quite possibly subscribe to your newsletter.

But here's the thing: Neither Jill nor Doug is real. They're made-up people, or *personas,* created by marketing or usability firms in order to go through your website to see whether your site is properly targeting its demographics. A persona can give you an idea of whether your website will work for your target demographic. A firm often designs seven to ten different personas that are then used as a preliminary test market for your website. These are people from different age groups, socioeconomic backgrounds, and ethnicities, and they go through your site and allow you to gather data on whether your pages are working the way you want them to or whether you're turning off the very people you want to entice. If your audience is the go-getter type like Jill, a long meandering trip to the conversion point is going to lose her early on. But rushing someone like Doug could make him uncomfortable and cause him to bail out, leaving a shopping cart full of unpurchased goodies behind.

If your site sells shoes, a persona can help you more effectively target your market because you can keep track of whether Jill is going through your site and actually making a purchase, as opposed to hitting your site and leaving immediately afterwards. We offer a lot more information about personas and creating them in Book V, Chapter 1.

A/B testing

One of the most commonly used tools for testing your website usability is *A/B testing.* It's like doing a science experiment. You test your old version of your website (Version A) with the new version (Version B) to see which one measures up better. A/B testing and multivariate testing (discussed in the following section) are somewhat complex, but we explain what they mean and how they can help. Afterward, we describe options to implement testing.

The big advantage of A/B testing is that you can send half your traffic to the page(s) with the proposed changes while sending the other half to the current page. That way, you can compare your current conversion rate for at least part of your site traffic in case some of the proposed changes aren't working. A/B testing is often the best choice for a page with lower traffic.

But you can't run off and do a hack-and-slash job on the test page and expect to get any sort of meaningful data out of it. Here are some guidelines to help you get meaningful, measurable results if you plan to run A/B tests on a website change or an email campaign:

✦ **Change only one variable at a time.** Figuring out what exactly is working for you is harder if you've changed several variables on the site.

✦ **Figure out the precise process for diverting traffic.** One of the problems in A/B testing is that some marketers don't understand how to divert traffic and don't get accurate traffic numbers.

✦ **Establish accurate measures of volume.** Doing a comparison test is hard if you don't know how many people you're testing.

✦ **Look for significant differences.** If you see a difference in the conversion rate for the B test, you need to ensure that this difference is significant. A miniscule change to your goal probably won't be worth the effort, whereas a significant change will.

✦ **Take the time to do a null test.** A *null test* is a test that you run on two A-version pages (pages you haven't made any changes to) in order to establish a baseline and make sure the traffic isn't coming in weird. This is to make sure that half your traffic is going to one page and the other half is going to the other page, and that you have enough people going into the test.

✦ **Run your test long enough to ensure results are real.** You won't get an accurate amount of data if you run the test only for a day or a week. Make sure to run it long enough to get enough data to do an accurate comparison, typically a month or more. Remember, with web analytics, the more time you take to do something right, the better your results are.

✦ **Run segmentation tests.** A *segmentation test* tests the variables in your incoming traffic (such as the demographics of that traffic) by asking users to answer a few questions. Really, you can test any variable as long as you set it up right. The more information you have on your different variables, the better you can target specific changes to your site to drive up your conversions.

We cover much more on the ins and outs of A/B testing in Chapter 3 of this minibook.

**Book VIII
Chapter 2**

**Tracking Behavior
with Web Analytics**

Multivariate testing

A/B testing is about measuring big changes to your site. It's comparing the old site with the completely new version. *Multivariate testing* is about testing all those smaller changes to your site, like the change to a certain font, or to a button instead of an arrow. Typically, you test many small changes to the same page at one time instead of two totally separate pages, as in A/B testing. Multivariate testing works better when a page has a large volume of traffic. If you are testing a medium- or low-volume page, use A/B tests instead.

Most of the testing tools involve copying and pasting a piece of JavaScript into the code of the pages that you are testing. The control code on the top of the HTML page tells you that people are trying to load the page. The tracking script at the bottom of the code tells you that the visitors saw the page, and then you have another code on the conversion page (whatever page the users view after they have completed a conversion) that tells you they converted and what version of the page they were looking at. If you do a test, each version of the landing page has a unique sticker for you to iden-tify it by. If you're doing the test with Google Analytics, after the test runs for a while, Google populates reports for you. Other programs work similarly.

Here are some quick guidelines to keep in mind when running your test:

+ **Test a small number of variations.** The rule of thumb is less than 100 variables per combination of tested pages.

+ **Test big changes.** If you can't see any difference between two variations in eight seconds, your visitors probably won't either and their reactions won't tell you anything. They can't react to what they don't notice.

+ **If conversions are relatively rare in your business, consider testing for early indicators.** If you're selling a $100,000 software package, for example, you won't have a high number of sales to test. Instead, optimize for conversion indicators such as request info, view product details, and so on.

+ **Don't jump to conclusions.** A two-week test is not enough time to gather your data. Run each test for at least one month, if not two.

Cookies

When we talk about cookies, we don't mean a tasty sugary snack. *Cookies* are little files that get saved in your browser to keep track of information on a particular site. A cookie is what enables you to automatically log on to your Facebook account regardless of whether you've closed your browser session or even logged off and powered down your computer.

Once upon a time, a server would send out web pages when they were requested without recording any data on who requested the page, where it went, or any other associated user behavior. Cookies were created to save this information. Cookies are used to enhance the browser experience, improve usability for customer interactions, increase purchase behavior, and improve commercial website performance by keeping track of what the user's doing.

Cookies are either first party or third party, depending on the type of website that sets them. A first-party cookie is set by the site that the user is visiting, such as `www.classiccarcustomization.com`. A third-party cookie is set by a third-party site, such as a web analytics vendor, that provides a service to the main website.

A first-party cookie can contain personal information such as username and a login ID so that users can be recognized when they visit a site. If cookies didn't store this data, websites would have to request it every time the users returned to the site.

A third-party cookie tracks a visitor's path through `www.classic carcustomization.com` so it can identify which pages work and which don't, helping optimize for better site performance. The ad network cookies track user behavior across multiple sites, helping them classify user behavior. This helps in the targeting of ads to user segments. For instance, frequent visitors of sports sites are given sports-relevant ads. Although anonymous, this multi-site gathering of visitor information has also caused some controversy regarding privacy violations.

Deleting third-party cookies
Your browser gives you options for deleting cookies. This, and the advent of antispyware software, has resulted in the deletion of third-party cookies. Cookie rejection is also being enabled by new software mechanisms that block cookies from ever being set on users' computers.

This is a slight problem in that mass cookie deletion and rejection can make it appear that a website's new visitors are increasing while returning visitors are decreasing, which is a change in visitor behavior that is pretty unlikely.

Solving the cookie dilemma
To fix this skew, client-side web analytics vendors have enabled their cookies to be set by their clients' websites, making them first-party cookies, which are less frequently deleted. Although this does not prevent all cookie-caused inaccuracies (users can still delete all cookies or use different computers), this can help.

An alternate solution suggested by Juniper Research is to use Adobe Flash *Local Shared Objects* (LSOs) as a cookie replacement or backup. Similar to a cookie, an LSO is a text file that can be read only by the website that creates it. There's an extra benefit to using LSOs: Browsers and antispyware programs can't delete them, and most users don't know how. Although this works for now, it won't be long before users figure out how to eliminate these as well.

The solution to the cookie dilemma may be to better describe the cookies: Some users see cookies as adding to the browser experience, whereas others see them as an invasion of their privacy. Users can easily get confused by the difference between first-party and third-party cookies — which one is helpful and which one is of questionable value? In the end, every user has to decide for herself whether to delete cookies based on the pros and cons.

Session IDs

Instead of using a cookie, you might be tempted to use a session ID. A session ID is a way of tracking users when they come to your website. Generally, we recommend that you don't use session IDs because they are assigned no matter who the visitor is, including a search engine robot. This means that every time a session ID is used, it is possible that the search engines will treat it as a new page, and you'll wind up with duplicate content that mucks with your rankings in the search engine. Additionally, a session ID is not very useful when it comes to measuring your website usability because a session ID tracks that user only for the duration of his visit to the site. A cookie remembers that user when he returns, whereas a session ID doesn't.

Overall, using cookies to track your visitors is much better, if they have cookies enabled in their browsers.

Tracking Conversions

Your website's objective is to make you money, not just sit out in cyberspace and look pretty. Each activity on your site should be subtly directing the visitor toward a conversion. A *conversion* is a term used by marketers to describe the final outcome of a site visit. As long as those visitors do what you want them to do, they've completed a conversion.

Before any further analysis can be done, you need to identify which processes on your website you want to measure and how your web analytics solution will help in the measurement.

As a rule of thumb, keep these three things in mind when you decide which processes to measure:

✦ **Contact:** Make sure that visitors can contact you if they have difficulty with the process.

✦ **Collect:** Make sure that you can collect the appropriate data when visitors complete the process so that you can retain the visitors in the future.

✦ **Competitors:** If visitors have difficulty on your site, find out whether they can complete a similar process on a competitor's site.

Before going into the details of conversion metrics, it is important to note that you are dealing with two types of conversions, your *website conversions* (conversions gained from your website) and your *marketing campaign conversions* (conversions of any kind in the bricks-and-mortar world). Because this book deals with the online aspect, we concentrate on website conversions.

So what should you be tracking on your site? We've put together a list of things you should be looking for. Feel free to add to this list as needed; this is just a jumping-off point for you to get started.

Measuring marketing campaign effectiveness

The first thing you should look at are your marketing campaigns. It's important to measure the effect of marketing campaigns on your website traffic. The following metrics are specific to marketing campaigns aimed at driving traffic to your site:

✦ **Campaign conversion rate:** Determines the effect of conversions from specific campaigns. Did the conversions rise due to the ads you placed on other websites or due to a grassroots viral marketing campaign, like These Come from Trees? (An environmental group asked its members to place These Come from Trees stickers in public restroom stalls in order to curb overuse of paper products — towels, toilet paper, and so on. These stickers included the URL of the organization's website, where it provided more information and stickers.)

✦ **Cost per conversion:** Figures the cost effectiveness for specific campaigns. You have a great idea for a marketing campaign, but giving away $20 bills stamped with your web address might cost more than the actual conversion you're aiming for. Make sure that you can afford the campaign before you start it.

✦ **Campaign ROI (return on investment):** Determines the cost effectiveness for specific campaigns. Is your campaign bringing in the conversions you need, or are you losing money?

- ✦ **Segment conversion rates:** Tracks conversion progress over time. Your conversions most likely won't change overnight. Watch them over a long period of time to make sure that your campaign is effectively working.

- ✦ **Percent of orders from new and repeat customers:** Determines the effectiveness of marketing or customer-retention programs. You want to attract new customers, yes, but you also want them to turn into repeat customers.

- ✦ **New and repeat customer conversion rates:** Helps understand barriers to online purchases. One repeat customer is worth more than a new customer because not only do repeat customers mean future conversions, they also cost less than new customers because you don't have to spend a whole lot to keep them.

- ✦ **Sales per visitor:** Measures marketing efficiency. How much is someone likely to buy? How little? Get an average so that you can figure out how to budget your campaign effectively.

Here are some key metrics you should track, regardless of whether your site is e-commerce, research, or any other kind of website:

- ✦ The conversion rates for any process that makes or saves money or that is critical to the customer experience

- ✦ The campaign conversion rate for current campaigns or the most expensive campaigns, if you have a lot of them

- ✦ The cost per conversion for the campaigns you decide to monitor

- ✦ The segment conversion rates for key or critical group conversions

Here are some specific metrics that e-commerce sites should be tracking:

- ✦ The site-wide conversion rate (all purchases to all visits or visitors)

- ✦ New and repeat site-wide customer conversion rates

- ✦ The percents of orders from new and returning customers

- ✦ The average order value, site-wide and for new and returning customers

- ✦ Sales per visitor (compare to site-wide conversion rate)

After you decide which site-wide processes you want to measure and how to measure them, the following metrics can help you understand visitor success or failure. These metrics follow whether a customer stays, searches, or actually makes a conversion:

- ✦ **Home to purchase:** The abandonment rate for visitors going through the sales path

- ✦ **Search to purchase:** The abandonment rate for visitors coming from a site search

+ **Special offer to purchase:** The effect of various merchandising and pricing options

+ **Lead generation:** The abandonment rate when personal data is requested

Establishing site objectives or goals and all the parts that make up these objectives (the who, how, where, what, and why) is essential when tracking the conversions on your site. One of these factors could contribute to the success of your campaign — or just as easily derail it.

Building conversion funnels

After your site objectives are established, you can measure your progress through the use of a conversion funnel. In Chapter 1 of this minibook, we define the four basic websites: e-commerce, content, lead generation, and self service. On an e-commerce site, a conversion is obviously a sale. For a content site, it might be the number of newsletter subscriptions. Lead-generation sites try to gather information for later contact. Self-service sites are targeted at solving a customer's problems, so the measure might be time spent on the site.

In the conversion funnel in Figure 2-1, each step in the sales process on the way to conversion is fraught with visitor drop-off. (Steps in the funnel differ based on the type of business and conversion that you're seeking.)

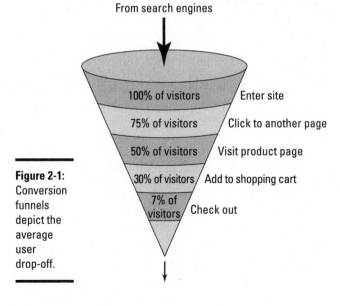

Figure 2-1: Conversion funnels depict the average user drop-off.

From search engines

100% of visitors — Enter site

75% of visitors — Click to another page

50% of visitors — Visit product page

30% of visitors — Add to shopping cart

7% of visitors — Check out

Each block on the conversion funnel becomes smaller as you go down the sales (or conversion) path. This represents the amount of users you lose along the way to a conversion, for whatever reason.

The point of using a conversion funnel is to figure out where you are getting the most drop-off. In a perfect world, there would be no conversion funnels because all visitors to your site would perform your desired action and you would have a conversion column. But because this isn't a perfect world, your main goal is for the drop-off rate to be as low as possible.

Measuring your website's conversion rate is a challenge because a number of steps lead to that final action, and sometimes visitors are thwarted in their quest to complete an intended action. You can hope that you lost them just because their browser crashed, but sometimes they simply didn't find what they were looking for, or the site was too confusing, or it took too long for them to get to their objective — and so they left. Additionally, many sites measure only their final conversion rate. This does not give webmasters the opportunity to improve their drop-off rates by analyzing the sales path and finding the bottlenecks in order to make the site improvements that result in higher conversions.

Don't measure your end-result conversion rate without tracking the *path* that your customers take to conversion.

Preventing conversion funnel drop-off

In a typical conversion funnel, visitors drop off along the way to the final step that completes the sale or achieves the desired action. The good news is that when your *analytics program* (such as Adobe Analytics or Google Analytics, which we discuss in Chapter 1 of this minibook) tracks the micro-steps required to reach the final conversion act, it reveals data that can be used to prevent drop-off. The analytics package you have does the work and the analysis so that you don't have to. Just be sure to implement the changes it recommends.

One of the things you can do is to eliminate all the unnecessary steps to visitor conversion to reduce the conversion funnel drop-off. The fewer steps needed for a visitor to convert, the greater the likelihood of a conversion. You should create an effective call-to-action for every step in the sales path. Your conversion rate reflects your ability to persuade visitors to complete their intended actions.

Analyzing your conversion funnel

Your conversion funnel is the path a user follows on your site on the way to a purchase. It's important to follow the conversion funnel closely and analyze where you're losing the most people by percentage. It's very unlikely that 100 percent of your visitors will continue on through every step, but you do want a high percentage of visitors to continue on your conversion path.

Say you have an e-commerce site that gets 2,000 visitors per month, your site has a three-step sales path, and your average sale is $11 per item. If half your site visitors enter the sales path, that means 1,000 prospects drop off at the first step. A 50 percent drop-off rate at the first step could be due to an impediment such as requiring site registration. If 40 percent of that total drops off at the second step, and 30 percent of that group completes the sale, you have $1,980 in sales at a 9 percent conversion rate because only 180 of the original 2,000 prospects made a purchase.

When people drop off, they have not found what they were looking for on your site. By identifying high abandonment pages, you can take a closer look to see what might be making visitors leave and test for ways that would make them want to stick around and continue on the conversion funnel. By properly analyzing this data, you can make sure you won't lose as many people along the conversion funnel. More people convert, which means more money for you.

Making site improvements

Using the math from the example in the preceding section, if you can improve the final step of the sales path by just 10 percent, it would bring you an additional $198 in sales, upping your conversion rate to 9.9 percent. However, if you can make improvements at the first step of the sales path, reducing your 50 percent drop-off rate to 25 percent, you can increase your sales by $5,940, resulting in a 36 percent conversion rate.

However, if you do not know what to measure and why, or you haven't a clue as to what indicators to evaluate in your analytics reports, you can't take the necessary actions to improve your site performance. So take the time to figure out the data to analyze based on your site objectives, and then follow up on the data revealed through the use of your analytics software.

Simply picking out indicators that look good at first glance — such as increasing numbers of referrals from Google and Yahoo or increasing the number of page views — might not help you improve site performance. It's not that these numbers are worthless; they just might not be the right metrics to improve your site. Knowing the basic analytic principles ensures that you know what metrics to check for when making your business decisions.

In the preceding sections in this chapter, we talk about overall site objectives, but you also need to consider objectives for the individual pages within your site, which we discuss in the following section.

Assigning web page objectives

Assign individual objectives to each page, especially the ones that require the user to perform an action. Every page should be designed to have a user perform an action, even if that action is something as simple as clicking over to the next page.

To effectively implement this approach, every page on your website that requires action should answer the following three questions:

✦ What action is required? Examples are clicking to the next page, playing a video, or reading the text on the website.

✦ Who must take that action?

✦ What information does your visitor need to take the required action?

By answering these questions, you can define your objectives and apply good analytics solutions to test and optimize your pages for improved results. The same principles you used for site optimization can also work for page optimization.

Tracking the Success of Your SEO Project

Besides watching your conversions, you still need to keep an eye on the big picture: Is the time, effort, and money you are putting into your SEO project actually bringing you a return? You need to know whether the keywords you are using are actually working out for you. Are they affecting your rankings in the search engines? Have your rankings gone up, stayed the same, or actually gotten worse? And in particular, has your traffic increased as a result of search engine traffic?

Determining success relies on tracking your keywords more effectively. *Keywords* are the search terms that users put into the search engines (we go over them in depth in Book II). When you are tracking keywords in order to see if they're working out for you, remember that the broad phrases aren't all you should be looking at, but also the more specific keywords and longer keyword phrases, called *long-tail keywords*. *Keyword phrases* are groups of three or more keywords that users put into a query window, such as [classic car customization Poughkeepsie].

By using analytics data in conjunction with ranking reports and keyword data provided by the search engines, you can keep track of which keywords are working for you to gain more conversions and which ones are just not working out at all. You can keep track of how much you are spending on these particular keywords (through ad campaigns and whatnot; see Book II for more details) and whether the ROI is really worth it.

Remember, if a keyword is not working out for you, don't be afraid to get rid of it and find a keyword that does.

SEO is much more nebulous when it comes to identifying and tracking the metrics. A good keyword might bring you more traffic, but if those users aren't giving you conversions, they're just using up server space and costing you time and money. That's why it's essential that you have relevant keywords and that you provide your users with the information or products you are advertising. For instance, if your keywords are [Classic car customization], your site should provide information on classic car customization.

There's also such a thing as too much information. The longer a person stays around your site, and the more she explores it, the more likely she is to provide you with a conversion. So do provide people with information, but don't do it all on one page. Spread it around your site, and make sure that your users have access to it.

Also keep in mind that SEO takes a while to fully work, so give it a decent amount of time before you really start to worry if you don't see a whole lot of change. The changes take time, so be prepared to be patient, and know that putting in the time and the effort is truly worthwhile.

Analyzing Rankings

Getting high rankings in a search engine is one thing. Say that you achieve a coveted second- or even first-place spot on the first page of Google results for the keywords you want. However, getting to the top of the search engine results page means nothing if it doesn't help your conversion rate or your ROI. You're not doing SEO to get high rankings; you're doing SEO to get more conversions.

A high ranking in the search engine results page only increases your traffic, and that's great if the conversions you are looking for happen to be a high volume of traffic. But if your traffic volume doesn't provide you with the conversions you need, and your bounce rate is pretty high, you need to figure out what's wrong with your site.

Analytics packages (such as those we talk about in Chapter 1 of this minibook) allow you to put these metrics next to one another; you can then pair that data with a ranking monitor so that you can see the amount of your conversions next to how you are ranking.

You also need to be tracking the paths your visitors took on the way to your site, so make sure that all your visitors have a cookie. That way, you can know which users arrived from the search engines and which ones came from outside links or from their own bookmarks. And if you know that, you can properly read the data coming in from the search engines. Also, be aware of seasonal trends in the search engines. Remember, some traffic is seasonal, especially around the holidays, so take that into consideration when you're watching your search engine rankings.

Chapter 3: Mastering SEO Tools and Reports

In This Chapter

✔ Getting started with conversion testing

✔ Getting to know page and site analysis tools

✔ Tracking conversions from multiple referral sources

✔ Seeing how your visitors travel through your site

In this chapter, we cover the nuts and bolts of conversion testing. We walk you through it, step by step, and hopefully demystify the process a little bit. We show you how to fix common conversion and usability problems, and we introduce you to some page and site analysis tools. Finally, we discuss how to use link analysis tools.

Getting Started with Conversion Testing

Say that you've gathered your data and done the proper analysis, and now you've decided that some things need to be changed on your website. Making major overhauls to your site requires A/B testing. *A/B testing* is testing the original version of the website (Version A) against the one you made the major changes to (Version B). The A/B test is a tool that tells you which changes have a better effect and to what degree.

We discuss A/B testing in Chapter 2 of this minibook, but in the following sections, we go a little more in-depth and tell you how to actually *do* an A/B test. Before we get started, here are some cardinal rules you need to keep in mind for running an A/B test:

✦ **Change only one variable at a time, especially when A/B testing involves major changes to your site.** If you change more than one variable at a time, you can't determine which variable is responsible for the change or to what degree. Systematic testing helps you isolate important variables.

✦ **Divert enough traffic to your test page for a valid sample.** The object of traffic diversion is to redirect a percentage of visitors through the page to which you made all those changes. Ideally, the percentage of traffic to be redirected can be easily changed without having to completely overhaul those pages.

✦ **Get a visitors-per-page count from your web analytics tool.** This ensures that you actually get the percentage of traffic you're expecting moving through your site based on the number of changes tested. For instance, if you expect to run half through Version A and half through Version B, you should see nearly equal numbers of visitors to the first page in the process. If you're running a three-way test (testing A/B/C pages), you should aim for a distribution of 33/33/34 percent of visitors running through each path.

✦ **Look for significant differences.** If you see a difference in the conversion rate for Version B, compared to Version A, you need to ensure this difference is significant (more than .5 percent) so that you can be certain it comes from the change you made to Version B. Smaller differences can be due to variations in your visitors or any other number of environmental factors. Keep running your test until all the changes can be attributed to the exact step that was tweaked, or until you are certain there was no change.

✦ **Take the time to do a null test.** A *null test* involves putting 50/50 traffic through two identical pages to be A/B tested. It's basically doing a control test for your science experiment. In this case, you replicate Page A, calling this copy Page B. Then, without making any changes to Page B, you test your analytics and conversions through both A and B, which should be equal. A null test verifies that you get the same conversion and abandonment rates and that your measurement tools are set up correctly. If you are not getting close to the same rates for both pages (about .5 percent), something is wrong, and your data from the A/B test will be skewed. If this happens, check that you are sending visitors into the tests exactly the same way and that you are running enough visitors through the test. Depending on your traffic volume, you need to attain a reasonable sample, and this can take time. You must run a null test to make sure the data you get back from the actual A/B test is accurate.

✦ **Run your test long enough to ensure results are real.** It takes time to gather good, solid data from an A/B test. For example, you may see trends in the first few hours that reverse themselves later. You need a representative sample before you can assume that Version B is better than Version A or that Version A is better than Version B.

✦ **Run segmentation tests.** *Segmenting* (dividing into like groups) the subjects that you're testing allows you to monitor their activities when they return to your site. This lets you target a group of visitors if it turns out that a good percentage of your B-page visitors (presuming that A/B test results favored B over A) return to the website within two months to make another purchase, especially if these were people who provided you with conversions.

The upside of A/B testing is that if your proposed changes don't work, not all your visitors are subjected to the bad changes, only those whom you put through the B page. This is better than just making the change without testing and crossing your fingers. The downside is that A/B testing is a long, complicated process that takes knowledge, precision, and time.

Because conversions are critical to your business's success, start up a program of A/B split testing before making final site changes. Test two different versions of your page when you're testing things like changes on a call-to-action landing page, one at a time. Table 3-1 shows the hypothetical results of such a test.

Table 3-1	Sample Results of an A/B Test		
	Page A (Original)	*Page B*	*Page C*
Percent of traffic received	34%	33%	33%
New sales generated	200	220	150
Percentage of change	N/A	10%	−25%

Getting ready to run a conversion test

You can use any of several different tools to run a test on pages of your website and compare which variation sees better conversions. Google Analytics has a feature for running A/B tests and *multivariate tests* (which are like an A/B test except that they test smaller details, like a different font color, instead of large changes, and you can test all variables at once with different permutations). In this section, we outline the broad steps you have to take before you run a test.

The first thing you need to do before running your test is to choose your test page. Not every single page needs to have a test run on it: You probably don't care about conversions from your About Us page, for example. To be a good candidate for testing, the page needs to offer an action the user can take, like purchasing, downloading, or signing up for something. The action can be as simple as a link that you want your users to click on — the point is that it has to be a measureable response.

For your first test, choose a landing page (the page that visitors first land on when they arrive at your website) that receives high volumes of traffic, like the top of a category or a pay per click (PPC) landing page. This lets you see meaningful results quickly.

The second step is choosing the objective of the test (or *experiment,* as it's called in the Content Experiments tool in Google Analytics that we walk you through in detail later in this chapter). Your objective is what you want to get out of the experiment, ranging from more conversions to fewer bounces, more pages viewed, and longer time spent on your site. If your test page is a *conversion page,* a page on which an action occurs that you want the user to take on your website, be it the aforementioned purchase, download, or sign-up, your objective for the test will most likely be more conversions.

When you're doing further, more in-depth testing, choose the conversion or user behavior you wish to track in order to measure the success of your test page. Remember, these tests are to figure out whether the changes you've made are successful from a user standpoint. And although the testing process is called conversion testing, you can also test for improvements to your visitors' behaviors, like staying on a page or the site as a whole longer.

The third step is to figure out which kind of test you want to run. Content Experiments, a free tool within Google Analytics that we cover in the following section, allows you to run an A/B or multivariate test. Depending on what kind of changes to your site you want to make, you can choose to run either an A/B test between two pages (for the big changes) or a multivariate test between many pages (for the small ones).

A/B tests compare the performance of two entirely different pages, which means trying out entirely different layouts, moving around sections of the page, or changing the overall look and feel of a page. A/B tests are simpler to run, and you can obtain results must faster.

Multivariate tests allow you to test content variations in different sections of your page simultaneously. So, instead of tracking one or two big changes, you can test two different headlines, three different images, and two different product descriptions. Obtaining results from these kinds of tests takes longer, but they're more flexible than A/B tests.

The fourth step is choosing the content you want to test. Within Content Experiments, you can use up to ten variations of your original page. For a multivariate test, for example, you might test the headline and an image to go with it. For an A/B test, you indicate your original page and your test page, as shown in Figure 3-1. The differences between your original page and test page in an A/B test can be on just about anything, such as which offer brings in more conversions: free phones or free kittens.

The fifth step is creating the actual content variations you want to test. For a multivariate test, for example, you could try a heading in a new font and test out some new wording and perhaps a different image as well (see Figure 3-2).

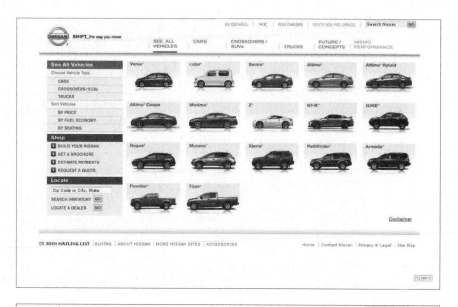

Figure 3-1:
For an A/B test, you run Version A (top) against Version B (bottom) to see which performs better.

Smaller changes like this should be tested with a multivariate test, not an A/B test, because you get better results.

For the A/B test, you need a Page A (your control page) and a Page B (the test page that has significant changes).

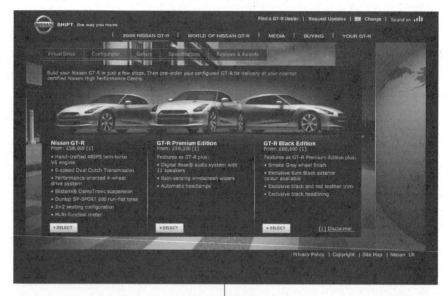

Page A-Original

Figure 3-2:
Multivariate
tests use
multiple
variables on
the same
page.

Page B-Test

During the experiment, your visitors see either your control page (A) or your test page (B). This way, you can test whether variations in the page lead to more conversions. Do people react differently with different images or text?

Or does rearranging your site differently lead to easier access for your users and more conversions for you?

The variations need to be *significantly* different than the original content. For example, you won't see much change if your headline changes from "Welcome!" to "Come on in!" Someone brand new to your page should be able to tell at a glance what's different about the page. Subtlety has no place in an A/B test.

The last step is deciding how much traffic you want for your test, the minimum length of time you want to run the experiment, and the confidence level you're comfortable with (Content Experiments lets you set this between 95 percent and 99.5 percent). You are running this test on your actual website, so you might not want to lose a whole lot of your site traffic. You can actually choose to limit what percent of your visitors see the new version of your page. But keep in mind that if you limit the amount of traffic to the test page, you'll have to wait a lot longer to get any sort of meaningful results from this test. We recommend running your test for at least a month to get any kind of decent results, and it may take even longer than that. Don't quit too soon and make a judgment based on early numbers.

Testing with Content Experiments

Content Experiments is a free tool that's included within Google Analytics (available at `www.google.com/analytics/`) that runs A/B and multivariate tests. We walk you through using this tool because it's quick, accurate, and free.

Set up your experiment

To start the testing process with Google Analytics Content Experiments, you need to first make sure that the Google Analytics tracking code is installed on all pages you're using in the test (see Chapter 1 of this minibook for these instructions). Then you need to do the following:

1. **Sign in to your Google Analytics account and select the site you're working on.**

   Click the Reporting tab, and then select Behavior and then Experiments from the left-hand menu.

2. **Click the Create Experiment button at the top of the page.**

   The Experiments list page, which displays a summary of all your experiments, appears. If this is your first experiment, your list is empty, as shown in Figure 3-3.

Create Experiment button

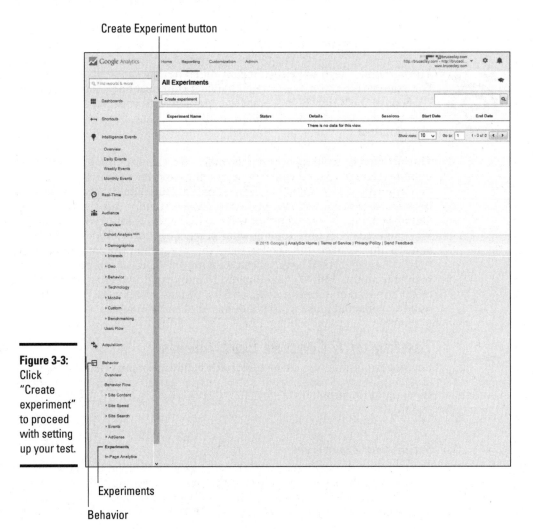

Figure 3-3:
Click
"Create
experiment"
to proceed
with setting
up your test.

Experiments

Behavior

The Create a New Experiment screen appears (see Figure 3-4).

3. **Name the experiment and select an objective along with the percentage of your traffic to serve the experiment.**

4. **Click Advanced Options to set the minimum length of time the experiment should run and your confidence threshold (your choices are 95, 99, or 99.5 percent confidence). Then click Next Step.**

5. **On the next screen that appears, enter the URLs of your original page and test variation page.**

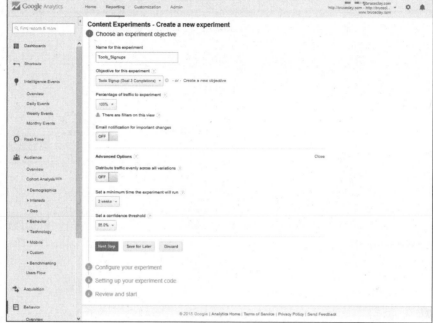

Figure 3-4:
Use the
Content
Experiments
Wizard to
start run-
ning a test
on your site.

If you're testing multiple variations of the page, click +Add Variation and enter another URL. You see a preview of each page, as shown in Figure 3-5. When you've finished adding up to ten test variations, click Next Step.

6. **Choose to add the Content Experiments code to your website.**

   Select Manually Insert the Code if you're comfortable with copying and pasting some code in the Head section of the original page and all variation pages. If you have a webmaster to do that kind of thing for you, tell Content Experiments to send that code to your webmaster by clicking the Send the Code to Webmaster button and providing your webmaster's email address.

7. **After the code has been added to the pages being tested, click Next Step.**

   Content Experiments validates that everything is set up right.

Review and start the experiment

After you've created your variations and tagged your pages, relax: The hard part's over. All you need to do now is turn the experiment on by clicking the Start Experiment button at the end of the Setup Wizard. But be warned: After

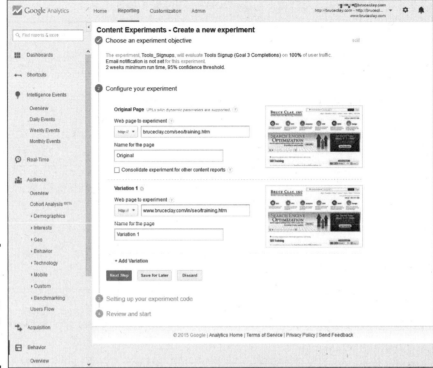

Figure 3-5:
Enter the
URLs of
your original
page and up
to ten test
pages.

you start running the experiment, you can't change any of the variables, so make sure that everything is as you want it to be before you start.

If you do find a problem, all you need to do is return to the experiment from the list page, and then click edit for any step in the wizard. But if you change the page URLs at this point, you have to go through and reinstall the code on the new pages and revalidate everything.

Before you click Start Experiment, you get one last chance to preview the alternate page variations that are displayed to visitors during the experiment. If anything needs to be changed, click edit to change the names, objectives, or page URLs.

Ready, set, go!

After you click Start Experiment, you are sent back to the Experiments list page.

You also see an additional section on the page describing the progress of this experiment, including the status, number of impressions, and start and end dates of the experiment. Your test page starts showing different variations immediately, but a delay of about an hour takes place before your reports start displaying data. The progress and duration of the experiment depends on how much traffic goes through your test and conversion pages.

After you've got some significant data, the reports have preliminary results ready for you. Click the experiment from the list to see the experiment's results.

Viewing your results

Be sure to check that visits and conversions are being recorded soon after starting your experiment. If you're not getting any visits or conversions, check the troubleshooting guide for some suggestions on what might be causing this error. Sometimes errors occur that don't show up until the experiment is actually running.

Hold off on checking your reports right away. Until a minimum amount of data has been collected, you get a message along the lines of Hold on There, Cowboy, We Don't Have a Complete Report Yet. (Well, okay, not literally, but you get the idea.) Check back in a day or two in order to see your results start coming in. With any test, you want to wait long enough to gather enough data for it to be meaningful. When you have enough data, you can check your reports, which look something like Figure 3-6.

Google Analytics support explains how to read results at `https://support.google.com/analytics/answer/1745152`. The report tells you:

✦ **Experiment status:** If an experiment is in progress, the status reads that you have no winner yet. If enough data has been gathered to meet the level of confidence you set at the outset of the test, a winner is announced.

✦ **Conversions and visits:** This is the number of conversions and visits a particular page generated.

✦ **Improvement:** The Compare to Original column displays the difference (positive or negative) between the conversion rate of the variation and the original.

✦ **Probability of outperforming original:** While the experiment is in progress, this column displays the probability that a combination will be more successful than the original version based on the results so far. The higher the percentage, the better the test page is doing.

With enough time and data, Content Experiments identifies the winning variation. It's all a matter of how long you run the experiment and how similar

Figure 3-6:
Reporting from Content Experiments provides the conversion rate of the original page and variations and predicts which is likely to perform best through the course of the test.

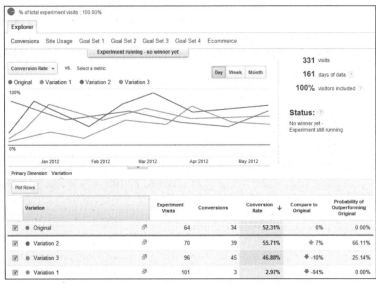

the variations are. If you've run the experiment for a long time and still don't have a clear winner, your variations might be too similar to get correct data, so you may need to make some tweaks and run another experiment.

To stop the experiment at any time, click the Stop Experiment button on the Experiment page.

Always be testing

One of the cardinal rules of analytics is that you must always be testing. Analytics experts tell you that if you're not constantly monitoring, testing, changing, and improving your pages based on your analytics, you'll miss out on huge opportunities.

Set up a system that detects high-performing pages and routinely performs an A/B or multivariate test on those pages. Test every product

launch page, your conversion points, your calls to action, your landing pages, and your buttons and fonts.

Never be satisfied with "good enough" on your website. As we describe in the appendix of this book, the more you test, the more you understand — so you'll be able to drive traffic and conversions better than your competitors.

Discovering Page and Site Analysis Tools

Without wisdom, data is just numbers. To use the powerful analytics tools at your disposal, you first need to know what you want your website visitors to do. This can be anything from purchasing products to signing up for a newsletter or just getting more traffic to your website. After you know what you are measuring, you can view how well you're doing in your analytics software.

Google Analytics is the free analytics package that we recommend using to see how your visitors are coming to your site and what they're doing after they get there. With Google Analytics, you can segment your view of visitors by where they came from; those segments are paid and organic Google search results, social networks, and other special campaigns that the website owner may define. To see your organic search traffic from both Bing and Yahoo, you look to the analytics reporting that's part of the free Bing Webmaster Tools. You can see your paid search traffic from the combined Yahoo and Bing ad networks in Bing Ads Reporting.

Viewing performance of paid search campaigns

When you run a pay per click (PPC) campaign, you spend money whenever potential clients click your advertisement. Because you're spending money, you want to know how much money or value you're getting back for that campaign. That's where PPC conversion reports come in.

PPC conversion reports tell you things like how many people are buying products. They can also be configured to tell you how much money you made from selling products to people who came from a PPC advertisement. For example, in Google Analytics, you can link your AdWords account, receive reports about your paid search campaigns, and find the information shown in Figure 3-7. For Bing Ads, analytics reporting is provided in Bing Ads Reporting (`https://secure.bingads.microsoft.com/`).

You need to tell Google AdWords and Bing Ads what your conversions are in order to get an accounting of conversions by visitors from search ad clicks. Read about setting up goals in AdWords in the Google support article at `https://support.google.com/adwords/answer/1722036`. Creating and tracking goals for Bing Ads is explained in this support article at `https://advertise.bingads.microsoft.com/en-uk/cl/256/training/campaign-analytics`.

You can drill down from your campaigns to your ad groups to your keywords, seeing the number of clicks an ad received, your ad's *click-through rate* (CTR), how much your *cost-per-click* (CPC) was, your conversion rate, and how much you made from that advertisement, reported as revenue.

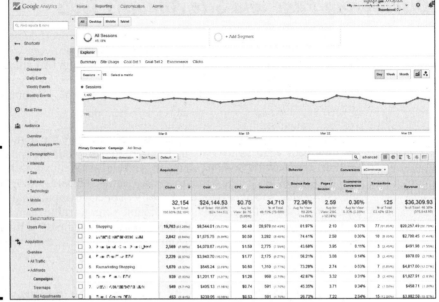

Figure 3-7:
Google
Analytics
is a source
of perfor-
mance data
about your
AdWords
campaigns.

With these types of reports, you can analyze your spending and your revenue based on PPC ads. This information helps you decide which keywords,
advertisements, and campaigns are working the best for you and which ones
are not working so well. With this information, you can optimize your PPC
campaigns by limiting your spending and maximizing your revenue based on
the spending constraint.

Measuring traffic and conversion from organic search

Measuring how much of your traffic and conversion is from *organic* (non-
paid) search is important because it tells you how much traffic and money
you are getting for your SEO efforts. Every SEO campaign costs you time and
money, so you want to know what you're getting back for it. Most analytics
software packages come with an out-of-the-box report for getting traffic from
organic search. Figure 3-8 is from Google Analytics.

Figure 3-9 shows a similar report from Bing Webmaster Tools. The graph
shows the number of clicks from a Bing organic search that a site received.
Below that, you can see a list of top pages receiving organic search traffic and the keywords the search visitors queried to see your site on a Bing
search results page.

Figure 3-8: This graph from Google Analytics shows the pages on the site that received the most visitors from Google organic search.

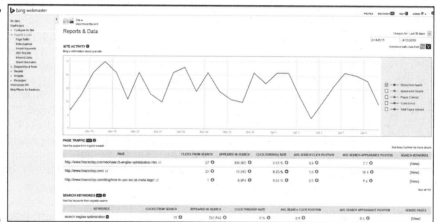

Figure 3-9: Bing Webmaster Tools reports site activity, page traffic, and search keywords from a Bing and Yahoo organic search.

Defining goals in Google Analytics

To get the most out of Google Analytics, define your conversions, called Goals in this analytics suite. You can choose from among four Goal types in Google Analytics:

✦ **Destination:** Triggers when a specific page loads because a goal action was completed, like a thank-you page

✦ **Duration:** Counted when a user is on the site for a specified amount of time or longer

✦ **Pages or screens per session:** Happens when a user views a specified number of pages or screens

✦ **Event:** Triggers when a defined action takes place, such as when a video is played or a specified link is clicked

Think of all the objectives you have for your website, and set up goals to track your visitors' completion of those objectives. If yours is an e-commerce site, set a Destination Goal linked to the thank-you page that shows up after a purchase is made. If a white paper download is a goal, set an Event Goal to trigger when the Download button is clicked. You have the option of assigning a monetary value to your goals, and if you do, Google Analytics reports dollar amounts attributed to traffic from different segments. With Goals defined, you can measure the value of paid and organic search and social media marketing efforts. For more on creating and managing Goals in Google Analytics, review the Google Support article here: `https://support.google.com/analytics/answer/1012040`.

Viewing traffic from social networks

Another visitor segment that you can home in on through Google Analytics (GA) is traffic from *social media*. Social media refers to any sort of online environment that allows social interaction, including blogs, social news sites such as Reddit (`www.Reddit.com`) and Digg (`www.Digg.com`), social networking sites such as Facebook (`www.facebook.com`), Twitter (`https://twitter.com`), and Google+ (`plus.google.com`). In Book VI, Chapter 5 you learn about building a community and brand awareness through content shared on social media. With the social reports in Google Analytic, you can see what pages shared in social media brought visitors to your site. If you've set up Goals in GA, you can even see whether these visitors *converted* (took any action you want visitors to take).

Figure 3-10 shows the social network referrals reported in Google Analytics. You can reach this report by going to Acquisition and then Social in the left navigation. Social networks bringing traffic to the site are listed in order of most pages viewed.

Seeing Visitor Paths through the Site

Now you know where visitors are coming from and whether a visitor converts. The final piece you can get from analytics is seeing how a visitor navigated through your site to wind up at her final destination. This helps you determine whether people are just searching through your site until they get something they are looking for or whether they are following a predetermined path that gets them to something you want them to get at.

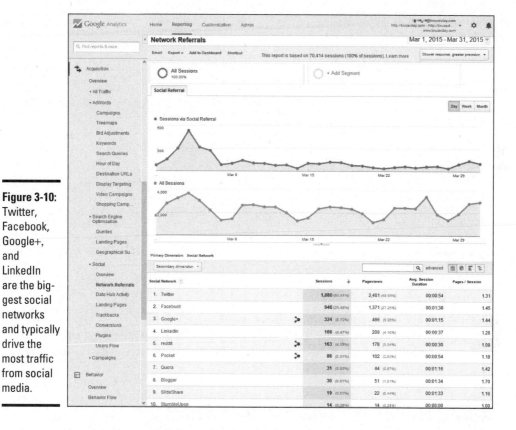

Figure 3-10:
Twitter,
Facebook,
Google+,
and
LinkedIn
are the biggest social
networks
and typically
drive the
most traffic
from social
media.

Google Analytics shows you the path of visitors through your site, a report that you can slice and dice a number of ways. The example in Figure 3-11 is the flow of visitors who entered a site through a social network. In this flow chart, you can see the most popular paths taken by visitors who landed on the site from a social network, with the flow from Twitter highlighted.

Go to Behavior and then Behavior Flow in Google Analytics' left navigation. The default view is the flow of visitors starting at the landing page they entered on. You can also view paths by these dimensions:

✦ Acquisition source (traffic type)

✦ Advertising (by ad content, ad group, ad campaign and ad keyword)

✦ Behavior (by defined Goals)

✦ Social referrals

Figure 3-11:
Behavior
Flow reports
in Google
Analytics
allow you to
track popu-
lar paths on
your site.

✦ Users (by browser, location, language, device, and many more
  subdimensions)

Get more on path reports, including how to set up advanced custom
dimensions, in Google Analytics support: `https://support.google.`
`com/analytics/answer/2519989`.

Understanding Abandonment Rates

On the flip side of knowing how users travel through your site after they get
there is learning when and from where they leave. *Abandonment rates* can be
broken up into two categories: how soon the visitors left your site and what
page they were on when they left your site. These both have different mean-
ings, and understanding what they mean is important.

When visitors leave your site, you naturally want to know why. When a visitor leaves after visiting a lot of pages or going through a process on your
website, that is when you want to know which page he left from. If he leaves
the site on the first page of his visit, the visitor is probably not satisfied
with your site at that time. Reasons for his exit can range from the site's not
answering a specific need of the user to a bad design that just makes the
visitor want to leave. Another reason is that the visitor came to your site for
only one thing, found it, and then left — which is often the case with a blog.
The percentage of visitors who leave after looking at only one page is called
the *bounce rate*.

An *exit page* is the last page the visitor was on before she left the site. Most users leave because they have not found what they were looking for, or they find your site hard to use and think they can find a better alternative. Note that in most cases, the exit page that the most visitors leave from is usually the page that contributes most to your bounce rate.

Both types of reports can be found in almost every analytics suite. Figure 3-12 shows an example of a Content Drilldown report in Google Analytics. The line graph has been set to the Bounce Rate metric and shows how often a visitor leaves after viewing only one page. In the table below the graph, you can see the bounce rate and exit rate of the pages listed. Examining these metrics on a page-by-page level can help you strengthen the weak points in your conversion funnel.

Figure 3-12:
Knowing your bounce rate and exit rate can help you fine-tune your conversion funnel.

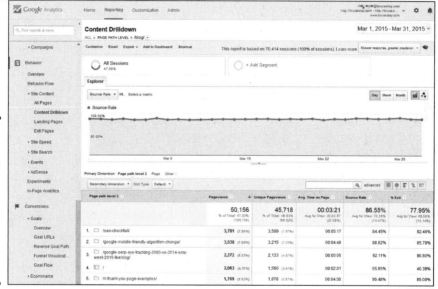

Book IX

International SEO

Contents at a Glance

Chapter 1: Discovering International Search Engines

In This Chapter

✓ Targeting international audiences

✓ Identifying opportunities

✓ Quantifying how many people search

Throughout this book, we talk mainly about what to do to optimize for search engines in the United States, but what about the international market? What about Europe, Latin America, and Asia? This minibook covers what you need to know about working on an international level.

In this chapter, you discover all the basics you need to know to start thinking globally. Cultures and languages vary across the globe, and if you don't properly adjust your market strategy for your international audiences, you risk failure.

You also need to be aware of the different opportunities in international search and how many people out there are using search engines. Not to worry: We have an overview all ready for you in this chapter.

Targeting International Users

Say that you decide to take your business to the international markets. You know that a market exists for classic car customization, and it will generate a whole lot more revenue for you and your company.

Before you get started, remember that when doing business in other countries, you have to be aware of laws other than those of the United States. Unfortunately, to make things difficult on all of us, there is no such thing as a standard international copyright law. National laws, to no one's surprise, apply only to businesses operating within that country. Two countries can barely agree on pizza toppings, metaphorically speaking, let alone a standard international law. Although international law goes beyond the scope of this book, we caution you to look into the laws governing copyright and business before entering an international market.

Along with the technicalities of international copyright laws, you have to think about certain challenges when you're gearing up to start working in the international markets. First of all, be aware of the different browsers that other countries use. Not all of them use Chrome or Mozilla Firefox, so when designing or tailoring your international website, you need to be aware of the constraints of whatever particular browser is popular in your target country or region. This is why good coding is so important. Remember to always test your web pages in a validator, such as the one at the World Wide Web Consortium's website, www.w3.org. (You can find more on validating your code in Book IV, Chapter 4.)

Second, the way people access the Internet varies across the globe. Mobile devices (smartphones) far exceed the number of desktop or laptop computers in developing countries. For example, in the world's most populous nation, China, 85.8 percent of the 649 million Internet users access the web with mobile devices, according to a report by the China Internet Network Information Center as of December 2014. To put those statistics in perspective, the number of Chinese Internet users already outnumbers the total U.S. population by two to one. Yet 649 million represents only 47.9 percent of China's population — so the Chinese market still has a lot of room to grow. Marketers who want to target China must focus on mobile apps and mobile-friendly websites. A mobile-focused strategy is essential for many other countries, as well.

In countries such as Indonesia, India, and others, Internet access is not a given. There are ongoing efforts by Google, Facebook, and other tech giants to expand the reach of the web in places where connections either don't exist or are very slow (2G speed, for example, compared to the 4G or 5G networks in the U.S.). If you hope to reach these markets with your online business, your site or application software needs to have streamlined code and small file sizes that can travel well through slow connections. In 2015, Google began using *transcoding* to simplify web pages when sending results to slow connections. Google has rolled this out in Indonesia, India, and Brazil so far. Transcoding drastically reduces the elements on a web page, removing large images and so forth, so it can load faster. Therefore, if you plan to do online business in these countries, we recommend that you trim your web pages down so that Google's transcoding hatchet doesn't have to butcher them too much.

Another thing you need to be aware of is any difference in currency. It affects shipping rates and the prices of the goods you're trying to sell. For example, at the time of this writing, 1 Euro is the equivalent of 1.07 United States dollars (USD), whereas 1 Japanese yen is the equivalent of .0083 USD. But the exchange rates fluctuate continually, so you need to revise accordingly. A good currency converter is available at XE (www.xe.com/ucc).

The language barrier is a fairly tricky one to navigate as well. Some countries have multiple languages spoken by the populace. For example, in the Netherlands, two main languages are spoken by the population, Dutch and Frisian, but most people speak English or German as well. Marketing in the correct language can be trickier than you'd think. Having local input is the best way to make sure you're getting it right.

Be especially aware of cultural dimensions within that language. Spanish is spoken in many different countries, but it has variations, and what can be a completely innocent word in one country can be a very nasty slang term in another. For example, in the U.S., when you want to determine what's causing a problem, you say you're trying to get to the "root" of the problem. In Australia, "root" is slang for something very different, and using it in a business meeting will probably get you accused of sexual harassment. Understanding the impact of culture on the language is equally important. In Japanese culture, 4 is an unlucky number (the way 13 is in America), so if your company has "four" in its title or you use it in advertisements, you might want to make a couple of tweaks if you're going to expand into the Japanese business market.

Some other issues to think about with language include

+ **Local terms:** Especially important if you hope to do local business within that country. Your classic-car customization site for southern Germany could use a listing of dealerships in Bavaria, for instance.

+ **Spelling and grammar differences:** The Spanish spoken in Spain and the Spanish spoken in Central or South America all have some key differences when it comes to spelling and grammar. For one thing, in Spain, Spanish makes use of verb conjugations for the plural second person, *vosotros,* whereas Spanish spoken in Mexico rarely uses it. French natives say that the dialect spoken in Quebec sounds "wrong" to them.

+ **Popular culture references:** Avoid dating yourself. Keep up on the pop culture trends in a country if you have a business that would be related (such as one that sells clothing). For example, a Bulgarian site would appear dated if it talked about a popular sitcom that hasn't been on the air in the United States in many years.

+ **Translation issues:** You risk a big hit to your credibility if you're not careful translating your website content from its original language to a new one. For example, in Wales, a website that had been improperly translated for a school listed its staff as a "stave made out of wood" in Welsh. We suggest adding someone who's fluent in both English and the language to which you're translating the site (and preferably someone actually from that country) to your content building and marketing process.

✦ **Vocal culture issues:** You may run into issues with languages that have different sounds than English. For example, Japanese has no "t" sound. The closest approximation is "tsu," so a word such as "fruit" would sound like "fruits" when pronounced in Japanese.

✦ **Visual design:** Figure out a country's particular design aesthetic. Study the visual culture of the target country. In both Japan and Korea, to look professional, your website needs a lot of bright colors and a busy page full of words, images, and links. Google's ultra-clean home page doesn't play well to that audience, but Yahoo's busy portal does. In England, however, a super busy and bright page is considered completely unprofessional. Similarly, color is an important consideration. In China, white is the color of death, much as black is here in the United States — probably not the best choice for your wedding site. Use red on your Chinese site instead because it represents joy in Chinese culture.

When you are doing keyword research, make sure to do it in the target language. Don't just copy/paste into an online translator to find keywords to try. You run the risk of missing out on nuances, subtleties, and all the cultural references you could be using in keywords, and you may run afoul of many tricky conjugation rules.

In order to truly succeed in a different language, we recommend you get experts in each country on your team. Do you have a German classic-car customization website? Hire someone from Germany who's an expert in classic cars. She can tell you about the different slang terms Germans use for cars, what kinds of cars are popular, and any of the cultural references you'd miss if you relied on just yourself and a German dictionary.

When translating the website copy you already have, consider language issues and don't try to translate your pages exactly from one language to another. To get the best final result for your foreign-language website, follow these steps:

1. **Break the original English down into main bullet points.**

2. **Have a professional translate this text into the second language.**

3. **Use that document to create your actual website text for your target language.**

Hire a marketer who's native to the language and region so that you know he's getting the tone and slang right. Web marketer Ian McAerin refers to this process as the *Symantec Expression Equivalency Document* (SEED) process.

If all else fails, use the local rule of thumb. Use local terms, local keywords, and local structure in order to truly succeed in your foreign market. People have started bandying about words such as *glocal*, which is defined as local-izing the global market.

The impact of languages and culture should not be underestimated. By understanding culture and languages, you can adapt better, succeed in your efforts to localize, and get more sales and respect. Showing an interest in communicating in the native language boosts interest in your company.

Domains and geolocating

Internationalization revolves around *domain* (where the site actually exists on the web), language, culture, and geolocation issues. *Geolocation* is the identification of a web page as belonging to or being relevant for a particular country. You also have to be aware of the country-code *top-level domain*, which is the last part of an Internet domain name — the letters that follow the final dot of any domain name. A country-code top-level domain (ccTLD) is specific to a particular country, such as .ca, .cn, .uk, and .mx. Be aware that ccTLDs are abbreviations in that country's language, so the ccTLD for Germany is actually .de, for *Deutschland*.

Creation and delegation of ccTLDs is performed by the Internet Assigned Numbers Authority, or IANA (www.iana.org). You can find a comprehensive list of ccTLDs on IANA's website at www.iana.org/domains/root/db.

The rules for obtaining a ccTLD are different for each country because each country can administer its own registered ccTLD as it chooses. You always need to do a little bit of research. For example, in order to obtain a .de (Deutschland, or Germany) ccTLD, you need to not only have your site hosted on a German server, but you have to be doing business in the country physically, as well. In Norway, a company can own only 20 domains. For more information on how to obtain a ccTLD, go to www.iana.org/domains/root/cctld.

Some countries have licensed their ccTLDs for worldwide commercial use. Tuvalu and the Federated States of Micronesia, small island countries in the South Pacific, have partnered with VeriSign and FSM Telecommunications, respectively, to license domain names that use the .tv and .fm ccTLDs to interested parties. For more information on country-code TLDs, check out Book VII, Chapter 2.

Search engines don't like to display duplicate content. If you have multiple domains that show the same page content, the search engines will display that page from only one domain. A search engine like Google may use a number of factors to decide which version of a page to display, including *link equity* (however many links lead to your site and how much authority they pass) on the page, opting for the page that has more links. Other signals that Google may take into account include the language on the page, the site's *IP address* (the location of the page on the web, called the "Internet Protocol" address) as well as the country targeting settings that a site owner indicates in Google Search Console. We tell you more about setting country and language targeting in Google Search Console in the "Single sites" section, later in this chapter.

Site architecture tips

To make your site accessible in the international market, you can follow some very simple architecture guidelines:

✦ **Have your site coded in UTF-8 (Unicode).** This is a type of code that allows your site to be translated into languages from around the globe. It is backwardly compatible with ASCII and it encodes up to four-byte characters.

✦ **Don't translate your *Meta tags and page titles* (HTML coding for your site that defines the characteristics of your page) from English to the language you're working in.** Work in the language itself and make all your tags individually. Plan to adjust for plurals, prepositions, special characters, and so on. Like your web page content, these are too important to just leave for a straight translation.

✦ **Adopt a global press-release strategy.** Many online press release portals exist for different languages. Sending out articles announcing news on your company or your products generates links and helps build your global presence.

✦ **Manage your 301s.** *301 Redirects* automatically send users from a URL that no longer exists to one that does. This is the only type of redirect that is considered to be search engine friendly. A typical global site has hundreds of links going to Page Not Found errors. Domains around the globe are often incorrectly set up, and *meta-refreshes* (having the page automatically reload) are often present, which are not SEO-recommended methods for handling page redirects. (For more on 301 Redirects, see Book VII, Chapters 3 and 4.)

✦ **Make sure that your URLs contain *keywords* (words that people search for by using search engines) for which you want to rank in that country.** Just like optimization in the United States, keywords in the URL help users identify your site as relevant and can promote recognition.

✦ **Link to other regional sites and seek to obtain inbound links from relevant regional sites as well.** Enhance your credibility with your international users.

✦ **Use experts for keyword research.** What do you do if there's no direct translation for a word? Employ someone fluent in that language to help you with the translation issues.

✦ **Use ccTLDs.** A *ccTLD* is the domain that relates to a particular country. Using a ccTLD more likely inspires users to trust your site.

✦ **Have a lot of content on your website that reads well to your target audience.** Use good, clean copy and make sure you're using the right character sets.

Identifying Opportunities for Your International Site

When you expand into the international market, you have three options when it comes to your site architecture: one site, multiple sites, or a combination of the two. With one site, you can take advantage of subdomains (smaller domains linked to bigger domains) and subdirectories that point to pages in different languages or are geared toward specific countries. Multiple sites require you to build an individual site for every country with a local ccTLD, preferably hosted in the country.

Each of these three options has its pros and cons. It's up to you to do the research and figure out what's best for your company in your target markets. However, you can understand the differences by reading the details we cover in the following sections.

Single sites

Having a single site and targeting using subdomains (such as `uk.myglobalsite.com`, `fr.myglobalsite.com`, `jp.myglobalsite.com`, and so on) provides you with several benefits. It's easy to set up, you only have to keep track of one server and one domain, and you can keep all your files in one place.

All the *incoming links* (links from outside sources) and all your web traffic point to one domain, rather than being split between two or more sites. Although lots of traffic doesn't necessarily mean a high conversion rate, it sure doesn't hurt.

In addition, if you use a single site, you will have more pages in the search engine's *index,* which is the search engine's database of web pages that it periodically searches to offer up to users for search queries. Grouping by language prevents duplicate content. Remember, search engines remove a site from their search results if they think it is duplicate content.

On the other hand, here are some disadvantages of a single-site approach:

If your home page is in the "wrong" language, it can be confusing for your international users. To avoid this problem, you would need to create an entry page that allows users to select what language they want to view the site in. These pages tend to be text-light, however, and not good for search engines.

Another disadvantage can be a home page that ranks highly in only one language. Having your site pop up high in the rankings for German is great, but what if you also want to do business in the English-speaking world and you're nowhere near the top 100 search results? You have to spend the same amount of effort on each section of your site, which can be time-consuming.

If you were to group by country, you are risking duplicate content. Although it's okay to have different pages in different languages, if you have separate pages for each Spanish-speaking country but don't provide unique content, the search engines read repeat pages as duplicate content and don't count them.

If you do decide that you want to maintain a single site, you can do some of the following:

✦ Specify the target country for each sub-domain by using Google Search Console. To set a geographic target, follow these steps:

1. *Sign in to Google Search Console by using your Google account* (`https://www.google.com/webmasters/tools/home`).

2. *Click the URL for the site that you want.*

3. *Click Search Traffic in the left navigation menu and then click International Targeting.*

4. *Click the Country tab and then use the drop-down selection menu to choose the country you want to target with this domain.*

✦ Redirect country-specific domains to the appropriate sub-domain or subdirectory.

✦ Make internal and external links language-appropriate and use the country-specific domains.

Multiple sites

Having multiple sites means that you set up a separate domain for each country. Expanding to new countries is technically easy. You can add sites one at a time, as needed, without impacting any of your current websites. Domains with local ccTLDs usually rank well in multiple country-specific search engines.

Certain countries require you to host your site on one of their servers in order to qualify for a ccTLD. But even if it's not a requirement, it may be a good practice if search engines try to match your server location to your physical location. However, search engines may decrease the weight of this ranking signal as more sites move to *cloud hosting* systems, where files and resources are stored and managed on virtual servers, to save costs.

But here are some of the disadvantages of a multiple site approach: The most obvious disadvantage is that maintenance is harder. Having more sites equals having more sites to update, more servers to troubleshoot, and more domains to keep registered. Additionally, you wind up putting in more time to your SEO. Having multiple sites means multiple SEO efforts. Dividing your time and resources could cause it to take longer for your main .com site to rise in the rankings.

With multiple sites, you're forced to target countries instead of languages. The world has many Spanish-speaking countries, for example, and maintaining a site focused on each and every country can get costly and time consuming.

Some tips for this approach include

✦ Target the country in Google Search Console, as outlined in the previous section.

✦ Make sure that external links have appropriate anchor text and link to the correct country-specific domains.

The blended approach

If you have an international site on the .com top-level domain, you can use a blended approach, which combines the methods used for both single and multiple sites. This approach might be the most realistic for worldwide presence. With this approach, you can start with a .com site and then build country-specific sites, as needed. Creating, maintaining, and updating this site setup can cost you, however, because you need to keep every site up-to-date and in step with all the others.

Here are some tips for implementing the blended approach:

✦ Specify countries in Google Search Console, but your international site — the one that serves any interest — should be left without a specific target country.

✦ Link your multiple country sites carefully and logically. External links should be logical. Keep the globally applicable content on the international site and country-specific information on country-specific sites.

You can use *IP sniffing* (using a program to analyze the traffic as it comes to your site) to automatically detect users' location and serve up a translation in the local language to direct them to the proper site. If you do that, always let them know that they are leaving the current domain and going to a new domain.

Realizing How People Search

In this section, we introduce you to how the rest of the world searches the web by discussing several internationally popular search engines. First up is Google, as shown in Figure 1-1. This figure shows the French, Japanese, and Brazilian versions of the site.

Figure 1-1: Google has sites for many international markets besides the flagship .com address.

Google is available pretty much everywhere. Here's a small sampling of the languages in which Google is available: Afrikaans, Amharic, Basque, Bihari, Chinese, Dutch, Finnish, Hindi, Kazakh, Malay, Norwegian, Quechua, Slovak, Tagalog, Twi, Urdu, Yiddish, and Zulu. This list is only a sample, but our point is that Google is available pretty much across the globe.

As for the other U.S. players, statistics from NetMarketShare as of May 2015 show that Yahoo makes up approximately 4 percent of the global search market worldwide, whereas Bing, has roughly twice that. Ask (www.ask. com in the U.S.) is a relatively minor player (with less than 1 percent). One extremely important thing to note here is that YouTube actually gets more searches per month than Yahoo.

Even search engines local to the target country are mostly *backfilled* (supplemented when the local engine's index doesn't have sufficient inventory) by Google's search index and paid ads.

Not every country uses Yahoo, Bing, or Google. Hold on tight: We're going to take a whirlwind tour around the global to look at some of the most important search engine brands outside the United States.

Baidu (www.baidu.com, shown in Figure 1-2) is the leading Chinese search engine for websites, audio files, and images. Baidu has an index of more than 740 million web pages, 80 million images, and 10 million multimedia files, and it attracts 5.5 million visitors annually.

Figure 1-2:
Baidu leads
search
engines in
China.

Yandex (www.yandex.com, shown in Figure 1-3), launched in 1997, is a Russian search engine and the largest Russian web portal. Its name comes from the phrase Yet Another Indexer.

Seznam (www.seznam.cz, shown in Figure 1-4) is a Czech search engine that has a customizable home page and other features such as email, maps, and a company database.

Naver (www.naver.com, shown in Figure 1-5) is the most popular search portal in South Korea. Naver was launched in June 1999, the first portal in Korea that used its own proprietary search engine. Naver received 2 billion queries in August 2007, accounting for more than 70 percent of all search queries in Korea and making it the fifth most-used search engine in the world, following Google, Baidu, Bing, and Yahoo.

Figure 1-3:
Yandex rules in Russian search engines.

Figure 1-4:
Seznam is a Czech search engine.

Najdi.si (`www.najdi.si`, shown in Figure 1-6) is a Slovenian search engine and web portal created by Interseek. It's the most-visited website in Slovenia.

Figure 1-5:
Naver is
the most
popular
search por-
tal in South
Korea.

Figure 1-6:
Nadji.si is a
Slovenian
search
engine.

These are just a sampling of the search engines across the world. So where do you want to advertise? Simple answer: maybe on all of them. You always want to be where your customers are looking for you. However, if that's too broad and a little daunting, narrow your target market by demographic or search engine. Start out small and then expand as time goes on (depending on your success in the international markets, of course).

It's time for a small, shameless plug: With the SEOToolSet (available in two versions, a free Lite version and a Pro version for just $89 a month from www.seotoolset.com), you can do three things for international search that make your international campaigns easier to manage:

✦ **Perform on-page SEO content analysis.** The Single Page Analyzer (available in its full-featured form in the free SEOToolSet Lite) supports about 20 languages. Use it to review how keywords are optimized on your page, with a natural language analysis that scores your content, makes suggested improvements, and visually maps your page themes.

✦ **Monitor keywords in a number of engines, including country-specific engines.** We think the Ranking Monitor (available only in SEOToolSet Pro) is a great tool, and not just because we built it. You can monitor your pages' rankings for your target keywords on search engines in close to 20 countries.

✦ **Share data with an international team.** With an unlimited number of users able to access and manage your projects, you can empower your multinational team with the data available through the SEOToolSet. Every report and interface can be displayed in 20 languages with the switch of a drop-down menu.

For more about the capabilities of the SEOToolSet, check out Book III, Chapter 2.

Chapter 2: Tailoring Your Marketing Message for Asia

In This Chapter

✔ Succeeding in Asia

✔ Discovering Japan

✔ Succeeding in China

✔ Finding out about South Korea

✔ Operating in Russia

The first stop on our world tour of online marketing in the international venue is the Asia region, which includes Japan, China, South Korea, and much of Russia. In Chapter 1 of this minibook, we briefly touch on the search engines popular in this region, along with a few tips and tricks for operating a website in those countries. In this chapter, we go into more depth on operating online in Asia. You discover tips on how to succeed in the targeted country, the demographics of the region, and any other hints we think would be useful to you along the way.

Succeeding in Asia

Starting a website or expanding your site into the Asian region can be a little daunting. Asian culture can be very different from Western culture, with nuances that can harm you and your company if you miss them, and that's not even considering the language barrier. Not to worry, though. We've put together a step-by-step getting-started guide for building or translating your site to work in the Asian markets.

One chapter in a book isn't enough to make you an expert in SEO for the Asian market. In fact, the most important message you should take away from this chapter is that there is no shortcut or substitute for research and local know-how.

Assessing your site's chances

Your first step is simple: Assess the usability of your translated site — is it going to work for your target country? What works in the U.S. might not work in Asia. If you want to work in any country other than your own, you should be hiring some people who are native speakers from the local markets. This doesn't have to be an expensive proposition. You might find some international students at your local college campus who want to earn a little money by looking over your translated site and pointing out anything you have missed. Look around and see who's available to you and get them to tell you everything they can about your new target market.

Just as you would analyze the market back home, you want to consider the viability of your niche when marketing in Asia. The trick here is that you're dealing with an entirely new culture. You need to find out what's popular before you can start selling it, after all. So maybe there's not a huge market for custom classic cars in Asia, but maybe you have a side operation that sells all sorts of classic-car memorabilia, including fuzzy dice. Through your research, you discover that, in Asia, they can't get enough fuzzy dice. You're in business! (Disclaimer: We made up this example. We really don't know whether anyone in any Asian country can't get enough fuzzy dice. But who doesn't love fuzzy dice?)

Sizing up the competition and sounding out the market

After you have your market, it's time to analyze your competition. Having figured out that there is a large market for fuzzy dice in Asia, you need to sit down and study how your competition is doing in the foreign market. Check out other sites that sell fuzzy dice, especially if they're local companies. This is where someone who speaks the language or knows the culture would come in very handy. All the tips and tricks from Book III come in especially handy here. Follow the same step-by-step procedure to gather and analyze information.

You'll have an easier time gathering information using the proper tools. Many SEO tools are available. We obviously recommend the SEOToolSet (www.seotoolset.com) from Bruce Clay, Inc. In SEOToolSet Pro, you can use the Single and Multi Page Analyzer tools to compare the optimization of top-ranked pages for your keywords, both general and localized. The SEOToolSet can be used in nearly 20 different languages, including Japanese and Russian. Find the top-ranking pages in your market for your target keywords and then include those URLs in your multipage comparison to see what patterns emerge from your competition. Another feature of the Pro version of SEOToolSet that's especially useful for a search marketing project outside the U.S. is the Ranking Monitor, which can be configured to track your pages' rankings for target keywords in the popular search engines of 17 countries, including Google Japan, Yahoo Japan, and Bing Japan.

After you sort out your competition, you need to broaden your research to the entire Asian market in order to plan your strategy and tactics. How does marketing work there? Who's online, and how are they searching? A quick search turns up these stats:

✦ China has 649 million Internet users, with the vast majority — 85.8 percent! — connecting via a mobile device. Users are overwhelmingly in the 15–34-year-old age group.

✦ In Japan, 86 percent of the population is online, which represents nearly 116 million people. The country has the fastest-aging population, and a demographic segment called the Baby Boomer Juniors, aged 28–37 years old, is responsible for much of the consumer spending.

✦ The Internet in South Korea is considered the fastest in the world. Most of the population is online, connecting to the lightning-fast Internet through mobile devices. North Korea's stats are largely unknown.

Determining your plan of attack

After you determine your suitability, competition, and strategy, you can move on to the actual implementation. Your next step is the planning phase: Here's where you create your Asian marketing plan.

If you have an *e-commerce site* (any website that sells a particular product or service, such as fuzzy dice), you need to start with Japan, and then expand into South Korea and China. However, if you're *branding* (establishing your name and associating it with your business, such as Nike or Xerox), you need to start with China, then move into South Korea, and then Japan.

Sound strange? It's really not. China is notorious for knock-off brands, so you should be starting there immediately if you want to expand your brand. In Japan, they tend to copy technology faster and to be conscious about brand, so you need to establish yourself as the authority product and then work on your branding so that you're recognized as the only brand to have.

Next, you need to know the search engines you'll be using. Google is used almost everywhere in the world, but certain search engines are actually more popular in a particular country or region. You need to know which search engines are the most prevalent in your target market, and look at getting *indexed* (getting your site into the search engine's database) as soon as you can. The search engine statistics look something like this:

✦ In Japan, Yahoo has 53 percent of the online market share, with Google the runner up at 40 percent.

✦ In China, Baidu (www.baidu.com) reigns as the major Chinese search engine and the fourth-most-used search engine in the world.

✦ In South Korea, Naver (www.naver.com, a Q&A formatted Korean search engine) claims nearly 80 percent of the Internet search market. Google has only 4 percent market share.

Use localized *keywords* (search terms), advertising copy, and *landing pages* (the page a user arrives on when he first visits your site). Do not use an unnatural mix of English and the local languages. Think of how amusing but untrustworthy misspelled signs or menus are. You might think a store offering "Creem donuts" is hilarious, but you probably wouldn't make a purchase from that store. The same is true when English speakers attempt to do business in other languages.

Building trust and face-to-face interaction are *huge* parts of selling yourself in the Asian market. Putting a face on your brand is very important, and you need to be selling yourself as much as your product. Be prepared to log some frequent flyer miles. Meeting with clients, vendors, and others you do business with face-to-face helps to establish trust.

You should also be monitoring your local competition. You're the foreigner, so you are starting at a disadvantage. Be looking for an edge: something that separates you from the local competition, but at the same isn't too foreign or untrustworthy.

In this chapter, we cover things that you should generally be aware of when you move into the Asian market. But each country has its own quirks and legal issues, so you need to do your research.

Discovering Japan

Japan has the third-largest economy in the world, following the United States and China. Japan has open markets that actively encourage foreign investment, which means that you can expand into the Japanese market slightly more easily than you can operate in some other Asian countries.

The most demanding shoppers in the world live in Japan. There is a huge market for brand-name services and goods, and the Japanese are very big on brand names as status symbols. Louis Vuitton, Vivienne Westwood, and others do a healthy share of business based on their brand names alone. During the global economic recession of 2008, it's said that the demographic group made of young working women 28–37 years old singlehandedly shored up Japan's economy with luxury brand purchases.

For much of the last 70 years, Japan led other countries in terms of personal savings. But an aging population is responsible for a decade of drawing down savings accounts. In 2014, for the first time since records were kept in 1955, the country's household savings rate (savings divided by disposable income plus pension payments) was –1.3 percent. Spending is strong, especially among the 13 percent of households with annual incomes above 10 million yen (approximately $80,000). For businesses vetting the viability of the Japanese market, note that another marked characteristic of the Japanese economy is an openness to foreign multinational companies that have evolved products and services for developed markets such as tech and advanced fields.

The Japanese are aware that the language of business on the Internet is English, but to do a good business with the Japanese, you have to be able to communicate in Japanese. The design aesthetic in Japan is also different from the Western one, and when you do business in another country, you should consider the local preferences of graphic design. Check out the site design of Yahoo Japan (`www.yahoo.co.jp/`) in Figure 2-1.

Figure 2-1 illustrates the preference in Japan for busy, interactive, and media-rich websites. Internet users in Japan are much more likely to trust a website that looks like this than one that looks much simpler.

To establish a web presence, get a `.jp` *domain* (the space your site occupies on the web, like a `.com`, or a `.net`, or in this case, `.co.jp`, `.or.jp`, or `.ne.jp`). Hosting your site on a server actually physically located in Japan is a good idea as well; however, the advent of *cloud computing* (storing, processing, managing, and hosting all files in a remote server) has made local hosting nice to have rather than a critical consideration. Be sure to include your contact info on your website, such as a number someone can call to receive information. Be sure that the person in charge of this phone line speaks Japanese and is able to answer any questions.

Figure 2-1:
The home page of Yahoo Japan has a lot more images and movement than Yahoo in North America.

As with starting a business in any foreign market, we recommend getting a person on the ground. Hire someone familiar with Japanese language and customs, and if at all possible, someone who actually lives in Japan. A local resident can help you navigate the differences between the Western world and Japan and help you achieve greater success in the long run.

Succeeding in China

China is a new frontier when it comes to the business world. It's also a tricky one to navigate. Not only do you have the language barrier and the cultural issues to work through, but you also have more extensive and stringent government regulations to deal with. However, China's economy is booming, and if you are willing to take the steps, now is a good time to get in the front door.

Internet searchers in China are very different from users in the United States or elsewhere. Two of the top ten Chinese website domains include numbers. Why? Because the Chinese language has 13,500 standardized characters. So, if you're designing a keyboard to have one key per character, the keyboard needs more than 13,000 keys! This is why businesses may find adopting the number platform beneficial.

You also definitely need to get a website domain within China's ccTLD (country code Top Level Domain) of `.cn` (or `.com.cn`, if you can). You also need to host your site in China to avoid gateway issues.

If you're getting started in search marketing (PPC or SEO) in China, start with Google, through its interface. Although it's not the dominant search engine in China, it's a good place to start your optimization campaign because Google China's rules are similar to its U.S. ones, and you can get your campaign up and running without having to jump too many hurdles.

The home page for Google China features a search box that drops down to offer a *guided search* (a search suggestion). Because the language has so many characters, the guided search helps users find information quickly.

Products that will help you understand your searchers and trends in the Chinese market are

✦ **Baidu Index:** The Baidu Index tool (`index.baidu.com/`) breaks down keyword-popular queries across all Baidu's products, including web, image, and video search and calculates how much user and media attention these terms are getting. This is a good way to do keyword research for up-and-coming trends and opportunities.

✦ **Drop-down keyword suggestions:** Because people in China often use *guided search* (in which the search engine makes suggestions based on your queries, much the same as Google Instant or Yahoo Suggests), search engine optimization is a little easier because search marketers know off the bat what queries searchers are using. Also, you can use Google China's Popular Searches function.

A site that might be worth checking out is Tom.com (`www.tom.com`), which is one of the top ten most popular websites in China (see Figure 2-2). This site features tons of links on the page without a search box above the fold. Users come here as a destination site, not to search.

Figure 2-2: Tom.com is among the top ten most popular sites in China.

Baidu (www.baidu.com), China's top search engine and its answer to Google and Bing, has made accommodations for Western businesses in recent years, with packages for paid search, display advertising, and an engine-specific SEO program, among others. Baidu Advertising offers two tiers of PPC management plans ($500 each month for the Lite package and $900 a month for the Comprehensive program). Funds can be paid via PayPal or wire transfer, and English-speaking support for account setup and management is now available. Find out all about these offerings at the English-language site https://www.baiduadvertising.com/.

Analytics-wise, Baidu and Yahoo provide no impression results. But Google Analytics is available in China. On Baidu, the paid listings are mixed in with the *organic* listings (search engine results that are not sponsored and which rank in a normal search of the index). *Long-tail search queries* (keywords, or search queries, made up of several words or a phrase) don't really exist in China because users don't do as many searches as Americans do. They rely more on guided search.

Here are some key observations on Baidu:

✦ It's the most popular search engine for lifestyle searches in China, but not for business. Google as well as China's second and third most popular search engines, Haosou (formerly known as 360; www.haosou.com/) and newcomer Sogou (www.sogou.com/), dominate searches in some verticals.

✦ Paid advertising campaigns overwhelmingly influence Baidu's results.

✦ Baidu has its greatest reach with young, lifestyle-centric searchers.

✦ Display advertising that charges by the page view, called CPM advertising (CPM stands for *cost per mille,* meaning cost per each thousand impressions), is most popular with Baidu.

✦ Baidu offers a unique (and expensive) product among the search engines — Baidu Brand Zone. A brand that purchases Baidu Brand Zone can have its logo and tailored content display whenever a brand's specified keywords are searched. It's expensive but draws a click-through rate of 50 percent. That's a big opportunity for brands with the budget to buy exposure in China.

Being a foreigner in China can be both a disadvantage and an advantage. Although people have the natural tendency to push back against the unfamiliar, in China, you have something of an advantage if you're an expert. When you come in to speak, if you have any kind of credentials, you're treated like a rock star. Additionally, by being a foreigner, you can get away with not knowing the customs at first. Be warned, however, that your grace period ends quickly, so be ready to adapt to Chinese culture.

The Chinese market has a few challenges that, although not unique to the country, are certainly worth knowing ahead of time:

+ **Budgets for local companies are small.** If you're a search marketer, you have to deal with less capital than you might have expected.

+ **Clients are very particular about their contacts in your business.** Have a point person who's extremely knowledgeable in the culture and can handle your business dealings in the local markets.

Business is very relationship-based in China. Good relationships are absolutely critical to success. You have to be introduced to the right people at the right places. Many Westerners underestimate exactly how important having good contacts is. This is true everywhere, but especially in China: It's about whom you know, how well you know them, and whom you work with.

Your employees make or break a deal in the long run. Most of the advertising in the Chinese market is branding, not trying to convert. If you do decide to tap into the Chinese market, make sure that you're willing to be flexible and do things its way.

When looking at hiring people abroad (and this includes all countries), be sure to check the following things:

+ Check the credentials for the people you're meeting.

+ Confirm that they're doing the work themselves, rather than outsourcing it.

+ Establish goals and document them in contracts.

+ Do periodic checks of the quality of the ads and the effectiveness of campaigns.

You should pick your teams based on their effectiveness. Offer incentives for employees to maintain loyalty. As with any business, a happy employee is an efficient and loyal employee. Pick your partners well and do a lot of research on their capabilities.

In China, Internet access via mobile devices is ubiquitous, with more than 85 percent of users connecting that way. The growth in search from smartphones is due to increased interest in the Internet and the government's heavy investment in network construction to make high-speed connectivity available. Remember the differences between desktop and mobile searches in regard to searcher intent and behavior, as we discuss in Book I, Chapter 3.

What does all this mean to the outside world? You have a lot of opportunities to market to the Chinese if you do it on its terms and within its comfort level. The keys to succeeding in China are relationships, patience, diligence, and an open mind. People in China have become comfortable with e-commerce in a very short time, with most users connecting through their mobile devices on the go. Keep this in mind as you expand into the Chinese market.

Finding Out about South Korea

When we talk about Korea, we focus on South Korea. North Korea is an unknown and politically hostile environment for pretty much all marketers, so we ignore them entirely. You should, too.

South Korea has an incredible infrastructure — claiming the title of the fastest Internet in the world, with projects in place to make it even faster in the next five years! Much of South Korea's population (82.5 percent) is online and searching. In terms of design aesthetic, a very busy-looking page gives you an advantage in South Korea because the population tends to prefer that style (a lot of color and text) for professional sites, so a Korean page can look a little something like Figure 2-3. Because of this push for color and content, Google's clean designs do very poorly in South Korea.

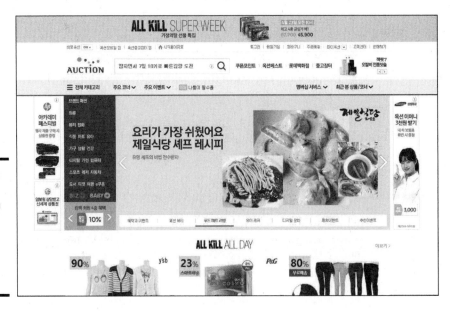

Figure 2-3: The typical Korean website uses a lot of images to engage users.

Operating in South Korea is like operating in Japan and China in that South Koreans prefer face-to-face interaction, and your success is a matter of establishing trust and accessibility. Get a .co.kr domain for your Korean site, and get started optimizing.

You absolutely must work to attract local links. Work on making connections, gaining trust and links, and getting the local search engines to recognize those things. International links are fine, but local links carry more weight in the long run. Remember, relevancy is always key and local is more relevant than non-local.

Naver (www.naver.com) is South Korea's biggest search engine. It currently commands a 73 percent share of desktop searches in the country, and holds a slightly bigger piece of the mobile search pie at 76 percent. The other contenders are Google with 9 percent of mobile search and Daum (www.daum.net) with 14.3 percent of South Korean mobile web searches.

When Naver was first launched, its founders discovered a real dearth of pages in the Korean language on the Internet. So Naver decided to create content and databases, so that when you would search in Korean, you would be able to find quality content. Naver set up Knowledge Search in 2002, enabling Koreans to help each other in a type of real-time question-and-answer platform. On average, 44,000 questions are posted each day, with about 110,000 returned answers. The tool allows users to ask just about any question, such as requests for recipes or how to subscribe to international magazines via the Internet, and get answers from other users. This tool was used by Yahoo as the inspiration for Yahoo Answers.

Operating in Russia

We include Russia in the marketing for Asian strategy for reasons of geography as well as strategy. Expanding to the Russian market is a lot like expanding into the Chinese market. In order to have a fully successful venture, you're going to need a person on the ground in Russia.

This means that you need someone who not only knows the language and culture but also actually lives and works there, to provide you with a bricks-and-mortar foothold in the country. Having someone who is based in Russia can also help in dealing with any legal or local bureaucratic issues that could spring up.

About 59 percent of Russia's population is online, which is about 84.4 million people. The largest search engine in Russia is Yandex (www.yandex.com, shown in Figure 2-4).

Figure 2-4:
Yandex is
Russia's
primary
search
engine.

Yandex was launched in 1997. The net income of the company in 2014 constituted $440 million USD. As for search engine market share, Yandex receives about 60 percent of searches in Russia, followed by Google at about 30 percent. One of Yandex's largest advantages is that it recognizes Russian inflection in search queries.

As with all the other countries we mention in this chapter, try to obtain a domain within the country's ccTLD and hire someone who lives and works in Russia to give you valuable credibility. You must do cultural research to pin down the right tone for your Russian audience.

Chapter 3: Staking a Claim in Europe

In This Chapter

✔ Succeeding in the European Union

✔ Knowing the legal issues in the EU

✔ Working in the United Kingdom

✔ Discovering France

✔ Operating in Germany

✔ Understanding the Netherlands

Across the pond from the United States lies the European Union (EU). The countries that belong to the EU are subject to certain laws and regulations, and all those countries are actually located within Europe itself.

Succeeding in the EU isn't as simple as copying and pasting your website into German or French and then hoping the traffic comes to you. You have to consider legal and cultural differences, along with the technical issues that come from running a website in another country. In this chapter, we talk about how to succeed in the European Union, some legal issues you should be aware of, and some specific facts about doing business in the United Kingdom, France, Germany, and the Netherlands that should give you a little more insight into the search markets in the European Union.

Succeeding in the European Union

You might think that getting started with the European Union would be pretty easy. It's actually not. For one thing, you have to remember that Europe comprises different countries with their own languages and customs, and their own markets for search engines. You can't create one website for the whole EU and then call it a day.

First, you need to figure out what countries you want to target. This is important in terms of tailoring your marketing campaign. Each country has its own language, culture, and social mores that you need to use when doing your keyword research. For example, in the United States, personal telephones are called *cell phones,* so when a user does a search, she most likely enters keywords such as [cellphone], [cell phone], [cellular phone], and the like. But in the United Kingdom, personal telephones are referred to as *mobiles.* So a U.K. user would, for the exact same product, use keywords like [mobile], [mobile telephone], and so on.

You also have to contend with the technical difficulties associated with obtaining and using a proper country code *top-level domain* (TLD; the letters that follow the final dot of any domain name, for example, .com or .net). A country-code top-level domain, or ccTLD, is a TLD that's specific to a certain country. The United States has .us, and the United Kingdom has .uk. Users within a specific country are much more likely to trust a website that's within their own country's ccTLD than one with a foreign ccTLD.

European users are also much more likely to trust a foreign website if it includes links to sites within their country, especially local links.

You can also use the free SEMToolBar from Bruce Clay, Inc., to help with your international SEO. It includes tools that enable you to do a local search in the area you're targeting so that you can see search results as someone would see them in Germany, even if you're sitting pretty in Denver. The toolbar supports 20 different languages, including French and German, so it's useful for your entire team, no matter where its members are based. The search is rerouted, using a proxy through a local IP address, so the search engine thinks you are located in the country you are searching for.

Knowing the Legal Issues in the EU

As a marketer to the EU, you benefit somewhat from the fact that all the member countries have agreed on standardized trade policies. However, one thing we have to stress is that the European Union is made up of many different countries, each with its own languages and laws.

For example, France is constantly suing Google over *pay per click (PPC) ads* (paid advertising that appears in the search results, for which advertisers pay a fee every time a user clicks each ad). In the United States, you can bid on a trademarked keyword and win it if you put up enough money (and the keyword is relevant to your company). In France, this is not the case, and several lawsuits have arisen over this issue. All the high courts in France (the Court of Nanterre, the Court of Paris, and the Court of Appeals of Versailles) have found that bidding on a copyrighted trademark is a copyright infringement.

However, according to the Cour d'Appel de Paris, the French courts have no jurisdiction if the ads in question lead only to websites owned by companies established outside France and appear only on google.co.uk, google.de, and google.ca, but not google.fr (decision of June 6, 2007, *Google Inc. and Google France versus Axa et al,* CRI 2007, 155 ff). This means that if you have an ad for a trademarked keyword, you can use it as long as you are not a French company and it doesn't appear on the French version of Google.

Another fun legal issue comes to us from Belgium. Several Belgian newspapers sued Google News for displaying and storing their content. A company called Copiepresse claimed that Google violated Belgian law by keeping archived versions of stories in its search cache and using headlines and excerpts within the Google News service. Google claimed that its activities fell under "fair use" laws, but a Brussels court didn't agree.

Because the legal system varies from country to country, you might want to hire a lawyer within the country you wish to be working in. You need someone who can help you with the ins and outs of that country's legal system.

Working within the United Kingdom

It's tempting to think that optimizing for the U.K. is going to be easy because you're at least working in the same language. "Aha!" you think, "The United Kingdom is a lot like America because English is the primary language of both." True — except that they're really not using the same language at all. English in the U.K. has a lot of spelling conventions that an American spell checker reads as misspelled (the "u" in words like *colour* and *favourable,* and an "s" rather than "z" in words like *customisation,* and so on). British English isn't exactly like American English, and you need to be well aware of that. There is no faster way to shoot down your credibility than forgetting cultural mores and language differences when working in another country.

It's not just spelling that's different. U.K. English often uses different words for everyday objects (a *cell phone* in the U.S. is called a *mobile* in the U.K., for instance) and different slang terms, and the same word can mean totally different things. These differences can be subtle, but they stick out like a sore thumb to a native. Blogs like Separated by a Common Language (http://separatedbyacommonlanguage.blogspot.com) are good resources for pinpointing the differences between British and American usage.

In the U.K., Google is the predominant search engine, even more so than in the United States, but here are some key differences:

✦ Google paid some outside agencies in the U.K. to bring people to AdWords (Google's PPC program), which created two types of PPC agencies in the U.K. — the *optimizers* (the ones that add value) and the *discounters* (agencies that rely on how much you can spend). Google has since stopped this practice.

✦ The U.K. has the Financial Services Authority (FSA), which is a body that regulates financial matters and financial companies like banks. Be aware that all it takes to cause you grief is an email to the FSA.

✦ In the U.K., people use different currencies because they are members of the EU, so you'll see euros and British pounds. Multi-currency transactions are difficult to manage and track.

When you use Google, you get two sets of search results. *Organic results* are the links that naturally match a user's search, and PPC results are the ads paid for by the advertising companies. When surveyed, more than 80 percent of U.K. respondents said that the organic results offered the best results. Only 6 percent in 2007 and 4.66 percent in 2008 answered that the paid search results gave the best results.

So, how much do U.K. firms spend on search engine optimization? Nine percent of U.K. firms are spending more than £1 million annually on paid search ads. One in six U.K. companies spends more than £50,000 on search engine optimization.

Compared to Internet users globally, U.K. users are quite confident online. They're not scared to give their credit card information to a brand they recognize. They're also a little more search engine savvy than a typical American user.

Certain Internet issues are of concern to the U.K. public:

✦ The U.K. has concerns about child safety issues, especially when it comes to online predators. Many people want to adopt a U.S.-like Amber Alert system, where automatic calls are sent out looking for missing children.

✦ Social networking sites can create problems at work, undermining employee relationships through gossip and also as a recruitment issue. People in the U.K. use social networking sites as much as Americans do. Unfortunately, this can be a bit of a problem for companies doing research on potential employees and finding, say, evidence of a potential employee doing questionable things on a social networking profile.

You need to be aware of two laws when you expand into the U.K. market. The first is the *John Doe law.* The term comes from an 18th-century law. This particular law lets court proceedings go ahead even when the identity of the person is unknown. When it comes to online marketing, after someone has obtained a court order, a plaintiff can go to the *ISPs* (Internet service providers) or even the search engines to prevent the defendant from entering sensitive information on a blog or website.

The second law is known as the *Spartacus Order.* The person responsible for anonymous activities must come forward and make himself known to the court, or he could be found in contempt of court — a whole extra set of charges that the offending party may want to avoid. This means that if someone files suit against you, even if she doesn't know who you are (using the John Doe law), and you fail to come forward, you're actually in danger of contempt of court. For online activities, in which the person behind a website may be unknown and untrackable, this is another level of trouble.

Discovering France

In France, more than 44 million people are connected via the Internet. But the digital economy makes up only 6 percent of the GNP (gross national product) in France, as opposed to 14 percent in the United States. More than 37 percent of the population uses search engines several times a week, whereas almost 50 percent uses them several times a month. Most users between 45 and 54 say they don't look past the first page of results, and women are less likely to go to the second page than men.

The search engine market in France looks something like this: Google is the biggest with 87 percent, and then Bing with 3 percent, Yahoo with 3 percent, Voila (`www.voila.fr`, a French search engine, shown in Figure 3-1) at 2 percent, with the rest of the pack making up the remaining 5 percent.

You have a couple of ways to use Google in France. You can use the French version of Google (`www.google.fr`) or you can use the English version (`www.google.com`) and ask for your results in French. Most people in France, not surprisingly, use the French version of Google. Many of the most visited sites within France are French-specific websites, such as Orange (`www.orange.fr`), Free (`www.free.fr`), PagesJaunes (`www.pagesjaunes.fr`), and Copains d'Avant (`http://copainsdavant.linternaute.com`). In 2008, French businesses planned to invest 29 percent of their resources in search marketing (22 percent was invested in 2007).

Figure 3-1:
Voila is
a French
search
engine.

The most-searched subject categories in France aren't much different than in the U.S.: entertainment, computers, and business. French searchers look for entertainment more than the U.S. markets do, however. The top search terms include [YouTube], [*jeux*] (games), and [*meteo*] (weather). This can be useful to you in terms of figuring out which keywords you want to target while working in France; however, remember that France is very strict about copyrighted keywords. You cannot use a copyrighted keyword that you do not own in any way. Although U.S. legislators have split on the issue, in France, nearly every case has gone the copyright holder's way. Copyrighted keywords cannot be used in metadata or to trigger paid search ads.

Seasons differ between countries. In the Unites States, the Christmas season officially begins the Friday after Thanksgiving. In other countries, the Christmas season can begin even earlier because there's not another holiday in the way. Travel is also different in France (where people typically have five weeks of paid vacation), so holiday-related search words are in high use. You need to adjust your marketing strategy to take advantage of these differences.

Online social networks are booming in France, and the traffic is proportionately huge compared to the United States. Skyrock (`http://fr.skyrock.com`), a French social networking site that's a lot like MySpace, is the big social media site (see Figure 3-2), and Copains d'Avant (`http://copainsdavant.linternaute.com`) is like Classmates.com for France, popular for reconnecting with old schoolmates and friends.

The French don't often use cell phones to conduct online searches. Fewer than 3 percent of mobile-phone users in France said they've used a phone to find information via search engines.

Here are some special French search engine issues you should keep in mind:

✦ You can submit your site's URL to most of the French search engines, but generally only if you have French-language content.

✦ If you put an accent on a word, it may change the meaning of the word. If you ignore accentuation, the French word for *diaper* is the same as for *making love.*

✦ Many French search engines analyze the word environment to determine the meaning of a word, even without accents, but results aren't perfect.

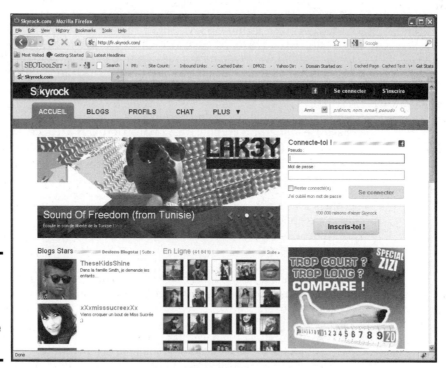

Figure 3-2:
Skyrock is
a popular
social net-
working site
for France.

Operating in Germany

Germany is a country of 82.3 million people. Of that number, 65 million people (79 percent) are online. The equivalent of $49 billion was spent online by Germans in 2007. As of 2009, Germany's GDP (gross domestic product) per capita was about $40,670. It's a pretty healthy economy.

The search engine landscape in Germany looks a little like this: Google Deutschland (`www.google.de`) has 95 to 98 percent market share. Germans use Yahoo and Ask.com, too, but they almost never use Bing. If you're going to operate in Germany, it's probably best to concentrate on Google Deutschland.

Local search, which is a search that is specifically targeted to businesses within the searcher's local area, is almost nonexistent in Germany. It's still in the starting stages, but it is growing.

Germany has 11 million `.de` domains. If you're thinking about going into Germany, you need to get a `.de` domain. Don't use a *subdomain* (a dependent domain set up within the primary domain, such as `de.classiccarcustomization.com`); it will not have as much success as a country-specific top-level domain.

To obtain a `.de` web address, you need to have a branch of your company physically operating in Germany, which means you need a local contact. The server that will be hosting your `.de` website must also physically reside in Germany. Remember when we said that the rules are different for every country? This is a good example.

Credit cards are just becoming popular in Germany. Not a whole lot of purchases are made with credit cards. (Many Germans are leery of giving out personal information over the Internet.) So make sure that they have an alternative way to pay in Germany if you are running an *e-commerce* (online retail) business.

Germans are also known to spend a lot of time researching. This is something to keep in mind if you're running a *research site* (a website geared toward providing information), as opposed to an e-commerce site; you might do well in Germany.

If you're running an e-commerce site in Germany, here are some steps you can take to ensure that the process is as easy as possible for both you and your German users:

✦ State on your landing page that you can ship worldwide and make it clear that it's easy for you to do so. A *landing page* is the page where a user arrives on your website. (See Book II, Chapter 4, Book III, Chapter 3, and Book IV, Chapter 5 for more information on landing pages.)

✦ Have a German bank account so that transferring money for purchases is as easy and hassle-free as possible.

✦ Obtain a German phone number that people can call to request more information if they need to. This is why having a physical location in Germany really helps, and not just in terms of obtaining a .de ccTLD.

In the German social networking arena, local companies are very strong, much stronger than the U.S. companies such as Facebook or MySpace. Important German social networking sites include studiVZ (www.studivz.net), a networking site for students that's similar to Facebook. Another important social networking site is Yigg (www.yigg.de), as shown in Figure 3-3. Yigg, which is similar to the U.S.'s Digg (www.digg.com), allows German users to vote on a particular news story. The more popular a news story becomes, the more likely it is to appear on the front page of the site.

The German language is much different than English. German has some common phrases, but for the most part, if you don't speak German, you're probably not going to understand it. German also has special characters that people in the U.S. aren't used to. You want to keep all this in mind when doing keyword research.

Figure 3-3:
Yigg is Germany's answer to U.S. social news networking sites such as Digg.

Understanding the Netherlands

In the Netherlands, about 88.6 percent of the population is online, which is the second-highest number of users online in the world and 11 percent more than the U.S. The Dutch also spend about $6 billion USD online, which makes them the fourth-largest market in Europe. Google commands 93 percent of the market.

When researching your keywords, be aware that Dutch is spoken by 15 million people in the Netherlands, which is the vast majority of the population. About 1 million speak Flemish, which refers to dialects of Dutch. Be aware that the paid search campaign you're running in one language won't work in the other. That being said, English is taught in all Dutch schools, and most of the population of the Netherlands is fluent in English.

Stemming (the difference between the ending of a word that makes it singular or plural) is one of the anomalies in the Dutch market. For example, a single tree in Dutch is *boom,* whereas more than one tree is *bomen.* This means for Dutch keywords, you would have to target both [boom] and [bomen]. As for all keyword research in languages not your own, we recommend that you employ someone who is fluent in your target language and preferably an actual resident of that country.

As for local search, the Netherlands has Marktplaats (`www.marktplaats.nl`; see Figure 3-4), which is its biggest online marketplace site. It's where a lot of the local search queries go.

Spam (sneaky or deceptive ways of fooling the search engines into giving a web page higher rankings) is unfortunately pretty common in the Netherlands. If some shady operator does a bit of no-frills spam and some aggressive link buying, he can rank pretty highly. People still do link farms too, so be wary when requesting links to your site. You can spot link farms a lot sooner than you could in the United States because only about 2 million Dutch websites exist.

Don't be tempted by those link farms, however. Remember that honesty is the best policy, and it's best to be operating aboveboard from the start. That way, when the Netherlands starts to clear out the spam in its search engines, you're in the clear and way ahead of the game.

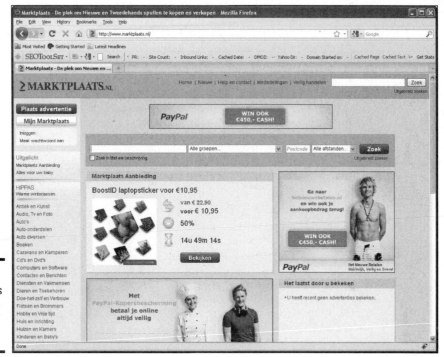

Figure 3-4:
Marktplaats
is Holland's
online mar-
ketplace.

Chapter 4: Getting Started in Latin America

In This Chapter

✔ **Succeeding in Latin America**

✔ **Using Google Search Console for geotargeting**

✔ **Making your website work in Mexico**

✔ **Operating in Brazil**

✔ **Discovering Argentina**

*L*atin America is an important stop on our search engine optimization (SEO) world tour. Latin America includes Mexico and both Central and South America. Keep in mind that, as with the Asian region (which we talk about in Chapter 2 of this minibook) and the European Union (discussed in Chapter 3 of this minibook), the Latin American region is made up of many different countries, all with different cultures, economies, and languages. Many countries in Latin America have Spanish as their dominant language, but not all. The biggest country in South America, Brazil, speaks Portuguese.

As always, you need to do research before you launch an online business in a particular country. Hiring someone with knowledge of the local language, customs, and legal ins and outs is also an invaluable asset to your company if you are looking to expand into the Latin American region. In this chapter, you find out a bit about operating in Latin America and discover some stats on a few countries in the area. Latin America is a pretty big place, so realize that we're giving you only a peek into the region.

Succeeding in Latin America

Latin America has a population that's hungry for everything the web has to offer. Latin American countries have more than 310 million Internet users, according to eMarketer. Although 51 percent of the population in Latin America is connected, Brazil alone makes up the bulk of the Internet population, housing one-third of Internet users. Latin America has the highest number of time spent online at 7.75 hours per day. These Internet users are highly mobile and social — 45 percent of users in the region connect to social networks on their mobile device, compared to the global average of 35.5 percent.

In 2013, 80 percent of Latin Americans said they shop online, with about a third of those users reporting that they shop on their phone and a quarter saying that they use a tablet. E-commerce sales in the region hit $70 billion in 2013. Latin American shoppers are comfortable paying with credit cards online, and the average employed Chilean is reported to have more than four credit cards!

In Latin America, language matters. Results differ by including accents or using the English- or Spanish-language versions of Google. When you're researching *keywords,* have someone who's from the country you're actually targeting help you, not just a generic Spanish speaker. The language has subtle variations based on both region and culture, and what might be a perfectly innocent word in one region might be an offensive slang term in another. For example, in Mexico, the term *cajeta* means a caramel dessert topping. In Colombia, it's slang for a bodybuilder, like "meathead" in English. In Costa Rica, it means a form of low-quality marijuana. But in Argentina, it refers to female private parts. Definitely *not* a mistake that you want to make! These are just some examples of regional differences. Obviously, you should take great care.

If you are going to be translating your site into Spanish to target Latin American users, do have a way of getting your products to your customers! Learn from the mistakes of Best Buy Español. In November 2007, this leading North American retailer translated its site into Spanish in order to target Spanish-speaking customers. Best Buy Español was then immediately *indexed* (included in a search engine's database of websites, which the search engines pull from when a user does a search) and got huge numbers of people visiting its sites. The problem was that it was showing up in the search engines in Spain and Latin America as well as in the United States, but Best Buy didn't have the ability to ship to those places! If you translate your website just for the U.S. Spanish-speaking population, be aware that you will probably draw traffic from these other countries. If you do, have a way to ship to them! Nothing is wrong with people wanting to buy things from you. Just make sure that you can provide what it is you are selling.

Also, do be aware that not all Latin American countries speak Spanish. Several countries, such as Brazil, use Brazilian Portuguese (distinct from that spoken in Portugal) as their primary language. Other countries still have a large native population that speaks their own diverse languages and dialects. Argentina, for instance, has a large German-speaking population and a large English-speaking population as well. This is something to look for when you do your research and to keep in mind when you target your keywords and create a version of your site to run in those countries.

As with expanding into any foreign market, hiring a legal expert who works in the country or region you are targeting is best. That expert helps you work out any legal issues, commerce headaches, or trade and tariff rules that you need to understand to do business in that country.

Geotargeting with Google Search Console

Google's Search Console is designed to help you build your site, but the package also has an option that allows you to associate a website with a particular country in order to enhance that website's presence in the particular country's local search results. (A *local search* is a search geared specifically toward a user's physical address, usually via the location of the server he's using.)

In geotargeting, Google looks at a couple of signals to determine where a site is located or what particular region it belongs to:

+ The server location of the website.

+ The top-level domain (TLD). A *domain* is the root part of a website address, such as `wiley.com`. The *TLD* is the part that identifies where the website is registered on the World Wide Web, marked by `.com`, `.net`, and so on. In the case of international domains, the TLDs (known as country code TLDs or *ccTLDs,* for short) identify the country where the domain was registered, such as `.us`, `.uk`, `.co.jp`, and so forth.

By using Google Search Console, you can do geotargeting even if your site is hosted in Colorado. If your website aims specifically for business in Argentina, you can use the tools to have your site appear in local searches for Argentina by setting it to that country in the Tools.

For more information on geotargeting by using Google Webmaster Central, go to the Google Search Console site at `www.google.com/webmasters/tools`.

Working in Mexico

Mexico has approximately 50 million Internet users, meaning more than 41 percent of the country is online, and the demand for broadband Internet services is increasing. Mexico ranks twelfth in the world in terms of personal computer Internet access via high-speed fixed Internet subscriptions. These fast connections enable residents to do online searches much more effectively. Telmex is de facto the only company that provides DSL connectivity in Mexico. The government used to own Telmex and had a complete monopoly. Although the company is now privately owned, it still has near-total control.

Mexico is a signing member of 12 separate trade treaties, the most important being the North American Free Trade Agreement (NAFTA). NAFTA is a trilateral trade bloc between Canada, the United States, and Mexico. This means that these three countries have agreed to eliminate tariffs, quotas, and preferences on most goods and services between them. Whatever your political views on NAFTA, it does make commerce between the United States and Mexico slightly easier if you are looking to create an e-commerce site that targets Mexico, as opposed to other Latin American countries.

As for the search engines, Google and Yahoo have versions for Mexican users: `www.google.com.mx` and `https://espanol.yahoo.com`. In fact, Google has a version for almost every Latin American country, including `www.google.com.ar` (**Argentina**), `www.google.com.co` (**Colombia**), `www.google.com.pe` (**Peru**), `www.google.com.ec` (**Ecuador**), `www.google.cl` (**Chile**), and so on.

For keyword research, add someone to your staff who both speaks Spanish and is actually from Mexico. This person can help you translate your website, pointing out cultural differences that a simple translator tool might miss and helping you effectively target your market.

You might also want to dip a toe into the YouTube (`www.youtube.com`) pool. Mexico and Brazil are the biggest consumers of YouTube in the world, and you have plenty of opportunity to connect with your users there. YouTube Mexico (`http://mx.youtube.com`) serves videos targeted at the Spanish-speaking market (see Figure 4-1).

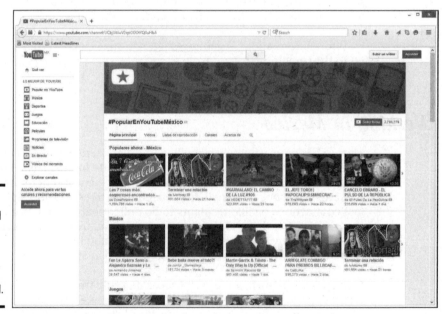

Figure 4-1: Mexico and Brazil are the biggest consumers of YouTube in the world.

To take advantage of YouTube's popularity to help promote your website, upload a few Spanish-language videos on YouTube Mexico, providing links back to your own site in the sidebar, and see where this takes you. YouTube can be a very effective tool in marketing your brand and reaching a completely new audience.

Operating in Brazil

Brazil has the largest Internet population of any country in Latin America, with a total of 113 million users at last count. Brazil is a country of about 200 million people, meaning that 56 percent of Brazil's population is online. In recent years, the increase in fixed telephone lines, cell phones, broadband access, and economic stability has afforded more Brazilians the opportunity to get online. In fact, the user growth from 2000 to 2013 was 2,095 percent. That's not a typo; it really does say that the growth exceeded two thousand percent.

A majority of the upper and middle classes in Brazil regularly use the Internet. Of the 56 percent of the population online, a large number of those people have purchasing power.

The Brazilian Internet Steering Committee has an online survey about Internet usage in Brazil. The site is available at `http://cetic.br/publicacoes`, in both English and Portuguese; however, survey data is provided only in Portuguese. Considering that you'll have a Portuguese speaker on your team to help you with language and marketing, you can make use of useful survey information like this when you're starting to figure out your keywords.

Brazil is one of the nine countries in which Google has launched a local version of YouTube. As we mention in the preceding section, uploading a few videos to this video-sharing site that include links back to your web pages can get you attention and bring you more traffic.

Facebook is the most popular social media site in Brazil, and the country tops the social network's list of highest active number of users. Brazil has 70 million active Facebook users, and as you know, using social media helps you be where your potential customers are, develop relationships, and promote brand awareness for your site. Search engine–wise, Google is the most popular.

Here are some other things to keep in mind while operating in Brazil:

✦ Don't just translate your ads into Portuguese. Take into account localisms and slang.

✦ Provide multiple payment systems, using both credit cards and Boleto, a local bank-invoicing system.

✦ If you're running an e-commerce site, be aware of the high taxes and duties that Brazil requires. Hire someone well-versed in Brazilian-commerce legal issues to help you out.

Discovering Argentina

Argentina is a Spanish-speaking Latin American country that has a large portion of its population online. The number of Internet users in the country has been estimated at 43 million in 2013, which is a whopping 75 percent of the total population. As of 2008, among the 7 million PCs registered in Argentina, the number of residential and business computers connected to the Internet totaled about 3.3 million, 92 percent of which were connected via broadband access to the Internet. Those without access to a PC at home can use Internet cafes called *locutorios,* so even those who don't own computers may still have online access.

The most popular search engine in Argentina is Google Argentina (www.google.com.ar), which gets 97 percent of searches.

There are also regional differences in language in Argentina. Argentinean Spanish is closer in pronunciation to Italian, and its speakers have a very distinct accent because of this. Italian is the second-most spoken language in Argentina, followed by German. In Argentinean Spanish, speakers also incorporate the usage of the pronoun *vos,* instead of *tu,* which is the informal "you." Only a few other Spanish-speaking countries use *vos,* including El Salvador and Honduras.

As we *always* recommend, if you intend to go international and target specific countries, hire someone from that country who can help you out with the language and cultural differences. Having someone who knows the ins and outs of the language and culture on your side makes the process of expanding into the international market a whole lot smoother for everyone involved.

Appendix: The Value of Training

In This Appendix

✔ **Making the most of industry conferences**

✔ **Choosing a conference: Small or big**

✔ **Getting the most out of conference networking**

✔ **Picking the right training courses**

✔ **Finding professional training**

✔ **Doing it yourself**

*T*hroughout this book, we walk you through the basics (and the not-so-basics) of search engine optimization (SEO). However, you can find plenty of opportunities out there for taking your SEO education even further. One of the best ways you can do this is through training.

You can go about achieving further training in one of several ways. You can attend Internet marketing industry conferences, such as SES Conference & Expo, Search Marketing Expo, Pubcon, or ad:tech. You can sign up for individual training courses, attend a training session, or have someone come out to help train you and your staff. There are courses for those who are seriously invested in SEO, and there are options for people who are just beginning to dabble. If you're wondering what to do in order to get further SEO training, not to worry; we have you covered in this appendix.

Making the Most of Industry Conferences

In 1999, the first Search Engine Strategy show (now called SES Conference & Expo) was launched to give search marketers a crash course in search engine optimization and how to get listed in the search engines. It was a fairly small and intimate gathering. But when Internet marketing and search engine optimization became viable tactics, this conference began to grow, with other large search conferences springing up, as well.

These conferences offered introductory sessions on a broad range of topics and let search marketers pick the sessions they thought were most important. These days, search marketers have a lot of choices when it comes to which search-marketing conference to attend. No matter what, the first rule is to bring a *lot* of business cards with you. You won't be sorry!

First off, you have the mainstays, such as

✦ **SES Conference & Expo:** This one happens all over the place, including San Francisco, New York, Chicago, Toronto, and other cities around the world. SES is purely about Internet marketing, and, of the larger conventions, it's the one most specialized toward search marketing. You can get more information at its website, www.sesconference.com.

✦ **Search Marketing Expo (SMX):** SMX is another popular search engine marketing (SEM) conference series. It boasts both major conferences (SMX East in New York, SMX West in San Jose, CA, and its flagship SMX Advanced in Seattle, WA), as well as smaller niche conferences targeted at specific topics (Local, Social Media, and so on). Its website is www.searchmarketingexpo.com.

✦ **Pubcon:** Pubcon is a large conference designed to meet the needs of webmasters. Topics tend to be in a wider range than SES or SMX, but it's still a niche show devoted to Internet marketing and webmastering. Here, you can find more information on how to run a website. The real gold of Pubcon is Pubcon Classic, a networking event held on the last day where all the real value is found. Pubcon takes place twice a year. For more information on these guys, check out www.pubcon.com.

✦ **ad:tech:** This large show also has conferences worldwide, with shows in New York, San Francisco, Chicago, London, Shanghai, Sydney, Hamburg, Paris, and Singapore. Its draw includes company executives from many major corporations. ad:tech is about Internet marketing as a whole, so it goes beyond just search engines or social networks. It incorporates a little bit of everything and focus on branding, marketing, and promotion. Search engine–specific marketing is definitely in the minority here, and the little bit that is discussed usually focuses on the PPC side of things. The conference often has few if any sessions that discuss SEO specifically. You can find more information at www.ad-tech.com.

Besides the stalwarts in the preceding list, you can find some smaller niche shows. These shows allow search marketers to network with a targeted group of their peers and dive into topics on a much more advanced level. Some of the more popular niche shows and educational opportunities include

✦ **SEMpdx:** These Portland-based mini-conferences happen fairly often. These guys are geared toward search engine marketing, specifically. If you're in the Pacific Northwest, they might be worth checking out (www.sempdx.org).

✦ **MozCon:** This conference draws Internet marketers to the technological hotbed of Seattle annually. It takes a more advanced look at Internet marketing disciplines from SEO to social media to community management and analytics. Read about this one at moz.com/mozcon.

✦ **SearchLove Conference:** With dates in Boston, San Diego, and London, this two-day conference looks at the Internet marketing spectrum, from search to content to paid promotions and more. Info is available at `www. distilled.net/events/`.

Smaller, focused events might be the way to go if you're considering SEO as a career. They give you more opportunity for networking than the larger shows, but *all* the shows strive to provide education and knowledge transfer.

Small versus large conferences

One advantage of a large conference is that it has something for everyone. Large conferences offer so many panels and sessions and information tracks that the hardest part can be choosing which session to attend. If you're just starting out in SEO, attend a big conference so that you can get exposure to a wide variety of disciplines. Internet marketing comes from discovering how to combine several disciplines for maximum efficiency. Search engine marketers can listen to the wise words of Google, whereas the social media marketers can go hang out with the people from Digg. On-demand marketers can go to TiVo. Brand managers know which ad networks are going to pay off big. A marketer should be able to find a way to use all these Internet marketing media elements in order to make his whole media campaign a success. Large conferences afford you the opportunity to sample each of the disciplines and add more ammo to your search-marketing arsenal.

Keep in mind that Internet marketing involves more than search engine optimization. At one conference, for example, attendees choose from panels on pay per click, web analytics, social media marketing, conversion rate optimization, site architecture and design, marketing for local businesses, and mobile platform marketing, in addition to search engine optimization. Even traditional media, such as television and print, have panel discussions devoted to them, especially in terms of digital advertising.

At a large conference, rather than hearing 15 speakers, you have the chance to hear 50. Speakers at big conferences will definitely expose you to ideas that have probably never occurred to you before. These conferences allow you to incorporate the best parts of their teachings into your new strategy.

But if you're looking to establish real connections, you want to pay close attention to the small-conference circuit. When you're in a room with 1,000 people, it's hard to actually talk to anyone. You're left looking up at the speakers on the stage, which, although informative, doesn't exactly create an optimal environment for sharing or networking.

At the smaller shows, it's different. The small group setting creates an environment where attendees aren't afraid to start up a conversation with the speaker. The benefit of smaller shows is that everyone is able to meet up at a central location after the sessions have ended and take part in the understanding that comes with sharing war stories with your peers and partaking in meaningful conversation. You can really find out what those around you do for a living, where they work, what their specialty is, what they hope to get out of the show, and more. Networking is about establishing relationships, and that's always best done in an intimate setting.

Another thing about smaller shows is that they give you a unique opportunity to get up close and personal with the speakers. In smaller shows, you get direct access to panelists during the sessions, lots of time to ask questions, and ample opportunity to hunt someone down during lunch or after hours for a quick chat. This is a key advantage for search marketers, especially those looking to expand their repertoire of SEO knowledge. What's also great about one-on-one time with the speakers is that they remember you later, so they might be willing to lend you a hand down the road. At a large conference, getting face time with your favorite speaker can be nearly impossible.

These smaller shows are also very topic-centric, focusing on smaller, niche aspects of search engine optimization and search engine marketing. Topic-centric shows help to spice up the speaker pool and ensure that attendees are always seeing something they have never seen before. For that reason, you want to carefully read a show's description before deciding to attend to make sure it lines up with what you're hoping to find out.

But although you might see the rising new voices at a niche conference, for the big names in SEO, you might want to lean toward the big conferences. Big conferences can afford to bring in the big-name panelists. Not only do you recognize the names of the speakers, but all the big companies know that they'll find an audience there. They know that at a big conference, they have the opportunity to reach thousands of people, which makes it worth their while to participate.

In the final balance, big or small, going to conferences can be a valuable investment of time and money for you and your company. Whether you're just starting out in SEO, seeking help with your website, or looking for new ideas as an SEO veteran, you're bound to get something out of your conference experience.

Networking effectively at conferences

SEO industry conferences are generally considered a must if you want to get anywhere with your brand and your site, mostly for conference networking. Networking is how you get clients, make contacts, and expand your sphere of influence. However, if you're a first-timer or somewhat introverted, it could be a little like your first day at a new school when you were a kid. The only difference is that, unlike back in grade school, you just spent a considerable amount of money to feel horribly uncomfortable.

At a conference, you have a lot of opportunities to make new connections. In your day-to-day existence, you probably don't run into anything like the variety of people that shows up for a large conference. Marketers, mid- to senior-level execs, reporters, and programmers — they all come to the big conferences to meet and greet.

You can't just hang around on the edges of things during conference time. Being shy hurts not only your personal reputation within the industry, but the brand of your company as well. So, when you're attending a conference, you have to put on your game face and master the tricks of making connections with ease.

Strategy 1: Show up prepared

One of the most effective ways to calm pre-show nerves is to show up prepared. Optimize your schedule by taking a look at the conference agenda a few days prior to the show and marking down everything you want to attend. Take care to check who's speaking at which sessions and consider whether you can benefit from a meet-and-greet. Create a list of everything you want to do and everyone you want to meet while you're at the conference. This list helps keep you on track in the midst of all the craziness and serves as motivation to get everything on your list covered.

Conferences are something of an endurance test, especially if you've never been to one before. Be prepared for the inevitable head explosion that hits near the end of the first day. Keeping a conference scorecard that lists the names of all the people you want to meet goes a long way in making sure you leave that conference feeling like you've accomplished something.

If you definitely want to meet certain people, research them so that you have something to talk about with them. Knowing your industry experts and what they specialize in (and what buttons to push) is always a good plan. Striking up a conversation is often as easy as knowing what to talk about. Your job at a conference is to engage those leaders you want to meet and ask them the questions that need asking.

Strategy 2: Start branding yourself before you get there

You can introduce yourself face-to-face much more easily when you have an established brand that you can lean on. A few weeks before conference time, start reaching out on the social networks and let people know you'll be there. Use Twitter to follow the conference's *hashtag* (a way of marking the subject of a tweet by using the pound or hash symbol), such as *#conference-name*. (You can usually find the conference's hashtag by following the official conference account, but sometimes attendees use a different hashtag.) Join that conference's Event page on Facebook. If the conference doesn't have an official Event page on Facebook, create one. Make plans to meet up with other attendees beforehand. Who can help you promote your company and your goals the most? Find out who they are before you go. You want to score some face time with those folks.

Use the lead-up time to the conference to start talking about the projects you're working on and generate some buzz. If you're going to be releasing a new blogging widget, plan the release date around the conference. Have something you can plug or a lead-in to a conversation. Have something to say before you start a cold conversation.

Strategy 3: Use the buddy system

One of the best ways to network and work a room is to attach yourself to someone who's an extrovert. Extroverts love meeting new people and love to walk you around and introduce you to everyone they know. It's perfect: You get to meet everyone in the room without ever having to actually introduce yourself. And if you've already established a brand for yourself beforehand, folks are excited to meet you and immediately bring you into the conversation.

Do beware when using the buddy system, though. Sticking with an extrovert is different than simply huddling in a corner with another nervous soul. Unless you have been surgically attached to the friend who dared come with you, you do not have to stand by her side the entire night. As comforting and warm and fuzzy as it feels, you want to avoid this at all costs. Doing so is a great way to ensure that you only speak to each other or to those you both know without ever meeting anyone new. The whole idea of networking is to get yourself out there and meet people whom you think can help you out, and vice versa. Step outside the box and take a chance on someone new.

Strategy 4: Have a gimmick

Regulars in the search engine optimization community have seen all kinds of unique attention-grabbing attempts on the conference grounds, including distinctive clothing — bright yellow shoes for one marketer, bright orange suits for another — and various forms of pretexts for getting photos (here, try on my silly hat so I can take a picture of you). These are all attention-getting gimmicks at conferences. Think of it as in-person link bait. It's all about grabbing people and striking up a conversation. Having a gimmick makes it easier for you to approach people and harder for them to ignore you.

If you were attending a networking event and a smiling face approached you and asked you to pose for a photo holding a potato, you'd do it, right? And after you agree, you open up the door for that person to hold a conversation with you and explain why you need to randomly have your photograph taken with a tuber. You'll also definitely remember that person when you spot him or her walking around the conference hall. That's the power of having a gimmick.

However, do be careful when using the gimmick technique: You have to walk a fine line between being funny and being annoying. Opt for something quirky and unobtrusive, such as handing out a T-shirt that promotes a cause benefitting someone other than yourself, such as a charity. Above all, keep in mind that if you think it might be offensive and obnoxious, it probably is, so don't do it.

Strategy 5: Don't use a gimmick

As effective as gimmicks can be, people sometimes grow tired of them. Your best bet is to be genuine and be yourself. Sometimes, a firm handshake and a warm smile are all you need to forge a real connection with someone.

The worst thing you can do is leave a conference with regrets. Meeting people and sharing work and life war stories are too valuable to pass up. When you meet someone at a conference, it's safe to say you have similar interests and are involved in the same industry. Strike up a conversation with that as your jumping-off point. When it comes to conference networking, there's no room for shyness. Be confident and willing to bust out of your shell.

Picking the Right Training Courses

You can find a wide variety of training options available for search engine optimization. But in picking the right courses for you, what should you be looking for? Ask yourself what you think you and your business need from the training. Is it enough to just learn the basics or should there be more to it than that? Should these classes convey search engine philosophy, as well as techniques for optimization? Should these classes set standards and test the knowledge you gain during them?

Here are some of the things you should be able to take away from a good training course:

+ **Fundamentals:** Any course that you take should give you a good grounding in the history and understanding of search engine optimization. It should discuss terminology, ranking factors, and all the components that make up a search engine–friendly web page. You should leave the class with a clear understanding of the basic methods of SEO.

✦ **Philosophy:** The instructor of any course you take should be upfront about the course's approach to search engine optimization and clearly define the reasoning behind the course's methods.

✦ **Ethics:** Any course should have a stated commitment to ethical *(white hat)* SEO. Both the industry and individuals benefit from ethics and good conduct, and these courses should require those practices from their students.

✦ **Something to hang on your wall:** This might seem frivolous, but having something physical to take away from any course is about more than just a pretty piece of paper. Certification from a respected authority serves as a reinforcement of the values and techniques reported in the class.

Beyond just making you better at SEO, better training courses raise the bar for all players. If you learn (and pass on) good solid techniques that adhere to ethical standards, everyone benefits. Where once few courses were available, a wide variety of choices is now available, and the hard part is finding the best one.

So, which is the right training course for you? You have three basic options: remote training, in-person destination training, and on-site training. We cover all three in the following sections.

Training remotely

You usually do remote training over the phone, online, by email, or through video lessons. Remote training is the most convenient of your training options, allowing you to do it from your home or office. It's also one of the cheapest methods. The price on this kind of training varies widely and runs from $250 to $3,000 per package, depending on the method, difficulty level, and length of the program. A few high-quality advanced search engine optimization courses are offered through remote training. But most of the programs available remotely are best for beginners who need to figure out the most basic SEO methodology and techniques.

Remote training works via video and online programs, which have the added benefit of allowing students to move at their own pace. Be aware that students can't receive lessons faster than the program schedule dictates, so those trainees who are a little more advanced than their peers might get impatient with the pace of the courses. Attendees also have limited opportunities to ask questions of instructors. To alleviate this problem, some of these remote programs host private discussion groups. With remote training, you also have less chance to personalize the training to your own website's needs, as compared to in-person and on-site SEO training courses.

MarketingProfs University is one remote location training service with courses that range from lead generation, email marketing, content marketing, analytics, social media, and small business marketing at www. marketingprofsu.com. One course, Search Marketing School, is a nine-class course that looks at how to build links, how to view analytics reports, and how to optimize your web presence to reach mobile users.

✦ **Subject matter:** In nine classes, Search Marketing School covers user-focused optimization, attracting links and attention from influencers, remarketing tactics, how to think about content, and Google Analytics basics.

✦ **Method:** Online, self-paced lessons with resources, available for 12 months after you register. You receive a certificate after you complete the course.

✦ **Cost:** MarketingProfs University's Search Marketing School costs $595.

✦ **Other info:** Search Marketing School is taught by many expert professionals who cover lessons in which they are recognized specialists. With the cost of the course, attendees also get a three-month subscription to MarketingProfs PRO, which comes with benefits such as online seminars and special industry reports.

Another remote training course is through Online Marketing Institute at www.onlinemarketinginstitute.org. Online Marketing Institute has a rich library of resources for motivated learners looking to expand their new media marketing skillset.

✦ **Subject matter:** There are basic, intermediate, and advanced courses in many categories, including digital marketing for the B2B space, content marketing, mobile marketing, social media marketing, analytics and testing, and search marketing, both paid and organic.

✦ **Method:** Hundreds of flexible, on-demand video classes taught by experts in each topic field.

✦ **Cost:** An annual subscription to OMI costs between $270 and $970, depending on the plan level. Monthly subscriptions are also available.

✦ **Other info:** Membership includes unlimited access to video classes with new courses on trending tactics released every month. OMI also has programs designed to keep agencies and small teams up to date on the latest online marketing tactics and channels.

Training around the country

If you want face-to-face basic and advanced SEM and SEO training courses, you can find several courses available across the United States. These courses usually cost anywhere from $750 to $2,000 per person, depending on their length and comprehensiveness. These courses are relatively cost-efficient, after you factor in travel expenses.

Location-based training provides opportunities to ask questions specific to your website, making it an opportunity for practical learning. In-person training addresses those who learn by visual and audio aids, as well as by application, as opposed to those who learn purely through visual means. Many courses include lab time for attendees to use SEO tools, sometimes included with the training package, on their own domain with the instructor available for help or suggestions.

SEOToolSet Training from Bruce Clay, Inc. (`www.bruceclay.com`) offers training courses regularly scheduled in California and annually around the world as published on the website:

+ **Subject matter:** Basic and advanced search engine optimization training course includes ample time for questions and answers, plus lab time to practice the techniques on your own site.

+ **Method:** Three-day basic course and one-and-a-half-day advanced certification course offered every other month.

+ **Cost:** $1,795 SEOToolSet Training; $1,195 Advanced Certification Course (which has SEOToolSet Training as a prerequisite).

+ **Location:** Simi Valley, California.

+ **Other info:** Designed for marketing and web design staff, IT professionals, and decision makers, the face-to-face training covers standard SEO practices and ethics issues, plus certification for those who complete the advanced course. Subscription to a Pro-level account for the SEOToolSet diagnostic tools is included with the course. Along with the Standard and Advanced courses held in Southern California, the company presents SEO workshops through its international offices in Japan, Switzerland, and India, as well as a stand-alone workshop in association with the SMX conference in Seattle, New York, and San Jose, CA.

Another option is Search Engine Academy's SEO Workshops, with basic, advanced and complete courses available (`www.searchengineacademy.com/seo-workshops/`):

+ **Subject matter:** Topics covered include keyword research, site architecture, copywriting, `Title` tags, `Meta` descriptions, links, publicity, social media, and measuring success with analytics.

+ **Method:** Two-day basic SEO workshop and three-day advanced SEO course.

+ **Cost:** $1,097 for the basic SEO workshop; $2,497 for the basic and advanced course together.

✦ **Location:** Locations in the United States include California, Colorado, Texas, Pennsylvania, and Florida.

✦ **Other info:** This course is geared toward new SEOs, Internet marketing managers, entrepreneurs, copywriters, and web designers. Through this hands-on training course, you can create an organic, site-specific SEO strategy.

Training on-site

On-site SEO training is the most expensive of all training methods, but it's also the most personalized method. On-site SEO training can be specifically tailored to your site and to your business's SEO and search engine marketing needs. On-site training can usually run you $150 to $500 an hour, with minimum time or minimum participant requirements. In order to get the most out of on-site training, come up with a list of expectations for your SEO campaign before you consult with several of these training companies to see what type of topics they cover. On-site training is the most useful if you plan to train many employees and perform all your business's SEO in-house. Most on-site training programs are tailored to a specific project, provide a syllabus of topics that are relevant to your objectives, and offer follow-up consultation.

SEOToolSet Training from Bruce Clay, Inc. (www.bruceclay.com) offers on-site training:

✦ **Subject matter:** An SEO training course customized to your organization's unique needs, audience, goals, and expertise level with ample time for questions and answers.

✦ **Method:** One- to three-day concentrated program that combines standard and advanced training.

✦ **Cost:** Average of $1,795 per student for a three-day program, plus travel-related expenses for the teaching staff.

✦ **Other info:** Designed for marketing and web-design staff, training covers standard SEO practices and ethics issues. Subscription to the SEOToolSet of diagnostic tools is included with the course. You can also get on-site SEO and SEM training if you want to train 24 or more employees.

You can also get on-site training from DISC (www.2disc.com/services/training/):

✦ **Subject matter:** In a personalized, company-specific manner, this training helps you discover your company's optimum ROI, benefits of PPC campaigns, how to write content, how to interpret analysis and reports, how to optimize your CMS, and how to conduct keyword research.

✦ **Method:** DISC evaluates your team, delivers training materials, performs a one- or two-day workshop at your location, and provides follow-up questions and answers.

✦ **Cost:** Packages range from $12,300 to $15,500, plus travel expenses.

✦ **Other info:** On-site and conference-style training allows businesses to train many employees at the same time in a comfortable environment, focusing on techniques personalized for your specific project. You receive detailed training materials that include step-by-step guidelines for performing essential SEO procedures. Packages are tailored to your business's needs. DISC also offers phone and email training.

From basic to advanced lessons offered at your desk or at your door, SEO training comes in all shapes, sizes, and price tags. You need to determine how training can help your business, and then choose the training method that best fits your needs.

Training for Professionals

When we talk about *professionals,* we mean people who already know more than a beginner's course of SEO and want to expand their general knowledge and expertise. The following sections can help people who take SEO very seriously and want to be on par with the experts in the field. In general, look over these sections if you make a living at providing SEO as a service.

Attending conventions

If you're a business person just getting your arms around search, in the big spender category, or looking for a way to immerse yourself in the search engine optimization field, the bigger, more general trade shows may work for you: the giant conventions such as ad:tech or Pubcon. But at some point, you want more than just the broad topics these conventions cover. You eventually reach a point where you need to become a true expert in your craft. At that point, you must start networking with those who can help you meet your goals. When you get to that level, the smaller, niche shows provide far more value. They're more approachable and provide a far better networking and educational environment.

Broad Internet marketing training may have had value when the industry was less competitive, but in order to compete today as an SEO, you have to know your stuff inside and out. In other words, you have to go beyond the introductory courses offered at the large shows. In this area, small, topic-focused shows thrive because they strip away that introductory-level material and get into the meat of the issues. Large shows such as ad:tech and SES simply can't provide that kind of depth because they have to cater to a beginner audience.

If you're looking to build your industry knowledge and expertise, seek out the small shows that emphasize the aspects that you want to dive into. Maybe you want to advance your branding techniques or dive further into networking via social media. The smaller shows are the ones that are going to really benefit you.

The sessions at the smaller, niche conferences are taught by the field experts. They are there to teach you real-life tactics, strategies, and methodologies so that you can go back and use what you have learned. Not only does this help you build your own set of SEO tools, but it also sets you up on your way to becoming an expert in a specialized field. This makes you invaluable in your home office and in the industry as well. You can gain fame by making yourself a noted expert in a singular field. As the industry matures, it's less about knowing a little bit about everything and more about becoming a specialist.

At these shows, you get speakers who can deliver success stories and anecdotes of failure, who can test a theory because they weren't constrained by budgets, and who are willing to tell you what happened because they're not afraid that it'll be revealing something. Listening to those who've gone before is a time-honored way to increase your knowledge and gain inspiration.

Getting advanced training

Another way to further your advanced SEO knowledge is to attend advanced training courses. We at Bruce Clay, Inc., offer an advanced SEO training course, and you can find advanced courses in Internet marketing disciplines for SEO and paid search through Search Engine Academy and other providers. When you do advanced training, you go beyond the basics of search engine optimization (such as finding out what a `Meta` tag is, for example) and really delve deep into the ins and outs of doing search engine optimization for you and your company. With advanced training, you find out more about how to read your competition and analyze your site, which means you can tell whether or not the changes you made to your site are actually working. This involves knowing what converts, and what ranks, and what draws in traffic. Seeing the complete picture is a must if you want to continue to work in search engine optimization.

You can find out more about advanced training courses at

✦ Learn with Google Webinars (`www.google.com/ads/experienced/webinars.html`) for continuing education in Google's advertising platforms

✦ Bruce Clay, Inc. (`www.seotoolset.com/training/courses.html`)

✦ Search Engine Academy (`www.searchengineacademy.com`)

Following trusted authorities

If you are looking to specialize in SEO, start following trusted authorities in the SEO field. Authorities can be individuals, companies, or websites, but what they have in common is that they're respected and they typically deliver solid, reliable information.

You can find several news-stream sites out there geared toward search engine optimization. These websites keep up with the latest SEO news and statistics, and they always provide reliable, helpful information (and sometimes some not-so-helpful information, so be discerning). Although this list by no means gives you all the resources out there, it does give you some good sites to start with:

+ **Search Engine Land (**`http://searchengineland.com`**):** A great resource, Search Engine Land (SEL) is a search engine marketing industry news site. This site can tell you the latest news out of Google, Yahoo, and Bing, among other search engines. The same company that runs SMX, one of the large SEO conferences, runs SEL, so it's a pretty trustworthy site.

+ **Search Engine Journal (**`searchenginejournal.com`**):** Covering search engine marketing industry news, publishing guides, and fostering a collaborative community of search marketing professionals.

+ **Search Engine Watch (**`searchenginewatch.com`**):** News and commentary on the latest Internet marketing strategies and happenings.

+ **Search Engine Roundtable (**`www.seroundtable.com`**):** A forum-based news site, the Search Engine Roundtable (SER) brings you the latest news from the forums, catching stuff that other news sites might miss.

Performing experiments

Performing experiments doesn't mean you get to play Mr. Mad Scientist with your company's website. For one thing, randomly changing elements here and there on the site can lead to a decrease in the site's rankings and a drop in conversions, which in extreme cases, could negatively impact your business and your job. But you need to know how to test the changes you make to the site in order to gain rankings, traffic, and, your ultimate goal, more conversions.

Figuring out SEO requires doing SEO because it's often a matter of trial and error. The online environment constantly changes (in terms of both competitors and search engine algorithms). Proper SEO takes time, diligence, and patience. Getting accurate test results takes a matter of months, not hours or days. You have to be willing to work and have the patience to watch your experiments to make sure that you're getting the results you want.

On the flip side, don't be afraid to continue to tweak things if your tests aren't giving you the results you want. Run several tests, rather than just one or two. Change one thing at a time. And if you get bad results, don't be afraid to change it back!

If you can't experiment on your own site, consider building another site just for the purposes of testing. Tinkering, playing, and all-around messing with your site is the only way to really be sure that what you're doing works. Take chances and see whether they pay off. Like gambling, don't bet what you can't afford to lose, but make sure that you're investing enough to make it all pay off in the end.

Getting Things Done for Do-It-Yourselfers

We cover what to do if you want to wade into the professional world of search engine optimization earlier in the preceding minibooks. But what do you do if you're a do-it-yourselfer just trying to make your website succeed? Say that you have your own classic-car customization website, and you and your brother *are* the company. Because your brother can't use a computer to save his life, the burden of running and maintaining your company's website falls on you. So, what can you do in terms of optimizing your own website? A few things, actually.

Training

Most training courses out there are aimed at the beginners. Take some time or make an investment in some basic training for search engine optimization. They're worth the time and effort, so go do some research into what's right for you. We list plenty of beginner training options in the section "Picking the Right Training Courses," earlier in this appendix. Focus on the ones that offer face time with a real expert and some kind of tangible metric for success.

Testing, testing, testing!

Like we say in the section "Performing experiments," earlier in this appendix, testing is one of the most important things you can do. Test your site to make sure that anything you've done to it, from tweaking your keywords to adding more Engagement Objects, is actually working the way you want it to.

This advice might seem like common sense, but some people think that they can just make changes across the board and see returns immediately. Your site is one of millions of sites, and being a top-ranked site takes time and effort. SEO requires fine-tuning, so if you add new keywords to your site, watch them! Study your rankings and your server logs to see whether traffic has gone up since you made the changes. Check whether this increased traffic has given you more conversions or whether the extra visitors simply arrive at your front page and then immediately navigate away.

Drawing traffic to your site is just one part of the process. You have to make money. If no one is coming to your site and asking you to customize a classic car for him or her, you need to do further tweaking to your site.

Networking

You also need to network. Start engaging other people who know and work in SEO. Hang around the forums that discuss SEO and go to Twitter to check out what other people are saying. Don't be afraid to ask for help or guidance if you're not quite sure what you're doing. But be aware that you need to take any advice you get with a grain of salt. Always test out the advice before you accept it as the gospel truth.

Go to conferences. Budget for a trip to attend one of the larger SEO trade shows, such as SES, SMX, Pubcon, or ad:tech. At these conferences, you can get your feet wet and do a little bit of networking. Make a list of things that you need help on, and then plan your schedule so that you can attend. Don't be afraid to talk to people; no one was born an expert in search engine optimization. They all once started where you are. Ask questions if you're lost and take plenty of notes! You can always expand your Internet marketing knowledge, so do your best sponge impersonation and soak up as much information as you can. Search conferences often offer, at an extra cost, conference-partnered one-day training classes before or after the convention, so plan to arrive a day early or stay a day after to take advantage of those training opportunities.

Be discerning about the information that you gather. SEO isn't an exact science, so you may get conflicting reports on what to do and what not to do.

Also, check out newsletters from reputable sources. Ask around and do your research to find some reliable sources. You can start with these free newsletters:

+ **Bruce Clay, Inc.'s SEO Newsletter:** `www.bruceclay.com/newsletter`
+ **The Moz Top 10:** `moz.com/moztop10`
+ **MarketingSherpa:** `www.marketingsherpa.com/newsletters.html`
+ **Search Engine Land's SearchCap:** `http://searchengineland.com/searchcap`

Knowing when to call in the experts

Unfortunately, almost inevitably in the course of your SEM campaign, you'll run into problems with your SEO that are beyond your scope of training and expertise. Find a mentor: someone who can help you out and guide you through the tricky world of search engine optimization. Make sure that you can trust your mentor and that she's a respected authority in her own right. You can hopefully meet someone who can become your mentor by checking out search marketing forums and Twitter feeds and by attending conferences.

Don't be afraid to ask for assistance. Call in a professional consultant if you need help. But remember: Be familiar with the technical side of your website and your SEO so that you can tell whether your consultant is taking you for a ride or giving you good advice. Be very particular. Someone can easily call himself a guru, but it's hard to actually earn that reputation. Make sure his walk matches his talk.

Index

Special Characters and Numerics

A

S

About the Author

Bruce Clay is founder and president of Bruce Clay, Inc., a global Internet marketing optimization firm. The company specializes in search engine optimization (SEO), search advertising (PPC), social media and content marketing, SEO-friendly web design and architecture, and SEO tools and education. Prior to launching Bruce Clay, Inc., in 1996, Clay operated as an executive with several high-tech businesses, with a far-reaching professional background in leading Silicon Valley firms. Bruce holds an MBA from Pepperdine University and a bachelor's in math and computer science from Western Illinois University. As an industry thought leader, Bruce is a frequent speaker at industry conferences, including SMX, ad:tech, Pubcon, Inc. Magazine's GrowCo, DOMAINfest, Affiliate Summit, and many others, both within the U.S. and internationally. He created and teaches SEOToolSet® Training, a weeklong, intensive SEO training course that has helped tens of thousands of students around the world through instruction in SEO best practices in a classroom setting for hands-on learning. His insights have been featured in publications such as the *Wall Street Journal, USA Today, PC Week, Wired Magazine, Smart Money, Huffington Post, Forbes,* and many more. Bruce hosts the search marketing podcast SEM Synergy, which airs on the iHeartRadio network. He is a former member of the Search Engine Marketing Professionals Organization (SEMPO) board of directors, and in 2013, Bruce received the Lifetime Achievement Award presented by the History of SEO advisory board.

Dedication

I dedicate this book to a wonderful industry that has kept me endlessly fascinated, to my talented team, without whom this book would not be so expertly prepared, and to Wendy, my beautiful wife and constant inspiration.

Author Acknowledgments

I wish to acknowledge the significant contributions of the following individuals: Virginia Nussey, Paula Allen, Kristi Kellogg, Chelsea Adams, Melanie Saxe, Gary Collins, Nasim Jafarzadeh, Mindy Weinstein, Maryann Robbins, Robert Ramirez, Johnny Lin, Michael Terry, John Alexander, and Aaron Landerkin. Validating and updating a large book takes several experts, and these are the experts who helped with this edition.

Publisher's Acknowledgments

Acquisitions Editor: Amy Fandrei

Project Manager, Development Editor, and Copy Editor: Susan Christophersen

Technical Editor: Michelle Krasniak

Editorial Assistant: Claire Brock

Sr. Editorial Assistant: Cherie Case

Production Editor: Antony Sami

Cover Image: © iStock.com/Magnilion; © iStock.com/jonathansloane

Apple & Mac

iPad For Dummies,
6th Edition
978-1-118-72306-7

iPhone For Dummies,
7th Edition
978-1-118-69083-3

Macs All-in-One
For Dummies, 4th Edition
978-1-118-82210-4

OS X Mavericks
For Dummies
978-1-118-69188-5

Blogging & Social Media

Facebook For Dummies,
5th Edition
978-1-118-63312-0

Social Media Engagement
For Dummies
978-1-118-53019-1

WordPress For Dummies,
6th Edition
978-1-118-79161-5

Business

Stock Investing
For Dummies, 4th Edition
978-1-118-37678-2

Investing For Dummies,
6th Edition
978-0-470-90545-6

Personal Finance

Personal Finance
For Dummies, 7th Edition
978-1-118-11785-9

QuickBooks 2014
For Dummies
978-1-118-72005-9

Small Business Marketing
Kit For Dummies,
3rd Edition
978-1-118-31183-7

Careers

Job Interviews
For Dummies, 4th Edition
978-1-118-11290-8

Job Searching with Social
Media For Dummies,
2nd Edition
978-1-118-67856-5

Personal Branding
For Dummies
978-1-118-11792-7

Resumes For Dummies,
6th Edition
978-0-470-87361-8

Starting an Etsy Business
For Dummies, 2nd Edition
978-1-118-59024-9

Diet & Nutrition

Belly Fat Diet For Dummies
978-1-118-34585-6

Mediterranean Diet
For Dummies
978-1-118-71525-3

Nutrition For Dummies,
5th Edition
978-0-470-93231-5

Digital Photography

Digital SLR Photography
All-in-One For Dummies,
2nd Edition
978-1-118-59082-9

Digital SLR Video &
Filmmaking For Dummies
978-1-118-36598-4

Photoshop Elements 12
For Dummies
978-1-118-72714-0

Gardening

Herb Gardening
For Dummies, 2nd Edition
978-0-470-61778-6

Gardening with Free-Range
Chickens For Dummies
978-1-118-54754-0

Health

Boosting Your Immunity
For Dummies
978-1-118-40200-9

Diabetes For Dummies,
4th Edition
978-1-118-29447-5

Living Paleo For Dummies
978-1-118-29405-5

Big Data

Big Data For Dummies
978-1-118-50422-2

Data Visualization
For Dummies
978-1-118-50289-1

Hadoop For Dummies
978-1-118-60755-8

Language & Foreign Language

500 Spanish Verbs
For Dummies
978-1-118-02382-2

English Grammar
For Dummies, 2nd Edition
978-0-470-54664-2

French All-in-One
For Dummies
978-1-118-22815-9

German Essentials
For Dummies
978-1-118-18422-6

Italian For Dummies,
2nd Edition
978-1-118-00465-4

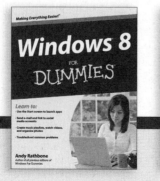 **Available in print and e-book formats.**

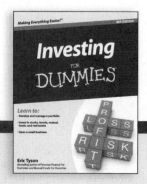 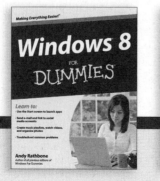  

Math & Science

Algebra I For Dummies,
2nd Edition
978-0-470-55964-2

Anatomy and Physiology
For Dummies, 2nd Edition
978-0-470-92326-9

Astronomy For Dummies,
3rd Edition
978-1-118-37697-3

Biology For Dummies,
2nd Edition
978-0-470-59875-7

Chemistry For Dummies,
2nd Edition
978-1-118-00730-3

1001 Algebra II Practice
Problems For Dummies
978-1-118-44662-1

Microsoft Office

Excel 2013 For Dummies
978-1-118-51012-4

Office 2013 All-in-One
For Dummies
978-1-118-51636-2

PowerPoint 2013
For Dummies
978-1-118-50253-2

Word 2013 For Dummies
978-1-118-49123-2

Music

Blues Harmonica
For Dummies
978-1-118-25269-7

Guitar For Dummies,
3rd Edition
978-1-118-11554-1

iPod & iTunes
For Dummies, 10th Edition
978-1-118-50864-0

Programming

Beginning Programming
with C For Dummies
978-1-118-73763-7

Excel VBA Programming
For Dummies, 3rd Edition
978-1-118-49037-2

Java For Dummies,
6th Edition
978-1-118-40780-6

Religion & Inspiration

The Bible For Dummies
978-0-7645-5296-0

Buddhism For Dummies,
2nd Edition
978-1-118-02379-2

Catholicism For Dummies,
2nd Edition
978-1-118-07778-8

Self-Help & Relationships

Beating Sugar Addiction
For Dummies
978-1-118-54645-1

Meditation For Dummies,
3rd Edition
978-1-118-29144-3

Seniors

Laptops For Seniors
For Dummies, 3rd Edition
978-1-118-71105-7

Computers For Seniors
For Dummies, 3rd Edition
978-1-118-11553-4

iPad For Seniors
For Dummies, 6th Edition
978-1-118-72826-0

Social Security
For Dummies
978-1-118-20573-0

Smartphones & Tablets

Android Phones
For Dummies, 2nd Edition
978-1-118-72030-1

Nexus Tablets
For Dummies
978-1-118-77243-0

Samsung Galaxy S 4
For Dummies
978-1-118-64222-1

Samsung Galaxy Tabs
For Dummies
978-1-118-77294-2

Test Prep

ACT For Dummies,
5th Edition
978-1-118-01259-8

ASVAB For Dummies,
3rd Edition
978-0-470-63760-9

GRE For Dummies,
7th Edition
978-0-470-88921-3

Officer Candidate Tests
For Dummies
978-0-470-59876-4

Physician's Assistant Exam
For Dummies
978-1-118-11556-5

Series 7 Exam For Dummies
978-0-470-09932-2

Windows 8

Windows 8.1 All-in-One
For Dummies
978-1-118-82087-2

Windows 8.1 For Dummies
978-1-118-82121-3

Windows 8.1 For Dummies,
Book + DVD Bundle
978-1-118-82107-7

ℯ Available in print and e-book formats.

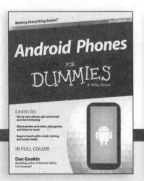

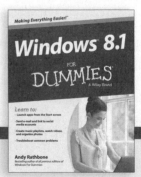

Available wherever books are sold. **For more information or to order direct visit www.dummies.com**

Take Dummies with you everywhere you go!

Whether you are excited about e-books, want more from the web, must have your mobile apps, or are swept up in social media, Dummies makes everything easier.

Leverage the Power

For Dummies is the global leader in the reference category and one of the most trusted and highly regarded brands in the world. No longer just focused on books, customers now have access to the For Dummies content they need in the format they want. Let us help you develop a solution that will fit your brand and help you connect with your customers.

Advertising & Sponsorships

Connect with an engaged audience on a powerful multimedia site, and position your message alongside expert how-to content.

Targeted ads • Video • Email marketing • Microsites • Sweepstakes sponsorship

Custom Publishing

Reach a global audience in any language by creating a solution that will
differentiate you from competitors, amplify your message,
and encourage customers to make a buying decision.

Apps • Books • eBooks • Video • Audio • Webinars

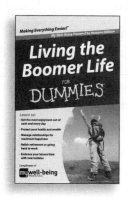

Brand Licensing & Content

Leverage the strength of the world's most popular reference brand to reach
new audiences and channels of distribution.

For more information, visit www.Dummies.com/biz

Dummies products make life easier!

- DIY
- Consumer Electronics
- Crafts
- Software
- Cookware
- Hobbies
- Videos
- Music
- Games
- and More!

For more information, go to **Dummies.com** and search the store by category.

FOR
DUMMIES

A Wiley Brand